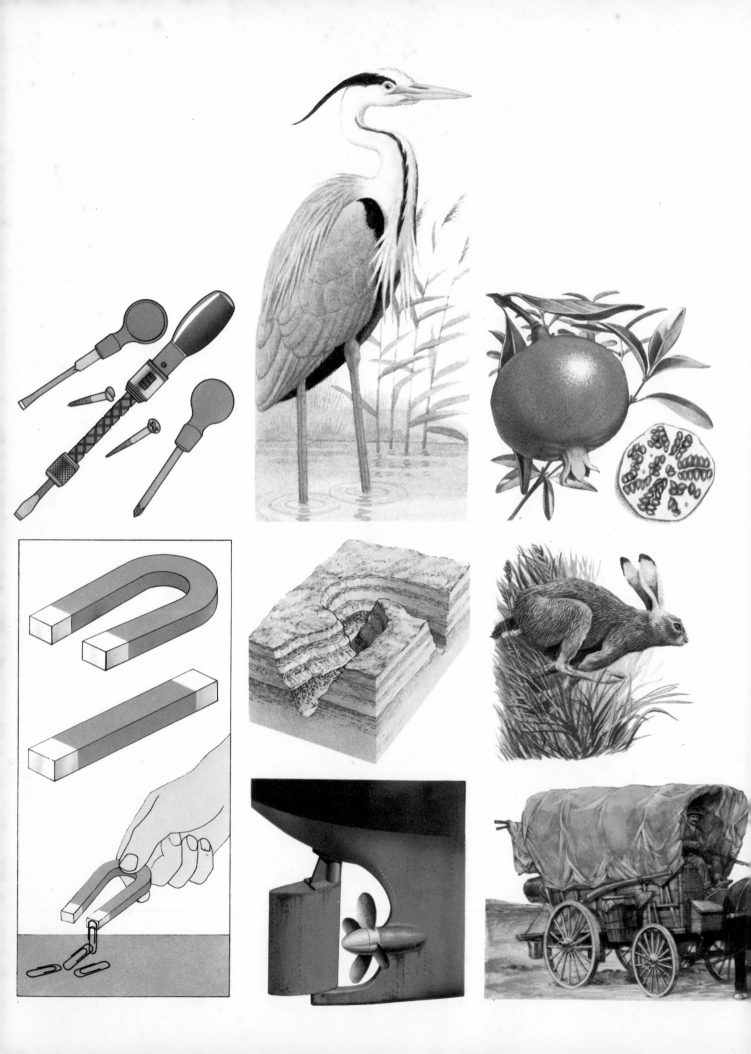

Illustrated
CHILDREN'S
DICTIONARY

Patrick Hanks B.A., Alan Isaacs B.Sc., Ph.D. and John Daintith B.Sc., Ph.D.
EDUCATIONAL CONSULTANT:
Mary Waddington M.A., Ph.D.

octopus

Introduction

This dictionary has been planned to help children from the age at which they are established readers until they are old enough to make full use of adult dictionaries. The vocabulary is that of pupils from their first years in junior school until their first year in secondary school – or the oldest class in middle schools.

To use a dictionary at all, children must have a minimal sight vocabulary, and so many words that appear in first reading books have been omitted, as have many simple three- and four-letter words, which children know and find easy to understand, read, and spell. Thus, the book does not contain a full vocabulary of all children in the age range.

Instead, it is designed to help children to read, to understand unfamiliar words, and to develop and increase their vocabulary and confidence in using words. It aims to support them in their efforts to write letters, stories, and accounts of events with increased imagination, understanding, and accuracy. The entries have been selected to reflect the language met in school and in everyday life and the meanings reflect current general usage.

The dictionary also aims to help children with their spelling and particular care has been taken to include difficult spellings and derivatives. For instance, many children can spell *begin*, but has *beginning* one *n* or two?

Finally, the book has been designed to resemble adult dictionaries in style and format. We hope that it will help to teach children to use dictionaries correctly and encourage them to consult dictionaries regularly, thus forming a habit that will be rewarding throughout a lifetime.

Compiled by Laurence Urdang Associates Ltd., Aylesbury

Contributors:

Della Summers
Carolyn Herzog
Jennifer Speake
William Gould
Elizabeth Martin
Judith Scott

Design: Logos Design, Windsor

Illustrators: Terry Allen Designs Ltd/Roger Courthold, Nick Skelton, Bob Stoneman; Barbosa, Patricia Capon, Roy Castle, Nigel Chamberlain, T. Crosby Smith, Karen Daws, Viv Donkin, Ian Garrard, Tony Gibbons, Donald Harley, Tim Hayward, Richard Hook, Mike Jaroszko, John Keay, Pavel Kostal, Jack Kunz, John Marshall, Donald Myall, David Nockels, Osborne/Marks, Stanley Paine, Gillian Platt, John Rignall, Ian Robertson, Sarson/Bryan, Doug Sheldrake, Michael Strand, Joan Thompson, George Thompson, David Warner, Phil Weare, Roy Wiltshire, Douglas Woodall.

This edition published 1980 by
Octopus Books Limited
59 Grosvenor Street, London W1

First published 1977 by
Sundial Books Limited as
The St Michael Illustrated Dictionary

© 1977 Hennerwood Publications

Reprinted 1981, 1982

ISBN 0 7064 0688 5

Printed in Czechoslovakia

50420/3

How to use this book

This dictionary contains a list of words together with their meanings and other information. A word, together with all its information, is called an *entry*. Below, you can find some typical dictionary entries with the kind of information given.

headword	**acorn** ('ākôn) *n.* the fruit of the oak tree, consisting of a smooth nut in a woody cup.
pronunciation	**hip**[1] (hip) *n.* the bony part of the body that sticks out below the waist.
	hip[2] (hip) *n.* a fruit of a rose that turns red when it is ripe.
definition	**ivory** ('īvəri) *n.* 1. the hard white bony substance of elephants' and walruses' tusks, used for making ornaments and piano keys. 2. a pale cream colour.
parts of speech	**jail** *or* **gaol** (jāl) *n.* a prison. —*vb.* to put in jail; imprison.
example sentence	**tang** (tañg) *n.* a strong taste or smell: *the wind had the salt tang of the sea.*
cross reference	**tangerine** (tanjə'rēn) *n.* a CITRUS fruit smaller than an orange and with a loose skin.

acorn

The headword The main words entered in the dictionary are called *headwords*. These are printed in large heavy type. The headword shows you how to spell the word. Sometimes the same spelling is given twice and numbers are added: **hip**[1] (part of the body) and **hip**[2] (fruit of a rose) are different words with widely different meanings, although they have the same spelling. Sometimes there is more than one way of spelling a word: **jail** and **gaol** are different spellings of the word meaning prison. In this dictionary we put the most common spelling first, but both are correct.

The pronunciation This comes after the headword and is placed in brackets. It tells you how to say (pronounce) the word, using some special symbols. Each symbol represents one – and only one – English sound. These are explained on page v.

The part of speech Words are classified into a few groups depending on how they are used in sentences. These are called parts of speech. An abbreviation, printed in sloping (italic) type, shows the part of speech of each word. Note that some words have more than one part of speech: **jail**, for example, is both a noun (*n.*) and a verb (*vb.*). Abbreviations used for parts of speech are:

noun	*n.*	pronoun	*pron.*
verb	*vb.*	preposition	*prep.*
adjective	*adj.*	interjection	*interj.*
adverb	*adv.*	conjunction	*conj.*

To find out more about these, look up the entries for noun, verb, and so on, in the dictionary.

The definition This is the part of the entry that tells you what the word means. Note that many

plural	**octopus** ('oktəpəs) *n., pl.* octopuses. a sea creature, ranging in size from 6 inches to 32 feet, with a soft rounded body and eight arms, each bearing rows of suckers.
comparative (prettier) superlative (prettiest) run-on	**pretty** ('priti) *adj.* prettier, prettiest. 1. pleasing to the eye or ear. 2. (informal) considerable: *after the crash the car was a pretty mess.* —*adv.* quite: *it hit him pretty hard.* — 'prettiness *n.*
sub-entry	**retire** (ri'tīə) *vb.* retiring, retired. 1. to give up full-time work because of age. 2. to withdraw; go away: *the runner retired from the race with a strained leg muscle.* re'tirement *n.* 1. the act of giving up work. 2. the state of being retired.
present participle (sowing) past tense (sowed) past participle (sown)	**sow**¹ (sō) *vb.* sowing, sowed, sown. to plant (seeds).

octopus

words have more than one meaning; **ivory**, for example, can be the material from elephants' tusks or the colour of elephants' tusks. Some definitions have an example sentence in italic type to help you understand the meaning or to show how the word is used. Words in capital letters, such as CITRUS in the entry for **tangerine**, are cross-references: they direct you to other headwords where you can get more information.

Plural nouns Sometimes the plural of a noun is written after the part of speech label to show its spelling: **octopuses**, for example, is the plural of **octopus**. This is only done when the plural spelling is unusual or difficult. Most English nouns form plurals by adding the letter -s (dogs, cats, etc.) or by adding -es (brushes, matches, passes, taxes, etc.) These plurals are not given in this dictionary.

Adjectives The spelling of adjectives can be changed when the adjective is used in comparing two or more nouns. Thus, one can say *this picture is prettier than that one* or *this is the prettier of the two pictures.* **Prettier** is called the *comparative* form of the adjective *pretty.* It is used when speaking of two objects. When three or more pictures are involved one can say *this picture is the prettiest.* **Prettiest** (meaning "most pretty") is the *superlative* form of the adjective *pretty.* Comparatives and superlatives are only given when they are difficult or unusual. Most words simply add -er and -est (hard, harder, hardest; strong, stronger, strongest).

Verbs Different forms of verbs are also given in this dictionary. The first form, ending in -ing, is the *present participle.* Thus, **playing** is the present participle of **play**. It is used with the verb *to be* to form different tenses of the verb, as in *I am playing next year* or in *he was sowing seeds yesterday.* The present participle is also a noun, as in *sowing takes place in the Spring.* The second form of the verb gives the *past tense* and *past participle.* The past tense is used in sentences such as *I played last year.* The *past participle* is the word used with the verb *to have* forming sentences such as *he has played.* It is also used with the verb *to be* to form passive sentences. For instance, **kicked**, the past participle of **kick**, is used in *the ball was kicked by the boy.* The past participle is also used as an adjective, as in *a kicked ball.*

Some verbs have a past tense that is different from the past participle. In these cases the past participle is given last. Thus, **sowed** is the past tense of **sow** (*I sowed the seeds*) and **sown** is the past participle (*I have sown the seeds*).

Different forms of the verb are shown only when they are difficult to spell. Otherwise they are formed simply by adding -*ing* and -*ed* to the verb (*walk, walking, walked; add, adding, added*; etc.).

Sub-entries These are words or phrases formed from the main entry and given their own definition: **retirement**, for example, is a sub-entry for the main headword **retire**. The mark (') in **re'tirement** is called a *stress mark* (see page v).

Run-ons Words formed from the main headword and given without a definition are called *run-on entries*. They are formed by adding common endings (suffixes) to the main headword and their meaning should be clear without any explanation. Some common endings used in this book are:

-ness   forms nouns from adjectives: prettiness – the state of being pretty.

-ly   forms adverbs from adjectives: happily – in a happy way.

-ation   forms nouns from verbs: separation – the act of separating or anything that has been separated.

-ful   forms adjectives from nouns: scornful – full of scorn; having scorn.

Pronunciation

The pronunciation of a word is the way it is said. In this dictionary a pronunciation is written in brackets after each headword. If you look at these you will see that some unfamiliar symbols are used. The purpose of these unfamiliar symbols is to ensure that each symbol represents one – and only one – English speech sound. Thus, letters that in English represent more than one sound are not used in the pronunciation guide. So we do not use *c*, because it could mean either *s* or *k*.

You may have noticed that the same letter is often given a different sound in different words: the *a* in *cat, rate,* and *farm* is sounded differently. These differences are shown by putting marks (accents) above the letters, as in ā and â.

Another feature of the pronunciation guide is that sometimes two letters are joined together as in c̦h or șh. This shows that the letters form one sound, as in *chin* and *shoe*.

The symbol ə (an e upside down) is used in many pronunciations. It represents an indistinct sound – for example the 'a' in *ago*, the 'o' in *lemon* and the 'e' in *agent* all have the same sound. The symbol is called *schwa*.

Finally, pronunciations contain a mark (') to show where the stress (or weight) is put in saying the word. Most words are pronounced in parts (syllables). The word *retire* has two syllables *re·tire* and the mark comes before the stressed syllable ri'tīə shows that the weight is put on the second part of the word: reTIRE.

The table below shows all the different sound symbols used in this dictionary with examples for words in which the sound occurs.

VOWELS		CONSONANTS	
a	c*at*	b	*b*at
ā	r*ate*	c̦h	*ch*in
â	f*a*rm	d	*d*og
e	g*e*t	d̦h	*th*en
ē	k*ee*p	f	*f*og
eə	th*ere*	g	*g*et
ēə	f*ear*	h	*h*ow
i	t*i*n	j	*j*oy
ī	*i*ce	k	*k*eep
iə	h*ere*	l	*l*ike
īə	ret*ire*	m	*m*y
o	j*o*g	n	*n*o
ō	g*o*	n̂g	si*ng*
ô	s*aw*	p	*p*ut
oi	b*oy*	r	*r*ace
ou	*ou*t	s	*s*ign
o͞o	t*oo*	șh	*sh*oe
o͝o	l*oo*k	t	*t*op
o͝oə	p*oor*	th	*th*in
u	h*u*sh	v	*v*ery
û	h*u*rt	w	*w*ag
ə	*a*go, *a*gent,	y	*y*ell
	san*i*ty, lem*o*n,	z	*z*oo
	circ*u*s	z̦h	mea*s*ure

A

abacus ('abəkəs) *n.* a device used for calculating, consisting of a frame in which parallel wires or rods are set with beads or counters that slide on them to indicate the quantities.

abandon (ə'bandən) *vb.* to give up or leave behind; surrender, desert, or forsake: *the crew abandoned the sinking ship.* **abandon oneself to** to yield completely to; give way to: *she abandoned herself to grief when her puppy died.* —*n.* carefree exuberance or delight. —**a'bandonment** *n.*

abbey ('abē) *n.* 1. a group of buildings housing a community of monks or nuns. 2. the church belonging or formerly belonging to such a community.

abbot ('abət) *n.* a man who is the head of a community of monks. See MONASTERY.

abbreviate (ə'brēviāt) *vb.* **abbreviating, abbreviated.** to shorten, e.g. for the sake of convenience. **abbrevi'ation** *n.* 1. a shortened form of a word, phrase, or title: *m.p.h. is an abbreviation for miles per hour.* 2. the act or an instance of abbreviating something.

abdicate ('abdikāt) *vb.* **abdicating, abdicated.** to give up a position of authority to another, esp. voluntarily —**abdi'cation** *n.*

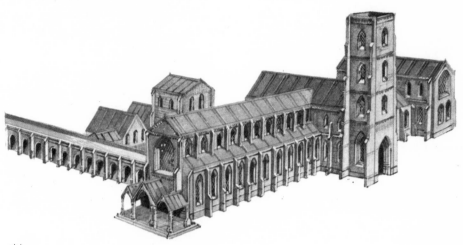

abbey

abdomen ('abdəmən) *n.* 1. the part of the human body between the chest and the hips, containing the stomach, liver, kidneys, intestines, and other organs; belly. 2. (in insects, crabs, etc.) the rear part of the body. —**abdominal** (ab'dominəl) *adj.*

able ('ābəl) *adj.* **abler, ablest.** 1. having the talent or opportunity to do something: *I am able to speak French fluently.* 2. generally capable; competent: *he is an able teacher and respected by his pupils.* **a'bility** *n.,pl.* **abilities.** talent or skill: *she has the ability to be a great singer.* '**ably** *adv.* competently.

abnormal (ab'nôməl) *adj.* not normal; unusual; unnatural. —**abnor'mality** *n.,pl.* **abnormalities.** —**ab'normally** *adv.*

aboard (ə'bôd) *prep.,adv.* on (a boat, train, or aeroplane).

abolish (ə'bolish) *vb.* to ban or do away with: *he believes prisons should be abolished.* **abolition** (abə'lishən) *n.* the act or an instance of abolishing; a formal ban.

aborigine (abə'rijini) *n.* 1. one belonging to the original or native race of a country. 2. **Aborigine** or **Aboriginal** a member of the race that originally inhabited Australia. —**abo'riginal** *adj.*

abrasion (ə'brāzhən) *n.* 1. the process of rubbing or scraping. 2. a graze or scratch. **a'brasive** *adj.* 1. irritating; harsh: *he has an abrasive personality.* 2. producing roughness, e.g. on a surface. *n.* a gritty substance for cleaning, grinding, or polishing.

abroad (ə'brôd) *adv.* 1. in or to a country other than one's own. 2. roaming about; at large: *the lions that escaped from the zoo are still abroad.*

abrupt (ə'brupt) *adj.* 1. sudden, sharp, or unexpected: *this play has an abrupt ending.* 2. rude; bad-mannered: *his manner was so abrupt that she was offended.* —**ab'ruptly** *adv.* —**ab'ruptness** *n.*

abscond (əb'skond) *vb.* to run away or go into hiding, esp. to escape from justice: *the treasurer absconded with the club's funds.*

absent ('absənt) *adj.* 1. not present; away. 2. lacking. **absent oneself** (ab'sent) to stay away deliberately: *he absented himself from school to watch football.* —**'absence** *n.*

absolute ('absəlōot) *adj.* 1. complete; total: *an absolute failure.* 2. unlimited; unconditional: *absolute power.* —**abso'lutely** *adv.*

absorb (əb'zôb) *vb.* 1. to soak up: *this material will absorb moisture.*

aborigine

1

2. to take in; understand: *she was able to absorb the lesson easily.* 3. to engage (one's whole attention): *the game absorbed him for over three hours.* —**ab'sorbent** *adj.* —**ab'sorption** *n.*

absurd (ab'sûd) *adj.* ridiculous, laughable, or silly: *we all laughed at her absurd suggestion.* —**ab'surdity** *n.,pl.* **absurdities.** —**ab'surdly** *adv.*

abundant (ə'bundənt) *adj.* plentiful; ample; lavish: *we have an abundant supply of food for the party.* —**a'bundance** *n.* —**a'bundantly** *adv.*

abuse *vb.* (ə'byo͞oz) **abusing, abused.** 1. to make the wrong use of: *he abused his position as manager by hiring only his relatives.* 2. to speak rudely to or insult (someone). —*n.* (ə'byo͞os) 1. misuse or ill treatment. 2. insulting language or behaviour. —**a'busive** *adj.* —**a'busively** *adv.* —**a'busiveness** *n.*

academic (akə'demik) *adj.* of or relating to a school, college, or university: *the academic year.* 2. theoretical; not concerned with practical matters. —*n.* a university teacher. —**aca'demically** *adv.*

accelerate (ak'selərāt) *vb.* **accelerating, accelerated.** to move or cause to move faster or happen sooner; speed up. —**ac'celerator** *n.* the pedal, lever, or other control used for changing the speed of an engine, esp. the pedal controlling the acceleration of a car; throttle. —**acceler'ation** *n.*

accent *n.* ('aksənt) 1. a way of speaking that indicates the speaker's nationality, region, social class, etc.: *a Scottish accent.* 2. the stress put on one syllable of a spoken word, e.g. 'umbrella' has the accent on the middle syllable. 3. a printed mark indicating a stressed syllable or musical note or (in some foreign languages) a particular vowel quality. —*vb.* (ak'sent) (also **accentuate**) to stress or emphasize.

accept (ək'sept) *vb.* 1. to take (something that is offered). 2. to agree or admit: *I accept that I was wrong.* **ac'ceptable** *adj.* worth accepting; satisfactory. —**ac'ceptance** *n.*

access ('akses) *n.* 1. the way in; approach: *the only access to the house was up a steep hill.* 2. the opportunity of using: *pianists need to have access to a good piano.* —**accessible** (ək'sesibəl) *adj.*

accessory (ək'sesəri) *n.,pl.* **accessories.** 1. an object or article used or worn in addition to something else, e.g. a handbag. 2. (law) a person guilty of helping in a crime.

accident ('aksidənt) 1. an unexpected and unpleasant event; a fall, car crash, etc. 2. a chance occurrence: *we met by accident.* —**acci'dental** *adj.* —**acci'dentally** *adv.*

acclaim (ə'klām) *vb.* to meet with shouts of approval; hail or applaud: *the astronauts were acclaimed as heroes.* —*n.* (also **acclamation**) enthusiastic approval; applause.

accommodate (ə'komədāt) *vb.* **accommodating, accommodated.** 1. to provide room for: *this hall can accommodate a thousand people.* 2. to adapt to the needs of: *this restaurant is unable to accommodate my tastes.* **accommo'dation** *n.* a place to live or stay in; lodgings.

accompany (ə'kumpəni) *vb.* **accompanying, accompanied.** to go with or attend. **ac'companiment** *n.* the musical support given to a soloist by another instrument, often a piano.

accomplish (ə'kumplish) *vb.* to achieve or complete successfully. **ac'complishment** *n.* 1. an achievement. 2. a skill or talent: *good aim in firing a gun is an accomplishment expected of a soldier.*

accordion

accordion (ə'kôdiən) *n.* a portable musical instrument operated by bellows. **piano accordion** an accordion with a small piano-like keyboard.

account (ə'kount) *n.* 1. a report or description of an event: *the critic gave a glowing account of the performance.* 2. a recorded count: *keep an account of all you spend.* 3. a statement of money owing; bill. 4. a banking arrangement by which money can be paid in or drawn out. 5. a credit arrangement by which goods or services are paid for at a later date: *we have an account at the bookshop.* 6. esteem or importance: *a mayor is usually a man of some account.* 7. **accounts** (*pl.*) written records of money received (credits) and paid out (debits). —*vb.* to consider or reckon: *he was generally accounted a good man.* **account for** to explain or answer for: *he could not account for his sudden fear.* **ac'countant** *n.* a person whose job is to keep or inspect business accounts. **ac'countancy** *n.* the work of an accountant.

accumulate (ə'kyo͞omyo͞olāt) *vb.* **accumulating, accumulated.** to pile up or collect: *over the years he accumulated a fortune.* —**accumu'lation** *n.*

accurate ('akyo͝orit) *adj.* 1. containing no mistakes; correct or right: *accurate typing.* 2. precise or exact: *Tom gave an accurate description of the thief.* —'**accuracy** *n.* —'**accurately** *adv.*

accuse (ə'kyo͞oz) *vb.* **accusing, accused.** to charge (someone) with doing wrong; blame. —**accusation** *n.*

ache (āk) *n.* a prolonged dull pain. —*vb.* **aching, ached.** to feel or produce an ache: *my head aches after exams.*

achieve (ə'chēv) *vb.* **achieving, achieved.** 1. to carry out successfully; accomplish. 2. to acquire, often with effort: *achieving success in life is rarely easy.* —**a'chievement** *n.*

acid ('asid) *n.* a chemical containing hydrogen, which is often very sour and corrosive and can form salts with metals and alkalis and turns LITMUS paper red. —*adj.* 1. tasting sour or sharp. 2. biting; sarcastic: *he had an acid wit.* —**acidity** (ə'siditi) *n.*

acknowledge (ək'nolij) *vb.* **acknowledging, acknowledged.** 1. to admit to be true, worthy, or valid; concede: *I acknowledged him the winner.* 2. to indicate that one has received something: *to acknowledge a letter.* 3. to indicate thanks or appreciation: *the actor acknowledged the applause by bowing.* 4. to show that one has noticed or recognized (somebody): *he acknowledged me with a cheerful smile.* —**ac'knowledgment** *or* **ac'knowledgement** *n.*

acorn

acorn ('ākôn) *n.* the fruit of the oak tree, consisting of a smooth nut in a woody cup.

acquaint (ə'kwānt) *vb.* (+ *with*) to make known or familiar to: *I will acquaint you with the facts.* **ac'quaintance** *n.* 1. a person one knows but who is not a close friend. 2. knowledge or familiarity: *his acquaintance with French is slight.*

acquire (ə'kwīə) *vb.* **acquiring, acquired.** to obtain or gain.

acquit (ə'kwit) *vb.* **acquitting, acquitted.** to declare (a person) not guilty of a charge. **acquit oneself** to play one's part: *in spite of the heat the team members acquitted themselves well.* —**ac'quittal** *n.*

acre (ākə) *n.* a measure of land covering 4840 square yards (about 4000 square metres).

acrobat ('akrəbat) *n.* a person who performs gymnastic tricks for entertainment. —**acro'batic** *adj.* —**acro'batics** *pl.n.*

action ('akshən) *n.* 1. the process of acting or doing or the state of being active. 2. something that is done; a deed; act: *I don't approve of his stupid action.* 3. a gesture or movement of the body. 4. the mechanism of a machine, clock, gun, etc. 5. a battle; fighting: *the main action of the war was a battle on the border between the two countries.* 6. a legal case or proceeding. 7. the events in a play, film, novel, etc.: *the action takes place in France at the beginning of the 18th century.*

active ('aktiv) *adj.* 1. energetic; busy; lively. 2. in operation; working. 3.

(grammar) indicating that the subject of a verb is doing something or performing an action, e.g. *painted* in the sentence *John painted the picture* is an active verb. Compare PASSIVE. **ac'tivity** *n.,pl.* **activities.** 1. movement; liveliness: *there was a lot of activity in the main hall.* 2. something that one does; an interest: *outside activities need not interfere with school work.* —**'actively** *adv.*

actor ('aktə) *n.* 1. a person who performs in a play or film. 2. a person who takes part in something: *who are the main actors in this scheme?* **actress** ('aktris) *n.* a female actor.

actual ('aktyooəl) *adj.* existing or real: *what are the actual facts of this case?* —**actu'ality** *n.* —**'actually** *adv.*

acute (ə'kyoōt) *adj.* 1. severely painful or distressing: *acute embarrassment.* 2. of grave importance; extremely serious: *an acute shortage of water.* 3. (of the senses) keen or sharp. 4. (of an illness or disease) quickly and suddenly reaching a crisis: *acute appendicitis.* Compare CHRONIC. **acute angle** an angle of less than 90°. See ANGLE. —**a'cutely** *adv.* —**a'cuteness** *n.*

adapt (ə'dapt) *vb.* 1. to adjust to new conditions or circumstances: *to adapt to a new climate.* 2. to change or alter for a specific purpose: *the author adapted his novel for the stage.* **a'dapter** *n.* a device used to alter a piece of machinery, apparatus, etc., so that it can be used for a purpose other than the one for which it was originally designed. —**a'daptable** *adj.* —**adaptation** (adap'tāshən) *n.*

adder ('adə) *n.* a small poisonous snake; viper.

adder

address (ə'dres) *n.* 1. the details of the exact location of a house, office, etc. 2. a public speech. —*vb.* 1. to write an address (def. 1) on a letter, parcel, etc. 2. to speak directly to: *he addressed the whole school.*

adequate ('adikwət) *adj.* just enough for one's needs; sufficient: *an adequate supply of food.* —**'adequacy** *n.* —**'adequately** *adv.*

adhere (əd'hiə) *vb.* **adhering, adhered.** 1. to stick to something. 2. to support: *I adhere to the principle of free speech.* **ad'herent** *n.* a supporter.

adhesion (əd'hēzhən) the process of sticking or adhering to something. **adhesive** (əd'hēziv) *adj.* 1. sticky. 2. able to stick to something. *n.* a substance used for sticking things together.

adjacent (ə'jāsənt) *adj.* next to; close to: *a house adjacent to a hospital.*

adjective ('ajiktiv) *n.* a word used to describe or modify a noun, e.g. 'red', 'small'. —**adjectival** (ajik'tīvəl) *adj.*

adjourn (ə'jûn) *vb.* to postpone or be postponed until a future occasion; suspend, defer, or put off: *the meeting was adjourned.* —**ad'journment** *n.*

adjust (ə'just) *vb.* 1. to alter or regulate: *if you adjust the controls the machine will work faster.* 2. to change or modify one's behaviour; adapt: *they adjusted to a new life in Australia.* —**ad'justable** *adj.* —**ad'justment** *n.*

administer (əd'ministə) *vb.* 1. to manage or control: *a deputy was appointed to administer the region.* 2. to hand out or dispense: *the court administers justice.* **adminis'tration** *n.* 1. the act of administering. 2. a government: *this administration has lasted six years.* —**ad'ministrative** *adj.* —**ad'ministrator** *n.*

admirable ('admərəbəl) *adj.* excellent; worthy of admiration: *an admirable achievement.* —**'admirably** *adv.*

admire (əd'mīə) *vb.* **admiring, admired.** to regard with respect or praise; appreciate or value: *she admires beautiful things.* See also ADMIRABLE. —**admiration** (admə'rāshən) *n.* —**ad'mirer** *n.*

admission (əd'mishən) *n.* 1. (also **admittance**) the power, right, or permission to enter a place. 2. an acknowledgment or confession.

admit (əd'mit) *vb.* **admitting, admitted.** 1. to permit entry or access: *the doorman has instructions to admit them both.* 2. to acknowledge or agree, often reluctantly, that something is true or right: *I admit that he is friendly, but I don't like him very much.* 3. to accept responsibility for something: *he was forced to admit his error.* —**ad'mittedly** *adv.*

adolescent (adə'lesənt) *n.* a person who is no longer a child but not yet an adult. —*adj.* growing from childhood to maturity. —**ado'lescence** *n.*

adopt (ə'dopt) *vb.* 1. to take legal responsibility for bringing up a child and acting as its parent. 2. to take up (a new idea, plan, fashion, etc.): *the committee voted to adopt the policy that was suggested by the President.* —**a'doption** *n.*

adore (ə'dô) *vb.* **adoring, adored.** 1. to love with extreme devotion. 2. to have a great liking for: *the miser so adores money that he cannot bear to part with it.* —**a'dorable** *adj.* —**adoration** (adô'rāshən) *n.*

adult ('adult, ə'dult) *n.* one who has grown up and reached maturity. —*adj.* mature; fully grown. —**adulthood** ('adulthŏŏd, ə'dulthŏŏd) *n.* the state of being grown up.

advance (əd'vâns) *vb.* **advancing, advanced.** 1. to move forward; progress: *the general commanded the army to advance across the bridge.* 2. to help the progress of; encourage: *the agreement did much to advance peace.* 3. to make a loan to: *the bank manager advanced him £1000.* —*n.* 1. a forward progression. 2. a loan or payment. 3. **advances** (*pl.*) gestures of friendship. **in advance** beforehand. —**ad'vancement** *n.*

advantage (əd'vântij) *n.* 1. a benefit or privilege: *the advantage of wealth.* 2. superiority over another: *the strong have a great advantage over the weak.* —**advantageous** (advən'tāj-əs) *adj.*

adventure (əd'venchə) *n.* an exciting, often dangerous, undertaking or experience. **ad'venturous** *adj.* bold or courageous. —**ad'venturer** *n.* —**ad'venturously** *adv.*

adverb ('advûb) *n.* a word used to modify a verb or adjective, usu. expressing a relation of time, place, manner, degree, etc., e.g. *quickly, happily.* —**ad'verbial** *adj.*

adversary ('advəsəri) *n.,pl.* **adversaries.** an enemy or opponent.

adverse ('advûs, əd'vûs) *adj.* acting against a person or thing; unfavourable: *adverse weather conditions prevented the race.*

advertise ('advətīz) *vb.* **advertising, advertised.** to give publicity to (something); make widely known. **advertisement** (əd'vûtizmənt) *n.* a public announcement on television, on hoardings, in newspapers, etc., designed to attract notice or to promote the sale of goods. —**'advertiser** *n.*

advice (əd'vīs) *n.* guidance or opinion that helps one to solve a problem, decide on a course of action, etc.

advise (əd'vīz) *vb.* **advising, advised.** 1. to counsel or give advice. 2. to notify: *he was asked to advise the police of his movements.* **ad'visable** *adj.* wise; to be recommended. —**ad'viser** *n.*

aeroplane ('eərəplān) *n.* (often shortened to **plane**) a propeller-driven or jet-driven aircraft kept in flight by the passage of air over its wings.

aerosol

aerosol ('eərəsol) *n.* 1. a mixture of very fine particles suspended in a gas. 2. (also **aerosol can, aerosol container,** etc.) a push-button container in which a liquid is kept under pressure, to be released in the form of a spray.

affair (ə'feə) *n.* 1. a public event or private matter; concern: *when I tried to help, he told me that it was his own affair.* 2. a romantic relationship, esp. one carried on outside one's marriage. 3. **affairs** (*pl.*) general business matters.

affect[1] (ə'fekt) *vb.* to cause a change; influence: *the weather will affect the success of the fair.*

affect[2] (ə'fekt) *vb.* to assume or feign (an attitude, emotion, etc.); pretend: *though she already knew what her birthday present was, she affected great surprise.* —**affectation** (afek'tāshən) *n.*

affection (ə'fekshən) *n.* a friendly or loving feeling; fondness. —**af'fectionate** *adj.* —**af'fectionately** *adv.*

affluent ('aflŏŏənt) *adj.* having great wealth. —**'affluence** *n.*

afford (ə'fôd) *vb.* 1. to have enough money or time for something: *we can't afford a new car.* 2. to be prepared or able to do something risky or potentially harmful: *I can't afford to risk letting John drive my car.*

afraid (ə'frād) *adj.* 1. frightened; scared; filled with fear or anxiety: *are you afraid of spiders?* 2. sorry; regretful: *I am afraid I can't help you to make up your mind.*

agent ('ājənt) *n.* 1. a person who acts on behalf of his firm or other people, usu. offering a special service: *a travel agent.* 2. a force or influence that produces a change: *a chemical agent.* **'agency** *n.,pl.* **agencies.** 1. a business employing agents who act on a client's behalf: *a detective agency.* 2. influence: *he gained his position through the agency of friends.*

aggravate ('agrəvāt) *vb.* **aggravating, aggravated.** 1. to make worse: *conditions on the crowded roads were aggravated by the snow.* 2. to annoy or irritate (someone). —**aggra'vation** *n.*

aggression (ə'greshən) *n.* 1. a feeling or show of violence or hostility. 2. a sudden attack. **ag'gressive** *adj.* 1. violent or threatening. 2. forceful: *an aggressive salesman can persuade people to buy against their will.* —**ag'gressively** *adv.* —**ag'gressiveness** *n.* —**ag'gressor** *n.*

agile ('ajīl) *adj.* quick-moving or active; deft or nimble: *though slow in body he had an agile mind.* —**'agilely** *adv.* —**a'gility** *n.*

agitate ('agitāt) *vb.* **agitating, agitated.** 1. to disturb or worry: *she became agitated when her son did not return from school.* 2. to stir or shake up (a liquid, etc.). **'agitator**

n. a person who encourages others to protest, go on strike, rebel, etc. —**agi'tation** *n.*

agony ('agəni) *n.,pl.* **agonies.** intense pain or suffering of the body or mind.

agree (ə'grē) *vb.* **agreeing, agreed. 1.** to feel the same way about something; share the same opinion: *I agree with you.* **2.** to consent to; approve: *the committee agreed (to) our plans.* **3.** to be consistent; correspond: *their stories don't agree.* **a'greeable** *adj.* pleasant or amiable: *an agreeable evening.* —**a'greeably** *adv.* —**a'greement** *n.*

agriculture ('agrikulchə) *n.* the practice or study of farming.

aid (ād) *vb.* to help or assist; support. —*n.* **1.** help or assistance; support: *foreign aid.* **2.** a person who gives help; a right-hand man.

air (eə) *n.* **1.** the invisible mixture of gases that surrounds the earth. It consists of a mixture of oxygen and nitrogen, with smaller amounts of other gases. **2.** a small movement of the air; a light breeze. **3.** appearance or character: *he had an air of confidence.* **4.** a tune or melody. **5. airs** (*pl.*) affected or snobbish behaviour: *he puts on airs.* —*vb.* **1.** to make (a room, hall, etc.) open to the air so as to make it cooler or fresher. **2.** to expose (sheets, clothes, etc.) to the air in order to remove all traces of dampness. **3.** to make known or publicize: *you can air your views at the meeting.*

aircraft ('eəkrâft) *n.,pl.* **aircraft.** any machine capable of flight in the air, including balloons, helicopters, gliders, and planes. **aircraft carrier** a large warship with a flat deck designed for the take-off and landing of aeroplanes.

airfield ('eəfēld) *n.* a place at which aircraft can take off and land, usu. with hard runways.

airport ('eəpôt) *n.* **1.** a place with runways, hangars, workshops, buildings, etc., for aeroplanes and for receiving and dispatching passengers and freight by air.

air raid a military attack by aircraft, usu. carrying bombs or rockets.

aisle (īl) *n.* **1.** the way leading down the centre of a church to the altar. **2.** a passageway separating rows of seats in a theatre, cinema, etc.

alarm (ə'lâm) *n.* **1.** a sound or sign made to warn others of approaching danger. **2.** a sudden fear or anxiety. —*vb.* to give a warning to or arouse a feeling of approaching danger in.

albatross ('albətros) *n.* a large white seabird, usu. found in the South Pacific.

albino (al'bēnō) *n.,pl.* **albinos.** a person or animal born with white skin and hair and pink eyes caused by absence of pigment.

album ('albəm) *n.* a book of blank pages used for displaying photographs, stamps, autographs, etc.

albino

alcohol ('alkəhol) *n.* a colourless liquid that forms the intoxicating content in drinks such as wine, beer, and spirits. **alco'holic** *adj.* of or containing alcohol. *n.* a person who regularly drinks alcoholic beverages so heavily that his health suffers; one addicted to alcohol. —**'alcoholism** *n.*

alcove ('alkōv) *n.* a space or recess set back in the wall of a room, sometimes containing a bed, a seat, or shelves.

alert (ə'lût) *adj.* **1.** watchful; wary; ready for action: *a good soldier remains alert at all times.* **2.** lively; wide awake; responsive.

algae ('aljē) *pl.n.,sing.* **alga** ('algə). a group of moisture-loving plants that includes seaweeds.

algebra ('aljibrə) *n.* a branch of mathematics that uses letters or sym-

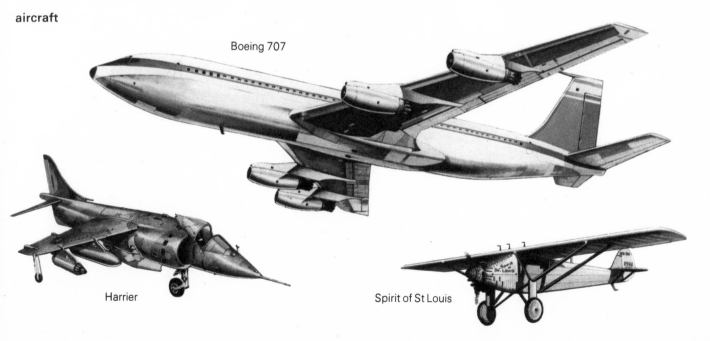
aircraft

Boeing 707

Harrier

Spirit of St Louis

alligator

bols in place of numbers in order to simplify complex calculations. —**algebraic** (aljə'brāik) *adj.*

alias ('āliəs) *n.* a false or assumed name. —*adv.* sometimes known as: *William Cody alias Buffalo Bill.*

alien ('āliən) *adj.* 1. foreign. 2. unnatural; contrary to: *violence is alien to her nature.* —*n.* a foreigner, usu. one living in a country not his own. '**alienate** *vb.* **alienating, alienated.** to lose the affection or interest of: *by her bad behaviour Anne alienated many of her friends.* —**alien'ation** *n.*

alight[1] (ə'līt) *adj.* 1. on fire. 2. bright; gleaming: *his face was alight with happiness.*

alight[2] (ə'līt) *vb.* **alighting, alighted** *or* **alit.** 1. to get down from a bus, train, etc. 2. (of winged creatures or anything airborne) to settle or take up a perch.

alkali ('alkəlī) *n.,pl.* **alkalis** *or* **alkalies.** a chemical such as soda or ammonia that forms salts with acids and turns LITMUS paper blue. —'**alkaline** *adj.*

allege (ə'lej) *vb.* **alleging, alleged.** 1. to assert or declare strongly: *he alleges he is a fine swimmer.* 2. to state as a fact (something that may prove to be untrue). —**allegation** (ali'gāshən) *n.*

allegiance (ə'lējəns) *n.* the loyalty and service due to a ruler, leader, or superior.

alliance (ə'liəns) *n.* 1. a friendly union of countries, families, or other groups. 2. an agreement (usu. between nations) to work together for a joint aim.

alligator ('aligātə) *n.* a large fish-eating REPTILE having a short broad head and rather uneven teeth. It lives in some lakes, swamps, and rivers of America and China.

allocate ('aləkāt) *vb.* **allocating, allocated.** to set aside (money, time, etc.) for a specific purpose; arrange as a person's share: *the judges allocated prizes to the three top sportsmen of the year.* —**allo'cation** *n.*

allot (ə'lot) *vb.* **allotting, allotted.** to deal out, distribute, or assign: *the teacher allotted us three hours of homework a week.* **al'lotment** *n.* a small plot of land rented out for growing different fruit, flowers, and vegetables.

allow (ə'lou) *vb.* 1. to permit. 2. to arrange to give (money, time, etc.): *they allowed us £5 towards expenses.* 3. to leave time or room for: *I allowed myself ten minutes to get to the station.* **al'lowance** *n.* a fixed sum of money given regularly for a special purpose: *a monthly clothes allowance.*

ally *vb.* (ə'lī) **allying, allied.** to unite or work together for a common purpose by means of a treaty or agreement. **allied to** connected with or related to. —*n.* ('alī) *pl.* **allies.** a country, person, or group that unites with others, esp. against a common enemy; friend.

almond ('âmənd) *n.* the edible nut found inside the stone of the fruit of the sweet almond tree. When ground, almonds form the main ingredient of MARZIPAN.

alphabet ('alfəbet) *n.* the set of letters, usu. in a particular order, used in a language. '**alphabetize** *vb.* **alphabetizing, alphabetized.** to arrange (names, words, etc.) so that

the first letters have the same order as the alphabet: *the words in this dictionary have been alphabetized.* —**alpha'betical** *adj.*

already (ôl'redi) *adv.* 1. by a certain time: *I have already eaten.* 2. so soon: *is it lunchtime already?*

altar ('ôltə) *n.* 1. the table found in the east end of Christian churches at which Holy Communion is celebrated. 2. a raised flat-topped structure such as a table or large rock on which offerings of wine, food, etc., and sometimes sacrifices of animals are made to a god.

alter ('ôltə) *vb.* to change; make or become different: *he has altered greatly since his recent illness.*

alternate *vb.* ('ôltənāt) **alternating, alternated.** to vary with something or between two choices: *she alternated between crying and laughing.* —*adj.* (ôl'tûnit) the second of every two: *they go to London on alternate weekends.* **alternative** (ôl'tûnətiv) *adj.* excluding another possibility; different: *an alternative method. n.* a choice: *you have no alternative but to come tomorrow.*

although (ôl'thō) *conj.* even though; in spite of the fact that: *Tom was given the prize, although he didn't deserve it.*

altitude ('altityōod) *n.* height above sea-level.

altogether (ôltə'gedhə) *adv.* entirely: *it's altogether too late to celebrate New Year's Eve on January 10th.*

aluminium (alyōo'miniəm) *n.* a strong lightweight silver-white metal

alphabet: Roman (top); Greek (centre); Hebrew (bottom).

extracted chiefly from the mineral bauxite and often used for making aircraft parts, technical instruments, kitchen equipment, etc. Chemical symbol: Al.

amateur ('amətə, 'amətʃə) *n.* a person who does something (esp. sport, acting, or playing a musical instrument) in his spare time out of interest, rather than for money.

amaze (ə'māz) *vb.* **amazing, amazed.** to astonish, bewilder, or surprise greatly: *the magician amazed us by pulling scarves out of his mouth.* —**a'mazement** *n.*

ambassador (am'basədə) *n.* 1. a minister sent to represent his country in a foreign land. 2. a messenger.

amber ('ambə) *n.* a hard brownish-yellow substance formed from resin produced by certain trees millions of years ago; it is used for decoration and jewellery. —*adj.* of the colour of amber.

ambiguous (am'bigyoōəs) *adj.* having more than one possible meaning, e.g. the sentence *blue man's bicycle for sale.* (Does it mean a blue man or a blue bicycle?) —**ambiguity** (ambi'gyoōiti) *n.,pl.* **ambiguities** anything that is ambiguous.

ambition (am'bishən) *n.* a strong desire for success, power, or fame, esp. in a job or any competitive activity. —**am'bitious** *adj.*

ambulance ('ambyoōləns) *n.* a van or other vehicle designed to carry sick or injured people to hospital.

ambush ('amboŏsh) *n.* a trap in which a force lies in wait to make an unexpected attack. —*vb.* to attack by surprise.

amenity (ə'mēniti) *n.,pl.* **amenities.** something in a place that makes life easy or convenient, e.g. good shops or a frequent bus service.

amethyst ('amithist) *n.* a clear purple or violet precious stone.

amiable ('āmiəbəl) *adj.* friendly, affectionate, or likable: *my father was an amiable man who never lost his temper.*

ammonia (ə'mōniə) *n.* a strong-smelling colourless gas made up of nitrogen and hydrogen and used in the manufacture of fertilizers.

ammunition (amyoō'nishən) *n.* materials such as gunpowder, bullets, shells, grenades, bombs, and rockets, which are used in a military attack.

amnesty ('amnisti) *n.,pl.* **amnesties.** a general pardon granted for crimes, esp. to political offenders.

amoeba (ə'mēbə) *n.* a tiny animal, visible only through a microscope, made up of only one cell, whose shape is always changing.

amount (ə'mount) *n.* quantity; sum; full value. —*vb.* (+ *to*) to add up to or equal: *the fund amounts to £20.*

amphibian (am'fibiən) *n.* 1. an animal able to live both on land and in water. 2. a tank or other vehicle adapted to travel on land and in water. —**am'phibious** *adj.*

amphitheatre ('amfithiətə) *n.* a round or oval open area or building in which seats are arranged in tiers around and above a central stage or arena, used for plays, games, etc., esp. in classical times.

ample ('ampəl) *adj.* 1. large or spacious: *the house has two ample living rooms.* 2. more than enough: *two cakes will be ample for me.*

amplify ('amplifī) *vb.* **amplifying, amplified.** 1. to enlarge or expand (a statement, description, etc.). 2. to make louder. **'amplifier** *n.* a piece of electrical equipment used to increase the sound volume of record players, musical instruments, etc.

amputate ('ampyoōtāt) *vb.* **amputating, amputated.** to cut off (a hand, arm, leg, etc.), usu. by a surgical operation. —**ampu'tation** *n.*

amuse (ə'myoōz) *vb.* **amusing, amused.** 1. to entertain or occupy pleasantly. 2. to make (a person) smile or laugh. —**a'musement** *n.*

anaesthetic (anis'thetik) *n.* a drug or other agent used to put a person to sleep or produce loss of feeling in a part of his body. Anaesthetics are used in surgical operations. **anaesthetize** (ə'nēsthətīz) *vb.* **anaesthetizing, anaesthetized.** to treat (a person or part of the body) with an anaesthetic. —**a'naesthetist** *n.*

analyse ('anəlīz) *vb.* **analysing, analysed.** 1. to examine or separate (something) into its parts in order to learn what it is made up of: *the*

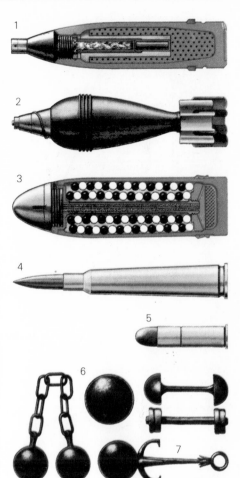

ammunition: 1 high explosive shell; 2 light mortar; 3 shrapnel shell; 4 high velocity rifle bullet; 5 revolver cartridge; 6 cannonball; 7 assortment of chain and bar shot.

chemist analysed the drink to see if it contained poison. 2. to study all the details of (something): *having analysed the situation I can see no easy solution.* **analysis** (ə'nalisis) *n.,pl.* **analyses** (ə'nalisēz). the act or result of analysing something.

anarchy ('anəki) *n.* a state of society without any law or government.

anarchist ('anəkist) *n.* a person who does not believe in government or authority. —**'anarchism** *n.*

anatomy (ə'natəmi) *n.,pl.* **anatomies.** 1. the study of the structure of the body. 2. the structure of the human body or an animal or plant. —**anatomical** (anə'tomikəl) *adj.* —**a'natomist** *n.*

ancestor ('ansestə) *n.* a person from whom one is descended, esp. a long-dead relative. —**an'cestral** *adj.* —**'ancestry** *n.,pl.* **ancestries.**

anchor: 1 admiralty type; 2 stockless.

anchor ('angkə) *n.* 1. a heavy metal object used for securing a ship to the sea bottom. 2. anything that ties down, fastens, or gives security. —*vb.* 1. to lower the anchor of (a ship, etc.). 2. to tie up or make secure.

ancient ('ānshənt) *adj.* 1. belonging to the earliest times: *an ancient tradition.* 2. very old: *an ancient man.* **ancient history** the study of Greek and Roman times up to the 5th century A.D.

anecdote ('anikdōt) *n.* a short and often funny story, esp. about a real event.

angel ('ānjəl) *n.* 1. (in the Christian and other religions) an immortal being acting as an attendant to God and a messenger between God and man, usu. represented in pictures as having human form and wings. 2. anyone thought of as being particularly good. —**angelic** (an'jelik) *adj.*

anger ('anggə) *n.* a feeling of fury or resentment caused by real or imagined wrong. —*vb.* to make angry; enrage: *her silence angered him.*

angle[1] ('anggəl) *n.* 1. a measure of the space between two straight lines extending from a common point. 2. the shape of a projecting corner. 3. a way of looking at things; viewpoint. **at an angle** slanting; diverging from a straight line. —*vb.* **angling, angled.** to point, divert, or propel at an angle: *the footballer angled the ball towards the goal.*

angle[2] ('anggəl) *vb.* **angling, angled.** 1. to fish with a rod and line. 2. (+ *for*) to invite or try for by sly or clever means: *he angled for a compliment.* —**'angler** *n.*

Anglican ('angglikən) *adj.* belonging to the Church of England. —*n.* a member of the Church of England.

angular ('anggyoolə) *adj.* 1. having or displaying angles or sharp edges. 2. bony; thin: *an angular face.* 3. acting or moving awkwardly; stiff.

animal ('animəl) *n.* 1. any living thing that is not a plant. 2. any living thing except a plant or human being. 3. a mammal, as distinguished from a reptile, fish, or bird.

animate *vb.* (an'imāt) **animating, animated.** 1. to give life to (something); make alive. 2. to make lively. —*adj.* (an'imit) alive; living: *plants are animate objects.* **animated** *adj.* (an'imātid) 1. full of life; lively. 2. appearing to be alive or moving: *an animated cartoon.*

ankle ('angkəl) *n.* the part of a person's leg between the foot and the shin.

annex (ə'neks) *vb.* 1. to join or add something to something larger or more important; unite. 2. to take political control or possession of (territory, another country, etc.): *the Emperor annexed a neighbouring state.* **annexe** *or* **annex** ('aniks) *n.* something that is added or joined, esp. a small building to a larger one: *a hotel annexe.*

annihilate (ə'nīəlāt) *vb.* **annihilating, annihilated.** 1. to destroy completely; obliterate: *the town was annihilated by enemy bombs.* 2. (informal) to defeat heavily; overwhelm: *the visiting football team annihilated the opposition.* —**annihi'lation** *n.*

anniversary (ani'vûsəri) *n.,pl.* **anniversaries.** a special day that marks an event, such as a wedding, that took place on that date in some previous year.

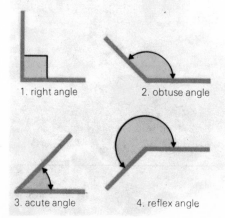

1. right angle   2. obtuse angle
3. acute angle   4. reflex angle

angle

announce (ə'nouns) *vb.* **announcing, announced.** 1. to tell or say publicly; proclaim. 2. to make known the arrival or presence of. 3. to make aware of through the senses: *the smell from the kitchen announced that lunch was ready.* **an'nouncer** *n.* someone who announces, esp. on radio or television. **the Annunciation** the angel Gabriel's act of telling the Virgin Mary that she was to become the mother of Jesus Christ. —**an'nouncement** *n.*

annoy (ə'noi) *vb.* to irritate, bother, disturb, or cause trouble. —**an'noyance** *n.*

annual ('anyooəl) *adj.* 1. concerning or relating to a year: *annual income.* 2. occurring or recurring every year; yearly: *an annual holiday.* 3. (of a plant) living for only one year or growing season. —*n.* 1. a plant living for only one year or growing season. 2. a yearly publication, such as a children's book containing stories, games, puzzles, and pictures. —**'annually** *adv.*

annunciation (ənunsi'āshən) *n.* See under ANNOUNCE.

anonymous (ə'noniməs) *adj.* 1. coming from an unknown or unnamed author or source: *an anonymous gift.* 2. undistinguished or unremarkable; lacking individuality: *the stranger is lost in the anonymous streets.* —**anonymity** (anə'nimiti) *n.* —**a'nonymously** *adv.*

anorak ('anərak) *n.* a warm waterproof jacket, usu. with a hood, designed to protect the wearer from cold and wind.

answer ('ânsə) *n.* a reply to a question, suggestion, etc.; response. —*vb.* make an answer to (a person or question). **'answerable** *adj.* (+ *for*) responsible.

ant (ant) *n.* any of several kinds of small insect that live in complex social groups.

antarctic (ant'âktik) *adj.* (sometimes **Antarctic**) of or relating to the cold region of the earth surrounding the South Pole. **Ant'arctica** *or* **the Antarctic** *n.* the snow-covered continent in which the South Pole lies. Compare ARCTIC.

antelopes

gerenuk

eland

hartebeest

impala

antelope ('antilōp) *n.* one of a large and varied family of hoofed animals that eat grass, have horns on their heads, and are found mainly in Africa and Asia.

antenna (an'tena) *n., pl.* **antennae** (an'tenē) one of two long thin feelers on an insect's head. They are used for smelling and touching.

anthem ('anthəm) *n.* a song or hymn, usu. expressing a particular sentiment such as praise, patriotism, etc.: *the national anthem.*

anthology (an'tholəji) *n.,pl.* **anthologies.** a collection of poems, stories, etc., often reflecting a particular theme: *an anthology of detective stories.*

anticlockwise (anti'klokwīz) *adv.* circling in the opposite direction to that in which the hands of a clock turn: *most screws are loosened by turning them anticlockwise.*

antifreeze ('antifrēz) *n.* a liquid with a low freezing point added to the radiator of a motor vehicle to prevent the water from freezing in very cold weather.

antique (an'tēk) *adj.* 1. of or belonging to the distant past; ancient. 2. (of an article, work of art, piece of furniture, etc.) of a period relatively much earlier than the present, esp. more than a hundred years old. —*n.* an article, work of art, piece of furniture, etc., that is antique: *that table made in 1760 is an antique, and is very valuable.*

antiseptic (anti'septik) *n.* a substance used to sterilize wounds, etc., by destroying the tiny organisms that cause infection. —*adj.* preventing infection.

antler ('antlə) *n.* one of the bony growths, usu. having branches, on the head of a deer. Antlers are cast off and grown again every year.

anvil ('anvil) *n.* an iron block on which metals, usu. heated until they are soft, can be beaten.

anxiety (aṅg'zīiti) *n.,pl.* **anxieties.** uneasiness or worry. —**anxious** ('aṅgkshəs) *adj.* —'**anxiously** *adv.*

apartment (ə'pâtmənt) *n.* a home consisting of a self-contained set of rooms within a house or building; flat.

apex ('āpeks) *n.* the top, tip, summit, or highest point of something: *the apex of a triangle.*

apology (ə'poləji) *n.,pl.* **apologies.** an admission of blame and expression of regret offered for some error, injury, offence, etc.: *he gave me an apology for his rudeness.* **a'pologize** *vb.* **apologizing, apologized.** to express an apology to someone. —**apologetic** (əpolə'jetik) *adj.*

apostle (ə'posəl) *n.* one of the original followers of Jesus Christ who spread his teaching; disciple.

apparatus (apə'ratəs) *n.,pl.* **apparatus** *or* **apparatuses.** a collection of instruments, tools, or other equipment used for a specific purpose, e.g. in a scientific experiment: *the photographer's apparatus.*

apparent (ə'parənt) *adj.* 1. capable of being clearly seen; visible. 2. capable of being easily understood; evident; obvious. 3. seeming; according to appearances: *he showed apparent distress at the news.*

appeal (ə'pēl) *n.* 1. an earnest request for help, mercy, etc. 2. an application to an impartial source to support a statement, settle an argument, etc. 3. (law) an application to a higher court to look again at the decision of a lower court. 4. attraction; interest: *this party has lost its appeal.* —vb. 1. to make an appeal for help or mercy or about a problem, argument, or decision. 2. (law) to make an appeal to a higher court. 3. to attract, be of interest, etc.: *the idea of a holiday appeals to me.*

appear (ə'piə) *vb.* 1. to become visible; come into sight: *she appeared in the distance.* 2. to give an impression; seem: *he appeared to be unwell.* 3. to be apparent or obvious: *it appears that we have missed the last bus.* 4. to make an appearance in public: *his new novel will appear in the spring.* 5. to come into existence: *legs appear in the tadpole when it is several weeks old.* —**ap'pearance** *n.*

appendix (ə'pendiks) *n.,pl.* **appendixes** *or* **appendices** (ə'pendisēz). 1. extra material at the end of a book or similar publication giving additional information, etc. 2. a narrow tubelike part of the digestive system, which now serves no apparent useful purpose but can become inflamed and painful. **appendicitis** (əpendi'sītis) *n.* a disease caused by inflammation of the appendix.

appetite ('apitīt) *n.* the desire for something to satisfy one's bodily needs, esp. for food and drink.

applaud (ə'plôd) *vb.* 1. to express approval, appreciation, or praise of someone, esp. by clapping the hands together. 2. to approve of or welcome: *they applauded his decision.* —**ap'plause** *n.*

apply (ə'plī) *vb.* **applying, applied.** 1. to request or offer oneself for consideration for a job, favour, etc.: *he applied for a pay rise.* 2. to be relevant or of practical use: *the rules do not apply to this game.* 3. to put something on top of something else; cover or bring into contact with: *they applied a new coat of paint.* 4. to devote to a particular use: *he applied his scientific knowledge to the problem.* 5. to connect or use (a word, description, etc.) with reference to a particular person or thing: *he applied his remarks to the whole school.* 6. to devote oneself diligently: *he applied himself to his work.* **applicant** ('aplikənt) *n.* someone who applies for a job, etc. —**applicable** ('aplikəbəl, ə'plikəbəl) *adj.* —**appli'cation** *n.*

appoint (ə'point) *vb.* 1. to select, nominate, or designate: *he was appointed chairman.* 2. to fix or determine, esp. by agreement: *they appointed next Thursday as the time for their meeting.* —**ap'pointment** *n.*

appreciate (ə'prēshiāt) *vb.* **appreciating, appreciated.** 1. to value or regard highly; esteem: *he appreciated their kindness.* 2. to be aware of: *they appreciated the difficulty of the task ahead.* 3. to increase in value. —**appreci'ation** *n.*

apprentice (ə'prentis) *n.* 1. a person who is learning a trade or craft, usu. receiving quite low wages in return for instruction from his employer: *a carpenter's apprentice.* 2. any beginner in a craft, skill, or profession. —**ap'prenticeship** *n.* a period served as an apprentice.

approach (ə'prōch) *vb.* 1. to come nearer or near to: *they approached the house.* 2. to make a proposal or advance to (someone): *he approached the sergeant with his plan.* —*n.* 1. the act of coming near: *their approach was very noisy.* 2. the means of access to a place, such as a road: *the approach to the house.* 3. the act or method of making contact with or presenting a proposal to someone or of dealing with a problem: *her approach to the job was original.*

appropriate *adj.* (ə'prōpriit) suitable or fitting: *his closing remarks were very appropriate.* —*vb.* (ə'propriāt) **appropriating, appropriated.** 1. to set aside, esp. for a particular purpose: *the university appropriated funds for the new building.* 2. to take over for oneself: *he appropriated the cricket bat and would let no one else use it.*

approve (ə'prōōv) *vb.* **approving, approved.** to agree to; officially confirm: *the committee approved their plans.* **approve of** to regard favourably; think well of: *he approved of her new dress.* **ap'proval** *n.* 1. the act of approving or agreeing. 2. official agreement or confirmation. **on approval** (of goods) allowed to be inspected or tested without obligation to buy.

approximate *adj.* (ə'proksimit) 1. nearly exact: *the approximate time.* 2. almost or very nearly the same as: *an approximate circle.* 3. rough or inaccurate: *an approximate total.* —*vb.* (ə'proksimāt) **approximating, approximated.** 1. to estimate; guess at: *we have approximated a solution to the problem.* 2. to approach or come near to in quality, amount, style, etc.: *his painting approximates that of Picasso.* —**ap'proximately** *adv.* —**approxi'mation** *n.*

apricot ('āprikot) *n.* a soft-skinned orange-coloured fruit, which is rather like a peach and related to the plum.

aqualung (ak'wəlung) *n.* a device used by underwater swimmers consisting of cylinders of compressed air connected to a face mask.

aquarium (ə'kweəriəm) *n.,pl.* **aquaria** (ə'kweəriə) *or* **aquariums.** a tank, bowl, or pond used to keep and display fish and other water creatures and plants.

aquatic (ə'kwatik, ə'kwotik) *adj.* living in or connected with water: *aquatic sports.*

aqueduct ('akwidukt) *n.* a channel or canal made for carrying water, often over a bridge across a valley.

aqueduct

arc (âk) *n.* 1. part of the circumference of a circle or of some other curved line. 2. anything bow-shaped. See GEOMETRY.

arch (âch) *n.* 1. a curved structure, often over an entrance or sometimes supporting a bridge, and generally made of stone or brick. 2. (also **archway**) a passageway or entrance with a curved roof. 3. the curved part of the sole of the foot between the ball and the heel. 4. anything that is curved like an arch. —*vb.* to form an arched shape: *the angry cat arched its back.*

archaeology (âki'oləji) *n.* the study of ancient or prehistoric times based on the evidence of relics and remains. —**archaeo'logical** *adj.* —**archae-'ologist** *n.*

archbishop (âch'bishəp) *n.* a bishop of the highest rank with authority over other bishops.

archer ('âchə) *n.* a person who shoots with a bow and arrows. '**archery** *n.* the art and practice of shooting with a bow and arrows.

architect ('âkitekt) *n.* a person who plans and designs buildings. '**architecture** *n.* 1. the art of building. 2. the style of building. —**archi'tectural** *adj.*

arctic ('âktik) *adj.* 1. (sometimes **Arctic**) of or relating to the cold region of the earth surrounding the North Pole. 2. extremely cold. **the Arctic** the area of ice-covered seas and islands in which the North Pole is situated. Compare ANTARCTIC.

area ('eəriə) *n.* 1. a region or district: *a country area.* 2. any space: *a shopping area.* 3. the general scope of a subject, field of study, or activity: *in the area of drama.* 4. the size of the surface of a square, circle, etc.

arena (ə'rēnə) *n.* 1. the central circular or oval area in a Roman AMPHITHEATRE or a modern sports stadium. 2. any area where action takes place: *the political arena.*

argue ('âgyoo) *vb.* **arguing, argued.** 1. to disagree or quarrel with someone. 2. to discuss (a matter, etc.) with someone. —'**argument** *n.*

arid ('arid) *adj.* 1. (of land) dry; parched; infertile or barren. 2. dull and uninteresting; fruitless. —**aridity** (ə'riditi) *or* '**aridness** *n.*

armour ('âmə) *n.* 1. protective covering, usu. made of metal and formerly worn to shield the body in battle. 2. heavy metal plates used to protect tanks, warships, etc.

army ('âmi) *n.,pl.* **armies.** 1. a nation's military force specially trained for war. 2. a huge throng: *an army of ants.*

arrange (ə'rānj) *vb.* **arranging, arranged.** 1. to put in order: *please arrange these flowers.* 2. to organize, fix, or plan: *I will arrange a trip to the beach.* 3. to adapt a musical composition for different instruments or voices. —**ar'rangement** *n.*

arrest (ə'rest) *vb.* 1. to seize (a suspected criminal) by warrant or other authority; take into custody. 2. to stop or check (movement, process, etc.): *the doctor was able to arrest the bleeding immediately.* 3. to capture and hold (a person's attention. etc.). —*n.* the act of arresting.

arrive (ə'rīv) *vb.* **arriving, arrived.** 1. to come to be present at a place or point in time; come to; reach. 2. (of a time) to be or come: *the day of the wedding at last arrived.* **ar'rival** *n.* 1. the act of arriving. 2. a person or thing that arrives.

arrow ('arō) *n.* 1. a thin straight stick or shaft sharpened to a point at one end with feathers at the other, which help to guide it through the air when shot from a bow. 2. a sign like an arrow used to indicate direction.

arsenic ('âsnik) *n.* a chemical element, greyish-white in colour, that is used in rat poisons, medicines, etc. Chemical symbol: As.

artery ('âtəri) *n.,pl.* **arteries.** 1. a vessel in the body that carries blood away from the heart. 2. the main channel in a series of smaller ones as in a road or drainage system. —**arterial** (â'tiəriəl) *adj.*

artful ('âtfəl) *adj.* 1. crafty; cunning: *the artful fox stole all the chickens.* 2. skilful or ingenious. —'**artfully** *adv.* —'**artfulness** *n.*

article ('âtikəl) *n.* 1. a piece of writing on a specific topic, esp. in a newspaper or magazine. 2. any individual object: *an article of furniture.* 3. (in some languages) a word that precedes and signifies a noun, as in English, 'the' (definite article) and 'a' or 'an' (indefinite article).

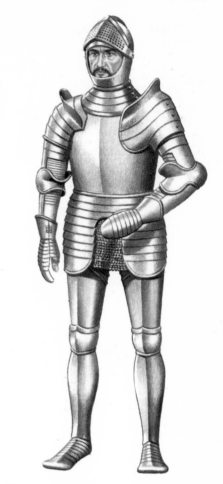

armour

artificial (âti'fishəl) *adj.* not made or occurring in nature; not natural. —**arti'ficially** *adv.*

artillery (â'tiləri) *n.* 1. large guns, cannons, and similar military weapons considered collectively. 2. the troops or the branch of an army responsible for such weapons: *the Royal Artillery.*

artist ('âtist) *n.* 1. a painter or sculptor. 2. a stage performer, such as a singer, musician, actor, etc. —**ar'tistic** *adj.* —**ar'tistically** *adv.*

ascend (ə'send) *vb.* 1. to move upward; climb. 2. to go upward along (a certain course): *they ascend the staircase.* **as'cent** *n.* 1. the act of going up. 2. a way of ascending. —**as'cension** *n.*

ash[1] (ash) *n.* 1. the fine powder or other material that is left after something has burnt. 2. the powdery lava emitted by an erupting volcano. 3. **ashes** (*pl.*) the remains of a body after it has been cremated. '**ashen** *adj.* pale, e.g. because of grief: *his face was ashen.*

ash

ash² (ash) *n.* 1. a DECIDUOUS tree common in Europe, North America, and parts of Asia, that bears black velvety buds in early spring, and has a tough grey-brown bark. 2. the wood of this tree used as timber.

ashamed (ə'shāmd) *adj.* 1. feeling shame, guilt, or embarrassment. 2. unwilling to do something through fear of disapproval: *he was ashamed to admit that he had lost his money.*

asparagus (ə'sparəgəs) *n.* a vegetable consisting of the young tender shoots (spears) of a plant of the lily family.

asphalt ('asfalt, 'asfelt, 'ashfelt) *n.* a substance made partly from earth minerals and partly from industrial materials, used to cover roads. —*vb.* to cover (a road) with asphalt.

aspirin ('asprin) *n.* a chemical substance usu. taken in white tablet form for the relief of headache, toothache, rheumatism, and other pains.

assassinate (ə'sasināt) *vb.* **assassinating, assassinated.** to kill a person of prominence, esp. for political or religious reasons. **as'sassin** *n.* a person who assassinates someone. —**assassi'nation** *n.*

assault (ə'sôlt) *n.* the act of attacking violently. —*vb.* to attack with violence.

assemble (ə'sembəl) *vb.* **assembling, assembled.** 1. to bring or gather together in one place. 2. to fit together the different parts of (a machine, model, etc.). **as'sembly** *n.,pl.* **assemblies.** a collection of people or things that have been assembled. **assembly line** (in a factory) an arrangement of machines and workers each performing separate tasks in the production of a particular article.

assess (ə'ses) *vb.* 1. to estimate (the value of income, property, etc.), e.g. for taxation or insurance purposes. 2. to determine the amount of (a fine, tax, etc.): *damages were assessed at £5000.* 3. to judge or evaluate: *he assessed the student's work.* —**as'sessment** *n.* —**as'sessor** *n.*

assist (ə'sist) *vb.* to help or aid (someone). —**as'sistance** *n.* —**as'sistant** *n.*

associate *vb.* (ə'sōsiāt) **associating, associated.** 1. to connect or relate in thought: *we associate war with suffering.* 2. to join as a friend, partner, etc.; keep company: *she only associates with the rich.* —*n.* (ə'sōsiit) a friend or colleague. —*adj.* (ə'sōsiit) 1. joined or related for companionship, business, etc.: *an associate partner.* 2. not possessing full rights or privileges: *an associate member.* **associ'ation** *n.* 1. the act of associating. 2. companionship. 3. a group of people joined together for some common purpose; organization; society: *a tenants' association.* **association football** see SOCCER. —**as'sociative** *adj.*

assorted (ə'sôtid) *adj.* consisting of various kinds: *assorted sweets.* **as'sortment** *n.* an assorted collection; mixture; range: *an assortment of different people.*

assume (ə'syōōm) *vb.* **assuming, assumed.** 1. to take for granted without being positive; presume; suppose: *I assumed he was coming.* 2. to take on (a new role, task, etc.): *she assumed leadership of the group.* —**assumption** (ə'sumpshən) *n.*

assure (ə'shŏŏə) *vb.* **assuring, assured.** 1. to declare positively so as to be believed: *they assured us that the bridge was safe.* 2. to ensure; make certain; guarantee: *his excellent performance assures him a place in the team.* **as'sured** *adj.* 1. made certain; guaranteed. 2. self-confident. **as'surance** *n.* 1. a positive statement giving confidence, encouragement, etc. 2. self-confidence; trust. 3. life insurance.

astonish (ə'stonish) *vb.* to amaze; surprise greatly. **as'tonishment** *n.* amazement.

astronaut ('astrənôt) *n.* a person who pilots, navigates, or is a member of the crew of a spacecraft. **astro'nautics** *n.* the science or study connected with the principles and techniques of space flight.

astronomy (ə'stronəmi) *n.* the study of the sun, moon, planets, and stars. —**as'tronomer** *n.* **astronomical** (astrə'nomikəl) *adj.* 1. connected with or used in astronomy: *an astronomical telescope.* 2. very large; great or considerable: *the expense was astronomical.*

athlete ('athlēt) *n.* a person trained and skilful in contests of strength, speed, endurance, etc., esp. in sports events, such as running, jumping, and throwing (track and field events). **athletic** (ath'letik) *adj.* 1. of or relating to an athlete or athletics. 2. strong, well-built, or agile. **ath'letics** *n.* a branch of sport consisting of track and field events.

atlas ('atləs) *n.* a collection of maps bound into a book.

atmosphere ('atməsfiə) *n.* 1. the layer of gas that surrounds the earth, consisting mainly of nitrogen and oxygen; the AIR. 2. the particular nature or quality of the air in an enclosed space: *a smoky atmosphere.* 3. the effect created by one's surroundings: *a calm atmosphere.* —**atmospheric** (atməs'ferik) *or* **atmos'pherical** *adj.*

atom ('atəm) *n.* one of the tiny particles of which all matter is formed. Every atom contains a NUCLEUS. **atom bomb** (also **atomic bomb**) a very powerful bomb whose force is created by the splitting of atoms. —**atomic** (ə'tomik) *adj.*

atrocious (ə'trōshəs) *adj.* 1. very cruel or brutal; wicked; evil: *an atro-*

cious crime had been committed. 2. (informal) bad; awful: *we had an atrocious time.* **atrocity** (ə'trositi) *n.,pl.* **atrocities.** a brutal or cruel act.

attach (ə'tach) *vb.* 1. to connect or fasten; join; fix: *he attached a new TV aerial to the roof.* 2. to assign or ascribe: *we don't attach much importance to trivial events.* **attached to** 1. personally involved with or fond of: *they were very attached to each other.* 2. appointed to a specific task or role: *he is attached to the British embassy in Washington.* —**at'tachment** *n.*

attack (ə'tak) *vb.* 1. to make a hostile and violent move against someone: *the enemy attacked unexpectedly.* 2. to criticize fiercely or harshly: *his statements were attacked by the press.* —*n.* 1. a hostile violent move: *an enemy attack.* 2. strong criticism. 3. a sudden violent spell of illness, pain, etc.

attain (ə'tān) *vb.* 1. to reach: *Bill has attained the age of 90.* 2. to accomplish: *the scientist attained fame while he was alive.*

attempt (ə'tempt) *vb.* to try; to make an effort (to do something). —*n.* 1. an effort or try. 2. an unsuccessful attack on someone's life: *a murder attempt.*

attend (ə'tend) *vb.* 1. to be present at (a meeting, school, etc.): *I attend classes three times a week.* 2. to wait on or serve: *a lady-in-waiting attends the Queen.* **attend to** 1. to listen to; pay attention. 2. to deal with; look after or manage: *we attend to 50 complaints a week.* **at'tendant** *n.* a person who looks after someone or something. —**at'tendance** *n.*

attention (ə'tenshən) *n.* 1. the concentration of one's mind on something or someone: *may I have your attention please!* 2. notice: *the strange noise attracted his attention.* 3. care or treatment; service: *this patient requires special attention.* —*interj.* 1. a military command to stand upright with the arms at the sides, heels together, and the head facing forwards. 2. a warning or request to take care, watch closely, listen carefully, etc. **at'tentive** *adj.* paying attention.

attic ('atik) *n.* a room directly under the roof of a house.

attitude ('atityōod) *n.* a particular belief, opinion, feeling, or type of behaviour towards someone or something: *her attitude towards him was one of curiosity.*

attract (ə'trakt) *vb.* 1. to draw or cause to draw closer; pull nearer. 2. to arouse the interest or claim the attention of: *her beautiful smile attracted him.* —**at'traction** *n.* —**at'tractive** *adj.*

auburn ('ôbən) *adj.* (esp. of hair) of a reddish-brown colour.

auction ('ôkshən) *n.* a public sale in which animals, houses, furniture, etc., are sold to the person who bids the most money. —*vb.* to sell by auction. **auction'eer** *n.* a person who conducts an auction and accepts bids for items being sold.

audience ('ôdiəns) *n.* listeners; spectators in a theatre, cinema, etc.

au pair (ō 'peə) *n.* a person, usu. a foreign girl learning English, who lives with a family and helps in the house in exchange for board and lodging and pocket money.

authentic (ô'thentik) *adj.* 1. true, reliable, or valid. 2. genuine or real: *the painting was not an authentic Picasso but a skilful forgery.* —**au'thentically** *adv.* —**authenticity** (ôthen'tisiti) *n.*

author ('ôthə) *n.* 1. a person who writes books that are published. 2. the originator or creator (of a plan, scheme, etc.).

authority (ô'thoriti) *n.,pl.* **authorities.** 1. the power or right to control, judge, or demand obedience. 2. sometimes **authorities** (*pl.*) a person or group, such as the government, police, etc., with such power. 3. an expert: *he is an authority on antiques.* **authorize** ('ôthərīz) *vb.* **authorizing, authorized.** to give (someone) power or authority; sanction. —**authori'zation** *n.*

autograph ('ôtəgrâf) *n.* a signature (esp. of a famous person) written in his own handwriting. —*vb.* to sign one's name: *the author autographed his latest book.*

automatic (ôtə'matik) *adj.* 1. (of a machine) able to operate independently; self-regulating. 2. occurring as a matter of routine, without conscious effort or thought. —*n.* a firearm capable of reloading itself and firing repeatedly when the trigger is pulled. **automation** (ôtə'māshən) *n.* the use of automatic machinery in industry. —**auto'matically** *adv.*

autumn ('ôtəm) *n.* the season following summer. —*adj.* (also **autumnal** (ô'tumnəl)) of or occurring in the autumn.

available (ə'vāləbəl) *adj.* able to be obtained or used: *are there any tickets available?*

avocado (avə'kâdo) *n.,pl.* **avocados.** (also **avocado pear**) a tough-skinned pear-shaped tropical fruit.

avocado

avoid (ə'void) *vb.* to keep or turn away from someone or something. —**a'voidance** *n.*

award (ə'wôd) *n.* something given as a token of honour; prize. —*vb.* to give (a prize, money, etc.): *the judges awarded him first prize.*

awe (ô) *n.* a sense of deep respect, fear, or wonder. —*vb.* **awing, awed.** to fill with awe. —**'awesome** *adj.*

awful ('ôfəl) *adj.* terrible; extremely bad: *that's an awful dress.* **'awfully** *adv.* very: *Donald is an awfully good pianist.*

awkward ('ôkwəd) *adj.* 1. clumsy; unskilful; not elegant. 2. badly designed: *an awkward shape.* 3. embarrassing or inconvenient: *an awkward silence.* 4. hard to deal with; difficult: *the boss is an awkward customer.* —**'awkwardly** *adv.* —**'awkwardness** *n.*

axe (aks) *n.* a sharp-bladed tool with a long wooden handle, usu. used for chopping wood. —*vb.* **axing, axed.** to cut down drastically on money spent on something: *student grants will be axed.* See TOOL.

axle ('aksəl) *n.* the rod or bar on which a wheel turns.

B

baboon (bə'boon) *n.* a large short-tailed monkey with a doglike face and large sharp teeth.

bachelor ('bachələ) *n.* 1. an unmarried man. 2. a person who has obtained his first degree at a university: *Bachelor of Science (BSc).*

backbone ('bakbōn) *n.* 1. the spine. 2. moral strength; courage: *a coward is a person with no backbone.*

backfire ('bakfīə) *vb.* **backfiring, backfired.** 1. (of a car engine) to produce an unexpected explosion of unburnt fuel in the exhaust pipe. 2. (of a plan) to fail and cause harm to the person who made it up.

background ('bakground) *n.* 1. that part of a scene that is furthest away from the observer. Compare FOREGROUND. 2. a person's past experience, family history, education, etc.: *she comes from a musical background.* 3. information that adds to one's understanding of a situation; context. **in the background** out of direct view; not prominent: *keep well in the background.*

backlog ('baklog) *n.* a large amount of work not yet done, unpaid debts, etc.

backward ('bakwəd) *adj.* 1. moving or directed towards the back: *a back-ward glance.* 2. slow to learn: *a backward child.* 3. (of a nation) undeveloped; uncivilized. 4. shy or reluctant. **'backwards** *or* **'backward** *adv.* 1. towards the back. 2. in reverse. 3. with the back end foremost. 4. into the past.

bacon ('bākən) *n.* the meat of a pig, taken from its back and sides and salted and dried.

bacteria (bak'tiəriə) *pl.n.* the tiny organisms belonging to the plant kingdom that cause decay and certain diseases. They also help to produce alcohol from sugar in making beer or wine. —**bac'terial** *adj.*

bade *or* **bad** (bad) *vb.* the past tense of BID (vb. defs. 4–6).

badger ('bajə) *n.* a dark grey burrowing animal related to the weasel, with a black-and-white-banded head. It is found in Europe, Asia, and North America. —*vb.* to pester; keep on at: *the children badgered him to tell them a story.*

badminton ('badmintən) *n.* a game similar to tennis but played on a shorter court, with a higher net and a shuttlecock instead of a ball.

baffle ('bafəl) *vb.* **baffling, baffled.** to bewilder; make (a person) feel puzzled and at a loss: *she was baffled by the corridors leading off in all directions.* —**'bafflement** *n.*

bagpipes ('bagpīps) *pl.n.* a musical instrument in which reed pipes are played by means of air supplied from a bag inflated by the player's mouth or by a pair of bellows held under the arm.

bail¹ (bāl) *n.* a sum of money paid to a law court in certain circumstances by or on behalf of a person accused of a crime, which allows him to leave prison. The money is forfeited if the person fails to appear at his trial. **go** *or* **stand bail (for)** to pay (a person's) bail. —*vb.* (+ *out*) 1. to secure (a person's) release from custody by paying

bail. 2. to rescue (someone) from an awkward or dangerous situation.

bail² (bāl) *n.* one of two small pieces of wood put on top of the three stumps in cricket.

bail³ *or* **bale** (bāl) *vb.* **bailing** *or* **baling, bailed** *or* **baled.** (often + *out*) to scoop (water) out of a boat. —*n.* (also **bailer**) a scoop used for bailing a boat.

bait (bāt) *n.* 1. scraps of meat or fish, worms, or imitation food put on a hook to attract and catch fish or in a trap to catch animals. 2. anything that attracts or tempts a person towards something. —*vb.* 1. to put bait on or in. 2. to tease and enrage.

balance ('baləns) *n.* 1. a device for weighing things, usu. having two dishes or pans hung from each end of a bar or beam supported at its exact centre. 2. the ability to stand upright; equilibrium: *it's easy to lose your balance on skates.* 3. a state in which differences have been evened out or all aspects agree and harmonize: *the right balance of high and low voices is important in forming a choir.* 4. the amount left over or due when money paid has been subtracted from money owing; remainder: *give me half now and you can pay the balance next week.* 5. the remainder of anything. 6. the part of a clock or watch that controls its speed. —*vb.* **balancing,**

bagpipes

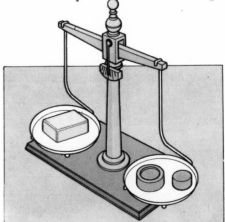
balance

14

balanced. 1. to place or keep or be placed or kept in a state of balance: *sealions balance balls on their noses; tightrope walkers balance on ropes.* 2. to even up; achieve a balance. **'balanced** *or* **well-'balanced** *adj.* even-tempered and in good mental health.

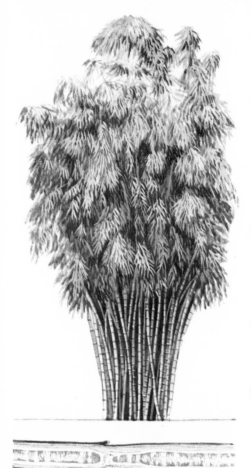

bamboo

balcony ('balkəni) *n.,pl.* **balconies.** 1. a narrow railed or walled platform built out from an upper floor of a building. 2. the gallery in a theatre or cinema.

bald (bôld) *adj.* 1. having no hair on the head. 2. lacking natural fur, feathers, leaves, etc.; bare. 3. without detail or disguise: *a bald statement.* —**'baldly** *adv.* —**'baldness** *n.*

bale[1] (bāl) *n.* a bundle of goods, esp. hay, wool, cotton, etc., packed for transportation. —*vb.* **baling, baled.** to make into bales.

bale[2] (bāl) *vb.* **baling, baled.** (usu. + *out*) 1. to parachute out of an aircraft in an emergency. 2. to abandon at the last minute: *just as the plans were completed, he baled out of the project.*

baleful ('bālfəl) *adj.* with evil intentions; harmful. —**'balefully** *adv.* —**'balefulness** *n.*

ballad ('baləd) *n.* 1. a simple poem that tells a story, usu. in a number of short verses. 2. a romantic song.

ballet ('balā) *n.* 1. a form of dancing in which intricate steps, exaggerated movements, and mime are used, often telling a story. 2. an entertainment or a piece of music written for such dancing.

balloon (bə'loon) *n.* 1. a prettily coloured rubber bag that may be blown up with air or other gas and used as a child's toy. 2. a gas-filled inflatable bag used for carrying a container of cargo or passengers through the atmosphere. —*vb.* 1. to swell or cause to swell like a balloon. 2. to travel by balloon.

ballot ('balət) *n.* 1. the card, sheet, or ticket used for voting. 2. a method of secret voting in which cards, etc., are put into a box (**ballot box**). 3. the voting process. —*vb.* to vote by means of a ballot.

bamboo (bam'boo) *n.* a tall grass that grows mainly in tropical regions, having stems used to make furniture, baskets, paper, etc.

banana (bə'nânə) *n.* 1. a long bow-shaped fruit grown in hot climates. It has a yellow or green skin surrounding a soft pulpy flesh. 2. the broad-leaved tree on which bananas grow.

band[1] (band) *n.* 1. a thin narrow strip of metal, rubber, etc., used to hold things together. 2. a strip of material used as a trimming, binding, or decoration, as in a waistband, headband, etc. 3. a coloured stripe. —*vb.* to put or place a band on something.

band[2] (band) *n.* 1. a group of people doing something together: *a band of actors.* 2. a number of musicians who play music for marching, dancing, or for outdoor entertainment. —*v.* (often + *together*) to unite in a band.

bandage ('bandij) *n.* a strip of material used to cover and protect a wound. —*vb.* **bandaging, bandaged.** to put a bandage on a wound.

banish ('banish) *vb.* 1. to expel (a person) from a country; drive into exile. 2. to send off; dismiss from one's mind. —**'banishment** *n.*

banjo ('banjō) *n.,pl.* **banjos.** a musical instrument like a guitar, used mainly in jazz or folk music and having a long neck, a round body, and a set of strings played by plucking.

banjo

bankrupt ('bangkrupt) *n.* a person unable to pay his debts and whose remaining money and possessions are legally removed so that they can be shared out fairly among his creditors. —*vb.* to make (someone) bankrupt. —*adj.* 1. declared to be a bankrupt; insolvent. 2. (of a business) failed or collapsed. 3. completely empty; devoid: *the play was bankrupt of ideas.* —**'bankruptcy** *n.,pl.* **'bankruptcies.**

banner ('banə) *n.* 1. a flag often bearing a slogan carried between two poles on a march or at a rally, sports match, etc. 2. a flag bearing a pattern, coat of arms, etc., carried on a single pole; standard. 3. a cause or faith.

banquet ('bangkwit) *n.* a large, often formal, feast. —*vb.* to be at or have a banquet.

baptism ('baptizəm) *n.* (in the Christian Church) a ceremony in which a person is christened and sprinkled with or plunged into water so that he may be cleansed of sin. **baptism of fire** 1. a soldier's first experience of war. 2. an unpleasant first experience. **baptize** ('baptīz) *vb.* **baptizing, baptized.** to perform a baptism on (someone).

barbarian (bâ'beəriən) *n.* an uncivilized or primitive person. —*adj.* rough and uncultured: *barbarian manners.* **barbaric** (bâ'barik) *adj.* 1. of or like a barbarian. 2. crude or vulgar in style, taste, etc. —**barbarism** ('bâbərizəm) *n.*

barbarity (bâˈbariti) *n.,pl.* **barbarities.** a brutal and savage act or practice; cruelty: *the barbarity of torture.* **barbarous** (ˈbâbərəs) *adj.* 1. savagely cruel or brutal; atrocious. 2. (of language) nonstandard; unrefined: *a barbarous form of English.*

barbecue (ˈbâbikyoō) *n.* 1. a meal usu. consisting of meat roasted over a charcoal grill and generally eaten out of doors. 2. an outdoor party at which barbecues are served. 3. an iron frame or grill over which barbecues are prepared. —*vb.* **barbecuing, barbecued.** to roast over a charcoal grill.

barber (ˈbâbə) *n.* a person whose job it is to cut men's hair and shave or trim their beards.

bare (beə) *adj.* 1. naked; uncovered: *bare feet.* 2. lacking equipment, decoration, furnishings, etc.: *the room was almost bare of furniture.* 3. scanty; mere: *a bare handful of people.* **lay bare** to uncover or expose (a secret, etc.). —*vb.* **baring, bared.** to uncover; reveal. ˈ**barely** *adv.* 1. nakedly; thinly; sparsely. 2. hardly; scarcely; only just: *there was barely enough to feed us all.* —ˈ**bareness** *n.*

bargain (ˈbâgən) *n.* 1. an agreement between two or more sides: *the bargain was that she would do the shopping if he would do the cooking.* 2. a surprisingly cheap purchase; a good buy. **drive a hard bargain** to stick persistently to one's prices or conditions. **into the bargain** in addition; on top of everything else. **strike** *or* **make a bargain** to reach agreement. —*vb.* (usu. + *with*) to discuss in order to make a bargain; negotiate. **bargain for** to expect or anticipate; be prepared for: *the tickets cost more than we bargained for.*

barge (bâj) *n.* 1. a low flat boat used on canals, rivers, and lakes for transporting goods. 2. an open low boat used for pageants or ceremonies on water. —*vb.* **barging, barged.** (+ *about, in, into,* etc.) to move clumsily or rudely: *stop barging about the house!*

bark[1] (bâk) *n.* 1. the loud abrupt cry made by dogs, foxes, seals, etc. 2. a sudden shout similar to a dog's: *he gave a bark of contempt.* —*vb.* to utter or make a bark. **bark up the wrong tree** to be mistaken or make efforts in the wrong direction.

bark[2] (bâk) *n.* the woody outer covering of a tree trunk and branches.

—*vb.* to scrape (one's skin); graze badly.

barley (ˈbâli) *n.* a grain-producing grass similar to wheat but with long feathery whiskers, used for food and in making beer and whisky.

barometer (bəˈromitə) *n.* an instrument for measuring atmospheric pressure, used to show changing weather conditions. —**barometric** (barəˈmetrik) *adj.*

barometer

baron (ˈbarən) *n.* a nobleman belonging to the lowest rank of the peerage.

barracks (ˈbarəks) *pl.n.* buildings for housing soldiers, often at an army camp.

barrel (ˈbarəl) *n.* 1. a cylindrical container often made of wooden slats bound with hoops, generally used for storing liquids. 2. the tubular metal part of a gun through which a bullet is fired.

barren (ˈbarən) *adj.* 1. (of land) unable to produce crops; infertile or arid. 2. unable to bear offspring. 3. useless; unprofitable: *a barren task.* —ˈ**barrenness** *n.*

barricade (ˈbarikād) *n.* a temporary makeshift barrier set up to block a street or passageway. —*vb.* **barricading, barricaded.** to obstruct in order to prevent access; block: *the men barricaded the door to keep the soldiers out.*

barrier (ˈbariə) *n.* 1. an obstacle such as a fence, wall, or gate, erected to prevent or control access and often used to mark a boundary or limit. 2. anything that prevents communication or progress: *a language barrier.*

barrow[1] (ˈbarō) *n.* a small handcart, esp. with one or two wheels, used for carrying loads.

barrow[2] (ˈbarō) *n.* a large mound of earth raised over a burial ground or grave in ancient times.

base[1] (bās) *n.* 1. the bottom, foundation, or support of something: *the base of a pillar.* 2. (also **basis**) the main ingredient or part of a mixture: *some paints have an oil base.* 3. a centre of operations for the army, navy, air force, business company, etc.: *a rocket base.* 4. BASIS (def.1.). 5. one of the positions to which the batter runs in baseball or rounders. —*vb.* **basing, based.** 1. to set up or establish a base. 2. to place or be placed in a military base. 3. to take as a basis or starting point: *she based her novel on her experiences in Africa.*

base[2] (bās) *adj.* low or mean; vile: *Judas was a base traitor.*

baseball (ˈbāsbôl) *n.* a game played in the U.S.A. by two teams of nine players each on a field with four bases arranged in a diamond pattern. After hitting the pitched ball with a bat, the batter attempts to run around the field and touch each base to score a run.

basement (ˈbāsmənt) *n.* the lowest storey of a building, usu. below ground level.

bashful (ˈbashfəl) *adj.* shy; hesitant; over-modest. —ˈ**bashfully** *adv.*

basic (ˈbāsik) *adj.* forming a basis or starting-point; fundamental or essential: *the basic cause of revolution is discontent.* —ˈ**basically** *adv.*

basis (ˈbāsis) *n.,pl.* **bases** (ˈbāsēz). 1. (also **base**) the foundation or principle on which something rests or can be developed: *their common interests gave them a firm basis for friendship.* 2. BASE[1] (n. def. 2).

bask (bâsk) *vb.* 1. to laze in the sunshine. 2. to revel or take delight in: *the winner basked in the applause.*

basketball (ˈbâskitbôl) *n.* a team sport played on a court with a wire hoop set at each end, the object being for each side of five players to toss the ball through the opponents' hoop as often as possible.

bass[1] (bās) *n.* the lowest male singing voice. —*adj.* 1. written for or sung by a bass. 2. lowest in sound in a class of musical instruments: *a bass trombone.*

bass² (bas) *n.* a sea or freshwater fish with large spiny fins.

bassoon (bə'sōōn) *n.* a musical wind instrument belonging to the oboe class, of which it is the largest member and the lowest in pitch.

baste (bāst) *vb.* **basting, basted.** to moisten (meat) with fat during cooking.

bat¹ (bat) *n.* a heavy wooden stick with a handle, used for striking a ball in games such as cricket and baseball. **off one's own bat** on one's own initiative; without guidance. —*vb.* **batting, batted.** to hit (a ball) with a bat. —**'batsman** *n.,pl.* **batsmen.**

bat² (bat) *n.* a small mouselike flying animal with wings of thin skin stretched over long thin bones.

batch (bach) *n.* 1. a quantity of bread, cakes, biscuits, etc., that have been prepared and baked at the same time. 2. a group of people or things taken as a set: *a batch of exam papers.*

baton ('baton) *n.* a short stick, esp. one used by a conductor to direct an orchestra or carried by an army or other officer as a symbol of his rank. A baton can also be passed between runners in a RELAY race.

batter¹ ('batə) *vb.* to beat savagely and repeatedly. **battering ram** see under RAM.

batter² ('batə) *n.* flour, milk, and eggs beaten together to form a mixture for pancakes, puddings, a coating for fish, etc.

battery ('batəri) *n.,pl.* **batteries.** 1. a device consisting of electric CELLs (def. 3) joined together to produce an electrical voltage. 2. a number of heavy guns firing from one place or the men in charge of them; artillery. 3. a series of boxes in which chickens can be cheaply reared and their eggs easily collected. 4. a large impressive set or series of anything: *a battery of cameras.* 5. the action, result, or crime of battering or beating.

battle ('batəl) *n.* 1. a violent fight or contest between enemies, esp. one using trained military forces. 2. any struggle: *a battle for higher wages.* —*vb.* **battling, battled.** 1. to fight

bassoon

fiercely: *they battled for control of the river.* 2. to struggle bravely; strive. **'battleship** *n.* a warship armed with heavy guns.

bay¹ (bā) *n.* a wide curved inlet of the sea or a lake.

bay² (bā) *n.* 1. an opening or recess in a wall or between two columns. 2. a special area set aside for parking or the loading and unloading of goods. **bay window** a window projecting out from a wall, forming a recess inside.

bay³ (bā) *vb.* (esp. of a hound picking up a scent) to bark deeply and repeatedly. —*n.* a continuous barking sound. **at bay** (esp. of a hunted animal) cornered and forced to turn and face the attacker. **hold** *or* **keep at bay** to keep at a distance; ward off.

bay⁴ (bā) *n.* a type of LAUREL whose pointed oval leaves are used to flavour food and were in ancient times woven into crowns for heroes.

bay⁵ (bā) *adj.* (of horses) of a reddish-brown colour. —*n.* a reddish-brown horse with a black mane and tail.

bayonet ('bāənit) *n.* a short steel blade fixed to the muzzle of a rifle.

beach (bēch) *n.* a stretch of sand lying beside the sea and forming part of the shore. —*vb.* to run or pull (a ship or boat) onto the beach.

beacon ('bēkən) *n.* 1. a hill-top or a fire lit on it to serve as a signal or warning. 2. a lighthouse or anything with a flashing light that warns of a danger at sea. **Belisha beacon** (bə'lēshə) a flashing orange light on top of a striped pole at a pedestrian crossing. (Named after Leslie Hore-Belisha, British Minister of Transport 1934–37.)

beak (bēk) *n.* 1. the nose and mouth of a bird; bill. 2. (slang) a MAGISTRATE.

beam (bēm) *n.* 1. a long horizontal piece of wood, metal, concrete, etc., used to bear the weight of the roof or floor of a building. 2. a ray of light, radio waves, etc. 3. the widest part of a ship. 4. a broad smile. **on one's beam ends** extremely poor. —*vb.* 1. to send out (rays of light or radio waves). 2. to smile radiantly.

bean (bēn) *n.* 1. any of several plants eaten as vegetables and having long seed-containing pods, e.g. runner bean, broad bean, soya bean. 2. the seed itself or any seed whose shape is similar, e.g. coffee bean. **full of beans** very cheerful; high-spirited.

bear¹ (beə) *vb.* **bearing, bore, borne** *or* (def. 4) **born.** 1. to carry or support; hold up: *the tallest man had to bear most of the weight.* 2. to have, show, or display: *the letter bore his signature.* 3. to tolerate or endure: *I could not bear to see her cry.* 4. to give birth to: *she is too young to bear a child.* 5. (of plants) to produce or yield: *the holly tree bears red berries.* **bear in mind** to take into account; remember. **bear out** to prove or confirm. **bear up** to keep one's courage. **bear with** to be patient and make allowances for. **'bearable** *adj.* tolerable; endurable. —**'bearer** *n.*

bear² (beə) *n.* a large brown-furred animal, found in parts of Europe, Asia, and America, that lives on both vegetation and meat. **Great Bear** and **Little Bear** two CONSTELLATIONs in the northern skies. Also called Ursa Major and Ursa Minor. **polar bear** a very large white bear found in the Arctic.

beard (biəd) *n.* 1. the hair growing on a man's face and chin. 2. anything resembling a beard, such as the tuft of hairs on a goat's jaw.

beauty ('byōōti) *n.,pl.* **beauties.** 1. the quality of being very pleasing to the senses, esp. to the eyes: *the beauty of the scenery.* 2. a person or thing that possesses this quality: *that new aeroplane is a beauty.* —**'beautiful** *adj.* —**'beautifully** *adv.*

beaver ('bēvə) *n.* a river animal of the rat family with webbed hind feet, a broad tail, and very sharp teeth, which it uses to cut down trees for building dams. It lives mainly in North America and is often trapped for its fur, which is used for making coats, hats, etc. **work like a beaver** (informal) to work hard and consistently at something.

beckon ('bekən) *vb.* to summon with a gesture of the hand or head.

bee (bē) *n.* an insect with a thick hairy body. Honey bees build HONEY-COMBS out of wax (see BEESWAX) and feed on NECTAR (from which they make honey) and pollen.

beech (bēch) *n.* 1. a DECIDUOUS tree with a smooth hard bark, shiny oval leaves, and small edible nuts. 2. the wood of this tree.

beef (bēf) *n.* the meat of the ox, bull, or cow. '**beefy** *adj.* **beefier, beefiest.** 1. containing or tasting like beef. 2. very strong; muscular. —'**beefiness** *n.*

beehive ('bēhīv) *n.* See HIVE.

beer (biə) *n.* an alcoholic drink made from barley, yeast, and hops.

beeswax ('bēzwaks) *n.* wax, made by honey bees, from which polishes, candles, etc. are made.

beet (bēt) *n.* 1. (also **sugarbeet**) a small plant whose white carrot-shaped root provides sugar. 2. (also **beetroot**) a similar plant whose red root is eaten as a vegetable.

beetle ('bētəl) *n.* 1. a type of insect with hard scaly wing-covers. 2. any other insect resembling this, e.g. the cockroach.

beetroot ('bētrōot) *n.* See BEET.

beg (beg) *vb.* **begging, begged.** 1. to ask people for money. 2. to ask (someone) for something or to do something, esp. with great emotion or feeling: *he begged her to forgive him.* 3. (of a dog) to sit on its haunches with its front paws raised. '**beggar** *n.* a person who begs for money. *vb.* to use up or go beyond the capacity of: *it beggars the imagination.*

behave (bi'hāv) *vb.* **behaving, behaved.** 1. to act or conduct oneself: *you are behaving like a baby.* 2. to act properly or correctly: *if you do not behave I shall be furious.* 3. to respond or react: *how does the fish behave if you throw it food?* **be'haviour** *n.* conduct or response.

beige (bāzh) *n.* a light creamy brown colour. —*adj.* having this colour.

belfry ('belfri) *n.,pl.* **belfries.** a tower or part of a church steeple in which the bells are hung. **have bats in the belfry** to be mad or insane.

belfry

belief (bi'lēf) *n.* 1. a feeling that something is real, right, or true; conviction: *it is my belief that honesty is the best policy.* 2. trust or confidence: *I have great belief in his ability as a lawyer.* 3. a religious doctrine or faith: *the Christian belief.*

believe (bi'lēv) *vb.* **believing, believed.** 1. to feel certain or be convinced of (the reality, rightness, or truth of something): *I believe in equality.* 2. to have trust or confidence in (someone or something). 3. to suppose: *I believe that you know Mrs Robinson.* **make believe** to imagine or pretend. '**make-believe** *n.* pretence.

bell (bel) *n.* 1. a hollow metal cup-shaped instrument, which is struck by a clapper or hammer to make a ringing sound. 2. anything bell-shaped, e.g. a bell-tent, bluebell, etc. **ring a bell** to strike one as familiar. **sound as a bell** completely healthy; in perfect working order.

bellow ('belō) *vb.* 1. to roar like a bull. 2. to shout in a loud deep voice. —*n.* an angry roaring noise.

bellows ('belōz) *pl.n.* a mechanical device for producing a strong blast of air for a fire or furnace or certain musical instruments such as the organ, bagpipes, etc.

belly ('beli) *n.,pl.* **bellies.** 1. (informal) the lower abdomen, stomach, or womb. 2. the bulging interior of a ship or the undercarriage of an aircraft. —*vb.* **bellying, bellied.** to bulge out or swell: *we could see*

the yacht's sails bellying out as it left the harbour.

belt (belt) *n.* 1. a strip of leather or other material worn around the waist. 2. a geographical region, esp. one with distinctive characteristics: *cotton belt.* **conveyor belt** a long continuous strip of rubber or other material that is kept moving by means of wheels or rollers and used in factories, etc., for carrying goods. —*vb.* 1. to fasten with a belt. 2. to beat with a belt; hit or strike. 3. (informal) to run or travel very fast: *the bus belted along the road.* 4. (+ *out*) to sing or play (something) on a musical instrument loudly and vigorously. **belt up** (slang) to stop talking or making a noise.

bench (bench) *n.* 1. a seat long enough for several people, often found in parks and other public places. 2. a work-table used by carpenters, mechanics, etc. **the Bench** (in a law court) a judge's seat, the judge himself, or judges, magistrates, etc., collectively. '**benchmark** *n.* a surveyor's mark on a rock or post, used as a reference point from which to measure distances or heights.

bend (bend) *vb.* **bending, bent.** 1. to force or be forced into a curved, angular, or other shape: *the circus strong man bent the iron bar into a hoop.* 2. to turn in a certain direction: *the road bends to the left.* 3. to apply one's energies to something: *we bent to the task of moving the log.* —*n.* 1. a curve: *a bend in the road.* 2. the act of bending or state of being bent.

benefit ('benifit) *n.* 1. something that acts as an advantage, does good, or gives pleasure: *he sang for the benefit of his friends.* 2. money paid by the state during periods of unemployment, sickness, etc. 3. a performance of a play, match, etc., the takings of which are given to charity or to one particular cause. —*vb.* 1. to do good. 2. to gain or profit from. —**bene'ficial** *adj.* acting to someone's good: *a beneficial climate.*

benevolent (bə'nevələnt) *adj.* kindly and helpful; acting for the benefit of other people. —**be'nevolence** *n.*

bent (bent) *vb.* the past tense and past participle of BEND. —*adj.* 1. curved or crooked: *a bent stick.* 2. (informal) dishonest. **bent on** determined: *bent on buying a car.* —*n.* a natural ability or interest: *my young brother has a musical bent.*

beret

beret ('berā) *n.* a flat round cap, usu. made of woollen material.

berry ('beri) *n.,pl.* **berries.** a small juicy fruit, usu. with seeds or pips.

berth (bûth) *n.* 1. a place in a dock where a ship is anchored. 2. a sleeping-place in a train, ship, etc. —*vb.* (of a ship) to dock.

besiege (bi'sēj) *vb.* **besieging, besieged.** 1. to lay SIEGE to (a town, city, etc.). 2. to crowd around (someone), esp. to ask numerous questions, make demands, etc.: *reporters besieged the film star.*

bet (bet) *vb.* **betting, bet.** 1. to make an agreement to risk money by guessing the outcome of an event: *Tim bet Jane that he could swim further underwater than she could.* 2. (informal) to be certain: *I bet he will forget to come.* —*n.* 1. the agreement to risk money on an uncertain event. 2. the money risked.

betray (bi'trā) *vb.* 1. to act against one's country, a friend, etc., by assisting an enemy. 2. to act disloyally by giving away a secret, breaking a promise, etc. 3. to reveal unintentionally. —**be'trayal** *n.* —**be'trayer** *n.*

bewilder (bi'wildə) *vb.* to perplex, lead astray, confuse, or puzzle: *you bewilder me with so many suggestions that I cannot decide what to do.* —**be'wilderment** *n.*

beyond (bi'yond) *prep.* 1. on the far side of: *you can see the hills beyond the river.* 2. outside the limits, scope, or range of; out of reach of: *that idea is beyond my understanding.* —*adv.* further away: *they travelled over the mountains and beyond.*

biannual (bī'anyŏoəl) *adj.* happening or occurring twice a year; half-yearly. —**bi'annually** *adv.*

bias ('bīəs) *n.* 1. a tendency or leaning: *he had a bias towards mathematics and wanted to be an accountant.* 2. a prejudice: *the woman had a bias against big dogs.* —*vb.* **biasing, biased.** to prejudice or influence: *propaganda tends to bias public opinion.*

bicycle ('bīsikəl) *n.* a pedal-operated vehicle having two wheels and a saddle-like seat for the rider. Often shortened to **bike.**

bid (bid) *vb.* **bidding, bid** (for defs. 1–2); **bidding, bade** *or* **bad, bidden** (for defs. 3–4). 1. to offer to buy something at a certain price, esp. at an auction. 2. to state one's price for doing a job. 3. to command: *we must do what he bids.* 4. to say as a greeting: *I bid you goodnight.* —*n.* the act of bidding; an offer. **'biddable** *adj.* willing to do what is asked. —**'bidder** *n.*

biennial (bī'eniəl) *adj.* 1. (of plants) lasting for two years. 2. happening once every two years. —*n.* a plant with a two-year life cycle, flowering and producing seeds in the second year. Compare ANNUAL and PERENNIAL. —**bi'ennially** *adv.*

bike (bīk) *n.* See BICYCLE.

bikini (bi'kēni) *n.* a brief two-piece swimsuit worn by women.

bill[1] (bil) *n.* 1. a list of costs or charges presented to a person for the goods or services he has received. 2. a draft of a proposed new law put before Parliament for debate. 3. a poster or public notice advertising some product or event.

bill[2] (bil) *n.* the beak of a bird.

billiards ('bilyədz) *n.* (Britain) a game played with long tapered poles (**billiard cues**) and one white and two red balls (**billiard balls**) on a rectangular table (**billiard table**) with six side-pockets.

bind (bīnd) *vb.* **binding, bound.** 1. to fix firmly by tying round with string, rope, etc. 2. to unite legally or morally; tie or put under an obligation: *marriage binds two people together.* 3. to put a border on (the edge of something), esp. to prevent fraying. 4. to stitch or glue together (one edge of a number of pages and covers) to form a

book. **'binder** *n.* 1. a man or machine that binds books. 2. a loose cover for holding and protecting sheets of paper, magazines, etc. **'binding** *n.* 1. the outside covers of a book. 2. a strip of material used to bind the edge of something.

binoculars (bi'nokyŏoləz) *pl.n.* an optical instrument for making distant objects seem larger and nearer containing a system of LENSes for magnifying the image.

binoculars

biography (bī'ogrəfi) *n.,pl.* **biographies.** the story of a person's life. —**bi'ographer** *n.* —**biographical** (bīə'grafikəl) *adj.*

biology (bī'oləji) *n.* the science and study of the function, structure, and development of animals and plants. —**biological** (bīə'lojikəl) *adj.* —**bio'logically** *adv.* —**bi'ologist** *n.*

birch (bûch) *n.* 1. a tree that grows in cool climates, the commonest variety being the silver birch, which has a silver and black patched bark. 2. a bunch of birch twigs bound together and used for beating someone as a punishment. —*vb.* to beat with a birch.

birth (bûth) *n.* 1. a baby's coming into the world. 2. the beginning of something.

biscuit ('biskit) *n.* 1. a flat crisp cake, often sweetened. 2. a light brown colour.

bishop ('bishəp) *n.* 1. a person of high rank in the Christian Church, in charge of all clerical matters in his area (diocese or **bishopric**) and with authority to ordain priests. 2. a chess piece that can move diagonally on the board.

bison

bison ('bīsən) *n.,pl.* **bison.** a large plant-eating animal, related to the ox, that lives in herds in North America. See also BUFFALO.

bit[1] (bit) *n.* 1. a small piece or amount of something: *a bit of money.* 2. a short time; moment.

bit[2] (bit) *n.* 1. the thin metal bar of a BRIDLE that is put in a horse's mouth. 2. a sharp-pointed boring tool fixed to the end of a drill. See TOOL.

bit[3] (bit) the past tense of BITE.

bite (bīt) *vb.* **biting, bit, bitten.** 1. to take hold of or cut into with the teeth as in eating or as a means of attack: *the vicious dog bit me on the leg.* 2. (esp. of insects) to sting: *he was bitten by a mosquito.* 3. to eat into; corrode: *acid bites into metals.* 4. to sink or cut into: *the wire bit into the soft wood.* 5. (esp. of fish) to take a baited hook. —*n.* 1. an instance or the act of biting. 2. a sting or wound caused by biting. 3. a piece or amount that has been bitten off: *a bite of apple.* 4. a sharp stinging sensation: *the bite of the wind.* 'biting *adj.* 1. causing a stinging pain: *a biting wind.* 2. sarcastic or hurtful: *a biting remark.*

bitter ('bitə) *adj.* 1. sour and sharp-tasting: *a bitter lemon.* 2. painful; causing suffering or distress: *a bitter experience.* 3. intensely hostile: *bitter enemies.* 4. biting: *a bitter wind.* 5. resentful through suffering: *the housewives became very bitter about rising prices.* —*n.* a kind of beer strongly flavoured with hops. —'bitterly *adv.* —'bitterness *n.*

blackberry ('blakbəri) *n.,pl.* **blackberries.** 1. a purplish-black edible berry. 2. the thorny bush on which these berries grow.

blackbird ('blakbûd) *n.* a European songbird, related to the thrush, with black plumage and a yellow bill.

blackmail ('blakmāl) *vb.* to obtain money or favours from (someone), by threatening to disclose a secret, reveal a past crime, etc. —*n.* 1. the act of blackmailing. 2. the money that is obtained from blackmailing. —'blackmailer *n.*

blackout ('blakout) *n.* 1. temporary loss of consciousness: *he suffered a blackout and could remember nothing that happened.* 2. an electricity failure; power cut.

bladder ('bladə) *n.* 1. the expanding bag in which liquid waste (urine) collects in human and animal bodies. 2. any inner inflatable bag: *the bladder of a football.*

blade (blād) *n.* 1. the narrow leaf of young grass, corn, etc. 2. the flat cutting part of a sword, knife, axe, etc. 3. a sword. 4. the wide flat part of an oar, propeller, etc.

blame (blām) *vb.* **blaming, blamed.** to attach guilt or responsibility to (a person or thing) for (a crime, etc.): *they blamed the weather for the failure of the horse show.* —*n.* responsibility for a fault, etc.

blank (blangk) *adj.* 1. not written on; unmarked: *a blank page.* 2. expressionless: *he looked blank when I told him my name.* 3. absolute; utter: *blank despair overwhelmed him.* **blank verse** non-rhyming verse. —*n.* 1. a space to be filled in, e.g. on a form. 2. a state of emptiness: *my mind was a blank.* 3. a cartridge without a bullet. —*vb.* (+ *out*) to cross out completely. —'blankly *adv.* —'blankness *n.*

blast (blâst) *n.* 1. a gust or sudden rush of wind, air, etc. 2. an explosion: *a blast of gunfire.* 3. a blare of trumpets, horns, etc. (at) **full blast** at top speed, loudest setting, or maximum activity. —*vb.* to break (something) or make a hole by setting off an explosion: *thieves had blasted the safe open.*

blaze[1] (blāz) *n.* 1. a burst or glow of bright flames or light. 2. a rush or outburst: *we finished the decorating in a blaze of activity.* —*vb.* **blazing, blazed.** 1. to flare or light up suddenly; burn, glow, or shine brightly. 2. to flare up with emotion: *she was blazing with rage.*

blaze[2] (blāz) *n.* 1. a white mark on the face of a horse or cow. 2. a white mark chipped or painted on a tree trunk. —*vb.* **blazing, blazed.** (usu. in **blaze a trail**) 1. to mark (a trail) by cutting blazes on trees. 2. to show the way or be a pioneer: *early spacemen blazed the trail to the moon.*

blaze

bleach (blēch) *vb.* to remove colour by the action of sunlight, chemicals, etc. —*n.* any substance that bleaches.

bleak (blēk) *adj.* 1. desolate, cold, or bare: *a bleak landscape.* 2. dreary; unpromising: *the future is bleak.* —'bleakly *adv.* —'bleakness *n.*

blemish ('blemish) *vb.* to spoil or damage; mar: *the scandal failed to blemish his reputation.* —*n.* 1. a mark, esp. on the skin that damages or spoils the look of something. 2. a fault, flaw, or defect: *a blemish in her character.*

blend (blend) *vb.* 1. to mix thoroughly; combine. 2. to merge: *chameleons change colour so as to blend into the background.* —*n.* 1. a mixture. 2. a shade of colour.

bless (bles) *vb.* 1. to wish heavenly happiness (on a person) by praying. 2. to make holy; consecrate. 3. to worship. 4. to feel grateful to: *I blessed my wife for remembering the cinema tickets.* **blessed** ('blesid) *adj.* 1. having been blessed; holy. 2. welcome: *after constant quarrelling blessed peace reigned at last.* '**blessing** *n.* 1. the giving of a prayer for God's favour. 2. anything bringing happiness; benefit: *television is a blessing for elderly people.* 3. approval: *the mayor gave his blessing to the tree-planting scheme.*

blew (bloo) *vb.* the past tense of BLOW[1].

blight (blīt) *n.* 1. a disease, fungus, or insect that attacks and destroys plants. 2. anything that has an unpleasant or destructive effect. —*vb.* to affect with or cause a blight.

blind (blīnd) *adj.* 1. unable to see. 2. hidden: *a blind entrance.* 3. heedless; not noticing: *she was blind to his faults.* 4. reckless; not thinking of the consequences: *blind panic seized him and he ran.* —*n.* a window shade, esp. one that rolls up. —*vb.* 1. to make blind. 2. to mislead: *his confident talk blinded us.* '**blindfold** *vb.* to cover (a person's eyes) with a handkerchief, scarf, mask, etc. —*n.* such a mask.

blink (blingk) *vb.* 1. to close and open the eyes quickly. 2. (of lights) to go on and off rapidly.

bliss (blis) *n.* perfect happiness. —'**blissful** *adj.* —'**blissfully** *adv.*

blister ('blistə) *n.* 1. a small fluid-filled swelling on the skin caused by a burn, rubbing, etc. 2. a small air pocket on a coat of paint, etc. —*vb.* to cause or come out in a blister. '**blistering** *adj.* 1. causing a blister. 2. extremely hot. 3. wounding or piercing: *a blistering attack.*

blitz (blits) *n.* 1. a sudden attack from the air; air raid. 2. a campaign for putting an end to something: *the townspeople decided to have a blitz on litter.* **the Blitz** the series of German air raids on Britain in 1940.

blizzard ('blizəd) *n.* a heavy snowfall accompanied by strong winds, greatly hampered visibility, and deep drifts.

bloat (blōt) *vb.* 1. to swell up; inflate. 2. (informal) to overfeed; stuff: *after a large meal I feel bloated.* 3. to puff up (with pride, vanity, etc.).

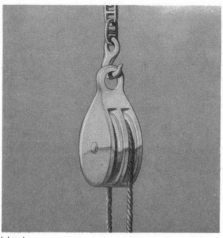
block

block (blok) *n.* 1. a solid, usu. rectangular piece of concrete, wood, stone, etc., esp. when used in building. 2. a large complex building having several storeys: *an office block.* 3. a number of buildings totally surrounded by streets: *once round the block.* 4. a device with pulleys for lifting heavy weights. 5. (also **blockage**) something that stops progress, flow, movement, etc.: *there's a block in the pipe.* —*vb.* to prevent or stop with a barrier: *ignorance blocks progress.*

blockade (blo'kād) *n.* the prevention by enemy forces of supplies getting in or out of a town, port, etc. —*vb.* **blockading, blockaded.** to conduct a blockade on (a town, port, etc.).

blond (blond) *adj.* 1. (of hair) golden or fair. 2. having golden or fair hair. **blonde** *n.* a woman with blond hair.

blood (blud) *n.* 1. the red liquid that is pumped round the body by the heart. See also CORPUSCLE. 2. descent or breeding: *she is of royal blood.* **bad blood** hostility: *there's bad blood between the sisters.* '**bloody** *adj.* **bloodier, bloodiest.** covered or stained with blood.

bloodshed ('bludshed) *n.* the spilling of blood by violent means.

bloodshot ('bludshot) *adj.* (of the eyes) red, esp. through tiredness.

bloom (bloom) *n.* 1. a flower head; blossom. 2. a fresh or healthy glow: *the bloom of her cheek.* 3. a state or condition of health or vigour: *the bloom of youth.* —*vb.* 1. to come into flower; blossom. 2. to glow with health, beauty, etc.

blossom ('blosəm) *n.* a flower or a mass of flowers, esp. of a fruit tree.

—*vb.* 1. to produce blossom; bloom. 2. to grow beautiful or attractive. 3. to reveal one's full talent; flourish.

blot (blot) *n.* 1. a mark or stain, esp. of a liquid: *an ink blot.* 2. fault; disgrace. —*vb.* **blotting, blotted.** 1. to make an ink stain (on something). 2. to stain or spoil: *his career was blotted by the scandal.* 3. to dab (ink, etc.) with absorbent paper (**blotting paper**) in order to dry it. 4. (+ *out*) to shut out or wipe out; obliterate: *the clouds were blotting out the sun.*

blow[1] (blō) *vb.* **blowing, blew, blown.** 1. (of the wind or air) to be in motion; move or flow. 2. to move or to be carried along by or as if by the force of the wind: *the washing was blown away.* 3. to send out a rush of air, esp. from the mouth: *blow out the candles.* 4. to produce sounds from (a wind or brass instrument, whistle, etc.): *he blew the trumpet.* 5. (of a tyre, fuse, etc.) to stop functioning suddenly; fail or perish. **blow over** to subside; pass: *this crisis won't blow over yet.* **blow up** 1. to inflate a balloon, tyre, etc. 2. to explode or cause an explosion. 3. (informal) to lose one's temper. 4. to enlarge (a photograph). —*n.* the act or an instance of blowing.

blow[2] (blō) *n.* 1. a hit with the fist, a weapon, etc.: *he knocked his opponent out with a single blow.* 2. a shock or setback; severe disappointment: *his death was a serious blow to their hopes.*

blubber ('blubə) *n.* the fatty layer between the skin and muscle of a whale, seal, or similar animal, from which oil is made. —*vb.* (informal) to cry noisily.

bluff (bluf) *vb.* to pretend confidently; mislead or deceive by behaving or acting boldly: *he bluffed his way out of the situation.* —*n.* the act or an instance of bluffing.

blunder ('blundə) *n.* a stupid or careless mistake. —*vb.* 1. to make a foolish or embarrassing mistake. 2. to stumble or wander about carelessly.

blunt (blunt) *adj.* 1. not sharp; having a dull or rough edge: *a blunt knife.* 2. forthright or outspoken: *a blunt reminder.* —*vb.* 1. to make (a knife, axe, etc.) blunt; dull. 2. to weaken or diminish: *smoking blunted my taste.* —'**bluntly** *adv.* —'**bluntness** *n.*

blur (blû) *n.* 1. something hazy, ill-defined, or indistinct: *the distant* *figure on the horizon was a blur.* 2. a smear or smudge. —*vb.* **blurring, blurred.** 1. to make or become hazy or indistinct: *the strong sun blurred his vision.* 2. to smear or smudge. 3. to confuse or disguise: *he deliberately blurred the facts.*

blush (blush) *vb.* to glow pink or red, esp. on the face through embarrassment. —*n.* 1. a pink glow, esp. on the face. 2. a rosy colour.

boar (bô) *n.* a male pig.

board (bôd) *n.* 1. a flat piece of hard material such as wood. 2. such a flat slab of wood, or other material used for a particular purpose: *an ironing board.* 3. any group of people who officially direct, control, or supervise something: *a board of directors.* **on board** on or in a train, ship, or aircraft. —*vb.* 1. to climb onto or enter (a ship, aircraft, train, etc.) 2. (often + *up*) to cover or enclose with boards: *he boarded up the window.* 3. to offer or receive accommodation, meals, etc., in return for payment; lodge.

boast (bōst) *vb.* 1. to speak with excessive vanity or pride, esp. about oneself; brag. 2. to have the distinction of possessing: *this house boasts a large garden.* —*n.* an act or instance of boasting. —**'boastful** *adj.*

body ('bodi) *n.,pl.* **bodies.** 1. the physical structure of a person or animal: *the human body.* 2. a corpse. 3. that part of a person or animal excluding the head, arms, and legs; trunk or torso. 4. a group of people taken collectively: *the main body of politicians.* 5. the main or major part of something: *the body of a church.* 6. a mass: *a body of water.* 7. substance or strength; dense consistency: *the vegetables gave the stew more body.* **'bodily** *adj.* of or relating to the body: *bodily needs. adv.* as a whole; completely: *he was removed bodily from the hall.*

bog (bog) *n.* a damp soggy area of ground; marsh. —*vb.* **bogging, bogged.** (usu. + *down*) 1. to sink in or as if in a bog: *the car was bogged down in the mud.* 2. (informal) to be unable to make progress in some activity: *I am bogged down with work.* —**'boggy** adj. **boggier, boggiest.**

boil[1] (boil) *vb.* 1. to change from a liquid to a gas when heated; bubble and produce steam. 2. to cook by boiling. 3. to become hot and red with emotion, esp. anger: *he was boiling*

with rage. **'boiler** *n.* any vessel or large container used for boiling or heating water, etc.

boil[2] (boil) *n.* an inflamed pus-filled sore or swelling of the skin.

bold (bōld) *adj.* 1. brave, daring, or courageous; fearless: *a bold explorer.* 2. direct or outspoken: *bold words.* 3. strong and firm: *bold handwriting.* —**'boldly** *adv.* —**'boldness** *n.*

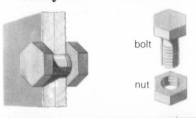

bolt

nut

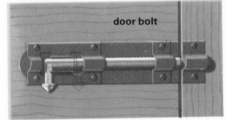

door bolt

bolt

bolt (bōlt) *n.* 1. a movable bar, usu. of metal, that slides into a socket to fasten a door, gate, etc. 2. any strong metal pin with a THREAD (def. 3) and a head at one end that may be tightened with a spanner to hold or secure parts of machines, etc. 3. a sudden dash or run. —*vb.* 1. to fasten with a bolt: *the machine is bolted to the floor.* 2. to run away in great haste; dash off. 3. to swallow (food) hurriedly.

bomb (bom) *n.* a weapon consisting of a metal container packed with explosive. —*vb.* to attack with bombs. **'bomber** *n.* 1. a person who uses bombs. 2. an aircraft used for dropping bombs.

bombard (bom'bâd) *vb.* 1. to use prolonged artillery fire against (an enemy position). 2. to pester or badger (someone) continually with questions or remarks: *he bombarded us with questions about our holidays.* —**bom'bardment** *n.*

bond (bond) *n.* 1. usu. **bonds** (*pl.*) chains or imprisonment. 2. something that joins or unites: *a strong bond of friendship between two people.* 3. a written promise, esp. concerning money, that must be kept by law. 4. a special paper issued by the government or a business promising to repay borrowed money at an agreed date.

bone (bōn) *n.* 1. the hard material that makes up the skeleton in animals. 2. a part of this skeleton. —*vb.* **boning, boned.** to remove the bones from meat or fish.

bonnet ('bonit) *n.* 1. a hat tied under the chin. 2. (in Scotland) a man's or boy's cap. 3. the front section of a car, usu. covering the engine.

boomerang ('boōmərang) *n.* a curved flat throwing stick used esp. by Australian Aborigines for hunting animals. If it misses its target it returns to the thrower.

boost (boōst) *vb.* 1. to lift by pushing from underneath. 2. to increase; raise: *the athlete's confidence was boosted by his win.* —*n.* a push forward. **'booster** *n.* 1. rocket used for launching a satellite or spacecraft. 2. an injection given to help keep up the strength of a vaccine injected at an earlier date.

border ('bôdə) *n.* 1. an edge or margin. 2. a frontier or boundary. 3. a narrow flower bed running along the edge of a lawn, path, etc. —*vb.* 1. to be next to: *my land borders on farmland.* 2. to be on the brink of; approach: *his jealousy bordered on madness.*

bore[1] (bô) *vb.* **boring, bored.** 1. to make a hole in: *woodworms bore into furniture.* 2. to drill: *the sea bed is being bored for oil.* —*n.* the inside diameter of a tube, drill, etc.

bore[2] (bô) *vb.* **boring, bored.** to make someone weary by being dull and tedious. —*n.* 1. a person who bores others by dull talk. 2. anything dull and tedious. —**'boredom** *n.*

born (bôn) *vb.* the past participle of BEAR[1] (for def. 4).

borne (bôn) *vb.* the past participle of BEAR[1] (for defs. 1–3, 5).

borrow ('borō) *vb.* 1. to take on loan. 2. to be lent money for paying back with interest. —**'borrower** *n.*

bosom ('boŏzəm) *n.* 1. the human breast: *he clasped his daughter to his bosom.* 2. the female breasts. 3. the very heart or centre of a person or thing. **bosom friend** a close friend.

boss[1] (bos) *n.* an employer, manager, or person in charge. —*vb.* 1. to order about. 2. to supervise; be in charge. **'bossy** *adj.* **bossier, bossiest.** fond of ordering others about.

boss² (bos) *n.* 1. a knob or stud, esp. one found in the centre of a shield. 2. any raised knoblike ornament or part, e.g. one concealing a joint in certain types of ceiling.

botany ('botəni) *n.* the study of plants. —**botanical** (bə'tanikəl) *adj.* —'**botanist** *n.*

bother ('bodhə) *vb.* 1. to annoy: *don't bother me while I'm working.* 2. to take trouble or make an effort: *don't bother to get up.* —*n.* 1. fuss or annoyance. 2. trouble or extra effort.

bough (bou) *n.* a tree branch.

boulder ('bōldə) *n.* a large rounded or smooth rock.

bounce (bouns) *vb.* **bouncing, bounced.** 1. to rebound or cause to rebound: *the ball bounced along the ground.* 2. to jump, move, or spring up and down. —*n.* 1. a rebound, spring, or lift. 2. vigour; energy.

bound¹ (bound) *vb.* the past tense and past participle of BIND. —*adj.* certain: *it's bound to rain soon.*

bound² (bound) *vb.* to leap or spring (along). —*n.* a leap or jump.

boundary ('boundəri) *n., pl.* **boundaries.** 1. the extreme edge or limit of something. 2. a frontier. 3. a score of 4 or 6 runs for a ball hit beyond the edge (**boundary**) of a cricket ground.

bouquet (boo'kā) *n.* 1. a bunch of flowers. 2. the quality of wine judged from its scent.

bout (bout) *n.* 1. a short period of activity; spell. 2. a fight or contest. 3. a fit or attack: *he had frequent bouts of coughing.*

boutique (boo'tēk) *n.* a shop, esp. one selling clothes.

bow¹ (bou) *vb.* 1. to nod the head or bend forward from the waist as a sign of reverence or acknowledgment. 2. to bend forward: *he bowed his head in shame.* 3. to give way or yield: *I will not bow to your demands.* —*n.* a bending of the head or body, usu. as a mark of respect.

bow² (bō) *n.* 1. a piece of flexible wood or metal drawn into a curve by a string stretched between the ends which is pulled taut to release arrows. 2. a curve or bend: *this wall has a slight bow in it.* 3. a stick with horse-hair strung from end to end, used in playing the violin. 4. a knot with two loops which pulls out easily, or any decorative looped knot or tie.

bow³ (bou) *n.* sometimes **bows** (*pl.*) the curved front or forward end of a boat. Compare STERN.

bowels ('bouəlz) *pl.n.* sometimes **bowel** (*sing.*) the long tubelike organs in the body through which food is absorbed into the blood.

bowl¹ (bōl) *n.* a basin or round deep-sided dish.

bowl² (bōl) *n.* 1. a heavy round ball used in games such as bowls, skittles, etc. 2. **bowls** (*sing.*) a game in which bowls are rolled across a level grass pitch (**bowling green**). —*vb.* 1. (cricket) to aim or throw a ball at the wicket. 2. (often + *out*) to get the batsman out by hitting the wicket with the ball. 3. to take one's turn in bowling, skittles, etc. **bowl over** 1. to knock over. 2. to surprise or over-whelm.

Braille

box¹ (boks) *n.* 1. a flat-bottomed container, often with a lid, and made of wood, metal, cardboard, etc. 2. an enclosed private set of seats in a theatre. **box office** the booking-office of a theatre or cinema.

box² (boks) *vb.* 1. to fight with the fists. 2. to hit, esp. on the ears. —*n.* a blow or hit. '**boxer** *n.* 1. a person who competes in boxing as a sport. 2. a large breed of dog with short smooth brown hair and a flattened face. '**boxing** *n.* a sport in which two people wearing padded gloves fight in a roped-off arena. (**boxing ring**).

box³ (boks) *n.* an evergreen shrub often used for garden hedges.

boycott ('boikot) *vb.* to refuse to handle (goods) or deal with (a person, country, etc.) on moral or political grounds. —*n.* the act or practice of boycotting.

brace (brās) *n.* 1. something that grips or holds firm; clamp. 2. a piece of iron or timber used to strengthen a building. 3. (esp. of game-birds) a pair or couple. 4. **braces** (*pl.*) straps worn over the shoulders to keep trousers up. **brace and bit** a carpentry TOOL used for drilling. —*vb.* **bracing, braced.** 1. to give support to; strengthen. 2. to prepare oneself; get ready to face.

bracelet ('brāslit) *n.* a decorative band, chain, etc., worn on the wrist.

bracket ('brakit) *n.* 1. a support for a shelf, lamp, etc., usu. fixed to a wall. 2. one of a pair of punctuation marks, that enclose information. 3. a grouping or scale: *the lower income bracket.* —*vb.* 1. to put into brackets. 2. to group together.

brag (brag) *vb.* **bragging, bragged.** to boast.

Braille (brāl) *n.* a type of printing for the blind, consisting of patterns of raised dots that can be read by touch.

brain (brān) *n.* 1. the soft mass of grey and white matter inside the skull of man and the higher animals. It is the centre of the nervous system, controlling thought, memory, bodily actions, etc. 2. also **brains** (*pl.*) intelligence or intellectual power: *he has a superb brain.* —*vb.* (slang) to hit (someone) violently on the head. '**brainy** *adj.* **brainier, brainiest.** intelligent or clever.

brainwashing ('brānwoshing) *n.* a method of gaining control of a person's mind to make him believe what one wants, sometimes by the use of drugs or torture.

brake (brāk) *n.* a device for slowing down or stopping a vehicle, usu. by pressure against some part of the wheels. —*vb.* **braking, braked.** to stop (a vehicle) by using the brake.

bramble ('brambəl) *n.* a form of prickly bush; the class of plant to which the blackberry belongs.

branch (brânch) *n.* 1. a part of a tree or other plant that comes from or is supported by the main body of the plant. 2. a subdivision or extension of something: *a branch of a bank.* —*vb.* (often + *off*) to turn or lead off in a different direction. **branch out** to extend one's activities.

brand (brand) *n.* 1. a tradename on manufactured goods, foodstuffs, etc.: *the best brand of butter.* 2. a mark on an animal showing ownership, often made with a hot iron (**branding iron**). —*vb.* 1. to mark with a brand. 2. to cause to be treated as a criminal, traitor, etc.: *his crime branded him forever.*

brandy ('brandi) *n.,pl.* **brandies.** a strong alcoholic drink, made by distilling the juice of grapes or other fruit.

brass (brâs) *n.* 1. a strong yellowish metal made from copper and zinc. 2. any article made of brass. 3. a collective term for musical instruments such as the trumpet, trombone, French horn, etc., which are usu. made of brass. —'**brassy.** *adj.* **brassier, brassiest.**

breach (brēch) *n.* 1. a gap made in a wall, dam, or other structure. 2. the breaking of a promise, law, etc.; violation or infringement. —*vb.* to make a breach in (something).

breadth (bredth) *n.* 1. width; broadness; the distance from one side of something to the other. 2. fullness of extent, scope, or range: *his works show great breadth.*

break (brāk) *vb.* **breaking, broke, broken.** 1. to come or cause to come to pieces: *the glass has broken.* 2. to damage; injure: *Lynn broke her leg.* 3. to discontinue completely: *he broke the bad habit.* 4. to force a way: *thieves have broken into the bank.* 5. to appear suddenly: *dawn is breaking.* **break down** to fail to work. —*n.* an action or instance of breaking. '**breakdown** *n.* a failure to work.

breast (brest) *n.* 1. the front of the body from the neck to the abdomen; chest. 2. the organ producing milk in women and some female animals.

breath (breth) *n.* 1. the air taken in or let out of the lungs. 2. a single intake of air: *he took a deep breath.* 3. a light movement of air: *a breath of wind.* 4. a faint trace or hint: *a breath of excitement.* —'**breathless** *adj.*

breathe (brēdh) *vb.* **breathing, breathed.** 1. to take in and let out air. 2. to utter very quietly: *she breathed a warning in his ear.*

breed (brēd) *vb.* **breeding, bred.** 1. to produce (offspring): *some animals do not breed in captivity.* 2. to mate and rear animals, usu. with careful attention to parentage, in order to produce good stock. 3. to cause or produce: *familiarity breeds contempt.* —*n.* a type or strain of animal: *a breed of cattle.* '**breeding** *n.* good manners and fine taste as produced by family influence and training; elegance. —'**breeder** *n.*

breeze (brēz) *n.* a gentle wind. **breeze in** *or* **out** (informal) to come in or out in a relaxed and high-spirited way. '**breezy** *adj.* **breezier, breeziest.** 1. windy, in a pleasant way. 2. casual and good-humoured: *Charles' breezy manner put people at ease.*

brew (brōō) *vb.* 1. to make (beer, etc.) by fermenting liquid from boiling hops together with yeast, malt, and sugar. 2. to make (tea, coffee, etc.). 3. (esp. referring to something unpleasant) to cause to or be about to happen: *a storm was brewing.* —*n.* any liquid that has been brewed. '**brewery** *n.,pl.* **breweries.** a place where beer is made. —'**brewer** *n.*

bridges

bribe (brīb) *n.* a present of money or items of value given to a person in order to gain information, favours, etc., illegally or dishonestly. —*vb.* **bribing, bribed.** to offer or give a bribe.

brick (brik) *n.* 1. a rectangular block made of fired or sunbaked clay, used in building. 2. anything similar to this in shape. —*vb.* (+ *up*) to seal or enclose with bricks: *they have bricked up the windows of that old house on the corner of the street.*

bride (brīd) *n.* a woman just married or about to be married. '**bridegroom** *n.* (often shortened to **groom**) a man just married or about to be married. —'**bridal** *adj.*

bridge (brij) *n.* 1. a structure built over a river, valley, road, etc., to allow the passage of people and traffic. 2. the upper part of the nose. 3. the raised part of a ship where the officer on watch is stationed. 4. a raised strip of wood on the body of a violin, cello, etc., over which the strings pass. —*vb.* **bridging, bridged.** to span; cross with or as if with a bridge.

bridge: 1 arch bridge; 2 girder bridge; 3 cantilever bridge; 4 suspension bridge.

bridle ('brīdəl) n. a leather head-harness for a horse, including the REINs and a BIT². —vb. **bridling, bridled.** 1. to put a bridle onto a horse. 2. to hold back, control, or restrain (one's feelings): he bridled his anger. 3. to lift the head and draw in the chin as an expression of scorn, resentment, etc.: she bridled at his sarcastic remark. '**bridlepath** n. a path suitable for horses but not vehicles.

brief (brēf) adj. short: a brief moment. —n. 1. (law) details concerning one side of a case given or offered to a barrister by a solicitor on behalf of his client. 2. a list of instructions or the outline of a plan to be acted upon. 3. **briefs** (pl.) very short tight-fitting underpants. —vb. to instruct or inform. '**briefcase** n. a flat case usu. made of plastic or leather, used for carrying papers. '**briefing** n. advice or instructions given in advance.

brigade (bri'gād) n. 1. a subdivision of an army, commanded by a brigadier, usu. made up of an infantry battalion, armour, and artillery. 2. any organized band or work-force: a fire brigade.

bright (brīt) adj. 1. giving off much light: a bright star. 2. (of colours) vivid: bright blue. 3. lively and intelligent; clever. '**brighten** vb. to make or become bright or brighter. —'**brightly** adv. —'**brightness** n.

brilliant ('brilyənt) adj. 1. extremely bright: brilliant sunshine. 2. highly intelligent: a brilliant scholar. 3. outstanding: a brilliant performance. —'**brilliance** n. —'**brilliantly** adv.

brim (brim) n. 1. the projecting edge of a hat. 2. the topmost edge of a cup or bowl. —vb. **brimming, brimmed.** to be full up to the brim with something; overflow.

brink (bringk) n. 1. the edge of something, usu. of a steep place and often over water. 2. the moment before a change of mood or events; verge: on the brink of tears.

brisk (brisk) adj. 1. with a quick smart movement: a brisk trot. 2. (of weather) healthy; cool and bracing. —'**briskly** adv. —'**briskness** n.

bristle ('brisəl) n. 1. a stiff short hair, esp. of an animal such as the pig. 2. anything resembling this, esp. as part of a toothbrush, hairbrush, etc. —vb. **bristling, bristled.** 1. (of the hair, bristles, etc.) to stand on end, often in

anger or fear. 2. to show a hostile reaction: John bristled when I suggested he might be wrong. 3. (+ with) to be full of (difficulties, etc.); teem with: the plan bristled with dangers.

brittle ('britəl) adj. (of glass, ice, bones, etc.) easily snapped or broken. —'**brittleness** n.

broad (brôd) adj. 1. wide: a broad river. 2. extensive: a broad range of goods. 3. (of opinions, views, attitudes, etc.) tolerant; liberal: a broad mind. 4. clear or obvious: a broad hint. 5. (of speech) having a strong regional dialect or accent: broad Scots. **in broad daylight** in plain view, with no attempt to conceal one's actions. '**broaden** vb. to make or become broader or wider. —'**broadness** n. See also BREADTH.

broadcast ('brôdkâst) vb. **broadcasting, broadcast** or **broadcasted.** 1. to transmit by television or radio. 2. to make widely known. —n. an instance or the action of broadcasting.

broccoli ('brokəli) n. a vegetable of the cabbage family with green or purple edible flowerheads.

brochure ('brōshyōōə) n. a printed booklet or pamphlet containing information or advertisements for a product, service, etc.

bronze (bronz) n. 1. a shiny reddish metal made of copper and tin. 2. a work of art made of bronze. —adj. made from or having the colour of bronze. —vb. **bronzing, bronzed.** to cover with or become the colour of bronze. **bronzed** adj. suntanned. **Bronze Age** a stage in the history of man during which he learnt to make tools, weapons, and ornaments from bronze. It occurred at different times in different parts of the world.

brooch (brōch) n. a piece of jewellery fixed onto clothing by a pin or clasp.

brood (brōōd) n. 1. the offspring of egg-producing animals, esp. birds. 2. (informal or humorous) the children in one's family. —vb. 1. (of a bird) to sit on eggs until they are hatched. 2. to think about something in a gloomy, bad-tempered way; sulk. '**broody** adj. **broodier, broodiest.** 1. (esp. of hens) tending to brood. 2. moody or sulky.

brow (brou) n. 1. the top or edge of a hill or cliff. 2. the forehead. 3. an eyebrow.

browse (brouz) vb. **browsing, browsed.** 1. to look through (books, shelves, etc.) in a leisurely and random way. 2. (of sheep, cattle, etc.) to feed off vegetation; graze.

bruise (brōōz) n. an injury in which the skin is discoloured but not broken. —vb. **bruising, bruised.** to suffer or cause to suffer a bruise.

brunette (brōō'net) adj. 1. (of hair) dark brown in colour. 2. having hair of this colour. —n. a woman with brunette hair.

brutal ('brōōtəl) adj. cruel and savage. —**brutality** (brōō'taliti) n.,pl. **brutalities.** —'**brutally** adv.

brute (brōōt) n. 1. any animal or beast, esp. a savage one. 2. a cruel or physically violent person. 3. anything that causes trouble or is difficult to handle: a brute of a car. —adj. purely physical: brute force. —'**brutish** adj.

bubble ('bubəl) n. a sphere of gas present in a liquid or found free with a thin liquid covering around it. —vb. **bubbling, bubbled.** 1. to produce bubbles. 2. to make the sound of bubbles rising and bursting; gurgle. 3. (of a person) to show happiness; sparkle.

buckle ('bukəl) n. a fastener made of metal, plastic, etc., with a spike attached to it, which passes through a hole in a belt, strip of material, etc. —vb. **buckling, buckled.** 1. to fasten with a buckle. 2. to crumple, collapse, or warp under pressure, heat, etc.

bud (bud) n. the small knob on a plant that will grow into a flower, leaf, or new branch. —vb. **budding, budded.** to put out buds; begin growing.

budget ('bujit) n. a financial statement or plan how one's money can be used or controlled. **the Budget** (in Britain) the budget concerning the government's and country's finances, presented by the Chancellor of the Exchequer to Parliament. —vb. to make a budget.

budgerigar ('bujərigâ) n. (often shortened to **budgie**) a small bird of the parrot family often kept as a pet.

buffalo ('bufəlō) n.,pl. **buffaloes** or **buffalo.** a large strong plant-eating animal with heavy curved horns. It is related to the ox, and is found mainly in India (water buffalo) and Africa (Cape buffalo).

buffet[1] ('bufit) *n.* a blow. —*vb.* to strike repeatedly; knock about.

buffet[2] ('bŏŏfā) *n.* 1. (at a wedding, party, etc.) refreshments set out on a bar or table for guests to help themselves. 2. a restaurant on a train or at a railway station that serves light snacks and drinks.

bug (bug) *n.* 1. any insect, esp. a flea or something similar. 2. (informal) a microbe, esp. one that can cause disease. 3. a concealed microphone or other device used to pick up conversations secretly. —*vb.* **bugging, bugged.** 1. (slang) to pester or annoy persistently. 2. to conceal a microphone or tape-recorder in a room, telephone, etc., to spy on people.

bugle ('byōōgəl) *n.* a brass musical instrument used for military signals and fanfares. —*vb.* **bugling, bugled.** to sound a bugle.

bugle

build (bild) *vb.* **building, built.** to construct; make something, e.g. a house, from an assortment of parts or materials.

bulb (bulb) *n.* 1. the swollen underground part of such plants as onions, daffodils, tulips, etc., that stores nourishment for new growth. 2. anything shaped like a bulb, e.g. an electric light bulb. —'**bulbous** *adj.*

bulge (bulj) *n.* a swelling or lump. —*vb.* **bulging, bulged.** to stick out.

bulk (bulk) *n.* 1. greatness of volume, size, or weight. 2. the main part: *the bulk of the work was completed today.* —'**bulky** *adj.* **bulkier, bulkiest.**

bull (bŏŏl) *n.* 1. the male of cattle, oxen, etc., and of certain other animals, e.g. the elephant or seal.

bulldozer

bulldozer ('bŏŏldōzə) *n.* a large heavy tractor used for clearing land, knocking down buildings, etc. '**bulldoze** *vb.* **bulldozing, bulldozed.** 1. to clear and level (land, etc.) using a bulldozer. 2. to get one's own way by using threats or violence; bully.

bullet ('bŏŏlit) *n.* a small metal pellet that is part of a CARTRIDGE and is usu. capable of killing or wounding when shot from a gun, etc.

bully ('bŏŏli) *n.,pl.* **bullies.** a person who uses force to frighten someone weaker than himself. —*vb.* **bullying, bullied.** to frighten or intimidate (a weaker person).

bump (bump) *vb.* to hit sharply, esp. with a bang: *he bumped his head on the low ceiling.* **bump into** 1. to knock into or collide with. 2. to 'meet' (someone) by chance: *I bumped into Jane on my way to Simon's party.* **bump off** (slang) to murder. **bump up** (informal) to increase the volume or amount of (something). —*n.* 1. a blow or dull thump caused by a collision. 2. a lump or swelling on the skin. 3. a bulge on the surface of something: *a bump in the road.* 4. a sudden jolt. —'**bumpy** *adj.* **bumpier, bumpiest.**

bumper ('bumpə) *n.* a bar at the back and front of motor vehicles, that is designed to weaken the force of a collision. —*adj.* unusually large: *because of the fine summer, we had a bumper crop of apples this year.*

bunch (bunch) *n.* 1. a cluster of fruit, small collection of flowers, etc. 2. a group of things or people gathered together. —*vb.* to gather together untidily in a group: *the papers were bunched together in a file, and we had difficulty in sorting them out.*

bundle ('bundəl) *n.* a collection of things held loosely together: *a bundle of firewood.* —*vb.* **bundling, bundled.** 1. to put together into a bundle. 2. to throw (something) untidily into something else: *he bundled his clothes into a suitcase.* 3. to go or send (someone) off hurriedly and without ceremony: *we bundled him into the car.*

bungalow ('bunggəlō) *n.* a single-storeyed house.

bunion ('bunyən) *n.* an inflamed swelling of a joint of the foot, usu. on the big toe.

bunk (bungk) *n.* 1. a sleeping-berth on a boat. 2. one of a pair of narrow beds often attached to a wall and placed one above the other.

buoy (boi) *n.* an anchored float, usu. coloured and sometimes bearing a coloured light, used to mark rocks or other hazards or to indicate the way into a harbour. —*vb.* 1. to mark with a buoy. 2. (+ *up*) to keep afloat or keep up.

spherical can mooring

buoy

buoyant ('boiənt) *adj.* 1. able to float or (of liquids) capable of supporting a floating object. 2. cheerful or lively. —'**buoyancy** *n.* —'**buoyantly** *adv.*

burden ('bûdən) *n.* 1. a heavy load. 2. a responsibility, task, duty, etc., that is difficult to bear: *the burden of work.* **beast of burden** an animal used mainly for carrying loads. —*vb.* to place a load or burden on (someone or something): *he burdened me with his worries.* —'**burdensome** *adj.*

bureau ('byŏŏərō) *n.,pl.* **bureaux** *or* **bureaus** ('byŏŏərōz). 1. a writing desk with drawers. 2. an office, agency, or government department concerned with specific activity: *a travel bureau.*

burglar ('bûglə) *n.* a person who breaks into and steals from a house, shop, etc. '**burglary** *n.,pl.* **burglaries.** the crime or act of breaking into a building in order to steal. '**burgle** *vb.* **burgling, burgled.** to commit burglary.

burial ('beriəl) *n.* the action or an instance of burying something, esp. a dead body at a funeral.

burn (bûn) *vb.* **burning, burnt** *or* **burned.** 1. to destroy or injure with heat, fire, etc. 2. to catch or be on fire; be destroyed or changed by fire. 3. to produce or suffer a stinging feeling on the skin because of or as if because of heat. 4. to be strongly affected by anger, passion, etc.: *he burned with rage.* —*n.* an injury on the skin, etc., produced by heat.

burrow ('burō) *n.* a hole or underground tunnel made by rabbits, moles, etc. —*vb.* to dig or tunnel underground.

burst (bûst) *vb.* **bursting, burst.** 1. to break open suddenly due to pressure or force: *the severe frost caused the pipes to burst.* 2. to do something suddenly and forcefully: *the wood burst into flames.* —*n.* a sudden outbreak: *a burst of applause.*

bury ('beri) *vb.* **burying, buried.** 1. to place (a dead person's body) in a grave at a funeral ceremony. 3. to place or hide something, esp. under the earth. **bury the hatchet** to make peace. See also BURIAL.

bush (bŏŏsh) *n.* a small woody plant: *a rose bush.* **the Bush** (chiefly in Australia) the large thinly populated uncultivated areas of countryside.

beat about the bush to take a long time to get to the point. '**bushy** *adj.* **bushier, bushiest.** 1. covered with bushes. 2. thick: *a bushy tail.*

business ('biznis) *n.* 1. commerce or trade: *the shipping business.* 2. a firm or organization engaged in supplying goods or services. 3. affair or concern: *it is not my business to interfere.* '**businessman** *n.,pl.* **businessmen.** (**businesswoman,** *pl.* **businesswomen**) someone engaged in business or commerce.

bust (bust) *n.* 1. the part of the body including the head, neck, and shoulders, often represented in a sculpture. 2. a woman's chest: *a 36-inch bust.*

bustle ('busəl) *vb.* **bustling, bustled.** to hurry; behave or move about in a brisk or energetic way. —*n.* the action or an instance of bustling.

busy ('bizi) *adj.* **busier, busiest.** occupied with a large number of jobs or duties. —*vb.* **busying, busied.** to keep (someone) busy or occupied.

butcher ('bŏŏchə) *n.* a person who slaughters animals or prepares and sells meat. —*vb.* 1. to slaughter animals. 2. to murder savagely and brutally. —'**butchery** *n.*

butler ('butlə) *n.* a male servant, esp. the head servant in a big house.

butt[1] (but) *n.* 1. the thicker or blunter end of something: *the butt of a rifle.* 2. the part of a cigarette or cigar left after most of it has been smoked.

butt[2] (but) *n.* a person who is an object of mockery, scorn, etc. —*vb.* (+ *onto*) to project onto or be adjacent to.

butt[3] (but) *vb.* 1. to push or ram with the head or horns. 2. (+ *in*) (informal) to interrupt or push one's way in.

butter ('butə) *n.* a soft fatty yellow foodstuff made from milk or cream. —*vb.* 1. to spread butter on something. 2. (+ *up*) (informal) to flatter (someone), usu. to obtain favours.

butterfly ('butəflī) *n.,pl.* **butterflies.** 1. an insect with large brightly coloured wings. 2. a stroke in swimming in which both arms are thrust through the water and brought forward above the water together.

buttock ('butək) *n.* either of the fleshy parts of the body at the back and lower end of the TRUNK.

button ('butən) *n.* 1. a small object on a jacket, shirt, dress, etc., that may be passed through a hole (**buttonhole**) to fasten the garment. 2. a small knob that is pressed with the finger to operate an electrical device. —*vb.* (often + *up*) to fasten (a jacket, etc.) with a button.

buttress ('butris) *n.* a structure built up against the outside wall of large buildings to support them. —*vb.* to support with or as if with a buttress.

buttress

buy (bī) *vb.* **buying, bought.** to give money or other payment in exchange for: *to buy some ice cream.* —*n.* something bought: *a bad buy.* '**buyer** *n.* a person who buys, esp. one who buys stock for a large shop.

buzz (buz) *n.* a low continuous humming sound, as of wasps, bees, machinery, etc. —*vb.* to make such a sound. '**buzzer** *n.* a device like an electric bell that makes a harsh buzzing sound.

bypass ('bīpâs) *n.* a road built to avoid a town centre. —*vb.* to go round or make a detour.

C

cabbage ('kabij) *n.* a green vegetable with large fleshy overlapping outer leaves·and round heart.

cabin ('kabin) *n.* 1. a simple hut or small house built of wood or other materials: *a log cabin.* 2. a living compartment on board ship. 3. (in an aircraft) the area occupied by the crew, passengers, or cargo. **cabin cruiser** a motorboat with living accommodation.

cabinet ('kabinit) *n.* a free-standing cupboard with drawers and often glass-fronted, usu. used for storing and displaying glass, china, ornaments, etc. **the Cabinet** (Britain) the inner circle of government consisting of people selected by the Prime Minister. It advises the monarch on government matters and meets privately to discuss administration, make policies, etc. **Shadow Cabinet** see under SHADOW.

cable ('kābəl) *n.* 1. a strong rope of wire, etc. 2. an anchor-chain or rope. 3. a wire or line, carried overhead, underground, or under the sea, along which telephone or telegraph messages or electrical power may be sent. 4. a telegram transmitted by cable. —*vb.* **cabling, cabled.** to send a telegram by cable.

cactus ('kaktəs) *n.,pl.* **cacti** ('kaktī) *or* **cactuses.** a fleshy plant, often covered in spiny prickles, that grows in very dry areas, being able to store its moisture for long periods.

cactus

cadet (kə'det) *n.* a young man who is training for a career in the armed forces or the police.

cafe *or* **café** ('kafā) *n.* a place where tea and coffee, snacks, etc., are served.

cafeteria (kafi'tiəriə) *n.* a self-service restaurant.

cage (kāj) *n.* 1. a framework of wood, wire, iron bars, etc., used for keeping animals or birds in captivity. 2. (in a mine) a lift. —*vb.* **caging, caged.** to place or keep in a cage.

calculate ('kalkyōōlāt) *vb.* **calculating, calculated.** 1. to work out mathematically; reckon. 2. to make an estimate; guess: *we calculated that there must have been about 500 people in the hall.* '**calculating** *adj* scheming or shrewd. —**calcu'lation** *n.*

calendar ('kaləndə) *n.* a chart of the months, weeks, and days of a particular year.

calf[1] (kâf) *n.,pl.* **calves** (kâvz). 1. the young of a cow. 2. the young of other mammals, such as elephants, deer, seals, and whales. **calf love** immature love in early youth.

calf[2] (kâf) *n.,pl.* **calves** (kâvz). the fleshy part of the back of the leg below the knee.

calorie *or* **calory** ('kaləri) *n.,pl.* **calories.** 1. a unit of heat; the amount of heat needed to raise one gram of water through one degree centigrade. 2. **Calorie** *or* **large calorie** 1000 calories; the unit for measuring energy produced by food. —**calo'rific** *adj.*

calve (kâv) *vb.* **calving, calved.** to give birth to a calf or calves.

calves (kâvz) *n.* the plural of CALF[1] and CALF[2].

camel ('kaməl) *n.* a large long-necked, heavy-footed, plant-eating animal with either one hump (Arabian camel *or* dromedary) or two (Bactrian camel), found mainly in the desert areas of the Middle East and Asia, and used mainly for carrying loads over long distances.

camera ('kamərə) *n.* an apparatus for taking photographs, consisting of a sealed box containing light-sensitive film and a shutter which opens very briefly to admit light through a LENS, thus producing an image on the film. **television camera** a device in which the television picture is formed before being broadcast. '**cameraman** *n.,pl.* **cameramen.** a person who operates a film or television camera. **in camera** (law) in private rather than in open court.

camouflage ('kaməōflâẓh) *n.* 1. the natural colouring or patterning of an animal that allows it to blend easily with its surroundings, thus hiding it from enemies. 2. (military) the dis-

camouflage

guising of buildings, vehicles, weapons, etc., so as to make them inconspicuous. —*vb.* **camouflaging, camouflaged.** to disguise something so that it is not easily seen.

camp (kamp) *n.* 1. the tents or temporary housing used by holidaymakers, an army, etc. 2. the area where the tents, etc., are placed. —*vb.* 1. to set up a camp or pitch one's tent at a camp. 2. (+ *out*) to sleep outside, usu. in a tent.

campaign (kam'pān) *n.* 1. a series of battles or planned military operations. 2. a lengthy and organized effort: *a campaign against litter.* —*vb.* to seek public support for a cause, political candidate, etc. —**cam'paigner** *n.*

canal (kə'nal) *n.* an artificial inland waterway used for transporting goods, for travel, or for irrigation.

canary (kə'neəri) *n.,pl.* **canaries.** a bright yellow songbird native to the Canary Islands but popular elsewhere as a pet.

cancel ('kansəl) *vb.* **cancelling, cancelled.** 1. to notify or state that something previously arranged will not be done, not take place, or is no longer required: *we cancelled our trip to France.* 2. to cross out or mark in some way (a ticket, cheque, postage stamp, etc.) to show that it cannot be reissued or used again. 3. (+ *out*) to prevent or destroy (something) by being equal or opposite to: *his handsomeness was cancelled out by his rudeness.*

cancer ('kansə) *n.* a disease in which cells grow abnormally on the skin or to form a tumour or swelling in an organ. Cancer often spreads to other organs in the body. —**'cancerous** *adj.*

candid ('kandid) *adj.* frank, open, and honest; not afraid to tell the truth; outspoken: *he admitted in his candid way that he detested the play.* **'candour** *n.* frankness; honesty. —**'candidly** *adv.*

candidate ('kandidāt) *n.* a person applying for a position or job, taking an examination, standing for election, etc.

candle ('kandəl) *n.* a long stick of wax, tallow, etc., containing a wick that draws up melted wax, which burns slowly to provide light. **burn the candle at both ends** to exhaust

canoe

oneself by working hard all day and going to bed late.

cane (kān) *n.* 1. the hollow woody stem of certain plants, e.g. bamboo, sugarcane, raspberry plants, etc. 2. a piece of cane used as a walking stick, for beating as a punishment, etc. —*vb.* **caning, caned.** to beat with a cane.

cannibal ('kanibəl) *n.* an animal that eats its own species, esp. a man-eating human. —**'cannibalism** *n.* —**canniba'listic** *adj.*

cannon ('kanən) *n.,pl.* **cannons** or **cannon.** a large gun mounted on a cart and having a barrel suitable for firing heavy objects (**cannonballs**). —*vb.* to crash into and bounce off again: *he cannoned into me as he ran down the street.*

canoe (kə'noō) *n.* a long thin boat propelled by paddles. —*vb.* **canoeing, canoed.** to paddle a canoe.

canon ('kanən) *n.* 1. a law or set of laws laid down by the Church. 2. a standard by which something is judged. 3. those books of the Bible or of a particular writer that are considered to be genuine. 4. a list of saints recognized by the Church. 5. a musical work in which all the parts overlap while having the same melody. 6. a church official.

canopy ('kanəpi) *n.,pl.* **canopies.** 1. a covering, esp. one supported above a throne or bed. 2. any shelter or protective cover. 3. the umbrella-shaped sail of a PARACHUTE.

canteen (kan'tēn) *n.* 1. a self-service restaurant attached to factories, schools, etc. 2. a small fitted case, esp. one designed to hold cutlery. 3. a water container for carrying on a long journey.

canter ('kantə) *n.* the running pace of a horse, slower and more relaxed than a gallop but faster than a trot. —*vb.* to move at a canter.

canvas ('kanvəs) *n.* 1. a rough strong cloth used according to thickness for sails, tents, shoes, the base for oil paintings, covers for lorries, etc. 2. an oil painting.

canvass ('kanvəs) *vb.* 1. to seek support or favours, esp. votes at an election. 2. to find out what support there is for a party, etc., by talking to people: *he canvassed opinion in the local pubs.* —**'canvasser** *n.*

canyon

canyon ('kanyən) *n.* a deep steep-sided valley often with a stream flowing through it.

capable ('kāpəbəl) *adj.* 1. able or qualified to do something: *John is capable of making a table but not anything more difficult.* 2. showing common sense and general practical ability: *Sally is a very capable girl.* **capa'bility** (kāpə'biliti) *n.,pl.* **capabilities.** 1. the quality of being capable. 2. an advantage.

cape[1] (kāp) *n.* a narrow pointed stretch of land jutting out into the sea or other body of water.

cape[2] (kāp) *n.* a loose fitting outer garment that has no sleeves and is worn over the shoulders.

capital ('kapitəl) *adj.* 1. most important; chief: *London is England's capital city.* 2. relating to financial capital: *capital investment.* 3. punishable by death: *murder is still a capital crime in some countries.* 4. indicating the large form of a letter of the alphabet used at the beginning of sentences, proper names, etc. 5. excellent; fine: *a capital idea.* —*n.* 1. a capital city: *Rome is the capital of Italy.* 2. the money needed for starting a company, etc., or investing in it in order to help it to grow. 3. (architecture) the top of a pillar. 4. a capital letter. **'capitalism** *n.* a social and economic system based on privately owned (rather than state-owned) commercial companies kept in existence by private investments and paying out part of their profits to the investors. —**'capitalist** *n.,adj.*

capsize (kap'sīz) *vb.* **capsizing, capsized.** 1. (of a boat) to overturn in water. 2. to overturn (a boat) in water: *the strong wind capsized the yacht.*

capsule ('kapsyōol) *n.* 1. a small protective container holding a dose of medicine. 2. a section of a spacecraft that contains the crew or vital machinery.

captain ('kaptin) *n.* 1. the leader of an organized group of people, such as a sports team or a ship's crew. 2. a rank in the army between lieutenant and major, or in the navy between commander and rear-admiral. —*vb.* to lead.

caption ('kapshən) *n.* 1. a title or heading. 2. a title, name, or other wording shown on the screen during a film or television programme. 3. a piece of writing associated with a picture or drawing that gives its title or describes it.

captive ('kaptiv) *n.* a person who has been taken prisoner. —*adj.* having been captured: *the captive soldiers were chained to the wall.* —**cap'tivity** *n.*

capture ('kapchə) *vb.* **capturing, captured.** to seize, take possession of, or take prisoner. —*n.* the action or an instance of capturing.

caravan

caravan ('karəvan) *n.* 1. a house on wheels designed to be pulled by a horse or motor vehicle. 2. a company of travellers in the East or North Africa travelling together for safety, usu. on camels in the desert.

carbohydrate (kâbō'hīdrāt) *n.* any of a large number of chemicals that make up plants and are important in the food of man and animals.

carbon ('kâbən) *n.* an element found as charcoal, graphite, diamond, and soot, present in coal and all living things.

care (keə) *n.* 1. concern; serious thought: *handle the box with care.* 2. guardianship; protection; love: *he left the parcel in his neighbour's care.* 3. worry; anxiety: *the cares of looking after them all made her ill.* —*vb.* **caring, cared.** 1. (+ *for*) to look after; show concern or love for: *nobody cared for the little girl.* 2. (usu. + *about*) to mind; be concerned: *I don't care what you think.* **'careful** *adj.* paying thoughtful attention to what one is doing, using, etc. **'carefully** *adv.* with care. **'careless** *adj.* 1. not paying proper attention to what one is doing; thoughtless. 2. lacking a sense of concern, love, or morality: *he was careless of her feelings.* —**'carelessly** *adv.*

career (kə'riə) *n.* 1. a job of work with opportunities for promotion to senior positions. 2. a headlong rush. —*vb* to rush madly and uncontrollably.

cargo ('kâgō) *n.,pl.* **cargoes.** the goods carried in the hold of a ship.

carnival ('kânivəl) *n.* 1. a festive procession or fair, esp. one set up during a public holiday for organized enjoyment. 2. noisy celebration or rejoicing. 3. the period of such activities, esp. in some countries, the short period before Lent.

carnivorous (kâ'nivərəs) *adj.* of animals (and some plants) that feed on meat.

carol ('karəl) *n.* a popular hymn or song, esp. one sung at Christmas or Easter.

carp (kâp) *n.* a large freshwater fish caught for food.

carpenter ('kâpintə) *n.* a man skilled in working with wood and making wooden articles, furniture, etc. —**'carpentry** *n.*

carriage ('karij) *n.* 1. a wheeled passenger-carrying vehicle pulled by horses. 2. one of the separate passenger coaches pulled by a railway engine and making up a train. 3. the way a person moves or carries his body: *the soldier had an upright carriage.*

cartoon (kâ'tōon) *n.* 1. a drawing showing a humorous scene, or a series of drawings telling a story in a newspaper or magazine. 2. the drawing of a design to be used for a painting or a tapestry.

cartridge ('kâtrij) *n.* 1. a metal or thick paper case holding the explosive and the bullet for a gun, etc. 2. (in certain types of pen) a plastic container for the ink. 3. see CASSETTE.

carve (kâv) *vb.* **carving, carved.** 1. to cut into or shape by cutting (wood, stone, etc.). 2. to produce by cutting or shaping in this way: *he carved a statue out of marble.* 3. to cut up (a roast or other meat) for serving.

case[1] (kās) *n.* 1. an instance or example of something. 2. the facts of a situation. 3. a legal action or the argument put forward by one of the parties in it. 4. (in some languages) the form of a noun or adjective which changes according to its grammatical function in a sentence.

case[2] (kās) *n.* 1. a box, chest, bag, etc., for holding or carrying things, esp. clothes, papers, etc. 2. any sort of container, esp. a protective one: *a watch case.* —*vb.* **casing, cased.** 1. to cover with or enclose in a case. 2. (slang) to examine or keep watch on (a building), esp. so as to find out how to break into or steal from it: *the criminal cased the bank.*

cats

bobcat

jaguar

tiger

Calico cat

Siamese cat

lion

Blue Persian cat

cash (kash) *n.* money in the form of coins and notes that can be used immediately. **petty cash** a small amount of money kept by a company for ordinary expenses, e.g. for buying postage stamps, etc. —*vb.* to change (a cheque, etc.) into cash.

casserole ('kasərōl) *n.* 1. a stewpot with a lid for use in an oven or on direct heat. 2. a stew of meat, gravy, and vegetables that has been cooked in a casserole.

cassette (kə'set) *n.* a small flat case containing a tape for a tape-recorder or a film for a camera.

cast (kâst) *vb.* **casting, cast.** 1. to throw. 2. to send out (a look, glance, etc.) at someone or something or in a certain direction. 3. to cause (light, a shadow, etc.) to fall upon something: *he cast a shadow on the wall in the moonlight.* 4. (+ *about*) to search in one's mind: *he cast about for an excuse for being late.* 5. to make from a mould: *he cast the statue in bronze.* 6. to assign parts to actors in a play. 7. (+ *on*) to start a row of stitches in knitting. 8. (+ *off*) to finish off knit-

ting stitches to form an edge. 9. (+ *off*) to untie (a boat) at the start of a voyage. —*n.* 1. the action of casting; a throw, esp: of a fishing line. 2. a list or group of characters in, or actors needed for, a play. 3. a model of something made from a mould. 4. (also **plaster cast**) a casing made from plaster of Paris and put on a broken limb while it is healing. 5. (also **worm cast**) the hard heap of earth brought up by an earthworm.

castanet

castanet (kastə'net) *n.* either one of a pair of shaped pieces of wood or ivory held in one hand and clicked together. They are used esp. in Spanish dance music.

caste (kâst) *n.* one of the divisions of Hindu society in India to which a person belongs as a result of his birth.

casual ('kazhyo͞oəl) *adj.* 1. not especially arranged or organized; happening by chance: *we paid a casual visit to our neighbours.* 2. informal; relaxed: *I wear casual clothes at the weekends.* —'**casually** *adv.*

casualty ('kazhyo͞oəlti) *n.,pl.* **casualties.** 1. an unlucky accident, usu. serious or fatal. 2. (military) any man lost because of death, desertion, injury, etc. 3. any person or thing killed, injured, or damaged purely by accident: *the hospital took in several casualties after the crash.*

cat (kat) *n.* any one of the family of warm-blooded furry flesh-eating animals that ranges in size from the cats that are kept as pets to tigers, lions, and jaguars.

31

catalogue ('katəlog) *n.* a list that is arranged in alphabetical or some other order, usu. with a short description of what is being listed. —*vb.* **cataloguing, catalogued.** to make a catalogue or enter (something) into a catalogue: *we catalogued all the books in our school library.*

catarrh (kə'tâ) *n.* the thick discharge produced by the tissues in the nose, throat, etc., when they are painfully inflamed, e.g. by a cold.

catch (kach) *vb.* **catching, caught.** 1. to lay hold of; seize or capture. 2. to stop and hold with the hand: *to catch a ball.* 3. to reach and get on to (a bus, train, etc.). 4. to be affected by (an infectious illness): *he caught a cold.* 5. (often + *up* or *up with*) to come near to or overtake (a person). 6. (+ *out*) to prove or discover that someone is lying or trying to deceive: *John said he had not stolen any apples but was caught out when one fell out of his pocket.* 7. (+ *on*) to become popular. 8. (+ *on*) to understand or realize. —*n.* 1. the action of catching or seizing; a capture. 2. something caught, esp. fish. 3. a fastener: *a catch on a window.* 4. a trick; drawback: *this is a genuine offer and there's no catch.* **'catchy** *adj.* **catchier, catchiest.** pleasant and easily learnt: *a catchy melody.*

caterpillar

caterpillar ('katəpilə) *n.* 1. the plump worm-like six-legged LARVA of a moth or butterfly. It feeds on leaves or other vegetation. 2. a vehicle for travelling over rough or snow-covered ground and having wheels that move inside an endless belt (**caterpillar track**).

cathedral (kə'thēdrəl) *n.* the chief church of a diocese in the charge of a bishop. Cathedrals are usually larger than ordinary churches.

cattle ('katəl) *pl.n.* 1. animals such as cows, oxen, buffaloes, etc. 2. the domestic cows and bulls used for milk and meat.

caught (kôt) *vb.* the past tense and past participle of CATCH.

cauliflower ('koliflouə) *n.* a plant of the cabbage family with a large hard compact white flowerhead that is eaten as a vegetable.

caution ('kôshən) *n.* 1. care taken to avoid danger. 2. a warning or reprimand. —*vb.* to warn (a person) to be sensible, careful, etc. **'cautious** *adj.* 1. prudent; careful. 2. timid; unadventurous. —**'cautiously** *adv.*

cavalry ('kavəlri) *sing.* or *pl.n.* the part of an army that fights on horseback; horse soldiers.

cease (sēs) *vb.* **ceasing, ceased.** to stop or come to an end: *fighting ceased completely.* **'ceasefire** *n.* a military agreement between sides to stop fighting at an appointed time; truce. **'ceaseless** *adj.* continuous.

cedar ('sēdə) *n.* a large spreading evergreen cone-bearing tree with tough sweet-smelling reddish wood. See CONIFER.

ceiling ('sēling) *n.* 1. the overhead surface of a room. 2. the highest possible limit: *most goods have a price ceiling.*

celebrate ('selibrāt) *vb.* **celebrating, celebrated.** 1. to mark a special occasion, esp. with a ceremony, party, etc.: *we usually celebrate Christmas at home.* 2. to perform solemnly (a religious ceremony). **'celebrated** *adj.* famous. —**cele'bration** *n.*

celebrity (si'lebriti) *n.,pl.* **celebrities.** 1. a person well known to the public for achievements in entertainment, sport, arts, etc. 2. fame.

celery ('seləri) *n.* a vegetable with long white stalks, which are eaten raw or cooked.

celestial (si'lestiəl) *adj.* appearing in or connected with heaven or the heavens: *a star is a celestial object.*

cell (sel) *n.* 1. a small, barely furnished room in a prison, monastery, etc. 2. the smallest unit of living matter capable of producing energy and reproducing itself, out of which all plants and animals are formed. 3. apparatus for producing electricity by chemical action, e.g. in a battery.

cellar ('selə) *n.* a windowless room below ground level, often used for storage.

cello ('chelō) *n.,pl.* **cellos.** a musical instrument of the violin family, pitched lower than the viola and higher than the double bass. Also called **violoncello** (vīələn'chelō). —**'cellist** *n.*

Celsius ('selsiəs) *n.* See CENTIGRADE.

cement (si'ment) *n.* 1. a mixture of burnt and powdered limestone and clay used as a building material that sets hard when combined with water. 2. any glue that sticks by setting hard. 3. a soft plastic material that sets hard to fill holes in teeth. —*vb.* 1. to cover or join together with cement. 2. to unite and confirm: *the holiday cemented their friendship.*

cemetery ('semitri) *n.,pl.* **cemeteries.** an area of land, not in the grounds of a church, that is used for burying the dead.

censor ('sensə) *n.* a person responsible for examining letters, plays, newspapers, films, etc., in order to remove from them anything he considers to be immoral, obscene, or secret. —*vb.* 1. to act as a censor. 2. to remove undesirable material from (a film, play, book, letter, etc.). **censorious** (sen'sôriəs) *adj.* tending to find fault; smugly disapproving. —**'censorship** *n.*

census ('sensəs) *n.,pl.* **censuses.** an official population count that sometimes includes details of housing, etc.

cent (sent) *n.* a small unit of currency in the United States and elsewhere; the 100th part of a DOLLAR.

centenary (sen'tēnəri) *n.,pl.* **centenaries.** the hundredth anniversary of an event. —*adj.* relating to a hundred year period or a hundredth anniversary: *centenary celebrations.*

centigrade ('sentigrād) *adj.* of a temperature scale that is divided into 100 degrees between the freezing point of water (0°) and its boiling point (100°). Also called **Celsius** ('selsiəs).

centimetre ('sentimētə) *n.* a unit of measure equal to one hundredth of a metre (0·3937 inches).

cello

centipede ('sentipēd) *n.* a small creature with a long body and many legs. See INVERTEBRATE.

centre ('sentə) *n.* 1. the middle. 2. the middle point, esp. of a circle or sphere. 3. a place where certain activities are based: *a shopping centre.* 4. a person or thing receiving a great deal of interest, attention, etc. 5. a player in some team games who occupies the middle position. **centre of gravity** the point at which a supported object will balance. —*vb.* **centring, centred.** 1. to place in the centre. 2. to concentrate upon: *all efforts were centred on rescuing people from the flood.* —*adj.* 1. of or placed at the centre. 2. (of a political party or opinion) moderate; not extreme. '**central** *adj.* 1. at the centre: *the central figure in the photograph.* 2. main or principal: *our central office is in New York.* 3. basic; most important: *the central issue.*

century ('senchəri) *n.,pl.* **centuries.** 1. a period of one hundred years. 2. (cricket) a hundred runs scored by one batsman. 3. (in ancient Rome) an army company consisting originally of a hundred men and commanded by an officer called a **centurion.**

cereal ('siəriəl) *n.* 1. a grass such as wheat, barley, oats, etc., that produces grains or seeds used for food. 2. a breakfast food containing wheat, etc.

ceremony ('seriməni) *n.,pl.* **ceremonies.** 1. a solemn act or ritual that follows a set pattern: *a wedding ceremony.* 2. formal behaviour; pomp. **ceremonial** (seri'mōniəl) *adj.* formal; used in ceremonies: *the mayor put on his ceremonial chain. n.* ritual performance: *when the ceremonial was over the feasting began.* —**cere'monially** *adv.* —**cere'monious** *adj.*

certain ('sûtən) *adj.* 1. particular; fixed: *the sun rises at a certain time.* 2. without any possible doubt. 3. accurate: *a certain aim.* 4. moderate: *we had a certain amount of snow.* '**certainly** *adv.* 1. without doubt. 2. indeed: *may I have a cake? certainly.* —'**certainty** *n.,pl.* **certainties.**

certificate (sû'tifikit) *n.* a written statement of proof of some fact or achievement: *a birth certificate states when and where one was born.*

certify ('sûtifī) *vb.* **certifying, certified.** 1. to declare as certain: *the man certified that he had not driven the car for a week.* 2. to declare in writing or by means of a certificate: *he was the certified owner of the car.* 3. to issue a certificate of insanity concerning (a patient).

chain (chān) *n.* 1. a length of connected metal links. 2. a series of connected things: *a chain of grocery stores.* 3. a unit of distance equal to 22 yards. 4. **chains** (*pl.*) imprisoning or restraining bands. '**chain-gang** *n.* a group of prisoners chained together for working outside the prison. **chain mail** flexible armour made of small metal links. **chain reaction** a series of events, each set off by the one before it. **chain smoker** a person who smokes continually. —*vb.* to fasten, connect, or imprison with a chain.

chalk (chôk) *n.* 1. soft white limestone rock found in cliffs, hills, etc., that is used for drawing and writing on blackboards. 2. a drawing or writing crayon made of chalk. **by a long chalk** by far: *it's not the best car by a long chalk.* —*vb.* 1. to write, mark, or cover with chalk: *he chalked a circle on the board.* 2. (+ *up*) to earn or notch up: *to chalk up a victory.* —'**chalky** *adj.* **chalkier, chalkiest.**

challenge ('chalinj) *vb.* **challenging, challenged.** 1. to invite, demand, or dare (a person) to take part (in a duel, argument, contest, etc.). 2. to question: *I challenged his right to be present.* 3. (of soldiers) to ask for identification: *the sentry challenged me at the gate.* —*n.* 1. the act of challenging. 2. any task, scheme, etc., in which a person can prove his skill, energy, imagination, etc.

chameleon (kə'mēliən) *n.* 1. a small lizard with an ability to change its colour to match its background. 2. a person who changes his behaviour and attitudes according to those of his companions.

chamois ('shamwâ) *n.,pl.* **chamois.** a small goatlike deer living in mountainous areas of Europe and Russia. **chamois, chammy,** *or* **shammy leather** (all pronounced 'shami) leather treated with special oil to make it flexible, originally obtained from the chamois. It is often used for cleaning windows.

champagne (sham'pān) *n.* a sparkling French white wine.

champion ('champiən) *n.* 1. a proved competition or contest winner. 2. an active supporter of a cause or person. —*vb.* to support (a cause, person, etc.) '**championship** *n.* 1. the position of being a champion. 2. support. 3. a series of contests to find an overall champion.

chandelier (shandə'liə) *n.* a holder hung from the ceiling with a number of branches to carry several lights.

channel ('chanəl) *n.* 1. a long narrow stretch of water; strait. 2. a course or route along which water flows. 3. a path by which news or information is passed or communicated. 4. usu. **channels** (*pl.*) methods of doing something: *he applied for permission through the usual channels.* 5. the wavelength or set of wavelengths used by a television company for its broadcasts. —*vb.* **channelling, channelled.** to send through or as if through a channel.

chant (chânt) *n.* 1. a tuneless song. 2. a simple tune of a few notes to which psalms are sung. —*vb.* 1. to sing a chant. 2. to speak rhythmically: *the girls were chanting skipping rhymes.*

chaos ('kāos) 1. a state or place of utter confusion: *the room was in chaos after the party.* 2. the huge disordered jumble of matter from which some religions suppose that the universe was formed. —**cha'otic** *adj.*

chapel ('chapəl) *n.* 1. a place for Christian worship attached to a school, university, etc. 2. a place of worship for Protestants outside the established church: *a Methodist chapel.* 3. a small area or room in a church set aside for private worship. See also CHURCH.

chapter ('chaptə) *n.* 1. a section of a book. 2. the members or organizers of a cathedral, monastery, etc. **chapter and verse** the exact details, esp. those that will back up or prove a statement.

33

character ('kariktə) *n.* 1. the collection of qualities which makes one thing different from another: *the character of a room changes when it is painted.* 2. the collection of qualities that makes one person different from another and helps to fix his individual nature. 3. moral or spiritual strength. 4. an unusual or eccentric person. 5. a person in a story, play, etc. 6. a symbol standing for a sound, group of sounds or words, etc. 7. any alphabetical symbol. **character'istic** *n.* a particular quality or feature: *the second-hand car had several unpleasant characteristics. adj.* typical: *the present was characteristic of his kind nature.* 'characterize *vb.* **characterizing, characterized.** to give a special quality to; distinguish; show the nature of.

charcoal ('châkōl) *n.* 1. the black substance, consisting of pure carbon, that is produced by the incomplete burning of wood or other living matter. 2. a drawing made in charcoal.

charge (châj) *vb.* **charging, charged.** 1. to attack with a forward rush. 2. to demand or require money in return for goods or services. 3. (+ *with*) to accuse (someone) of something: *he was charged with murder.* 4. to fill with electricity: *to charge a battery.* 5. (+ *with*) to place a duty, responsibility, etc., upon (someone). 6. to note down (something) to be paid for later: *charge it to my account.* —*n.* 1. a forward-rushing attack. 2. (esp. of services rather than goods) the money to be paid; price. 3. an accusation or criticism: *a charge of stupidity.* 4. control or guardianship: *I'm in charge here.* 5. the amount of explosive to be let off at one blast. 6. the amount of electricity or energy in something. 'charger *n.* 1. a horse formerly used in battle. 2. a device for charging (def. 4) a battery. —'chargeable *adj.*

charity ('chariti) *n.,pl.* **charities.** 1. generosity and kindness towards others, esp. the poor. 2. an organization providing money, often given to it by the public, to finance projects for relieving poverty.

charm (châm) *n.* 1. the pleasantness or beauty that makes a person or place attractive: *that area of Italy is full of charm.* 2. often **charms** (*pl.*) such an attractive quality considered separately: *he was pleased by her many charms.* 3. an object, phrase, etc., supposedly having magic powers or bringing good luck: *a lucky charm.*

—*v.b.* 1. to please. 2. to work magic upon (someone). 'charming *adj.* pleasant; attractive.

chart (chât) *n.* 1. a drawing, table, or graph giving information on something. 2. a map, esp. of a sea area. —*vb.* to make a chart of or plan out, as on a chart.

charter ('châtə) *n.* an official paper granting someone certain special rights. —*vb.* 1. to give (someone) a charter. 2. to hire (a bus, aircraft, etc.) for a special purpose.

chatter ('chatə) *vb.* to talk quickly and foolishly.

chauffeur ('shōfə, shō'fû) *n.* a person hired to drive his employer's private car. **chauffeuse** (shō'fûz) *n.* a woman chauffeur.

cheetah

cheap (chēp) *adj.* 1. costing little money. 2. poor in quality or value: *cheap rubbish.* 3. unkind; lacking tact: *a cheap joke.* 'cheapen *vb.* to make cheap.

cheat (chēt) *vb.* to trick (someone); act dishonestly, esp. regarding money, the rules of a game, etc. —*n.* a person who cheats.

check (chek) *vb.* 1. to stop or restrain. 2. to make sure about the correctness of (a fact, etc.). 3. to mark with a pattern of squares: *a checked coat.* 4. (chess) to threaten one's opponent's king. —*n.* 1. the action or an instance of checking; a restraint, investigation, etc. 2. a pattern of squares, as on cloth. 3. the threat to a king at chess. —*adj.* patterned in squares. 'checkmate *n.* (chess) the final threat to an opponent's king, from which there is no escape. *vb.* **checkmating, checkmated.** to threaten (a king) thus. 'checkout *n.* the place in a supermarket where one pays for things bought.

cheek (chek) *n.* 1. the side of the face between the eye and the jaw. 2. rudeness or impertinence. **cheek by jowl** side by side; close together. **turn the other cheek** to refuse to react against insults, etc. **tongue in cheek** mockingly; jokingly. 'cheeky *adj.* **cheekier, cheekiest.** saucy; cheerfully impolite. —'cheekily *adv.* —'cheekiness *n.*

cheer (chiə) *n.* 1. a state of pleasant comfort; happiness or gladness. 2. a shout of joy, approval, encouragement, etc. —*vb.* 1. to comfort or encourage. 2. to give a shout of joy, approval, encouragement, etc. 3. (+ *up*) to make or become happy again. —'cheerful *adj.* —'cheerfully *adv.* —'cheerfulness *n.*

cheese (chēz) *n.* a food made from the solid fatty part of milk (curd). **cheesed off** (slang) bored or fed up.

cheetah ('chētə) *n.* an animal belonging to the cat family and closely resembling the leopard, but having longer legs. It is found in parts of Asia and Africa and is famous for its great speed.

chef (shef) *n.* the head cook in a restaurant.

chemical ('kemikəl) *adj.* concerning or connected with the science or processes of chemistry. —*n.* a substance made by or used in chemistry. —'chemically *adv.*

chemist ('kemist) *n.* 1. an expert in the science of chemistry. 2. a shopkeeper selling drugs, medicines, cosmetics, etc. **chemistry** *n.* the science concerned with the elements and compounds that make up different substances and their properties, reactions, and effects.

cheque (chek) *n.* a written order from a customer to his bank, generally using a printed form supplied by the bank, to pay a certain sum of money from his account to the person or firm mentioned. 'chequebook *n.* a book of blank cheques supplied by a bank.

cherry ('cheri) *n.,pl.* **cherries.** the small round red, yellow, or black stone-fruit of the cherry tree. —*adj.* bright red.

chess (ches) *n.* a game played by two people, each moving sixteen pieces (**chessmen**) on a board having 64 black and white squares (**chessboard**).

chest (chest) *n.* 1. the upper front part of the human body. 2. a large wooden box used for storage, etc. **get (something) off one's chest** to speak openly and frankly about (a problem, worry, etc.). **chest of drawers** a piece of furniture with several drawers used for storing linen, clothes, etc.

chestnut ('chesnut) *n.* 1. the smooth shiny edible brown nut of the sweet chestnut tree, that grows inside a prickly green case. 2. (also **conker**) the inedible nut of the horse chestnut tree. 3. a horse of a reddish-brown colour. 4. an old and well-worn question, joke, etc. —*adj.* of a rich reddish-brown colour.

chew (choo) *vb.* 1. to crush or grind between the teeth. 2. (+ *over*) to muse or ponder: *give me time to chew over the plan.* 3. (+ *up*) to destroy or ruin (something) as if by chewing; mangle: *the machine chewed up my ticket.* —*n.* the action or an instance of chewing.

chicken ('chikin) *n.* 1. a domesticated bird whose flesh and eggs are used as food. 2. (slang) a young or inexperienced person. 3. (slang) a coward.

chestnut

chimpanzee

count one's chickens before they are hatched to rely on something that has not yet happened. **chickenpox** a mild disease that usu. affects children, causing itchy spots all over the body. —*adj.* (also **chicken-hearted**) cowardly.

chief (chēf) *n.* the head or leader of a group, society, tribe, etc. —*adj.* main; most important. —**'chiefly** *adv.*

chilblain ('chilblān) *n.* a sore and itchy swelling generally found on the hands and feet and caused by intense cold or bad circulation of the blood.

chill (chil) *n.* 1. a sharp or sudden feeling of coldness: *a chill in the air.* 2. a feverish cold. —*vb.* to make or become cold or colder: *the orange juice was chilled.* **'chilly** *adj.* **chillier, chilliest.** 1. rather cold. 2. unwelcoming, unfriendly: *a chilly reception.* —**'chilliness** *n.*

chime (chīm) *n.* the sound produced by a striking bell or clock. —*vb.* **chiming, chimed.** 1. to ring out like a bell. 2. (+ *in*) to interrupt or break into a conversation.

chimney ('chimni) *n.* an open hollow pillar-like structure built above a house, factory, etc., to allow smoke to escape from a fire, etc., inside. **chimney pot** a small pottery or metal pipe that fits on top of a chimney. **chimney sweep** a person who cleans the soot from chimneys.

chimpanzee (chimpan'zē) *n.* a small African ape resembling but smaller than a gorilla.

chin (chin) *n.* the part of the face below the mouth. **keep one's chin up** to remain cheerful in difficult circumstances.

china ('chīnə) *n.* 1. very fine fragile pottery first made in China. 2. plates, cups, etc., collectively. —*adj.* made of china.

chinchilla (chin'chilə) *n.* 1. a South American animal that looks like a squirrel. 2. the thick soft pale grey fur of this animal, which is highly valued for coats, etc.

chink[1] (chingk) *n.* a narrow crack or slit, esp. one with light showing through it.

chink[2] (chingk) *vb.* to make a sound like that of coins or glasses struck together. —*n.* a chinking sound.

chip (chip) *n.* 1. a small piece or splinter of wood, stone, china, etc., that has been broken or cut off. 2. a crack or mark on a piece of crockery, glass, etc., caused by chipping. 3. a small stick of deep-fried potato. 4. a counter or token used in gambling. **a chip off the old block** a person who is very like one of his parents. **have a chip on one's shoulder** to bear a grudge or feel great resentment about something. —*vb.* **chipping, chipped.** 1. to crack or cause to crack. 2. to remove chips from (an object). 3. to cut (potatoes) into chips. 4. (+ *in*) to interrupt. 5. (+ *in*) (informal) to give or contribute money to a fund, outing, etc.

chisel ('chizəl) *n.* a long metal TOOL with a sharp edge, used for shaping wood, stone, or metal. —*vb.* **chiselling, chiselled.** to shape or cut with a chisel.

chivalry ('shivəlri) *n.* the qualities of honour, courage, kindness, etc., that knights in the Middle Ages were expected to have. —**'chivalrous** *adj.*

choice (chois) *n.* 1. the action or an instance of choosing: *a difficult choice.* 2. the thing chosen: *her final choice.* 3. the range or variety available: *a wide choice of dresses.* —*adj.* **choicer, choicest.** excellent: *a choice cut of meat.*

choir (kwīə) *n.* 1. a group of singers, esp. one that takes part in the services at a church; chorus. 2. that part of a church usu. used by the singers.

choke (chōk) *vb.* **choking, choked.** 1. to block or prevent air from entering the windpipe of (a person). 2. to be unable to breathe or swallow; suffocate: *he choked on a fish bone.* 3. to be unable to speak because of the strength of one's feelings. 4. to block or stop up a passage, space, etc.; obstruct: *weeds choked the drains.* —*n.* a device in a car's engine to decrease the amount of air taken in when it is cold.

choose (chōoz) *vb.* **choosing, chose, chosen.** 1. to select; pick out. 2. to wish; decide: *I did not choose to come here, I obeyed his order.* '**choosy** *adj.* **choosier, choosiest.** (informal) very fussy.

chop (chop) *vb.* **chopping, chopped.** 1. to cut with a heavy blow, as with an axe. 2. to cut up into small pieces: *chop the parsley.* —*n.* 1. a short sharp cut or blow. 2. a piece of pork or mutton containing part of a rib-bone. '**chopper** *n.* 1. a heavy axe with a large flat blade. 2. (informal) a helicopter.

chopstick

chopstick ('chopstik) *n.* one of two small wooden, plastic, or ivory sticks, both held in one hand and used by the Chinese for eating food.

choral ('kôrəl) *adj.* connected with, adapted for, or sung by a choir: *choral music.*

chord (kôd) *n.* 1. a combination of three or more musical sounds played or sung together. 2. a straight line passing through two points on a circle or curve.

chore (chô) *n.* 1. a dull or boring but necessary task. 2. an odd job.

chorus ('kôrəs) *n.,pl.* **choruses.** 1. a company of singers or dancers, esp. those who support the soloists in an opera, ballet, etc. 2. a choir. 3. a section of a song that is usu. repeated at the end of each verse. —*vb.* to say or sing all together: *the children chorused their thanks for the party.*

chose (chōz) *vb.* the past tense of CHOOSE.

chosen ('chōzən) *vb.* the past participle of CHOOSE.

christen ('krisən) *vb.* 1. (in the Christian Church) to baptize and give a name to (someone). 2. to choose a name for.

Christian ('krischən) *n.* a person who believes in and follows the teachings of Jesus Christ. —*adj.* 1. of or relating to Christianity. 2. notable for the Christian virtues of kindness, generosity, etc. **Christianity** (kristi'aniti) *n.* the Christian faith based on the teachings of Jesus Christ.

chronic ('kronik) *adj.* 1. (of a disease, illness, etc.) long-lasting and continuous. 2. (informal) very severe: *a chronic housing shortage.* 3. (slang) dreadful; very bad: *her singing was chronic.* —'**chronically** *adv.*

chronicle ('kronikəl) *n.* often **chronicles** (*pl.*) a list or book of past events, usu. arranged in order of time: *she read the chronicles of the local archaeological society.* —*vb.* **chronicling, chronicled.** to record in a chronicle.

chrysalis ('krisəlis) *n.* the PUPA of a moth or butterfly.

chrysanthemum (kri'santhəməm) *n.* one of a family of autumn-flowering garden plants, usu. with large red, white, or gold blooms.

chuckle ('chukəl) *vb.* **chuckling, chuckled.** to laugh quietly in a gently cheerful way. —*n.* a quiet laugh.

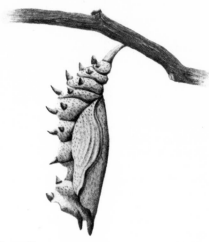
chrysalis

chunk (chungk) *n.* a large thick piece or slice: *a chunk of meat.* '**chunky** *adj.* **chunkier, chunkiest.** 1. in a chunk or chunks. 2. knitted in thick wool: *a chunky pullover.*

church (chûch) *n.* (often **Church**) 1. a building used for Christian and other religious services. 2. a particular group of Christians following its own interpretation of Christ's teachings: *the Methodist Church.* 3. all clergymen considered as a single group. 4. the career of a clergyman. '**churchyard** *n.* the burial ground surrounding a church. Compare CEMETERY.

churn (chûn) *n.* the container in which milk or cream is stirred or beaten to make butter. —*vb.* (often + up) to shake or beat violently; stir up: *the horses' hoofs churned up the mud.*

cider ('sīdə) *n.* an alcoholic drink made from the fermented juice of apples.

cinema ('sinimə) *n.* 1. a theatre or other building where films are shown. 2. the art or industry of film-making, or films collectively: *she has written a book on the cinema.*

circle ('sûkəl) *n.* 1. an area enclosed by a curved line, which is at every point the same distance away from the centre; a ring. See GEOMETRY. 2. a group of people with the same interests: *a literary circle.* 3. a recurring series of events; cycle. **vicious circle** a difficult situation from which there is no escape because the necessary methods of removing the difficulty lead back to it. —*vb.* **circling, circled.** 1. to surround with a ring. 2. to go round: *the kitten nervously circled the sleeping dog.*

circuit ('sûkit) *n.* 1. the route or way around a course or area that has been marked out; lap: *the players made a quick circuit of the football pitch.* 2. the path taken by an electric current. 3. a number of places, e.g. cinemas or law courts, that are linked in some way; chain.

circular ('sûkyoolə) *adj.* 1. in the shape of a circle or ring; round: *a circular table.* 2. tending to bring one back to the original starting point: *a circular argument.* **circular saw** an electrically powered saw that is round or disc-shaped with a sharp-toothed edge. —*n.* a printed letter, notice, advertisement, etc., sent to a large number of people.

circumference (sə'kumfərəns) *n.* 1. the boundary line of a circle or circular area; perimeter. 2. the length of this line. See GEOMETRY.

circumstances ('sûkəmstənsiz) *pl.n.* the conditions or facts connected with a person, event, etc.: *what were the circumstances of the accident?*

circus ('sûkəs) *n.,pl.* **circuses.** 1. a travelling show with performing animals, acrobats, clowns, etc. 2. a central arena as in a Roman amphitheatre. 3. (Britain) a circular area or place in a town or city where several main streets meet: *Oxford Circus.*

citizen ('sitizən) *n.* a person who enjoys the rights or privileges of a particular city, town, or country: *a French citizen.* —'**citizenship** *n.*

citrus ('sitrəs) *n.* a family of trees, consisting of the orange, lemon, grapefruit, etc., that grow in warm climates. —*adj.* of or relating to such trees or their fruit.

city ('siti) *n.,pl.* **cities.** a large or important town, esp. one with special rights or status, and usu. having a cathedral. **the City** the area of London that contains the Bank of England, the Stock Exchange, etc., and is the financial and commercial centre of the country.

civic ('sivik) *adj.* of or relating to the affairs of a city or citizenship: *a civic hall.*

civil ('sivəl) *adj.* 1. of or relating to the state, cities, citizens, etc., esp. as distinguished from the Church or the army, navy, or air force. 2. polite or courteous: *a civil answer.* **civil ser-**

vant a person employed by the official administration of a country (**civil service**), which serves the government. **civil war** a war between members or parties of the same state or country.

civilian (si'vilyən) *n.* a person who is not in the armed forces. —*adj.* of or relating to a person or life outside the armed forces: *civilian clothes.*

civilize ('sivilīz) *vb.* **civilizing, civilized.** to bring (a people or nation) out of a primitive or savage condition by the introduction of education, law, government, trade, etc. **civili'zation** *n.* 1. the act or process of civilizing a people or nation. 2. a society, nation, or empire having a highly developed cultural, social, economic, and political structure. '**civilized** *adj.* 1. having been civilized. 2. well-bred or polite.

claim (klām) *vb.* 1. to demand or take possession of (something) as one's right. 2. to insist that something is true: *he claims to be 100 years old.* —*n.* 1. a demand or the thing claimed. 2. an area of unused land marked out by a settler or miner for future use. '**claimant** *n.* one who claims something, esp. land or a title.

clamp (klamp) *n.* a tool or device that can be tightened to grip, secure, or hold something together. —*vb.* to grip or **hold** (something) in or as if in a clamp. **clamp down on** (informal) to exercise authority or discipline in order to stop or reduce (crime, protest, etc.)

clarinet

clarinet (klari'net) *n.* a musical instrument of the woodwind family in which a single reed set in the mouthpiece vibrates the air in a tube. —**clari'nettist** *or* **clari'netist** *n.*

clash (klash) *vb.* 1. to bang two or more things together or collide, making a loud harsh metallic sound: *their swords clashed.* 2. to disagree very strongly; conflict: *these two colours clash violently.* 3. (of events) to coincide. —*n.* the action, the sound, or an instance of clashing.

clasp (klâsp) *n.* 1. a small fastening, such as a hook, pin, or buckle, generally made of metal and often used in jewellery. 2. a firm handshake or grip. —*vb.* to grasp or hold (something) tightly.

class (klâs) *n.* 1. a group or set of people, animals, plants, objects, words, etc., having common qualities or characteristics: *mammals form a class of the animal kingdom.* 2. a category or grade: *first class.* 3. a group of children or students who are taught together: *the art class.* 4. (informal) excellence; fine style or quality: *this chess-player has great class.* —*vb.* to place in or regard as belonging to a particular class or group.

classic ('klasik) *adj.* (also '**classical**) 1. (esp. of art or literature) of the very highest or finest class or standard: *a classic novel.* 2. (of well-established practices or traditions) serving as a model or guide: *a classic example.* 3. relating to or typical of ancient Greek or Roman culture or art: *the classic style of painting.* —*n.* 1. a work of art that has been regarded as one of the best of its kind for a long time. 2. an ancient Greek or Roman writer or book.

classical ('klasikəl) *adj.* 1. (of a work of art) based on traditional forms; balanced and restrained. 2. (also **classic**) of or in accordance with ancient Greek or Roman style in art, literature, architecture, etc. **classical music** music that is regarded as serious and conforms to recognized or established aesthetic standards, esp. when compared with pop music, jazz, etc.

classify ('klasifī) *vb.* **classifying, classified.** to put in order; sort or arrange into classes or groups: *we classify the books according to their subjects.* —**classifi'cation** *n.*

clause (klôz) *n.* 1. a sentence or part of a sentence containing a subject and a verb, as in *here is the house* (main clause) *where Joan lived last year* (subordinate clause). 2. a single paragraph in a legal document.

claw (klô) *n.* a sharp curved nail on the foot of birds and certain animals. —*vb.* to scratch, tear, or pull at (something) with nails or claws.

clay (klā) *n.* a heavy, smooth type of earth or mud that holds together when wet and hardens when baked, used for making pots, bricks, etc.

clench (klench) *vb.* to close (one's fists or teeth) very tightly.

clergy ('klûji) *n.* vicars, bishops, etc., considered collectively or as a special group. '**clergyman** *n.,pl.* **clergymen.** a member of the clergy.

clerk (klâk) *n.* 1. an office or shop employee who deals with records, papers, and documents. 2. a person who keeps the records, etc., at a law court. 3. (also **town clerk**) the chief administrator on a town or other local council.

cliff (klif) *n.* a steep rock face, esp. a high one.

climate ('klīmit) *n.* 1. the general weather conditions of a country. 2. a general set of circumstances, attitudes, or opinions: *the political climate.* —**climatic** (klī'matik) *adj.*

climax ('klīmaks) *n.* 1. a point of greatest excitement, intensity, etc.: *the music rose to its climax.* 2. the last part of something; end or finale. —cli'**mactic** *adj.*

climb (klīm) *vb.* to go up; ascend: *he climbed the tree.* —*n.* 1. the act or an instance of climbing. 2. a slope: *the hill was a steep climb.* '**climber** *n.* a person who climbs mountains, cliffs, etc., for sport.

cling (kliñg) *vb.* **clinging, clung.** 1. to hold on tightly: *the monkey clung to his trainer's coat.* 2. to stay with: *the smell of the cheap scent clung to him all day.* 3. (of thin clothes, etc.) to fit closely, showing. the shape of the body.

clinic ('klinik) *n.* 1. a place that people visit to receive medical or dental treatment. 2. a private nursing home. '**clinical** *adj.* 1. clean and hygienic. 2. excessively clean and bare: *the tidy living-room had an unfriendly, clinical atmosphere.*

clip (klip) *vb.* **clipping, clipped.** 1. to trim or shorten. 2. to nick or cut (tickets, etc.), with a punch. 3. to fasten tightly: *he clipped the papers together.*

4. to hit or strike. —*n.* an object used for fastening things together, esp. papers or women's hair. '**clippers** *pl. n.* a tool for cutting hair, grass, claws, etc.

cloak (klōk) *n.* a long outer garment worn wrapped round the shoulders, for outdoor use. —*vb.* to hide or cover with or as if with a cloak. '**cloakroom** *n.* a place where coats, umbrellas, etc., are left.

clock

clock (klok) *n.* an instrument for measuring time. '**clockwise** *adv.* circling in the direction in which the hands of a clock turn: *most screws are tightened by turning them clockwise.* —*adj.* characterized by moving in this direction: *the clockwise motion of the sun.*

clockwork ('klokwûk) *adj.* 1. working like a clock, i.e. by the slow unwinding of a tightly coiled spring. 2. precise; regular: *the display was planned with clockwork precision.* **go like clockwork** to happen exactly according to plan, without any difficulties.

clog (klog) *n.* 1. a shoe with a wooden sole. 2. a wooden shoe traditionally worn in Holland. —*vb.* **clogging, clogged.** to block up: *the drain was clogged with dead leaves.*

cloister ('kloistə) *n.* a covered place for walking along the side of a building, often built around courtyards of monasteries.

cloth (kloth) *n.* 1. material or fabric. 2. a piece of material serving any of several purposes, e.g. cleaning or covering.

clothe (klōdh) *vb.* **clothing, clothed.** 1. to provide with clothes; dress. 2. to cover: *he clothed his real feelings in polite words.*

cloud (kloud) *n.* 1. a visible mass of water vapour in the form of tiny droplets or ice crystals in the sky. 2. a mass of dust, smoke, etc. 3. a cause of gloom, darkness, or disgrace: *he left under a cloud.* —*vb.* 1. (+ *over*) to become full of clouds. 2. to make dark or gloomy. 3. to make sad or difficult to understand. —'**cloudy** *adj.* **cloudier, cloudiest.**

clown (kloun) *n.* 1. a fool or jester in a circus or pantomime. 2. an ignorant person who acts foolishly, esp. without realizing it. —*vb.* to act like a clown.

club (klub) *n.* 1. a heavy stick used as a weapon. 2. a stick used in games such as golf to hit the ball. 3. an association or group of people with a common interest, and often rules of membership. —*vb.* **clubbing, clubbed.** to hit with a club. **club together** to join together.

clue (klōo) *n.* a hint or suggestion leading to the solution of a problem: *the police found a clue to the murderer's identity.* **clued up** (slang) aware of what is going on, esp. in regard to current fashion, methods, etc. '**clueless** *adj.* (informal) lacking common sense.

clump (klump) *n.* 1. a cluster or group of bushes, trees, etc. 2. a mass of anything. 3. (informal) a hit or blow. —*vb.* to tread loudly and heavily.

clumsy ('klumzi) *adj.* **clumsier, clumsiest.** 1. awkward; lacking in grace. 2. embarrassing; tactless: *a clumsy apology.*

clung (kluñg) *vb.* the past tense and past participle of CLING.

cluster ('klustə) n. a group of closely associated things; bunch. —vb. to gather or be gathered into a cluster.

clutch (kluch) vb. (often + at) to catch hold of (something) tightly. —n. 1. often **clutches** (pl.) power or influence: in the clutches of the enemy. 2. a grip or grasp.

coach (kōch) n. 1. a bus for long-distance or private journeys. 2. a railway carriage for passengers. 3. a passenger vehicle drawn by several horses. 4. a person who gives individual tuition, or who trains an athletics team. —vb. to teach or train.

coal (kōl) n. a hard, usu. black, mineral composed mainly of carbon and formed under heat and pressure from plants that decayed millions of years ago. It is used as a fuel.

coarse (kôs) adj. 1. (of cloth, etc.) rough. 2. having or showing a lack of good manners, etc.: coarse behaviour. 'coarsen vb. to make or become coarse or coarser.

coast (kōst) n. the part of a land or island that meets the sea; shore. 'coastguard n. a government officer whose duty is to keep watch on the sea, esp. to prevent smuggling or to help ships in difficulty. 'coastline n. the shape of a coast. **the coast is clear** there is no danger near. —vb. 1. to move or work in a relaxed way. 2. (of a car) to be driven without using the engine.

coax (kōks) vb. to persuade by flattery or kindness.

cobra ('kōbrə) n. a highly poisonous African and Asian snake. Some cobras have the power to spit their venom at their prey.

cobweb ('kobweb) n. the web spun by a spider.

cock (kok) n. 1. a male chicken. 2. a male bird of any species: a cock pheasant. 3. (also **stopcock**) a device for regulating the flow of liquid, esp. water. —vb. to set (one's hat) at a slanting angle.

cocktail ('koktāl) n. a short drink mixed from several alcoholic ingredients.

cocoa ('kōkō) n. 1. chocolate powder made from the crushed beans of a tree (the cacao tree). 2. the drink made from this powder. ·

coconut ('kōkənut) n. the large round fruit of a tall tropical tree (**coconut palm**), that has a very hard hairy shell, an inner lining of soft sweet white flesh, and a whitish sweet juice (**coconut milk**).

cocoon (kə'kōōn) n. the silky ball spun by silkworms and other insect-grubs, into which the grub retires in order to grow into a winged adult.

cod

cod (kod) n.,pl. **cod.** a large sea-fish of the northern Atlantic, important as food. **codliver oil** an oil obtained from cod and used as medicine.

code (kōd) n. 1. a system for transmitting messages briefly or secretly. 2. a set of signals for sending messages: morse code. 3. an organized system of rules governing behaviour, etc.

coffee ('kofi) n. 1. a drink made by pouring boiling water onto roasted and ground coffee beans. 2. the tropical tree that produces these beans.

coffin ('kofin) n. a long wooden chest, wider at one end than the other, in which a dead body is laid for burial in the ground.

cog (kog) n. 1. any of several teeth on the rim of a wheel in a machine that can engage with similar teeth on other wheels and thus cause these wheels to turn and make the machine work. 2. a wheel having such teeth on its rim.

coil (koil) vb. to curl or cause to curl round and round in circles: the snake coiled its body around the tree. —n. a length of rope, wire, etc., that has been coiled or made into a spiral shape.

coin (koin) n. a flat piece of metal, used as money, having a government stamp on it. —vb. 1. to make or pro-

duce (money). 2. to earn (a great deal of money) by some activity. 3. to invent (a new word or phrase).

collapse (kə'laps) vb. **collapsing, collapsed.** 1. to give way; fall to the ground: he collapsed in the street. 2. (of balloons, etc.) to lose air suddenly; shrink down. 3. to fold up or cause to fold up; push or be pushed inwards. 4. (of hopes, etc.) to fail. —n. the action or an instance of collapsing. —col'lapsible adj. able to be folded into a smaller space.

collar ('kolə) n. 1. the part of a shirt, jacket, etc., that encloses the neck. 2. a leather band round a dog's neck. 'collar-bone n. either of two prominent bones at the base of the neck, joining the breastbone and the shoulder-blades. —vb. 1. (informal) to seize (someone) by the collar. 2. (informal) to stop (someone) for a particular purpose.

collect vb. (kə'lekt) 1. to find and bring together (stamps, coins, etc.). 2. to get (contributions). 3. to assemble or cause to assemble: a large crowd collected to see the parade. —n. ('kolikt) a short prayer to be said at a special time or season. **col'lection** n. 1. the act of collecting. 2. a group of things that have been collected together.

college ('kolij) n. 1. a place where one can continue one's education or obtain a professional training after leaving school. 2. a body of scholars or students forming part of a university. 3. any of several famous public schools.

collide (kə'līd) vb. **colliding, collided.** (often + with) to run into; crash: the two cars collided with each other. —**collision** (kə'lizhən) n.

colon ('kōlən) n. a punctuation mark(:) ranked between the semi-colon and the full stop and used to introduce an illustration or an example, or to balance two parts of a sentence.

colonel ('kûnəl) n. an army officer ranking above a major and below a brigadier and commanding a regiment.

colony ('koləni) n.,pl. **colonies.** 1. an area ruled by another country. 2. a group of foreigners in a country. 3. any group living together: a colony of ants. 'colonist n. a member of a colony. —**colonial** (kə'lōniəl) adj. —co'lonially adv.

colour ('kulə) *n.* 1. the appearance that light of a certain WAVELENGTH or combinations of wavelengths presents to the human eye. Light of a long wavelength is red and light of short wavelength is blue. 2. the appearance of an object described in terms of the type of light it reflects: *green is the colour of grass.* 3. the appearance of the face, esp. the red colour caused by anger, shame, etc. 4. paint or dye. 5. **colours** (*pl.*) the flag of an army, regiment, etc. —*vb.* 1. to treat with colour; paint. 2. to become red in the face, e.g. because of shame or anger. —'**coloured** *adj.* —'**colourless** *adj.*

column

column ('koləm) *n.* 1. a pillar, usu. with a decorated top. 2. a line of men, army vehicles, etc. 3. a list of figures for adding up. 4. a vertical section of print in a newspaper, book, etc. 5. anything rising straight up: *a column of smoke.*

comb (kōm) *n.* 1. a toothed device for getting tangles out of the hair or for cleaning it. 2. the red fleshy crest on the heads of domestic fowls and other birds. —*vb.* 1. to apply a comb to (one's hair, etc.). 2. to search very thoroughly: *they combed the countryside for escaped prisoners.*

combat *n.* ('kombat) a battle or fight. —*vb.* ('kombat, kəm'bat) to do battle against.

combine *vb.* (kəm'bīn) **combining, combined.** to mix or join together. —*n.* ('kombīn) 1. a group of people brought together for a special purpose, esp. concerning business, politics, or finance. 2. (also **combine harvester**) a machine that combines the reaping and threshing of grain. **combi'nation** *n.* 1. the action or

result of combining. 2. the group of people or things combined.

combustion (kəm'buschən) *n.* 1. the action of burning. 2. the chemical or physical process connected with burning. **com'bustible** *adj.* able to be burnt.

comedy ('komidi) *n.,pl.* **comedies.** a play that is light and amusing and generally has a happy ending. **comedian** (kə'mēdiən) *n.* 1. a comic actor. 2. a writer of comedies. See also COMIC.

comet ('komit) *n.* any of several objects moving around the sun, consisting of a bright head and a very long tail.

comfort ('kumfət) *n.* 1. freedom from pain, worry, hunger, poverty, etc. 2. help or kindness for someone in distress. 3. something that provides help or relief: *a hot drink is a comfort on a cold day.* —*vb.* to provide comfort. '**comfortable** *adj.* 1. providing comfort. 2. feeling at ease, free from pain, etc. —'**comfortably** *adv.*

comic ('komik) *adj.* (also **comical**) funny; humorous. —*n.* 1. (also **comic strip**) a group of drawings that tell a story. 2. a newspaper containing such drawings. 3. a comic entertainer.

comma ('komə) *n.* a punctuation mark (,) used to show a slight break in a sentence.

command (kə'mând) *vb.* 1. to give an order to (someone). 2. to lead. 3. to look out over: *the house on the cliff commanded a fine view.* —*n.* 1. an order: *he gave out his commands.* 2. the position of giving orders: *I am in command.*

commence (kə'mens) *vb.* **commencing, commenced.** to begin; start. —**com'mencement** *n.*

commend (kə'mend) 1. to give approval to; praise. 2. to entrust; give into someone's care. **com'mendable** *adj* praiseworthy.

comment ('koment) *n.* a statement or opinion about something; remark. —*vb.* (often + *about* or *on*) to make a comment or say as a comment. **commentary** ('komentəri) *n.,pl.* **commentaries.** 1. a spoken description of a sporting event broadcast on radio or television. 2. the descriptive notes about the text of a book. '**commentator** *n.* a person who provides a commentary.

commerce ('komûs) *n.* business or trade, esp. on a large scale. **com'mercial** *adj.* 1. of or relating to trade or commerce. 2. able to be sold or to make money: *a commercial pop record. n.* an advertisement on radio or television.

commission (kə'mishən) *n.* 1. a military officer's post or a paper confirming this. 2. payment made to a salesman or saleswoman depending on the amount of goods that he or she sells. 3. a special job given to someone. 4. a group of people given power to carry out a special duty, esp. an investigation: *a government commission.* —*vb.* to pay (someone) to do a special job: *he was commissioned to write a symphony.*

commit (kə'mit) *vb.* **committing, committed.** 1. to do (something), esp. a crime or foolish action. 2. to entrust; give (something) up to someone's care or charge. **com'mitment** *n.* 1. a promise. 2. complete devotion.

comet

committee (kə'miti) *n.* a group of people chosen by a larger group and given authority to carry out certain duties, such as the administration of a society, etc.

common ('komən) *adj.* 1. usual; normal; most often seen, met with, etc.: *a cold is common illness.* 2. shared: *common knowledge.* 3. impolite or ill-mannered. —*n.* an open area of land for use by everyone.

commonplace ('komənplās) *adj.* not very unusual; not out of the ordinary: *the daisy is a very commonplace flower.*

Common Market an economic and trading association of nine European countries (Italy, France, West Germany, Belgium, the Netherlands, Luxembourg, and (since 1973) Britain, Eire, and Denmark), established in 1958. It is also called the European Economic Community (EEC).

commonwealth ('komənwelth) *n.* 1. the entire body of people in a country or state. 2. (usu. **Commonwealth**) a federation of colonies or former colonies, esp. those belonging to Britain.

commotion (kə'mōshən) *n.* a noisy, rushing, sometimes violent movement or disturbance.

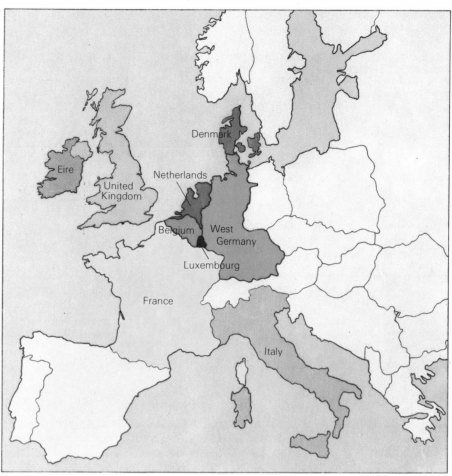
Common Market

communicate (kə'myōōnikāt) *vb.* **communicating, communicated.** 1. (+ *with*) to get in contact with. 2. (+ *to*) to pass (information, etc.) on to. 3. to pass (illness or disease) on to: *parrot fever is a disease that can be communicated to human beings.* **communi'cation** *n.* 1. the action of communicating. 2. something that is communicated, esp, a letter.

community (kə'myōōniti) *n.,pl.* **communities.** 1. a group of people living together, esp. in a village, town, etc. 2. the act of sharing or state of being shared.

commuter (kə'myōōtə) *n.* a person living outside the large town or city where he works, and travelling in every day. **com'mute** *vb.* **commuting, commuted.** 1. to travel to work as a commuter. 2. to reduce the severity of (a punishment, etc.).

compact *adj.* (kəm'pakt) occupying little space; tightly packed; condensed. —*n.* ('kompakt) 1. an agreement, bargain, or treaty. 2. a flat, usu. circular box containing a woman's face powder and puff.

companion (kəm'panyən) *n.* 1. a person with whom one keeps company: *a travelling companion.* 2. a person one likes to be with; friend. 3. someone hired to help or look after a sick or elderly person.

company ('kumpəni) *n.,pl.* **companies.** 1. the state or condition of having another person in one's presence. 2. a business; firm. 3. a small group of soldiers; sections of an army. 4. any group of people.

compare (kəm'peə) *vb.* **comparing, compared.** 1. (+ *with* or *to*) to judge one thing as being like another. 2. (often + *with*) to discover the similarities and differences between one thing and another. **comparative** (kəm'parətiv) *adj.* 1. of or concerning the action of comparing. 2. approximate: *comparative safety.* *n.* a form of an adjective, e.g. *bigger* is the comparative of *big.* **comparison** (kəm'parisən) *n.* the action or an instance of comparing.

compartment (kəm'pâtmənt) *n.* 1. a separate section of a container. 2. a part of a railway passenger coach.

compass ('kumpəs) *n.* 1. an instrument that indicates direction, consisting of a magnetized needle that always points north. 2. also **compasses** (*pl.*) a geometrical instrument used for drawing circles and arcs. 3. range; scope.

compass

compel (kəm'pel) *vb.* **compelling, compelled.** to make or force (someone) to do (something); bring pressure upon: *he compelled her to come with him.*

compete (kəm'pēt) *vb.* **competing, competed.** (+ *against, with,* etc.) 1. to take part in a game, sport, etc. 2. to match or rival. **competition** (kompi'tishən) *n.* 1. the act of competing. 2. a game, etc., in which one competes. **competitor** (kəm'petitə) *n.* a person who competes.

complain (kəm'plān) *vb.* 1. to express one's annoyance about something unjust or wrong. 2. to talk about a pain one is suffering from: *she complains of a headache.* **com'plaint** *n.* 1. the action or an instance of complaining. 2. an illness.

complement ('komplimənt) *n.* 1. the amount necessary to make something complete. 2. the second part of a sentence containing verbs like 'be' or 'seem', e.g. *a student* in the sentence *Sue is a student.* 3. the full number of officers and men on a ship.

complete (kəm'plēt) *adj.* 1. full or finished; needing nothing more. 2. total: *complete silence.* —*vb.* **completing, completed.** to make complete. —**com'pletion** *n.*

complex ('kompleks) *adj.* not simple; complicated. —*n.* 1. a large set of connected parts, esp. buildings, etc.: *a sports complex was planned for the school.* 2. a mental or psychological condition. —**com'plexity** *n., pl.* **complexities.**

complexion (kəm'plekshən) *n.* 1. the appearance of the face or skin: *a soft complexion.* 2. the appearance of a situation: *that puts a different complexion on matters.*

complicate ('komplikāt) *vb.* **complicating, complicated.** to make (something) difficult or much less simple: *uncertainty over the weather complicated our plans for a picnic.* —**compli'cation** *n.*

compliment *n.* ('komplimənt) 1. an expression of admiration, respect, or praise. 2. **compliments** (*pl.*) a formal expression of greetings: *my compliments to your wife, Sir John.* —*vb.* ('kompliment) 1. to express admiration; pay a compliment to: *he complimented her on her cooking.* 2. to congratulate. **compli'mentary** *adj.* 1. of or expressing a compliment; admiring. 2. free of charge.

compose (kəm'pōz) *vb.* **composing, composed.** 1. to make up out of several parts: *a string quartet is composed of two violins, one viola and one cello.* 2. to write (music, poetry, a letter, etc.). 3. to calm: *she tried to compose herself for her difficult task.* 4. to arrange and prepare (printing type) before printing. **com'poser** *n.* a writer of music. **composition** (kompə'zishən) *n.* something composed, esp. a musical or literary piece. **compositor** (kəm'pozitə) *n.* a person who sets up printing type.

compound[1] *n.* ('kompound) 1. something formed by combining two or more ingredients, elements, etc. 2. (chemistry) a substance formed by the combination of two or more elements and having properties different from those of these elements: *water is a compound of two elements called hydrogen and oxygen.* —*vb.* (kəm'pound) 1. to mix or combine. 2. to increase or be increased: *the farmer's misfortunes were compounded by the heavy rainfall.* —*adj.* ('kompound) composed of two or more parts, ingredients, etc.

compound[2] ('kompound) *n.* an enclosure in which prisoners of war, workers, etc., are held or housed.

compulsion (kəm'pulshən) *n.* 1. the act of compelling or the state of being compelled. 2. a strong obsession, urge, etc. **com'pulsive** *adj.* of or reflecting a strong urge: *he was a compulsive gambler.* **com'pulsory** *adj.* required by law or some other authority.

compute (kəm'pyoot) *vb.* **computing, computed.** to calculate; work out. **com'puter** *n.* an electronic device able to carry out highly complex mathematical calculations, at great speed, according to instructions that are fed into it. —**computation** (kompyoo'tāshən) *n.*

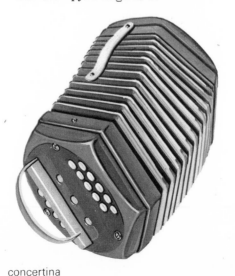

concertina

comrade ('komrid) *n.* 1. a companion or friend. 2. a term of address used esp. in Communist countries to replace 'Mr', 'Sir', 'Mrs', or 'Madam'. —**'comradeship** *n.*

concave (kon'kāv) *adj.* (esp. of a lens or mirror) curving or bulging inwards. —**concavity** (kon'kaviti) *n., pl.* **concavities.**

conceal (kən'sēl) *vb.* 1. to hide or keep out of sight: *her face was concealed under a mask.* 2. to keep secret: *he concealed the fact that he already knew the girl.* —**con'cealment** *n.*

conceit (kən'sēt) *n.* excessive love and admiration of oneself; vanity. —**con'ceited** *adj.*

concentrate ('konsəntrāt) *vb.* **concentrating, concentrated.** 1. to direct thoughts or actions to one particular subject: *to concentrate on a problem.* 2. to increase the strength or intensity of. 3. to bring to a particular point: *most of the population is concentrated heavily in the cities.* —**concen'tration** *n.*

concentric (kən'sentrik) *adj.* (of two or more circles or spheres) having a common central point, one circle or sphere lying within the other. See GEOMETRY.

concern (kən'sûn) *n.* 1. something in which one has an interest, share, etc.; affairs; business. 2. anxiety; worry: *she showed great concern over the fate of the dog.* 3. a manufacturing or commercial firm; business: *he works for a shipping concern.* —*vb.* 1. to involve or be of interest or importance: *I am concerned with local politics.* 2. to worry or feel anxious: *I am concerned about her health.*

concert ('konsût) *n.* a musical entertainment given by an orchestra, soloist, etc., before a large audience. **concerted** (kən'sûtid) *adj.* done with all persons involved working together: *a concerted effort.*

concertina (konsə'tēnə) *n.* a small accordion.

conclude (kən'klood) *vb.* **concluding, concluded.** 1. to finish; come or bring to an end: *he concluded his speech.* 2. to draw an impression or opinion: *may we conclude from your silence that you agree?* 3. to bring to a decision; settle: *they concluded a defence treaty.* **con'clusion** *n.* 1. the end or final part of something. 2. a result or outcome. 3. a deduction; inference: *she came to the conclusion that he was ill.* **con'clusive** *adj.* decisive or convincing: *conclusive evidence.*

concrete ('konkrēt) *adj.* 1. firm or real. 2. made of concrete. —*n.* a hard material made by mixing sand, water, cement, pebbles, etc., together, used esp. in building.

concussion (kən'kushən) *n.* shock produced by a blow on the head, e.g. after a fall or collision, sometimes involving a jarring of the brain.

condemn (kən'dem) *vb.* 1. to sentence: *the judge condemned him to five years' imprisonment.* 2. to express very severe disapproval of; criticize strongly: *he condemned her action.* 3. to declare (a building) no longer safe or fit for use. —**condemnation** (kondem'nāshən) *n.*

condense (kən'dens) *vb.* **condensing, condensed.** 1. to pack into a smaller space; make compact, small, etc. 2. (of a gas) to cool to liquid form. 3. to cut (a story, article) to shorter length. **conden'sation** *n.* 1. the action or process of condensing. 2. the condensed state or something in that state, e.g. water from water vapour: *there was condensation on the bathroom window.*

condition (kən'dishən) *n.* 1. state of being; situation: *the goldfish bowl was in poor condition because it had not been cleaned out.* 2. a state of health: *she suffers from a nervous condition.* 3. a necessary, agreed, or appropriate state; requirement or term: *conditions of surrender.* —*vb.* 1. to determine or limit. 2. to make terms or conditions. 3. to train (a person or animal) always to respond in the same way to certain treatment or actions: *the dog was conditioned to bark when he saw a bone.* **con'ditional** *adj.* depending on, containing, or imposing a condition or conditions: *the offer of a job was conditional on good references.* —**con'ditionally** *adv.*

conduct *vb.* (kən'dukt) 1. to guide or lead: *he conducted the blind man across the road.* 2. to manage or control (a meeting, business). 3. to control (an orchestra, choir, etc.) by indicating time with one's hands or a stick called a baton. 4. to be able to transmit or pass on (heat, electricity, etc.): *a metal spoon conducts heat more quickly than a wooden one.* —*n.*

('kondukt) behaviour: *disobedience shows bad conduct.* **con'ductor** *n.* 1. a person who controls an orchestra or choir. 2. a person who collects fares on a bus. 3. something that transmits heat, electricity, etc.

cone (kōn) *n.* 1. a solid pointed object on a circular base. See GEOMETRY. 2. (also **cornet**) a biscuit made in this shape and filled with icecream. 3. the scaly fruit of certain trees such as the pine or fir. Each of the scales has a seed. See CONIFER.

conference ('konfərəns) *n.* a meeting for discussion, consultation, etc.

confess (kən'fes) *vb.* 1. to admit or acknowledge: *she confessed her dislike of his plan.* 2. to declare (one's sins) to a priest. —**con'fession** *n.*

confide (kən'fīd) *vb.* **confiding, confided.** to trust someone with a secret, etc.; entrust. **confidant** *or* **confidante** ('konfidant) *n.* someone to whom secrets, feelings, etc., are confided. **confidence** ('konfidəns) *n.* 1. trust or belief in someone or something: *I have confidence in his ability.* 2. self-assurance: *he stepped onto the stage with great confidence.* 3. a secret. **in confidence** told as a secret or private matter. **confidence trick** a swindle or deception. **'confident** *adj.* showing confidence; bold, assured, or positive. **confidential** (konfi'denshəl) *adj.* secret or characterized by secrecy: *a confidential message.*

confine *vb.* (kən'fīn) **confining, confined.** 1. to imprison. 2. to set limits or bounds to (something). **be confined** (of a woman) to give birth to a baby. —*n.* ('konfīn) a limit or boundary. **con'finement** *n.* 1. imprisonment. 2. the period during which a woman gives birth to a child.

confirm (kən'fûm) *vb.* 1. to provide a good reason for: *your wet umbrella confirms my suspicion that you have been out in the rain.* 2. to make (something) certain: *a letter confirmed his appointment.* 3. to make firm or more firm; strengthen: *the news confirmed his determination.* 4. to admit (a baptized person) as a full member of the church at a special religious service. —**confir'mation** *n.*

confiscate ('konfiskāt) *vb.* **confiscating, confiscated.** to seize, esp. legally or officially: *the teacher confiscated the child's chocolate.* —**confis'cation** *n.*

cone

conflict *n.* ('konflikt) 1. an argument, disagreement, or quarrel: *a conflict of opinion.* 2. a war or battle, esp. a prolonged struggle. —*vb.* (kən'flikt) 1. to clash or disagree. 2. to do battle; fight.

conform (kən'fôm) *vb.* 1. to act according to certain rules of behaviour: *John would not conform to the rules of the club.* 2. to agree with or be similar to: *the shape of the house did not conform to the plans.* **con'formist** *n.* a person who behaves in the same way as everyone else. **con'formity** *n.* the act or an instance of conforming.

confront (kən'frunt) *vb.* 1. to stand before (an enemy or opponent); face boldly. 2. to meet or face up to (a difficulty or problem).

confuse (kən'fyooz) *vb.* **confusing, confused.** 1. to bewilder, perplex, or muddle: *if you all talk at once you will confuse me.* 2. to throw into disorder; jumble: *you've confused all my exam papers.* —**con'fusion** *n.*

congratulate (kən'gratyoolāt) *vb.* **congratulating, congratulated.** to compliment (someone) on success, good fortune, etc. **congratu'lation** *n.*

congregate ('konggrəgāt) *vb.* **congregating, congregated.** to gather together or assemble; collect. **congre'gation** *n.* 1. the action or an instance of congregating. 2. the whole group of worshippers in a church or parish.

congress ('konggres) *n.* 1. a series of meetings for discussion between representatives of different societies, professions, etc.: *a congress of dentists was held at the college last summer.* 2. **Congress** the law-making assembly of the United States, consisting of the Senate and the House of Representatives. —**congressional** (kən'greshənəl) *adj.*

conifers

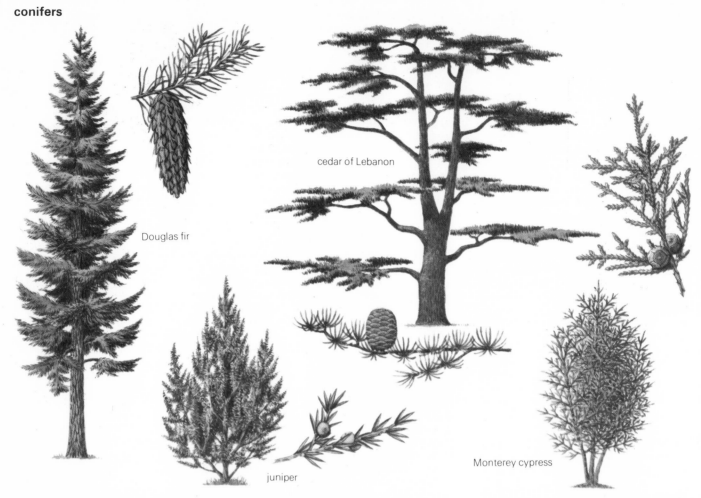

Douglas fir

cedar of Lebanon

juniper

Monterey cypress

conifer ('konifə) *n.* a class of tree, including the pine and fir, that produces fruit in the form of cones.

conjunction (kən'juṇgkshən) *n.* a word such as *and* or *but* used to link other words or phrases.

conjurer ('kunjərə) *n.* a magician.

connect (kə'nekt) *vb.* 1. to join together or link up: *the mechanic connected the trailer to the lorry.* 2. to associate or be associated: *I always connect lavender with Norfolk.* —**con'nection** *n.*

conquer ('koṇgkə) *vb.* 1. to win a victory over; subdue or gain by force: *they conquered new territory.* 2. to overcome (difficulty, etc.): *he conquered all his fears.* **conquest** ('koṇgkwest) *n.* a person, thing, or country conquered: *he surveyed his conquests.*

conscience ('konshəns) *n.* the ability to recognize a distinction between right and wrong: *my conscience will not let me deceive you.* **conscientious** (konshi'enshəs) *adj.* guided by conscience; extremely careful, reliable, and scrupulous. —**consci-'entiously** *adv.*

conscious ('konshəs) *adj.* 1. fully aware of one's own sensations, etc. 2. mentally awake and alert. 3. deliberate and intentional: *his words were a conscious attempt to start a fight.* **'consciousness** *n.* 1. the state of being fully awake and alert. 2. the mind. —**'consciously** *adv.*

consent (kən'sent) *vb.* to agree or approve; assent. —*n.* permission; approval: *the headmaster willingly gave his consent to the plan.*

consequence ('konsikwəns) *n.* 1. an outcome, effect, or result: *the trick had an unfortunate consequence.* 2. importance, significance, or distinction: *a person of great consequence.* **'consequent** *adj.* following; being the result of. —**'consequently** *adv.*

conservative (kən'sûvətiv) *adj.* 1. tending or preferring to preserve existing institutions, conditions, etc.; resisting change. 2. cautious or moderate: *a conservative estimate.*

conserve (kən'sûv) *vb.* **conserving, conserved.** 1. to protect or keep safe (something highly valued); preserve. 2. to store up for later use: *conserve your energy for tomorrow's race.* **conser'vationist** *n.,adj.* (of) a person who wishes to protect and preserve natural resources, the countryside, animals, etc. —**conser'vation** *n.*

consider (kən'sidə) *vb.* 1. to think about carefully; contemplate. 2. to look upon; regard as: *I consider him a fool.* 3. to be kind and thoughtful; regard: *he never considered his mother.* **con'siderable** *adj.* 1. fairly large or great: *a considerable amount.* 2. important: *he was a considerable artist.* **con'siderate** *adj.* kind and thoughtful. **consider'ation** *n.* 1. kindness or thoughtfulness. 2. attention: *I will give the matter careful consideration.* 3. something taken or to be taken into account: *the cost of the plan was the most important consideration.* 4. a reward, payment, etc.: *for a small consideration he will take you there.*

consist (kən'sist) *vb.* 1. to be composed of: *the programme consists of* *three short ballets.* 2. to be contained or based in. **con'sistency** *n.,pl.* **consistencies.** 1. texture, density, firmness, etc.: *mix the ingredients to a thick consistency.* 2. constancy; lack of variation. **con'sistent** *adj.* 1. logically in agreement with: *his statement was not consistent with the facts of the case.* 2. unchanging; constant: *he showed a consistent dislike of her.* —**con'sistently** *adv.*

consonant ('konsənənt) *n.* 1. a speech sound made by blocking the passage of one's breath with the tongue or lips. 2. a letter representing such a sound: *b, d, g, l, m are all consonants.* Compare VOWEL.

conspicuous (kən'spikyōōəs) *adj.* noticeable, striking, or eye-catching: *he was conspicuous in the crowd because of his height.*

conspire (kən'spīə) *vb.* **conspiring, conspired.** to plot or agree together, esp. in secret, to do something illegal, evil, etc.: *Guy Fawkes conspired with his friends to blow up Parliament.* **conspiracy** (kən'spirəsi) *n.,pl.* **conspiracies.** —**con'spirator** *n.*

constable ('kunstəbəl) *n.* a policeman of the lowest rank, esp. a uniformed policeman on patrol.

constant ('konstənt) *adj.* fixed or unchanging; invariable. —*n.* something that is unchanging or fixed. —'**constancy** *n.* —'**constantly** *adv.*

constellation (konstə'lāshən) *n.* a pattern or grouping of stars.

construct (kən'strukt) *vb.* to build, create, or put (something) together. **con'struction** *n.* 1. the action or an instance of constructing. 2. anything constructed; structure, building, etc. 3. an explanation or interpretation: *there is only one construction that can be put on his conduct.* 4. (grammar) a form of words used in a sentence. 5. a special drawing made in geometry. **con'structive** *adj.* 1. of, relating to, or tending to construct. 2. helpful; positive. —**con'structively** *adv.*

consult (kən'sult) *vb.* 1. to ask for help, advice, an opinion, etc. 2. to refer to for information, etc.: *to consult a dictionary.* 3. (+ *with*) to discuss something (with one's colleagues, etc.). **con'sultant** *n.* a specialist who gives professional advice, help, etc. —**consultation** (konsəl'tāshən) *n.* the act of seeking professional advice or the occasion on which this is done.

consume (kən'syōōm) *vb.* **consuming, consumed.** 1. to use up. 2. to drink or eat up: *he consumed two whole cakes.* 3. to waste or squander (money, etc.). 4. to destroy or be destroyed: *the building was consumed by fire.* **con'sumer** *n.* a person who buys and uses goods and services. **consumption** (kən'sumpshən) *n.* the action or an instance of consuming.

contact *n.* ('kontakt) 1. the act or state of touching, meeting, etc. 2. a useful acquaintance; connection: *he has contacts in politics.* 3. the state of being in communication: *don't forget to get in contact with us.* **contact lenses** thin curved discs of plastic or glass worn on the eyeballs to correct faulty eyesight. —*vb.* ('kontakt, kən'takt) 1. to touch or to bring into contact: *his hand contacted the cold steel.* 2. to communicate with.

contagious (kən'tājəs) *adj.* 1. (of a disease) passed on by touch or close contact. 2. able to be spread to other people: *fear is contagious.*

contain (kən'tān) *vb.* 1. to hold or have inside: *the bottle contains a pint of milk.* 2. to include: *our team contains two fast forwards.* 3. to keep in check; restrain: *he was unable to contain his feelings.* **con'tainer** *n.* a box, tin, etc., for holding something.

content[1] ('kontent) *n.* 1. usu. **contents** (*pl.*) all that is held in a container, area, etc.: *the contents of my room are in a mess.* 2. usu. **contents** (*pl.*) the chief topics, chapters, items, or subject of a book, etc. 3. the volume or amount that can be held in a container, area, etc: *the bottle has a content of two pints.*

content[2] (kən'tent) *adj.* (also **contented**) 1. satisfied; pleased: *he is content to stay at home.* 2. agreeing. —*vb.* to satisfy or please. —**con'tentment** *n.*

contest *n.* ('kontest) a struggle for victory, superiority, a prize, etc.: *a hard contest between the two tennis players.* —*vb.* (kən'test) 1. to fight or struggle against; dispute: *I'll contest that decision.* 2. to fight or struggle for: *he contested the leadership.* —**con'testant** *n.*

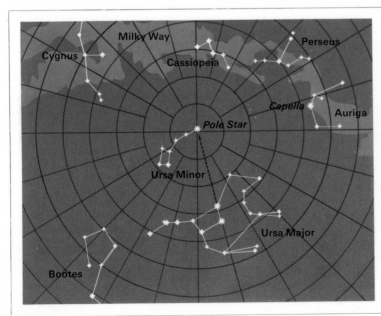
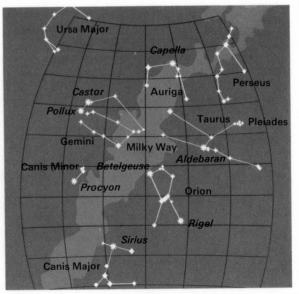

constellation

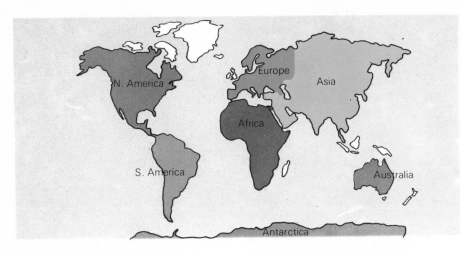

continent

continent ('kontinənt) *n.* one of the seven great divisions of land on the earth's surface (Asia, Africa, Europe, Australia, Antarctica, North America, and South America). **the Continent** the mainland of Europe. —**continental** (konti'nentəl) *adj.*

continue (kən'tinyoo) *vb.* **continuing, continued. 1.** to last; endure: *the drought continued for four years.* **2.** to carry on again or take up again; resume: *the show will continue after an interval.* **3.** to remain or stay: *John will continue as our team captain.* **4.** to extend or stretch out: *let's continue the trench.* **con'tinual** *adj.* without interruption; never stopping: *the continual roar of the waves.* **con'tinuous** *adj.* connected or uninterrupted: *a continuous stream of traffic.* —**con'tinually** *adv.* —**con'tinuously** *adv.*

contract *n.* ('kontrakt) an agreement between two or more people or groups, esp. a written legal agreement. —*vb.* (kən'trakt) **1.** to draw or be drawn together; make or become shorter, smaller, etc.; shrink. **2.** to start (an illness): *he contracted measles.* **3.** to form an agreement.

contradict (kontrə'dikt) *vb.* **1.** to be inconsistent with or state the opposite of; deny. **2.** to deny or speak against (the statements, comments, etc., of another or oneself): *you always contradict your father.* **contra'diction** *n.* the action or an instance of contradicting. —**contra'dictory** *adj.*

contrary *adj.* **1.** (kən'treəri) stubborn; perverse: *she is a very contrary child.*

contrast *n.* ('kontrâst) **1.** difference; dissimilarity. **2.** a person or thing that

is very different from another: *she's a contrast to her brother.* **3.** the use of dissimilar colours, etc., e.g. in painting. —*vb.* (kən'trâst) to compare (several people or things) in order to demonstrate or discover the differences between them.

contribute (kən'tribyoot) *vb.* **contributing, contributed.** (usu. + *to*) **1.** to give (money, help, etc.) to a good cause: *we all contributed 50p to the appeal fund.* **2.** to write for a book, magazine, etc. **3.** to have a share in; play a part in: *human error contributed to the disaster.* —**contribution** (kontri'byooshən) *n.* —**con'tributor** *n.* —**con'tributory** *adj.*

control (kən'trōl) *vb.* **controlling, controlled. 1.** to have power over; command. **2.** to restrict, restrain, or check. —*n.* **1.** power; command. **2.** restriction; restraint: *his temper is out of control.* **3.** an instrument or device for controlling a machine, etc. —**con'troller** *n.*

convenient (kən'vēnyənt) *adj.* **1.** well-situated; handy: *a convenient location.* **2.** in accordance with one's needs; suitable: *a convenient arrangement.* **con'venience** *n.* **1.** the state of being convenient. **2.** something that is useful or convenient, esp. an aid or facility.

convent ('konvənt) *n.* **1.** a community of nuns. **2.** the buildings in which this community lives. **3.** a girls' school run by nuns.

convention (kən'venshən) *n.* **1.** something or a way of doing something that is generally accepted; custom; usage. **2.** general agreement. **3.** a conference or meeting. —**con'ventional** *adj.*

converge (kən'vûj) *vb.* **converging, converged.** to come together; meet at a certain place: *parallel lines never converge.* —**con'vergence** *n.*

converse (kən'vûs) *vb.* **conversing, conversed.** to talk together informally. **conversation** (konvə'sāshən) *n.* an informal discussion. —**conver'sational** *adj.*

convert *vb.* (kən'vût) **1.** to change or transform: *they converted the old barn into a house.* **2.** to change or cause to change in religious belief, etc.: *the people were converted to Christianity.* —*n.* ('konvût) a person whose principles, religious beliefs, etc., have been changed: *he is a recent convert to Christianity.* —**con'version** *n.* —**con'vertible** *adj.*

convex (kon'veks) *adj.* (esp. of a lens or mirror) curving or bulging outwards.

convict *vb.* (kən'vikt) to prove or declare guilty of an offence. —*n.* ('konvikt) a person convicted of a crime and serving a prison sentence. **con'viction** *n.* **1.** the act of proving or declaring a person guilty of a crime. **2.** a firm belief.

convince (kən'vins) *vb.* **convincing, convinced.** to make (someone) believe something; persuade: *he convinced her that she was wrong.* **con'vincing** *adj.* believable; able to convince. —**con'vincingly** *adv.*

cool (kool) *adj.* **1.** fairly cold; not hot. **2.** feeling or producing coolness: *a cool dress.* **3.** unfriendly: *a cool welcome.* **4.** calm: *keep cool in an emergency.* **5.** (slang) excellent; fine. —*vb.* **1.** (sometimes + *down*) to make or become cool. **2.** (+ *off* or *down*) to become calmer.

cooperate (kō'opərāt) *vb.* **cooperating, cooperated.** to act as a single group; work together. **co'operative** *adj.* intending to or willing to cooperate. *n.* a business in which profits are shared amongst members. —**cooper'ation** *n.*

cope (kōp) *vb.* **coping, coped.** (+ *with*) to handle successfully; deal with: *an astronaut has to cope with weightlessness.*

copper[1] ('kopə) *n.* **1.** a reddish-brown metallic element used for wiring, plumbing, etc. Chemical symbol: Cu. **2.** a copper coin, esp. (Britain) an old penny. —*adj.* made of copper.

copper² ('kopə) *n.* (slang) a policeman.

copy ('kopi) *vb.* **copying, copied.** 1. to imitate. 2. to produce an exact likeness or second example of; reproduce: *copy this poem.* —*n.,pl.* **copies.** 1. an imitation or reproduction. 2. one of an edition of a book, magazine, etc.

coral ('korəl) *n.* the hard material forming sea reefs and formed from the skeletons of very small sea creatures.

coral

cord (kôd) *n.* 1. a thick string consisting of several twisted or woven strands. 2. something resembling a cord: *the spinal cord.* 3. a fabric, such as corduroy.

corduroy ('kôdəroi) *n.* 1. a strong fabric having raised lines and grooves on its surface. 2. **corduroys** (*pl.*) trousers made of corduroy.

core (kô) *n.* 1. the central part of something. 2. the basic or most important part of anything; heart: *we have now reached the core of the problem.* 3. the middle of an apple or similar fruit, containing the seeds or pips. —*vb.* **coring, cored.** to remove the core from (apples, etc.).

cork (kôk) *n.* 1. the light outer bark of a type of oak tree. 2. a piece of this used for stopping up bottles. —*vb.* (sometimes + *up*) to stop up with a cork.

corn¹ (kôn) *n.* 1. wheat, barley, etc., or the grain obtained from them. 2. (also **Indian corn**) (chiefly U.S.) maize. '**corny** *adj.* **cornier, corniest.** (informal) old-fashioned or unoriginal. '**sweetcorn** *n.* a sweet type of maize whose seeds are used as a vegetable.

corn² (kôn) *n.* a small painful area of hardened skin esp. on the foot, caused by pressure or rubbing.

corner ('kônə) *n.* 1. the place where two lines or surfaces meet. 2. the place where two roads meet or one road turns at a sharp angle. —*vb.* 1. to prevent from escaping. 2. to go round a corner: *the car corners badly.*

coroner ('korənə) *n.* an officer of a county, etc., who organizes INQUESTs into unexplained or sudden deaths.

corporal ('kôpərəl) *n.* a rank in the army or air force directly below that of sergeant.

corpse (kôps) *n.* a dead body.

corpuscle ('kôpəsəl) *n.* one of the microscopic cells found in blood. The white corpuscles help the body to fight infection, while the smaller red corpuscles carry oxygen.

correct (kə'rekt) *adj.* 1. having no mistakes; accurate: *a correct answer.* 2. right: *a correct conclusion.* 3. observing the usual rules or conventions: *correct behaviour.* —*vb.* to make correct. —**cor'rection** *n.*

corridor ('koridə) *n.* 1. an enclosed passageway in a building with rooms on one or both sides. 2. a similar passageway in a train linking compartments. 3. a narrow strip of land or air space, forming an access route for a country through neighbouring countries, often unfriendly ones.

corrode (kə'rōd) *vb.* **corroding, corroded.** to wear or be worn away; eat or be eaten into: *acid corrodes metal.* —**cor'rosion** *n.*

corrupt (kə'rupt) *vb.* 1. to have an evil or destructive influence on: *some think that violence on television corrupts young people.* 2. to make rotten or foul. —*adj.* dishonest or untrustworthy. —**cor'ruption** *n.*

cosmetic (koz'metik) *n.,* often **cosmetics** (*pl.*). a substance, such as lipstick, hair spray, etc., used for improving the skin or hair or making them more beautiful. —*adj.* relating to or acting like a cosmetic.

costume ('kostyōōm) *n.* 1. a set of clothes worn by an actor or a person in fancy dress. 2. any clothing or a set of clothes: *Elizabethan costume.* 3. a woman's suit. 4. (also **swimming costume**) a swimsuit.

cosy ('kōzi) *adj.* **cosier, cosiest.** snug, warm, and comfortable. —*n.* a cover for keeping a teapot or boiled egg warm. —'**cosily** *adv.* —'**cosiness** *n.*

cottage ('kotij) *n.* a small, simple residence.

cotton ('kotən) *n.* 1. the soft white furry substance obtained from the seed pods of the cotton plant, which grows in warm climates. 2. thread or cloth made from cotton.

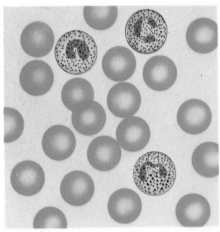
corpuscle

cough (kof) *vb.* to force air from the lungs in a sudden noisy burst. —*n.* the action or an instance of coughing.

council ('kounsəl) *n.* 1. a group of people who meet to discuss, organize, and decide on important matters. 2. a group elected to organize the affairs of a town, county, district, or parish.

counsel ('kounsəl) *n.* 1. guidance or advice. 2. a barrister. —*vb.* to advise.

count (kount) *vb.* (sometimes + *up*) 1. to recite the cardinal numbers in the correct order: *count to fifty.* 2. (sometimes + *up* or *out*) to work out (the number of objects, items, etc., in a set) by counting: *count the cards in your hand.* 3. to come into consideration; be important: *a good education still counts.* —*n.* the action or an instance of counting. '**countdown** *n.* a count of the time before a spacecraft launch, made backwards and ending at zero.

counter¹ ('kountə) *n.* a table in a shop or similar place, at which goods are bought, etc.

counter² ('kountə) *n.* 1. a person or machine that counts or adds up. 2. a small, flat, usu. round piece of plastic, metal, etc., used in a game.

county ('kounti) *n.,pl.* **counties.** 1. one of the areas into which some countries or states are divided for administrative purposes. 2. the people who live in a county. —*adj.* 1. of or connected with a county. 2. (informal) upper-class.

country ('kuntri) *n.,pl.* **countries.** 1. a nation. 2. the area away from a city or village, where houses and other buildings are far apart.

couple ('kupəl) *n.* 1. two; a pair. 2. a man and woman who are married, engaged, courting, etc. 3. a pair of people dancing together. 4. (informal) a few; small number: *I'll see you in a couple of weeks.* —*vb.* **coupling, coupled.** to join together two things, esp. railway carriages.

courage ('kurij) *n.* bravery, usu. in the face of danger or misfortune.

course (kôs) *n.* 1. a route or direction: *the earth follows a course around the sun.* 2. forward movement; passage of time: *much building was done during the course of the following year.* 3. a method of action. 4. a piece of ground used for sport: *a golf course.* 5. a part of a meal: *soup is the first course.* 6. a series: *a course of driving lessons.* —*vb.* **coursing, coursed.** 1. to move or circulate quickly: *blood courses through one's body.* 2. to hunt (hares) with greyhounds for sport.

crab

court (kôt) *n.* 1. an enclosed ground marked out for certain ball games: *a tennis court.* 2. a group of buildings round an open space (**courtyard**). 3. the official home of a king or queen and his or her attendants (**courtiers**). 4. a place, often open to the public, where legal cases are heard and judged. —*vb.* 1. (of a man) to be friendly with (a woman) and hope to marry her. 2. to try to win (a person's favour or attention). 3. to risk: *the girl was courting disaster by playing on the broken swing.*

courteous ('kûtiəs) *adj.* polite, well-mannered, and considerate. '**courtesy** *n.* politeness; consideration for other people.

cousin ('kuzin) *n.* the son or daughter of one's aunt or uncle.

cover ('kuvə) *vb.* 1. (often + *up*) to put one thing over another in order to protect or hide it. 2. to lie or be spread on: *snow covered the ground.* 3. to conceal: *he covered his embarrassment by coughing.* 4. to extend or stretch over: *the farm covers forty acres.* 5. to include or deal adequately with: *I hope I have covered everything.* 6. to aim a weapon at. —*n.* 1. something that covers. 2. a book or magazine binding. 3. shelter or concealment: *the small bushes gave little cover.* 4. an activity or organization that conceals some other, possibly illegal, activity: *his business journeys were a cover for smuggling.* 5. military support.

coward ('kouəd) *n.* a person who lacks courage and is easily frightened. '**cowardice** *n.* the behaviour of a coward. —'**cowardly** *adj.*

crab (krab) *n.* a seashore animal having eight legs, two powerful front claws, and a hard shell.

crack (krak) *n.* 1. a line appearing in a breakable object as the result of a sharp blow, exposure to heat, etc. 2. a small hole, as in a wall. 3. a sudden sharp noise: *the crack of a pistol.* 4. (informal) a sharp blow: *a crack on the shin.* 5. (informal) a humorous or sarcastic remark. —*vb.* 1. to cause or get a crack: *the cup cracked.* 2. to make or cause to make a sudden noise: *Steve cracked the whip.* 3. (informal) to strike (someone) a sharp blow. 4. (informal) to make a humorous or sarcastic remark. 5. (often + *up*) (informal) to suffer strain. 6. to break open (a safe).

craft (krâft) *n.* 1. a skill or ability, e.g. in art, work done by hand, etc. 2. a job requiring such skill. 3. cunning or cleverness. 4. (*pl.* **craft**) a boat, ship, aeroplane, or spaceship. '**craftsman** *n.,pl.* **craftsmen.** a skilled or talented workman. '**crafty** *adj.* **craftier, craftiest.** clever; cunning.

cram (kram) *vb.* **cramming, crammed.** 1. to fill completely: *his pockets were crammed with apples.* 2. to study very hard at the last minute: *Dave crammed for the geography test.*

cramp (kramp) *n.* a sudden severe muscular pain.

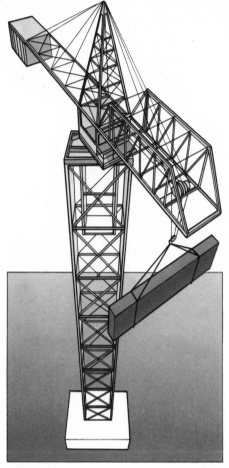
crane

crane (krān) *n.* 1. a type of large water bird related to the heron. 2. a machine for raising heavy weights. —*vb.* **craning, craned.** to stretch (one's neck) in trying to see something.

crash (kra sh) *n.* 1. a harsh loud sound; clash. 2. a collision or accident involving one or more vehicles. —*vb.* to have or cause to have a crash.

crater ('krātə) *n.* 1. the hole in the top of a volcano through which smoke and lava emerge during an eruption. 2. a hole in the ground caused by an explosion. 3. a saucer-shaped depression on the moon, often very large and often surrounded by very high ground.

crawl (krôl) *vb.* 1. to move along on one's hands and knees or on one's stomach. 2. to move very slowly: *the traffic crawled along.* —*n.* 1. the act of crawling. 2. a way of swimming in which a person pulls himself along by alternate movements of his arms over his head.

craze (krāz) *n.* an activity, etc., followed by many people with considerable enthusiasm for a short time; fashion. —*vb.* **crazing, crazed.** to make mad. '**crazy** *adj.* **crazier, craziest.** 1. mad. 2. (usu. + *about*) very interested in: *crazy about pop music.*

cream (krēm) *n.* 1. the thick fatty substance in milk that rises to the top. 2. any substance made from, containing, or resembling cream: *face cream.* 3. the very best of something: *the cream of the navy.* 4. a colour between white and yellow. —*adj.* 1. made from or resembling cream. 2. having the colour cream. —*vb.* to make (food) smooth like cream: *she creamed the potatoes.*

crease (krēs) *n.* 1. a line produced in paper or cloth by folding it. 2. (cricket) a line on the pitch showing the batsman or bowler where to put his feet. —*vb.* **creasing, creased.** to have or cause to have creases.

create (kri'āt) *vb.* **creating, created.** to bring into existence; make: *God created heaven and earth.* **cre'ation** *n.* 1. the act of creating or something created. 2. (often **Creation**) the whole world or universe. **creature** ('krēchə) *n.* 1. any living animal. 2. a person for whom one feels pity or scorn: *a poor creature.*

credible ('kredibəl) *adj.* able to be believed: *his story is not credible.* —**credi'bility** *n.* —'**credibly** *adv.*

credit ('kredit) *n.* 1. just praise or acknowledgment: *give him credit for his achievement.* 2. confidence or trust placed in a buyer who receives goods before paying for them. 3. money or paments received. —*vb.* 1. to believe. 2. (+ *with*) to accept someone as having some quality, etc.: *he did not credit her with any intelligence.* '**creditable** *adj.* worthy. —'**creditably** *adv.*

creek (krēk) *n.* 1. a narrow channel carrying away water from a main river. 2. (U.S.) a small river or stream.

creep (krēp) *vb.* **creeping, crept.** 1. to move along gradually, silently, and secretly. 2. (of plants) to spread along the ground or up a wall. '**creeper** *n.* a type of plant that grows along the ground or up a wall.

crept (krept) *vb.* the past tense and past participle of CREEP.

crescent ('kresənt) *n.* the thin curved shape that the moon has when less than half its surface appears to be lit by the sun as viewed from earth. —*adj.* of, resembling, or describing this shape.

crescent moon

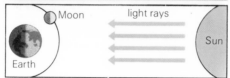

crescent

crest (krest) *n.* 1. the top of something, such as a wave or hill. 2. a group of feathers sticking upwards on a bird's head. 3. a special mark or design used by a family, business firm, etc., e.g. on letters.

crevice ('krevis) *n.* a deep narrow crack.

crew (krōō) *n.* all the men, except the captain, employed to take care of the management of a ship or aircraft.

cricket[1] ('krikit) *n.* a game played by two teams of eleven players each, in which a batsman tries to protect his wicket by striking away a ball aimed at it by a bowler on the opposing team, and also attempts to win points for his side by running from one end of the pitch to the other after the ball has been struck. —'**cricketer** *n.*

cricket[2] ('krikit) *n.* a small insect that makes a distinctive sound by rubbing its wings together.

crime (krīm) *n.* 1. an act that is against the law: *bank robbery is a serious crime.* 2. an evil act; sin: *war is a crime against humanity.* **criminal** ('kriminəl) *n.* a person who commits a crime. *adj.* of crime: *he had a criminal record.*

crimson ('krimzən) *n.* a deep red colour. —*adj.* having this colour. —*vb.* to make or become red.

cringe (krinji) *vb.* **cringing, cringed.** 1. to shrink away in fear: *the dog cringed under the whip.* 2. to fawn or act in a slavish way: *the villain cringed servilely to get his own way.*

cripple ('kripəl) *n.* a lame person; someone who cannot walk properly. —*vb.* **crippling, crippled.** 1. to make lame. 2. to hold back progress or reduce the efficiency of (something): *production at the new factory was crippled by strikes.*

crisis ('krīsis) *n.,pl.* **crises** ('krīsēz). 1. an emergency. 2. a critical state of affairs; a time of political, economic, or social difficulty: *an international crisis.* 3. a turning point in the course of a serious illness.

crisp (krisp) *adj.* 1. hard and crunchy: *crisp biscuits.* 2. fresh or bracing; pleasantly cold: *a crisp morning.* 3. abrupt; brisk: *a crisp reply.* —*n.* a thin slice of potato fried quickly in hot deep fat. —*vb.* to make or become crisp. —'**crisply** *adv.* —'**crispness** *n.*

critic ('kritik) *n.* 1. a person who judges something or someone, esp. in a disapproving way: *the new housing plans had many critics.* 2. a person who judges literature, music, art, etc., esp. for a living: *an art critic.* '**critical** *adj.* 1. of a critic or criticism: *critical opinion.* 2. fault-finding: *why are you so critical of everything I do?* 3. at a crisis: *the injured man is in a critical condition.* '**criticize** *vb.* **criticizing, criticized.** 1. to give an opinion. 2. to find fault with; blame. '**criticism** *n.* —'**critically** *adv.*

crockery ('krokəri) *n.* cups, saucers, plates, and dishes; china.

crocodile ('krokədīl) *n.* 1. a large REPTILE similar to the ALLIGATOR but with a longer narrower snout and even teeth. It is found in Africa, Asia, Australia, and Central America. 2. leather made from the skin of a crocodile, used for shoes, bags, belts, etc. 3. (informal) a double line of people one behind the other, esp. schoolchildren.

crook (krŏŏk) *n.* 1. anything that is curved or bent: *the crook of an umbrella.* 2. a long stick with a curved hook at the top, formerly used by shepherds. 3. (slang) a criminal, esp. one who cheats or swindles. —*vb.* to curve or bend. '**crooked** *adj.* 1. not straight. 2. dishonest; criminal: *a crooked deal.* —'**crookedly** *adv.* —'**crookedness** *n.*

crop (krop) *n.* 1. the produce from a cultivated field, such as vegetables, fruit, etc. 2. the gullet of a bird, where food is stored and broken up to make it easier to digest. 3. (also **riding crop**) a short stick with a loop on the end used in riding. 4. a very short hair style. —*vb.* **cropping, cropped.** 1. to harvest or reap (crops). 2. to cut (hair) very short. 3. (of animals) to feed on (plants): *the horse cropped the grass by the roadside.*

crow

cross[1] (kros) *adj.* feeling or expressing bad temper.

cross[2] (kros) *n.* 1. any two intersecting lines (×, +). 2. a wooden stake driven into the ground, with another nailed across it near the top, on which condemned men were once executed. 3. the symbol of Christianity. 4. a crucifix. 5. a cross-shaped monument, usu. of stone, e.g. one that marks a grave. 6. a cross-shaped decoration in metal presented as an honour for some service or act of bravery: *the Victoria Cross.* 7. an animal or plant of mixed breed: *a mule is a cross between a donkey and a horse.* —*vb.* 1. to go from one side to the other: *we crossed the road.* 2. (+ *out* or *off*) to draw a line across or through: *she crossed her name off the list.* 3. to breed from two different animals or plants in order to obtain a new type. 4. to anger or thwart. —*adj.* angry; annoyed. **cross reference** a reference or note directing a reader to another section of a book, index, etc., where further information is to be found. **cross section** 1. a view of something or a diagram representing such a view obtained by cutting part of it away, esp. to show how it is constructed. 2. a small number of items taken to represent the larger group of which they are members: *a cross section of the population.*

cross-eyed ('krosīd) *adj.* with one or both eyes looking inwards.

crossroads ('krosrōdz) *pl.n.* a place where two or more roads cross.

crossword ('krosûd) *n.* (also **crossword puzzle**) a puzzle made up of squares in which words are to be filled in according to clues given in a numbered table.

crouch (krouch) *vb.* 1. to squat or bend down. 2. to bow low or stoop. —*n.* a squatting position.

crow[1] (krō) *n.* a bird with black plumage and a dark bill.

crow[2] (krō) *vb.* **crowing, crowed** *or* (for def. 1) **crew.** 1. (esp. of a cock) to utter a shrill cry. 2. to boast triumphantly: *he crowed about winning the race.* —*n.* the cry of a cock.

crow-bar ('krōbâ) *n.* a heavy iron bar used as a lever.

crowd (kroud) *n.* a large number of people in one place. —*vb.* 1. (of people) to gather together in a mass. 2. to press uncomfortably close to (someone): *don't crowd me!* 3. to pack into a confined space.

crown (kroun) *n.* 1. a head covering, usu. a circle of gold or silver decorated with precious stones, worn by a king or queen, esp. at ceremonial occasions. 2. any head covering resembling this: *a crown of laurels.* 3. the top part of the head or the head itself. 4. top of a hat. 5. the top of a hill, mountain, etc. 6. (formerly) a British coin worth five shillings (25p). —*vb.* 1. to place a crown upon (someone's head). 2. to make (someone) king or queen. 3. (slang) to hit (someone) over the head.

crude (krōod) *adj.* 1. rough; unfinished: *a crude drawing.* 2. vulgar: *a crude joke.* 3. raw: *crude oil.* —'**crudely** *adv.* —'**crudity** *n.*

cruel ('krōoəl) *adj.* taking pleasure in causing pain or suffering; unkind. —'**cruelly** *adv.* —'**cruelty** *n.*

crumb (krum) *n.* 1. a very small piece of bread, cake, etc. 2. any very small amount: *a crumb of comfort.*

crumble ('krumbəl) *vb.* **crumbling, crumbled.** to break up into small pieces; disintegrate or decay. —'**crumbly** *adj.*

crush (krush) *vb.* 1. to squeeze hard, esp. causing injury. 2. to crease (a fabric). 3. to squash into a small space. 4. to defeat. —*n.* a dense crowd of people.

crust (krust) *n.* 1. the hard crisp outer part of bread and other food. 2. any similar covering: *a crust of ice formed on the puddle.*

crutch (kruch) *n.* 1. a specially shaped wooden or metal stick designed to help a cripple or injured person to walk. 2. a support or aid: *she was a crutch to her sick sister.*

crystal ('kristəl) *n.* 1. a kind of rock that looks like clear glass. 2. the definite flat-sided regular shape natural to many solid substances: *sugar crystals.* 3. fine quality glassware. —*adj.* clear and bright, like crystal.

cube (kyōob) *n.* 1. a solid block with six equal square sides. 2. (mathematics) the product of a number multiplied by itself twice: *the cube of 4 is 64 (4 × 4 × 4).* '**cubic** *adj.* 1. with the shape of a cube. 2. of the measurements of volume.

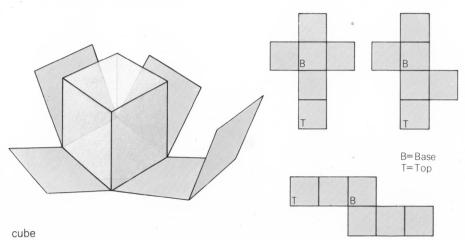

cube

B=Base
T=Top

cubicle ('kyōōbikəl) *n.* a small area of a larger room, curtained off or divided from the rest: *the changing room has eight cubicles.*

cuckoo ('kŏŏkōō) *n.* a small bird that has a call that sounds like its name. The female cuckoo usu. lays her eggs in other birds' nests.

cucumber ('kyōōkumbə) *n.* 1. a long fleshy green-skinned fruit used in salads or for pickles. 2. the creeping plant on which these fruits grow.

cuff (kuf) *n.* a band of material sewn at the end of a sleeve to make it fit round the wrist.

culprit ('kulprit) *n.* a person who is guilty of some crime or sin.

cultivate ('kultivāt) *vb.* **cultivating, cultivated. 1.** to prepare and use (land) to grow crops. 2. to train (the mind). 3. to encourage: *I cultivated her friendship.* —**culti'vation** *n.*

culture ('kulchə) *n.* 1. all the customs, beliefs, and arts of a particular people: *we are studying Chinese culture.* 2. high development of civilized human powers: *a man of great culture.* 3. the growing or developing of something, either by natural or artificial means: *the culture of pearls.* 'cultured *adj.* possessing culture. —'cultural *adj.* —'culturally *adv.*

cunning ('kuniñg) *adj.* clever in a sly underhand way.

cupboard ('kubəd) *n.* a closet, either built into the wall or made as a separate piece of furniture, containing shelves for storing food, clothes, etc.

curate ('kyōōərit) *n.* a junior priest, who usu. assists another priest in his duties.

curator (kyōō'rātə) *n.* an official in charge of a museum or art gallery.

cure (kyōō) *vb.* **curing, cured. 1.** to heal; make (a sick person) better. 2. to preserve (meat, fish, skins) by drying, smoking, or salting. —*n.* something that restores health.

curious ('kyōōəriəs) *adj.* 1. eager to find out; inquisitive: *the curious child was always asking questions.* 2. strange; unusual; odd. **curiosity** (kyōōəri'ositi) *n.,pl.* **curiosities. 1.** eagerness to find out. 2. a rare or strange object: *he brought several curiosities back from his travels.*

curl (kûl) *vb.* 1. to form (hair) into ringlets or coils. 2. (often + *up*) to twist (something) into a spiral; coil: *the heat made the papers curl up.* —*n.* a spiral coil, esp. a curve of hair. —'curly *adj.* **curlier, curliest.**

currant ('kurənt) *n.* 1. a small seedless dried grape, like a raisin, used in cooking. 2. a small round berry that is red, white, or black.

current ('kurənt) *n.* 1. a flowing stream of water, gas, etc. 2. the flow of electricity. 3. a general trend or movement: *the current of opinion.* —*adj.* 1. generally used or accepted. 2. of the present time.

curry ('kuri) *n.,pl.* **curries.** a spicy Indian dish, containing meat or vegetables, prepared in a sauce seasoned with **curry powder** (a mixture of spices), and served with rice. —*vb.* **currying, curried.** to make a curry of.

curse (kûs) *vb.* **cursing, cursed. 1.** to express a wish to bring harm upon (someone). 2. to use bad language. —*n.* a word or phrase expressing a wish to harm someone or something.

curtain ('kûtən) *n.* a hanging piece of cloth or other material used to shut out the light coming through a window, divide part of a large room, etc.

curve (kûv) *n.* a line, stretch of road, etc., that is not straight and keeps constantly bending in a particular direction. —*vb.* **curving, curved.** to have or cause to have a curved shape.

cushion ('kŏŏshən) *n.* a pad made of cloth, leather, plastic, etc., stuffed with soft material, such as feathers, and used for sitting or lying on.

custard ('kustəd) *n.* a pale yellow mixture of sweetened eggs and milk that is boiled or baked, and served as a pudding or as a sauce on sweet dishes.

custom ('kustəm) *n.* 1. a social habit, practice, or pattern of behaviour that members of a group are expected to observe; tradition: *it is the custom to give presents at Christmas.* 2. an individual habit: *it was her custom to go abroad every year.* 3. patronage of a business or shop by persons (**customers**) who regularly trade there. 4. **customs** (*pl.*) taxes or duty due on goods imported into a country and the official body responsible for collecting them. 'customary *adj.* usual.

cutlery ('kutləri) *n.* implements such as knives, forks, and spoons.

cycle ('sīkəl) *n.* 1. a sequence of events, small units of time, etc., that is periodically repeated. 2. a bicycle. —*vb.* **cycling, cycled.** to ride a bicycle. **cyclic** ('sīklik, 'siklik) *adj.* repeated in cycles. 'cyclist *n.* a person who rides a bicycle.

cyclone ('sīklōn) *n.* a violent tropical storm.

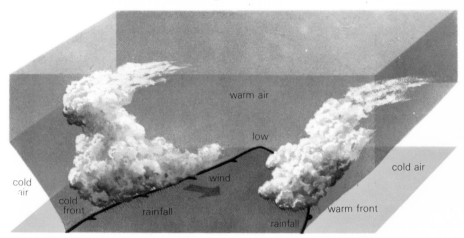

cyclone

cygnet ('signit) *n.* a young swan.

cylinder ('silində) *n.* 1. a solid or hollow circular body with round flat ends and straight sides. See GEOMETRY. 2. a cylinder-shaped part of an engine. 3. the rotating part of a revolver, containing the bullets. —**cy'lindrical** *adj.*

cymbal ('simbəl) *n.* one of a pair of round metal plates making up a musical instrument. Cymbals are clashed together to make a ringing noise.

cypress ('sīprəs) *n.* a type of CONIFER.

51

D

dabble ('dabəl) *vb.* **dabbling, dabbled.** 1. to splash (one's fingers or toes) lightly in water. 2. (often + *in*) to engage in an activity, hobby, or interest with only casual concern. —'**dabbler** *n.*

daffodil

daffodil ('dafədil) *n.* a garden plant grown from a bulb, having a yellow flower with a trumpet-shaped centre.

dagger ('dagə) *n.* a short knifelike stabbing weapon with a sharp pointed blade. **look daggers at** to look at (a person) with anger; scowl.

daily ('dāli) *adj.* occurring or appearing every day. —*n.,pl.* **dailies.** 1. a newspaper published every weekday. 2. (also **daily help**) a woman who comes on weekdays to a private house, shop, office, etc., in order to clean it.

dainty ('dānti) *adj.* **daintier, daintiest.** 1. small, delicate, and neat in appearance. 2. of delicate taste; delicious. —*n.,pl.* **dainties.** something dainty or special, esp. food. —'**daintily** *adv.* —'**daintiness** *n.*

dairy ('deəri) *n.,pl.* **dairies.** 1. a room or building on a farm where milk is kept and butter and cheese are made. 2. a shop that sells milk and its products (butter, cheese, etc.). **dairy farm** a farm producing milk, butter, eggs, cheese, etc.

daisy ('dāzi) *n.,pl.* **daisies.** 1. a field flower with a yellow centre and radiating white petals. 2. one of many similar kinds of garden flower, usu. with white, red, pink, or yellow petals.

dam (dam) *n.* 1. a barrier built across a stream, river, lake, etc., to obstruct or control the flow of water, e.g. to irrigate the land or to produce electricity. 2. a reservoir of water created by a dam. —*vb.* **damming, dammed.** 1. to build a dam across. 2. to stop (a flow of water, tears, blood, etc.); keep in check or control.

damage ('damij) *n.* 1. harm or injury causing loss of value, usefulness, or efficiency. 2. **damages** (*pl.*) money awarded by a court as compensation for loss or injury. —*vb.* **damaging, damaged.** to injure, harm, or spoil.

damn (dam) *vb.* 1. to condemn to hell; curse. 2. to criticize severely. 3. to ruin the hopes or chances of. —*interj.* an expression of impatience or annoyance. —**damnable** ('damnəbəl) *adj.* —**dam'nation** *n.*

damp (damp) *adj.* slightly wet; moist. —*n.* 1. (also **dampness**) humidity or moisture. 2. undesirable moisture on walls or other surfaces. —*vb.* (also **dampen**) 1. to make slightly wet; moisten. 2. to check or restrain (spirits, action, etc.); discourage. 3. (often + *out*) to stifle or extinguish (fire). '**damper** *n.* 1. anything that discourages or depresses. 2. a felt pad in a piano that stops the vibration of the strings.

dandruff ('dandrəf) *n.* small white scales found on the scalp and in the hair.

danger ('dānjə) *n.* 1. risk of being harmed, injured, or killed; peril. 2. somebody or something that causes danger or harm. —'**dangerous** *adj.* —'**dangerously** *adv.*

dangle ('danggəl) *vb.* **dangling, dangled.** to hang loosely or swing back and forth.

dare (deə) *vb.* **daring, dared.** 1. to have enough courage to do something: *he didn't dare to move.* 2. to challenge (someone) to show his courage: *I dare you to jump.* —*n.* a challenge to someone to show his courage.

dam

dark (dâk) *adj.* 1. having little or no light; dim; gloomy. 2. being of a deep colour or shade that has some black in it. 3. (of hair or the complexion) brown or black. 4. secret: *keep it dark.* 5. wicked: *dark thoughts.* **dark room** a room that is made completely dark, in which photographic films can be developed. —*n.* (also **darkness**) 1. absence of light; blackness. 2. night time: *I'm not afraid of the dark.* **in the dark** still ignorant or unaware of something. '**darken** *vb.* to make or become dark or darker. '**darkly** *adv.* mysteriously or sinisterly: *he said darkly that there was more in the story than appeared on the surface.*

darn (dân) *vb.* to mend a hole (in socks, knitwear, etc.) by sewing it with interwoven rows of wool or thread. —*n.* the hole or area repaired in this way. —*interj.* a mild expression of impatience or annoyance.

dart (dât) *n.* 1. a small metal or wooden arrow, esp. one thrown by hand at a circular target (**dartboard**) in the game of **darts.** 2. a quick dash. 3. a short tapered seam used to shape a bodice, etc., in dressmaking. —*vb.* to move forward for a short distance suddenly and very fast.

date¹ (dāt) *n.* 1. the time or period, expressed as day, month, year, on which any event takes place. 2. an appointment to meet on a specific day. **'out-of-'date** *adj.* old-fashioned. **'up-to-'date** *adj.* modern. —*vb.* **dating, dated.** 1. to mark (a letter, etc.) with the date. 2. to make an appointment with, esp. with a member of the opposite sex. 3. to estimate how old something is: *the archaeologist dated the vase to an early period.* 4. to show signs of age: *many fashions date quickly.* **'dated** *adj.* old-fashioned.

date² (dāt) *n.* the sweet sticky oval fruit of the date palm tree.

daughter ('dôtə) *n.* a female child or person in relation to her parents.

dawdle ('dôdəl) *vb.* **dawdling, dawdled.** to move slowly, wasting time.

dawn (dôn) *n.* 1. sunrise. 2. the beginning of anything. —*vb.* 1. to begin to grow light or appear. 2. (+ *on*) to become gradually clear to: *as he spoke, it dawned on me that his accent was French.*

day (dā) *n.* 1. the period of 24 hours in which the earth makes one turn round its axis. 2. the light part of this period.

daze (dāz) *vb.* **dazing, dazed.** to stun and confuse: *the uproar of the big city dazed the old man.* —*n.* the state of being bewildered.

dazzle ('dazəl) *vb.* **dazzling, dazzled.** 1. to blind temporarily with bright light. 2. to stun with great beauty, brilliance, etc.: *a dazzling performance of Shakespeare.*

dart

dead (ded) *adj.* 1. without life; having died. 2. dull; boring. 3. no longer in use: *a dead language.* **dead end** a road, path, etc., with only one way in and out. **dead heat** a race in which two or more people are equal winners. —*n.* those who have died. —*adv.* 1. completely: *dead tired.* 2. (informal) absolutely: *dead right.* **'deadly** *adj.* **deadlier, deadliest.** likely to cause death: *arsenic is a deadly poison.* *adv.* (informal) extremely: *deadly boring.*

deadline ('dedlīn) *n.* the time by which a job must be finished.

deadlock ('dedlok) *n.* the point in a situation where no progress, e.g. towards settling a dispute, can be made.

deaf (def) *adj.* 1. unable to hear at all. 2. refusing to listen: *he was deaf to her pleading.* **'deafen** *vb.* to make partly or temporarily unable to hear: *he was deafened by the noise of the traffic.* —**'deafness** *n.*

deal (dēl) *vb.* **dealing, dealt** (delt). 1. to hand out, divide, or deliver: *she dealt the playing cards.* 2. (+ *with*) to do business with: *my family has dealt with your firm for years.* 3. (+ *with*) to manage or handle: *I will deal with him!* —*n.* 1. quantity; amount: *I had a good deal of trouble finding the house.* 2. bargain; arrangement.

dear (diə) *adj.* 1. beloved; highly thought of. 2. expensive; costly. —**'dearly** *adv.* —**'dearness** *n.*

death (deth) *n.* the end of life; condition of being dead. **at death's door** about to die. **death trap** a building, car, etc., with serious hidden dangers. —**'deathly** *adj.*

debate (di'bāt) *n.* formal discussion or argument between several consecutive speakers in front of an audience. —*vb.* **debating, debated.** to discuss formally or consider: *she debated whether to buy the dress.*

debris ('debrē) *n.* scattered rubbish, wreckage, or fragments.

debt (det) *n.* something that is owed to another: *I owe you a debt of gratitude for your kindness.* **in debt** owing money. **bad debt** debt that is likely never to be paid. —**'debtor** *n.*

decade ('dekād) *n.* a period of ten years: *the years between 1960 and 1970 is the decade referred to as the sixties.*

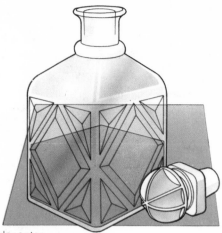

decanter

decanter (di'kantə) *n.* a fancy glass bottle into which wine, spirits, etc., are poured for serving.

decay (di'kā) *vb.* to rot or waste away: *sugar can cause teeth to decay.* —*n.* state of rottenness or gradual decline.

deceive (di'sēv) *vb.* **deceiving, deceived.** to mislead, cheat, or lie to: *though a cunning liar, he could not deceive his mother.* **deceit** (di'sēt) *n.* (also **deception**) cheating; the act or practice of deceiving. —**de'ceitful** *adj.* —**de'ceitfully** *adv.*

decent ('dēsənt) *adj.* 1. modest; respectable. 2. sufficient: *a decent portion.* 3. kind: *it was decent of you to give us all supper.* —**'decency** *n.* —**'decently** *adv.*

deception (di'sepshən) *n.* a deliberately misleading act or the practice of misleading by tricks. **de'ceptive** *adj.* likely to mislead; giving a false impression: *this is a deceptive dress—I'm really quite fat.*

decide (di'sīd) *vb.* **deciding, decided.** to make up one's mind; choose or settle.

deciduous (di'sidyŏŏəs) *adj.* (of a tree, etc.) shedding its leaves every year: *the oak is a deciduous tree.* Compare EVERGREEN.

decimal ('desiməl) *adj.* of or based on units of 10 or tenth parts. —*n.* a part of a whole number expressed in tens or tenth parts, e.g. 3·5 (three and a half) is a decimal. Whole numbers and parts are separated by the **decimal point,** e.g. 6·4 is the decimal equivalent of six and four-tenths. **decimali'zation** *n.* the conversion from another system to a decimal system of units of money, weight, etc.

deer

moose

red deer

fallow deer

decipher (di'sīfə) *vb.* to work out the true meaning of (a piece of writing that is written in code, another alphabet, or just badly written): *can you decipher Tom's writing?*

decision (di'sizhən) *n.* 1. the act of deciding. 2. judgment or course of action decided upon. 3. firmness and strength of character: *he acted with great decision on all occasions.* **decisive** (di'sīsiv) *adj.* final, firm, and positive.

deck (dek) *n.* 1. the platform or floor of a ship, bus, etc. 2. a pack (of cards). **deck chair** a folding canvas chair often available for hire on the beach, etc. —*vb.* to adorn or decorate.

declare (di'kleə) *vb.* **declaring, declared.** 1. to announce publicly or formally: *I declare Jones the winner.* 2. to state firmly. 3. to admit one has (taxable goods) when going through customs on entering a country. 4. (cricket) to end an innings before all 10 wickets have fallen. **declaration** (deklə'rāshən) *n.* 1. the act of declaring. 2. a formal or legal statement or announcement.

decline (di'klīn) *vb.* **declining, declined.** 1. to become gradually less or worse. 2. to refuse, esp. politely. 3. to slope downwards. —*n.* 1. a gradual lessening, worsening, or downward turn: *a decline in moral standards.* 2. a downward slope.

decorate ('dekərāt) *vb.* **decorating, decorated.** 1. to make more beautiful by adding ornaments, etc.; adorn: *on Christmas Eve the children helped to decorate the tree.* 2. to paint or wallpaper (a room). 3. to award (someone) an honour or medal in recognition of courage, etc. —**deco'ration** *n.* —'**decorative** *adj.*

decoy *n.* ('dēkoi) 1. a person or thing used to lure persons away from what they are seeking, to distract attention, etc. 2. a model of an animal, duck, etc., used to attract animals to where the hunters are. —*vb.* (di'koi) to deceive or trap in this way.

decrease *vb.* (di'krēs) **decreasing, decreased.** to grow less; diminish. —*n.* ('dēkrēs) 1. the process of growing less. 2. the amount by which a thing is lessened.

decrepit (di'krepit) *adj.* old and worn out: *Mary's bicycle was so decrepit she had to throw it away.*

dedicate ('dedikāt) *vb.* **dedicating, dedicated.** 1. to consecrate for a holy purpose: *the church is dedicated to St. Joseph.* 2. to devote wholly and exclusively: *this department is dedicated to scientific research.* 3. to inscribe (a book, piece of music, etc.) to someone as a mark of respect. '**dedicated** *adj.* devoted and hard-working: *a dedicated nurse.* —**dedi'cation** *n.*

deduct (di'dukt) *vb.* to subtract or take away. —**de'duction** *n.*

deed (dēd) *n.* 1. an act or action: *Peter's good deed for the day was to visit his grandmother.* 2. a legal document to prove ownership.

deep (dēp) *adj.* 1. going very far down: *a deep pool.* 2. wide: *a deep shelf.* 3. low in pitch: *a deep voice.* 4. dark in colour: *deep blue.* 5. strong; intense: *deep sadness.* 6. far-reaching: *a deep thinker.* —*adv.* very far: *deep into the forest.* **deep freeze** a refrigerator for storing food for long periods.

at a very low temperature. **deep-'freeze** *vb.* **deep-freezing, deep-froze, deep-frozen.** to freeze (food) thus. —**'deeply** *adv.* —**'deepness** *n.* See also DEPTH.

deer (diə) *n.,pl.* **deer.** a four-footed grass-eating animal, the male of which has antlers that are shed every year.

defeat (di'fēt) *vb.* 1. to beat in a battle, game, etc.; overcome; conquer. 2. to frustrate, thwart, or prevent success in: *to give way now would defeat your purpose.* —*n.* the loss of a battle, game, etc. **de'featist** *n.* a person who accepts defeat too easily.

defect *n.* ('dēfekt) a flaw; fault. —*vb.* (di'fekt) to run away from one's country or duty. —**de'fective** *adj.*

defence (di'fens) *n.* 1. protection against attack. 2. something used for this. 3. a legal case for proving the innocence of a defendant. 4. the players in or games, e.g. football, who try to prevent goals being scored. **de'fensible** *adj.* able to be defended; justified. **de'fensive** *adj.* intended to defend or ward off an attack. —**de'fensively** *adv.*

defend (di'fend) *vb.* 1. to protect against attack; keep safe. 2. to speak to prove someone's innocence in a law court. **de'fendant** *n.* a person called to a court of law to answer charges.

defer (di'fû) *vb.* 1. to put off; postpone. 2. to yield to someone's opinion.

defiance (di'fīəns) *n.* the act of defying; bold, often foolhardy opposition or disobedience. —**de'fiant** *adj.* —**de'fiantly** *adv.*

definite ('definit) *adj.* 1. clear; firm: *a definite outline of a footprint.* 2. firm: *let's make a definite plan to meet on Thursday.* —**'definitely** *adv.*

definition (defi'nishən) *n.* 1. an explanation of the meaning of a word or phrase. 2. degree of clearness: *the photo lacks definition.* **definitive** (di'finitiv) *adj.* needing no further work or explanation: *the definitive edition of Shakespeare.*

deflate (di'flāt) *vb.* **deflating, deflated.** to let out air or gas from (a tyre, balloon, etc.). **de'flation** *n.* (economics) the general fall in prices caused by lessening of the amount of money that people have to spend. Compare INFLATION.

deform (di'fôm) *vb.* to spoil the natural shape or look of; disfigure: *his right hand was deformed in an accident.* **de'formity** *n.,pl.* **deformities.** a misshapen part of the body.

defy (di'fī) *vb.* **defying, defied.** 1. to refuse to obey. 2. to challenge; dare: *I defy you to prove me wrong!* 3. to resist; prevent: *the beauty of the mountains defies description.*

degree (di'grē) *n.* 1. a unit for measuring heat; one of the divisions on a scale of temperature: *32 degrees Fahrenheit (freezing point) is equivalent to 0 degrees centigrade.* 2. the unit for measuring angles; there are 360 degrees in one complete turn. 3. amount or extent. 4. an award given to a person who attains a certain standard of knowledge at a university, etc.

dejected (di'jektid) *adj.* depressed, cast down; gloomy. —**de'jection** *n.*

delay (di'lā) *vb.* to take a long time; be slow or make (something) late. —*n.* 1. the act of making late. 2. amount of time lost.

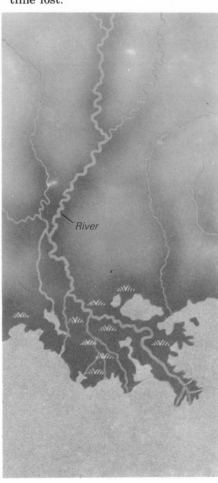
delta

delegate *vb.* ('deligāt) **delegating, delegated.** to entrust (another person) with (a task, message, etc.). —*n.* ('deligit) a representative sent to a conference or meeting. **dele'gation** *n.* a group of delegates.

deliberate *adj.* (di'libərit) 1. not accidental; intentional. 2. careful or cautious; unhurried: *a deliberate pace.* —*vb.* (di'libərāt) **deliberating, deliberated.** to consider possible courses of action. —**de'liberately** *adv.* —**deliber'ation** *n.*

delicate ('delikit) *adj.* 1. pretty and fragile. 2. weakly; liable to sickness. 3. requiring careful handling: *a delicate situation.* **'delicacy** *n.,pl.* **delicacies.** a rare food. —**'delicately** *adv.*

delicious (di'lishəs) *adj.* 1. extremely good to eat. 2. very pleasant to the senses: *a delicious scent of violets.* —**de'liciously** *adv.*

delight (di'līt) *n.* 1. great pleasure or enjoyment. 2. something causing delight. —*vb.* to give or get great pleasure or enjoyment. —**de'lightful** *adj.* —**de'lightfully** *adv.*

delinquent (di'lingkwənt) *n.* (also **juvenile delinquent**) a young person who has broken the law. —*adj.* failing in one's duty, esp. breaking the law. —**de'linquency** *n.*

deliver (di'livə) *vb.* 1. to take (letters, goods, etc.) to the correct address. 2. to save; rescue. 3. to say (a speech, sermon, sentence on a criminal, etc.). 4. to bring (a baby) into the world: *her baby was delivered last Saturday.* 5. to aim or launch (a blow, etc.). —**de'livery** *n., pl.* **deliveries.**

delta ('deltə) *n.* the triangular area where a river divides into branches as it reaches the sea.

deluge ('delyōōj) *n.* 1. a flood or heavy storm. 2. an overwhelming amount: *a deluge of letters.* —*vb.* **deluging, deluged.** to cover with or as if with a flood.

demand (di'mând) *vb.* to ask for strongly. —*n.* 1. a firm or urgent request. 2. requirement; need: *the demand for holidays abroad has increased.*

demolish (di'molish) *vb.* 1. to destroy completely; tear down. 2. to disprove forcibly (someone's argument, etc.). —**demolition** (demə'lishən) *n.*

demonstrate ('demənstrāt) *vb.* **demonstrating, demonstrated.** 1. to show how to do something, how a machine works, how to prove a geometric theorem, etc. 2. to take part in a demonstration. **demon'stration** *n.* 1. the act of demonstrating. 2. a meeting or rally held to protest against or support something, usu. a political cause. **demonstrative** (di'monstrətiv) *adj.* showing one's feelings; warm and affectionate. —'**demonstrator** *n.*

denial (di'nīal) *n.* 1. a refusal. 2. the action or an instance of denying.

denote (di'nōt) *vb.* **denoting, denoted.** 1. to be a sign of; to show: *red often denotes danger.* 2. to be a symbol of: *'r' denotes the radius.*

dense (dens) *adj.* 1. solid; closely packed. 2. heavy in proportion to volume: *oil is less dense than water, so it floats on its surface.* 3. (informal) rather slow-witted. —'**density** *n.,pl.* **densities.** 1. the state or quality of being dense: *the density of the crowd increased.* 2. (physics) the ratio of weight to volume. —'**densely** *adv.*

dent (dent) *n.* a hollow or groove in a surface, resulting from being hit by something with a blunt edge. —*vb.* to make a dent in.

dental ('dentəl) *adj.* relating to the teeth.

dentist ('dentist) *n.* a person who specializes in the care of the teeth.

deny (di'nī) *vb.* **denying, denied.** 1. to say that something is non-existent or not true: *she denied all knowledge of the plot.* 2. to deprive of; refuse: *they deny admittance to children.* See also DENIAL.

depart (di'pât) *vb.* 1. to go away (from); leave. 2. (+ *from*) to change (from the usual thing that is done); veer (from the truth). **de'partment** *n.* a section or subdivision of a large store, country, school, college, etc. —**de'parture** *n.*

depend (di'pend) *vb.* (+ *on*) 1. to rely on. 2. to be decided or affected by: *the harvest will depend on the weather.* **de'pendable** *adj.* reliable; trustworthy. **de'pendant** (also **dependent**) *n.* a person who relies on another for support, e.g. one's children. **de'pendence** *or* **de'pendency** *n.* 1. a state of relying. 2. a colonial territory. **de'pendent** *adj.* (+ *on*) 1. relying on. 2. related to.

deport (di'pôt) *vb.* to send (a foreigner) out of the country, usually because he has committed a political or criminal offence.

deportment (di'pôtmənt) *n.* the manner in which a person moves, stands, or behaves; carriage or bearing.

deposit (di'pozit) *n.* 1. a layer of a substance left by nature; accumulation: *a deposit of mud.* 2. money put in a bank. 3. a first part payment on an article. —*vb.* to put or place. **de'positor** *n.* a person who puts a deposit of money in a bank.

depot ('depō) *n.* 1. a warehouse, esp. a military one. 2. a bus garage. 3. a military training centre. 4. ('dēpō) (U.S.) a bus or railway station.

depress (di'pres) *vb.* 1. to make miserable or unhappy. 2. to press (a switch, etc.) down. **de'pression** *n.* 1. a feeling of sadness and unhappiness. 2. a slackening off in trade, accompanied by high unemployment; slump. 3. low pressure in the atmosphere, usu. producing rain and high winds. 4. a hollow, e.g. in the ground.

deprive (di'prīv) *vb.* **depriving, deprived.** (+ *of*) to take away: *prison deprives people of their freedom.* **de'prived** *adj.* lacking normal comforts, rights, etc.: *he felt deprived because he had very little money.* —**deprivation** (depri'vāshən) *n.*

depth (depth) *n.* 1. the state of being deep. 2. often **depths** (*pl.*) the most severe or intense stage: *the depths of despair.* **in depth** in detail. **out of one's depth** in a situation beyond one's capabilities.

deputy ('depyŏŏti) *n.,pl.* **deputies.** 1. a person appointed to stand in for someone else: *a deputy sheriff.* 2. one of a group of people chosen to represent the views of others. **depu'tation** *n.* a group chosen by a larger group to speak for or represent it. '**deputize** *vb.* **deputizing, deputized.** to do something for or in the name of someone else: *the secretary deputized for her boss at the meeting.*

derelict ('derilikt) *adj.* deserted, abandoned, or neglected and allowed to fall into ruin: *a derelict house.*

descend (di'send) *vb.* 1. to move or slope downwards: *we descended the hill; the road descends into the valley.* 2. (+ *from*) to have as an ancestor. 3. (+ *upon* or *on*) to attack or swoop down on. 4. (+ *to*) to lower oneself or stoop to: *don't descend to bullying.* **de'scendant** *n.* a person descended from others. **de'scent** *n.* 1. a movement downwards. 2. ancestry.

describe (di'skrīb) *vb.* **describing, described.** 1. to state what someone or something is or was like. 2. to form the shape of (a geometrical figure): *to describe an arc.* —**description** (di'skripshən) *n.* —**de'scriptive** *adj.*

desert[1] ('dezət) *n.* a large barren usu. sandy region with little vegetation or water.

desert[2] (di'zût) *vb.* 1. to abandon or forsake; go away from: *all his friends have deserted him.* 2. (of a soldier, etc.) to leave one's post; run away. —**de'serter** *n.* —**de'sertion** *n.*

deserve (di'zûv) *vb.* **deserving, deserved.** to have a right or be entitled to; merit: *he deserved promotion.* **deservedly** (di'zûvidli) *adv.* rightly; justifiably.

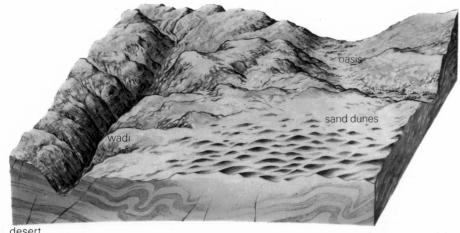

desert

design (di'zīn) *n.* 1. a preliminary sketch, outline, or plan for a building, machine, etc. 2. a pattern; ornamentation. **by design** deliberately or intentionally. **have designs on** (informal) to have evil or selfish intentions towards. —*vb.* to make a preliminary sketch; plan. **de'signing** *adj.* artful or very cunning. —**de'signer** *n.*

desire (di'zīə) *n.* a strong longing, wish, or craving; passion. —*vb.* **desiring, desired.** to wish or long for. —**de'sirable** *adj.*

desk

desk (desk) *n.* a table-like piece of furniture often with drawers, used esp. in offices and schools for writing or drawing on.

despair (di'speə) *n.* a state or feeling of total hopelessness. —*vb.* to abandon hope.

despatch (di'spach) *n.,vb.* See DISPATCH.

desperate ('despərit) *adj.* 1. acting or feeling reckless because of despair. 2. causing despair: *a desperate situation has arisen.* —'**desperately** *adv.* —**desperation** (despə'rāshən) *n.*

despise (di'spīz) *vb.* **despising, despised.** to feel contempt or scorn for: *he despises cowards.* **despicable** (di'spikəbəl) *adj.* to be despised.

despite (di'spīt) *prep.* in spite of; in the face of: *despite your behaviour, you may go to the beach.*

despondent (di'spondənt) *adj.* downcast; in low spirits.

dessert (di'zût) *n.* a sweet course served at the end of the meal: *trifle is my favourite dessert.*

destination (desti'nāshən) *n.* a place to which someone or something is going.

destiny ('destini) *n.,pl.* **destinies.** a predetermined course of events; fate: *it was his destiny to die young.*

destroy (di'stroi) *vb.* to ruin or spoil completely: *fire destroyed the new building.* **de'stroyer** *n.* a high-speed naval warship used to defend larger ships. **destructible** (di'struktibəl) *adj.* able to be destroyed. **destruction** *n.* the act or an instance of ruining completely. **de'structive** *adj.* —**de'structively** *adv.*

detach (di'tach) *vb.* to separate (a part) from a larger whole; unfasten; remove. **de'tached** *adj.* without bias or special interest. **de'tachment** *n.* 1. aloofness; lack of involvement. 2. a section of an army separated for a special mission.

detail ('dētāl) *n.* 1. a very small precise part of something. 2. a group of soldiers selected to do a particular job. —*vb.* 1. to describe or list (every part). 2. to select and order (someone) to do a particular job.

detect (di'tekt) *vb.* to discover by careful examination. **de'tective** *n.* a person who hunts for evidence, usu. to solve crimes and catch the criminal. —**de'tection** *n.* —**de'tector** *n.*

deter (di'tû) *vb.* **deterring, deterred.** to prevent or discourage (someone) from doing something because of its unpleasant results; put off. See also DETERRENT.

detergent (di'tûjənt) *n.* a strong cleaning or washing substance, esp. one used in place of soap for washing dishes and clothes.

deteriorate (di'tiəriərāt) *vb.* **deteriorating, deteriorated.** to make or become worse: *the old cottage had deteriorated because no one lived in it.* —**deterio'ration** *n.*

determine (di'tûmin) *vb.* **determining, determined.** 1. to decide; settle on: *we determined to go.* 2. to affect conclusively: *our refusal was determined by her rudeness.* 3. to establish or settle the facts about (something): *the explorers determined the course of the river.* **de'termined** *adj.* trying hard to get what one wants; resolute. —**determi'nation** *n.*

deterrent (di'terənt) *n.* something that deters, e.g. a weapon so powerful that it deters other countries from making war: *the hydrogen bomb is the ultimate deterrent.*

detest (di'test) *vb.* to hate greatly; loathe.

detour ('dētŏŏə) *n.* a route other than the usual or direct route: *we had to make a detour to avoid the floods.*

devastate ('devəstāt) *vb.* **devastating, devastated.** to destroy completely; make waste; ruin: *the floods devastated the whole countryside.* '**devastating** *adj.* extremely effective: *a devastating nuclear attack.* —**devas'tation** *n.*

develop (di'veləp) *vb.* 1. to grow or cause to grow and change; become larger, improved, etc. 2. to treat (photographic film) with chemicals so that the picture appears on it. —**de'veloper** *n.* —**de'velopment** *n.*

device (di'vīs) *n.* 1. a mechanical instrument; gadget: *he invented a device for lifting cattle onto ships.* 2. a cunning trick or plan. 3. a badge or motto.

devil ('devəl) *n.* 1. an evil spirit. 2. a mischievous or evil person. **the Devil** the chief wicked spirit who tries to possess men by evil; Satan. —*vb.* **devilling, devilled.** to prepare (eggs, etc.) using hot spices.

devote (di'vōt) *vb.* **devoting, devoted.** (+ *to*) 1. to give up (one's time, etc.) completely to. 2. to dedicate to: *a fund devoted to children overseas.* **de'voted** *adj.* very fond or loving: *a devoted wife.* —**de'votion** *n.*

devour (di'vouə) *vb.* 1. to eat hungrily. 2. to look at or read in a desiring way: *he devoured the car with his eyes.*

dew (dyōō) *n.* drops of moisture that form out of the atmosphere as the air cools towards the early morning and are found on surfaces of leaves, etc.

diagnosis (dīəg'nōsis) *n.,pl.* **diagnoses** (dīəg'nōsēz). (medicine) the finding out by a doctor of what disease or injury a person has. **diagnose** ('dīəgnōs) *vb.* **diagnosing, diagnosed.** 1. to find out (what illness a person has). 2. to guess at (what is wrong with something).

diagonal (dī'agənəl) *adj.* slanting from or as if from one upper corner of a rectangle to the opposite lower one. —*n.* such a line. See GEOMETRY.

diagram ('dīəgram) *n.* a line drawing used to show how something works, is built, etc.

dial

dial ('dīəl) *n.* 1. the face of a clock or watch. 2. any face with numbers or markings on it for measuring electricity, pressure, etc., usu. by means of a movable pointer. —*vb.* **dialling, dialled.** to select (numbers on a dial), esp. to make a telephone call.

dialect (dīəlekt) *n.* a way of speaking the language of a country that is typical · in pronunciation, words, and sometimes grammar, for a particular group of speakers.

dialogue ('dīəlog) *n.* a conversation between two or more people: *writing good dialogue is the playwright's art.*

diameter (dī'amitə) *n.* 1. a line through the centre of a circle from one side to the other. 2. the thickness of something round: *the diameter of a pipe.* See GEOMETRY.

diamond ('dīəmənd) *n.* 1. a very hard clear precious stone. 2. a four-sided figure like a squashed square. 3. **diamonds** (*pl.*) a suit of playing cards marked with such figures.

diary ('dīəri) *n.,pl.* **diaries.** 1. a personal account of daily events and thoughts. 2. a book marked out in days and with the date.

dice (dīs) *pl.n.,sing.* **die** (dī). small cubes with from one to six dots marked on each side, thrown in games of chance. —*vb.* **dicing, diced.** to cut (food) into small cubes.

dictate *vb.* (dik'tāt) **dictating, dictated.** 1. to order; command. 2. to say (something) aloud so that another person can write it down. —*n.* ('diktāt) an order: *the dictates of one's conscience.* **dic'tator** *n.* a ruler of a nation who has complete power. —**dic'tation** *n.*

dictionary ('dikshənəri) *n.,pl.* **dictionaries.** a book in which words are listed in alphabetical order and either explained or defined or given an equivalent in another language. Some dictionaries are illustrated.

die[1] (dī) *vb.* **dying, died.** 1. to stop living; perish. 2. to fade away; subside: *her anger died.*

die[2] (dī) *n.* 1. any mechanical device for cutting out, stamping, or shaping, e.g. for putting a raised design onto a coin. 2. an instrument for cutting the spiral thread on screws, etc.

diesel ('dēzəl) *n.* 1. an engine that uses **diesel oil,** which is compressed until it is so hot it burns and drives the engine. 2. a lorry, train, etc., using diesel oil.

diet ('dīət) *n.* 1. the food that a person normally eats. 2. special selection of food eaten to lose weight, etc. —*vb.* to eat only certain food in order to lose weight.

differ ('difə) *vb.* 1. to be unlike. 2. to disagree. **'difference** *n.* 1. the state of being unlike. 2. amount between two different numbers. 3. disagreement; argument. **'different** *adj.* 1. unlike. 2. (informal) exciting and unusual. —**'differently** *adv.*

difficult ('difikəlt) *adj.* 1. not easy; requiring effort to do, understand, etc.; hard. 2. awkward to get on with; uncooperative. —**'difficulty** *n.,pl.* **difficulties.**

digest (dī'jest) *vb.* 1. to convert (food) into substances that the body can absorb and use. 2. to understand; take in: *he digested the news after a few minutes.* **di'gestible** *adj.* able to be digested. —**di'gestion** *n.*

dice

digit ('dijit) *n.* 1. a finger or toe. 2. a whole number below ten. **digital clock** a clock showing the time in figures, e.g. 12.42.

dignity ('digniti) *n.,pl.* **dignities.** 1. calm composed seriousness; noble or important bearing. 2. a title or honour. **'dignified** *adj.* calm; stately. **'dignify** *vb.* **dignifying, dignified.** to bestow dignity on: *the king dignified the gathering by his presence.*

dike (dīk) *n.* See DYKE.

dilapidated (di'lapidātid) *adj.* run down through neglect or age: *a dilapidated house.* —**dilapi'dation** *n.*

dilute (dī'lyōōt) *vb.* **diluting, diluted.** 1. to make weaker or thinner by adding water, etc.: *he diluted the paint.* 2. to reduce the strength, intensity, etc., of. —**dilution** (dīlōōshən) *n.*

dim (dim) *adj.* **dimmer, dimmest.** 1. lacking in brightness; gloomy. 2. indistinct: *a dim outline.* 3. (also **dim-witted**) slow-witted. **take a dim view of** to disapprove of. —*vb.* **dimming, dimmed.** to become or make dim. —**'dimly** *adv.* —**'dimness** *n.*

dimension (dī'menshən) *n.* 1. size or measurement. 2. the characteristic of length, area, or volume: *a line has one dimension, a square has two dimensions, and a cube has three dimensions.* 3. importance; scope.

diminish (di'minish) *vb.* to make or become smaller; reduce in size, scope, etc.: *the firm's profits diminished.*

dinghy ('dinggi) *n.,pl.* **dinghies.** any small rowing or sailing boat.

dingy ('dinji) *adj.* **dingier, dingiest.** dull or dark with age, dirt, etc.; faded; shabby: *a dingy carpet.* —**'dinginess** *n.*

dinosaur ('dīnəsô) *n.* one of the giant reptiles that existed from about 200 to 65 million years ago.

diocese ('dīəsis) *n.* the district under the authority of a bishop.

diploma (di'plōmə) *n.* a certificate to show that someone has reached a required degree of knowledge or skill in a subject.

direct (dī'rekt) *adj.* 1. not stopping or turning off; straight: *a direct route.* 2. honest; frank: *a direct remark.* —*vb.* 1. to show the way to: *can you direct* me to the station? 2. to manage; control. 3. to cause to head for or aim at. 4. to turn (one's attention). **di'rection** *n.* 1. angle of movement towards a place; way. 2. instruction; order. 3. control or management. **di'rectory** *n.,pl.* **directories.** a list of names and addresses: *the telephone directory.* —**di'rectly** *adv.* —**di'rectness** *n.* —**di'rector** *n.*

disability (disə'biliti) *n.,pl.* **disabilities.** lack of a physical or mental ability; handicap; incapacity: *being short is a disability if you want to become a policeman.* **disable** (dis'ābəl) *vb.* **disabling, disabled.** to make (someone or something) unable to function. **dis'abled** *adj.* crippled.

disadvantage (disəd'vântij) *n.* any unfavourable condition, situation, etc.; drawback: *his size put him at a disadvantage in the fight.*

disagree (disə'grē) *vb.* **disagreeing, disagreed.** 1. to differ in opinion; fail to agree. 2. to quarrel. 3. (+ *with*) to cause sickness in: *seafood disagrees with me.* **disa'greeable** *adj.* unpleasant, cross, or bad-tempered. —**disa'greement** *n.*

disappear (disə'piə) *vb.* 1. to vanish; cease to be visible. 2. to cease to exist; become extinct: *dinosaurs disappeared millions of years ago.* —**disap'pearance** *n.*

disappoint (disə'point) *vb.* to fail to fulfil expectations, arrangements, etc.; let down: *they were disappointed when he refused their invitation.* —**disap'pointment** *n.*

disapprove (disə'prōōv) *vb.* **disapproving, disapproved.** (+ *of*) to consider wrong; condemn.

disarm (dis'âm) *vb.* 1. to remove weapons from; render harmless or defenceless: *he disarmed his enemy with one blow.* 2. to rid of suspicion, etc., by charm: *she disarmed him with a happy smile.* —**dis'armament** *n.*

disaster (di'zâstə) *n.* a very unfortunate event, result, or situation. —**dis'astrous** *adj.* —**dis'astrously** *adv.*

disc (disk) *n.* 1. a flat circular object. 2. (informal) a gramophone record: *don't forget to bring your discs to the party.*

discard (dis'kâd) *vb.* to throw away; reject as unwanted.

disciple (di'sīpəl) *n.* a follower, esp. of a religious leader, who tries to spread his teaching.

discipline ('disiplin) *n.* 1. training to obey or behave well, esp. through strictness and punishment. 2. orderly behaviour. 3. a subject of study. —*vb.* **disciplining, disciplined.** 1. to train. 2. to punish.

disclose (dis'klōz) *vb.* **disclosing, disclosed.** to reveal (a secret, etc.). —**dis'closure** *n.*

discount *n.* ('diskount) a reduction in a price, given e.g. to those who buy in bulk or to attract customers. —*vb.* (dis'kount) to reject as being untrue, worthless, or invalid; disbelieve: *we discounted his story.*

discourage (dis'kurij) *vb.* **discouraging, discouraged.** 1. to take away courage or confidence from. 2. to prevent or try to prevent (someone) from carrying out a particular intention. —**dis'couragement** *n.*

discover (dis'kuvə) *vb.* to reveal, find, or find out (something that was hidden or previously unknown): *Columbus discovered America in 1496.* —**dis'coverer** *n.* —**dis'covery** *n.,pl.* **discoveries.**

discriminate (dis'krimināt) *vb.* **discriminating, discriminated.** 1. to see a difference between one thing and another; distinguish: *to discriminate right from wrong.* 2. (+ *against*) to make an unfair distinction; act in a biased way. —**discrimi'nation** *n.*

discus ('diskəs) *n.,pl.* **discuses.** a stone, wood, or metal disc used in throwing competitions.

discuss (dis'kus) *vb.* to exchange ideas on a particular subject; talk over. —**dis'cussion** *n.*

disease (di'zēz) *n.* 1. illness or disorder of health. 2. a specific illness. —**dis'eased** *adj.*

disgrace (dis'grās) *vb.* **disgracing, disgraced.** to bring shame and dishonour to. —*n.* 1. a state of shame or dishonour. 2. anything that is shameful. —**dis'graceful** *adj.* —**dis'gracefully** *adv.*

disguise (dis'gīz) *vb.* **disguising, disguised.** to change the appearance, sound, or flavour of (something) in order to conceal its true identity, etc. —*n.* anything that serves to disguise.

disgust (dis'gust) *n.* an intense dislike or loathing, e.g. strong enough to produce feelings of sickness; revulsion. —*vb.* to offend strongly; sicken. —**dis'gusting** *adj.*

dish (dish) *n.* 1. a shallow bowl or plate of china, glass, wood, etc., used for serving food. 2. a particular kind of food: *what is your favourite dish?* **dish out** (informal) to hand out; distribute.

disinfect (disin'fekt) *vb.* to cleanse in order to kill or get rid of germs. **disin'fectant** *n.,adj.* (any chemical agent) that destroys germs.

disintegrate (dis'intigrāt) *vb.* **disintegrating, disintegrated.** to fall apart; break or collapse into small pieces. —**disinte'gration** *n.*

dislike (dis'līk) *vb.* **disliking, disliked.** to find (something) very unpleasant. —*n.* an idea that something is unpleasant: *a dislike of sleeping in the open.*

dinosaur

dismal ('dizməl) *adj.* gloomy, dreary, or unhappy. —'**dismally** *adv.*

dismay (dis'mā) *vb.* to cause worry or alarm; discourage or sadden. —*n.* loss of hope or courage; alarm; worry: *the news filled him with dismay.*

dismiss (dis'mis) *vb.* 1. to send away; give (soldiers, a class, etc.) permission to leave. 2. to end the employment of. 3. to put (something) out of one's mind. —**dis'missal** *n.*

dispatch *or* **despatch** (dis'pach) *vb.* 1. to send (someone) off quickly to a place. 2. to settle quickly: *to dispatch a business matter.* 3. to kill; execute. —*n.* 1. message; report. 2. speed and efficiency.

dispense (dis'pens) *vb.* **dispensing, dispensed.** 1. to distribute or deal out. 2. to administer (justice, etc.). 3. to prepare (medicines). 4. (+ *with*) to cease using. **dis'pensable** *adj.* not absolutely necessary or needed. **dis'pensary** *n.,pl.* **dispensaries.** a place where medicines are prepared. **dispen'sation** *n.* 1. the act of dispensing. 2. permission to do something that is normally forbidden, esp. according to ecclesiastical law.

disperse (dis'pûs) *vb.* **dispersing, dispersed.** to scatter in different directions: *the high wind soon dispersed the smoke.* —**dis'persal** *or* **dis'persion** *n.*

display (dis'plā) *vb.* 1. to put on show; exhibit. 2. to show or reveal: *the pianist displayed his talent with a brilliant performance.* —*n.* an exhibition, demonstration, etc.

dispose (dis'pōz) *vb.* **disposing, disposed.** (+ *of*) to get rid of: *how can we dispose of these empty boxes?* **dis'posed** *adj.* willing or likely; inclined: *he is not disposed to be friendly.* **disposition** (dispə'zishən) *n.* one's natural qualities or character: *a nervous disposition.*

dispute *vb.* (dis'pyoot) **disputing, disputed.** 1. to argue or debate strongly. 2. to question the truth or validity of; contest. —*n.* ('dispyoot) a disagreement or quarrel.

disqualify (dis'kwolifī) *vb.* **disqualifying, disqualified.** to take away the rights or privileges of, usu. because a law or rule has been broken: *the court disqualified him from driving.* —**disqualifi'cation** *n.*

disregard (disri'gâd) *vb.* to ignore or pay no attention to. —*n.* indifference; lack of care or attention.

dissolve (di'zolv) *vb.* **dissolving, dissolved.** 1. to melt in a liquid; to be or cause to be absorbed into a liquid: *sugar dissolves in hot coffee.* 2. to melt; change into a liquid: *the snow dissolved.* 3. to end: *to dissolve a partnership.*

dissuade (di'swād) *vb.* **dissuading, dissuaded.** (+ *from*) to persuade not to do (something). —**dis'suasion** *n.*

distant ('distənt) *adj.* 1. far away in space or time. 2. related, but not in a close way: *a distant relative.* 3. reserved; unfriendly; aloof. '**distance** *n.* 1. amount of space between two places or time between two events. 2. unfriendliness. —'**distantly** *adv.*

distil (dis'til) *vb.* **distilling, distilled.** to heat a liquid or solid and then allow the vapour produced to cool and form a pure or more concentrated liquid. **di'stillery** *n.,pl.* **distilleries.** a place in which alcoholic beverages, e.g. whisky and gin, are produced. —**dis'tiller** *n.*

distinct (dis'tiṅgkt) *adj.* 1. separate; having differences that mark out and set something apart. 2. clear; easily heard, seen, or understood. 3. definite: *a distinct possibility of rain.* **dis'tinction** *n.* 1. difference, esp. between things that are similar: *what is the distinction between a raven and a crow?* 2. excellence; superiority. —**dis'tinctive** *adj.* —**dis'tinctively** *adv.* —**di'stinctly** *adv.*

distinguish (dis'tiṅggwish) *vb.* 1. to recognize a difference; make a distinction. 2. to see or hear clearly; make out; recognize: *can you distinguish your friend in this crowd?* **distinguish oneself** to bring credit or honour to oneself; excel. **dis'tinguished** *adj.* well-known and honoured.

distract (dis'trakt) *vb.* 1. to attract the attention, concentration, etc., of (someone) from what he is doing. 2. to disturb or upset greatly: *they were distracted by grief.* —**dis'traction** *n.*

distress (dis'tres) *n.* suffering, esp. mental; grief; pain. —*vb.* to cause to suffer distress: *we were distressed by the news.*

distribute (dis'tribyoot) *vb.* **distributing, distributed.** 1. to give out

or share amongst many; divide up. 2. to spread or scatter over an area: *the leaflets were distributed from the air.* —**distri'bution** *n.* —**dis'tributive** *adj.* —**dis'tributor** *n.*

district ('distrikt) *n.* a division of land, e.g. into a county, borough, state, etc., for administrative, electoral, or other purposes.

disturb (dis'tûb) *vb.* 1. to interrupt (a person, the silence, etc.). 2. to disarrange; disorder. 3. to cause worry or trouble to. —**dis'turbance** *n.*

ditch (dich) *n.* a long hollow channel dug in the earth, used for drainage, etc.; trench. —*vb.* (informal) to throw away; discard: *all the original plans were ditched.*

ditto ('ditō) *n.* the same as stated above. Used in lists to avoid repeating the same information and indicated by **ditto marks** ("").

divan (di'van) *n.* a bed without sides, headboard, or footboard, that can be used as a seat during the day.

dive (dīv) *vb.* **diving, dived.** 1. to throw oneself into water, esp. head first. 2. to move downwards suddenly and quickly. 3. to reach for, into, etc., suddenly: *he dived into his pocket for money.* —*n.* the act of diving.

divert (dī'vût) *vb.* 1. to turn aside, e.g. from a course or plan. 2. to entertain; amuse. —**di'version** *n.*

divide (di'vīd) *vb.* **dividing, divided.** 1. to separate or become separated into parts. 2. to give out; share. 3. to calculate how many times one number is contained in another. 4. to cause disagreement between. **division** (di'vizhən) *n.* 1. the act of dividing. 2. a part or section, e.g. of an army. 3. the point at which something divides. 4. disagreement. 5. a vote in Parliament. **divisible** (di'vizibəl) *adj.* able to be divided: *28 is exactly divisible by 4 and 7.*

dividend ('dividənd) *n.* 1. a number to be divided. 2. a shareholder's profit.

divine (di'vīn) *adj.* 1. of or like a god. 2. (informal) wonderful; lovely. —*n.* a priest, clergyman, etc.

divorce (di'vôs) *n.* 1. the legal ending of a marriage. 2. any complete separation. —*vb.* **divorcing, divorced.** to end one's marriage. **divorcee** (divô'sē) *n.* a divorced person.

dogs

Old English Sheepdog

Greyhound

Labrador

Pekingese

divulge (dī'vulj) *vb.* **divulging, divulged.** to reveal or make public (something previously unknown or secret); disclose: *Tom divulged Mary's secret passion.*

dizzy ('dizi) *adj.* **dizzier, dizziest.** 1. feeling an unbalanced or spinning sensation; giddy. 2. liable to cause giddiness: *a dizzy height.* —'**dizzily** *adv.* —'**dizziness** *n.*

docile ('dōsīl) *adj.* easily managed or taught. —**docility** (dō'siliti) *n.*

dock[1] (dok) *n.* a place where ships and boats are tied up for loading, repair, etc. —*vb.* 1. to enter or cause to enter a dock. 2. (of spacecraft) to link in space. '**docker** *n.* person who loads ships, etc.

dock[2] (dok) *n.* a small enclosed space in a courtroom where the accused is placed during his trial: *the prisoners in the dock looked scared.*

dock[3] (dok) *vb.* 1. to cut (a tail, etc.) short. 2. to deduct a part from (wages). —*n.* the part of the tail left after clipping.

doctor ('doktə) *n.* 1. a person professionally qualified to practise medicine; physician. 2. a person who has been awarded one of the highest degrees conferred by a university. —*vb.* 1. to give medical treatment to. 2. (informal) to alter; falsify: *he doctored the entry date on the passport.* 3. (informal) to remove the reproductive organs of (a male animal): *I have had my cat doctored.*

doctrine ('doktrin) *n.* a particular principle or system of belief, esp. an official or established one.

document *n.* ('dokyŏŏmənt) a written paper, esp. an official one providing evidence. —*vb.* ('dokyŏŏment) to support or prove by documentary evidence. **docu'mentary** *adj.* relating to documents. *n.,pl.* **documentaries.** a film presenting a factual account of something: *a documentary about schools.*

dodge (doj) *vb.* **dodging, dodged.** 1. to move aside quickly to avoid (a blow, etc.). 2. to avoid cleverly or by trickery: *his answers dodged the question.* —*n.* the act of dodging.

dog (dog) *n.* any one of the family of warm-blooded flesh-eating animals many kinds of which are kept as pets. Wolves are a type of wild dog. —*vb.* **dogging, dogged.** to follow closely.

dogma ('dogmə) *n.* a principle or belief that is accepted as true.

dogwood ('dogwŏŏd) *n.* a small tree that is grown for ornament. It has dark red branches and its leaves turn bright red in the autumn.

dole (dōl) *n.* (usu. **the dole**) the regular state payment of hardship money to the unemployed. —*vb.* **doling, doled.** (+ *out*) (informal) to share out.

doll (dol) *n.* a toy that looks like a human being.

dollar ('dolə) *n.* a unit of currency in the United States, Canada, Australia, and elsewhere.

dolphin ('dolfin) *n.* an animal found in the Mediterranean and Atlantic, that looks like a large fish but breathes air and is very intelligent.

dome

dome (dōm) *n.* a roof like a hollow half sphere.

domestic (də'mestik) *adj.* 1. of the home or household affairs. 2. living with man; tame: *the cat is a domestic creature.* 3. of the affairs of one's own country: *domestic policies.* —*n.* a household servant. —**domesticity** (dōmes'tisiti) *n.*

dominate ('domināt) *vb.* **dominating, dominated.** 1. to be the strongest force in; control. 2. to be the most important or noticeable feature or person in: *the Eiffel Tower dominates the Paris skyline.* —'**dominant** *adj.* —**domi'nation** *n.*

domino ('dominō) *n.,pl.* **dominoes.** a small flat oblong piece of wood or plastic marked with spots, used in playing the game **dominoes.** Usually the wood is stained and the spots are painted white.

donate (də'nāt) *vb.* **donating, donated.** to give, esp. to charity. '**donor** *n.* a person who gives for a charitable or humane cause: *blood donor.* —**do'nation** *n.*

donkey ('doñgki) *n.* a long-eared sure-footed animal of the horse family used chiefly as a beast of burden; ass.

doodle ('dōōdəl) *vb.* **doodling, doodled.** to scribble or draw, usu. while thinking about something else. —*n.* an idle scribble or drawing. —'**doodler** *n.*

doom (dōōm) *n.* 1. unpleasant fate or destiny. 2. death: *the wild animal fell to its doom.* —*vb.* to condemn to death, ruin, failure, or misfortune.

dope (dōp) *n.* 1. (slang) drugs, esp. those sold illegally or given illegally to racehorses. 2. (informal) detailed or advance information. 3. (informal) a stupid person. 4. a thick varnish used for waterproofing aircraft, etc. —*vb.* **doping, doped.** to drug. '**dopey** *or* '**dopy** *adj.* **dopier, dopiest.** (informal) 1. half asleep; half-conscious. 2. stupid; dim-witted.

dormouse ('dômous) *n.,pl.* **dormice** ('dômīs). a small furry squirrel-like animal with a bushy tail, found mainly in Europe. It is usu, nocturnal and hibernates in winter.

dose (dōs) *n.* an amount of medicine to be taken at one time.

double ('dubəl) *adj.* 1. twice as much. 2. paired; matching: *double doors.* 3. for two people: *a double bed.* —*adv.* 1. twice: *double the price.* 2. in two: *fold the blanket double.* —*n.* 1. an amount that is twice as much. 2. a person or thing that looks exactly like another. 3. **doubles** (*pl.*) (in tennis, etc.) a match with two players on each side. —*vb.* **doubling, doubled.** 1. to make or become double. 2. to fold or bend

dormouse

into two. **double back** to turn back, esp. to mislead pursuers. **double up** (*or* **over**) to bend the body, esp. through pain. —'**doubly** *adv.*

double-cross (dubəl'kros) *vb.* to trick (someone) by pretending to do but not doing what has been agreed; cheat, betray, or deceive. —*n.* the act of double-crossing.

doubt (dout) *vb.* 1. to tend not to believe; be uncertain: *I doubt if he will come.* 2. to distrust; suspect: *I doubt his motives.* —*n.* often **doubts** (*pl.*) uncertainty, fear, distrust, or suspicion. —'**doubter** *n.* —'**doubtful** *adj.* —'**doubtfully** *adv.*

dough (dō) *n.* thick mixture of flour with water, milk, eggs, and other ingredients that is is baked to make bread, pastry, etc.

doughnut ('dōnut) *n.* a type of bun made of dough and fried in fat. It usually has a hole through its centre or is filled with jam.

dove (duv) *n.* a bird of the pigeon family that is a symbol of peace and (in the Christian religion) of the Holy Spirit.

downcast ('dounkâst) *adj.* 1. discouraged; disappointed. 2. turned down: *downcast eyes.*

downfall ('dounfôl) *n.* 1. sudden collapse or ruin, esp. of a ruler. 2. something causing failure: *untidiness was her downfall.* 3. heavy shower of rain or snow.

downpour ('dounpô) *n.* a very heavy rain storm.

downright ('dounrīt) *adj.* 1. absolute; complete: *the expedition was a downright disaster.* 2. honest; frank. —*adv.* thoroughly; completely: *downright dishonest.*

dowry ('douri) *n.* the money or property that a wife gives to a husband when they marry.

doze (dōz) *vb.* **dozing, dozed.** 1. to sleep lightly, waking often. 2. (often + *off*) to fall asleep, esp. unintentionally. —*n.* a short light sleep. '**dozy** *adj.* **dozier, doziest.** 1. sleepy; drowsy. 2. (informal) dull-witted. —'**dozily** *adv.* —'**doziness** *n.*

dozen ('duzən) *n.* a set of twelve: *a dozen eggs.* **a baker's dozen** thirteen.

drab (drab) *adj.* **drabber, drabbest.** dull-coloured or dreary; dull; shabby. —'**drably** *adv.* —'**drabness** *n.*

draft (drȧft) *n.* 1. a rough sketch or plan; outline: *the first draft of a play.* 2. (esp. in the U.S.) a group of men called upon for military service, etc. —*vb.* 1. to draw up (plans, etc.). 2. to choose for or assign to a special purpose, esp. military service. See also DRAUGHT.

drag (drag) *vb.* **dragging, dragged.** 1. to pull or haul, esp. along the ground. 2. to move or happen slowly or tediously: *time often drags before a holiday.* 3. to search (a river, etc.), by pulling nets along the bottom. —*n.* 1. something that pulls a person down or holds him back. 2. (slang) a bore; nuisance. 3. (slang) a puff on a cigarette.

dragon

dragon ('dragən) *n.* a mythical fire-breathing winged reptile with a scaly skin.

dragonfly ('dragənflī) *n., pl.* **dragonflies** a type of large colourful winged insect that breeds in water.

dragoon (drə'gōōn) *n.* a type of cavalry soldier in the British Army. —*vb.* to force (someone) to do something: *we were dragooned into helping with the decorating.*

drain (drān) *n.* 1. a channel or pipe for carrying away waste matter, such as sewage. 2. anything that uses up money, energy, etc. —*vb.* 1. (sometimes + *off*) to channel or draw off (excess liquid). 2. to empty into a larger stretch of water: *the Nile drains into the Mediterranean Sea.* 3. to exhaust; use up. —'**drainage** *n.*

drainpipe ('drānpīp) *n.* a pipe carrying water from a roof.

dram (dram) *n.* one-sixteenth part of an ounce.

drama ('drȧmə) *n.* 1. a play for stage, radio, or television. 2. plays in general; the theatre. 3. an emotional or exciting scene; stir. **dramatic** (drə'matik) *adj.* 1. of or relating to drama. 2. exciting or vivid: *a dramatic landscape.* **dramatics** *pl.n.* 1. the staging of plays. 2. a fit of over-emotional behaviour. **dramatize** ('dramətīz) *vb.* **dramatizing, dramatized.** 1. to describe in an exaggerated or dramatic way: *the explorer dramatized the journey's dangers.* 2. to turn (a novel, poem, etc.) into a play. —**dramati'zation** *n.*

drape (drāp) *vb.* **draping, draped.** 1. to hang or arrange cloth so that it falls in loose folds. 2. to place one's arms or legs around something loosely or casually: *she draped herself around the statue for the photograph.*

drastic ('drastik) *adj.* highly effective or severe: *drastic action must be taken to save whales from extinction.* —'**drastically** *adv.*

draught (drȧft) *n.* 1. a current of air inside a room, chimney, etc. 2. a drink or gulp: *a draught of beer.* 3. the depth of water required to float a boat. 4. **draughts** (*pl.*) a board game for two people played with 24 counters on a board marked out with 64 squares (**draughtboard**). **draught animal** an animal, e.g. a horse or ox, used for pulling heavy loads. '**draughty** *adj.* **draughtier, draughtiest.** full of draughts (def. 1).

draw (drô) *vb.* **drawing, drew, drawn.** 1. to pull in a specified direction: *the man drew me to one side.* 2. to move: *she drew near.* 3. to pull out: *the dentist drew a tooth.* 4. to get or obtain: *he drew the money out of the bank.* 5. to pull (a weapon) from a sheath or holster. 6. to pick or choose (a team, winning tickets, a playing card, etc.). 7. to attract: *he drew my attention to the time.* 8. to take in: *he drew a deep breath.* 9. to make a picture or design in pencil, etc. 10. to obtain equal points or goals in a game or contest; tie. 11. (+ *out*) to make or become longer in time. 12. (+ *out*) to persuade (a person) to talk or express his feelings. 13. (+ *up*) to set out or draft (a document, plans, etc.). 14. (+ *up*) to come to a halt. **draw a blank** to fail to find out or obtain. —*n.* 1. an attraction: *the exhibition was a big draw.* 2. the selection of the winning tickets in a lottery. 3. the selection of players for a team. 4. a competition in which none of the competitors is declared the outright winner.

drawback ('drôbak) *n.* a disadvantage or hindrance; inconvenience.

drawbridge ('drôbrij) *n.* 1. a bridge, across the moat of a castle, that can be drawn up to prevent access. 2. a bridge on a river or canal that can be pulled up to allow ships to pass.

drawer ('drôə) *n.* 1. a lidless boxlike compartment that slides in and out of a piece of furniture. 2. **drawers** (*pl.*) underpants or knickers.

drawl (drôl) *vb.* to speak very slowly, exaggerating the vowel sounds. —*n.* drawling or slow speech.

drawn (drôn) *vb.* the past participle of DRAW. —*adj.* tired or tense, as with worry, pain, etc.

dread (dred) *n.* great fear, alarm, or anxiety. —*vb.* to feel anxious and apprehensive; fear. '**dreadful** *adj.* unpleasant; very bad; frightening. '**dreadfully** *adv.* 1. extremely: *dreadfully tired.* 2. terribly or horribly.

dream (drēm) *n.* 1. a sequence of pictures that pass through the mind during sleep. 2. the state of being lost in thought and seeming not to notice one's surroundings. 3. an ambition or desire. —*vb.* **dreaming, dreamed** *or* **dreamt** (dremt). to see in or have a dream. —'**dreamer** *n.* —'**dreamily** *adv.* —'**dreaminess** *n.* —**dreamy** *adj.* **dreamier, dreamiest.**

dreamt (dremt) *vb.* the past participle of DREAM.

dreary ('driəri) *adj.* **drearier, dreariest.** 1. dull; gloomy: *a dreary view of factories.* 2. boring; tedious. —'**drearily** *adv.* —'**dreariness** *n.*

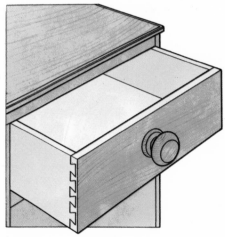
drawer

dredge (drej) *vb.* **dredging, dredged.** to remove silt, mud, or other substances from the bottom of the sea, a river, etc. —*n.* a device for doing this. '**dredger** *n.* a ship used for dredging.

dregs (dregz) *pl.n.* 1. particles left at the bottom of a container of wine, coffee, etc. 2. the worthless parts, e.g. of life.

drench (drench) *vb.* to wet thoroughly; soak: *the heavy rain drenched her.*

dress (dres) *vb.* 1. to put on clothes or to clothe. 2. to decorate (a shop window, Christmas tree, etc.). 3. to clean and bandage (a wound). **dress up** to put on or wear formal clothes or fancy dress. —*n.* 1. a woman's or girl's one-piece garment with a top and skirt. 2. clothing; costume: *informal dress.* '**dressing** *n.* 1. a seasoned sauce made to put on foods, esp. used for salad. 2. a bandage, ointment, etc., used for cleaning and covering wounds. '**dressy** *adj.* **dressier, dressiest.** (informal) stylish.

dresser ('dresə) *n.* a kitchen sideboard with shelves, cupboards, and drawers.

dresser

dribble ('dribəl) *vb.* **dribbling, dribbled.** 1. to allow SALIVA to escape from the mouth; slobber. 2. to trickle. 3. to send a ball forward while running, using short kicks or hits. —*n.* 1. the saliva dribbled from the mouth. 2. the act of dribbling a ball.

dried (drīd) *vb.* the past tense and past participle of DRY.

drift (drift) *vb.* 1. to be carried along by wind or water. 2. to move into something without resistance: *they drifted into poverty.* 3. to wander aimlessly. 4. to leave a set course. —*n.* 1. a slow surface movement of the sea or sand, caused by wind or currents: *the North Atlantic Drift.* 2. a movement off course by a ship or aircraft due to wind or currents. 3. a slow general movement; trend. 4. (also **snowdrift**) a deep layer of snow. 5. (informal) general meaning: *do you get the drift of what I'm saying?* —'**drifter** *n.*

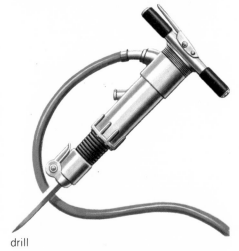

drill

drill¹ (dril) *n.* 1. a TOOL or machine used for boring holes in wood, teeth, etc. 2. a repetitive military training exercise involving marching and the handling of weapons. 3. disciplined instruction: *fire drill.* —*vb.* 1. to bore (a hole). 2. to train, instruct, or exercise by practice.

drill² (dril) *n.* a shallow trench or furrow in the ground in which seeds are planted.

drip (drip) *vb.* **dripping, dripped.** to fall or let fall in drops. —*n.* 1. a series of drops or the sound made as they fall. 2. (slang) a silly or weak person.

drive (drīv) *vb.* **driving, drove, driven** ('drivən). 1. to push, press, or urge on or forward. 2. to control, transport, or travel in a car, bus, etc. 3. to force; compel: *he was driven to sell the house.* 4. to send; render: *the noisy aircraft drove him mad.* 5. (+ home) to knock into position. 6. (+ home) to emphasize strongly. **drive at** to hint at; imply. —*n.* 1. a thrust, stroke, or blow. 2. energy and ambition. 3. a campaign: *the government drive to improve housing conditions.* 4. a journey made in a car, etc. 5. (also **driveway**) a private road leading up to a house or other building. 6. the apparatus for changing power into movement in a machine: *this car has front-wheel drive.* —'**driver** *n.*

drizzle ('drizəl) *n.* very light rain. —*vb.* **drizzling, drizzled.** to rain lightly and steadily.

drone¹ (drōn) *n.* 1. a stingless male bee that produces no honey. 2. an idle person.

drone² (drōn) *vb.* **droning, droned.** 1. to make a dull low continuous humming or buzzing noise. 2. to speak in a dull monotonous voice. 3. to continue in a boring way: *work droned on.* —*n.* 1. a droning sound. 2. a part of the BAGPIPES.

droop (drōop) *vb.* to sag; hang limply, bend over, or flag: *the flowers drooped because they had no water.* *n.* a drooping movement or position, e.g. of plants.

drop (drop) *n.* 1. a small round or tear-shaped blob or spot of liquid. 2. a small amount of liquid: *just a drop, please.* 3. anything resembling a drop: *a cough drop.* 4. a sudden fall or decrease. 5. a sudden fall between a high and lower level: *a steep drop.* —*vb.* **dropping, dropped.** 1. to fall or let fall: *he dropped the ball.* 2. (sometimes + off) to decrease. 3. to give up, stop, omit, or abandon: *he was dropped from the team.* 4. (+ off) to fall asleep. **drop out** to give up; withdraw. '**dropout** *n.* a person who has abandoned an educational course, conventional way of life, etc.

drought (drout) *n.* a prolonged period in which little or no rain falls, causing water shortages.

drove (drōv) *vb.* the past tense of DRIVE.

drown (droun) *vb.* 1. to die or kill by suffocating in water or other liquid. 2. to drench or flood. 3. to muffle or prevent (something) being heard: *the noise of the party was so great that his words were drowned.*

drowse (drouz) *vb.* **drowsing, drowsed.** to be half-asleep or sleepy; doze. —*n.* a state of sleepiness. —'**drowsily** *adv.* —'**drowsiness** *n.* —**drowsy** *adj.* **drowsier, drowsiest.**

drug (drug) *n.* 1. any chemical substance used to treat a disease or disorder. 2. a chemical substance whose overuse or misuse causes addiction. —*vb.* **drugging, drugged.** to administer drugs to, usu. with the intention of putting to sleep or harming.

drum (drum) *n.* 1. a musical instrument consisting of a skin stretched over a hollow body and struck with sticks (**drumsticks**). 2. a large cylindrical container, esp. for oil. —*vb.* **drumming, drummed.** to beat (the fingers) rhythmically on a surface.

drum

drunk (drungk) *vb.* the past participle of DRINK. —*adj.* (also **drunken**) having drunk so much alcohol that behaviour and speech are affected.

dry (drī) *adj.* **drier, driest.** 1. not wet or damp. 2. having little or no rainfall. 3. shrewd: *a dry sense of humour.* —*vb.* **drying, dried.** to make or become dry. —'**drily** *adv.*

dual ('dyōōəl) *adj.* double.

duchess ('duchis) *n.* 1. the wife or widow of a DUKE. 2. a woman equal in rank to a DUKE.

duck[1] (duk) *n.* a flat-billed web-footed water-bird.

duck[2] (duk) *vb.* to bend down or lower the head quickly, esp. to avoid something.

duct (dukt) *n.* 1. a tube carrying fluid somewhere, esp. in the body. 2. a pipe enclosing electric wires.

due (dyōō) *adj.* 1. owing; to be paid: *the rent is due.* 2. deserved, fair, or proper: *due respect.* 3. expected: *when is the bus due?* **in due course** eventually. **due to** because of. —*n.* 1. that which is owed or deserved: *we must give him his due.* 2. **dues** (*pl.*) a fee; subscription. —*adv.* directly; straight: *due north.* —'**duly** *adv.*

duel ('dyōōəl) *n.* (formerly) a sword or pistol fight between two men to settle a quarrel or decide a point of honour, usu. organized according to strict rules. —*vb.* **duelling, duelled.** to fight a duel. —'**dueller** *or* '**duellist** *n.*

duet (dyōō'et) *n.* a work for two singers or instrumentalists.

duke (dyōōk) *n.* a nobleman next down in rank to a prince. —'**dukedom** *n.*

dull (dul) *adj.* 1. not bright; cloudy. 2. boring; uninteresting. 3. blunt; not sharp: *a dull ache.* 4. stupid; slow: *a dull student.* 5. indistinct; deadened: *a dull thud.* —*vb.* to make or become dull. —'**dullness** *n.* —'**dully** *adv.*

dumb (dum) *adj.* 1. unable or unwilling to speak. 2. (informal) stupid. —'**dumbly** *adv.* —'**dumbness** *n.*

dummy ('dumi) *n.,pl.* **dummies.** 1. a model, copy, or substitute, e.g. a figure used to display clothes. 2. a rubber teat for a baby to suck. —*adj.* substitute; imitation.

dump (dump) *n.* 1. a pile of rubbish, abandoned objects, etc. 2. (slang) a boring or depressing place. **down in the dumps** feeling miserable. —*vb.* to throw away or throw down.

duck

dune (dyōōn) *n.* a hill of light sand, formed by the wind, usu. on a beach or in a desert.

dungeon ('dunjən) *n.* an underground prison, esp. below a castle.

duplicate *vb.* ('dyōōplikāt) **duplicating, duplicated.** 1. to make a copy of. 2. to imitate very closely. —*n.* ('dyōōplikit) something exactly like another. —*adj.* exactly like something else. '**duplicator** *n.* a machine that makes copies, usu. of letters or documents. —**dupli'cation** *n.*

dusk (dusk) *n.* twilight; the darkening of the day just before night. '**dusky** *adj.* **duskier, duskiest.** darkish.

dust (dust) *n.* fine dry particles of earth, etc. —*vb.* 1. to wipe or sweep dust from (furniture). 2. to sprinkle lightly, e.g. with flour. —'**dusty** *adj.* **dustier, dustiest.**

duty ('dyōōti) *n.,pl.* **duties.** 1. something a person knows he must do because it is right, because it is part of his job, etc. 2. tax on goods sold, brought into a country, etc. '**dutiful** *adj.* keen to do one's duty.

dwarf (dwôf) *n.,pl.* **dwarfs** *or* **dwarves.** an abnormally short person, animal, or plant. —*vb.* to make look small; overshadow: *the skyscraper dwarfed the surrounding buildings.*

dwell (dwel) *vb.* **dwelling, dwelt.** to reside; live (at); inhabit. **dwell on** to consider or speak about at length; linger over; emphasize: *he dwelt on his problems.* '**dwelling** *n.* a residence; place where someone lives.

dwindle ('dwindəl) *vb.* **dwindling, dwindled.** to grow gradually less; decline in importance or greatness.

dye (dī) *n.* a substance used to colour cloth, hair, etc. —*vb.* **dyeing, dyed.** to change the colour of, using a dye. —'**dyer** *n.*

dyke *or* **dike** (dīk) *n.* a bank of earth, etc., built along the edges of a sea or river, esp. to prevent flooding.

dynamite ('dīnəmīt) *n.* a highly explosive material, usu. used packed in sticks, esp. in mines.

dynamo ('dīnəmō) *n.,pl.* **dynamos.** a rotating machine that converts mechanical power into electrical power.

E

eager ('ēgə) *adj.* keen; impatiently enthusiastic: *he was eager to leave.* —'**eagerly** *adv.* —'**eagerness** *n.*

eagle ('ēgəl) *n.* the largest bird of prey, usu. brown or black in colour, with long broad wings and tail, feathered legs, strong sharp hooked beak, and talons. It is noted for its very high flight and its habit of nesting in very high and inaccessible places.

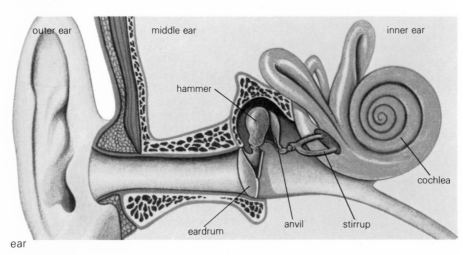

ear

ear (iə) *n.* either of the two bodily parts, one each side of the head, with which sounds are picked up; one of the organs of hearing.

earl (ûl) *n.* 1. the title of a British nobleman. 2. a person holding this title: *Walter Devereux was the first earl of Essex.* —'**earldom** *n.*

early ('ûli) *adj.* **earlier, earliest.** 1. near the beginning of something: *early music.* 2. before an agreed or suitable time: *an early arrival.* —*adv.* 1. at or near the beginning. 2. too soon.

earn (ûn) *vb.* to gain (something) in return for work or as a direct result of some action, etc. '**earnings** *pl.n.* wages; regular payment for work.

earnest ('ûnist) *adj.* 1. deeply serious or sincere: *his earnest wish was to help her.* 2. needing serious thought and concern: *an earnest endeavour.*

earth (ûth) *n.* 1. (also **Earth**) the third planet from the sun; the planet on which we live. 2. soil; dust or dirt. '**earthenware** *n.* pottery made of baked clay. *adj.* made of such pottery. '**earthquake** *n.* a violent shaking or cracking of the earth's crust. '**earthly** *adj.* connected with or appearing in the world; not heavenly.

ease (ēz) *n.* freedom from worry, difficulty, or effort; comfort. **with ease** without difficulty. **at ease.** 1. not worried or uncomfortable. 2. (military) an order for soldiers to stand in a formal relaxed position after standing at attention. —*vb.* **easing, eased.** 1. to make easier or provide relief, e.g. from pain, etc. 2. to relax; be comfortable. 3. to move gently: *he eased the plant into the pot.*

easel ('ēzəl) *n.* a frame, usu. of wood, upon which a blackboard or painter's canvas can be mounted.

east (ēst) *n.* 1. the direction in which one turns to see the sunrise. 2. the part of a country lying in this direction. —*adj.* lying in or towards the east: *the east side.* —*adv.* towards the east: *moving east.* '**eastern** *adj.* of or in the east.

easy ('ēzi) *adj.* **easier, easiest.** 1. not difficult; simple. 2. free from worry; comfortable. **take things easy** to make no special effort. —'**easily** *adv.* —'**easiness** *n.*

eavesdrop ('ēvzdrop) *vb.* **eavesdropping, eavesdropped.** to listen to or overhear private conversation. —'**eavesdropper** *n.*

ebb (eb) *n.* the movement of a tide backwards away from a beach or shore.

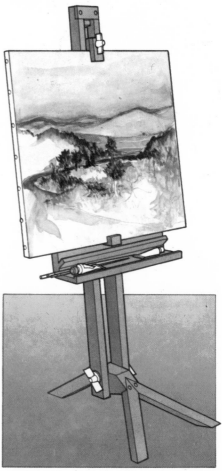

easel

ebony ('ebəni) *n.* a very hard, valuable, usu. black wood from a tree found mainly in India. —*adj.* 1. made from ebony. 2. of the colour or toughness of ebony.

eccentric (ek'sentrik) *n.* a person who behaves in an unusual, strange way. —*adj.* irregular; strange. —**ec'centrically** *adv.* —**eccentricity** (eksen'trisiti) *n.,pl.* **eccentricities.**

echo ('ekō) *n.,pl.* **echoes.** 1. the repetition of a sound produced by the reflection of sound waves from a wall, cliff, etc. 2. any repetition or imitation. 3. a reminder. —*vb.* **echoing, echoed.** to produce or return as an echo.

eclipse (i'klips) *vb.* **eclipsing, eclipsed.** 1. to hide the light from (the sun or moon). 2. to become more powerful, better known, etc., than someone else. *n.* a time when the moon moves between the earth and the sun and blocks off its light (**eclipse of the sun**), or when the earth moves between the sun and the moon (**eclipse of the moon**).

economy (i'konəmi) *n.,pl.* **economies.** 1. the way in which a country manages its money and industries. 2. the state or condition of a country's money, etc. 3. a way of saving money. **economic** (ēkə'nomik) *adj.* 1. relating to a country's economy. 2. saving money. **eco'nomics** *sing.n.* the science concerning business and money and the best way to manage them. **eco'nomical** *adj.* 1. using little, esp. using little money: *an economical holiday.* 2. brief: *an economical account.* **economize** (i'konəmīz) *vb.* **economizing, economized.** to keep low the amount of money one spends.

edge (ej) *n.* 1. the outer part of something, lying away from the centre. 2. the sharp side of a knife, razor blade, sword, etc. **on edge** nervous or worried. —*vb.* **edging, edged.** (+ *away, away from, towards,* etc.) to move very slowly, esp. to move sideways. **'edgeways** or **'edgewise** *adv.* with the edge first; sideways.

edible ('edibəl) *adj.* suitable for eating.

edit ('edit) *vb.* 1. to prepare (someone else's writing) for publication. 2. to organize the contents of and run (a magazine or newspaper). **'editor** *n.* a person who edits. **edi'torial** *adj.* of a person who edits. *n.* a newspaper article written by the editor.

edition (i'dishən) *n.* a set of identical books printed at the same time.

educate ('edyŏŏkāt) *vb.* **educating, educated.** to instruct, train, or teach (a person), esp. at a school. —**edu'cation** *n.* —**edu'cational** *adj.*

eel

eel (ēl) *n.* a long snakelike fish.

effect (i'fekt) *n.* 1. the result of some action or event. 2. **effects** (*pl.*) one's belongings or possessions. **ef'fective** *adj.* having an effect, esp. a good one. **ef'fectual** *adj.* useful; effective.

efficient (i'fishənt) *adj.* working or functioning well without wasting effort or time. —**ef'ficiency** *n.*

effort ('efət) *n.* 1. use of one's strength or energy, e.g. in working, facing a problem, etc. 2. an attempt: *he made no effort to escape.*

egg[1] (eg) *n.* 1. a hard-shelled object produced by female birds and inside which young birds develop. 2. a similar object produced by insects, snakes, lizards, etc. 3. a hen's egg, or part of it, used as food.

egg[2] (eg) *vb.* (+ *on*) to urge or encourage someone: *they egged on the youngest boy to ring the doorbell.*

eject (i'jekt) *vb.* to throw or cast out: *lava and flames were ejected from the volcano.* —**e'jection** *n.*

elaborate *adj.* (i'labərit) complicated: *an elaborate design.* —*vb.* (i'labərāt) **elaborating, elaborated.** to work out in great detail.

elastic (i'lastik) *n.* a stretchable substance, usu. made from rubber or other material. —*adj.* 1. containing or using elastic. 2. able to be stretched or extended: *the time allowed for this job is very elastic.*

elbow ('elbō) *n.* the bending joint in the middle of the arm. —*vb.* to hit or push with the elbow. **elbow one's way** (often + *through, past,* etc.) to clear a path for oneself by elbowing.

elect (i'lekt) *vb.* 1. to choose, esp. by voting for a person to act as one's representative. 2. to decide. —**e'lection** *n.*

electricity (ilek'trisiti) *n.* a form of energy produced by the presence or motion of charged particles such as electrons or protons. **e'lectric** *adj.* 1. operated by or resulting in electricity: *an electric light.* 2. emotionally very strong: *an electric atmosphere.* **e'lectrical** *adj.* 1. relating to electricity: *an electrical fault.* 2. requiring electricity to operate: *an electrical appliance.*

elegant ('eləgənt) *adj.* 1. (esp. of clothes) in good taste, esp. according to the fashions of the time. 2. graceful or beautiful. —**'elegance** *n.* —**'elegantly** *adv.*

element ('eləmənt) *n.* 1. something forming part of a larger thing. 2. a chemical substance that cannot be split into other substances: *oxygen and iron are elements.* 3. a heating device in a kettle, fire, etc. **elementary** (elə'mentəri) *adj.* simple; basic.

elephant

elephant ('eləfənt) *n.* an animal of Africa and India whose nose and front teeth are extended into a long trunk and tusks. Elephants are the largest land animals.

eliminate (i'limināt) *vb.* **eliminating, eliminated.** to reject; remove, esp. from a competition. —**elimi'nation** *n.*

elm (elm) *n.* 1. a tall tree grown for shade or decoration. 2. the wood of this tree, used for furniture. —*adj.* made from or concerning elm.

elope (i'lōp) *vb.* **eloping, eloped.** (of a young man or woman) to run away to marry without the approval of one or both sets of parents. —e'**lopement** n.

embark (em'bâk) vb. 1. to go on board a ship at the start of a voyage. 2. (+ on or upon) to begin; start: *he embarked on his new career in teaching.* —embar'**kation** n.

embarrass (em'barəs) vb. **embarrassing, embarrassed.** to cause (someone) to feel uncomfortable, worried, etc. —em'**barrassment** n.

embassy ('embəsi) n.,pl. **embassies.** 1. a place where the ambassador and other diplomats representing a foreign country live and work. 2. a job in which someone represents a foreign country.

embrace (em'brās) vb. **embracing, embraced.** 1. to take in one's arms, usu. as a sign of affection. 2. to accept willingly: *he embraced Christianity.* 3. to include: *the book embraces many interesting ideas.* —n. the act of embracing; a hug.

embroidery

embroider (em'broidə) vb. 1. to decorate with ornamental designs in needlework. 2. to exaggerate or add invented detail to (a story, etc.). —em'**broidery** n.

embryo ('embriō) n.,pl. **embryos.** 1. a child or animal at the earliest stages of development inside the mother. 2. the beginning or earliest stage of an idea, project, etc. —**embryonic** (embri'onik) adj.

emerald ('emərəld) n. a rare green precious stone used in jewellery. —adj. 1. made of emerald. 2. having the colour of emerald.

emerge (i'mûj) vb. **emerging, emerged.** 1. to appear; come out: *the moon emerged from behind the clouds.* 2. to develop: *new problems emerge every day.* —e'**mergence** n. —e'**mergent** adj.

emergency (i'mûjənsi) n.,pl. **emergencies.** an unexpected or sudden event, situation, etc., requiring immediate action.

emigrate ('emigrāt) vb. **emigrating, emigrated.** to leave one country or region to settle in another. **emigrant** ('emigrənt) adj.,n. (of) a person who emigrates. —emi'**gration** n.

eminent ('eminənt) adj. 1. high in rank or reputation; distinguished. *Dickens was an eminent author.* 2. remarkable: *he showed eminent courtesy.* —'**eminence** n. —'**eminently** adv.

emit (i'mit) vb. **emitting, emitted.** 1. to send or be sent out: *she emitted a scream.* 2. to give out (radiation or other energy). —e'**mission** n.

emotion (i'mōshən) n. 1. a strong feeling, such as love, fear, hate, joy, etc. 2. an agitated state of mind; excitement or passion: *her voice trembled with emotion.* —e'**motional** adj.

emperor ('empərə) n. the supreme ruler of an empire. **empress** ('empris) n. 1. a female emperor. 2. an emperor's wife.

emphasis ('emfəsis) n.,pl. **emphases** ('emfəsēz). 1. importance or prominence given to anything by calling attention to it in some way. 2. the act of calling attention to something: *he laid emphasis on the word by repeating it.* 3. vigour; intensity of expression, action, etc.: *he spoke well and with great emphasis.* **emphasize** ('emfəsīz) vb. **emphasizing, emphasized.** to give emphasis to. **emphatic** (em'fatik) adj. 1. using emphasis. 2. striking; clear. —em'**phatically** adv.

empire ('empīə) n. a number of countries or states ruled over by a single person or government.

employ (em'ploi) vb. 1. to use the services of or provide work for (a person or persons): *that builder employs sixty men.* 2. to make use of: *I employ my spare time in playing the guitar.* **em-ploy'ee** n. a person working for another person or a firm in exchange for wages. **em'ployment** n. 1. work. 2. the act of employing or the state of being employed. —em'**ployer** n.

empress ('empris) n. See EMPEROR.

empty ('empti) adj. **emptier, emptiest.** 1. containing nothing: *an empty box.* 2. unoccupied: *an empty house.* 3. worthless: *empty promises.* —vb. **emptying, emptied.** to make or become empty: *empty the bucket.* —'**emptiness** n.

emu

emu ('ēmyōō) n. a large non-flying bird of Australia similar to the ostrich.

enable (en'ābəl) vb. **enabling, enabled.** to give (someone) the power, ability, or chance to do something: *the money he earned enabled him to have a holiday.*

enamel (i'naməl) n. 1. a glossy material used as a protective or decorative coating on metal or pottery. 2. a paint or varnish resembling this. 3. the hard outer covering on teeth. —adj. of, resembling, or coated with enamel.

enchant (in'chânt) vb. 1. to cast a spell over (someone or something); bewitch. 2. to delight or charm: *the actors enchanted the audience with their performance.* —en'**chanting** adj. —en'**chantment** n.

enclose (in'klōz) vb. **enclosing, enclosed.** 1. to shut in; surround: *the garden was enclosed by a high wall.* 2. to send in the same envelope or package as that containing the main letter, etc.: *I enclosed a cheque with the letter.* 3. to contain or hold. **enclosure** (in'klōzhə) n. 1. the act of enclosing or the state of being enclosed. 2. an area of land surrounded by a fence or wall.

encore ('onkô) n. (in a concert, etc.) a repeat of a piece as demanded by the audience.

encounter (in'kountə) *vb.* 1. to meet unexpectedly. 2. to come across or struggle against (difficulties, opposition, etc.). —*n.* 1. a casual or unexpected meeting. 2. a hostile meeting; combat or battle.

encourage (in'kurij) *vb.* **encouraging, encouraged.** to urge on by giving support, approval, etc.; inspire with hope or confidence. Compare DISCOURAGE. —**en'couragement** *n.*

encyclopedia (ensīklə'pēdiə) *n.* a book or set of volumes giving information on all branches of knowledge or all aspects of one subject, usu. arranged in alphabetical order. —**encyclo'pedic** *adj.*

endeavour (en'devə) *vb.* to make an effort or attempt; try: *I will endeavour to be there on time.* —*n.* a strenuous effort or the use of it: *after great endeavour they reached the hilltop.*

endure (en'dyŏŏə) *vb.* **enduring, endured.** 1. to suffer or bear: *he endured great pain.* 2. to last or continue: *their love endured for a lifetime.* —**en'durance** *n.*

enemy ('enəmi) *n.,pl.* **enemies.** 1. a person who hates an opponent and wishes to harm him. 2. a hostile nation or its armed forces; an opponent in war. 3. anything that threatens to harm or destroy: *fear is the great enemy.* —*adj.* of or belonging to a hostile force.

energy ('enəji) *n.,pl.* **energies.** 1. force; strength; vigour: *he had the energy to walk for miles without tiring.* 2. (physics) the capacity to do work. 3. power supplied by coal, gas, electricity, etc. **energetic** (enə'jetik) *adj.* having plenty of energy. —**ener'getically** *adv.*

enforce (en'fôs) *vb.* **enforcing, enforced.** to put into effect (a decision, law, etc.). —**en'forcement** *n.*

engage (en'gāj) *vb.* **engaging, engaged.** 1. to agree to pay for the services of (a person, etc.); employ. 2. to reserve or book for future use. 3. to attract or occupy (one's interest or attention). 4. to fit; lock; match: *the wheel cogs of the machine engaged.* 5. to begin a battle with (an enemy). **en'gaged** *adj.* 1. (of a man and woman) intending to marry. 2. (of a telephone line) already in use. 3. (of a toilet) occupied. **en'gagement** *n.* 1. the act of engaging. 2. a promise to marry. 3. a battle.

car (internal combustion) engine

aeroplane (jet) engine

engine

engine ('enjin) *n.* a machine that drives or pulls a car, train, etc.

engineer (enji'niə) *n.* 1. a person employed on any of several practical scientific activities. —*vb.* to make up (a clever plan). **engi'neering** *n.* an applied science involving the techniques of the engineer.

engrave (en'grāv) *vb.* **engraving, engraved.** to cut (words, a design, etc.) into (stone or metal). **en'graving** *n.* 1. the art of doing this. 2. a picture or design produced by engraving a piece of metal and printing it on paper.

enigma (i'nigmə) *n.* a person or thing that cannot be easily understood; puzzle. —**enigmatic** (enig'matik) *adj.* —**enig'matically** *adv.*

enjoy (en'joi) *vb.* 1. to obtain a pleasant or happy feeling from something or doing something: *I enjoy riding.* 2. to have the benefit of: *I enjoy good health.*

enlarge (en'lâj) *vb.* **enlarging, enlarged.** 1. to make bigger, esp. to make a larger print by magnification from (a photograph). 2. (+ *on* or *upon*) to give further details about. —**en'largement** *n.*

enlighten (en'lītən) *vb.* to help (someone) to increase his knowledge or understanding. **en'lightened** *adj.* intelligent or civilized. **en'lightenment** *n.* the act of enlightening or state of being enlightened.

enlist (en'list) *vb.* 1. to enter or be entered into the army, navy, or air force. 2. to obtain (help): *he enlisted my aid in doing his homework.*

enormous (i'nôməs) *adj.* very big; huge. **e'normity** *n.,pl.* **enormities.** 1. very great evil or wickedness. 2. a great crime. —**e'normously** *adv.*

enquire (en'kwiə) *vb.* **enquiring, enquired.** to seek information from someone. **enquire after** to ask about someone. **en'quiry** *n.,pl.* **enquiries.** a request for information. See also INQUIRE.

enrage (en'rāj) *vb.* **enraging, enraged.** to cause to be very angry.

enrol (en'rōl) *vb.* **enrolling, enrolled.** to place someone's name or have one's name placed on a list of members. —**en'rolment** *n.*

ensure (en'shŏŏr) *vb.* **ensuring, ensured.** to make certain: *he ensured his success by practising hard.*

enterprise ('entəprīz) *n.* 1. willingness or ability to do something unusual: *she showed great enterprise by organizing a charity walk.* 2. a commercial business undertaking.

entertain (entə'tān) *vb.* 1. to provide amusement or distraction for (an audience). 2. to be prepared to think about: *I wouldn't entertain such an idea.* —**enter'tainer** *n.* —**enter'tainment** *n.*

enthusiasm (in'thyōōziazəm) *n.* very great interest, eagerness, or keenness. **en'thuse** *vb.* **enthusing, enthused.** to feel or express enthusiasm. **en'thusiast** *n.* someone full of enthusiasm. —**enthusi'astic** *adj.*

entice (en'tīs) *vb.* **enticing, enticed.** (+ *into*) to encourage someone to do something, esp. something bad.

entire (en'tīə) *adj.* whole; complete; total: *Richard ate an entire cake.* —**en'tirely** *adv.* —**en'tirety** *n.*

entreat (en'trēt) *vb.* to appeal to or beg (someone) to do something: *I entreat you to help me.* **en'treaty** *n.,pl.* **entreaties.** an appeal; prayer.

envelop (en'veləp) *vb.* to cover or surround totally: *smoke enveloped the scene.*

envelope ('envələp) *n.* a rectangular packet made of paper that is used for carrying letters and cards by post.

envelope

environment (en'vīrənmənt) *n.* the surroundings, situation, or circumstances in which a person or thing exists. —**environ'mental** *adj.*

envy ('envi) *n.* the feeling suffered by a person because of not being able to have what another person possesses or experiences; jealousy. —*vb.* **envying, envied.** to feel envy: *John envied Alan's new bicycle.*

epidemic (epi'demik) *n.* a disease that affects many people at the same time.

episode ('episōd) *n.* 1. one of several sections of a story published in a periodical or broadcast over radio or television. 2. an event: *a sad episode in someone's life.*

epitaph ('epitâf) *n.* a memorial inscription (sentence, poem, etc.) carved on a dead person's gravestone or tomb.

epoch ('ēpok) *n.* a period in history, geology, etc., esp. one during which something important happens.

equal ('ēkwəl) *adj.* the same; (esp. of figures) coming to the same amount: *2 plus 3 equals 5.* —*vb.* **equalling, equalled.** 1. to come to an equal amount. 2. to make (something) equal to something else. **equality** (i'kwoliti) *n.* the state of being equal, esp. of having the same rights as other people. **'equalize** *vb.* **equalizing, equalized.** to be or cause to be equal; balance. —**'equalizer** *n.*

equate (i'kwāt) *vb.* **equating, equated.** 1. to consider or think of as equal. 2. to balance equally. **e'quation** *n.* a mathematical expression in algebra in which one side is equal to the other and there is at least one unknown quantity, as in $x + 1 = 3$.

equator (i'kwātə) *n.* an imaginary line around the earth exactly halfway between the North and South Poles.

equinox ('ēkwinoks) *n.* 1. the two times during the year (in spring and autumn) when day and night are of equal length. 2. the two points reached during these times by the sun as it appears to move around the earth.

equip (i'kwip) *vb.* **equipping, equipped.** to provide or supply with the apparatus, etc., necessary for some activity: *they equipped the soldiers with weapons for the battle.*

e'quipment *n.* things with which someone or something can be equipped.

equivalent (i'kwivələnt) *adj.* matching something in effect or meaning: *10° Centigrade is equivalent to 50° Fahrenheit.* —**e'quivalence** *n.*

era ('iərə) *n.* a period of time, esp. an age of history; epoch: *the Christian era.*

erase (i'rāz) *vb.* **erasing, erased.** 1. to rub out (a mark, esp. a pencil mark). 2. to remove: *erase the memory from your mind.* **e'raser** *n.* (U.S.) a rubber for erasing pencil or pen marks. —**erasure** (i'rāzhə) *n.*

erect (i'rekt) *adj.* upright; vertical or straight. —*vb.* to build; put up. —**e'rection** *n.* —**e'rectly** *adv.*

ermine

ermine ('ûmin) *n.* 1. a stoat in winter. 2. the white fur grown by a stoat during the winter. —*adj.* trimmed with or made of ermine.

erode (i'rōd) *vb.* **eroding, eroded.** to wear down slowly or eat away over a long period: *water eroded the rock.* —**e'rosion** *n.*

err (û) *vb.* 1. to make a mistake. 2. (formerly) to commit a crime or sin.

errand ('erənd) *n.* 1. a journey made in order to carry news or a message from one place to another. 2. a trip made, e.g. to a shop, to get or buy something: *will you run an errand for me?*

error ('erə) *n.* a mistake.

erupt (i'rupt) *vb.* to burst out unexpectedly: *lava erupted from the volcano.* —**e'ruption** *n.*

escalator

escalator ('eskəlātə) *n.* a staircase moving either up or down on a power-driven endless track.

escape (i'skāp) *vb.* **escaping, escaped.** 1. to get free from prison, danger, etc. 2. to avoid; elude: *Jim escaped his teacher's attention.* **es'capism** *n.* the avoidance of all the problems of life and reality. —**es'capist** *n.,adj.*

escort *vb.* (is'kôt) to go along with a person to a place as a protector, guard, or companion. —*n.* ('eskôt) a person or group who escorts someone.

espionage ('espiənâzh) *n.* spying.

essay *n.* ('esā) 1. a piece of writing; written composition: *write an essay on fishing.* 2. an attempt: *his first essay as a professional footballer was a failure.* —*vb.* (e'sā) to try; attempt.

essence ('esəns) *n.* 1. the most important part or quality of a thing. 2. the concentrated form of a plant, drug, etc.: *vanilla essence.* **essential** (i'senshəl) *adj.* completely necessary and important. *n.* an essential part of something. —**es'sentially** *adv.*

establish (i'stablish) *vb.* 1. to organize, create, or set up: *to establish new laws.* 2. to prove: *can you establish that this is your own car?* **es'tablishment** *n.* the action of establishing or something that is established, e.g. an organization or business.

estate (i'stāt) *n.* 1. everything a person owns; possessions: *she left her whole estate to her sister.* 2. a large piece of land owned by one person. 3. (also **housing estate**) a piece of land on which a number of privately or publicly owned houses stand.

estimate *vb.* ('estimāt) **estimating, estimated.** to guess; judge: *he estimated that there were 30 people in the room.* —*n.* ('estimit) 1. a guess or judgment. 2. a statement of the probable cost of some work, service, etc. **esti'mation** *n.* a judgment or guess.

estuary ('estyŏoəri) *n.,pl.* **estuaries.** the mouth of a river, extending into the sea.

eternal (i'tûnəl) *adj.* lasting forever; never ending: *he swore eternal loyalty.* —**e'ternally** *adv.* —**e'ternity** *n.,pl.* **eternities.**

evade (i'vād) *vb.* **evading, evaded.** to escape from or avoid: *he evaded my question by changing the subject.* —**e'vasion** *n.* —**e'vasive** *adj.*

evangelist (i'vanjəlist) *n.* 1. a person who spreads Christian religion in a vigorous way, esp. through public meetings. 2. **Evangelist** any of the four gospel writers, Matthew, Mark, Luke, and John. —**e'vangelism** *n.*

evaporate (i'vapərāt) *vb.* **evaporating, evaporated.** to change from a liquid to a vapour. —**evapo'ration** *n.*

even ('ēvən) *adj.* 1. level; smooth: *an even surface.* 2. equal; matching: *the two boxers were even after the first round.* **get even with** to pay (someone) back for harm or injury. **even number** any of the numbers that can be exactly divided by 2, e.g. 2, 4, 6, 8, etc.

event (i'vent) *n.* something taking place at a certain time; an action or occurrence.

eventual (i'venchŏoəl) *adj.* forming a result; final. **eventu'ality** *n.,pl.* **eventualities.** something that might occur; possible result. **e'ventually** *adv.* at last; finally.

evergreen ('evəgrēn) *n.* a tree that does not shed its leaves in winter: *the fir tree is an evergreen.* —*adj.* of or concerning such a tree. Compare DECIDUOUS.

evict (i'vikt) *vb.* to remove (someone) from his home by legal methods or force. —**e'viction** *n.*

evidence ('evidəns) *n.* a set of facts that support or disprove a case, esp. a legal case. **'evident** *adj.* clear; obvious: *it is evident that you are ill.* —**'evidently** *adv.*

evil ('ēvil) *adj.* morally very bad; wicked. —*n.* 1. the state of being evil. 2. anything causing injury or harm: *poverty is a great evil.*

evolution (ēvə'lŏoshən) *n.* a process of evolving; development: *the evolution of road transport in Britain.*

evolve (i'volv) *vb.* **evolving, evolved.** to change gradually from an early form over a long period; develop: *it has been proved that men evolved from apes.*

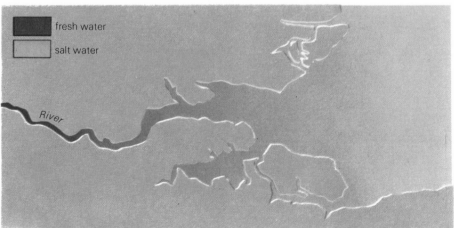

estuary

ewe

ewe (yōō) *n.* a female sheep.

exact¹ (ig'zakt) *adj.* accurate, correct, or precise. **ex'actly** *adv.* correctly; accurately. *interj.* quite right (used to indicate agreement).

exact² (ig'zakt) *vb.* to raise (money) by putting taxes on things. **ex'action** *n.* 1. the action of exacting money. 2. taxes put on things to raise money.

exaggerate (ig'zajərāt) *vb.* **exaggerating, exaggerated.** to make something appear bigger, better, etc., than it really is: *John exaggerated when he said that he had caught a hundred fish.* —**exagger'ation** *n.* —**ex'aggeratedly** *adv.*

examine (ig'zamin) *vb.* **examining, examined.** 1. to look at closely or thoroughly; inspect or investigate. 2. to put questions to (a student, pupil, etc.) in order to test his knowledge. **ex'aminer** *n.* someone who sets examinations. **exami'nee** *n.* a person being examined, esp. a student or pupil. —**exami'nation** *n.*

example (ig'zâmpəl) *n.* 1. a person or thing that represents a class or group of similar people or things: *lions and tigers are examples of wild animals.* 2. an action or form of behaviour worth copying or someone who provides this. **make an example of** to punish (someone) in order to show others what will happen if they copy him. **set an example** to act or behave well as a model for others.

exasperate (ig'zâspərāt) *vb.* **exasperating, exasperated.** to annoy very much: *I was exasperated by the little girl's stupidity.* —**exasper'ation** *n.*

exceed (ek'sēd) *vb.* to go beyond: *do not exceed 30 miles per hour.*

excel (ek'sel) *vb.* **excelling, excelled.** to be very good, e.g. in an activity; do better than other people: *she excels at swimming.* **excellent** ('eksələnt) *adj.* very good or fine. **'excellence** *or* **'excellency** *n.* 1. the quality of being excellent. 2. a term of address used to certain high-ranking officials, e.g. a foreign ambassador.

except (ek'sept) *prep.* (often + *for*) leaving out; not including or considering: *everyone came to the party except Bill.* —*vb.* to leave out; exclude. **ex'ception** *n.* something outside or beyond what is allowed or usual. —**ex'ceptional** *adj.* —**ex'ceptionally** *adv.*

excess *n.* (ek'ses) 1. the state of exceeding or going beyond what is suitable or right: *he eats to excess.* 2. an amount or quantity that exceeds what is necessary, suitable, usual, etc.: *an excess of energy.* —*adj.* ('ekses, ek'ses) beyond what is needed, suitable, or usual: *excess weight.* **ex'cessive** *adj.* greater in amount, quantity, etc., than is usual.

exchange (eks'chānj) *vb.* **exchanging, exchanged.** to give one thing in return for another: *he exchanged his old car for a new one* —*n.* 1. the act or an instance of exchanging. 2. a place where things are bought and sold: *people buy and sell financial shares at a stock exchange.*

excite (ek'sīt) *vb.* **exciting, excited.** to awaken (strong feelings or emotions, esp. of interest, anger, etc.) in (someone): *the news excited her.* —**ex'citement** *n.*

exclaim (eks'klām) *vb.* to shout in surprise, anger, etc. **exclamation** (eksklə'māshən) *n.* a shout.

exclude (iks'klōōd) *vb.* **excluding, excluded.** to leave out; not consider or take account of: *he was excluded from the journey because of his age.* **ex'clusion** *n.* the act of excluding or state of being excluded. **ex'clusive** *adj.* 1. excluding something. 2. including only a few people or things; selective: *this club is exclusive.*

excursion (ek'skûzhən) *n.* a trip or journey, esp. a special trip organized for pleasure: *we went on an excursion to the seaside.*

excuse *vb.* (ek'skyōoz) **excusing, excused.** 1. to forgive: *the teacher excused him for being late.* 2. to give reasons for some wrong behaviour or

action: to excuse a person's rudeness. 3. to allow (someone) to be absent: *he excused her from school.* —*n.* (ek'skyōos) a reason given for something that might be thought wrong or bad.

execute ('eksikyōot) *vb.* **executing, executed.** 1. to kill (someone) according to a law: *they executed him for treason.* 2. to perform (a task or duty): *he executed his task with great efficiency.* —**exe'cution** *n.*

executive (eg'zekyōotiv) *n.* 1. a person who organizes or administers a company or business firm. 2. a group responsible for organizing the work of a government, large association, union, or society.

exempt (eg'zempt) *adj.* (+ *from*) legally excluded from some law, rule, duty, etc.: *he is exempt from income tax.* —*vb.* to exclude (someone) in this way: *they exempted him from paying the usual fee.*

exercise ('eksəsīz) *vb.* **exercising, exercised.** 1. to train or move the various parts of the body in order to build up one's strength, improve one's health and appearance, etc., e.g. by playing sport. 2. to use (one's power or authority). —*n.* 1. the act of exercising; the process of training or building up one's body. 2. a piece of work done at school.

exert (ig'zût) *vb.* to bring into active operation or put into vigorous action (power, pressure, influence, etc.): *he exerted all his strength to move the rock.* **exert oneself** to make a vigorous effort; struggle or strive. —**ex'ertion** *n.*

exhaust

exhaust (ig'zôst) *vb.* 1. to use up or consume entirely: *we have exhausted* our supply of food. 2. to use up the energy of; wear out: *I exhausted myself climbing the hill.* 3. to say, write, or find out everything possible or necessary about (something): *after writing three pages he had exhausted the subject.* —*n.* gases or steam given off by an engine, or the pipe through which the gases are expelled. **ex'haustive** *adj.* thorough: *an exhaustive search.* —**ex'haustion** *n.*

exhibit (eg'zibit) *vb.* 1. to put on show; expose to view; present for inspection: *to exhibit paintings in public.* 2. to make plain; display: *he exhibited delight at the suggestion.* —*n.* 1. an object placed on show. 2. (law) a document or article produced in court as evidence: *the revolver was the first exhibit.* **exhi'bition** *n.* 1. a public presentation or show (of works of art, etc.). 2. a demonstration or public display. **to make an exhibition of oneself** to behave in such a way as to cause ridicule.

exile ('egzīl) *n.* 1. prolonged enforced separation from one's native land or home: *she was sent into exile.* 2. a person living in exile. —*vb.* **exiling, exiled.** to send into exile; banish from one's native land.

exist (eg'zist) *vb.* 1. to be or live. 2. to continue to be or live over a period of time: *we existed on very little food.* 3. to occur or be found: *great poverty still exists in some parts of the world.* —**ex'istence** *n.* —**ex'istent** *adj.*

exit ('eksit) *n.* 1. a way out of a building or enclosure. 2. a departure, esp. the departure from the stage of an actor in a play, etc. —*vb.* to leave or depart; go out.

expand (ik'spand) *vb.* 1. to enlarge in size, volume, extent, etc.: *water expands on freezing.* Compare CONTRACT. 2. to spread out. 3. to develop; express in detail: *she expanded her notes into an essay.* —**ex'pansion** *n.* —**ex'pansive** *adj.*

expanse (ek'spans) *n.* a wide open space or area of water, sky, land, etc.

expect (ik'spekt) *vb.* 1. to look forward to or consider likely: *I expect him to be here soon.* 2. to require or look for: *I expect complete obedience.* 3. to suppose: *I expect you are tired.* **expectation** (ekspek'tāshən) *n.* 1. the act of expecting. 2. something one expects or hopes for; a hope. —**ex'pectancy** *n.* —**ex'pectant** *adj.* —**ex'pectantly** *adv.*

expedition (ekspi'dishən) *n.* an organized journey made, usu. to a distant place, for a specific purpose. —**expe'ditionary** *adj.*

expel (ek'spel) *vb.* **expelling, expelled.** 1. to drive out or away with force; *we shall expel the invaders from our country.* 2. to dismiss (from a club, community, school, etc.): *they expelled the student from college.* See also EXPULSION.

expend (ek'spend) *vb.* to use up (money, energy, etc.). **ex'penditure** *n.* 1. the act of expending. 2. the amount of money that is spent or used up.

expense (ek'spens) *n.* 1. cost or charge. 2. the occasion or cause for spending money: *a holiday abroad can be a great expense.* 3. **expenses** (*pl.*) money spent, esp. during the course of a job: *she was paid a salary plus expenses.* **at someone's** or **something's expense** to someone's or something's disadvantage: *the work had to be done very quickly at the expense of quality.* **ex'pensive** *adj.* very highly priced. —**ex'pensively** *adv.*

experience (ek'spiəriəns) *n.* 1. a particular event or series of events that happen to or have a personal effect on someone: *driving fast can be a frightening experience.* 2. the process of gaining knowledge and skill in life or in some activity, occupation, etc.: *he has business experience.* —*vb.* **experiencing, experienced.** to meet with; undergo; feel: *she experienced great joy.* —**ex'perienced** *adj.*

experiment (ek'sperimənt) *n.* a test or trial carried out in order to discover something unknown or to test or prove a principle or theory. —*vb.* to make an experiment; test something out. —**experi'mental** *adj.* —**ex'perimenter** *n.*

expert ('ekspût) *n.* a person having special skill or knowledge in some particular subject. —*adj.* 1. possessing special skill or knowledge; taught by practice: *an expert marksman.* 2. coming from or produced by an expert. —**expertise** (ekspû'tēz) *n.* —'**expertly** *adv.*

explain (ek'splān) *vb.* 1. to make clear or understandable. 2. to account for; give meaning to: *how do you explain your behaviour?* **explanation** (eksplə'nāshən) *n.* the act or an instance of explaining.

explode (ek'splōd) *vb.* **exploding, exploded.** 1. to blow up or cause to blow up: *the bomb exploded after hitting the ground.* 2. to show sudden strong emotions: *she exploded with anger.* See also EXPLOSION.

exploit *n.* ('eksploit) a daring or bold action, achievement, etc. —*vb.* (ek'sploit) 1. to employ or use, esp. for profit. 2. to take advantage of in a selfish way. —**exploi'tation** *n.* —**ex'ploiter** *n.*

explore (ek'splô) *vb.* **exploring, explored.** 1. to travel through (a region, country, etc.) for the purposes of discovery. 2. to look into closely; examine thoroughly. —**explo'ration** *n* —**exploratory** (ek'splorətəri) *adj.* —**ex'plorer** *n.*

explosion

explosion (ek'splōzhən) *n.* a sudden, violent, loud, and often destructive bursting or breaking out. **ex'plosive** *adj.* capable of exploding or being exploded. *n.* an explosive substance.

export *vb.* (ek'spôt, 'ekspôt) to take or send (manufactured goods, etc.) out of a country for sale abroad. —*n.* ('ekspôt) 1. the act or process of exporting. 2. an item that is exported. —**expor'tation** *n.* **exporter** (ek'spôtə, 'ekspôtə) *n.* a person who exports goods.

expose (ek'spōz) *vb.* **exposing, exposed.** 1. to lay open (to danger, harm, etc.): *the army exposed itself to attack from the rear.* 2. to uncover: *he exposed his back to the sun.* 3. to put on show; display. 4. to make known; reveal or disclose: *the newspaper exposed the man as a fraud.* 5. to subject (a photographic film or plate) to the action of light. **ex'posure** *n.* 1. the action or an instance of exposing or being exposed. 2. the effects on the body of being without shelter or protection from severe weather.

express (ek'spres) *vb.* 1. to put into words: *to express one's ideas.* 2. to reveal or communicate: *he expressed his anger by striking the table.* —*adj.* 1. clearly or definitely expressed: *express instructions.* 2. special; particular: *for an express purpose.* 3. travelling fast and directly: *express delivery.* —*n.* 1. a fast train or coach. 2. a system of sending letters, parcels, etc., quickly.

expression (ek'spreshən) *n.* 1. an act or instance of expressing: *the expression of an opinion.* 2. a display of emotion or feeling: *the expression on someone's face.* 3. a particular phrase or form of words: *a slang expression.* **ex'pressive** *adj.* serving to express or having the force of expression: *an expressive gesture.*

expulsion (ek'spulshən) *n.* an instance of being expelled.

exquisite (ek'skwizit) *adj.* 1. charming, excellent, perfect, or refined: *exquisite workmanship.* 2. showing delicate understanding or fine judgment: *an exquisite ear for music.* 3. (of pain or pleasure) sharp; strongly felt. —**ex'quisitely** *adv.* —**ex'quisiteness** *n.*

extend (ek'stend) *vb.* 1. to increase in length, either in time or space: *we extended the pathway by 2 metres.* 2. to stretch out: *her land extends to the foot of the hills.* 3. to hold out (a hand, arm, etc.). 4. to offer; give: *to extend one's thanks.*

extension (ek'stenshən) *n.* 1. act of extending. 2. the additional part of something produced by extending. 3. an extra telephone in a house or building.

extensive (ek'stensiv) *adj.* 1. of a great area: *extensive grounds.* 2. thorough; comprehensive: *she has extensive knowledge.* —**ex'tensively** *adv.*

extent (ek'stent) *n.* 1. great length or area; expanse. 2. scope; range. 3. amount or degree.

exterior (ek'stiəriə) *n.* the outside of something, e.g. a building, person, etc.: *the exterior of a house.* —*adj.* occurring on or relating to the outside of something: *an exterior section.*

exterminate (ek'stûmināt) *vb.* **exterminating, exterminated.** to kill or destroy completely; put an end to: *all the rats in the house have been exterminated.* —**extermi'nation** *n.* —**ex'terminator** *n.*

external (ek'stûnəl) *adj.* coming from, occurring on, or connected with the outside of a person or thing. —**ex'ternally** *adv.*

extinct (ek'stiṅkt) *adj.* (of an animal, plant, etc.) no longer in existence; having died out entirely: *the dodo was a bird that became extinct in the 17th century.* —**ex'tinction** *n.*

extinguish (ek'stiṅggwish) *vb.* to put out (a fire or something similar to fire): *they extinguished the flames with water.* —**ex'tinguishable** *adj.*

extol (ek'stol) *vb.* **extolling, extolled.** to praise highly.

extra ('ekstrə) *adj.* additional; more, esp. more than expected: *an extra helping of potatoes.* —*n.* 1. an additional thing or part. 2. (cricket) a run added on to the team's total but not the batsman's score. 3. a late or additional edition of a newspaper, esp. one published to give news of a major event.

extract *n.* ('ekstrakt) 1. a part removed or chosen from a whole, e.g. an excerpt from a film, story, play, etc. 2. a substance obtained from food, etc.: *malt extract.* —*vb.* (ek'strakt) 1. to draw (a part from a whole); select. 2. to remove (a tooth). —**ex'traction** *n.*

extraordinary (ek'strôdinəri) *adj.* very unusual; strange; amazing. **ex'traordinarily** *adv.* 1. unusually; strangely. 2. very: *that's extraordinarily kind of you.*

extravagant (ek'stravəgənt) *adj.* 1. spending too much money; wasteful. 2. beyond what is sensible: *Bill has some very extravagant ideas.* —**ex'travagance** *n.*

extreme (ek'strēm) *adj.* 1. at the furthest outer limits of something: *the extreme south of the country.* 2. on or over the limit of what is acceptable, reasonable, etc.: *extreme political measures.* 3. of the highest degree: *extreme heat.* —*n.* a limit. **in the extreme** in the highest degree. **go to extremes** to take extreme action in order to do or gain something. **go to the other extreme** to act or behave in a way exactly opposite to what one has formerly done. **ex'tremism** *n.* the holding of extreme, often violent or revolutionary political views. **ex'tremist** *adj.,n.* (of) someone who holds extreme political views. **extremity** (ek'stremiti) *n.,pl.* **extremities.** 1. the very end of something. 2. danger, poverty, or a similar extreme situation. 3. **extremities** (*pl.*) the toes or fingers.

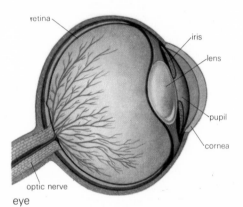

eye

eye (ī) *n.* 1. the part of the body that perceives light; the organ of sight. 2. something like an eye, e.g. the hole in the end of a needle through which the thread passes, or a mark on a potato. **keep an eye on** to keep a watch over. **more than meets the eye** more than there appears to be. **see eye to eye (with)** to agree (with). **set** *or* **lay eyes on** to see. —*vb.* **eying** *or* **eyeing, eyed.** to look at or examine carefully, esp. with desire.

eyeball ('ībôl) *n.* the coloured ball-like part of the eye, containing the pupil, through which light enters.

eyebrow ('ībrou) *n.* the hairy ridge above the eye.

eyelash ('īlash) *n.* a collection of short hairs growing from the eyelid.

eyelid ('īlid) *n.* a protective piece of skin that is lowered in closing the eye and when blinking.

eyewitness (ī'witnis) *n.* a person who is present at and observes an event, esp. an accident or crime.

F

fable ('fābəl) *n.* a story, esp. one that teaches a lesson about life. Aesop's fables are about animals. **fabulous** ('fabyŏŏləs) *adj.* 1. (informal) wonderful; excellent. 2. spoken of in fables: *the unicorn is a fabulous monster.*

fabric ('fabrik) *n.* 1. cloth or material. 2. the material that something is made out of: *the main fabric of the building was wood.*

facade (fə'sâd) *n.* 1. the front view or face of a building. 2. an outward appearance, esp. a false or misleading one: *beneath his cold facade he was very friendly.*

face (fās) *n.* 1. the front part of the head, including the eyes, nose, and mouth. 2. a look or expression of the face: *a sad face.* 3. the front or prominent part or surface of something: *the face of a clock.* 4. the outward appearance of something: *the face of the town is changing.* 5. (informal) boldness: *he had the face to challenge my decision.* **face to face** in direct contact; opposite. **on the face of it** according to how something is seen; apparently. **show one's face** to make an appearance; be seen. —*vb.* **facing, faced.** 1. to turn or be turned towards; look at: *face me when I'm talking to you.* 2. to have the front towards; to be opposite: *the house faces the street.* 3. to meet directly; confront: *to face facts.* 4. to provide with a covering surface: *to face brick with a layer of plaster.* **face up to** to confront realistically; meet: *face up to the situation.* **'facial** *adj.* of or relating to the face. *n.* (informal) a massage or other treatment for making the face more beautiful, healthy, etc. —**'facially** *adv.*

fact (fakt) *n.* anything that is known to be true: *it is a fact that World War II began in 1939.* —**'factual** *adj.*

faction ('fakshən) *n.* 1. a group of people having a common aim, esp. a small group within a political party, etc., that disagrees with the aims of that party. 2. internal conflict or disagreement.

factor ('faktə) *n.* 1. a fact, esp. one of several connected with a subject or matter: *we must consider several factors in trying to solve this problem.* 2. one of several numbers or quantities which when multiplied together produce a given number: *5 and 3 are factors of 15 because 5 × 3 is equal to 15.*

factory ('faktəri) *n.,pl.* **factories.** a building or group of buildings in which things are manufactured

facade

faculty ('fakəlti) *n.,pl.* **faculties.** 1. any inborn ability of a living creature: *man has the faculty of hearing.* 2. any mental or physical ability or power: *she has a faculty for both mathematics and tennis.* 3. the teaching staff of a department of a college or university: *the history faculty.*

fad (fad) *n.* a fashion or craze; something of interest for a short time.

fade (fād) *vb.* **fading, faded.** 1. to become or make less bright; lose colour: *that dress will fade if you wash it in hot water.* 2. to wither or lose strength: *the flowers have faded.* 3. to disappear gradually: *the music faded away.*

Fahrenheit ('farənhīt) *adj.* of a temperature scale on which the freezing point of water is set at 32° and the boiling point at 212°. Compare CENTIGRADE.

fail (fāl) *vb.* 1. to be unsuccessful in an attempt. 2. to stop working properly: *the radio has failed.* 3. to disappoint or be disappointing: *you have failed me.* 4. to lose strength; fade. **'failure** *n.* 1. the action or an instance of failing. 2. a person or thing that fails.

faint (fānt) *adj.* 1. lacking in brightness; dim; unclear; *the sky had a faint glow.* 2. feeble or weak; lacking strength. —*vb.* to lose consciousness for a short time. —**'faintly** *adv.*

fair[1] (feə) *adj.* 1. free from bias; just: *a fair decision.* 2. having light-coloured skin, hair, etc. 3. attractive; pleasant-looking. 4. of moderate ability or achievement: *she's a fair swimmer.* 5. according to the rules; properly performed, done, etc.: *a fair tackle.* 7. (of weather) fine and clear. **fair and square** 1. honest. 2. directly or accurately: *the boxer hit his opponent fair and square on the jaw.* **'fairly** *adv.* 1. justly. 2. without cheating; legitimately: *he won fairly.* 3. moderately: *a fairly good game.*

fair[2] (feə) *n.* 1. a temporary show with amusements, exhibits, contests, etc. 2. a show, market, or exhibition: *an antique fair.*

fairy ('feəri) *n.,pl.* **fairies.** an imaginary tiny person with magical powers. —*adj.* of or concerning fairies. **fairy tale** 1. a story involving magic and fairies. 2. an invented or imaginary story or account.

faith (fāth) *n.* 1. a belief in something that cannot be proved true: *faith in magic.* 2. confidence or trust: *I have faith in your judgment.* 3. a religion or other belief: *the Christian faith.* **in good faith** honestly and sincerely. 'faithful *adj.* 1. steady, honest, and loyal. 2. sticking closely to the truth, an original, etc.; accurate: *he gave a faithful account of the accident.* —'faithfully *adv.* —'faithfulness *n.*

fake (fāk) *vb.* **faking, faked.** 1. to forge (something) and pass it off as true, real, etc.: *he faked the painting.* 2. to pretend: *he faked illness to avoid working.* —*n.* a forgery or deliberate deception. —*adj.* false or fraudulent: *a fake painting.*

falcon ('fôlkən) *n.* a bird of prey belonging to the hawk family, with a powerful curved beak and hooked claws, often used for hunting other birds or small animals.

fall-out ('fôlout) *n.* radioactive dust, etc., that falls onto the surface of the Earth after a nuclear explosion.

false (fôls) *adj.* 1. not true: *a false account of the event.* 2. treacherous or untrustworthy: *a false friend.* 3. not real; artificial: *a false nose.* 'falsehood *n.* a deliberate lie. **falsify** ('fôlsifī) *vb.* **falsifying, falsified.** to alter (something) in order to deceive: *to falsify evidence.* —'falsely *adv.* —'falsity *n.*

falter ('fôltə) *vb.* 1. to act or speak with hesitation. 2. to lose balance, confidence, etc., for a moment: *the boy faltered on the narrow ledge and lost his balance.*

fame (fām) *n.* the quality of being widely known by many people: *Winston Churchill achieved fame in his own lifetime.* See also FAMOUS.

familiar (fə'milyə) *adj.* 1. commonly known; recognizable; not strange: *a familiar face.* 2. relaxed; informal. 3. (+ *with*) having good knowledge of something; well acquainted: *I'm not familiar with his books.* —*n.* a close friend. **fa'miliarize** *vb.* **familiarizing, familiarized.** (+ *with*) 1. to make acquainted with something. 2. to make (something) well known. —**familiarity** (fəmili'ariti) *n.*

family ('famili) *n.,pl.* **families.** 1. a group of individuals who have a common ancestor or who are related by marriage. 2. any related group.

famine ('famin) *n.* 1. a widespread severe shortage of food, esp. one causing many people to starve to death. 2. an extreme shortage of anything: *a potato famine.*

famous ('fāməs) *adj.* well known; having FAME.

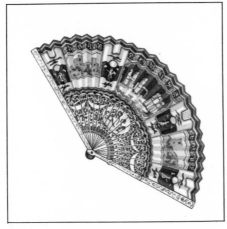

fan

fan[1] (fan) *n.* 1. a semicircular object made of feathers, paper, etc., that a person waves in order to produce a cooling draught. 2. any device for producing a draught or movement of air, e.g. for heating, cooling, etc. 3. anything resembling a fan in its shape or action. —*vb.* **fanning, fanned.** 1. to move air with a fan. 2. to cool or refresh with a fan. 3. to move with an action like a fan: *he fanned the air with his hand.*

fan[2] (fan) *n.* a devoted and enthusiastic admirer. **fan club** an organized group of admirers.

fanatic (fə'natik) *n.* a person who supports a political or religious cause with uncontrollable or violent enthusiasm. —*adj.* (also **fanatical**) concerning or typical of a fanatic. —**fa'naticism** *n.*

fancy ('fansi) *n.,pl.* **fancies.** 1. an idea or impression; one's imagination. 2. a desire or interest: *a pretty dress took her fancy.* —*vb.* **fancying, fancied.** 1. to have an idea or impression; imagine: *I fancy I know that man.* 2. to desire; want: *I fancy an apple.* —*adj.* **fancier, fanciest.** pretty; not plain or ordinary: *fancy dress.* —*interj.* an exclamation of surprise. 'fanciful *adj.* produced in the imagination; not real.

fanfare ('fanfeə) *n.* a short tune played on a trumpet or bugle as a signal, etc.

fang (fang) *n.* any of the long sharp teeth of an animal, such as a wolf or snake.

fantastic (fan'tastik) *adj.* 1. of or happening in fantasy; unreal. 2. (informal) wonderful; excellent. —**fan'tastically** *adv.*

fantasy ('fantəzi) *n.,pl.* **fantasies.** 1. a very strange or unreal experience, dream, or idea. 2. strangeness; unreality. Also (less common) **phantasy.** 'fantasize *vb.* **fantasizing, fantasized.** to make up a dream or fantasy.

fare (feə) *n.* 1. money paid for a journey by bus, taxi, train, etc. 2. a bus or taxi passenger. 3. (old-fashioned) food or drink. —*vb.* **faring, fared.** to progress; get on: *I fared badly in the examinations.* **fare'well** *interj.,n.* goodbye.

far-fetched (fâ'fecht) *adj.* very difficult to believe and therefore probably untrue: *she gave a rather far-fetched excuse for being late.*

farther ('fâdhə) *adv.* at a greater distance; to a greater degree: *the farther you go, the longer it will take you to get back.* —*adj.* more distant: *the farther house on the street is ours.*

fascinate ('fasināt) *vb.* **fascinating, fascinated.** to attract all or most of the attention or interest of (a person): *he was fascinated by her beautiful eyes.* —**fasci'nation** *n.*

fashion ('fashən) *n.* 1. a style or activity that attracts general interest or enthusiasm for a short period; trend. 2. an activity, style of dress, etc., that is modern or up to date. 3. a way of doing something; manner. 4. a kind; type. —*vb.* to make or produce: *the chair was fashioned out of wood.*

fast[1] (fâst) *adj.* 1. moving or able to move very quickly: *a fast car.* 2. allowing speedy movement: *a fast road.* 3. (of a clock) ahead of the right time. —*adv.* 1. at high speed: *don't drive too fast.* 2. firmly; soundly: *fast asleep.* 3. firm. 4. loyal: *a fast friend.* 5. fixed; not easily removed: *fast colours do not run when washed.* 6. firmly stuck: *glue will hold the pieces fast.*

fast[2] (fâst) *n.* 1. the action of refusing to eat. 2. a period during which no food is eaten, esp. for religious reasons. —*vb.* to take part in a fast; do without food.

fasten ('fâsən) vb. to fix or be fixed firmly; hold or be held in place: *this shirt fastens up the front.* '**fastener** or '**fastening** n. a device used to fasten clothes.

fatal ('fātəl) adj. causing death; mortal: *a fatal wound.* **fa**'**tality** n.,pl. **fatalities.** a person who dies in an accident, battle, etc. —'**fatally** adv.

fate (fāt) n. a power supposed to control people's lives and futures; fortune; destiny. '**fated** adj. brought about by fate; not able to be avoided: *it was fated that we should meet.* '**fateful** adj. decided by fate and usu. having unpleasant results.

fathom ('fadhəm) n. a unit of length, used to measure the depth of the sea, equal to 6 ft (approximately 1·8 m). —vb. to discover the meaning of; get to understand thoroughly.

fatigue (fə'tēg) n. 1. tiredness. 2. (military) a non-military task, e.g. cleaning floors, washing windows, etc. —vb. **fatiguing, fatigued.** to make tired: *we were fatigued by a hard day's work.*

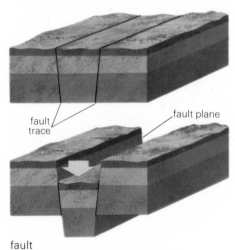

fault trace
fault plane
fault

fault (fôlt) n. 1. a mistake; error. 2. something that prevents something from being perfect or working properly: *there is a fault in the car's engine.* 3. (geology) a crack in the earth's crust. **at fault** in error; wrong. **find fault with** to criticize; find mistakes. —vb. to discover mistakes in: *we could not fault her singing.* —'**faulty** adj. **faultier, faultiest.**

favour ('fāvə) n. 1. a kind action done to or for someone: *he did him a favour by lending him a book.* 2. kind treatment or receiving such treatment: *he hopes to win the king's favour.* 3. excessive or unfair kindness

to someone: *he showed favour to Bill by giving him easy jobs.* 4. a badge or ribbon showing the wearer's loyalty to a party, team, etc. —vb. to support; show favour to. '**favourable** adj. giving support; helpful. '**favourite** adj.,n. (something) that is liked best of all. —'**favourably** adv.

fawn[1] (fôn) n. 1. a young deer. 2. a light brown colour. —adj. having a light brown colour: *a fawn coat.*

fawn[2] (fôn) vb. (usu. + on) 1. to act in a slavish way in order to win someone's favour. 2. (of dogs) to show affection for (a human), esp. by wagging the tail, licking, etc.

fear (fiə) n. 1. the feeling or state of being afraid. 2. a worry or cause for worry. 3. deep respect or awe, esp. towards God. **for fear of** in order to avoid: *he wouldn't go out for fear of catching a cold.* —vb. to show fear of or for.

feast (fēst) n. 1. a rich or ceremonial meal, entertainment, etc.; banquet. 2. a special day on which a religious or other event is remembered. —vb. 1. to attend a feast or banquet. 2. to dine well or richly.

feat (fēt) n. a great deed or action.

feather ('fedhə) n. one of the light objects that form the outer covering of birds. **as light as a feather** very light. **birds of a feather** people of the same character or type.

feature ('fēchə) n. 1. a distinguishing mark or characteristic; important element. 2. often **features** (pl.) part of the face: *he had rugged features.* 3. a special article in a newspaper or magazine. —vb. **featuring, featured.** 1. to have or show as a feature. 2. to draw attention to (something); make prominent.

federation (fedə'rāshən) n. 1. a group of connected states, societies, etc., organized together. 2. the formation of such a group.

fee (fē) n. a payment made to someone for a job or service.

feeble ('fēbəl) adj. weak. —'**feebly** adv. —'**feebleness** n.

feed (fēd) vb. **feeding, fed.** 1. to provide (a person or animal) with food. 2. (+ on) to eat: *horses feed on hay.* 3. to supply: *he fed paper into the machine.* —n. 1. the action or an instance of

giving or taking food: *the baby is given four feeds each day.* 2. food for chickens and other farm animals. 3. the part through which material is passed into a machine.

feel (fēl) vb. **feeling, felt.** 1. to touch, esp. with the hands, or experience: *she felt the sun on her back.* 2. to think; be of the opinion that: *I felt that he was wrong.* —n. 1. the impression of something to the touch: *the feel of soft silk.* 2. familiarity: *I don't yet have the feel of this job.* '**feeler** n. a long jointed organ sticking out of an insect's head; antenna. '**feeling** n. 1. the ability to feel. 2. an emotion or an opinion based on emotion.

feet (fēt) n. the plural of FOOT.

feline ('fēlīn) adj. of or like a cat. —n. a cat or a member of the cat family.

fellow ('felō) n. 1. (informal) a man: *a nice fellow.* 2. a companion; friend. 3. a senior member or research worker of a college or learned society. —adj. being a companion: *one's fellow workers.* '**fellowship** n. 1. friendship; companionship. 2. a group or society.

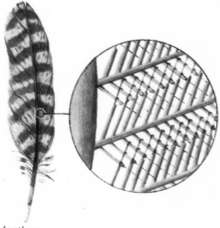

feather

felt[1] (felt) n. a tough material made from wool matted together. —adj. made of felt.

felt[2] (felt) vb. the past tense and past participle of FEEL.

female ('fēmāl) adj. of or concerning a woman or the sex that corresponds to that of women in animals, birds, etc. —n. a female animal.

feminine ('feminin) adj. 1. of, relating to, or suitable for a woman or girl: *feminine clothes.* 2. (grammar) denoting a gender (class of nouns) that concerns women or includes nouns of a specially defined type. 3. indicating a noun of this gender. —*n.* the feminine gender. **femi'ninity** *n.* the quality of being feminine.

fence[1] (fens) *n.* 1. a wooden or metal framework used for enclosing or dividing an area of land. 2. (informal) a person who buys and sells stolen property. **sit on the fence** to avoid showing support for either side in an argument. —*vb.* **fencing, fenced** (often + *off*) to separate or surround with a fence.

fence[2] (fens) *vb.* **fencing, fenced.** to fight with swords as a sport.

fern (fûn) *n.* a green non-flowering plant with large feathery leaves.

ferocious (fə'rōshəs) *adj.* fierce; aggressive and untamed. —**fe'rociously** *adv.* —**ferocity** (fə'rositi) *n.*

ferret ('ferit) *n.* a small aggressive animal of the weasel family used for driving out rabbits and rats from their burrows. —*vb.* 1. to use a ferret in hunting. 2. (+ *out*) (informal) to search out or discover (information, facts, etc.).

ferry ('feri) *n.,pl.* **ferries.** a boat, plane, etc., that transports passengers and goods back and forth over a relatively short distance between two places. —*vb.* **ferrying, ferried.** to carry (passengers and goods) by ferry.

fertile ('fûtīl) *adj.* 1. able to produce plants, fruit, etc., easily: *fertile land.* 2. able to have children or young. 3. producing many ideas: *a fertile imagination.* **fertilize** ('fûtilīz) *vb.* **fertilizing, fertilized.** to make fertile. '**fertilizer** *n.* a chemical or other substance used to make land fertile. —**fertili'zation** *n.*

fester ('festə) *vb.* 1. (of a sore or wound) to produce pus. 2. to rot or decay. 3. to cause feelings of bitterness; rankle.

festival ('festivəl) *n.* an occasion for public celebration or enjoyment. 2. a series of events or performances: *a music festival.*

fetch (fech) *vb.* 1. to get and carry back. 2. to be sold for: *the painting fetched £10,000.* **fetch up with** 1. to meet. 2. to strike against.

fete (fāt) *n.* a festival or outdoor entertainment, often one organized to raise money for something. —*vb.*

feting, feted. to welcome (an important or popular person) with public celebrations.

feud (fyōod) *n.* a bitter and long-standing quarrel between two people or groups. —*vb.* to conduct a feud.

feudal ('fyōodəl) *adj.* concerning a way of life in the Middle Ages in which people were able to live and work on land in return for services given to the overlord who owned the land. —'**feudalism** *n.*

fever ('fēvə) *n.* 1. an abnormally high body temperature. 2. any of several diseases normally associated with a very high temperature. 3. a state of great excitement or agitation. —'**feverish** *adj.* —'**feverishly** *adv.* —'**feverishness** *n.*

fiancé (fi'ânsā) *n.* a man engaged to be married. **fiancée** (fi'ânsā) *n.* a woman engaged to be married.

fiasco (fi'askō) *n.,pl.* **fiascos.** a disastrous or complete failure: *because of the rain the outdoor show was a fiasco.*

fig

fibre ('fībə) *n.* 1. a fine thread or a threadlike part or structure. 2. any substance composed of threads. '**Fibreglass** *n.* (trademark) glass spun into fibres and used in making cloth, lightweight car bodies, boat hulls, etc. **moral fibre** strength of character; courage.

fiction ('fikshən) *n.* literature consisting of matter produced by the writer's imagination: *novels are works of fiction.* **fictitious** (fik-'tishəs) *adj.* false; made up.

fiddle ('fidəl) *n.* (informal) 1. a violin or similar musical instrument. 2.

cheating or an instance of cheating, usu. in a minor way. —*vb.* **fiddling, fiddled.** (informal) 1. to play a fiddle. 2. to cheat. 3. (often + *with*) to touch or play with, esp. nervously. —'**fiddler** *n.*

fidget ('fijit) *vb.* to move about or play with or touch things in a nervous or restless way. —*n.* a person who fidgets.

field (fēld) *n.* 1. a piece of enclosed land where crops are grown, animals grazed, etc. 2. an area or district from which industrial raw material is obtained: *an oilfield.* 3. a piece of land used for a special purpose: *a sports field.* 4. a branch of learning, experience, or knowledge: *the field of jazz.* —*vb.* (cricket) to take up a position in the field in order to stop or catch the ball hit by the batsman. '**fielder** *n.* a person who fields. **field glasses** binoculars. **a field day** an enjoyable time.

fiend (fēnd) *n.* 1. an evil spirit; devil or demon. 2. an evil or wicked person. —'**fiendish** adj. —'**fiendishly** *adv.*

fierce (fiəs) *adj.* 1. aggressive and savage: *a fierce lion.* 2. angry, forceful, or dangerous: *a fierce attack.* —'**fiercely** *adv.* —'**fierceness** *n.*

fiery (fīəri) *adj.* **fierier, fieriest.** 1. of or resembling fire. 2. easily made angry; quick-tempered.

fig (fig) *n.* a soft pear-shaped fruit produced by a small tree (**fig tree**), growing in warm countries, and eaten fresh or in dried form.

fight (fīt) *n.* 1. a combat between two or more people using their fists or weapons. 2. a boxing match. 3. any battle or hard struggle. —*vb.* **fighting, fought.** (often + *with* or *against*) 1. to take part in a fight. 2. to struggle hard.

figure ('figə) *n.* 1. a symbol used to represent anything other than a letter, esp. a number from 0 to 9. 2. any geometrical drawing, or a diagram or illustration, as in a book or magazine. 3. a form or shape; the outline of something, esp. a human body. 4. the human form: *she has a slender figure.* 5. a person, esp. an important one: *Cromwell was an important figure in British history.* 6. a representation of something in painting, sculpture, etc., esp. of the human form. 7. the price of something: *I bought my bookcase at a low* *figure.* —*vb.* **figuring, figured. 1.** to use numbers to find the answer to a problem; calculate. **2.** to be portrayed; feature: *his mother figures in most of his paintings.* **figurative** ('figyŏŏr-ətiv) *adj.* (of words) not used in a literal sense, e.g. the adjective *cool* used of a person's temperament. **'figurehead** *n.* **1.** an ornamental figure, such as a statue, placed on the prow of a ship. **2.** a person who is nominally presiding over or in charge of something but has no real responsibility or authority.

filament ('filəmənt) *n.* **1.** a thin thread. **2.** a metal wire in an electric light bulb that is made to glow brightly.

file[1] (fīl) *n.* **1.** a folder containing papers arranged in correct order. **2.** a cabinet or drawer containing such papers or folders in a particular arrangement. **3.** a line of people or things arranged one behind the other (in **single file**). —*vb.* **filing, filed. 1.** to place or arrange in a file. **2.** to send in (a newspaper story). **3.** to march or walk in a file.

file[2] (fīl) *n.* **1.** a tool for smoothing or cutting metal, etc., having a working surface covered with many small ridges or teeth. —*vb.* **filing, filed.** to cut or smooth with a file.

fillet ('filit) *n.* a thick piece of fish or meat without bones. —*vb.* to remove the bones from (a piece of fish or meat).

film (film) *n.* **1.** a thin coating of anything: *a film of oil on water.* **2.** a thin sheet of any material. **3.** a usu. tranparent strip or roll of material coated with a light-sensitive chemical and used in photography. **4.** a moving picture on a cinema screen prepared from film used in a special camera. —*vb.* **1.** to cover with a film. **2.** to make a moving film of.

filter ('filtə) *n.* **1.** a device for removing solid material from a liquid by allowing only the liquid to pass through. **2.** a device used on a camera that allows only a certain colour of light to reach the film. —*vb.* **1.** to pass through a filter. **2.** (often + *out*) to remove with a filter. **3.** (+ *through* or *down*) to move or come gradually: *news of the accident filtered through.*

filth (filth) *n.* **1.** unpleasant dirt. **2.** something disagreeable or disgusting. —**'filthy** *adj.* **filthier, filthiest.**

fin (fin) *n.* any of the parts projecting from the body of a fish, dolphin, whale, etc., that are used to control movement.

final ('fīnəl) *adj.* **1.** coming at or marking the end of something; last. **2.** conclusive; not to be questioned or changed: *the referee's decision is final.* —*n.* the last game in a competition played to decide the overall winner. **'finalize** *vb.* **finalizing, finalized.** to make the final arrangements or changes in something; complete. —**finality** (fi'naliti) *n.* —**'finally** *adv.*

finance ('fīnans, fi'nans) *n.* **1.** the handling of money in business or other public matters. **2.** often **finances** (*pl.*) the money needed or used for something. —*vb.* **financing, financed.** to provide money for (a plan, scheme, business, etc.). **financial** (fi'nanshəl) *adj.* concerning money. **financier** (fī'nansiə) *n.* a person concerned with money.

fine[1] (fīn) *adj.* **1.** excellent; very good: *a fine man.* **2.** pretty; attractive: *a fine girl.* **3.** delicate or thin; easily broken or damaged: *a fine thread.* **4.** made up of small particles: *a fine powder.* —*adv.* very well: *Tim gets on fine with his new team.* **'finery** *n.* decorative rich-looking clothes, jewels, etc.

fine[2] (fīn) *n.* a sum of money that a court of law or other authority compels a person to pay as a punishment for an offence. —*vb.* **fining, fined.** to punish (someone) by making him pay a sum of money: *the judge fined him £20.*

finger ('fiṅggə) *n.* **1.** any of the flexible jointed parts of the hand joined to the palm opposite the thumb. **2.** anything resembling a finger in shape or function. —*vb.* **1.** to touch or handle (something) with the fingers. **2.** to play (a musical instrument) with the fingers. **keep one's fingers crossed** to wish or hope for something. **not lift a finger** to do absolutely nothing; make no effort.

fingerprint *n.* the impression left on an object by the pattern of ridges on the tips of the fingers and thumb. *vb.* to take the fingerprints of.

fingertip *n.* the very end of a finger. **have at one's fingertips** to have readily available.

finish ('finish) *vb.* **finishing, finished. 1.** (sometimes + *off* or *up*) to bring or come to an end. **2.** (+ *with*) to have no more to do with; be no longer friendly with: *I have finished with him.* **3.** (+ *with*) to have no further need of: *I have finished with the bathroom.* —*n.* **1.** a polished surface: *a smooth finish.* **2.** an end or point at which something ends.

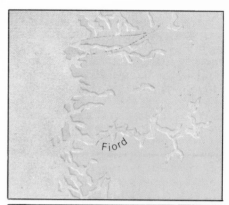

fiord

fiord *or* **fjord** (fyôd) *n.* a long channel of the sea stretching far inland, esp. in Norway.

fir (fû) *n.* **1.** an evergreen cone-bearing tree. **2.** the wood of this tree.

fire (fīə) *n.* **1.** heat, light, flames, and smoke produced by burning. **2.** a collection of coal, wood, paper, etc., that is set burning for warmth. **3.** an electrical, gas, or oil-powered device for warming a room, esp. one with a visible glowing part in it. **4.** shooting with guns. **5.** enthusiasm or passion. —*vb.* **firing, fired. 1.** to shoot (a gun). **2.** to set burning. **3.** to fill with enthusiasm, passion, etc.: *the leader's speech fired them with enthusiasm.* **4.** (slang) to dismiss (someone) from a job.

firework ('fīəwûk) *n.* a cardboard container filled with gunpowder and other chemicals, that makes a loud bang or displays brightly coloured lights when burnt.

firm[1] (fûm) *adj.* 1. strong; hard. 2. fixed; not easily moved. **stand firm** to stand still and not yield.

firm[2] (fûm) *n.* a business or company.

first (fûst) *adj.,adv.* before everyone or everything else. —*n.* a person or thing that is first: *this car was the first of its kind.*

first aid emergency treatment or care given to an injured person.

fish (fish) *n.,pl.* **fishes** *or* **fish.** any of numerous types of animal living in seas or rivers, swimming by means of fins, and breathing through gills. —*vb.* to catch fish. **'fisherman** *n.,pl.* **fishermen.**

fist (fist) *n.* the hand with the fingers closed tightly upon the palm.

fit[1] (fit) *adj.* **fitter, fittest.** 1. suitable; appropriate. 2. strong and healthy. —*vb.* **fitting, fitted.** 1. to be suitable for: *he does not fit the job at all.* 2. to be the right size for: *this coat fits me perfectly.* 3. to put into place or position: *he fitted a new light bulb in the bedroom.* **'fitter** *n.* 1. a mechanic who fits machine parts or equipment together. 2. a person who fits clothes on people at a shop.

fit[2] (fit) *n.* 1. a sudden attack of illness, often connected with uncontrollable movements of the body. 2. a sudden attack of anything: *a fit of coughing.* **have a fit** (informal) to be greatly shocked: *he had a fit when he saw the electricity bill.* **by fits and starts** accompanied by frequent interruptions. **'fitful** *adj.* with many stops and starts. —**'fitfully** *adv.*

fix (fiks) *vb.* 1. to place firmly in position; stick or fasten. 2. to make certain; settle: *to fix the date for a wedding.* 3. (sometimes + *up*) (informal) to arrange: *to fix a meeting.* 4. to mend; repair. 5. to make (a colour on cloth) stable; prevent from fading. 6. (slang) to arrange dishonestly, esp. by bribery. —*n.* (informal) 1. a difficult situation. 2. a trick. **fixed** *adj.* 1. sure; certain. 2. immovable. **'fixture** *n.* 1. an item of equipment fixed or fitted, e.g. to a wall. 2. a sporting or other traditional event, esp. one happening regularly on the same date.

Union Jack   Stars & Stripes
flag

flabby ('flabi) *adj.* **flabbier, flabbiest.** soft or limp to the touch; not firm: *he has flabby muscles from lack of exercise.* —**'flabbily** *adv.* —**'flabbiness** *n.*

flag[1] (flag) *n.* a piece of cloth bearing a design, usu. attached to a pole, staff, or cord by one edge and used as a symbol, signal, decoration, etc. —*vb.* **flagging, flagged.** 1. to decorate, signal, warn, communicate, etc., with or as if with a flag. 2. (usu. + *down*) to wave to (a passing car, train, etc.) in order to make it stop.

flag[2] (flag) *vb.* **flagging, flagged.** 1. to hang loosely; droop. 2. to fade or lose vigour; weaken: *his spirits flagged towards the end of the game.*

flair (fleə) *n.* natural talent or ability; aptitude: *she had a flair for cooking.*

flake (flāk) *n.* a small thin piece of something, often a piece broken off; chip: *a flake of stone.* —*vb.* **flaking, flaked.** 1. (often + *off*) to peel off in tiny flakes. 2. to form into flakes. **flake out** (informal) to collapse from exhaustion or tiredness. —**'flaky** *adj.* **flakier, flakiest.**

flamboyant (flam'boiənt) *adj.* outrageously bold or brilliant; showy; striking: *he was noticeable because of his flamboyant clothes.* —**flam'boyance** *n.* —**flam'boyantly** *adv.*

flame (flām) *n.* 1. a flickering light or glow produced when something burns. 2. anything like a flame in brilliance or intensity: *the sunset was a flame of colour.* **in flames** ablaze. —*vb.* **flaming, flamed.** 1. to burn or glow with flames; blaze. 2. to burn or glow with strong emotion: *his eyes flamed with anger.*

flamingo (flə'minggō) *n.,pl.* **flamingos** *or* **flamingoes.** a long-legged wading bird with pale pink feathers, a long neck, and a bent bill.

flank (flangk) *n.* 1. the fleshy part of the body between the sides of the hips and the ribs. 2. the side of anything. 3. the right- or left-hand side of an army or group of soldiers. —*vb.* 1. to place or be located at the side of. 2. to attack or menace (an army, etc.) at its flank. 3. to protect or guard on the flanks.

flannel ('flanəl) *n.* 1. a warm loosely-woven cloth of wool or wool blended with some other material. 2. a small piece of rough cotton cloth or similar material used in washing. —*vb.* **flannelling, flannelled.** to wash or rub with a flannel.

flap (flap) *vb.* **flapping, flapped.** 1. to flutter or cause to flutter, esp. making a noise; wave: *the sail flapped in the breeze.* 2. to wave or move up and down: *the bird flapped its wings.* 3. (informal) to panic. —*n.* 1. any broad flat part that hangs loosely attached by one side only: *the flap of a letter box.* 2. the movement or noise made by something flapping. 3. (informal) a state of distress, emergency, or panic: *the unexpected visitors sent her into a flap.*

flare (fleə) *vb.* **flaring, flared.** 1. to burn very brightly. 2. to blaze suddenly and brightly. 3. to burst into activity, anger, etc. 4. to spread outwards or widen: *her skirt flared at the hem.* —*n.* 1. a flickering flame or a sudden bright burst of light. 2. such a light or a device producing it used as a distress signal, warning, etc. 3. a sudden violent outburst: *a flare of anger.* 4. a curve outward: *the flare of a trumpet.*

80

flash (flash) *n*. 1. a sudden bright flare of light lasting for only a moment: *a flash of lightning*. 2. a brief item of news. 3. a moment; instant: *he did it in a flash*. —*vb*. 1. to give out a flash, esp. repeatedly: *the lighthouse beacon flashed all night*. 2. to pass before or into one's sight or mind very suddenly or quickly: *the racing car flashed past*. 3. (often + *around*) (informal) to display; show: *he flashed his money around*. —*adj*. (informal) showy or gaudy. **'flashy** *adj*. **flashier, flashiest.** 1. gaudy; showy. 2. sparkling or twinkling. —**'flashily** *adv*. —**'flashiness** *n*.

flashbulb ('flashbulb) *n*. a small glass bulb used in photography to light up the subject by a bright flash of light.

flashlight ('flashlīt) *n*. 1. a small torch. 2. a light with a flashbulb used in photography.

flask (flâsk) *n*. a container for liquids made of metal, glass, etc.

flat[1] (flat) *adj*. **flatter, flattest.** 1. even; level; smooth. 2. dull; uninteresting: *a flat performance*. 3. spread out or levelled. 4. absolute; complete: *a flat refusal*. 5. (of a tyre) deflated by damage or wear. 6. (of soft drinks or beer) having lost its sparkle. 7. (of a note) lowered from its ordinary pitch by an interval of a semitone: *E flat*. 8. out of tune by being too low in pitch. —*adv*. 1. in or into a horizontal position: *he fell down flat*. 2. completely; absolutely: *I'm flat broke*. 3. exactly: *she finished in ten minutes flat*. **flat out** at maximum speed or effort. —*n*. 1. a flat object, surface, part, etc. 2. low-lying land, esp. a marsh. 3. a deflated tyre. 4. (music) a note that is flat. **'flatten** *vb*. to make or become flat.

flask

flat[2] (flat) *n*. a set of rooms, usu. on one floor only, making up a complete dwelling or home.

flatter ('flatə) *vb*. 1. to praise or compliment, esp. insincerely. 2. to give undue praise to. 3. to suit or show to advantage: *pink flatters you*. 4. to persuade (oneself) of something: *he flattered himself that he would get the job*. —**'flattery** *n*.

flavour ('flāvə) *n*. 1. the special taste of something. 2. a special quality: *the song had a nautical flavour*. —*vb*. to give a flavour to: *she flavoured the meat with garlic*.

flea (flē) *n*. a small wingless blood-sucking insect living on the bodies of animals and sometimes humans. **a flea in one's ear** a sharp scolding.

fleck (flek) *n*. a spot or mark; speck: *a fleck of paint*. —*vb*. to mark with a fleck or flecks; speckle.

fled (fled) *vb*. the past tense and past participle of FLEE.

flee (flē) *vb*. **fleeing, fled.** 1. to run away from (danger, a threat, etc.); take flight from. 2. to go swiftly or quickly.

fleece (flēs) *n*. the coat of wool covering a sheep or similar animal. —*vb*. **fleecing, fleeced.** 1. to shear the wool from (a sheep). 2. (informal) to rob or cheat; swindle.

fleet[1] (flēt) *adj*. rapid or swift.

fleet[2] (flēt) *n*. 1. the entire navy of a country or all the ships under a single command: *the French fleet*. 2. a number of ships, cars, etc., travelling together or under a single ownership: *a fleet of taxis*.

fleeting ('flēting) *adj*. passing very quickly: *I had only a fleeting look at the man because he was running quickly*. —**'fleetingly** *adv*.

flesh (flesh) *n*. 1. the soft tissues that cover the bones of an animal, consisting mainly of muscle and fat. 2. the meat of animals used as food. 3. the soft inner part of fruit and vegetables. —**'fleshy** *adj*. **fleshier, fleshiest.**

flew (floo) *vb*. the past tense of FLY[1].

flex (fleks) *vb*. to bend. —*n*. an insulated and flexible electric cable. **'flexible** *adj*. 1. able to be bent

without breaking. 2. willing to adapt: *he was flexible enough to try any job*. 3. able to be modified or changed; used for a number of applications. —**flexi'bility** *n*. —**'flexibly** *adv*.

flick (flik) *vb*. 1. to strike lightly and quickly. 2. to move or remove (something) with a jerky stroke: *to flick a speck of dust from clothing*. —*n*. a light sudden movement. **the flicks** (informal) the cinema or a cinema film show.

flea

flicker ('flikə) *vb*. 1. to burn with or give out an irregular wavering light: *the candle flickered in the draughty corridor*. 2. to make or cause to make brief fluttering movements; quiver: *her eyelashes flickered in surprise*. —*n*. 1. an unsteady flame or light. 2. a brief display of movement or emotion: *a flicker of hope*.

flier ('flīə) *n*. a person or thing that flies.

flies (flīz) *pl.n.* the plural of FLY[2].

flight (flīt) *n*. 1. the motion, power, or act of flying. 2. a journey by aeroplane or spacecraft. 3. the act of fleeing; running away; escaping. 4. a series of steps or stairs between two landings. 5. the feathers on an arrow or dart that make it fly straight. —*vb*. to attach feathers as flights to an arrow, etc.

flimsy ('flimzi) *adj*. **flimsier, flimsiest.** 1. (of materials) thin; lacking strength; easily destroyed: *flimsy curtains*. 2. weak and insubstantial: *flimsy evidence*. —**'flimsily** *adv*. —**'flimsiness** *n*.

flinch (flinch) *vb*. to draw back in pain or fear. —*n*. the act of flinching.

fling (fliŋ) *vb.* **flinging, flung.** 1. to throw or hurl (something) violently: *he flung the money on the floor.* 2. to absorb oneself in some activity enthusiastically and wholeheartedly: *she flung herself into her work.* —*n.* 1. an energetic or violent movement. 2. (also **Highland fling**) a vigorous Scottish dance.

flint (flint) *n.* 1. a type of hard dark stone. 2. a hard material in a cigarette lighter that produces a hot spark.

flipper ('flipə) *n.* 1. a broad flat limb of some animals such as seals, penguins, etc., adapted for swimming. 2. one of a pair of broad flat pieces of rubber roughly resembling this, worn on the feet by swimmers, divers, etc.

flit (flit) *vb.* **flitting, flitted.** 1. to move rapidly from one object or place to another; dart: *bees flit from flower to flower.* 2. to pass quickly. 3. (also **do a moonlight flit**) to move out secretly from a house, hotel, etc., in order to avoid paying one's debts. —*n.* 1. a light rapid movement. 2. (also **moonlight flit**) a secret hasty departure.

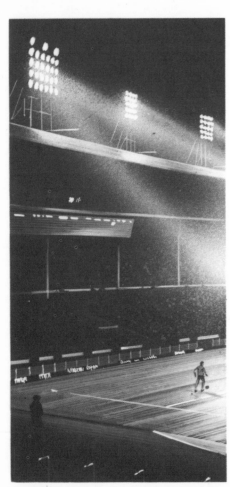

floodlight

float (flōt) *vb.* 1. to move along or be supported on the surface of a liquid, gas, or other fluid. 2. to cause to float. —*n.* 1. a piece of cork, plastic, etc., floating on water to mark a fisherman's line and indicate, by bobbing, a bite. 2. a supply of small change (money) used for general purposes. 3. a decorated vehicle used in a procession.

flock (flok) *n.* a collection of sheep, goats, or birds. —*vb.* to move in a crowd: *the people flocked into the street to see the queen.*

flog (flog) *vb.* **flogging, flogged.** 1. to punish (someone) by beating; cane or whip. 2. (informal) to sell: *he flogged me a new car.*

flood (flud) *n.* 1. a body of water covering a large area of normally dry land after severe rain, etc. 2. a large amount of anything: *a flood of letters.* —*vb.* to cause (dry land) to be covered with water.

floodlight ('fludlīt) *n.* a powerful light used at night to light up buildings, sports events, etc. —*vb.* **floodlighting, floodlit.** to light with a floodlight.

floor (flô) *n.* 1. the part of a building or room upon which people walk. 2. a storey in a building: *the first floor.* —*vb.* to knock (someone) down: *he floored him with a blow on the jaw.*

flop (flop) *vb.* **flopping, flopped.** 1. to fall untidily or without control: *he flopped into his seat.* 2. to fail. —*n.* the action or an instance of flopping.

flounder[1] ('floundə) *vb.* to struggle awkwardly or helplessly; be in or move with difficulty.

flounder[2] ('floundə) *n.* a common flatfish, used for food.

flour (flouə) *n.* powdered wheat or similar cereal used for making bread, pastry, etc.

flourish ('flurish) *vb.* 1. to grow or live; be active. 2. to make large gestures with; wave: *he flourished his handkerchief.* —*n.* 1. a large gesture; wave. 2. a curve or bold stroke, e.g. in handwriting or painting.

flow (flō) *vb.* 1. (of liquid) to move along; run down under the influence of gravity. 2. to move like a liquid: *time flows along.* —*n.* the movement of a liquid.

flower ('flouə) *n.* a colourful part in some plants that contains the plant's reproductive organs; a bloom or blossom. —*vb.* to produce flowers.

flown (flōn) *vb.* the past participle of FLY[1].

flu (floo) *n.* See INFLUENZA.

flue (floo) *n.* a passage or pipe for carrying air or gases.

fluent ('flooənt) *adj.* 1. able or competent in a foreign language: *she is fluent in French.* 2. flowing; not hesitant: *a fluent speaker.* —'**fluency** *n.* —'**fluently** *adv.*

fluff (fluf) *n.* small bits of fibre, etc., that stick to cloth, collect in pockets, etc. —*vb.* (informal) to fail at; make a mess of: *the actor fluffed his lines.*

fluid ('flooid) *n.* a liquid or gas. —*adj.* 1. of or like a fluid; not solid. 2. (of arrangements or plans) not settled; easily changed. —**flu'idity** *n.*

flung (fluŋ) *vb.* the past tense and past participle of FLING.

flush (flush) *vb.* 1. to go red in the face; blush. 2. to be affected greatly by some emotion: *he flushed with pride.* 3. to drive away or make clean with a powerful flow of water. 4. (often + *out*) to force (a hunted animal) out of hiding. —*n.* 1. a blush; redness of complexion. 2. a rush of emotion. 3. a rushing flow. —*adj.* 1. rich; wealthy. 2. level or even: *the door is flush with the wall.*

flute (floot) *n.* 1. a tubular musical wind instrument usu. equipped with keys, held horizontally, and played by blowing across the mouth-hole. 2. any sort of whistle.

flute

flowers

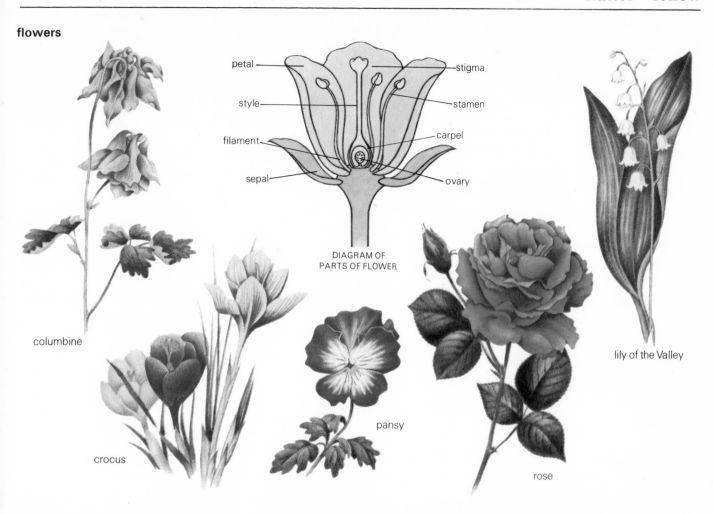

petal

style

filament

sepal

stigma

stamen

carpel

ovary

DIAGRAM OF
PARTS OF FLOWER

columbine

crocus

pansy

rose

lily of the Valley

flutter ('flutə) *vb.* to move or flap quickly and lightly. —*n.* 1. any light quick movement. 2. excitement or confusion: *a flutter of activity.* 3. (informal) a small bet on a horserace.

fly[1] (flī) *vb.* **flying, flew, flown.** 1. to move through the air without touching the ground: *bats and most birds and insects can fly.* 2. to control (an aeroplane) in flight. 3. to move quickly; rush. **'flier** *or* **'flyer** *n.* an aircraft pilot.

fly[2] (flī) *n.,pl.* **flies.** 1. a small winged insect. There are many kinds of fly, including the common housefly. 2. a lure of feathers made to resemble a fly and used as a bait in fishing.

foal (fōl) *n.* a newly born horse, mule, etc. —*vb.* to give birth to a foal.

foam (fōm) *n.* a large quantity of tiny bubbles produced on the surface of a liquid; froth. —*vb.* to produce foam.

focus ('fōkəs) *n.,pl.* **focuses.** 1. the point at which rays of light meet after passing through a lens or being reflected from a specially shaped

mirror. 2. the central point or figure in something. —*vb.* 1. to bring to a focus. 2. to concentrate on. **'focal** *adj.*

fog (fog) *n.* 1. a thick mist or cloud at ground level occurring when a layer of hot moist air meets a layer of cold. 2. any mist or something that seems like a fog. —**'foggy** *adj.*

foil[1] (foil) *n.* 1. thin flexible material made of rolled and hammered metal: *tin foil.* 2. a person or thing serving by contrast to make another person or thing appear good, clever, etc.: *the man in the audience was a perfect foil for the comedian.*

foil[2] (foil) *vb.* to prevent (someone) from achieving his aim; thwart.

foil[3] (foil) *n.* a thin light flexible sword with a button on its point.

fold[1] (fōld) *vb.* to bend (paper, cloth, etc.) with one side overlapping the other. —*n.* a crease produced by folding. **'folder** *n.*

fold[2] (fōld) *n.* a fenced enclosure for holding sheep.

foliage ('fōliij) *n.* the leaves of trees and other plants.

folk (fōk) *n.,pl.* **folk** *or* **folks.** 1. people in general, often those belonging to one tribe or area. 2. **folks** (*pl.*) (informal) one's parents or relatives. —*adj.* of or concerning the common people: *folk music.*

follow ('folō) *vb.* 1. to go or come after (a person or thing) in space or time. 2.

foil

to chase; pursue; hunt. 3. to understand; comprehend. 4. to act in agreement with: *to follow advice*. 5. to be interested in: *he follows hockey*. —'**follower** *n.*

folly ('foli) *n.,pl.* **follies.** 1. foolishness; foolish words or actions. 2. an expensive and useless building.

font

font (font) *n.* a basin in a church filled with water for baptisms.

fool (fool) *n.* a person who acts stupidly or absurdly; idiot. —'**foolish** *adj.* —'**foolishly** *adv.* —'**foolishness** *n.*

foolproof ('foolproof) *adj.* totally reliable or easy; unable to go wrong.

foot (foot) *n.,pl.* **feet.** 1. the part of the body at the bottom of the leg upon which a person or animal walks. 2. the base or lowest point of anything: *the foot of the mountain*. 3. the bottom end of the leg of a piece of furniture. 4. a unit of length equal to 12 inches (30·5 cm) or one third of a yard. 5. a division of a line of verse.

football ('footbôl) *n.* 1. SOCCER. 2. (U.S.) a game similar to RUGBY FOOTBALL between two teams of eleven players each who try to kick or carry the ball into the goal area of their opponents. 3. the large inflated ball used in these games.

footlight ('footlīt) *n.* one of the row of lights at the front of the stage.

forbid (fə'bid) *vb.* **forbidding, forbade** *or* **forbad, forbidden.** to order (someone) not to do something; prevent (an action) by an explicit order: *she forbade her son to stay out late at night*. **for'bidding** *adj.* producing fear or worry.

force (fôs) *n.* 1. violence: *the police used force to open the door*. 2. strength or power: *the force of the wind*. 3. an organized group of people: *the police force*. 4. (physics) the influence on an object that causes it to move, change its motion, or stop. —*vb.* **forcing, forced.** 1. to use strength on. 2. to compel to do something. 3. to produce unnaturally rapid growth in (a plant). —'**forceful** *adj.* —'**forcefully** *adv.* —'**forcefulness** *n.*

forceps ('fôseps) *n.,pl.* **forceps.** an instrument used by surgeons for grasping and holding a bodily organ, etc., esp. during an operation.

forecast ('fôkâst) *n.* a statement or report about what is likely to happen in the future; prediction: *a weather forecast*. —*vb.* **forecasting, forecast.** to made a forecast; predict.

forefinger ('fôfiṅgə) *n.* the finger that one usu. uses to point with; index finger.

foreground ('fôground) *n.* 1. the front part of a scene; the part that is nearest the observer. Compare BACKGROUND. 2. the front or foremost part of anything: *he is in the foreground of English literature*.

forehead ('forid) *n.* the front of the head; the part of the face between the eyebrows and the hair.

foreign ('forin) *adj.* coming from abroad; not native to the country in which it is found. '**foreigner** *n.* a foreign person.

foreman ('fômən) *n.,pl.* **foremen.** 1. a person in charge of a group of workers at a factory, building site, etc. 2. the man who speaks on behalf of a jury in a legal case.

foresee (fô'sē) *vb.* **foreseeing, foresaw, foreseen.** to see or know beforehand that something will happen; prophesy or predict something. '**foresight** *n.* the ability to foresee future events.

forest ('forist) *n.* a large collection of trees; woodland or jungle. '**forester** *n.* an official responsible for the management and protection of woodland. '**forestry** *n.* forest management and protection.

forfeit ('fôfit) *vb.* to give up something as a punishment, esp. according to rules or a law: *he forfeited his turn in the game because he cheated*. —*adj.*

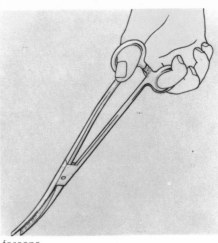
forceps

lost or taken away as a punishment: *the traitor's lands will be forfeit*.

forge[1] (fôj) *n.* 1. a furnace used for heating metal objects and beating them into shape. 2. a workshop where this is done. —*vb.* **forging, forged.** 1. to make on a forge. 2. to make or imitate (something) with the intention of deceiving someone. '**forgery** *n.,pl.* **forgeries.** 1. the crime of imitating something to deceive someone. 2. an imitation made with the intention of deceiving; a fake.

forge[2] (fôj) *vb.* **forging, forged.** (+ *ahead*) to move ahead in a determined way.

forget (fə'get) *vb.* **forgetting, forgot, forgotten.** (often + *about*) to put out of one's memory, usu. unintentionally; fail to remember: *she soon forgot about the accident*.

forgive (fə'giv) *vb.* **forgiving, forgave, forgiven.** 1. to pardon (someone who has done wrong). 2. to ignore (a wrong or bad action done by someone): *please forgive my mistake*. —**for'giveness** *n.*

fork (fôk) *n.* 1. an instrument with two or more pointed parts (prongs) used in eating, serving, holding, etc., solid food. 2. a larger similar-shaped instrument used for turning over soil in a garden. 3. a point at which a road or path divides into two.

forlorn (fə'lôn) *adj.* alone and in distress; lost. **a forlorn hope** an attempt that is bound to fail.

form (fôm) *n.* 1. shape or a shape; outline: *the human form*. 2. a type or kind: *various forms of speech*. 3. a class in a school. 4. a way of doing things; accepted custom: *a matter of* *form.* 5. an official paper with spaces to be filled in by a person: *an application form.* 6. the performance or ability of a racehorse, athlete, or other type of competitor: *the horse's past form is excellent.* —*vb.* to produce or be produced. **for'mation** *n.* 1. the process or an instance of forming. 2. a shape. 3. the grouping together of aircraft in flight: *close formation.* **'formative** *adj.* of or during the time when something, esp. a person's character, is being formed.

formal ('fôməl) *adj.* done in the correct, approved, or official manner. **for'mality** *n.,pl.* **formalities.** 1. the state of being formal. 2. a formal or official process, custom, or method.

former ('fômə) *adj.* concerning or belonging to an earlier time; previous. —**'formerly** *adv.*

forsake (fə'sāk) *vb.* **forsaking, forsook, forsaken.** to leave, give up, or abandon: *he forsook his family.*

fort (fôt) *n.* a castle or other building defended against enemy attacks; fortress.

forthright ('fôthrīt) *adj.* bold and frank in speech: *the president made a forthright speech.*

fortify ('fôtifī) *vb.* **fortifying, fortified.** 1. to build a protective wall, ditch, etc., around (a place) so it can be defended: *they fortified the top of the hill.* 2. to build up (someone's strength, spirits, or reputation): *the hot meal in camp fortified the climbers.* **fortifi'cation** *n.* 1. the act of fortifying a place. 2. usu. **fortifications** (*pl.*) walls, ditches, etc., built for defence.

fortress ('fôtris) *n.* a strongly defended building; fort.

fortune ('fôtyŏon) *n.* 1. luck or chance affecting the events of a person's life: *good fortune.* 2. a large amount of money: *he made a fortune as an architect.* **'fortunate** *adj.* lucky; having or causing good fortune. —**'fortunately** *adv.*

forward ('fôwəd) *adj.* 1. moving towards, facing, or situated at the front: *a forward seat on a bus.* 2. bold, esp. too bold: *that girl is very forward.*

'forwards *or* **'forward** *adv.* in the direction of the front; ahead; forth: *the car moved forwards.*

fossil ('fosəl) *n.* the remains of an ancient animal or plant or a piece of rock bearing its imprint. **'fossilize** *vb.* **fossilizing, fossilized.** to make into a fossil.

foster ('fostə) *vb.* 1. to help to grow or develop: *to foster a love of music.* 2. to care in one's own home for (a child from another family). —*adj.* concerning, related by, or used for the process of fostering: *foster parents.*

fought (fôt) *vb.* the past tense and past participle of FIGHT.

foul (foul) *adj.* 1. filthy; dirty; polluted: *a foul sewer.* 2. morally intolerable; disgusting: *a foul crime.* —*n.* (sport) a move, stroke, etc., that breaks the rules. —**'foully** *adv.* —**'foulness** *n.*

found (found) *vb.* 1. to establish; bring into being: *the society was founded in 1876.* 2. to base: *the theory was founded on the belief that the Earth*

fort

was flat. **foun'dation** *n.* 1. the act of founding. 2. usu. **foundations** (*pl.*) the base of a building.

fountain ('fountin) *n.* a decorative jet or pattern of jets of water.

fowl (foul) *n.,pl.* **fowl** or **fowls.** any bird, esp. a domestic one, e.g. a chicken, turkey, or goose.

fox

fox (foks) *n.* 1. a bushy-tailed, doglike, reddish-brown animal that kills domestic birds and is hunted for sport. 2. a cunning person. —*vb.* to deceive.

foxglove ('foksgluv) *n.* a tall poisonous plant having purplish bell-shaped flowers.

foyer ('foiā) *n.* the entrance hall of a large public building, esp. a cinema or hotel.

fraction ('frakshən) *n.* 1. any quantity that is not a whole number, e.g. a half or a quarter. 2. a small part of a whole.

fracture ('frakchə) *n.* a break, esp. a break in a bone. —*vb.* **fracturing, fractured.** to break (a bone): *he fractured his wrist.*

fragile ('frajīl) *adj.* easily broken or damaged; delicate: *that glass is fragile.* —**fragility** (frə'jiliti) *n.*

fragment ('fragmənt) *n.* a small piece broken off or separated from the whole object: *after the explosion there were fragments of glass all over the road.* —**'fragmentary** *adj.*

fragrant ('frāgrənt) *adj.* producing a pleasant smell; scented. —**'fragrance** *n.* —**'fragrantly** *adv.*

frail (frāl) *adj.* 1. easily broken, dam-

aged, or destroyed; delicate; fragile. 2. weak; easily tired: *a frail old man.* —**'frailty** *n.*

frame (frām) *n.* 1. a structure of wood, metal, etc., usu. rectangular in shape, used to enclose and provide a firm border for a picture, window, etc. 2. the skeleton or supporting structure of a human or animal body or a building. —*vb.* **framing, framed.** 1. to provide with a frame. 2. to shape or form (words, ideas, etc.). 3. to bear false witness against (someone) in order to incriminate him.

framework ('frāmwûk) *n.* 1. a supporting structure for a building, machine, etc. 2. the basic or main ideas, actions, etc., of something: *the framework of society.*

frank (frangk) *adj.* direct and straightforward: *a frank statement.* —**'frankly** *adv.* —**'frankness** *n.*

frankfurter ('frangkfətə) *n.* a reddish sausage made from minced beef, cereals, preservatives, etc.; hot dog.

frantic ('frantik) *adj.* in a great state of agitation; distracted with worry, excitement, etc. —**'frantically** *adv.*

fraud (frôd) *n.* 1. a crime involving trickery or deception in order to obtain money, etc. 2. a person or thing that is not genuine; impostor.

fray (frā) *vb.* to unravel or become unravelled, esp. by rubbing or wearing away material: *the sleeves of his jacket are badly frayed.*

freak (frēk) *n.* 1. an abnormal, usu. deformed living creature; monster. 2. an irregular or unusual event, mood, or object. 3. an unconventional or unusual person. —*adj.* unusual; irregular. —**'freakish** *adj.* —**'freaky** *adj.* **freakier, freakiest.**

freckle ('frekəl) *n.* any of the brownish marks on the skin of fair people produced through exposure to the sun. —*vb.* **freckling, freckled.** to become covered with freckles.

free (frē) *adj.* **freer, freest.** 1. not under external control: *nobody is free to do what he likes.* 2. not in prison: *the criminal is still free.* 3. costing no money: *the air we breathe is free.* 4. generous; liberal: *he is free with his money.* 5. not occupied in business; without duties: *I am free until two o'clock.* —*vb.* **freeing, freed.** to set free. —**'freedom** *n.*

freeze (frēz) *vb.* **freezing, froze, frozen.** 1. to become or make very cold. 2. to make (a fluid) solid by lowering its temperature. 3. (of a fluid) to become solid in this way. 4. (+ *over*) (of water) to become covered with ice. 5. to stand very still. 6. to fix (prices or wages) at a certain level. —*n.* the action or an instance of freezing, esp. of fixing prices or wages: *a pay freeze.* **'freezer** *n.* a special refrigerator for storing food at low temperatures.

freight (frāt) *n.* 1. the transport of goods by road, rail, air, or sea. 2. the goods being thus transported. —*vb.* to load (a ship) with freight. **'freighter** *n.* a ship carrying freight.

frenzy ('frenzi) *n.,pl.* **frenzies.** a condition of an uncontrollable or mad excitement, passion, fear, joy, etc. —**'frenzied** *adj.* —**'frenziedly** *adv.*

frequent *adj.* ('frēkwənt) occurring regularly or often. —*vb.* (fri'kwent) to go to (a place) often. **'frequency** *n.,pl.* **frequencies.** 1. the condition or fact or being frequent. 2. (physics) the rate or regularity of the movement of a radio signal, alternating electric current, etc. —**'frequently** *adv.*

fresh (fresh) *adj.* 1. new or having the qualities of newness: *fresh paint.* 2. not stale or preserved in a tin or packet: *fresh fruit.* 3. (informal) bold; cheeky. 4. (of water) not salty. 5. healthy; bright; clean. 6. (of a breeze) strong. **'freshen** *vb.* to make or become fresh. —**'freshly** *adv.* —**'freshness** *n.*

fret[1] (fret) *vb.* **fretting, fretted.** to make or become anxious or irritable.

fret[2] (fret) *n.* 1. (also **fretwork**) an angular design on wood, etc. 2. any of the raised pieces of metal, wood, etc., crossing the neck of a guitar, etc., against which the strings are pressed to produce different tones. —*vb.* **fretting, fretted.** to provide with frets or fretwork. **'fretsaw** *n.* a thin saw for doing delicate work.

friar ('frīə) *n.* a member of one of several Roman Catholic religious organizations or groups.

friction ('frikshən) *n.* 1. the force that tends to prevent sliding and causes heat or wear when objects are rubbed together. 2. angry disagreement.

friend (frend) *n.* a person whom one knows and likes. —**'friendliness** *n.* —**'friendly** *adj.* —**'friendship** *n.*

frieze

frieze (frēz) *n.* a long narrow decorated band or border near the top of a wall in a room or building.

frigate ('frigit) *n.* a small fast warship, often used to escort and protect other ships.

fright (frīt) *n.* 1. fear, esp. sudden fear. 2. a sudden unexpected shock. 'frighten *vb.* to make afraid; cause fear in. 'frightening *adj.* producing fear. 'frightful *adj.* terrible; awful; unpleasant. —'frighteningly *adv.* —'frightfully *adv.*

frill (fril) *n.* 1. a decorative edging made from material fixed along one side and left loose and wavy on the other. 2. an ornamental or useless addition. 'frilly *adj.* frillier, frilliest. (also frilled) having frills.

fringe (frinj) *n.* 1. a decorative edge made of loose hanging threads, often gathered into bunches. 2. the hair hanging down over the forehead and cut short. 3. the outer parts of something: *the fringes of civilization.* —*vb.* fringing, fringed. to provide with a fringe.

frog (frog) *n.* a small animal able to live both in water and on land and noted for its ability to jump quite long distances. **a frog in one's throat** a soreness, blockage, or swelling in the throat preventing clear speech. 'frogman *n.,pl.* frogmen. a diver.

front (frunt) *n.* 1. the leading part, surface, or side of anything. 2. the part of a building containing the main door and having a facade. 3. the part of a town or city facing the sea or a river. 4. the part of a battle area closest to the enemy. 5. a legal organization concealing the activities of a criminal one. 6. a group of polit-ical parties acting as one. —*vb.* (of a building) to face onto (something); to be at the head of. 'frontage *n.* the length of the side of a building along a street. **in front (of)** before; at the head (of). **put on a bold (** *or* **good) front** to act or appear brave or successful when one is not.

frontier ('fruntiə) *n.* 1. the boundary between one country or state and another. 2. often **frontiers** (*pl.*) any limiting boundary: *the frontiers of science.*

frost (frost) *n.* 1. a weather condition occurring when the temperature falls below the freezing point of water. 2. a thin covering of icy particles formed from condensed water vapour in the air at night during such weather. 'frostbite *n.* injury to parts of the body caused by exposure to extreme cold. —'frostbitten *adj.* —'frosty *adj.* frostier, frostiest.

froth (froth) *n.* foam: *froth on the surface of beer.* —*vb.* (sometimes + *up*) to produce froth. —'frothy *adj.* frothier, frothiest.

frown (froun) *n.* a sad, worried, or angry expression of the face, usu. with wrinkling of the forehead. —*vb.* to make a frown.

froze (frōz) *vb.* the past tense of FREEZE.

frozen ('frōzən) *vb.* the past participle of FREEZE.

fruit (frōot) *n.* 1. the parts of a plant containing the seeds. These parts in some plants, e.g. apples, bananas, etc., can be eaten. 2. something gained as the result of hard work, long careful handling, development, etc.: *the fruits of one's labour.* —*vb.* (of plants) to bring forth fruit. 'fruiterer *n.* a fruit-seller. 'fruitful *adj.* 1. producing much fruit. 2. producing great reward. 'fruitless *adj.* 1. producing no fruit. 2. achieving nothing; futile. fru'ition *n.* a condition of successful conclusion. 'fruity *adj.* fruitier, fruitiest. 1. tasting of fruit. 2. (of a voice) deep.

frustrate (frus'trāt) *vb.* frustrating, frustrated. 1. to deprive of or keep from completion or success; make futile: *all our plans were frustrated by the bad weather.* 2. to cause (someone) to be angry because of failure, a handicap, etc.: *his blindness frustrated him.* —frus'tration *n.*

fry[1] (frī) *vb.* frying, fried. to cook in hot fat or oil. **frying pan** *n.* a container used for frying.

fry[2] (frī) *pl.n.* tiny fish newly hatched out of their eggs. **small fry** (informal) 1. unimportant people. 2. children.

fuchsia

fuchsia ('fyōoshə) *n.* a popular garden plant producing fine drooping flowers.

fuel ('fyōoəl) *n.* 1. any material that can be converted into energy for operating a machine, providing heat, etc., usu. by the process of burning: *coal and oil are important fuels.* —*vb.* fuelling, fuelled. to provide with fuel.

fugitive ('fyōojitiv) *n.* a person who is running away, esp. someone trying to escape legal punishment or someone in search of freedom, such as a refugee.

fulcrum ('foolkrəm) *n.,pl.* fulcrums *or* fulcra ('foolkrə). the point of rest or support on which a lever turns; balancing point, as in a see-saw.

fulfil (fŏol'fil) vb. **fulfilling, fulfilled.**
1. to bring to completeness or actual existence: to fulfil a promise. 2. to perform (one's duty) correctly and completely. —**ful'filment** n.

full (fŏol) adj. 1. having no room for any more; completely filled: a full cup of coffee. 2. containing a large amount or number: the water is full of fish. 3. rich; plentiful: a full crop. 4. well-rounded in form: a full face. 5. of the greatest size, amount, etc.: at full speed. —'**fully** adv. — '**fullness** n.

fumble ('fumbəl) vb. **fumbling, fumbled.** to make clumsy or awkward movements with the hands; handle clumsily: he fumbled for his keys.

fume (fyŏom) n. usu. **fumes** (pl.) gas, smoke, or vapour, esp. when unpleasant or dangerous: the fireman was almost overcome by fumes. —vb. **fuming, fumed.** 1. to produce fumes. 2. to be very angry: my father was fuming because I came home late.

function ('fungkshən) n. 1. the purpose or usual duty of a person or thing. 2. a formal public event, e.g. a fete or banquet. —vb. 1. to perform the duty of; serve as: the kitchen also functions as a dining room. 2. to operate; work: this machine is not functioning.

fund (fund) n. 1. often **funds** (pl.) money needed for something: the committee is trying to raise funds. 2. a large amount of something: he has a fund of knowledge. —vb. to provide money for.

funeral ('fyŏonərəl) n. the religious ceremony concerning the burial or cremation of a dead person at a cemetery, etc. —adj. of or connected with a funeral. **funereal** (fyŏo'niəriəl) adj. gloomy; dark.

funfair ('funfeə) n. a fair full of various amusements and shows.

fungus ('funggəs) n.,pl. **funguses** or **fungi** ('funggī). a plant that lives on other plants or on rotting plant material: mushrooms and toadstools are fungi.

funnel

funnel ('funəl) n. 1. an open-ended, typically cone-shaped object through which liquid can be poured into a container with a narrow opening. 2. a large chimney-like object, e.g. on a steamship, through which smoke and steam escape. —vb. **funnelling, funnelled.** to pass through a funnel.

funny ('funi) adj. **funnier, funniest.** 1. amusing; humorous. 2. strange; odd. **funny bone** a part of the elbow which, when struck, produces a sharp tingling pain. —'**funnily** adv.

fur (fû) n. 1. the hair of certain animals, e.g. cats. 2. the skin of an animal, e.g. an ermine or mink, with the fur on it, used for clothes. 3. a garment made of or lined with fur. 4. a substance produced inside a kettle, etc., when hard water is boiled in it regularly. 5. a coating sometimes formed on the tongue during an illness. '**furry** adj. **furrier, furriest.** 1. or or like fur. 2. covered with fur. **furred** adj. covered with fur.

furious ('fyŏoriəs) adj. See FURY.

furnace ('fûnis) n. a structure in which a very hot fire can be made to heat a building, melt metals, etc. It usu. has a chimney to take away the burnt gases.

furnish ('fûnish) vb. to provide a room, house, or flat with tables, chairs, beds, curtains, etc. '**furniture** n. objects used for furnishing.

furrow ('furō) n. 1. a trench cut along a field by a plough, into which seeds are sown. 2. a fold in the skin of a person's forehead, e.g. when frowning. —vb. to make a furrow or furrows in.

further ('fûdhə) adj. 1. situated at or travelling to a greater distance. 2. additional: further work is required. —adv. 1. at or to a greater distance: I can't walk any further. 2. to a greater degree; additionally. —vb. to advance; push forward: his father helped to further his career. '**furtherance** n. development.

fury ('fyŏoəri) n.,pl. **furies.** 1. rage or violence. 2. an instance of this. —'**furious** adj. —'**furiously** adv.

fuse (fyŏoz) n. 1. a part of an electric circuit that is designed to blow (i.e. melt) and break the circuit if the electric current becomes too great. 2. a length of cord, etc., ignited at one end to set off an explosive connected to the other. —vb. **fusing, fused.** 1. (of an electric circuit or appliance) to break down because a fuse has blown. 2. to melt. 3. to weld or be welded together under extreme heat. '**fusion** n. a joining together.

fuselage ('fyŏozəlâzh) n. the outer body or structure of an aircraft, excluding the wings and the tail.

fuss (fus) n. unnecessary or excessive worry, excitement, attention, etc. —vb. 1. (often + over) to make a fuss: she fussed over her hair. 2. to disturb or excite (someone); cause (someone) to make a fuss. —'**fussy** adj. **fussier, fussiest.**

futile ('fyŏotīl) adj. having no useful result; achieving nothing: a futile effort. —**futility** (fyŏo'tiliti) n.

future ('fyŏochə) n. 1. the time or set of events that will follow the present. 2. a life or career that is yet to come: you have a great future. 3. (grammar) the tense used for verbs describing actions that will happen after the present (**future tense**). —adj. 1. describing time or events that will follow the present. 2. of or concerning the future tense in grammar.

G

gable ('gābəl) *n.* the triangular upper section of the side wall of a building formed by the two parts of a sloping roof.

gadget ('gajit) *n.* any sort of tool, machine, or device: *a gadget for opening bottles.* '**gadgetry** *n.* a large number of gadgets.

gag (gag) *n.* a piece of cloth stuffed into someone's mouth to keep him from making any sounds. —*vb.* **gagging, gagged.** to keep (someone) quiet with a gag.

gaiety ('gāiti) *n.* cheerfulness; light-heartedness.

gain (gān) *vb.* 1. to get or obtain (what one wants or hopes for): *to gain good examination results.* 2. to win: *to gain first prize.* 3. (often + *on*) come closer to or overtake: *looking back he saw that his opponent was gaining on him.* 4. (of a clock) to show a time later than the real time. —*n.* profit; advantage.

gait (gāt) *n.* a way of walking: *he had an awkward gait.* '**gaiters** *pl.n.* ankle or leg coverings of cloth or leather, fastened by buttons.

galaxy ('galəksi) *n.,pl.* **galaxies.** any of the huge collections of thousands of millions of stars scattered throughout space. **the Galaxy** the collection of stars to which the sun belongs; Milky Way. —**galactic** (gə'laktik) *adj.*

gale (gāl) *n.* a very powerful or strong wind.

gallant ('galənt) *adj.* 1. brave. 2. (usu. of men in relation to women) polite or keen to show admiration or affection.

gallery ('galəri) *n.,pl.* **galleries.** 1. a narrow passage or corridor, sometimes open on one side. 2. a narrow platform projecting from a wall and running around the inside or outside of a building. 3. an extended balcony in a theatre, usu. containing the cheapest seats. 4. a room or building used for putting works of art on show: *an art gallery.*

galley

galley ('gali) *n.* a large single-decked ship used in ancient times, usu. propelled by means of a large number of oars rowed by slaves or prisoners.

gallon ('galən) *n.* a measure of liquid equal to eight pints (4·546 litres).

gallop ('galəp) *vb.* 1. (of a horse) to move at high speed. 2. to ride at high speed: *the cowboy galloped through the town on his horse.* —*n.* the action or an instance of galloping.

gallows ('galōz) *n.* a stout wooden scaffold from which a criminal was hanged.

galore (gə'lô) *adv.* abundantly; in plenty: *there were flowers galore growing in his garden.*

galoshes (gə'loshiz) *pl.n.* rubber or plastic shoes worn over other shoes to keep them dry or clean.

galumph (gə'lumf) *vb.* to walk in a triumphant way: *Patrick galumphed in boasting about his new car.*

galvanize ('galvəniz) *vb.* **galvanizing, galvanized.** 1. to shock with electricity. 2. to startle into sudden action. 3. to coat (metal) with zinc to protect it.

gamble ('gambəl) *vb.* **gambling, gambled.** to take a risk, esp. on a game, horserace, etc., in order to gain money or some other advantage: *he gambles at the casino.* —*n.* the action or an instance of gambling. —'**gambler** *n.*

gambol ('gambəl) *vb.* **gambolling, gambolled.** to skip about; frolic: *lambs gambolled in the fields.*

game (gām) *n.* 1. a competition, as in a sport, played according to rules. 2. a self-contained part of a tennis or bridge match: *the tennis champion lost the first set six games to three.* 3. birds or animals hunted for sport and usu. used as food. 4. **games** (*pl.*) a series of competitions: *the Olympic Games.* **the game is up** no further action is possible. —*adj.* eager or bold. —*vb.* **gaming, gamed.** to gamble.

gamekeeper ('gāmkēpə) *n.* a person who takes care of game hunted for sport.

game reserve *n.* an area set aside for the protection of wild animals.

gamma rays (gamə rāz) *pl.n.* rays similar to X-rays.

gammon ('gamən) *n.* 1. smoked ham. 2. the lower part of a side of bacon.

gamut ('gamət) *n.* a range or scale; a spread of varying emotions or things: *a gamut of emotions.*

gander ('gandə) *n.* a male goose.

gang (gan͡g) *n.* 1. a group of criminals: *the gang robbed the bank.* 2. a group of workmen: *a road gang.* 3. (informal) a group of friends: *I saw the gang last night.* '**gangster** *n.* a criminal, esp. a member of a gang.

gangway ('gan͡gwā) *n.* 1. a passage between two rows of seats; aisle. 2. a movable bridge from a ship to the shore allowing passengers to get on or off the ship.

gaol (jāl) *n.,vb.* See JAIL.

gape (gāp) *vb.* **gaping, gaped.** 1. to open the mouth wide, esp. in surprise. 2. to do this while staring at something. —*n.* an act of gaping.

garage ('garâzh) *n.* 1. a building or covered area where a car may be kept when not in use. 2. a place where petrol is bought or where repair work is done on cars.

garden ('gâdən) *n.* 1. a place, esp. a piece of ground next to a house, where flowers, fruit, and vegetables are grown. 2. usu. **gardens** (*pl.*) a public park or open area in a city. '**gardener** *n.* a person who takes care of a garden. '**gardening** *n.* the action or an instance of taking care of a garden.

gargle ('gâgəl) *vb.* **gargling, gargled.** to wash the inside of the mouth or throat by filling the mouth with liquid, leaning the head back, and breathing out to cause the breath to bubble through the liquid. —*n.* the action or an instance of gargling.

gargoyle

gargoyle ('gâgoil) *n.* a metal or stone figure of a very ugly man or animal whose mouth forms the end of a spout

for carrying rainwater off the roof of a building.

garlic ('gâlik) *n.* a plant with an onion-like root having a strong taste and smell and used in cooking.

garment ('gâmənt) *n.* (formal) an item of clothing.

garrison ('garisən) *n.* a group of soldiers staying in a town, fort, etc., to protect it or keep control of it against enemy forces. —*vb.* to provide with a garrison.

garter ('gâtə) *n.* a strip or band of elastic material worn around the leg to hold up a sock or stocking.

gas (gas) *n.* 1. the state of a substance that is produced when a liquid is heated beyond its boiling point; a substance, such as air, in which the atoms or molecules are sufficiently far apart to move freely so that they occupy all the space available to them. 2. the inflammable substance supplied to homes for cooking, heating, etc. —*vb.* **gassing, gassed.** to kill or injure (a person or animal) with harmful gas. —'**gaseous** *adj.*

gash (gash) *n.* deep cut, esp. a wound in someone's flesh. —*vb.* to make or cause a gash in something.

gasoline ('gasəlēn) *n.* (U.S.) PETROL.

gasp (gâsp) *n.* a sudden sucking in of the breath, as in surprise, pain, etc. —*vb.* 1. to produce a gasp. 2. to breathe quickly, esp. when fighting for air. 3. to say with a gasp.

gate (gāt) *n.* 1. a type of door into a field, garden, etc., usu. in the form of a metal or wooden frame. 2. any structure like a gate: *the gate of the fortress.* 3. the people who pay to enter a sports ground. 4. (also **gate money**) the total of the money paid by such people.

gatecrash ('gātkrash) *vb.* (slang) to attend an event without paying a fee or without having been invited. —'**gatecrasher** *n.*

gather ('gadhə) *vb.* 1. to come or bring together; assemble: *a crowd gathered.* 2. to pick up and collect together: *to gather flowers.* 3. to be led to understand: *I gather you're from abroad.* 4. (of a wound) to swell as a result of becoming poisoned. '**gathering** *n.* 1. a crowd; assembly. 2. a poisoned swollen wound.

gaudy ('gôdi) *adj.* **gaudier, gaudiest.** bright and showy: *he wore a rather gaudy shirt.*

gauge (gāj) *n.* 1. a device for measuring something: *a pressure gauge.* 2. a measure of something, esp. of the distance between railway lines: *narrow gauge.* —*vb.* **gauging, gauged.** 1. to measure with a gauge. 2. to estimate; guess: *I gauged her to be about 16.*

gaunt (gônt) *adj.* thin; having the appearance of being ill or hungry. —'**gauntly** *adv.*

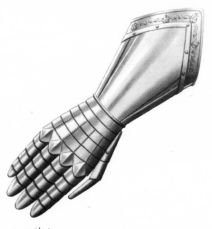

gauntlet

gauntlet[1] ('gôntlit) *n.* a strong glove protecting the hand and wrist, esp. as worn by a knight in armour.

gauntlet[2] ('gôntlit) *n.* used in the phrase **run the gauntlet.** 1. to run between two lines of people who strike out at one as one passes. 2. (often + *of*) to make oneself open to blame or criticism: *to run the gauntlet of public opinion.*

gauze (gôz) *n.* 1. very thin fine cloth through which it is possible to see. 2. fine wire netting resembling this. —'**gauzy** *adj.* **gauzier, gauziest.**

gawky ('gôki) *adj.* **gawkier, gawkiest.** awkward in movement or behaviour; clumsy. —'**gawkiness** *n.*

gay (gā) *adj.* cheerful; happy; lively. —'**gaily** *adv.* See also GAIETY.

gaze (gāz) *vb.* **gazing, gazed.** to stare or look at; fix one's eyes upon something or look in a certain direction. —*n.* a long look or stare.

gazelle (gə'zel) *n.* a type of small ANTELOPE, particularly graceful in its movements.

gear (giə) *n.* 1. a device, often a toothed wheel that connects with a similar wheel, to change the speed or direction of rotation of a shaft in a machine. 2. tools, etc., for a job.

geese (gēs) *n.* the plural of GOOSE.

gelatine *or* **gelatin** ('jelətin) *n.* a substance used in cooking. It can be melted in boiling water and forms a jelly upon cooling.

gelignite ('jelignīt) *n.* a type of explosive used esp. for blasting rock, etc.

gem (jem) *n.* 1. a precious stone, such as a diamond; jewel. 2. something thought of or valued very highly.

gender ('jendə) *n.* (grammar) a class of nouns: *woman, mare, and cow are nouns of the feminine gender.*

gene (jēn) *n.* one of the tiny units by means of which the characteristics of an animal or plant are passed from parents to offspring. **genetics** (jə'netiks) *sing.n.* the science concerned with the study of genes.

general ('jenərəl) *adj.* 1. of, concerning, or applied to most or all persons and things; common. 2. showing no details; vague: *a general idea.* —*n.* a high-ranking military officer. **'generalize** *vb.* **generalizing, generalized.** to make a vague statement intended to include every case. **generali'zation** *n.* a vague general statement. **'generally** *adv.* usually.

generate ('jenərāt) *vb.* **generating, generated.** to produce, create, or cause: *the television lights generated a great deal of heat.* **gener'ation** *n.* 1. all the people born at or about the same time: *the younger generation.* 2. the period between the beginning of one generation and the beginning of the next, usu. about 30 years.

generous ('jenərəs) *adj.* 1. giving freely: *generous people.* 2. plentiful: *a generous helping.* —**generosity** (jenə'rositi) *n.* —**'generously** *adv.*

genius ('jēniəs) *n.,pl.* **geniuses.** 1. brilliant intelligence, originality, or imagination. 2. a person having these qualities.

gentile ('jentīl) *n.* a person who is not a Jew, esp. a Christian. —*adj.* of or concerning a gentile.

gentle ('jentəl) *adj.* 1. pleasantly soft or kind; not rough, harsh, etc. 2. well-born; noble.

genuine ('jenyo͞oin) *adj.* real; not forged: *a genuine painting by Rembrandt.*

geography (ji'ogrəfi) *n.,pl.* **geographies.** the study of the earth's physical characteristics, industries, population, etc. —**geographic** (jiə-'grafik) *or* **geo'graphical** *adj.*

geology (ji'oləji) *n.,pl.* **geologies.** the study of the rocks and layers of which the earth is made. —**geologic** (jiə'lojik) *or* **geo'logical** *adj.* —**ge'ologist** *n.*

geometry (ji'omitri) *n.* the branch of mathematics concerned with the properties of triangles, rectangles, circles, spheres, cubes, etc. —**geometric** (jiə'metrik) *or* **geo'metrical** *adj.*

geometry

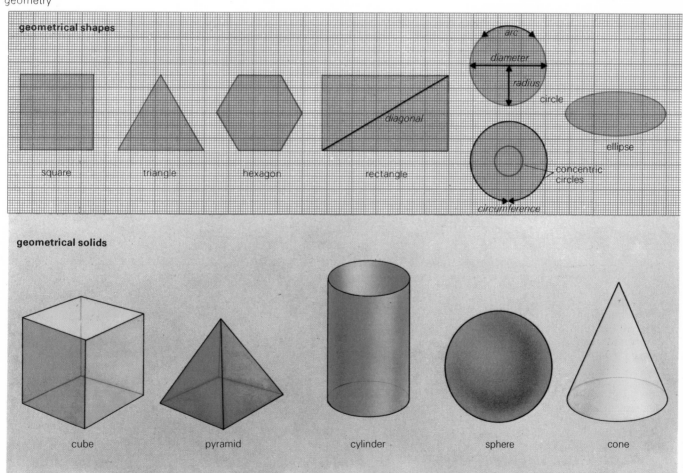

91

geranium (jə'rāniəm) *n.* any of a number of plants bearing red, white, or pink flowers and grown for show.

germ (jûm) *n.* 1. a very tiny plant found in or on other bodies. Germs often cause disease. 2. a starting point: *the germ of an idea.*

germinate ('jûmināt) *vb.* **germinating, germinated.** 1. (of seeds) to begin to grow by taking root and producing shoots. 2. to make (seeds) begin to grow. 3. to develop.

gesture ('jeschə) *n.* 1. a movement of the head, hands, etc., indicating or conveying an idea or emotion: *he shook his head in a gesture of refusal.* 2. any movement or action indicating intention, attitude, etc.: *a gesture of goodwill.* —*vb.* **gesturing, gestured.** to make a gesture.

geyser ('gēzə) *n.* 1. a natural spring in a volcanic area providing hot water and steam. 2. a device for heating water.

geyser

ghost (gōst) *n.* 1. the soul or spirit of a dead person that is believed to be capable of haunting living people. 2. a shadow or pale likeness of something: *a ghost of an idea.*

giant ('jīənt) *n.* 1. an imaginary human being of great height, size, strength, etc. 2. a person or thing of exceptional talents: *Bach is a giant among composers.* —*adj.* huge; enormous.

gibbon ('gibən) *n.* a slender ape with long arms that lives in trees in southern Asia and the East Indies.

giddy ('gidi) *adj.* **giddier, giddiest.** 1. having or causing a dizzy or light-headed feeling: *he felt giddy after*

glacier

climbing to the top of the tree. 2. impulsive or frivolous: *a giddy adventure.* —'**giddily** *adv.* —'**giddiness** *n.*

gift (gift) *n.* 1. a present; something freely given. 2. a natural talent or ability: *she has a gift for painting.*

gigantic (jī'gantik) *adj.* huge or enormous. —**gi'gantically** *adv.*

giggle ('gigəl) *vb.* **giggling, giggled.** to laugh in a silly manner. —*n.* a silly laugh. —'**giggler** *n.* —'**giggly** *adj.*

gild (gild) *vb.* to cover or coat with gold dust, gold leaf, gold paint, etc.

gill[1] (gil) *n.* the delicate organ of breathing of fish and certain other animals that live in the water.

gill[2] (gil) *n.* a liquid measure equal to one fourth of a pint.

gilt (gilt) *n.* gold leaf or gold paint. —*adj.* 1. having the colour of gold. 2. (also **gilded**) covered in gold.

gimmick ('gimik) *n.* a method, esp. an unusual or silly one, used to attract attention, gain publicity, etc.: *free glasses are the shop's latest gimmick to attract customers.*

gin (jin) *n.* an alcoholic drink made from grain and often flavoured with the oil of juniper berries.

ginger ('jinjə) *n.* a tropical plant whose spicy underground stems are used in cooking. —*adj.* 1. containing ginger. 2. of the colour of ginger; reddish brown. —*vb.* (+ *up*) (informal) to liven up. '**gingerly** *adv.* cautiously or warily.

Gipsy *or* **Gypsy** ('jipsi) *n.,pl.* **Gipsies** *or* **Gypsies.** a member of a group of

nomadic people who came from India into Europe about 600 years ago. —*adj.* of or like a Gipsy. Often written **gipsy** or **gypsy.**

giraffe (ji'râf) *n.* an African animal having a very long neck and legs and a coat with regular dark brown markings.

girder ('gûdə) *n.* any horizontal beam of steel, wood, etc., used as a main support in building, etc.

girdle ('gûdəl) *n.* 1. a band, belt, etc., worn around the waist. 2. an undergarment designed to support or hold in the abdomen.

glacier ('glasiə) *n.* a large mass of ice produced by a build-up of snow and slowly moving down a mountain or towards the sea. —**glacial** ('glāsiəl) *adj.*

glad (glad) *adj.* **gladder, gladdest.** 1. happy; pleased; delighted. 2. causing joy or pleasure: *glad tidings.* —'**gladly** *adv.* —'**gladness** *n.*

gladiator ('gladiātə) *n.* an armed slave or captive who fought other

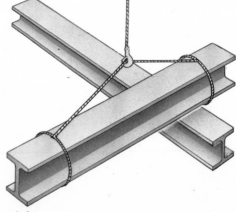

girder

gladiators, wild animals, etc., to entertain an audience in ancient Rome.

glamour ('glamə) *n.* charm, beauty, attractiveness, etc., esp. of a simply external kind. **'glamorize** *vb.* **glamorizing, glamorized.** to make more attractive, etc. —**'glamorous** *adj.* —**'glamorously** *adv.*

glance (glâns) *vb.* **glancing, glanced.** 1. to look briefly or quickly at, towards, through, etc. 2. (+ *off*) to strike against (something) and fly off at a narrow angle. —*n.* 1. a brief look. 2. a deflection.

gland (gland) *n.* any of various bodily organs that pass natural substances directly into the blood or pass substances out of the body through special tubelike passages called ducts, e.g. the pancreas. —**'glandular** *adj.*

glare (gleə) *n.* 1. a bright dazzling light. 2. something resembling this in appearance, nature, etc.: *the glare of publicity.* 3. a fierce or angry stare. —*vb.* **glaring, glared.** 1. to shine with a dazzling light. 2. to stare fiercely or angrily.

glass (glâs) *n.* 1. a hard transparent breakable substance. 2. something made of glass, e.g. a drinking container. 3. (also **looking glass**) a mirror. 4. the amount contained in a glass drinking vessel: *a glass of milk.* 5. **glasses** (*pl.*) a pair of glass lenses held in a frame and worn over the eyes to aid bad sight; spectacles. —*adj.* made of or fitted with glass. **'glasshouse** *n.* a GREENHOUSE.

glaze (glāz) *n.* a smooth glassy surface or coating, such as the finish given to pottery or porcelain. —*vb.* **glazing, glazed.** 1. to give a smooth shiny surface to. 2. to fit or cover with glass. **'glazier** *n.* a person who fits panes of glass, e.g. for windows.

gleam (glēm) *n.* 1. a flash or beam of light. 2. a faint glow. 3. a slight or faint appearance; glimmer: *a gleam of hope.* —*vb.* to glow or catch the light, giving off a gleam or gleams.

glide (glīd) *vb.* **gliding, glided.** to move gently and smoothly. —*n.* an effortless movement. **'glider** *n.* an aircraft without an engine, kept in flight by draughts of air. **'gliding** *n.* the sport of flying a glider.

glimmer ('glimə) *vb.* 1. to shine faintly with an unsteady flickering light. 2. to appear dimly. —*n.* 1. a dim

flickering light. 2. a faint appearance; flicker: *a glimmer of hope.*

glimpse (glimps) *n.* 1. a brief and temporary view or sight of something: *I caught a glimpse of the train.* 2. a vague idea; hint. —*vb.* **glimpsing, glimpsed.** 1. to obtain a brief view of. 2. to gain a vague idea of.

glisten ('glisən) *n.* to reflect the light, as when wet or polished: *after the shower the leaves glistened on the trees.*

glitter ('glitə) *vb.* to sparkle with a changing or flashing light: *the tinsel glittered on the Christmas tree.* —*n.* a splendid or sparkling appearance, light, etc. **'glittering** *adj.* 1. shining or sparkling. 2. splendid; fine: *a glittering success.*

gloat (glōt) *vb.* to take delight in or rejoice over wealth or over another's misfortune. —*n.* the act or an instance of gloating.

globe (glōb) *n.* 1. an object shaped like a ball; SPHERE. 2. an object of this shape used to represent the earth and

having the continents and seas shown on its surface.

gloom (gloom) *n.* 1. deep shadow or near darkness; dimness. 2. despair or depression; melancholy. —**'gloomy** *adj.* **gloomier, gloomiest.** —**'gloomily** *adv.* —**'gloominess** *n.*

glory ('glôri) *n.,pl.* **glories.** 1. honour; distinction; admiration. 2. brightness; splendour; brilliance. 3. praise or worship. —*vb.* **glorying, gloried.** (+ *in*) to rejoice in; take pride in: *he gloried in his success.* **'glorify** *vb.* **glorifying, glorified.** to praise or worship. **'glorious** *adj.* splendid; wonderful. —**glorifi'cation** *n.*

glow (glō) *vb.* 1. to emit a steady light. 2. to burn without flames. 3. to feel warmth. 4. to appear bright, lively, etc.: *she glowed with pride.* —*n.* 1. the light given out by a bright or burning object or substance. 2. a feeling of warmth. **'glowing** *adj.* 1. giving off a glow. 2. brilliant; fine; splendid: *glowing reports of someone's success.*

glucose ('glookōz) *n.* a type of sugar found in many fruits.

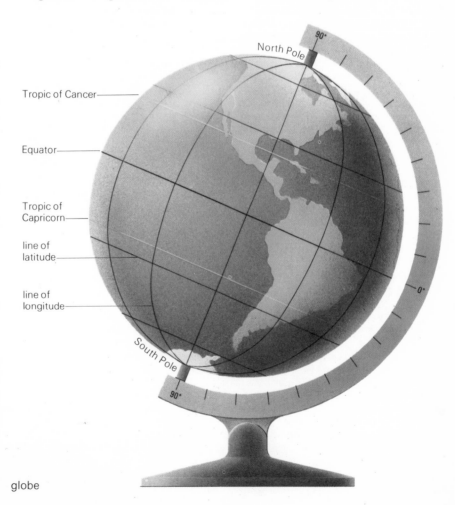

globe

93

glue (gloo) *n.* a substance for sticking things together. —*vb.* **gluing, glued.** 1. to stick or fasten with glue. 2. to be, stay, or put very close to something: *he is glued to the television.*

gnarled (nâld) *adj.* rugged in appearance: *a gnarled tree trunk.*

gnash (nash) *vb.* to force or grind (one's teeth) together in anger or pain.

gnat (nat) *n.* a tiny flylike insect related to the mosquito, the female of which is a bloodsucker.

gnaw (nô) *vb.* 1. to bite or nibble persistently; wear away: *the rats had gnawed through the floor.* 2. to trouble or worry: *the problem gnawed at his conscience.*

gnome (nōm) *n.* a type of fairy, usu. described as a tiny old man, said to live underground and guard the treasures of the earth.

gnu (noo) *n.,pl.* **gnus.** a large antelope having an ox-like head, curved horns, and a long tail, that lives in the plains of south and east Africa.

goad (gōd) *vb.* to cause (someone) to become angry, esp. angry enough to commit some bad action; provoke. —*n.* 1. a pointed stick for driving cattle. 2. any means of provocation.

goal (gōl) *n.* 1. an area marked by posts, lines, nets, etc., towards which players in some games, e.g. football and hockey, kick or direct a ball. 2. the action of directing a ball to or over a goal or the score made by doing this. 3. an end or aim; ambition: *his goal was to become a millionaire.* **'goalkeeper** *n.* a player in football, hockey, etc., whose job is to defend the goal.

goat (gōt) *n.* a sure-footed hairy animal having horns and a beard, closely related to the sheep, and often kept as a domestic animal.

gobble ('gobəl) *vb.* **gobbling, gobbled.** (often + *up*) to eat hurriedly.

god (god) *n.* 1. a being regarded as having power over nature and the affairs of men. 2. an image or other object worshipped as a symbol of supreme power; an idol. 3. **God** (in Christianity and some other religions) the one supreme being, creator and ruler of the unverse. **goddess** ('godis) *n.* a female god.

gold (gōld) *n.* 1. a heavy, yellowish, very highly valued metal used in jewellery, industry, and commerce, and formerly used for coins. Chemical symbol: Au. 2. a yellowish colour. —*adj.* 1. made of gold. 2. (also **golden**) of the colour gold.

goldfish ('gōldfish) *n.* a small yellow or orange fish of the carp family, often kept in aquariums and pools.

golf (golf) *n.* an outdoor game in which the player uses a number of clubs with wooden or metal heads to hit a small ball, using as few strokes as possible, into a series of holes set into the ground along a **golf course** with obstacles between them.

gong (gong) *n.* a metal disc, usu. made of brass or bronze, that produces a hollow vibrating note when struck.

goose (goos) *n.,pl.* **geese.** 1. a wild or domesticated web-footed swimming bird, usu. larger than a duck and having a longer neck. 2. the female bird as distinguished from the male (GANDER). 3. a silly or foolish person.

gooseberry

gooseberry ('goozbəri) *n.,pl.* **gooseberries.** a small, rather acid-tasting fruit that grows on a prickly bush.

gorge (gôj) *n.* 1. a narrow steep-sided valley, often having a stream running through it. 2. food that has been swallowed. —*vb.* **gorging, gorged.** (+ *on*) to swallow or eat greedily: *he gorged himself on apple pie.*

gorgeous ('gôjəs) *adj.* 1. splendid or very beautiful. 2. highly enjoyable: *a gorgeous meal.* —**'gorgeously** *adv.*

gorilla (gə'rilə) *n.* the largest of the apes, a plant-eating animal found in equatorial Africa. When upright, it stands six feet tall.

gospel ('gospəl) *n.* 1. the teaching of Christ. 2. the story of Christ's life and teaching, as told in the New Testament books of Matthew, Mark, Luke, and John. 3. one of these books.

gossip ('gosip) *n.* 1. idle talk, esp. about the private affairs of other people; rumour. 2. casual conversation. 3. a person who spreads rumours. —*vb.* to talk gossip.

govern ('guvən) *vb.* 1. to rule with authority: *to govern a country.* 2. to influence; guide; control: *the reasons governing his actions were clear.* 3. to hold in check; curb: *try to govern your impatience.* **'government** *n.* 1. political administration and rule. 2. the system by which a community, country, etc., is governed. 3. the body of persons responsible for a country's government. **'governor** *n.* 1. a person who directs or controls an institution, society, etc.: *a prison governor.* 2. the ruler appointed to govern a province, town, etc.

grace (grās) *n.* 1. ease or elegance in manner, movement, or form. 2. (in Christian religion) the love and favour freely granted by God to men. 3. an allowance of time to carry out some task: *he gave the boy three days' grace to finish his work.* 4. a term of address used to or in reference to a duke, duchess, or archbishop. —*vb.* **gracing, graced.** to favour or honour: *the princess graced the party with her presence.* **'graceful** *adj.* elegant or beautiful. **gracious** ('grāshəs) *adj.* 1. kind; courteous. 2. characterized by good taste or elegance: *gracious living.* —**'gracefully** *adv.* —**'graciously** *adv.*

grade (grād) *n.* 1. quality, value, or rank. 2. (U.S.) a class or form at school. —*vb.* **grading, graded.** 1. to organize into a series of grades; place in order of quality, value, etc.; sort or classify. 2. to judge or mark (an essay, examination, etc.).

gradient ('grādiənt) *n.* a slope or a degree of slope: *the steep gradient forced the train to go slowly.*

gradual ('gradyooəl) *adj.* happening or moving by slow degrees or very gently. —**'gradually** *adv.*

grain (grān) *n.* 1. the seed of one of the cereal plants (oats, wheat, barley, etc.). 2. corn in general. 3. any small hard particle: *a grain of sand.* 4. a tiny amount: *a grain of sense.* 5. a very small unit of weight equal to one seven-thousandth of a pound. 6. the arrangement of fibres in wood, as indicated by surface markings.

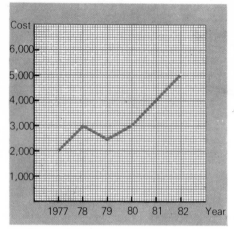

graph

gram *or* **gramme** (gram) *n.* the metric unit of mass or weight, approximately equal to one twenty-eighth of an ounce.

grammar ('gramə) *n.* 1. the description and classification of sounds and words in a language and the ways in which they are arranged and modified to form sentences. 2. a book about the grammar of a certain language: *a French grammar.* 3. speech or writing that agrees with accepted standards or rules: *bad grammar.* —**grammatical** (grə'matikəl) *adj.* —**gram'matically** *adv.*

grand (grand) *adj.* 1. very great in size or appearance. 2. magnificent; splendid: *the palace was very grand.* 3. very high in rank or dignity; of great importance: *a grand duke.* 4. noble or admirable. 5. complete or final: *he added up the figures to find the grand total.* '**grandstand** *n.* the principal seating area at a sports stadium or racecourse. —*n.* a grand PIANO. —'**grandly** *adv.* '**grandness** *or* **grandeur** ('grandyə) *n.*

grant (grânt) *vb.* 1. to give, esp. formally: *the king granted a new charter.* 2. to agree to: *he granted her request.* 3. to admit as true: *I grant you that point.* —*n.* something given formally such as a right, a piece of land, or a sum of money.

grape (grāp) *n.* a green or purple berry that grows in clusters on vines and is eaten as fruit and used to make wine.

grapefruit ('grāpfrŏot) *n.,pl.* **grapefruit** *or* **grapefruits.** a large round yellow-skinned edible CITRUS fruit

with an acid-tasting juicy flesh.

graph (grâf) *n.* a diagram showing by means of curves, lines, etc., how one quantity or factor changes with respect to another. **graphic** ('grafik) *adj.* 1. of, concerning, or shown on a graph, diagram, or drawing. 2. vivid; clear. —'**graphically** *adv.*

grasp (grâsp) *vb.* 1. to seize or try to seize with the hands or fingers. 2. to understand: *do you grasp my meaning?* —*n.* 1. the act of seizing. 2. a hold or grip: *he held me in his grasp.* 3. the ability to understand: *this book is beyond my grasp.* '**grasping** *adj.* greedy: *a grasping landowner.*

grasshopper ('grâshopə) *n.* plant-eating insect having strong hind legs with which it leaps considerable distances and which it rubs against its wings to produce a ticking sound.

grate[1] (grāt) *vb.* **grating, grated.** 1. to rub together with a harsh scraping noise: *the knife grated against the plate.* 2. to reduce to small pieces by rubbing against a rough cutting surface: *she grated a carrot.* 3. (+ *on*) to have an irritating effect: *his constant chatter grates on my nerves.*

grate[2] (grāt) *n.* 1. a metal framework, esp, of iron, for holding burning fuel in a fireplace, furnace, etc. 2. (also **grating**) a framework of bars used as a guard, cover, etc. 3. a fireplace.

grateful ('grātfəl) *adj.* thankful to someone for benefits received, kindness, etc.: *I am grateful for all your help.* —'**gratefully** *adv.* —**gratitude** ('gratityŏod) *or* '**gratefulness** *n.*

grave[1] (grāv) *n.* 1. a pit or hole in the earth in which a dead body is buried. 2. any place of burial; tomb. '**gravestone** *n.* a slab of stone placed over a grave and carved with the name and birth and death dates of the person buried there. '**graveyard** *n.* a cemetery; burial ground.

grave[2] (grāv) *adj.* 1. serious or solemn in manner or expression. 2. important; involving serious matters: *grave news.* —'**gravely** *adv.*

gravel ('gravəl) *n.* small stones and pebbles; a mixture of these with sand, used for making paths and roads. —*vb.* **gravelling, gravelled.** to cover with gravel. —'**gravelly** *adj.*

gravity ('graviti) *n.* 1. (also **gravitation**) the force that holds or pulls

objects down towards the earth. 2. seriousness; importance.

graze[1] (grāz) *vb.* **grazing, grazed.** 1. (of cattle, sheep, etc.) to feed on growing grass or pasture. 2. to cause cattle, sheep, etc., to feed on pasture or grassland. '**grazing** *n.* pasture.

graze[2] (grāz) *vb.* **grazing, grazed.** 1. to rub lightly against in passing: *the car grazed the wall as it turned the corner.* 2. to scrape the skin from: *I fell and grazed my knee.* —*n.* a slight scratch on the skin.

grease (grēs) *n.* 1. soft animal fat. 2. any fatty or oily substance, usu. used to reduce friction between the moving parts of a machine, etc. —*vb.* **greasing, greased.** to cover with grease. —'**greasy** *adj.* **greasier, greasiest.**

greed (grēd) *n.* excessive desire, esp. for food or money. '**greedy** *adj.* **greedier, greediest.** (often + *for* or *of*) excessively eager for (food, money, praise, etc.). —'**greedily** *adv.*

greenfly ('grēnflī) *n.,pl.* **greenfly** *or* **greenflies.** a small green insect that sucks the sap from the stems and leaves of plants.

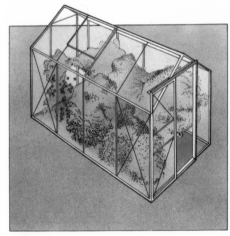

greenhouse

greenhouse ('grēnhous) *n.* a building, mainly made of glass, for the protection and cultivation of plants.

greet (grēt) *vb.* 1. to address (someone) with a special form of words when meeting; welcome: *we greeted our guests cheerfully.* 2. to meet with or receive: *her speech was greeted with applause.* '**greeting** *n.* the words or actions of someone who greets.

grenade (grə'nād) *n.* 1. a small explosive shell thrown by hand or shot from a rifle. 2. a glass container that shatters and sends out chemicals, such as tear gas, when thrown.

grew (groo̅) *vb.* the past tense of GROW.

greyhound ('grāhound) *n.* a tall slender short-haired DOG, noted for its great speed and keen sight.

grid (grid) *n.* 1. a framework of crossed bars; grating. 2. a network of cables and pipes carrying electricity, gas, etc., throughout a region. 3. a set of numbered squares on a map to indicate the accurate position of a place.

grief (grēf) *n.* 1. deep sorrow or distress over affliction or loss. 2. a cause or source of such distress.

grieve (grēv) *vb.* **grieving, grieved.** (often + *over*) to feel or cause to feel deep sorrow or grief: *he grieved over the death of his friend.* '**grievance** *n.* 1. a real or imagined wrong; complaint. 2. a state of resentment. '**grievous** *adj.* extremely serious; severe: *grievous injuries.*

grill (gril) *n.* 1. a kitchen device in which meat, fish, or vegetables are cooked on a metal grid directly under or over a source of heat. 2. a dish of meat, fish, etc., cooked in this way. —*vb.* to cook using a grill.

grille

grille (gril) *n.* a gridlike screen or barrier usu. made of metal and often of decorative design.

grim (grim) *adj.* **grimmer, grimmest.** stern; fierce; bitter or harsh: *he worked with grim determination.* —'**grimly** *adv.* — '**grimness** *n.*

grime (grīm) *n.* dirt, dust, etc., sunk into the surface of something or into

one's skin. —'**grimy** *adj.* **grimier, grimiest.** —'**griminess** *n.*

grin (grin) *vb.* **grinning, grinned.** to show the teeth when smiling. —*n.* the action or an instance of grinning.

grind (grīnd) *vb.* **grinding, ground.** 1. to crush into powder or tiny particles: *to grind coffee.* 2. to sharpen, shape, or smooth by means of friction: *to grind a knife.* 3. to rub (one's teeth) together, making a harsh scraping sound. 4. to work or study very hard. 5. (+ *down*) to wear down or oppress.

grip (grip) *vb.* **gripping, gripped.** 1. to take a firm hold of; grasp. 2. to capture the interest or attention of (someone): *the story gripped me right to the end.* —*n.* 1. a firm hold; grasp. 2. an understanding: *he has a good grip on the subject.*

gristle ('grisəl) *n.* a whitish elastic substance found in meat.

grit (grit) *n.* 1. small particles of stone or sand. 2. (informal) courage. —*vb.* **gritting, gritted.** to cover with grit: *they gritted the roads to prevent accidents on the icy surface.* —'**gritty** *adj.* **grittier, grittiest.** —'**grittiness** *n.*

groan (grōn) *n.* a low sound of distress, pain, disappointment, etc. —*vb.* 1. to make the sound of a groan. 2. (of things) to be overloaded or weighed down: *the table groaned with food.*

grocer ('grōsə) *n.* a shopkeeper who sells tea, sugar, jam, tinned and packaged foods, washing powder, and other household goods. '**grocery** *n.,pl.* **groceries.** 1. a grocer's shop or business. 2. **groceries** (*pl.*) goods bought from a grocer's shop.

groin (groin) *n.* 1. the line along which the top of either thigh meets the abdomen. 2. the curved line where two vaulted arches meet.

groom (groo̅m) *n.* 1. a person who takes care of the horses at a stable. 2. a bridegroom. See BRIDE. —*vb.* 1. to brush and clean the hair of a horse, dog, cat, etc. 2. to make oneself tidy or smart.

groove (groo̅v) *n.* a narrow channel or furrow on the surface of an object: *a groove on a record.*

grope (grōp) *vb.* **groping, groped.** 1. to move or search by feeling rather than looking. 2. to make progress in a slow or hesitant manner: *to grope*

towards an understanding of a problem. —'**gropingly** *adv.*

gross (grōs) *adj.* 1. whole; entire; without anything being taken away: *a gross wage.* Compare NET². 2. very large or fat, often unpleasantly.so. 3. rude; vulgar: *gross language.* —*n.* 1. the total amount of something. 2. a batch of 144 (12 dozen) items. —*vb.* to have as one's total earnings, before taxation: *he grosses £6000 a year.* —'**grossly** *adv.*

grotesque (grō'tesk) *adj.* 1. absurd or fantastically ugly; unnatural. 2. (in art) decorated with fantastic or monstrous human and animal forms intertwined with foliage.

ground[1] (ground) *n.* 1. the land surface of the earth. 2. soil: *fertile ground.* 3. the surface of cloth, a flag, etc., esp. in respect of its colour: *her dress had blue flowers on a white ground.* 4. often **grounds** (*pl.*) a cause; basic reason: *he left his job on the grounds that he was underpaid.* 5. **grounds** (*pl.*) the land surrounding a large house, etc. —*vb.* 1. to keep (an aircraft pilot) from flying, esp. for medical reasons. 2.(+ *on*) to use (something) as a reason or basis for (some action): *his decision to leave was grounded on fear.*

ground[2] (ground) *vb.* the past tense of GRIND. —*n.* usu. **grounds** (*pl.*) something ground up or the remains of something ground up: *coffee grounds.*

group (groo̅p) *n.* a number of people or things considered together; assembly or collection. —*vb.* (often + *together*) to form into a group.

grouse

grouse[1] (grous) *n.,pl.* **grouse.** a bird with feathered legs and red or brown plumage, found mainly on open moorland in northern regions and hunted for sport and food.

grouse[2] (grous) *vb.* **grousing, groused.** (informal) to grumble; complain. —*n.* (informal) an instance of grousing; complaint.

grovel ('grovəl) *vb.* **grovelling, grovelled.** 1. to crawl face downwards in humility, fear, or flattering respect in front of someone; fawn. 2. to act as if one were doing this.

grow (grō) *vb.* **growing, grew, grown.** 1. to get bigger; develop. 2. to become: *to grow tired.* 3. (+ *on* or *upon*) to become acceptable or enjoyable to someone: *that song's growing on me.* **grow up** to become an adult; mature. **'grown-up** *n.* an adult. **growth** (grōth) *n.* 1. the process or amount of development or growing. 2. something that has grown, esp. something that develops in or on the body because of disease.

growl (groul) *vb.* 1. (of a dog) to make a deep angry throaty noise. 2. to express angrily or aggressively: *he growled an order.* —*n.* the sound of a growl.

grub (grub) *n.* 1. the wormlike form of certain insects; LARVA. 2. (slang) food. —*vb.* **grubbing, grubbed.** to search for something by or as if by digging; dig up or uproot. **'grubby** *adj.* **grubbier, grubbiest.** *adj.* dirty.

grudge (gruj) *vb.* **grudging, grudged.** to be jealous or resentful of: *I don't grudge him his wealth.* —*n.* an instance or cause of resentment. **bear a grudge against** to be jealous or resentful of: *I bear a grudge against him for making me lose my job.*

gruesome ('grōōsəm) *adj.* horrifying; terrible to see. —**'gruesomely** *adv.* —**'gruesomeness** *n.*

grumble ('grumbəl) *vb.* **grumbling, grumbled.** 1. to complain. 2. to murmur in indistinct low sounds. —*n.* 1. the action or an instance of grumbling; complaint or murmur. 2. a rumble. —**'grumbler** *n.*

grunt (grunt) *n.* 1. a low short murmured sound: *he gave a grunt of agreement.* 2. the sound made by a pig. —*vb.* to make the sound of or express with a grunt.

guarantee (garən'tē) *n.* 1. a promise, esp. a formal or official one, that something will be done, will work

properly, etc.: *the radio was sold with a guarantee.* 2. a promise to accept responsibility for the actions, genuineness, or honesty of a person or thing. —*vb.* **guaranteeing, guaranteed.** to provide a guarantee for (a person or thing).

guinea pig

guard (gâd) *vb.* 1. to watch over; defend; protect. 2. to keep as a prisoner; prevent from escaping. —*n.* 1. a person or group who guards. 2. the action or an instance of guarding: *the police set a guard around the building.* 3. a man who looks after a train. 4. a defence or protection. **off (one's) guard** not watchful; unawares. **on (one's) guard** keeping watch. **'guardian** *n.* a person who takes responsibility for an orphan.

guerrilla *or* **guerilla** (gə'rilə) *n.* a fighter who is not part of a regular army but carries on war in small secret bands.

guess (ges) *n.* an opinion, judgment, or estimate that one cannot be certain about. —*vb.* to make a guess about something.

guest (gest) *n.* 1. a visitor or a person invited to someone's home. 2. a person staying at a hotel, etc.

guide (gīd) *vb.* **guiding, guided.** 1. to point out the way to; lead, as an expedition or tour. 2. to advise. —*n.* 1. a person acting as a guide: *the guide showed us around the museum.* 2. something, e.g. a book, providing information or advice. 3. **Guide** (also **Girl Guide**) a member of an international organization that teaches girls to look after themselves and to help others. **'guidance** *n.* advice.

guild (gild) *n.* 1. an association of people with similar jobs or interests

set up to help and protect its members. 2. one of many such organizations formed in England during the Middle Ages.

guillotine ('gilətēn) *n.* 1. a mechanical device fitted with a blade and used mainly in France for executing people by cutting their heads off. 2. a device for cutting or trimming paper. —*vb.* **guillotining, guillotined.** to execute by guillotine.

guilt (gilt) *n.* 1. the condition of being responsible for a crime or wrong. 2. the feeling connected with this: *full of guilt.* **'guilty** *adj.* **guiltier, guiltiest.** responsible for a crime or wrong. —**'guiltily** *adv.* —**'guiltiness** *n.*

guinea pig (ginē) 1. a small ratlike animal with no tail often kept as a pet or used in scientific experiments. 2. any person or animal used in a scientific or other test.

guitar (gi'tâ) *n.* a stringed musical instrument having a wooden body curving inward at the centre and a narrow wooden neck crossed by small ridges called frets. It is plucked with the fingers.

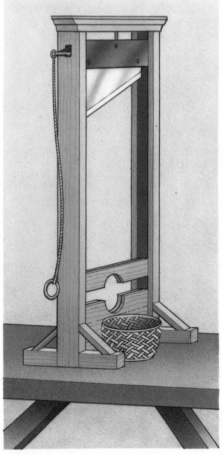
guillotine

gulf (gulf) *n*. 1. an abyss; chasm. 2. a stretch of sea partly surrounded by land. 3. any wide gap or space.

gull (gul) *n*. (also **seagull**) a type of seabird having webbed feet, a white front, a greyish back, and long greyish wings. Gulls live mainly on fish.

gullet ('gulit) *n*. the tube along which food is transferred from the mouth to the stomach; throat.

gullible ('gulibəl) *adj.* easily deceived or tricked: *a gullible customer.* —**gulli'bility** *n*.

gulp (gulp) *vb*. 1. to swallow quickly: *he gulped his food.* 2. to swallow as a sign of nervousness, fright, or surprise: *he gulped when he saw how big his opponent was.* —*n*. an instance of gulping.

gum[1] (gum) *n*. the soft flesh surrounding the base of a tooth.

gum[2] (gum) *n*. 1. a thick substance used as glue and obtained from certain trees. 2. a sweet made from such

a substance: *chewing gum.* 3. (also **gum tree**) a tree producing gum. **'gumboots** *pl.n.* knee-high rubber boots. **up a gum tree** in a difficult situation. —*vb*. **gumming, gummed.** 1. to stick with gum. 2. (+ *up*) (slang) to ruin, confuse, or make a mess of: *you've gummed up the television.*

gurgle ('gûgəl) *n*. a bubbling noise, as of boiling liquid. — *vb*. **gurgling, gurgled.** to make or seem to make the sound of a gurgle.

gush (gush) *vb*. 1.(often + *out, forth,* etc.) (of liquid) to rush out of somewhere in a flood. 2. to release (liquid) in a rushing flood. 3. to talk enthusiastically. —*n*. 1. the action or an instance of gushing. 2. the liquid that gushes. 3. a flow of enthusiastic talk.

gust (gust) *n*. 1. a sudden strong burst of wind, rain, smoke, sound, etc. 2. a burst of passion or emotion. —*vb*. (of the wind) to blow in gusts.

gusto ('gustō) *n*. forceful or hearty keenness or enthusiasm: *he sang out with gusto.*

gut (gut) *n*. 1. the channel along which food travels through the body; intestine. 2. material prepared from the intestines of an animal, e.g. a sheep, and used for strings for violins, tennis-rackets, etc. 3. **guts** (*pl.*) (slang) courage. —*vb*. **gutting, gutted.** 1. to remove the insides from (a fish). 2. to burn completely the inside of: *fire gutted the flat.*

gutter ('gutə) *n*. 1. a drainage channel at the side of a road or street for carrying away surface water. 2. a similar channel running around a roof.

gymkhana (jim'kânə) *n*. an outdoor sports show devoted mainly to events involving horse-riding.

gymnasium (jim'nāziəm) *n*. a special room or building fitted out with equipment for physical exercise. **gymnast** ('jimnast) *n*. someone who performs physical exercises as a sport. **gym'nastic** *adj.* of or connected with physical exercises. **gym'nastics** *sing.n.* the sport involving such exercises.

Gypsy ('jipsi) *n*. See GIPSY.

gymnastics

rings

high bar

beam

H

habit ('habit) *n.* 1. a regularly repeated action, esp. one that one does without really thinking about it: *he has the habit of taking a walk on Sundays.* 2. a special form of clothing worn for a particular reason: *a monk's habit.* '**habitat** *n.* the natural surroundings of plants or animals: *tigers have a jungle habitat.* **habitual** (hə'bityŏŏəl) *adj.* of or by habit.

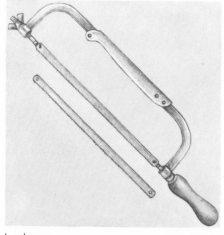
hacksaw

hacksaw ('haksô) *n.* a saw for cutting metal. It has a replaceable blade.

haddock ('hadək) *n.* a deep-sea fish like a cod but smaller. It is found esp. in the eastern Atlantic around Britain, and is often eaten smoked.

hail[1] (hāl) *vb.* 1. to greet or call to (someone). 2. to come from a particular place: *he hails from Texas.* —*n.* a shouted greeting.

hail[2] (hāl) *n.* 1. balls of ice made from raindrops frozen together in a thundercloud and falling as a shower. 2. a shower of small missiles: *a hail of bullets.* —*vb.* to fall as hailstones.

hair (heə) *n.* 1. a thin growth like a thread on an animal's skin. 2. the mass of these growing on a human head. —'**hairy** *adj.* **hairier, hairiest.** —'**hairiness** *n.*

hair-raising ('heərāziñg) *adj.* very frightening.

half (hâf) *n.,pl.* **halves.** one of two equal parts into which a thing is divided. —*adj.* of a half.

half-hearted *adj.* not very enthusiastic: *they gave the team half-hearted support.*

half-truth *n.* a statement that is partly true but is not the whole truth, esp. a statement made to deceive someone.

halibut ('halibət) *n.* the largest of the flatfishes, living on the bottom of the North Atlantic and Pacific Oceans. It is a greatly valued food.

hall (hôl) *n.* 1. a building used for public gatherings, concerts, etc. 2. a large public room in a building. 3. a big house or other dwelling. 4. the entrance passage of a private house or flat.

hallmark ('hôlmâk) *n.* a mark used by government offices for stamping silver or gold in order to indicate its quality.

halo ('hālō) *n.,pl.* **haloes** *or* **halos.** 1. a circle of light around the head of a saint, esp. in religious pictures. 2. a circle of light around any heavenly body, such as the moon.

halt (hôlt) *vb.* to stop or cause to stop, esp. on a journey. —*n.* 1. a temporary stop on a journey. 2. a small stopping-place on a railway.

halter ('hôltə) *n.* a rope or strap to fit around the head or neck of a horse or other tame animal.

halve (hâv) *vb.* **halving, halved.** to divide into two equal parts.

ham (ham) *n.* 1. meat from the thigh of a pig. 2. the thigh and buttocks of a human or animal. 3. (informal) an actor who overacts.

hamburger ('hambûgə) *n.* a flat round cake of minced beef, often eaten grilled or fried in a split bread roll.

ham-fisted (ham'fistid) *adj.* clumsy.

hamlet ('hamlit) *n.* a small group of houses in the country, smaller than a village.

hammer ('hamə) *n.* 1. a TOOL, usu. with a wooden handle and metal head, used for hitting nails and flattening or breaking wood, metal, etc. 2. one of the three small bones in the middle ear that transmit sounds to the inner ear. —*vb.* to hit, join, or shape (nails, metal, etc.).

hammock ('hamək) *n.* a bed made of strong cloth or netting. It is hung between two supports and can swing freely between them.

hamper[1] ('hampə) *vb.* to hinder by getting in the way of (someone or something); to restrict: *their progress was hampered by their loads.*

hamper[2] ('hampə) *n.* a large basket with a lid: *a picnic hamper.*

hamster ('hamstə) *n.* a small furry animal with a short tail and pouched cheeks, often kept as a pet.

hamstring ('hamstriñg) *n.* a cord (tendon) connecting the muscle with the leg bone in the back of the knee.

hand (hand) *n.* 1. the part of the human body below the wrist. 2. a

halo

worker: *a factory hand.* 3. a pointer on a clock, watch, etc. 4. a style of writing. —*vb.* (often + *over*) to give. **hand down** to pass on, esp. to an heir.

handcuff ('handkuf) *n.* one of a pair of locking metal bracelets joined by a short chain, used by police to restrict a prisoner's movements. —*vb.* to put (someone) in handcuffs.

handicap ('handikap) *n.* a problem or circumstance tending to hold a person back, esp. a physical disability: *John's deafness is a handicap to him.* —*vb.* **handicapping, handicapped.** 1. to hold back or restrict. 2. to create an infirmity or disability in (a person).

handkerchief ('hangkəchif) *n.* a piece of cloth or tissue-like paper used for cleaning the nose, wiping up perspiration, etc.

handle ('handəl) *vb.* **handling, handled.** 1. to control or touch with the hands: *she handled the glass carefully.* 2. to deal with (a person, subject, business, etc.): *he handled his staff with tact.* —*n.* that part of a tool, object, etc., intended to be grasped or held by the hand, e.g. doorhandle.

handsome ('hansəm) *adj.* 1. pleasing to look at, esp. used of a good looking man. 2. ample in quantity; generous: *a handsome donation.* —'**handsomely** *adv.*

handy ('handi) *adj.* **handier, handiest.** 1. useful: *a handy tool.* 2. clever at using one's hands. 3. readily available: *keep the first-aid kit handy.*

hang (hang) *vb.* **hanging, hung** or (for def. 2) **hanged.** 1. to hold or be held from above only, esp. so as to swing loosely. 2. to kill (a person) by suspending him by a rope around his neck. **hang about** to remain waiting: *we hung about in the garage while the car was being mended.* **hang back** to be unwilling to act; hesitate. **hang onto** to refuse to let go of. **hang up** to end a telephone conversation by replacing the receiver.

hangar ('hangə) *n.* 1. a covered shed for sheltering aircraft. 2. an aircraft workshop.

happen ('hapən) *vb.* 1. to take place; occur: *what happened yesterday?* 2. to take place by chance: *I happened to see Carol last night.* 3. to become of: *what happened to you when you left?* **happen on** or **upon** to come across by accident: *he happened on a clearing in the wood.* '**happening** *n.* an event.

happy ('hapi) *adj.* **happier, happiest.** 1. expressing or feeling joy. 2. lucky: *that was a happy win.* —'**happily** *adv.* —'**happiness** *n.*

harass ('harəs) *vb.* to pursue or attack continually; pester. —'**harassment** *n.*

harbour ('hâbə) *n.* 1. a place of shelter for ships on a sea coast. 2. any place of refuge or safety. —*vb.* 1. to give protection to (someone). 2. to keep (an idea, a feeling, etc.) in one's mind: *he harboured dreams of riches.*

hard (hâd) *adj.* 1. solid; firm. 2. difficult to understand or deal with: *a hard problem.* 3. cruel: *a hard man.* 4. violent: *a hard blow.* 5. energetic: *a hard worker.* —*adv.* 1. in a firm way. 2. with difficulty. 3. strenuously. 4. forcefully; violently: *to hit hard.* '**harden** *vb.* 1. to make or become hard or harder. 2. to make or become insensitive or indifferent. —'**hardness** *n.*

hardly ('hâdli) *adv.* scarcely: *he hardly moved an inch.*

hardship ('hâdship) *n.* something that is difficult to bear, esp. poverty, pain, hunger, etc.

hardware ('hâdweə) *n.* man-made metal goods; ironmongery.

hardy ('hâdi) *adj.* **hardier, hardiest.** able to survive hardship; tough: *a hardy child.* —'**hardily** *adv.* —'**hardiness** *n.*

hare (heə) *n.* a wild animal similar to a rabbit but larger, with long ears and powerful hind legs.

hare

harm (hâm) *n.* 1. injury; damage. 2. moral evil; wrong. —*vb.* to injure physically or mentally. '**harmful** *adj.* having a hurtful effect. —'**harmfully** *adv.* '**harmless** *adj.* not having a hurtful effect. —'**harmlessly** *adv.*

harmonica (hâ'monikə) *n.* a musical wind instrument consisting of reeds set in a box and sounded by blowing or sucking air over them. It is also called a mouth organ.

harmony ('hâməni) *n.,pl.* **harmonies.** 1. musical notes sounded together to make chords. 2. agreement. '**harmonize** *vb.* **harmonizing, harmonized.** to be in harmony. —**harmonious** (hâ'mōniəs) *adj.* —**har'moniously** *adv.*

harness ('hânis) *n.* the leather straps and metal parts used to attach a work animal to a plough, carriage, etc. —*vb.* to put a harness on (an animal).

harp

harp (hâp) *n.* a large stringed musical instrument. The strings are usu. made of wire, and they are plucked by the player's fingers.

harpoon (hâ'pōōn) *n.* a spearlike weapon with a rope attached to one end. It is shot from a gun or thrown by hand and used for spearing and capturing whales, fish, and seals. —*vb.* to use a harpoon to kill (whales, fish, etc.).

harsh (hâsh) *adj.* 1. unpleasant to any of the senses: *harsh sounds.* 2. cruel: *he is a harsh man.* —'**harshly** *adv.* —'**harshness** *n.*

harvest ('hâvist) *n.* 1. the gathering in of ripe crops. 2. the crops so gathered. 3. the time of year when crops are gathered. 4. the results of actions, esp. the rewards of hard work. —*vb.* 1. to gather in crops. 2. to obtain the results of one's deeds, esp. as reward or punishment.

haste (hāst) *n.* 1. speed of movement or action. 2. excessive hurrying, often resulting in rashness. **hasten** ('hāsən) *vb.* to move or cause to move very speedily. —'**hasty** *adj.* **hastier, hastiest.** —'**hastily** *adv.* —'**hastiness** *n.*

hatch[1] (hach) *vb.* 1. to cause (chicks, snakes, etc.) to be born from eggs. 2. (of young birds, snakes, etc.) to break out of their eggs. 3. to think up (a plan): *they hatched a plot.* '**hatchery** *n.,pl.* **hatcheries.** a place where young (chicks, fish, etc.) are reared from eggs.

hatch[2] (hach) *n.* 1. a trapdoor in a floor or roof. 2. an opening in a wall between rooms through which goods can be passed.

hatchet ('hachit) *n.* a small axe with a short handle, usu. held in one hand.

hate (hāt) *vb.* **hating, hated.** to have an extreme dislike or loathing for (someone or something): *he hates war.* —*n.* 1. (also **hatred**) the emotion or feeling of extreme dislike; loathing. 2. the object of the hatred or dislike: *oranges are one of my pet hates.* —'**hateful** *adj.* —'**hatefully** *adv.* —'**hatefulness** *n.*

hat-trick ('hattrik) *n.* 1. (cricket) taking three wickets with successive balls. 2. a similar sequence of three successes in another sport or activity.

haughty ('hôti) *adj.* **haughtier, haughtiest.** being overproud of oneself and scornful of others; arrogant: *the haughty princess looked down on her servants.* —'**haughtily** *adv.* —'**haughtiness** *n.*

haul (hôl) *vb.* to pull in or up; drag or carry something along: *we hauled the boat out of the water.* —*n.* 1. a strong pull; tug. 2. something obtained by effort: *the thieves got a good haul.* 3. a distance, esp. one that is long or difficult: *it was a long haul up the hill.* '**haulage** *n.* 1. the transport of goods. 2. the charge made for transporting goods. '**haulier** *n.* a person or company that transports goods.

haunch (hônch) *n.* the fleshy rear part of human beings and animals between the ribs and the thighs.

haunt (hônt) *vb.* 1. (of ghosts) to cause trouble or disturbance by lingering in a place after death. 2. to visit (a place) often: *he haunted the football club.* 3. to fill (the mind) repeatedly: *the song haunted her.* —*n.* a place visited often by a particular person. '**haunted** *adj.* visited by ghosts and spirits: *a haunted house.*

hatchet

haven ('hāvən) *n.* 1. a place where ships may stay protected from rough weather, etc. 2. any place of safety.

haversack ('havəsak) *n.* a canvas bag made to be carried on a person's back and used by walkers, soldiers, etc.

havoc ('havək) *n.* complete destruction usu. caused by a huge force, e.g. the weather, a mob of people: *the gale caused havoc.*

hawk[1] (hôk) *n.* a bird of prey with broad wings, strong curved beak, and powerful clawed feet.

hawk[2] (hôk) *vb.* to offer (goods) for sale in the street, esp. by taking them from house to house.

hawthorn ('hôthôn) *n.* a thorny shrub of the rose family with pink or white flowers and small red berries.

hay (hā) *n.* grass cut and dried and used for feeding cattle, etc.

hayfever ('hāfēvə) *n.* an unpleasant allergic reaction suffered by some people if they breathe in pollen, dust, etc. Hayfever causes sneezing and a runny nose, and is common when hay is being cut.

hazard ('hazəd) *n.* 1. something causing danger of injury or damage: *an icy road is a hazard to traffic.* 2. luck. 3. a dice game. —*vb.* 1. to expose to danger or damage: *to hazard one's safety.* 2. to take a chance with; risk: *I'll hazard a guess.* —'**hazardous** *adj.* —'**hazardously** *adv.*

haze (hāz) *n.* a thin mist caused by smoke, water vapour, or dust in the air: *a heat haze.*

hazel ('hāzəl) *n.* 1. a tree or bush on which grow small edible nuts (**hazelnuts**). 2. a light reddish brown colour. —*adj.* reddish brown.

head (hed) *n.* 1. the part of the body above the neck containing the eyes, mouth, nose, etc. 2. anything like a head in shape, function, or position. 3. the most important person. —*vb.* 1. to be a leader of: *she headed an inquiry into the disaster.* 2. (+ *for*) to move in a particular direction: *let's head for home.*

headline ('hedlīn) *n.* the title of a newspaper story, esp. one printed in large type on the front page.

headquarters ('hedkwôtəz) *n.* the place from which an organization or operation is controlled.

headstrong ('hedstrong) *adj.* not easily guided or controlled; obstinate.

heal (hēl) *vb.* to make or become well, esp. after an injury.

health (helth) *n.* a state of physical or mental well-being, esp. being free from illness. '**healthy** *adj.* **healthier, healthiest.** having or encouraging good health.

hear (hiə) *vb.* **hearing, heard** (hûd). to become aware of sounds through the ears. '**hearing** *n.* 1. the ability to hear. 2. a trial in a court of law.

hearse (hûs) *n.* a vehicle for transporting the coffin of a dead person.

101

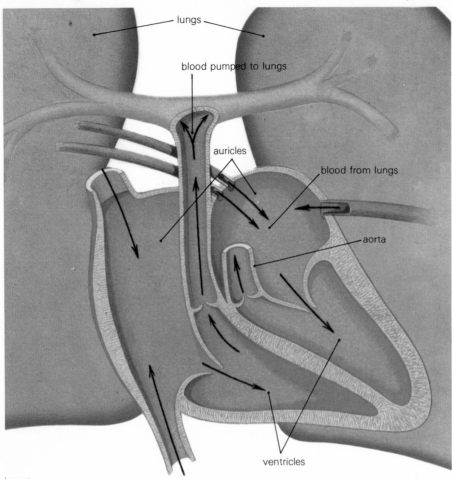

lungs

blood pumped to lungs

auricles

blood from lungs

aorta

ventricles

heart

heart (hât) *n.* 1. the part of the body that pumps blood. 2. the centre of the emotions. 3. the centre of any activity, organization, etc. '**heartless** *adj.* unkind. '**hearty** *adj.* **heartier, heartiest.** 1. strong. 2. (of meals) big. —'**heartily** *adv.* '**heartbroken** *adj.* very sad.

heather ('hedhə) *n.* a hardy evergreen shrub that grows plentifully on heathland.

heather

heaven ('hevən) *n.* 1. (in religious belief) the place where God and his angels live and to which the souls of dead people go. 2. usu. **heavens** (*pl.*) the sky. 3. any delightful place or event. —'**heavenly** *adj.*

heavy ('hevi) *adj.* **heavier, heaviest.** 1. difficult to lift: *a heavy sack.* 2. more than average: *a heavy rainfall.* —'**heavily** *adv.* —'**heaviness** *n.*

hedge (hej) *n.* a fence or boundary formed by bushes or trees planted close together to make a barrier. —*vb.* **hedging, hedged.** 1. to form a fence with bushes or trees. 2. to avoid being committed: *he hedged on the issue.*

heed (hēd) *vb.* to pay careful attention to (someone or something). '**heedful** *adj.* careful. —'**heedfully** *adv.* '**heedless** *adj.* unthinking; careless. —'**heedlessly** *adv.*

heel (hēl) *n.* 1. the rounded back part of a human foot. 2. the part of a sock or stocking covering it. 3. the part of a shoe underneath it.

height (hīt) *n.* 1. the distance between the top and bottom of anything: *the man was 6 feet in height.* 3. often **heights** (*pl.*) a high place. 4. a high point, esp. of success: *he died at the height of his fame.* '**heighten** *vb.* 1. to make or become higher. 2. to make (something) more intense or dramatic: *the sun heightened the beauty of the lake.*

heir (eə) *n.* someone who receives a person's property, etc., after that person's death. '**heiress** *n.* a female heir.

heirloom ('eəloॉom) *n.* an object, esp. a valuable one, that has been owned by a family for many years and handed down from one generation to the next generation.

helicopter ('helikoptə) *n.* an aircraft powered by long blades that turn horizontally on top of it.

hell (hel) *n.* (in religious belief) a place of punishment for wicked souls after death. —'**hellish** *adj.* —'**hellishly** *adv.* —'**hellishness** *n.*

helm (helm) *n.* the steering wheel or TILLER of a ship.

helmet ('helmit) *n.* a hard hat (usu. metal) that prevents injuries to the head.

help (help) *vb.* 1. to aid or assist. 2. to avoid: *I couldn't help laughing.* 3. to aid recovery from: *the medicine helped the cough.* —*n.* 1. an act of helping or assisting. 2. someone who gives assistance. '**helping** *n.* 1. an act of giving help. 2. a portion of food. —'**helpful** *adj.* —'**helpfully** *adv.* —'**helpless** *adj.* —'**helplessly** *adv.*

hem (hem) *n.* the edge of a garment that has been made by turning over and stitching down the raw edge of the material. —*vb.* **hemming, hemmed.** to make a hem.

hemisphere ('hemisfiə) *n.* half a sphere, esp. half the Earth: *Australia is in the Southern Hemisphere.*

hen (hen) *n.* an adult female bird, esp. a domestic fowl.

herald ('herəld) *n.* a messenger or carrier of news. —*vb.* to proclaim or announce. '**heraldry** *n.* the study of family histories, esp. in reference to the granting of family badges (coats of arms). —**heraldic** (he'raldik) *adj.*

herb (hûb) *n.* 1. a plant commonly used in cooking to flavour food, e.g.

heron

parsley, sage, etc. Herbs are also used in making medicine and perfumes. 2. any plant that dies after flowering and does not have a woody stem.

herd (hûd) *n.* a group of animals of the same species that keeps together while eating, sleeping, etc. —*vb.* 1. to come or cause to come together into a large group. 2. to drive (animals). **'herdsman** *n.,pl.* **herdsmen.** a man in charge of a herd.

heritage ('heritij) *n.* something that can be handed down from one generation to the next.

hermit ('hûmit) *n.* a person who lives alone, esp. a holy man. **'hermitage** *n.* a hermit's dwelling.

hero ('hiərō) *n.,pl.* **heroes.** 1. a man of great bravery, admired and respected by all. 2. the main male character in a play or book. **heroine** ('herōin) *n.* 1. a brave, daring woman. 2. the main female character in a play or book. —**heroic** (hi'rōik) *adj.* —**he'roically** *adv.* —**heroism** ('herōizəm) *n.*

heron ('herən) *n.* a big bird that lives

near water. It has a long, slender bill for catching fish, a long neck, and long legs for wading.

herring ('heriñg) *n.,pl.* **herrings** or **herring.** a small bony sea fish that is often eaten pickled or salted. **red herring** something introduced to distract attention from the main subject under discussion.

hesitate ('hezitāt) *vb.* **hesitating, hesitated.** 1. to hang back or pause: *he hesitated before jumping.* 2. to show signs of uncertainty: *he hesitated when telling us his tale.* —**'hesitant** *adj.* —**'hesitantly** *adv.* —**hesi'tation** *n.*

hexagon ('heksəgən) *n.* a six-sided shape, usu. with sides of equal length. —**hexagonal** (hek'sagənəl) *adj.*

hibernate ('hībənāt) *vb.* **hibernating, hibernated.** (of some animals such as squirrels and hedgehogs) to spend the winter in very deep sleep. —**hiber'nation** *n.*

hiccup ('hikəp) *n.* often **hiccups** (*pl.*) a jerky uncontrollable catching of breath, with a cough-like noise. —*vb.* **hiccupping, hiccupped.** to have an attack of hiccups.

hide[1] (hīd) *vb.* **hiding, hid, hidden** or **hid.** 1. to keep secret or prevent from being seen or known; conceal: *he hid the fact that he knew her.* 2. to put or keep out of sight: *the trees hid the houses from view.*

hide[2] (hīd) *n.* 1. the skin of an animal, usu. a large animal. 2. an animal skin treated for use in making clothing, shoes, bags, etc.; leather. **'hiding** *n.* a beating.

hideous ('hidiəs) *adj.* horrible or frightful; shocking to the senses or emotions: *the hideous crime shocked the whole town.* —**'hideously** *adv.* —**'hideousness** *n.*

hieroglyphic (hīərə'glifik) *n.* (also **hieroglyph**) a symbol or picture representing a word or sound, esp. in the writing (**hieroglyphics**) of the ancient Egyptians. —*adj.* of, relating to, or written in hieroglyphics.

high (hī) *adj.* 1. long from top to bottom; tall: *a high tower.* 2. much above ground or sea level: *he was high in the air.* 3. extending a specified distance upwards: *the tree is five feet high.* 4. relatively large or great in degree, intensity, importance, or

amount: *high prices.* 5. (of food) slightly tainted or decomposed. 6. (of sound, a note, etc.) at the upper end of the musical scale. —*adv.* at or to a high place, level, degree, etc.: *he reached high.* —*n.* something that is high: *prices reached a new high.* **'highly** *adv.* 1. very much. 2. with great respect, admiration, etc.: *we think highly of our teacher.* 3. at a high price. See also HEIGHT.

highway ('hīwā) *n.* a main route, esp. a road between towns. **'highwayman** *n.,pl.* **highwaymen.** (formerly) a robber, esp. one on horseback, who steals from travellers on public roads.

hijack ('hījak) *vb.* to seize control of or steal (an aircraft, motor vehicle, etc.).

hike (hīk) *vb.* **hiking, hiked.** to go on a long walk through the countryside, esp. for pleasure. —*n.* a long walk.

hill (hil) *n.* 1. a little mountain. 2. a slope up or down, e.g. on a road.

hilt (hilt) *n.* the handle of a weapon or tool, esp. of a sword or dagger. **to the hilt** completely: *he was armed to the hilt.*

hinder ('hində) *vb.* to cause delay or difficulty to; hamper: *pouring rain hindered us in painting the house.* —**'hindrance** *n.*

hinge (hinj) *n.* 1. a movable joint by which two things, e.g. a door and its frame, are connected, allowing one or both to turn or move. 2. a similar natural joint, e.g. in the knee. 3. something upon which other events, actions, etc., depend. —*vb.* **hinging, hinged.** 1. to turn on, supply with, or attach a hinge. 2. to depend or cause to depend: *the plan's success hinges on John.*

hieroglyphic

hint (hint) *n.* 1. an indirect suggestion: *he dropped the hint that he wanted a new pen.* 2. a very slight amount: *a hint of garlic.* —*vb.* to make a hint or give a hint of.

hip[1] (hip) *n.* the bony part of the body that sticks out below the waist.

hip[2] (hip) *n.* a fruit of a rose that turns red when it is ripe.

hippopotamus

hippopotamus (hipəˈpotəməs) *n.,pl.* **hippopotamuses** *or* **hippopotami** (hipəˈpotəmī) often shortened to **hippo**. a large plant-eating African animal with a tough hairless skin and short legs. It spends much time almost submerged in water.

hire (hīə) *vb.* **hiring, hired.** 1. to engage the services or use of (someone or something) for payment: *he hired a boat.* 2. to grant the use or services of (someone or something) for payment. —*n.* 1. the act of hiring. 2. the price paid or asked for hiring. **hire purchase** a system that enables people to buy large objects by paying for them with many small payments at regular intervals.

hiss (his) *vb.* to make a noise like the letter 's', as a snake does, esp. as a sign of anger or contempt. —*n.* a hissing sound.

history (ˈhistəri) *n.,pl.* **histories.** 1. branch of knowledge dealing with the past. 2. an account of past events relating to a particular nation, person, etc.: *a history of France.* **historian** (hiˈstôriən) *n.* a person who studies history. **historic** (hiˈstorik) *adj.* having important connections with the past. **hisˈtorical** *adj.* concerning history. —**hisˈtorically** *adv.*

hit (hit) *vb.* **hitting, hit.** 1. to strike or knock against: *he hit his head on the ceiling.* 2. to achieve (a desired target): *he hit the jackpot.* 3. to affect badly: *the manager's illness hit the business hard.* —*n.* 1. a blow or stroke, esp. one that reaches its target: *she scored three hits.* 2. (informal) popular success: *the song was a hit.*

hitch (hich) *vb.* 1. to move or pull something with a jerk: *he hitched his trousers up.* 2. to tie up or fasten: *she hitched the horse to the rail.* —*n.* 1. a knot that can be quickly tied and untied: *a clove hitch.* 2. a delay. 3. a jerking movement.

hitchhike (ˈhichhīk) *vb.* **hitchhiking, hitchhiked.** to travel by walking along roads and taking free rides offered by the drivers of passing vehicles.

hive (hīv) *n.* 1. a special box in which bees live and store their honey. 2. a busy scene: *a hive of activity.*

hoard (hôd) *vb.* to collect and store, esp. in a secret place: *the squirrel hoarded nuts.* —*n.* a hidden store (of food, money, etc.).

hoarding (ˈhôding) *n.* a large board in a public place on which advertising posters are displayed.

hoarse (hôs) *adj.* (of a voice, speech) husky; not clear. —ˈ**hoarsely** *adv.* —ˈ**hoarseness** *n.*

hoax (hōks) *n.* a trick or practical joke involving a trick. —*vb.* to play a practical joke on (someone).

hobby (ˈhobi) *n.,pl.* **hobbies.** a favourite leisure-time activity: *Jack's hobby is stamp-collecting.*

hobbyhorse (ˈhobihôs) *n.* a toy made of a wooden horse's head stuck on a pole.

hockey (ˈhoki) *n.* a game played on a field by two teams of eleven players each. Sticks with curved ends are used to hit a small hard ball into the opposing team's goal. **ice hockey** a similar game played on ice by teams of six players with a rubber disc (puck).

hoe (hō) *n.* a TOOL used for breaking up large lumps of soil. It consists of a blade attached to a long handle. —*vb.* **hoeing, hoed.** to use a hoe.

hog (hog) *n.* 1. a pig. 2. (informal) a greedy person. **go the whole hog** to carry an action to its limit. —*vb.* **hogging, hogged.** to eat, consume, use, or take greedily.

hoist (hoist) *vb.* to pull up (a flag, sail, etc.), esp. by means of ropes and pulleys: *the sailors hoisted the mainsail.* —*n.* a device for lifting heavy goods.

hold (hōld) *vb.* **holding, held.** 1. to grasp and keep a grip on something: *he held a pipe between his teeth.* 2. to keep in place or give support to: *this pillar holds the whole building up.* 3. to have or keep in one's possession or control: *they held the fort against many attacks.* 4. to contain or be able to contain: *this box holds all my marbles.* 5. to have (an opinion): *I hold that the earth is flat.* 6. (+ *back*) to stop (someone) from doing something. 8. (+ *up*) to stop a person, vehicle, etc., with the intention of stealing: *the robbers held up a lorry.* 9. (+ *up*) to delay or stop. **hold by** to follow, stick to, retain (an opinion): *I hold by your decision.* **hold forth** to make a long speech. **hold on** *or* **out** to endure; stay in position: *they held out despite many attacks.* **hold with** to agree with: *I do not hold with his new ideas.* —*n.* 1. a grasp: *he had a firm hold on the rope.* 2. an influence over

hobbyhorse

honeycomb

someone: *she has a hold over him.* 3. storage space for goods below the deck of a ship. '**hold-up** *n.* 1. an armed robbery. 2. a delay.

hole (hōl) *n.* 1. a space, gap, or hollow. 2. an awkward or difficult situation: *having lost my money, I was in a nasty hole.* —*vb.* **holing, holed.** 1. to make a hole in (something): *he holed his trousers on the fence.* 2. (golf) to hit the ball into the hole: *he holed in one shot.*

holiday ('holidā) *n.* often '**holidays** (*pl.*) a time in which one does not have to work, go to school, etc.

hollow ('holō) *n.* a space or groove in a solid object. —*adj.* 1. empty or with the centre scooped out: *a hollow tree trunk.* 2. sunken: *his eyes were hollow.* —*vb.* to make a hollow; scoop out.

holly ('holi) *n.,pl.* **hollies.** a small tree with dark green, prickly leaves and red berries, used for decoration at Christmas.

holy ('hōli) *adj.* **holier, holiest.** 1. having special religious importance. 2. deeply religious: *St. Peter was a holy man.* '**holiness** *n.* the quality of being holy.

home (hōm) *n.* 1. the place where one lives. 2. the place where one was born and bred. 3. any place where people or animals are looked after: *a home for the aged.* —*adj.* 1. connected with one's home: *what is your home address?* 2. not foreign: *we found a home market for our goods.* —*adv.* 1. to or towards one's home: *he came home late.* 2. strongly touching one's feelings: *the photograph brought John's death home.* —*vb.* **homing, homed.** to move naturally towards one's home. '**homesick** *adj.* wishing one were at home. —'**homeless** *adj.*

honest ('onist) *adj.* trustworthy; not likely to cheat or tell lies. —'**honestly** *adv.* —'**honesty** *n.*

honey ('huni) *n.* 1. yellow, sweet, sticky, edible syrup made by bees from the NECTAR inside flowers. 2. a much loved person or thing.

honeycomb ('hunikōm) *n.* the mass of six-sided cells made of wax in which bees store honey.

honeymoon ('hunimōōn) *n.* the holiday that the bride and groom traditionally take directly after their wedding. —*vb.* to spend a honeymoon.

honeysuckle ('hunisukəl) *n.* a climbing plant with delicate sweet-smelling yellow, pink, and red flowers.

honour ('onə) *n.* 1. a strict standard of morals and behaviour. 2. title, privilege, award, etc., given as a mark of respect. —*vb.* to express respect for (someone): *they honoured her for her medical work.* '**honourable** *adj.* having the quality of honour. —'**honourably** *adv.*

hood (hōōd) *n.* 1. a piece of clothing that covers the head and neck. It is often attached to a coat. 2. the folding roof of an open motorcar.

hoof (hōōf) *n.,pl.* **hooves.** the hard natural covering on the foot of certain animals, e.g. cows, horses, etc.

hook (hōōk) *n.* 1. a curved piece of wood, metal, etc. for hanging or catching something: *a coat hook.* 2. a bent wire, usu. with a barb, for catching fish. 3. (sport) a short, swinging blow with the arm bent. —*vb.* 1. to curve into a hook; bend. 2. to catch (a fish). 3. to fasten or attach: *this dress hooks up at the back.*

hooligan ('hōōligən) *n.* a member of a rough gang.

hoop (hōōp) *n.* a large circular band of metal, wood, etc.

hoot (hōōt) *n.* the cry of an owl, or a similar deep, hollow noise. —*vb.* 1. to make a noise like an owl's hoot. 2. to sound a motorcar horn.

hop[1] (hop) *vb.* **hopping, hopped.** 1. to jump on one foot. 2. (of animals) to jump on two legs at once. —*n.* 1. a short jump. 2. an unbroken journey or stage of a journey: *she flew from Rome to Oslo in one hop.*

hop

hop[2] (hop) *n.* a climbing plant that produces green cone-shaped flowers used in brewing beer.

hope (hōp) *vb.* **hoping, hoped.** 1. to wish for or desire. 2. to expect. —*n.* 1. a wish or desire. 2. something that one trusts will happen: *he has a hope of winning.* 3. a person or thing trusted or relied on by others. —'**hopeful** *adj.* —'**hopefully** *adv.* —'**hopefulness** *n.* —'**hopeless** *adj.* —'**hopelessly** *adv.* —'**hopelessness** *n.*

horde (hôd) *n.* a very large crowd

horizon (hə'rīzən) *n.* the line at which the sky and the ground or sea seem to meet. **horizontal** (hori'zontəl) *adj.* 1. parallel to the horizon. 2. level.

horn (hôn) *n.* 1. a bony, pointed growth on the head of a cow, goat, etc. 2. the substance of which horns are made, often used to make other objects: *the knives have handles of horn.* 3. a type of brass musical instrument: *French horn.* '**horny** *adj.* **hornier, horniest.** hard like horn.

hornet ('hônit) *n.* a large type of wasp with a powerful sting.

horror ('horə) *n.* 1. a feeling of terror or disgust: *I was filled with horror.* 2. something that causes fear, disgust, etc.: *the horrors of war.* '**horrible** *adj.* 1. shocking; causing fear: *a horrible crime.* 2. very unpleasant: *a horrible smell.* '**horrid** *adj.* 1. disgusting; repulsive. 2. mean; nasty. '**horrify** *vb.* **horrifying, horrified.** to disgust; cause shock or fear. —'**horribly** *adv.*

horse (hôs) *n.* 1. a large four-legged animal, used for riding, carrying goods, pulling carts, etc. 2. a large wooden box with a padded top used in gymnastics.

hose[1] (hōz) *n.* stockings; socks.

hose[2] (hōz) *n.* a long easily bent tube through which water is passed for watering gardens, putting out fires, etc. —*vb.* **hosing, hosed.** to spray with water from a hose.

hospitable (ho'spitəbəl) *adj.* offering a friendly welcome to visitors and treating them well. —**hos'pitably** *adv.*

hospital ('hospitəl) *n.* a place in which people who are ill can be cared for by doctors, surgeons, nurses, etc.

hospitality (hospi'taliti) *n.* friendly and generous treatment of guests, esp. in one's home.

host[1] (hōst) *n.* 1. a man who receives guests. 2. a plant or animal on which another plant or animal, a PARASITE, depends for its existence. **'hostess** *n.* 1. a female who receives guests. 2. a woman who looks after the passengers in an aeroplane.

host[2] (hōst) *n.* a large number of people or things gathered together.

hostage ('hostij) *n.* a person who is kept as a prisoner until the person holding him receives money or some other thing he wants.

hostel ('hostəl) *n.* 1. a building where students live. 2. a building where people with very little money can stay overnight: *a youth hostel.*

hostile ('hostīl) *adj.* 1. of or concerning an enemy: *the spy crossed into hostile territory.* 2. unfriendly: *he was hostile to new ideas.* **hostility** (ho'stiliti) *n.,pl.* **hostilities.** unfriendliness; hatred. 2. (*pl.*) acts of war.

hot (hot) *adj.* **hotter, hottest.** 1. having a high temperature; giving off, having, or feeling heat. 2. (of food) having a strong, burning taste. 3. (informal) dangerous or uncomfortable: *the stolen goods were too hot to handle.* 4. very recent; having just come from: *the news was hot off the press.* —*vb.* **hotting, hotted.** (+ *up*) 1. to become or make hotter. 2. to make more exciting. **'hotly** *adv.* angrily.

hotel (hō'tel) *n.* a building where travellers can sleep and eat.

hound (hound) *n.* a dog trained for hunting, esp. a foxhound. —*vb.* to chase or worry persistently: *the outcast was hounded from town to town.*

hovercraft

hour (ouə) *n.* 1. one of the twenty-four equal parts of a day; sixty minutes. 2. **hours** (*pl.*) a period of time, esp. regular working time: *her hours are from 9.00 till 5.00.* 3. any particular time: *the hero of the hour.* —**'hourly** *adj.,adv.*

house *n.* (hous), *pl.* **houses** ('houziz). 1. a building for people to live in. 2. the audience in a theatre. 3. the law-making assembly of a country, e.g. the House of Commons. 4. a family considered as ancestors and descendants: *the house of Tudor.* **keep house** to look after household affairs. —*vb.* (houz) **housing, housed.** 1. to provide with a house or shelter. 2. to act as a house for: *the old kettle housed the robin very well.*

household ('houshōld) *n.* all the people who live in one house.

housewife ('houswīf) *n.,pl.* **housewives.** a married woman who looks after her house and family.

hover ('hovə) *vb.* 1. to stay suspended in the air above one place. 2. to linger around close by.

hovercraft ('hovəkrâft) *n.* a vehicle that moves at high speed on a cushion of air just above the surface of the ground or water.

howl (houl) *vb.* to make a long, wailing sound: *wolves howl.* —*n.* a prolonged wailing cry. **'howler** *n.* (slang) a stupid blunder.

hub (hub) *n.* 1. the solid middle part of a wheel where it is joined to the AXLE. 2. main point of activity, interest, etc.: *Rome was the hub of a great empire.*

huddle ('hudəl) *vb.* **huddling, huddled.** to gather together into a group, esp. for warmth or out of fear. —*n.* a closely packed group.

huge (hyōoj) *adj.* enormous; very large.

hull (hul) *n.* the body of a ship or boat including the sides and bottom, but excluding anything above the deck.

hum (hum) *vb.* **humming, hummed.** 1. to make a singing noise with the lips together. 2. to make a buzzing, vibrating noise: *bees hummed in the* *garden.* —*n.* any humming noise.

human ('hyōomən) *adj.* belonging to or concerning men and women. —*n.* a human being; a person. **humanity** (hyōo'maniti) *n.* 1. mankind; the human race. 2. kindness; the quality of being HUMANE. 3. human nature.

humane (hyōo'mān) *adj.* 1. kind; sympathetic. 2. minimizing the amount of pain to be suffered: *a quick death is more humane than a slow one.* —**hu'manely** *adv.*

humble ('humbəl) *adj.* 1. having a low opinion of oneself. 2. having a low or poor position. —*vb.* **humbling, humbled.** to make humble; humiliate. —**'humbly** *adv.*

humid ('hyōomid) *adj.* (esp. of the weather) damp. —**hu'midity** *n.*

humour ('hyōomə) *n.* 1. the quality in an action, writing, etc., that causes amusement. 2. a mood or temper: *he is in a good humour.* **sense of humour** the ability to laugh at life and oneself. —*vb.* to please (someone) by adapting to his mood or opinions: *he humoured his old uncle by agreeing with him.* —**'humorous** *adj.* —**'humorously** *adv.*

hump (hump) *n.* 1. a large rounded lump as on a camel's back. 2. a small rise in the ground.

hunch (hunch) *vb.* to curve or bend in: *he hunched his shoulders against the cold wind.* —*n.* (informal) a feeling or guess without proper logical basis: *I had a hunch that you would visit us today.*

hundredweight ('hundridwāt) *n.* (often written **cwt.**) 112 pounds in weight.

hung (hung) *vb.* the past tense of HANG.

hunger ('hunggə) *n.* 1. the uncomfortable or painful feeling caused by lack of food. 2. the strong desire for food or other much longed-for things. —*vb.* 1. to feel hungry. 2. to wish strongly for something. **'hungry** *adj.* **hungrier, hungriest.** 1. feeling hunger. 2. having a strong need or wish. —**'hungrily** *adv.*

hunt (hunt) *vb.* 1. to search carefully. 2. to chase and kill (wild animals) for food, sport, etc. 3. to drive off: *the rogue was hunted out of town.* —*n.* 1. a chase. 2. a careful search.

hurdle ('hûdəl) *n.* 1. a light fence that can be easily moved. 2. any obstacle that has to be surmounted before further progress can be made. —*vb.* **hurdling, hurdled.** (athletics) to run in a race in which hurdles are placed across the course (**hurdle race**).

hurl (hûl) *vb.* to throw or cause to be thrown violently or with great force.

hurricane ('hûrikən) *n.* an enormously strong wind, esp. one developing over the North Atlantic Ocean.

hurry ('huri) *vb.* **hurrying, hurried.** 1. to act or move with speed. 2. to act or urge to act hastily or without due thought: *she hurried them into a decision.* —*n.* 1. the need to hurry through eagerness, lack of time, etc. 2. unnecessary speed of action: *what is the hurry?* —**'hurriedly** *adv.*

hurt (hût) *vb.* **hurting, hurt.** 1. to injure; cause mental or physical pain or distress. 2. to feel sore or painful.

husband ('huzbənd) *n.* a man who has a wife. —*vb.* to save, esp. by using carefully: *we husbanded our water in the desert.*

hush (hush) *vb.* 1. to make quiet; calm. 2. (+ *up*) to prevent (something) from becoming known. —*n.* stillness.

husk (husk) *n.* the dry protective covering of a seed. —*vb.* to remove husks from (seeds).

husky[1] ('huski) *adj.* **huskier, huskiest.** 1. (of a voice) deep and rough, esp. because of a dry throat. 2. (of a man) big and strong. —**'huskiness** *n.*

husky[2] ('huski) *n.,pl.* **huskies.** a strong dog with a thick coat, used by Eskimos to draw sledges.

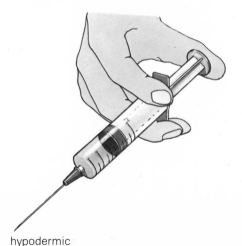
hypodermic

hustle ('husəl) *vb.* **hustling, hustled.** to push along roughly.

hutch (huch) *n.* a box with wire netting on one or more sides, used esp. for housing small animals, e.g. rabbits.

hyacinth ('hīəsinth) *n.* a plant that grows thick clusters of small sweet-smelling flowers. Hyacinths grow from bulbs.

hydrogen ('hīdrəjən) *n.* a gas that has no taste, smell, or colour. It combines with OXYGEN to form water. Chemical symbol: H.

hyena

hyena (hī'ēnə) *n.* a flesh-eating dog-like animal with very powerful jaws and large shoulders. Hyenas live in Africa and Asia.

hygiene ('hījēn) *n.* actions that must be carried out to encourage good health and prevent disease. —**hy'gienic** *adj.* —**hy'gienically** *adv.*

hymn (him) *n.* a song of praise, esp. to God.

hyphen ('hīfən) *n.* the sign (–), used in compound words, e.g. multi-coloured, or for indicating that a word has been split up at the end of a line.

hypnotize ('hipnətīz) *vb.* **hypnotizing, hypnotized.** to cause (someone) to fall into a state like a deep sleep in which his actions are controlled by the person who has hypnotized him. **hypnotic** (hip'notik) *adj.* causing a sleep-like state. **'hypnotist** *n.* a person who hypnotizes another. —**hyp'notically** *adv.*

hypodermic (hīpə'dûmik) *n.* an instrument used by doctors and nurses to give injections below the surface of the skin.

I

ice (īs) *n.* frozen water. —*vb.* **icing, iced. 1.** to keep or make (something) cold by adding ice: *she iced the drinks.* **2.** to cover (a cake) with a sugary coating (**icing**). **3.** (often + *up* or *over*) to become coated with ice: *the lake iced up.* **break the ice** to do or say something that puts people at ease. **'icy** *adj.* **icier, iciest. 1.** covered with ice. **2.** as cold as ice. —**'icily** *adv.* —**'iciness** *n.*

iceberg ('īsbûg) *n.* a huge mass of ice, broken off a GLACIER or ice sheet. It floats in the sea and is a danger to ships.

iceberg

icicle ('īsikəl) *n.* a thin stick of ice formed by water that has frozen while dripping.

idea (ī'diə) *n.* a thought; a plan or picture formed in the mind.

ideal (ī'diəl) *adj.* perfect; completely suitable: *the flat was ideal for two people.* —*n.* an idea, situation, person, etc., regarded as perfect or the best possible. **i'dealism** *n.* the pursuit of noble or excellent aims or standards. **i'dealist** *n.* a person who pursues or values such aims. —**ideal'istic** *adj.* —**i'deally** *adv.*

identical (ī'dentikəl) *adj.* the same in all respects: *the police stopped him, as his car was identical with the stolen one.* —**i'dentically** *adv.*

identify (ī'dentifī) *vb.* **identifying, identified. 1.** to recognize and give a name to (a specific person or thing): *he could identify the lost puppy.* **2.** (+ with) to sympathize with or join: *she identifies with the prisoners.* **3.** to mark: *the badge identifies a member of our club.* —**identifi'cation** *n.*

identity (ī'dentiti) *n.,pl.* **identities. 1.** exactly who somebody is or what something is: *the identity of the masked man is not known.* **2.** complete sameness or likeness: *the identity of the twins causes confusion.*

idiom ('idiəm) *n.* **1.** a phrase whose meaning is difficult to tell from the meanings of the words in it. For example, *to let the cat out of the bag* is an idiom meaning to tell a secret. **2.** a particular style of language: *Shakespeare's idiom.* —**idio'matic** *adj.* —**idio'matically** *adv.*

idiot ('idiət) *n.* **1.** a person who is lacking in mental abilities, usu. from birth. **2.** someone who behaves in a foolish manner: *he was an idiot to buy that old car.* —**'idiocy** *n.* —**idiotically** (idi'otikli) *adv.*

idle ('īdəl) *adj.* **idler, idlest. 1.** not working or being used; unemployed: *the machines lay idle.* **2.** lazy. **3.** worthless: *idle chatter.* —*vb.* **idling, idled. 1.** to spend time being idle: *she idled away the afternoon.* **2.** (of an engine) to be running without driving the machinery. —**'idleness** *n.* —**'idly** *adv.*

idol ('īdəl) *n.* **1.** an image of a god used in worship. **2.** a person (esp. an entertainer) who is greatly admired: *a film idol.* **idolatry** (ī'dolətri) *n.* the practice of worshipping images. **'idolize** *vb.* **idolizing, idolized.** to worship idols.

idyll ('idil) *n.* a short description, esp. in poetry, of a country scene. **i'dyllic** *adj.* simple and pleasant.

igloo ('iglōō) *n.,pl.* **igloos.** a dome-shaped Eskimo house made out of blocks of hard-packed snow or ice.

ignite (ig'nīt) *vb.* **igniting, ignited. 1.** to burst into flames: *the petrol ignited as the cigarette fell into it.* **2.** to cause (something) to explode or begin to burn, usu. by using a spark. **ignition** (ig'nishən) *n.* **1.** an instance of igniting. **2.** the electrical system in a car engine, rocket, etc.

ignorant ('ignərənt) *adj.* **1.** generally ill-informed; not knowledgeable. **2.** not aware of a particular fact or facts: *we are ignorant of the cause of the disaster.* —**'ignorantly** *adv.*

ignore (ig'nô) *vb.* **ignoring, ignored.** to pay no attention to (someone or something): *she ignored her mother's advice.*

ill (il) *adj.* physically or mentally unwell. **ill at ease** nervous or anxious. **'illness** *n.* sickness; disease.

illegal (i'lēgəl) *adj.* not allowed by the law: *it is illegal to park here.* **ille'gality** *n.,pl.* **illegalities.** something that is illegal. —**il'legally** *adv.*

illegible (i'lejibəl) *adj.* unable to be read: *illegible handwriting.*

illuminate (i'lōōmināt) *vb.* **illuminating, illuminated. 1.** to cast light on (something); light up: *the lamp illuminates the room.* **2.** to explain something clearly: *he illuminated the meaning of the play.* **illumi'nation** *n.*

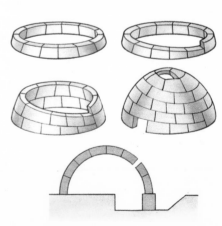

igloo

1. light 2. **illuminations** (*pl.*) an ornamental display of lights: *the fun-fair illuminations.*

illusion (i'loozhən) *n.* a false idea, esp. one based on something one has perceived through the senses: *the water in the desert was an illusion.* Although line b looks longer than line a, that is an optical illusion.

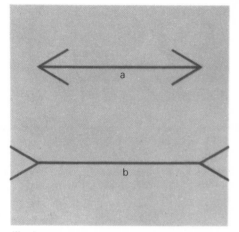
illusion

illustrate ('iləstrāt) *vb.* **illustrating, illustrated.** 1. to provide (a book) with pictures. 2. to explain with the help of pictures. **'illustrator** *n.* a person who draws pictures for a book. —**illus'tration** *n.*

image ('imij) *n.* 1. a mental picture: *the poem gave a gloomy image of city life.* 2. a statue or painting of a god or saint for worship. 3. a symbol: *the moon is an image of changeability.* 4. the aspect of personality presented to other people: *he had a bad public image.*

imagine (i'majin) *vb.* **imagining, imagined.** 1. to make or have a mental picture of: *I can imagine how sad you feel.* 2. to suppose: *I imagine it will be all right.* 3. to invent. **im'aginable** *adj.* able to be imagined. **im'aginary** *adj.* having no existence outside the mind; not real. **imagi'nation** *n.* 1. the mind's power to invent and picture things, esp. in artistic and poetic matters. 2. fanciful invention. **im'aginative** *adj.* 1. having or resulting from a strong mental creative ability. 2. given to daydreaming. —**im'aginatively** *adv.* —**im'aginativeness** *n.*

imitate ('imitāt) *vb.* **imitating, imitated.** 1. to try to behave or appear like someone or something else; MIMIC. 2. to make a close copy of (something). —**imi'tation** *n.*

immaculate (i'makyoolit) *adj.* without spot or stain; clean and tidy: *he was wearing an immaculate suit for the interview.* —**im'maculately** *adv.* —**im'maculateness** *n.*

immature (imə'tyooə) *adj.* youthful; not fully developed: *his behaviour is very immature.* —**imma'turity** *n.*

immediate (i'mēdiit) *adj.* 1. happening without delay: *an immediate answer.* 2. concerning the present time: *our immediate course of action.* 3. next or nearest: *my immediate neighbour.* 4. direct: *the immediate cause of the trouble.* —**im'mediacy** *n.* —**im'mediately** *adv.*

immense (i'mens) *adj.* very large; not easily measurable: *the Sahara is an immense desert.* —**im'mensely** *adv.* —**im'mensity** *n.*

immerse (i'mûs) *vb.* **immersing, immersed.** 1. to dip under the surface of a liquid: *she immersed her hands in water.* 2. to involve deeply; absorb: *I immersed myself in the travel book.* —**im'mersion** *n.*

immigrate ('imigrāt) *vb.* **immigrating, immigrated.** to come into a country where one was not born in order to settle there permanently. —**'immigrant** *n.* —**immi'gration** *n.*

immobile (i'mōbīl) *adj.* not moving or incapable of movement: *the car stood immobile through lack of petrol.* **im'mobilize** *vb.* **immobilizing, immobilized.** to make incapable of moving or of being moved. —**immo'bility** *n.* —**immobili'zation** *n.*

immoral (i'morəl) *adj.* contrary to what are considered the proper standards of personal and social behaviour. —**immo'rality** *n.*

immortal (i'môtəl) *adj.* 1. not having to suffer death. 2. remembered or admired for all time: *the immortal plays of Shakespeare.* —*n.* 1. a being that will always exist. 2. a person of enduring fame. —**immor'tality** *n.* —**im'mortally** *adv.*

immune (i'myoōn) *adj.* 1. protected from a disease (often by VACCINATION or INOCULATION). 2. not affected by peoples' remarks, etc., or by any other outside influence: *he was immune to all criticism.* **immunize** ('imyooniz) *vb.* **immunizing, immunized.** to protect from disease: *we were immunized against measles.* —**im'munity** *n.,pl.* **immunities.**

imp (imp) *n.* 1. a little devil or wicked spirit. 2. (informal) a mischievous child. —**'impish** *adj.*

impact ('impakt) *n.* 1. the blow of a body in motion striking another; collision: *the car hit the wall with a tremendous impact.* 2. an influence: *the impact of new ideas changed their lives.*

impartial (im'pâshəl) *adj.* without showing favour to one side or another; just: *he was an impartial judge.* —**impartiality** (impâshi'aliti) *n.* —**im'partially** *adv.*

impatient (im'pāshənt) *adj.* 1. showing lack of patience; unable to wait, listen, etc., calmly. 2. (+ *of*) intolerant: *impatient of new ideas.* 3. (+ *for*) restlessly eager: *she was impatient for adventure.* —**im'patience** *n.* —**im'patiently** *adv.*

impede (im'pēd) *vb.* **impeding, impeded.** to obstruct or hinder: *their progress was impeded by thick jungle.*

impediment (im'pedəmənt) *n.* 1. an obstacle or hindrance. 2. a physical defect, esp. a disorder preventing ease in speaking: *a speech impediment made him shy.*

imperative (im'perətiv) *adj.* 1. urgently necessary: *it is imperative that the message reaches them today.* 2. commanding: *the officer in charge addressed his troops in imperative tones.* —**im'peratively** *adv.*

imperfect (im'pûfikt) *adj.* having faults or defects: *imperfect eyesight can be helped by wearing glasses.* **imperfect tense** (in grammar) the past tense denoting action going on but not completed, e.g. *he was walking.* —**imper'fection** *n.* —**im'perfectly** *adv.*

imperial (im'piəriəl) *adj.* of, like, or relating to an empire, emperor, or empress: *the imperial throne.* **im'perialism** *n.* the policy of extending the rule of an empire or nation over other countries. **im'perialist** *n.* a person who believes in and supports imperialism.

impersonal (im'pûsənəl) *adj.* 1. not connected with any individual person: *as an outsider, I can give an impersonal opinion.* 2. having little or no concern for individual feelings: *an impersonal government department.* —**imperson'ality** *n.* —**im'personally** *adv.*

impersonate (im'pûsənāt) *vb.* **impersonating, impersonated.** to pretend to be (some other person) by assuming his character, appearance, or manner: *he escaped from prison by impersonating one of the guards.* —**imperson'ation** *n.*

impertinent (im'pûtinənt) *adj.* 1. rude; impudent: *his impertinent remarks annoyed me.* 2. not relating to the matter in hand; irrelevant: *impertinent details.* —**im'pertinence** *n.* —**im'pertinently** *adv.*

impetuous (im'petyŏŏəs) *adj.* acting rashly; over-eager; impulsive: *he regretted his impetuous remarks when he saw that he had upset his friends.* —**impetu'osity** *n.* —**im'petuously** *adv.*

imply (im'plī) *vb.* **implying, implied.** 1. to suggest without directly stating; hint: *he implied that I was lying.* 2. to involve necessarily: *a competition implies competitors.* —**impli'cation** *n.*

import *vb.* (im'pôt) to bring (something) into a country from somewhere else. —*n.* ('impôt) 1. often **imports** (*pl.*) goods imported from another country. 2. the meaning or significance of something: *the import of her words troubled me.*

important (im'pôtənt) *adj.* 1. of great significance, effect, etc.: *she wrote an important book on the subject.* 2. of great authority: *an important official.* —**im'portance** *n.* —**im'portantly** *adv.*

impossible (im'posibəl) *adj.* 1. not possible; not capable of existing, being done, or being true. 2. hopelessly unsuitable or objectionable: *an impossible person.* —**impossi'bility** *n.* —**im'possibly** *adv.*

impostor (im'postə) *n.* someone who deceives by pretending to be someone else.

impress (im'pres) *vb.* **impressing, impressed.** 1. to produce a deep effect (esp. on the mind or feelings): *his knowledge will impress you.* 2. to mark by pressure: *I impress the design in the soft wax.* **im'pression** *n.* 1. a strong effect produced on the mind. 2. the immediate effect left in the mind by a person, experience, etc.: *my impression of him was unfavourable.* 3. a vague, uncertain memory. 4. a mark produced by pressure: *there was a clear impression of a foot in the sand.* **im'pressionable** *adj.* easily influenced. **im'pressive** *adj.* capable of producing a deep effect: *an impressive speech.* —**im'pressively** *adv.*

imprint *n.* ('imprint) a mark made by pressure: *the imprint of a hoof in the mud.* —*vb.* (im'print) 1. to make a mark on (something) by pressure; stamp. 2. to fix in the mind.

impromptu (im'promptyŏŏ) *adj.* done without preparation; improvised: *an impromptu speech.*

improve (im'prŏŏv) *vb.* **improving, improved.** to make or become better in quality. **improve upon** to produce something better than: *I can't improve upon that.* —**im'provement** *n.*

improvise ('imprəvīz) *vb.* **improvising, improvised.** 1. to speak or perform without previous preparation: *she improvised a tune on the violin.* 2. to make (a substitute for something) from materials available: *they improvised a sail for their boat from an old sack.* —**improvi'sation** *n.*

impudent ('impyŏŏdənt) *adj.* disrespectful; rude. —**'impudence** *n.* —**'impudently** *adv.*

impulse ('impuls) *n.* 1. a force acting on the mind or body, causing a particular result: *he spoke bitterly under the impulse of disappointment.* 2. a sudden inclination to do something: *I had an impulse to hit him.* 3. a single movement of electrical current in one direction. —**im'pulsive** *adj.*

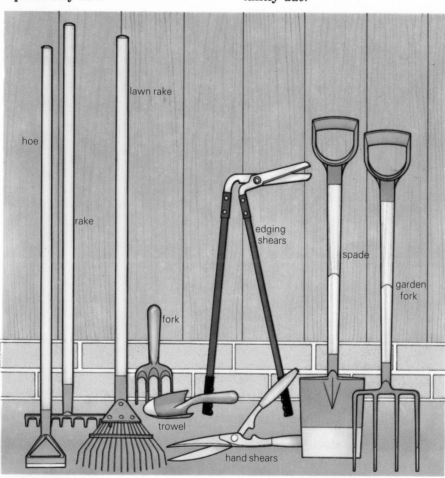

implements

implement *n.* ('implimənt) a tool, utensil, or instrument: *agricultural implements.* —*vb.* ('impliment) to fulfil or perform: *his plans were soon implemented.* —**implemen'tation** *n.*

implore (im'plô) *vb.* **imploring, implored.** to ask earnestly; entreat: *they implored him to have mercy.*

impose (im'pōz) *vb.* **imposing, imposed.** 1. to put upon by authority or force: *I shall impose severe penalties.* 2. (+ *upon* or *on*) to take unfair advantage of (patience, kindness, etc.): *he imposed upon our friendship.* **im'posing** *adj.* making a strong impression on the mind. —**imposition** (impə'zishən) *n.*

inaugurate (i'nôgyŏŏrāt) *vb.* **inaugurating, inaugurated.** 1. to begin or open in a formal manner: *the Queen inaugurated the conference.* 2. to install (a person) in office with formal ceremony: *we shall inaugurate the new president today.* —**in'augural** *adj.* —**inaugu'ration** *n.*

incense[1] ('insens) *n.* a substance that is burned to produce sweet-smelling fumes, esp. during religious ceremonies.

incense[2] (in'sens) *vb.* **incensing, incensed.** to inflame with anger; enrage: *your carelessness incenses people.*

incentive (in'sentiv) *n.* something that provides a strong reason for action; motive: *money and power were the incentives that kept him working.*

incessant (in'sesənt) *adj.* going on without interruption; continual: *I could not study because of their incessant chattering.* —**in'cessantly** *adv.*

inch (inch) *n.* a measure of length. There are twelve inches in one foot.

incident ('insidənt) *n.* 1. an occurrence, esp. something of minor importance that happens in connection with something else: *various incidents caused delays on the journey.* 2. an event involving hostility: *an international incident that could lead to war.* **inci'dental** *adj.* happening in connection with something else but of less importance: *the fact we had met was incidental.* —**inci'dentally** *adv.*

incite (in'sīt) *vb.* **inciting, incited.** to urge (someone on to do something): *he incited them to refuse to work.* —**in'citement** *n.*

incline *vb.* (in'klīn) **inclining, inclined.** 1. to have a preference for; be disposed: *I incline to the belief that he is lying.* 2. to lean or slant: *the road inclines steeply upward.* —*n.* ('inklīn) a slope: *the horses struggled up the incline.* —**incli'nation** *n.*

include (in'klōōd) *vb.* **including, included.** to take in as part of something: *he was included in the team to play cricket on Sunday.* —**in'clusion** *n.* —**in'clusive** *adj.*

income ('inkum) *n.* the financial gain that comes from work, business, investment, etc. **income tax** a government tax on a person's annual income.

incorporate (in'kôpərāt) *vb.* **incorporating, incorporated.** 1. to combine in one body or mass: *flour, water, and yeast are incorporated in the dough.* 2. to contain as a part: *the book incorporates some very good ideas.* —**incorpo'ration** *n.*

increase *vb.* (in'krēs) **increasing, increased.** to make or become greater in size: *the tree's height increased with age.* —*n.* ('inkrēs) 1. growth. 2. the amount by which something grows. —**in'creasingly** *adv.*

incredible (in'kredəbəl) *adj.* 1. impossible to believe. 2. (informal) very surprising. —**in'credibly** *adv.*

incriminate (in'krimənāt) *vb.* **incriminating, incriminated.** to say or suggest that (someone) is guilty of wrongdoing: *the evidence incriminates the entire class.*

incubate ('inkyŏŏbāt) *vb.* **incubating, incubated.** to keep at the right temperature for aiding development, esp. in hatching eggs. **'incubator** *n.* an apparatus in which a steady temperature is maintained for hatching eggs, for rearing weak babies, etc. —**incu'bation** *n.*

indefinite (in'defənit) *adj.* not fixed or certain; vague: *she said that she would be away for an indefinite length of time.* —**in'definitely** *adv.*

indelible (in'deləbəl) *adj.* unable to be removed or rubbed out: *indelible stains.* —**in'delibly** *adv.*

independent (indi'pendənt) *adj.* 1. not relying on or influenced by others. 2. not subject to another's authority: *an independent state.* —*n.* (politics) a person who acts and votes without being a member of any party. —**inde'pendence** *n.* —**inde'pendently** *adv.*

index ('indeks) *n., pl.* **indexes** (or, esp. for def. 4., **indices** ('indisēz)). 1. an alphabetical list of things in a book, showing the numbers of the pages on which they are mentioned. 2. anything that gives a sign or indication. 3. a pointer or hand on an instrument, scale, etc. **index finger** the finger nearest the thumb on either hand.

indicate ('indikāt) *vb.* **indicating, indicated.** 1. to point out: *he indicated the road we should follow.* 2. to show or be a sign of: *their smiles indicated friendliness.* **'indicator** *n.* a flashing light on a motor vehicle that shows which way it is going to turn. —**indi'cation** *n.*

indifferent (in'difərənt) *adj.* 1. not caring; unconcerned: *they were indifferent to my problems.* 2. undistinguished in quality: *he gave an indifferent performance at the concert last night.* —**in'difference** *n.* —**in'differently** *adv.*

indigestion (indi'jeschən) *n.* 1. difficulty in digesting food. 2. pain caused by this.

indignant (in'dignənt) *adj.* affected by mingled anger and scorn, usu. caused by something unjust or bad: *I was indignant at his accusations.* —**in'dignantly** *adv.* —**indig'nation** *n.*

indigo ('indigō) *n.* a dark blue dye obtained from the leaves of various plants. —*adj.* deep violet-blue in colour.

individual (indi'vidyŏŏəl) *adj.* 1. relating to, or provided for, one only: *each person had his individual place at table.* 2. unique or unusual: *she has some highly individual ideas.* —*n.* any single person, animal, plant, etc.: *he was an unpleasant individual.* —**individu'ality** *n.* —**indi'vidually** *adv.*

induce (in'dyōōs) *vb.* **inducing, induced.** 1. to persuade or influence (someone to do something): *they induced him to betray his friends.* 2. to cause: *the noise induced a headache.* —**in'ducement** *n.*

index finger

indulge (in'dulj) *vb.* **indulging, indulged.** 1. to yield to the wish or desires (of oneself or another person): *Mike's mother indulges him too much.* 2. (+ *in*) to enjoy freely: *I indulged in an enormous meal.* —**in'dulgence** *n.* —**in'dulgent** *adj.* —**in'dulgently** *adv.*

industry ('indəstri) *n., pl.* **industries.**
1. manufacture or trade in general. 2.
any particular branch of manufacture, trade, or business: *the steel industry.* 3. steady application to work: *they worked with great industry.* —**industrial** (in'dustriəl) *adj.*

ineffectual (ini'fektyo͞oəl) *adj.*
unsuccessful; futile: *his attempts to persuade us to go for a long walk were ineffectual.* —**ine'ffectually** *adv.*

inert (i'nût) *adj.* 1. without life or energy. 2. (chemistry) not likely to combine or react with another chemical. **inertia** (i'nûshə) *n.* state of being without energy. —**in'ertly** *adv.*

inevitable (in'evitəbəl) *adj.* unavoidable; certain to happen or come. —**inevita'bility** *n.* —**in'evitably** *adv.*

infamous ('infəməs) *adj.* of very bad reputation; famed for being evil: *an infamous murderer.* —**'infamously** *adv.* —**'infamy** *n.*

infant ('infənt) *n.* a baby or young child. —*adj.* very young. —**'infancy** *n.*

infantry ('infəntri) *n.* soldiers who normally fight on foot (not in tanks, aircraft, or ships).

infect (in'fekt) *vb.* 1. to pass a disease on to (someone else). 2. to influence (someone) in a bad way. —**in'fection** *n.* —**in'fectious** *adj.*

inferior (in'fiəriə) *adj.* 1. of lower quality. 2. lower in rank: *police constables are inferior to police sergeants.* —*n.* someone of lower rank. —**inferi'ority** *n.*

infiltrate ('infiltrāt) *vb.* **infiltrating, infiltrated.** 1. to pass or cause to pass into by filtering: *the poison infiltrated the water supply.* 2. to place agents secretly in a rival organization or amongst enemies. —**infil'tration** *n.*

infinite ('infinit) *adj.* without any limit or boundary.

infinitive (in'finitiv) *n.* the form of a verb not made particular as to subject or object, e.g. *to walk, to run.*

inflame (in'flām) *vb.* **inflaming, inflamed.** 1. to make (part of the body) hot, swollen, and painful. 2. to arouse (temper, passion, or desire). **inflammatory** (in'flamətəri) *adj.*

likely to arouse anger. **in'flammable** *adj.* likely or able to burn easily. —**inflam'mation** *n.*

inflate (in'flāt) *vb.* **inflating, inflated.** to fill (a balloon, tyre, etc.) with gas or air. **in'flation** *n.* 1. the act of inflating. 2. an increase in the usual price of goods and services, causing the cost of living to rise. —**in'flationary** *adj.*

inflict (in'flikt) *vb.* to cause (something unpleasant) to happen to another person: *the boys inflicted a beating on the bully.* —**in'fliction** *n.*

influence ('inflo͞oəns) *vb.* **influencing, influenced.** 1. to affect (decisions, actions, etc.). 2. to persuade or convince (somebody). —*n.* 1. the ability to affect people, objects, events, etc. 2. a force affecting the mind or feelings. —**influ'ential** *adj.*

influenza (inflo͞o'enzə) *n.* (often abbreviated to **flu**) a common and unpleasant disease, passed on from one person to another, and causing a high temperature, runny nose, sore throat, etc.

infantry

inform (in'fôm) *vb.* to pass facts on to (another person). **in'formant** *n.* a person who informs. **in'former** *n.* a person who passes on damaging facts to harm someone else. **infor'mation** *n.* the facts that are passed on. —**in'formative** *adj.*

informal (in'fôməl) *adj.* without ceremony: *he had an informal meeting with the mayor yesterday.* —**in'formally** *adv.*

infra-red (infrə'red) *adj.* (of light waves, etc.) too long to be seen by the human eye; found below red in the visible colour SPECTRUM.

infuriate (in'fyo͞oəriāt) *vb.* **infuriating, infuriated.** to arouse anger in (someone): *John's whining infuriates me.* —**infuri'ation** *n.*

ingenious (in'jēniəs) *adj.* 1. clever at inventing things, solving problems, etc. 2. cleverly made or designed: *ingenious plans.* —**in'geniously** *adv.* —**ingenuity** (inji'nyo͞oiti) *n.*

ingredient (in'grēdiənt) *n.* a substance that forms part of a mixture: *flour is an ingredient of bread.*

inhabit (in'habit) *vb.* to live in. —**in'habitant** *n.*

inherit (in'herit) *vb.* 1. to receive (money or goods) from the estate of someone who has died: *she inherited her mother's jewels.* 2. to have looks, skills, or habits in common with an ancestor: *he inherited his father's red hair.* —**in'heritance** *n.*

initial (i'nishəl) *n.* the first letter of a word, esp. of a name: *Howard Alec Jones has the initials H.A.J.* —*adj.* to do with the first stages of. —*vb.* **initialling, initialled.** to sign (a document) using only one's initials, not one's entire signature. —**in'itially** *adv.*

initiate (i'nishiāt) *vb.* **initiating, initiated.** 1. to begin; take the first steps in (a project or plan). 2. to instruct (someone) in the basic ideas of (a subject of study, secret society, etc.). —*n.* a beginner who has taken the first steps. —**initi'ation** *n.*

initiative (i'nishətiv) *n.* 1. the very first step in a new policy or action: *Alan took the initiative.* 2. the ability to begin things or make changes.

inject (in'jekt) *vb.* 1. to force (something) into (something else): *in some* *engines fuel is injected at high pressure.* 2. to push a liquid under someone's skin through a hollow needle. —**in'jection** *n.*

injure ('injə) *vb.* **injuring, injured.** 1. to damage (the body). 2. to do an injustice or cause other damage to (someone). —**injurious** (in'jōōəriəs) *adj.* —**in'juriously** *adv.* '**injury** *n.,pl.* **injuries.**

ink (iṅgk) *n.* a black or coloured liquid used for writing, drawing, or printing. —*vb.* to smear or cover with ink. —'**inky** *adj.* **inkier, inkiest.**

inmate ('inmāt) *n.* one who lives in an INSTITUTION or shares a lodging house: *when I was in hospital I played chess with the other inmates.*

innate (i'nāt) *adj.* inborn; natural: *some animals have an innate ability to swim.*

inner ('inə) *adj.* 1. inside; further in. 2. private; personal: *inner thoughts.*

innocent ('inəsənt) *adj.* 1. free from guilt or fault. 2. inexperienced; without cunning. —*n.* 1. a blameless person. 2. a simple person who does not suspect another's motives. —'**innocence** *n.* —'**innocently** *adv.*

innovate ('inəvāt) *vb.* **innovating, innovated.** to make changes by introducing a new idea or method. —**inno'vation** *n.*

inoculate (i'nokyōōlāt) *vb.* **inoculating, inoculated.** to inject a living, but weakened, disease-carrying VIRUS into (someone's body). The body's own defences learn how to kill the weak virus and can react against a strong virus for some time afterwards. —**inocu'lation** *n.*

inquest ('inkwest) *n.* a legal inquiry by a CORONER into the causes of a person's death.

inquire (in'kwīə) *vb.* **inquiring, inquired.** to ask questions about; look into or investigate. See also ENQUIRE. **in'quiry** *n.,pl.* **inquiries.** an investigation, esp. a public one. **inquisitive** (in'kwizitiv) *adj.* always asking questions, esp. about other people's business. —**in'quisitively** *adv.* —**in'quisitiveness** *n.*

inscribe (in'skrīb) *vb.* **inscribing, inscribed.** to write, mark, carve, or engrave words upon. —**inscription** (in'skripshən) *n.*

red ants

hornet

pond skater

swallowtail butterfly

insect ('insekt) *n.* any creature that has no backbone, a body in three parts (head, thorax, abdomen), and three pairs of jointed legs. **in'secticide** *n.* a chemical made to kill insects.

insert (in'sût) *vb.* 1. to put inside: *he inserted the coin into the drinks machine.* 2. to place something extra in or among: *the teacher inserted three words into my sentence.* —**in'sertion** *n.*

insight ('insīt) *n.* an understanding that goes deeper than normal: *my day at the farm gave me an insight into a farmer's life.*

insist (in'sist) *vb.* to demand urgently and firmly: *when my new iron broke, I insisted upon having my money back.* —**in'sistence** *n.* —**in'sistent** *adj.* —**in'sistently** *adv.*

insolent ('insələnt) *adj.* rude; disrespectful; insulting. —'**insolence** *n.* —'**insolently** *adv.*

insomnia (in'somniə) *n.* inability to sleep. **in'somniac** *n.* a person who frequently cannot sleep.

inspect (in'spekt) *vb.* to examine carefully, esp. looking for faults. **in'spector** *n.* 1. an official responsible for examining and checking. 2. a rank in the British police forces, next above sergeant. —**in'spection** *n.*

inspire (in'spīə) *vb.* **inspiring inspired.** to stir up noble or creative thoughts, feelings, or actions in someone: *the general's bravery inspired his soldiers.* —**inspiration** (inspi'rāshən) *n.*

install (in'stôl) *vb.* 1. to place or fix into position for use: *the plumber installed our new sink.* 2. to place (someone) ceremoniously in an official job or position. **installation** (instə'lāshən) *n.* 1. the act of installing. 2. something that has been installed: *a radar installation.*

instalment (in'stôlmənt) *n.* 1. an amount of money paid at intervals, esp. to pay off part of a larger debt or loan. 2. a single episode in a series or serial.

instance ('instəns) *n.* an example or particular case: *the soldier's rescue of his wounded friend was an instance of great courage.*

instant ('instənt) *n.* a brief or particular moment of time. —*adj.* 1. immediate. 2. urgent: *we were in instant need of help.* —'**instantly** *adv.*

instep ('instep) *n.* the arched top of the foot, between the ankle and toes.

instinct ('instiṅgkt) *n.* a tendency or ability to act in a certain way, that has not been, or cannot be, taught: *cats find their way home by instinct, even if they are taken miles away.* —**in'stinctive** *adj.* —**in'stinctively** *adv.*

113

institute ('instityoot) *vb.* **instituting, instituted.** to start (a process, system, etc.); establish (an organization). —*n.* an organization set up to study or promote a particular cause: *she works at the institute for medicine.*

institution (insti'tyooshən) *n.* 1. an organization, or its buildings, devoted to a public or social cause. 2. a long-standing custom. **insti'tutional** *adj.* 1. of institutions. 2. lacking in homely comforts or privacy.

instruct (in'strukt) *vb.* 1. to teach; train. 2. to inform. 3. to give orders. —**in'struction** *n.* —**in'structor** *n.*

instrument ('instrōomənt) *n.* 1. a tool or object used for doing work, esp. in science or medicine. 2. a device for making musical sounds. **instru'mental** *adj.* 1. serving as an instrument or means. 2. of musical instruments. —**instru'mentally** *adv.*

insulate ('insyōolāt) *vb.* **insulating, insulated.** to seal off; protect against heat, cold, electrical current, etc. '**insulator** *n.* a device, often made of glass, pottery, or plastic, which will hold a live electrical wire without passing its current to earth. —**insu'lation** *n.*

insult *vb.* (in'sult) to make hurtful or rude remarks to or about (someone). —*n.* ('insult) a hurtful or rude remark.

insurance (in'shōoərəns) *n.* arrangement to ensure that in the event of loss (damage, fire, death, etc.) another person or company will pay a sum of money as COMPENSATION. **in'sure** *vb.* **insuring, insured.** 1. to make a contract whereby COMPENSATION will be paid if property or life is lost or damaged. 2. to make or be safe against.

intact (in'takt) *adj.* whole; undamaged: *the car was intact after the accident.*

integrate ('intəgrāt) *vb.* **integrating, integrated.** 1. to make available to people of all races and social groups: *our sports club is integrated.* 2. to bring together into a whole. **inte'gration** *n.* act of making (schools, social facilities, etc.) available to all races.

integrity (in'tegriti) *n.* complete honesty.

intellect ('intəlekt) *n.* brains; clever-ness: *the new teacher was a person of great intellect.* **intel'lectual** *adj.* concerned with using the mind: *chess is an intellectual game. n.* a clever person who is good at using his or her brains. —**intel'lectually** *adv.*

intelligence (in'telijəns) *n.* 1. the ability to think quickly and adapt to new circumstances. 2. high intellectual ability. 3. news, esp. secret information of military importance. **in'telligent** *adj.* 1. able to think well. 2. (of plans, ideas, etc.) well thought out. —**in'telligently** *adv.*

intend (in'tend) *vb.* to mean; plan: *she intended to return early, but was delayed.*

intense (in'tens) *adj.* 1. extreme or very great: *intense heat.* 2. (of people) apt to feel or express emotions very strongly. **in'tensify** *vb.* **intensifying, intensified.** to make intense or more intense. **in'tensive** *adj.* 1. thorough: *an intensive medical check-up.* 2. concentrated on one particular point: *an intensive study.* —**in'tensely** *adv.* —**in'tensity** *n.* —**in'tensively** *adv.*

intent (in'tent) *adj.* (often + *or*) with the mind firmly fixed on something. —*n.* an aim or purpose.

intention (in'tenshən) *n.* a purpose or desire. **in'tentional** *adj.* done on purpose. —**in'tentionally** *adv.*

intercept (intə'sept) *vb.* to catch (someone or something) on the way to somewhere else. —**inter'ception** *n.*

interest ('intrest) *n.* 1. the desire to be involved with or know about something: *his interest was aroused by this incident.* 2. something that one is involved with: *though confined to a wheelchair he had plenty of interests.* 3. a private advantage, esp. a monetary one: *they put their own interest before the public good.* 4. a sum of money charged periodically by a lender in return for use of a sum of money lent or invested. —*vb.* to involve or be concerned.

interfere (intə'fiə) *vb.* **interfering, interfered.** 1. (of people) to meddle with. 2. to cause disturbance to (sound or radio waves): *passing traffic can interfere with radio reception.* —**inter'ference** *n.*

interim ('intərim) *n.* an interval. —*adj.* temporary: *he gave us an interim report while the full report was being prepared.*

interior (in'tiəriə) *adj.* inside; the further in of two. —*n.* 1. the inner part of something. 2. the home affairs or inland regions of a country.

interjection (intə'jekshən) *n.* 1. a remark put in while someone else is speaking: *interjections from the audience interrupted his speech.* 2. (grammar) a natural exclamation, e.g. *hey! phew!* etc. classified as a part of speech. **inter'ject** *vb.* to interrupt suddenly with an exclamation or remark.

interlude ('intəlood) *n.* 1. a happening, often amusing in character, that is not part of the main course of events. 2. an interval between two acts of a play, opera, etc.

intermediate (intə'mēdiit) *adj.* coming between two places, grades, or points in time; in between: *the Express does not stop at intermediate stations.*

intermission (intə'mishən) *n.* a brief pause or rest, esp. between two parts of a play.

internal (in'tûnəl) *adj.* 1. situated inside something else: *the internal organs of the body.* 2. concerning the inner part or workings of something: *this is an internal matter and does not concern outsiders.* 3. to do with the domestic affairs of a country: *internal politics.* —**in'ternally** *adv.*

international (intə'nashənəl) *adj.* 1. between nations: *the international telephone exchange.* 2. of many nations: *an international gathering.* —*n.* someone qualified to compete in sport at an international level. —**inter'nationally** *adv.*

interpret (in'tûprit) *vb.* 1. to translate the words of a speaker into a different language, sentence by sentence. 2. to explain, bring out, or understand the meaning of (a play, writings, dreams, etc.). **in'terpreter** *n.* someone who translates for a speaker. —**interpre'tation** *n.*

interrupt (intə'rupt) *vb.* 1. to break in while someone else is speaking. 2. to interfere with so as to stop (the flow of traffic, an electric current, etc.). —**inter'ruption** *n.*

intersect (intə'sekt) *vb.* (of roads, railways, etc., also of lines, surfaces, and solids) to cross or overlap one another. **inter'section** *n.* the point at which two lines cross.

interval ('intəvəl) *n.* a pause between two events, esp. the time between two acts at the theatre. **at intervals** from time to time.

intervene (intə'vēn) *vb.* **intervening, intervened.** to come between, esp. between two people who are quarrelling, with the aim of making peace. —**intervention** (intə'venshən) *n.*

interview ('intəvyōō) *n.* a pre-arranged formal meeting, esp. one to decide on someone's suitability for a job. —*vb.* to question (someone) at an interview.

intestine (in'testin) *n.* often **intestines** (*pl.*) the long twisty tubelike part of the body through which food is passed after it has been digested in the stomach, from which it is absorbed into the body. —**in'testinal** *adj.*

intimate ('intimət) *adj.* 1. very close and familiar: *intimate friends.* 2. private; personal: *an intimate diary.* —*n.* a close friend. —**'intimacy** *n.* —**'intimately** *adv.*

intricate ('intrikət) *adj.* 1. delicate and complicated: *an intricate design.* 2. difficult to understand: *an intricate plot.* —**'intricacy** *n.,pl.* **intricacies.** —**'intricately** *adv.*

intrigue *vb.* (in'trēg) **intriguing, intrigued.** 1. to plot: *the army intrigued against the government.* 2. to arouse the interest of: *the rumour intrigues me.* —*n.* (in'trēg, 'intrēg) a secret plan or business.

introduce (intrə'dyōōs) *vb.* **introducing, introduced.** 1. to start; bring into use or consideration. 2. to present (two people) to each other formally. —**introduction** (intrə'dukshən) *n.* —**intro'ductory** *adj.*

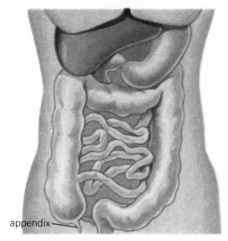

appendix—

intestine

intrude (in'trōōd) *vb.* **intruding, intruded.** to come into a place or another person's company uninvited. —**in'trusion** *n.*

invade (in'vād) *vb.* **invading, invaded.** 1. to enter and overrun (another country) with an army. 2. to intrude on (another person's privacy). —**in'vasion** *n.*

invalid[1] ('invəlid) *n.* a person in need of nursing because of illness or injury. —*vb.* to remove from active service because of sickness or injury: *he was invalided out of the army.* —*adj.* ill.

invalid[2] (in'valid) *adj.* not valid; with no legal value: *the cheque was invalid without his signature.*

invaluable (in'valyōōəbəl) *adj.* too valuable to be measured: *she was an invaluable help in organizing the jumble sale.*

invent (in'vent) *vb.* 1. to design (something new) or discover (a new way of doing something). 2. to make up (a plausible excuse, etc.). —**in'vention** *n.* —**in'ventive** *adj.* —**in'ventor** *n.*

invertebrate (in'vûtibrət) *n.* an animal with no backbone. —*adj.* having no backbone.

invest (in'vest) *vb.* (+ *in*) 1. to put money into the full or partial purchase of an interest in a company, product, work of art, etc., in the expectation of an increase in its value. 2. (informal) to buy: *I want to invest in a new coat.*

investigate (in'vestigāt) *vb.* **investigating, investigated.** to inquire carefully into (a problem, crime, etc.). —**investi'gation** *n.* —**in'vestigator** *n.*

invite (in'vīt) *vb.* **inviting, invited** 1. to ask (someone) formally to come to a meal, party, etc. 2. to cause or attract: *his strange new shoes invited teasing.* **in'viting** *adj.* attractive; tempting. —**invi'tation** *n.*

invoice ('invois) *n.* a bill; a list of goods sent and services rendered, with prices.

invertebrates

spider

jellyfish

earthworm

centipede

involve (in'volv) *vb.* **involving, involved.** 1. to include; entangle in (a mystery, a plot, etc.). 2. to make necessary; entail: *learning Arabic involves a great deal of hard work.* —**in'volvement** *n.*

iodine ('īədēn) *n.* 1. a chemical element found in seaweed. Chemical symbol: I. 2. a brown strong-smelling medicine used as an ANTISEPTIC.

ion ('īən) *n.* an electrically charged atom.

iris ('īris) *n.* 1. a plant that has long sword-shaped leaves and handsome flowers, usu. of purple, blue, yellow, or white. 2. the coloured circular part of the eye surrounding the PUPIL.

iris

iron ('īən) *n.* 1. the most common metallic chemical element. It is greyish white in colour. Chemical symbol: Fe. 2. an object made of iron. 3. a household device with a flat lower surface used to smooth clothes after they have been washed. **Iron Age** a stage in the development of man during which he learnt to make tools, weapons, and ornaments from iron. It occurred at different times in different parts of the world. —*adj.* 1. made of iron. 2. hard and not easily broken: *he has an iron will.*

Iron Curtain 1. the frontier set up by Russia and allied countries against the rest of the world, forming a barrier against free communications and trade. 2. any similar barrier.

irony ('īrəni) *n.,pl.* **ironies.** 1. saying the opposite of what one means, for the sake of emphasizing one's meaning. 2. the arrival of a hoped-for event too late or at a bad moment. —**ironic** (ī'ronik) *adj.* —**i'ronically** *adv.*

irrational (i'rashənəl) *adj.* not reasonable. **ir'rationally** *adv.*

irregular (i'regyŏolə) *adj.* 1. not regular or according to the usual standards; uneven. 2. (grammar) of word patterns not formed according to the usual rules. **irregulars** *pl.n.* troops who are not in regular service. —**irregu'larity** *n.,pl.* **irregularities.** —**ir'regularly** *adv.*

irrelevant (i'reləvənt) *adj.* pointless; not relating to the matter in hand: *he tried to prolong the meeting by asking irrelevant questions.* —**ir'relevance** *or* **ir'relevancy** *n.*

irresistible (iri'zistəbəl) *adj.* too strong to be resisted: *the cakes were an irresistible temptation to the hungry child.* —**irre'sistibly** *adv.*

irresponsible (iri'sponsibəl) *adj.* 1. (of behaviour) thoughtless; done without regard to the consequences. 2. (of people) not to be trusted; unreliable. —**irresponsi'bility** *n.*

irrigate ('irigāt) *vb.* **irrigating, irrigated.** to supply water to (fields and crops) by means of manmade channels, dams, etc. —**irri'gation** *n.*

irritate ('iritāt) *vb.* **irritating, irritated.** 1. to annoy. 2. to make (an itch or a sore place) worse. —**irritable** ('iritəbəl) *adj.* —**irri'tation** *n.*

island ('īlənd) *n.* any area of land entirely surrounded by water.

isle (īl) *n.* an island, esp. a small one (often used in the names of places): *the Isle of Wight.*

isolate ('īsəlāt) *vb.* **isolating, isolated.** to take or put (something) apart from other things; separate. **'isolated** *adj.* 1. far from other people. 2. single; unique: *an isolated case of measles.* —**iso'lation** *n.*

issue ('ishŏo) *vb.* **issuing, issued.** 1. to come out from; emerge. 2. to hand out; distribute. —*n.* 1. the act of giving or sending out: *the commander ordered an issue of food to his men.* 2. something sent or given out: *have you seen the new issue of the magazine?* 3. an outcome or result: *he did not know the issue of the discussion.*

isthmus ('isməs) *n.,pl.* **isthmuses.** a narrow piece of land with water on two sides that joins together two larger areas of land: *the Isthmus of Panama.*

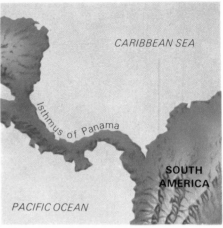

isthmus

italic (i'talik) *adj.* 1. of a style of printing type with sloping letters: *this sentence is printed in italic type.* 2. of a style of handwriting with narrow letters that slope to the right. **italics** *pl.n.* italic print or handwriting.

itch (ich) *n.* 1. a tickling feeling on the skin that makes one want to scratch. 2. a nagging desire: *I have an itch to visit India.* —*vb.* to have or feel an itch. —**'itchiness** *n.* —**'itchy** *adj.* **itchier, itchiest.**

item ('ītəm) *n.* 1. one article from a list, collection, etc.: *one item is missing.* 2. a short piece of information or news, esp. in a newspaper. **'itemize** *vb.* **itemizing, itemized.** to make a list of items.

ivory ('īvəri) *n.* 1. the hard white bony substance of elephants' and walruses' tusks, used for making ornaments and piano keys. 2. a pale cream colour.

ivy ('īvi) *n.,pl.* **ivies.** an evergreen plant with shiny, often star-shaped leaves that climbs up and covers walls, trees, etc.

ivy

J

jab (jab) *vb.* **jabbing, jabbed.** to thrust (something pointed) sharply into or at something else: *he jabbed the knife into the wood.* —*n.* 1. a quick thrust; poke. 2. (informal) an injection: *have you had a flu jab?*

jack (jak) *n.* 1. a tool or machine for raising cars or other heavy objects short distances. 2. **jacks** (*pl.*) a game in which small pieces of metal (**jacks**) are picked up while the player bounces a small rubber ball. 3. a playing card with the picture of a young man (knave) on it. —*vb.* (often + *up*) 1. to raise with a jack. 2. (informal) to increase (prices, wages, etc.): *they've jacked up the cost of petrol again.*

jackal ('jakəl) *n.* a wild dog of Africa and Asia that hunts in packs at night and often eats animals killed by larger beasts of prey.

jacket ('jakit) *n.* 1. a short coat, usu. extending only down to the waist or seat. 2. an outer covering: *the book jacket was made of plastic.*

jade (jād) *n.* a hard, usu. pale green stone that is much prized for ornaments, esp. in China.

jaded ('jādid) *adj.* tired or worn out, as by overwork or overuse: *she had a jaded look after her long journey.*

jagged ('jagid) *adj.* (of a line or edge) having sharp, irregular points or notches: *the broken bottle had a jagged edge.*

jail *or* **gaol** (jāl) *n.* a prison. —*vb.* to put in jail; imprison.

jar[1] (jâ) *n.* a container made of glass, pottery, etc., usu. with a wide mouth.

jar[2] (jâ) *vb.* **jarring, jarred.** 1. to jerk or jolt: *he jarred my elbow.* 2. to cause an unpleasant, grating noise or effect: *his voice jarred (on) my nerves.* 3. to conflict: *his ideas jarred with my plans.* —*n.* 1. a jolt or jerk. 2. an unpleasant shock. 3. an unpleasant, grating noise.

jackal

jargon ('jâgən) *n.* 1. language that is full of scientific or technical words. 2. (informal) any speech or writing that is difficult to understand because it uses unnecessarily difficult words.

jaundice ('jôndis) *n.* a sickness that tints the skin, whites of the eyes, and body fluids yellow. —*vb.* **jaundicing, jaundiced.** to prejudice.

jaunt (jônt) *n.* a short journey made for pleasure: *let's go for a jaunt in the country.* —*vb.* to go on a short pleasure trip.

jaunty ('jônti) *adj.* **jauntier, jauntiest.** lively or carefree: *he has a jaunty look.*

javelin ('javəlin) *n.* a light spear for throwing, now used in athletics competitions.

jaw (jô) *n.* 1. either of the two bones that form the frame of the mouth and in which the teeth are set. 2. the lower part of the face. 3. **jaws** (*pl.*) anything resembling a pair of jaws in shape or function, such as the parts of a tool used for gripping.

jazz (jaz) *n.* a type of music that originated amongst black people in America. It has strong rhythms with the beat on notes that normally would not be accented.

jealous ('jeləs) *adj.* 1. envious of another person's advantages: *Tony is jealous of Susie's wealth.* 2. afraid that someone one loves will love another person more than oneself: *when Julie saw John talking to her sister, she became jealous.* 3. watchful and alert in guarding something: *a jealous guardian of freedom.* —'**jealously** *adv.* —'**jealousy** *n.,pl.* **jealousies.**

jeans (jēnz) *pl.n.* a pair of trousers, usu. made out of tough cotton cloth and worn for heavy work and as informal leisure wear.

jeep (jēp) *n.* a strong motor vehicle used by farmers, soldiers, etc., for driving over rough country.

jeep

jeer (jiə) *vb.* to say or shout unkind things about someone; mock: *they jeered the blind man when he fell down.* —*n.* a mocking cry; taunt.

jelly ('jeli) *n.,pl.* **jellies.** 1. sweet food usu. made from fruit juice and sugar, and eaten on bread. 2. a pudding made of flavoured gelatine. —*vb.* **jellying, jellied.** to make into, put into, or become jelly.

jellyfish ('jelifi̱sh) *n.* any of various soft boneless sea animals that have a jelly-like body and (usu.) tentacles.

jeopardy ('jepədi) *n.* danger; risk. '**jeopardize** *vb.* **jeopardizing, jeopardized.** to risk (something); endanger.

jerk (jûk) *vb.* to pull, twist, or move abruptly or suddenly: *she jerked her hand away from the fire.* —*n.* a sudden movement such as a twitch or quick pull.

jest (jest) *vb.* 1. to make jokes. 2. (+ *at*) to scoff: *the girls jested at their brother.* —*n.* 1. a joke. 2. something or someone to scoff at. '**jester** *n.* a person who jests, esp. one who was paid to amuse a noble household in former times.

jet[1] (jet) *n.* 1. a stream of gas, liquid, or small particles shot out from a narrow opening: *a jet of hot steam burst from the pipe.* 2. a nozzle or other device through which fluid, gas, etc., is shot: *the jets on the gas cooker are blocked.* 3. an aeroplane driven by jet engines that thrust the aircraft forward by shooting out a stream of gas or liquid in the opposite direction. —*vb.* **jetting, jetted.** to shoot out forcefully in a stream.

jet[2] (jet) *n.* hard black mineral like a stone, often cut and highly polished for jewellery.

jetty ('jeti) *n.,pl.* **jetties.** 1. a wooden or stone structure sticking out from the shore into a lake, river, sea, etc., to protect a harbour or beach from the force of currents and waves. 2. a similar structure to which boats can be tied.

jewel ('jōōəl) *n.* 1. a precious stone, e.g. a diamond, that has been cut and polished; gem. 2. an ornament made of gems. 3. a person or thing that is valued highly. '**jeweller** *n.* a person who makes, sells, or repairs jewellery. '**jewellery** *n.* ornaments of metal set with real or fake gems.

jigsaw puzzle ('jigsô) a puzzle consisting of a picture mounted on cardboard or wood and cut up into small curved pieces. The pieces must be fitted together to make the complete picture.

jingle ('jiṅggəl) *n.* 1. a clinking sound. 2. a short song or rhyme, esp. one used in advertisements. —*vb.* **jingling, jingled.** to clink and tinkle.

job (job) *n.* 1. a trade or profession: *she got a good job as a teacher.* 2. a particular piece of work: *can you do a job for me?* 3. (informal) an effort: *they had a job deciding.*

jockey ('joki) *n.* a person who rides racehorses for a living. —*vb.* to trick or cheat. **jockey for position** to use clever tactics to gain an advantage.

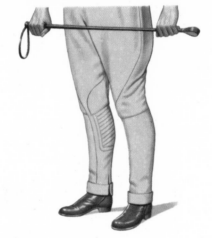

jodhpurs

jodhpurs ('jodpəz) *pl.n.* riding trousers that are wide round the thigh and hip, and tight-fitting from knee to ankle.

jog (jog) *vb.* **jogging, jogged.** 1. to bump; jolt: *you jogged my elbow.* 2. to run at a slow steady pace.

join (join) *vb.* 1. to unite or connect: *the Panama Canal joins the Atlantic to the Pacific Ocean.* 2. to come together or merge. 3. to become a member of: *she joined a club.* **join up** to enlist in one of the armed services. —*n.* a place where two things meet or are joined. '**joiner** *n.* a skilled carpenter. **joint** *n.* 1. a structure that connects two bones in the body: *the knee joint connects the shin and thigh bones.* 2. the point at which two or more things are joined, or the method of joining them: *carpenters use various types of joint.* 3. a large chunk of meat cut for cooking. *adj.* shared; done by two or more people: *joint owners.*

joke (jōk) *n.* 1. a short funny story. 2. (often **practical joke**) an amusing trick played on another person to make him look foolish. 3. something said or done in fun. —*vb.* **joking, joked.** 1. to make jokes. 2. to say (something) in fun. '**joker** *n.* 1. a person who loves playing or telling jokes. 2. a playing card, usu. with a jester's head on it.

jolly ('joli) *adj.* **jollier, jolliest.** full of cheerfulness and high spirits; good-natured. —'**jollity** *n.,pl.* **jollities.**

jolt (jōlt) *vb.* to jerk or bump: *the train jolted and stopped.* —*n.* a sudden bump or jerk.

jostle ('josəl) *vb.* **jostling, jostled.** to push roughly; shove: *we were jostled by the crowd.*

journal ('jûnəl) *n.* 1. a magazine or newspaper, usu. on a special subject. 2. a full daily diary. '**journalism** *n.* the job of writing for, editing, and publishing newspapers, magazines, etc. —'**journalist** *n.*

journey ('jûni) *n.* a long trip. —*vb.* to travel.

joust (joust) *vb.* to fight in armour on horseback with lances, as knights did in the Middle Ages. —*n.* a jousting contest.

jovial ('jōviəl) *adj.* hearty and jolly. —**jovi'ality** *n.* —'**jovially** *adv.*

joy (joi) *n.* 1. great happiness or pleasure. 2. a cause of happiness or pleasure: *your singing is a joy to hear.* —'**joyful** *adj.* —'**joyfully** *adv.*

jubilee ('jōōbilē) *n.* a celebration to mark a special anniversary. **silver** (**golden, diamond**) **jubilee** a twenty-fifth (fiftieth, sixtieth) anniversary.

judge (juj) *n.* 1. the official in charge of court cases, who decides on and announces punishments. 2. any person appointed to give a decision or ruling in a contest or dispute. 3. a person qualified to form an opinion: *she is a good judge of character.* —*vb.* **judging, judged.** 1. to act as a judge. 2. to form an opinion about: *I judge his age to be about fifty.* '**judgment** or '**judgement** *n.* 1. a law court's final decision, sentence, or ruling. 2. the ability to look at things in a critical and discerning way. 3. opinion: *in my judgment this man is not to be trusted.*

judo

judo ('jōōdō) *n.* Japanese form of fighting without weapons, rather similar to wrestling.

jug (jug) *n.* a container with a handle and lip or spout, used for holding and pouring liquids.

juggernaut ('jugənôt) *n.* (informal) a huge noisy lorry, often with a trailer.

juggle ('jugəl) *vb.* **juggling, juggled.** to do tricks that involve throwing, catching, and balancing numbers of balls, bottles, rings, etc.

juice (jōōs) *n.* liquid found in meat, fruit, and vegetables, that runs out when the substance is cooked, crushed, etc. —'**juiciness** *n.* —'**juicy** *adj.* **juicier, juiciest.**

juke-box ('jōōkboks) *n.* a coin-operated machine for playing popular music.

jumble ('jumbəl) *n.* an untidy collection of goods; confusion. **jumble sale** a sale of various unwanted articles. —*vb.* **jumbling, jumbled.** to mix up.

junction ('juñgkshən) *n.* 1. a place where two or more roads, railway lines, etc., meet or cross. 2. the act, instance, or method of joining or being joined: *the leak began at the junction of two pipes.*

jungle ('juñggəl) *n.* 1. a dense, wild, tropical forest. 2. an area of life that is fiercely competitive and ruthless: *the world of business is a jungle.*

junior ('jōōniə) *adj.* 1. younger. 2. lower in rank or less experienced: *a junior partner.* —*n.* a lower-ranking, younger, or less experienced person.

junk[1] (juñgk) *n.* rubbish; something worthless or useless: *that car is complete junk.*

junk[2] (juñgk) *n.* a Chinese ship with large sails.

jury ('jōōəri) *n.,pl.* **juries.** twelve people chosen from all areas of life who listen to evidence in a law court and decide whether the person being

junk

tried is guilty or not guilty. '**juror** *n.* a member of a jury.

just (just) *adj.* 1. fair; not taking sides: *a just decision.* 2. honourable; upright: *a just ruler.* 3. suitable; deserved: *a just reward.* —*adv.* 1. exactly: *the bell rang just as the door opened.* 2. barely; hardly: *I just had time to comb my hair.* 3. a moment ago: *he's just gone.* 4. a short time or distance: *it's just round the corner.* '**justly** *adv.* fairly; with justice.

justice ('justis) *n.* 1. sense of fairness. 2. fair treatment: *the expelled student demanded justice.* 3. the carrying out of the law: *not all thieves are brought to justice.* 4. a judge.

justify ('justifī) *vb.* **justifying, justified.** to have or give good reason for: *can you justify such an outrageous lie about us?* —'**justifiable** *adj.* —**justifi'cation** *n.*

jut (jut) **jutting, jutted.** (often + *out*) to stick out or stand out: *the hills jutted out against the sky.*

jute (jōōt) *n.* 1. strong fibre used to make rope or coarse canvas. 2. the Asian plant from which this fibre comes.

juvenile ('jōōvənīl) *n.* a young person or animal. —*adj.* 1. relating to or intended for children. 2. (of behaviour) childish.

K

kaleidoscope (kə'lĭdəskōp) *n.* an instrument with small pieces of coloured glass or plastic at one end. When viewed through a hole at one end, pieces of mirror inside reflect snowflake-like patterns.

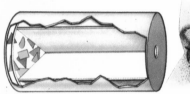

kaleidoscope

kangaroo (kaṅggə'rōo) *n.* an Australian animal that carries its young in a pouch and bounds along on powerful hind legs, using its long tail as a balance.

karate (kə'râti) *n.* Japanese form of fighting without weapons. Fighters use sharp blows, esp. from the side of the hand and forearm.

keel (kēl) *n.* the central bottom part of a boat running the length of the boat. **on an even keel** steady. —*vb.* (+ *over*) 1. to capsize: *the boat keeled over in the high wind.* 2. (informal) to fall down.

keen (kēn) *adj.* 1. (often + *on*) very interested (in). 2. acute or active: *a keen sense of responsibility.* 3. sharply edged; cutting: *a keen winter wind.* —'**keenly** *adv.* —'**keenness** *n.*

kennel ('kenəl) *n.* 1. a small hut for a dog. 2. often **kennels** (*pl.*) a place where dogs are bred.

kerb (kûb) *n.* the edging of a path or pavement: *don't step off the kerb without looking out for cars.*

kernel ('kûnəl) *n.* 1. the soft part of a nut inside its hard shell. 2. a grain (of wheat, corn, etc.).

kettle ('ketəl) *n.* a closed metal pot with a spout and handle, used for boiling water.

key (kē) *n.* 1. a shaped piece of metal used to open and close locks. 2. something similar in shape or function. 3. something that explains or solves: *the key to the mystery.* 4. a means of attaining success: *work is the key to success.* 5. a part of a machine or musical instrument that is pressed down to operate the machine: *typewriter keys.* 6. a musical scale: *the tune was written in the key of B flat.* —*adj.* very important; vital.

keyboard ('kēbôd) *n.* the part of a machine or musical instrument on which keys are situated: *a piano keyboard.*

khaki ('kâki) *n.* 1. a dull brown colour. 2. a thick cotton cloth in this colour, used esp. for soldiers' uniforms to provide camouflage.

kibbutz (ki'bŏots) *n.,pl.* **kibbutzim** (ki'bŏotsim). a farming settlement in Israel. The land is owned jointly, and everyone who lives on the kibbutz shares in the work and profits.

kidnap ('kidnap) *vb.* **kidnapping, kidnapped.** to steal a human being, often for ransom. —'**kidnapper** *n.*

kidney ('kidni) *n.* one of the two bean-shaped organs in the body that filter waste matter from the bloodstream and turn it into liquid waste matter.

kiln (kiln) *n.* a furnace or large oven used in various manufacturing processes, e.g. for baking or drying bricks, pottery, corn, etc., or for burning lime.

kilogram ('kiləgram) *n.* a unit for measuring weight in the metric system. It is equal to 1000 grams (about 2 pounds 3 ounces). It is now replacing the pound.

kilometre (ki'lomitə) *n.* a unit for measuring length in the metric system. It is equal to 1000 metres (about 0·67 mile).

kilowatt ('kiləwât) *n.* a unit for measuring electrical power. A kilowatt is equal to 1000 watts.

kilt (kilt) *n.* a short pleated skirt, usu. TARTAN, originally worn by Highland Scotsmen.

kind[1] (kīnd) *adj.* gentle; friendly. —'**kindness** *n.*

kind[2] (kīnd) *n.* a sort, variety, or type: *there are several kinds of musical instruments.*

king (kiṅg) *n.* 1. the male ruler of a nation. 2. a man who leads or is the most important in his business, work, etc. 3. a playing card with the picture of king. 4. a chess piece to be defended against checkmate. '**kingdom** *n.* a state having a king or queen at its head.

kingfisher ('kiṅgfishə) *n.* a bird with a long pointed beak and brilliantly coloured feathers. It feeds on fish that it obtains by diving.

kingfisher

kiosk ('kēosk) *n.* a small hut in a public place used as a shop or for some other particular purpose: *a telephone kiosk.*

kipper ('kipə) *n.* a fish, esp. a HERRING, split open, dried, salted, and used for food.

kitchen ('kiçhən) *n.* a place where food is prepared and cooked.

kite (kīt) *n.* 1. a toy made of paper or cloth stretched over a light frame for flying in the air at the end of a long string. 2. a bird of the hawk family that hunts other birds.

knack (nak) *n.* the special ability to do something; skill: *she has the knack of making people happy.* '**knick-knack** *n.* a small ornament of furniture, dress, or food.

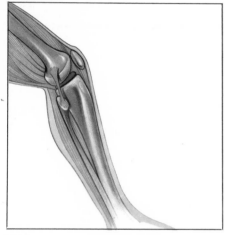
knee

knee (nē) *n.* the joint in the human leg between the thigh and shin bones. '**kneecap** *n.* the flat round bone in front of the knee.

kneel (nēl) *vb.* **kneeling, knelt.** to bend the legs and rest on the knees.

knew (nyoō) *vb.* the past tense of KNOW.

knickers ('nikəz) *pl.n.* short trousers worn as an undergarment by women and covering from waist to thigh.

knife (nīf) *n.,pl.* **knives.** a cutting instrument made of a blade with one edge sharpened and set either in a handle or a machine. —*vb.* **knifing, knifed.** to cut or stab with a knife.

knight (nīt) *n.* 1. a soldier of high rank who fought on horseback in the Middle Ages. 2. a man with the title 'Sir'. 3. a chess piece in the shape of a horse's head. —*vb.* to make (someone) a knight. —'**knighthood** *n.*

knit (nit) *vb.* **knitting, knitted** *or* **knit.** 1. to form fabric by closely interlocking loops of wool on two or more long straight needles or a machine. 2. to make or become well joined: *her broken leg knitted well in three months.* '**knitting** *n.* a piece of work in process of being knitted.

knob (nob) *n.* 1. a rounded handle: *the tuning knob fell off the old radio.* 2. a small lump, e.g. of sugar or coal.

knock (nok) *vb.* 1. to hit with a hard sharp blow. 2. (of an engine) to rattle as a result of faulty mechanism. 3. (slang) to run down; belittle. **knock off** to stop working. —*n.* a short sharp blow (on a door or other surface). '**knocker** *n.* 1. a person who knocks. 2. a shaped piece of metal attached to a door so that people can strike it to attract attention.

knockout ('nokout) *n.* 1. the blow that knocks a boxer down and makes him unable to get up again before the referee has counted to ten. 2. a tournament in which competitors play no more once they have lost a match.

knot (not) *n.* 1. a fastening made of tightly tied loops of thread or string. 2. any similar lump or tangle. 3. a measure of speed at sea, equal to one nautical mile (6080 feet) per hour. 4. a compact group of persons or things. 5. a hard lump in a sawn piece of timber. —*vb.* **knotting, knotted.** to tie in knots.

know (nō) *vb.* **knowing, knew, known.** 1. to be acquainted with; to be familiar with: *I know John and he would not lie.* 2. to be certain about: *I know you have made a mistake.* **knowledge** ('nolij) *n.* information; a body of facts gained from experience. '**knowledgeable** *adj.* well informed.

knuckle ('nukəl) *n.* any of the bony joints in a finger or between the finger and hand. **knuckle down to** to turn one's attention and energy to. **knuckle under** to submit; give way.

koala (kō'âlə) *n.* a small bearlike animal that lives in Australia. It eats eucalyptus leaves and carries its young in a pouch under its body.

koala

L

label ('lābəl) *n.* a small piece of card, cloth, etc., attached to an object to give information about the object: *the label in the shirt had Tom's name on it.* —*vb.* **labelling, labelled.** to attach a label to (something).

laboratory (lə'borətəri) *n.,pl.* **laboratories.** a building or room equipped for carrying out scientific experiments, research, and tests: *a hospital laboratory can test people's blood.*

labour ('lābə) *n.* 1. hard work, esp. physical work done for money. 2. people who do hard work for a living: *there was not enough labour on the building site.* 3. the pains and effort undergone in giving birth. —*vb.* 1. to work hard mentally or physically. 2. to have difficulty in doing, moving, etc.: *the old car laboured up the hill.* —**laborious** (lə'bôriəs) *adj.*

labyrinth ('labərinth) *n.* 1. a complicated arrangement of passages, streets, etc. 2. the inside part of the ear.

lace (lās) *n.* 1. a delicate patterned net-like material, used for decorating dresses, underwear, etc. 2. a piece of string that is threaded through holes to hold two pieces of material, leather, etc., together. —*vb.* **lacing, laced.** 1. to tie up by means of laces. 2. to thread a lace through holes. —**'lacy** *adj.* **lacier, laciest.**

lack (lak) *n.* shortage or absence of something much needed or wanted. —*vb.* to be without (something): *all we lack is fine weather.*

ladder ('ladə) *n.* 1. a device of metal or wooden bars, fixed one above the other between two parallel poles. It is used for climbing up the outside of buildings, trees, etc. 2. a ladder-like flaw in stockings or tights caused by a broken thread. —*vb.* to make a flaw in (stockings or tights).

lady ('lādi) *n.,pl.* **ladies.** 1. (polite) any woman. 2. a woman of high social rank. 3. a woman with good manners.

ladybird

ladybird ('lādibûd) *n.* a small flying beetle, usu. red or yellow, with black spots.

lag¹ (lag) *vb.* **lagging, lagged.** to drop behind: *he was lagging at the end of the long walk.* —*n.* a delay; time lapse: *after the overture there was a lag before the play started.*

lag² (lag) *vb.* **lagging, lagged.** to wrap thick material around (hot water pipes, boilers, etc.) to prevent loss of heat. **'lagging** *n.* any material used for this purpose.

lagoon (lə'gōon) *n.* a shallow enclosed stretch of water partly cut off from the sea by coral reefs or sandbanks.

lagoon

laid (lād) *vb.* the past tense of LAY¹.

lain (lān) *vb.* the past tense of LIE².

lake (lāk) *n.* a large stretch of water surrounded by land.

lamb (lam) *n.* 1. a young sheep. 2. the meat from a young sheep. 3. (informal) a very gentle and defence-less person. —*vb.* to give birth to lambs.

lame (lām) *adj.* 1. crippled or injured usu. in the legs or feet and so unable to walk properly. 2. feeble: *a lame excuse.* —*vb.* **laming, lamed.** to make (someone) lame. **lame duck** a helpless feeble person. —**'lamely** *adv.* —**'lameness** *n.*

lamp (lamp) *n.* a device that produces light by means of electricity, oil, etc.

lance (lâns) *n.* a long spearlike weapon with a sharp metal point used in the past by mounted soldiers.

land (land) *n.* 1. dry, solid part of the earth's crust. 2. a country: *the land of Norway.* 3. the people of a country: *the whole land rejoiced.* 4. that part of a country devoted mainly to farming: *he returned from Chicago to the land.* —*vb.* 1. to arrive on land from water or the air: *the aeroplane landed.* 2. (fishing) to catch (a fish). 3. to get into a situation or place: *his temper landed him in prison.* 4. (informal) to get or win: *he landed a big contract.*

landlord ('landlôd) *n.* 1. a man who owns property and lets other people (tenants) occupy it in return for money (rent). 2. a man in charge of a public house. **'landlady** *n.,pl.* **landladies.** a female landlord.

landmark ('landmâk) *n.* 1. something immovable that is clearly visible and serves as a guide to travellers. 2. something that marks the boundary of a piece of land. 3. something that marks a major change or turning point: *the invention of the internal combustion engine was a landmark in history.*

landscape ('landskāp) *n.* 1. a stretch of countryside seen from one position. 2. a picture of such a view. —*vb.* **landscaping, landscaped.** to improve the appearance of (land) by planting trees, lawns, etc.

landslide ('landslīd) *n.* 1. the fall of a mass of rocks and earth down a steep slope. 2. an overwhelming majority of votes in an election: *the government won a landslide victory at the last election.*

lane (lān) *n.* 1. a narrow country road. 2. a route which aeroplanes and ships regularly use. 3. the part of a road marked out for traffic moving in a particular direction.

language ('laṅggwij) *n.* 1. spoken or written human speech. 2. any particular form of this used for communication between people. 3. a way of expressing feelings or thoughts without words: *sign language.* **strong** *or* **bad language** swearing.

lantern

lantern ('lantən) *n.* a case, usu. of glass and metal, often made to be carried by hand, and intended to protect the light inside it.

lap[1] (lap) *n.* the area between the front part of the waist and the knees of a seated person.

lap[2] (lap) *vb.* **lapping, lapped.** 1. to take (liquid) into the mouth by scooping it up with the tongue: *the cat lapped the milk.* 2. (+ *up*) (slang) to accept (something) eagerly: *he lapped up the story.*

lap[3] (lap) *n.* one circuit of a race track. —*vb.* **lapping, lapped.** 1. to place or be placed so as to lie partly over something else. 2. (athletics) to overtake (competitors) still completing a previous lap.

lapse (laps) *n.* 1. a slight and easily made mistake: *a lapse of memory.* 2. a departure from good conduct: *a lapse into crime.* 3. that which has passed: *a time lapse.* —*vb.* **lapsing, lapsed.** 1. to fail to keep to accepted standards: *he lapsed into crime.* 2. to become void: *my television licence has lapsed.*

lard (lâd) *n.* soft white pig fat often used in cooking. —*vb.* to grease (food) with fat before cooking to improve its flavour.

large (lâj) *adj.* big or bigger than usual: *a large meal.* **at large** 1. free: *the lion was at large.* 2. everyone or everything together: *people at large.* '**largely** *adv.* mainly. —'**largeness** *n.*

lark[1] (lâk) *n.* one of several kinds of small dull-coloured bird, noted for its song.

lark[2] (lâk) *n.* a bit of fun; romp. —*vb.* (usu. + *about* or *around*) to frolic: *stop larking around and finish the job.*

larva ('lâvə) *n.,pl.* **larvae** ('lâvē). an insect in the form that it takes immediately after it hatches from the egg. Larvae often look very different from the adult insects.

lash (lash) *vb.* **lashing, lashed.** 1. to strike violently and repeatedly, esp. with a whip or stick: *he lashed the horse.* 2. to work (someone) into a temper, frenzy, etc.: *he lashed them into a fury.* 3. to attack in writing, speech, etc. 4. to move from side to side in a restless violent manner: *he lashed about in bed.* 5. to tie: *she lashed the dog to the post.* —*n.* 1. a whip made from a thong attached to a handle. 2. a blow from a lash or whip. 3. an EYELASH.

lasso (la'sōō) *n.,pl.* **lassos.** a long rope with a loop at one end, used by cowboys to catch animals. —*vb.* **lassoing, lassoed.** to catch (a horse, calf, etc.) with a lasso.

last[1] (lâst) *adj.* 1. coming at the end. 2. most recent: *his last holiday.* 3. remaining: *her last penny.* 4. least satisfactory: *the last place to go.* **the last word** 1. decisive point in an argument. 2. (informal) the newest thing: *the last word in cars.* **the last straw** the final unbearable thing in a series of annoyances. —*adv.* 1. after everyone or everything else: *he spoke last.* 2. most recently: *she was last seen in Paris.* **at last** eventually; finally.

last[2] (lâst) *vb.* 1. to remain. 2. to survive in good repair. —*n.* that which is left; remainder.

latch (lach) *n.* a fastener made from a bar that drops into a notch to close doors, windows, or gates. —*vb.* to fasten with a latch.

latchkey ('lachkē) *n.* a key that releases or opens a latch, usu. one that is used to open a front door: *don't forget your latchkey if you go out.*

late (lāt) *adj.* **later, latest.** 1. arriving or happening after the expected time. 2. coming near the end. 3. recently dead: *the late Mr. Smith.* —*adv.* 1. after the expected time. 2. towards the end of a period. '**lately** *adv.* not long ago. —'**lateness** *n.*

latent ('lātənt) *adj.* present but not able to be seen; hidden or concealed: *Tom has considerable latent ability.*

lathe (lādh) *n.* a machine that holds a piece of metal or wood and turns it around at speed so that a stationary cutting tool can be held against it in order to shape it.

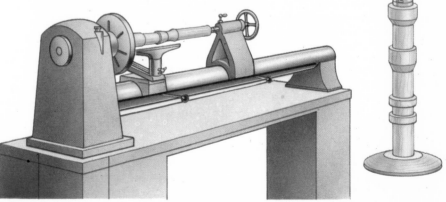

lathe

lather ('lâdhə) *n.* 1. bubbly foam made by soap and water. 2. the foam caused by heavy sweat. —*vb.* 1. to make lather. 2. to cover with lather.

latitude ('latityōod) *n.* 1. the distance north or south of the equator. Latitude is measured in degrees and each degree equals about 69 miles: *the latitude of Peking is forty degrees north.* 2. freedom from restrictions: *the pupils are given more latitude in the sixth form.*

latter ('latə) *adj.* 1. the second of two. 2. more recent. '**latterly** *adv.* of late; recently.

laugh (lâf) *vb.* to express merriment, joy, scorn, etc., by smiling and making other movements or sounds. **laugh up** *or* **in one's sleeve** to be secretly amused. **laugh off** to dismiss (something) as unimportant. —*n.* 1. the act or sound of laughing. 2. (slang) something which causes amusement: *her hat was a laugh.* '**laughable** *adj.* likely to make people laugh; ridiculous: *his dancing was laughable.* '**laughter** *n.* continuous laughing.

launch[1] (lônch) *vb.* 1. to send off (a ship, rocket, etc.) esp. for the first time. 2. to start (a course of action, a career, etc.): *Peter launched out into business on his own.*

launch[2] (lônch) *n.* an open motorboat used mainly in harbours and on rivers or lakes.

launderette (lôndə'ret) *n.* a shoplike business with several coin-operated washing machines and (usu.) tumble dryers.

laundry ('lôndri) *n.,pl.* **laundries.** 1. a place where clothes and bedclothes are washed and (usu.) ironed. 2. the clothes that are laundered. '**launder** *vb.* to wash (clothes).

laurel ('lôrəl) *n.* a small evergreen tree with smooth shiny leaves that have long been the symbol of victory and honour. **rest on one's laurels** to be satisfied with the success one has gained already and to cease to strive for more.

lava ('lâvə) *n.* 1. melted rock flowing from an erupting volcano. 2. rock formed by cooled and hardened lava.

lavatory ('lavətəri) *n.,pl.* **lavatories.** 1. a room fitted with a toilet. 2. the toilet itself.

lavender

lavender ('lavəndə) *n.* 1. a plant with pale purple strong-smelling flowers used to make scents, lavender water, etc. 2. pale purple colour.

lavish ('lavish) *adj.* 1. generous; extravagant. 2. produced or producing in excess; abundant. —*vb.* to give generously; waste.

law (lô) *n.* 1. a rule or set of rules laying down what may and may not be done by people: *laws of a country.* 2. the basic facts and principles: *laws of science.* 3. the legal profession. 4. (informal) the police; a policeman. '**lawful** *adj.* obeying or allowed by law. —'**lawfully** *adv.*

lawn (lôn) *n.* a stretch of ground in a garden with very closely cut grass growing on it.

lawyer ('lôyə) *n.* a member of the legal profession whose job is to advise people about the law and to represent people in court.

lay[1] (lā) *vb.* **laying, laid.** 1. to put down, fasten, or place in a certain position: *he laid the cutlery on the table.* 2. (of birds) to produce eggs. **lay it on** (informal) to flatter; overstate something.

lay[2] (lā) *adj.* 1. of someone who is not in holy orders. 2. nonprofessional: *in lay opinion, doctors often do not explain things sufficiently clearly to their patients.* '**laity** *n.* all the people who are not clergymen. —'**layman** *n.,pl.* **laymen.**

layer ('lāə) *n.* 1. a single coating or thickness: *layers of paint.* 2. a hen that lays eggs. 3. a twig or other part of a plant pressed into the ground to take root. —*vb.* 1. to form layers. 2. to make a plant layer.

lazy ('lāzi) *adj.* **lazier, laziest.** idle; not liking activity. **laze** *vb.* **lazing, lazed.** to be idle. —'**lazily** *adv.* —'**laziness** *n.*

lead[1] (lēd) *vb.* **leading, led.** 1. to guide esp. by walking ahead of (someone or something). 2. to live or experience: *she led a happy life.* 3. to be a way to: *jealousy leads to hate.* 4. to be the first, best, etc: *she led the class.* **lead the way** to act as guide. —*n.* 1. the most important position: *a famous actor took the lead.* 2. the ability to act first and make others follow: *we followed his lead.* 3. a clue or hint: *the murder weapon gave the police a lead.* 4. a cord by which dogs are led. '**leader** *n.* someone who leads or guides. —'**leadership** *n.*

lead[2] (led) *n.* 1. a very heavy soft grey metal, used for making water pipes. It melts and bends easily. Chemical symbol: Pb. 2. the black substance inside a pencil.

leaf (lēf) *n.,pl.* **leaves.** 1. the flat green part of plants that grows from the stem. 2. a sheet of paper. —*vb.* (+ *through*) to turn over (pages of a book, magazine) rapidly.

league (lēg) *n.* 1. an agreement, esp. between nations. 2. an association with members who have interests in common. **in league** plotting together: *the detective is in league with the thieves.*

leak (lēk) *vb.* 1. to pass slowly through a hole, crack, etc.: *the icecream leaked out of the packet.* 2. to become known by accident: *the news leaked out.* —*n.* 1. a crack, hole, etc., through which fluids or gases leak. 2. the revealing of news that should have been kept secret. '**leakage** *n.* the act of leaking. —'**leakiness** *n.*

lean[1] (lēn) *vb.* **leaning, leant** (lent) *or* **leaned.** 1. to slope or slant: *the old house leans to the left.* 2. to rely on for support: *she leaned heavily on the stick.*

lean[2] (lēn) *adj.* 1. thin; having no fat: *lean meat.* 2. (of soil, food, etc.) poor: *a lean income.* —'**leanness** *n.*

leap (lēp) *vb.* **leaping, leapt** (lept) *or* **leaped.** 1. to spring up. 2. to react suddenly, often with a start. —*n.* a jump. **by leaps and bounds** very fast.

leapfrog ('lēpfrog) *n.* a game in which players take turns in jumping over other players' bent backs.

leapt (lept) *vb.* the past tense and past participle of LEAP.

leap year a year that has 366 days. Leap years occur every four years and in a leap year February has 29 days.

learn (lûn) *vb.* **learning, learnt** *or* **learned.** 1. to acquire knowledge, skills, etc. 2. to find out: *he learnt the truth.* 3. to commit (something) to one's memory: *she learnt the poem.* **'learning** *n.* 1. the process of gaining knowledge, skills, etc. 2. knowledge obtained by studying.

lease (lēs) *n.* an agreement by which one person lets another occupy his house, land, etc., for a certain number of years in return for money. —*vb.* **leasing, leased.** to rent (property) on a lease.

least (lēst) *adj.* smallest. —*adv.* to the smallest degree: *he was least loved of all.* —*n.* the smallest amount.

leather ('ledhə) *n.* animal skin treated so as to be tough but soft and used to make shoes, bags, coats, etc. —**'leathery** *adj.*

leave[1] (lēv) *vb.* **leaving, left.** 1. to go away from (a place or situation). 2. to allow to remain behind: *she left the box on the table.* 3. to give in a will: *he left the house to his wife.* 4. to have (a number) left over: *two from four leaves two.*

leave[2] (lēv) *n.* 1. permission to do or not to do something. 2. permission to be absent, usu. for a holiday: *the soldiers were on leave.*

lectern ('lektən) *n.* a sloping surface or stand on which a reader, preacher, or lecturer places a book, notes, etc.

lectern

lecture ('lekchə) *n.* 1. an educational speech to a class or audience: *a lecture on Africa.* 2. a warning. —*vb.* **lecturing, lectured.** 1. to give a lecture. 2. to rebuke.

led (led) *vb.* the past tense and past participle of LEAD[1].

ledge (lej) *n.* 1. a narrow shelf that sticks out from a wall. 2. a rocky shelf projecting from the side of a cliff or steep slope. .

ledger ('lejə) *n.* a book containing a record of all sums of money coming in or going out of a business.

leek (lēk) *n.* a winter vegetable similar to an onion in taste and having a white edible stem and broad green leaves. It is the national emblem of Wales.

left[1] (left) *vb.* the past tense and past participle of LEAVE[1].

left[2] (left) *adj.* on the west side of your body as you face north. —*n.* the left side or direction.

legal ('lēgəl) *adj.* 1. concerning the law: *legal papers.* 2. allowed by law: *smoking is legal.* **'legalize** *vb.* **legalizing, legalized.** to make (something) legal. —**legali'zation** *n.*

legend ('lejənd) *n.* a story handed down, usu. by word of mouth, for many years, sometimes based on truth but sometimes just an imaginary tale. —**'legendary** *adj.*

legible ('lejibəl) *adj.* something clear enough to be read: *neat writing is usually legible.* —**'legibly** *adv.*

legion ('lējən) *n.* 1. a division of the army in ancient Rome, consisting of about 5000 soldiers on foot and horseback. 2. a huge number. **'legionary** *n.,pl.* **legionaries.** a Roman soldier.

leisure ('lezhə) *n.* a time for relaxing and enjoying oneself; spare time: *Henry spends most of his leisure out on his bicycle.* **'leisurely** *adj., adv.* without haste.

lemon ('lemən) *n.* 1. a yellow CITRUS fruit with sour juice. 2. the tree on which lemons grow. —*adj.* 1. made or tasting of lemons. 2. pale yellow.

lend (lend) *vb.* **lending, lent.** 1. to allow the use of (something) for a time to someone else. 2. to give: *the music lent gaiety to the evening.*

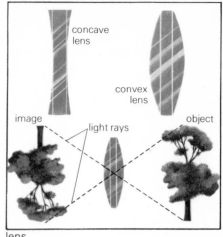
lens

length ('length) *n.* 1. the distance from one end to another of a thing: *the length of a river.* 2. distant in time from the beginning to the end: *the length of a day.* 3. a measured piece of something: *a length of material.* **go to great lengths** to make an extraordinary effort to do something. **at length** 1. eventually. 2. in great detail. **'lengthen** *vb.* to make or become long or longer. —**'lengthiness** *n.* See also LONG.

lens (lenz) *n.* 1. a piece of glass or clear plastic with surfaces curved to move light rays closer together or further apart. Lenses are used in magnifying glasses, telescopes, spectacles, and microscopes. 2. the part of the eye that focuses the light rays entering the eye.

lent (lent) *vb.* the past tense and past participle of LEND.

leopard ('lepəd) *n.* a large wild animal belonging to the cat family and having a golden-brown coat with black spots. Leopards kill other animals for food.

lemon

leprosy ('leprəsi) *n.* crippling skin disease, now mainly confined to tropical countries. **'leper** *n.* a person suffering from leprosy. —**'leprous** *adj.*

less (les) *adj.* not as much: *she eats less food than her brother.* —*adv.* to a smaller extent: *he tried eating less.* —*n.* a smaller amount: *he earned less this year.* **'lessen** *vb.* to make or become small or smaller. **'lesser** *adj.* 1. smaller of two. 2. less in extent, amount, etc.

lesson ('lesən) *n.* 1. something learnt at school or college: *a science lesson.* 2. anything taught by experience: *the accident taught Peter a lesson.*

let (let) *vb.* **letting, let.** 1. to permit; allow. 2. to hire (property) for rent: *she let her house to some students.* 3. (+ *down*) to disappoint. **let on** (slang) to reveal (a secret). **let slip** (informal) to release (information) by accident. **let up** to lessen (one's efforts).

lethal ('lēthəl) *adj.* deadly; able to kill: *a lethal weapon.* —**'lethally** *adv.*

letter ('letə) *n.* 1. a symbol representing a speech sound: *there are 26 letters in the English alphabet.* 2. a written message sent from one person to another.

lettuce ('letis) *n.* a plant that has large bright green leaves commonly eaten in salads.

level ('levəl) *adj.* 1. with a flat surface; even. 2. at the same distance or height. —*n.* 1. height: *the flood reached the level of the window sills.* 2. any level surface: *sea level.* —*vb.* **levelling, levelled.** to flatten.

lever ('lēvə) *n.* 1. a bar or other tool used to raise things or force things open. 2. a bar or rod by which a machine is operated. —*vb.* to use a lever to do or move (something). **'leverage** *n.* force obtained by using a lever.

levy ('levi) *vb.* **levying, levied.** 1. to collect (taxes, fines) by force or authority. 2. to call up (men) to become soldiers. —*n.,pl.* **levies.** men or money collected by levying.

liar ('līə) *n.* someone who does not tell the truth.

liberal ('libərəl) *adj.* 1. generous: *a liberal helping of cake.* 2. broadminded; tolerant: *a man of liberal*

lifeboat

views. —*n.* a member of a moderate political party that advises reform. **'liberalize** *vb.* **liberalizing, liberalized.** to make liberal or more liberal. **liberali'zation** *n.* act of making more liberal. —**'liberalism** *n.*

liberate ('libərāt) *vb.* **liberating, liberated.** to set free; release: *the police liberated the hostages.* —**liber'ation** *n.* —**'liberator** *n.*

liberty ('libəti) *n.,pl.* **liberties.** 1. freedom to act without government control: *liberty is much prized in democratic countries.* 2. political freedom of a country: *the colonists fought for their liberty.* 3. a rude or disrespectful act: *he took a terrible liberty with the headmaster by asking for a day off.*

library ('lībrəri) *n.,pl.* **libraries.** 1. a collection of books, journals, etc., owned by a person or institution. 2. a room or building where books are kept, and people can go to read them or borrow them. **librarian** (lī'breəriən) *n.* a person in charge of a library.

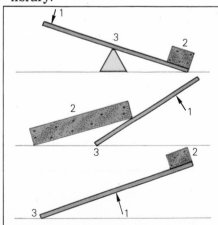
lever: 1 effort; 2 load; 3 fulcrum.

lice (līs) *n.* the plural of LOUSE.

licence ('līsəns) *n.* 1. a paper, cardboard disc, etc., proving that a tax has been paid: *dog licence.* 2. excessive or unreasonable freedom of action.

license ('līsəns) *vb.* **licensing, licensed.** 1. to grant a licence (def. 1). 2. to give (someone) permission to do something.

lichen ('līkən) *n.* a plant that grows on trees, rocks, etc., and looks like a flat, slightly rough, green, grey, brown, or yellow patch.

lick (lik) *vb.* 1. to move one's tongue across (something). 2. to eat or drink something by making similar movements. 3. (informal) to defeat. —*n.* 1. act of licking with the tongue. 2. a block of salt or other minerals for cattle to lick.

lid (lid) *n.* 1. a cover used to close open vessels. 2. the movable skin that covers the eyes to close them.

lie¹ (lī) *vb.* **lying, lied.** to say something that one knows is not true. —*n.* an untrue statement. **white lie** a lie used so as not to hurt somebody's feelings.

lie² (lī) *vb.* **lying, lay, lain.** 1. to be in a horizontal position; stretch out flat. 2. to be in a fixed position: *America lies across the Atlantic Ocean from Britain.* **take (something) lying down** to show no resistance: *he took this insult lying down.* **lie in** to stay in bed longer than usual. **lie low** to keep quiet; hide. **lie in wait for** to hide in order to make a surprise attack upon (someone).

lieutenant (lef'tenənt) *n.* a junior officer in the army or navy.

life (līf) *n.,pl.* **lives.** 1. quality that enables animals and plants to grow and reproduce. 2. the period between birth and death, or between start and finish. 3. a way of living: *a monk's life is a hard one.* 4. activity; bustle: *there is no life in this town.* 5. a book about a certain person. 6. energy; liveliness: *her presence gave new life to the party.*

lifeboat ('līfbōt) *n.* a small boat often carried aboard ships and used for rescuing people in case of a shipwreck.

lifeguard ('līfgâd) *n.* a very good swimmer employed at beaches and swimming pools to rescue swimmers who get into difficulties.

lilac

lift (lift) *vb.* to raise from a lower to a higher level. —*n.* 1. a device for carrying goods or people up and down a building. 2. a ride in somebody else's vehicle: *John gave Mary a lift to the station.*

ligament ('ligəmənt) *n.* white connecting tissue that joins bones to each other and holds organs in place.

light¹ (līt) *n.* 1. a form of energy that affects one's eyes, making possible the sense of sight. 2. rays of energy from a fire, lamp, candle, the sun, etc. 3. something that produces light rays, e.g. a candle, lamp, torch, etc. —*vb.* **lighting, lit** *or* **lighted.** 1. to set alight; cause to burn: *she lit the bonfire.* 2. to burn or start to burn: *the bonfire lit after three attempts to start it.* 3. (+ *up*) to show interest or pleasure: *his face lit up when his mother gave him a new watch.* —*adj.* 1. bright and clear; not dark. 2. pale in colour. '**lighten** *vb.* to make or become light or lighter. '**lighter** *n.* a small device that produces a flame for lighting cigarettes, cigars, etc.

light² (līt) *adj.* 1. not heavy; easy to lift or handle. 2. (of food) easy to digest. 3. mild; not severe: *the light fall of snow did not block the roads.* '**lighten** *vb.* to make or become less heavy. '**lightly** *adv.* 1. not heavily; not pressing hard: *the ladder rested lightly against the wall.* 2. nimbly; in an agile way: *he hopped lightly across the stepping-stones.* 3. not seriously; without complaining: *she treated the accident lightly.*

lighthearted ('līt'hâtid) *adj.* happy; carefree. —'**light'heartedly** *adv.* —'**light'heartedness** *n.*

lighthouse ('līthous) *n.* a tall, tower-like building, built near or just off the coast, with a powerful flashing lamp at the top to warn or guide ships or warn of obstructions.

lightning (lītniñg) *n.* a sudden brilliant flash of light in the sky caused by electricity in the clouds.

lightweight ('lītwāt) *n.* 1. a boxer weighing between 126 and 135 pounds. 2. anything below normal weight. —*adj.* 1. not heavy. 2. unimportant: *he has written three lightweight novels.*

like¹ (līk) *adj.* similar to or the same as: *this cloth feels like silk.*

like² (līk) *vb.* **liking, liked.** to enjoy; be fond of: *I like icecream.* **likes** *pl.n.* things one enjoys: *icecream is one of my likes.* '**liking** *n.* fondness. —'**likable** *or* '**likeable** *adj.*

likely ('līkli) *adj.* **likelier, likeliest.** 1. expected: *it is likely that I shall return soon.* 2. possibly or apparently suitable: *the man who applied for the job is a likely young fellow.* **most** *or* **very likely** probably: *I shall very likely be back soon.* —'**likelihood** *or* '**likeliness** *n.*

lilac ('līlək) *n.* a small tree that has clusters of sweet-smelling purple or white flowers.

lily ('lili) *n.,pl.* **lilies.** 1. a plant, grown from a bulb, that has white or coloured flowers. 2. any plant like a lily: *water lily.*

limb (lim) *n.* 1. a part of the body that is attached to, but not part of, the trunk, e.g. a leg. 2. a large branch of a tree.

lime¹ (līm) *n.* a white powdery substance made by burning limestone

and used as a fertilizer or in cement.

lime² (līm) *n.* a small oval pale green CITRUS fruit with acid-tasting juice.

limelight ('līmlīt) *n.* 1. a powerful lamp, used in lighting the stage of a theatre. 2. the centre of attention.

limerick ('limərik) *n.* a funny poem five lines long. Lines 1, 2, and 5 have one rhyme, and lines 3 and 4 another. There was a young lady of Riga. Who went for a ride on a tiger. They returned from the ride. With the lady inside. And a smile on the face of the tiger.

limit ('limit) *n.* 1. a place, point, or line that cannot or may not be passed: *the limit of man's endurance.* 2. also **limits** (*pl.*) boundary: *the limits of the area.* —*vb.* to put a limit or limits to; restrict: *we must limit the amount we eat in order to stay healthy.*

limousine ('limǝzēn) *n.* a large luxurious motorcar.

limp¹ (limp) *vb.* to move unsteadily or unevenly usu. because of an injured foot or leg. —*n.* a halting or unsteady step; lameness.

limp² (limp) *adj.* not firm or crisp; flabby: *limp lettuce.*

limpet ('limpit) *n.* a small soft-bodied sea creature that lives in a shell and is able to cling very tightly to any surface on which it settles.

limpet

line¹ (līn) *n.* 1. a thin mark which may be straight or curved: *he drew a line across the page.* 2. a boundary or border. 3. a geometric figure having length but not breadth. 4. a wrinkle or fold: *lines of worry on someone's brow.* 5. a row of people or things: *a line of soldiers.* 6. a single row of words on a page, in a poem, etc. 7. a short letter: *just a line to say I arrived safely.* 8. a succession of ancestors; family: *his is an aristocratic line.* 9. any course, route, or direction: *a line of action.* 10. a career or hobby. 11. **lines** (*pl.*) the speeches delivered by an actor in a play. 12. **lines** (*pl.*) the outline or contour of any object, esp. when judging whether it is pleasing: *the new car has nice lines.* **bring** or **come into line** 1. to make or become like others of the same type. 2. to behave or cause to behave in an acceptable way. **draw the line (at)** set the limits (for): *the gang robbed people but drew the line at murder.* **get out of line** to be disobedient. **railway line** a track along which railway trains run. **read between the lines** to discover a hidden meaning in a message, etc. **toe the line** to obey accepted laws, policies, etc. —*vb.* **lining, lined.** 1. to mark with a line. 2. to form a row or rows along: *crowds lined the streets.* **line up** to gather or be gathered into rows.

line² (līn) *vb.* **lining, lined.** to cover the inside of (a coat, box, room, etc.) with some material. **line one's pockets** to make money, often by dishonest means. **'lining** *n.* material used to cover the inside of something, esp. a coat.

linear ('liniə) *adj.* 1. composed of, concerning, or depending mainly on lines: *linear art.* 2. straight; not curved: *linear motion.*

linen ('linin) *n.* 1. cloth woven from flax fibres. 2. the household items made or formerly made from linen cloth, e.g. sheets, tablecloths, serviettes, and clothes.

liner ('līnə) *n.* a ship, esp. a large passenger ship, controlled by a shipping line and usually sailing regularly on the same voyage.

linger ('liŋgə) *vb.* 1. to delay or move slowly: *he lingered on his way to school.* 2. to remain.

link (liŋk) *n.* 1. one of the rings in a chain. 2. anything that connects or holds things together. —*vb.* to join, esp. with a link.

linoleum (li'nōliəm) *n.* a tough, hardwearing material used to cover floors.

lion ('līən) *n.* a big fierce golden-brown cat that eats other animals and lives wild in Africa and southeast Asia. The fully grown male has a shaggy mane of hair which frames his face. **'lioness** *n.* a female lion.

lip (lip) *n.* 1. the fold of pink flesh above or below the mouth. 2. the edge or rim of something: *the lip of a jug.* 3. (informal) impudent and disrespectful talk. **pay lip service to** to express admiration, respect, etc., insincerely.

liquid ('likwid) *n.* a substance that is neither a solid nor a gas and is able to flow freely, e.g. oil, water. —*adj.* in the form of a liquid. **'liquidize** *vb.* **liquidizing, liquidized.** to make into a liquid.

liquor ('likə) *n.* an alcoholic drink, e.g. brandy.

liquorice ('likəris) *n.* 1. a sweet substance usu. coloured black and used to make sweets and medicines. 2. the plant whose roots produce liquorice.

lisp (lisp) *n.* a speech habit that causes people to make a *th* sound when they try to make a *s* sound: *to lithp.* —*vb.* to speak with a lisp.

list (list) *n.* a series of names, things, etc., set down one after the other: *a shopping list.* —*vb.* to write down or state a list.

listen ('lisən) *vb.* to make a conscious effort to hear: *she listened to the lesson.*

listless ('listlis) *adj.* lacking energy or interest; indifferent: *the heat made everyone listless.* —**'listlessly** *adv.* —**'listlessness** *n.*

lit (lit) *vb.* the past tense and past participle of LIGHT¹.

literal ('litərəl) *adj.* 1. exactly following the words of a text: *I made a literal translation into Italian.* 2. unimaginative or lacking in artistic expression; ignoring symbolism: *a literal interpretation of the Bible.* —**'literally** *adv.*

literature ('litərəchə) *n.* 1. creative written works of permanent value or interest. 2. written works on a particular subject: *historical literature.* 3. leaflets or other printed matter given out to people for advertising purposes. **literary** ('litərəri) *adj.* of or connected with literature.

litmus ('litməs) *n.* a vegetable dye that is blue in an ALKALI solution and turns red in an ACID solution. **litmus paper** a paper soaked in litmus and used to test whether substances are acids or alkalis.

litre ('lētə) *n.* a unit for measuring fluids in the metric system. One litre equals about 1·75 pints. It is now being used in place of the pint for many purposes.

litter ('litə) *n.* 1. rubbish dropped in public places. 2. straw or other material used as bedding for animals. 3. a number of kittens, puppies, etc., produced at one birth. 4. a stretcher on which injured people are carried. —*vb.* to make untidy by carelessly throwing rubbish around: *don't litter the room with your sewing.*

little ('litəl) *adj.* **littler, littlest** or **less, least.** 1. small in size. 2. short. —*adv.* to a small extent; hardly at all: *he talks little.* —*n.* 1. a small amount. 2. a short distance or time.

live¹ (liv) *vb.* **living, lived.** 1. to have life; remain alive: *he lived through the war.* 2. to occupy: *she lived in a flat.* 3. (+ *on* or *by*) to support oneself; depend on something for survival: *he lived on his savings.* 4. to spend one's life in a certain way. **live and let live** to be tolerant of other people. **live up to** to be worthy of. **living** *n.* one's means of keeping alive.

liner

live[2] (līv) *adj.* 1. alive: *a live fish.* 2. charged with electricity: *a live rail.* 3. (of a television or radio programme) broadcast while being performed; not pre-recorded.

lively ('līvli) *adj.* **livelier, liveliest.** 1. cheerful. 2. lifelike. —**'liveliness** *n.*

liver ('livə) *n.* 1. the large reddish-brown organ in the body that helps the stomach digest food. 2. animal's liver used for food.

livestock ('līvstok) *n.* animals such as cows, sheep, and pigs that are raised on a farm for profit.

lizard ('lizəd) *n.* 1. a reptile with four legs and a long body and tail covered in scales. 2. the leather made from this reptile's skin.

load (lōd) *n.* 1. something that is carried; a burden, esp. if heavy or big: *a load of sand.* 2. a weight on the mind; a worry. —*vb.* 1. (often + *on* or *up*) to put a load or burden into a vehicle or onto someone's back. 2. to put ammunition into (a gun). 3. to put film into (a camera).

loaf[1] (lōf) *n.,pl.* **loaves.** 1. a lump of bread dough baked in one piece. 2. a quantity of food shaped like a bread loaf: *a meat loaf.*

loaf[2] (lōf) *vb.* (informal) to be idle: *he loafed in the garden all summer.*

loan (lōn) *n.* 1. something lent or borrowed, esp. money lent for a certain time in return for payment. 2. the act of lending something. —*vb.* to lend.

loathe (lōdh) *vb.* **loathing, loathed.** to hate very strongly: *he loathes greasy food.*

loaves (lōvz) *n.* the plural of LOAF[1].

lobby ('lobi) *n.,pl.* **lobbies.** 1. an entrance hall. 2. a group of people who try to put pressure on government members to vote in a particular way. —*vb.* **lobbying, lobbied.** to try to get one's way by forming a lobby (def. 2): *the villagers lobbied for better bus services.*

lobster ('lobstə) *n.* an edible sea creature, with a dark coloured shell and five pairs of legs, with very large claws on the front pair. The shell turns bright red when it is cooked.

local ('lōkəl) *adj.* belonging to one particular place: *the local shops.*

lizard

lo'cality *n.,pl.* **localities.** place; area: *our home is in a beautiful locality.*

locate (lō'kāt) *vb.* **locating, located.** 1. to find or note the position of (something): *he located the mine field.* 2. to be positioned or placed: *the church was located on a hill.* **lo'cation** *n.* 1. a place where something is positioned. 2. a place, esp. a place outside the studio where scenes from a film are made: *they shot the skiing scene on location in Switzerland.* 3. the act of locating something.

lock[1] (lok) *n.* 1. a device for securing a door, box, desk, etc., so it cannot be opened without a key. 2. a grip or hold in wrestling. 3. a system of watertight gates in a canal enabling the level of the water between them to be raised or lowered. 4. the full extent to which a motorcar's steering wheel will turn. **lock, stock, and barrel** entirely. —*vb.* 1. to fasten with a lock. 2. to become fixed or immovable: *the wheel locked and would not budge.*

lock[2] (lok) *n.* a piece of hair; a curl.

locker ('lokə) *n.* a box or small cupboard in a public place, e.g. a railway

station, in which people can leave their possessions and lock them up safely.

locust ('lōkəst) *n.* an insect, similar to the grasshopper, that sometimes occurs in great numbers in many parts of the world, destroying crops.

lodge (loj) *n.* 1. a small country house or hut used as a base for sporting activities: *a fishing lodge.* 2. a small house at the gateway of a large estate. 3. a local branch of a secret society such as the Freemasons. 4. a beaver's nest. —*vb.* **lodging, lodged.** 1. to stay in a house, esp. temporarily as a paying guest. 2. to become firmly fixed: *the arrow lodged in the tree.* 3. to put forward formally (a complaint, statement). 4. to offer (someone) a place to stay, usu. in return for payment: *she lodged an old lady.* **'lodger** *n.* someone who pays to live in part of another person's house. **'lodgings** *pl.n.* rented rooms in a private house.

loft (loft) *n.* 1. an attic; room or space just under the roof of a house, church, stables, etc. 2. a pigeon house.

lofty ('lofti) *adj.* **loftier, loftiest.** 1. very high: *a lofty tree.* 2. noble; dignified: *the hero had lofty ideals.* —**'loftiness** *n.*

log (log) *n.* a rough thick chunk of tree-trunk or branch. —*vb.* **logging, logged.** 1. to cut down trees and chop up the wood into logs. 2. to record (an event, etc.) in an official book.

loiter ('loitə) *vb.* to delay; linger idly: *Tom loiters on his way to school.*

lonely ('lōnli) *adj.* **lonelier, loneliest.** 1. sad because alone: *I was lonely when my friends left town.* 2. away from others: *a lonely tree.*

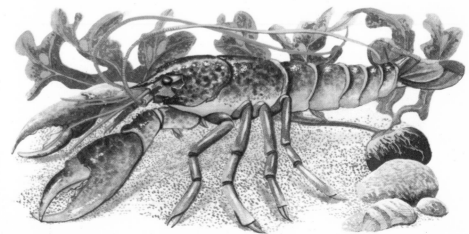
lobster

long¹ (loñg) *adj.* 1. great in length or distance; not short. 2. being great in length of time: *a long day.* 3. being of a certain measurement in length: *the car is twelve feet long.* —*adv.* 1. for a long time. 2. for a certain time: *it rained all day long.* See also LENGTH.

long² (loñg) *vb.* (+ *for*) to want (something) very badly; desire: *he longed for water.* '**longing** *n.* the state of wanting something badly.

longitude ('lonjityōod) *n.* the distance east or west of an imaginary line on the earth's surface drawn between the North Pole and the South Pole and passing through Greenwich, England. Longitude is measured in degrees: *the longitude of Seville is six degrees east.*

longwinded ('loñg'windid) *adj.* (of a speech, letter) tediously long.

look (lŏok) *vb.* 1. to observe, study, or watch: *he looked at the flowers.* 2. to appear; seem: *she looked a mess.* 3. to face: *the palace looked northwards.* **look after** to take care of. **look down on** (also **look down one's nose at**) to regard with scorn or disapproval. **look forward** to expect with pleasure. **look the other way** to pretend not to see. **look up to** to respect (someone). —*n.* 1. the act of looking. 2. expression: *a naughty look.*

lookout ('lŏokout) *n.* 1. the act of keeping watch for someone or something. 2. a person who keeps watch. 3. the place from which the person on the watch looks out. 4. (slang) problem; worry: *finding the money is his lookout.*

loom¹ (lŏom) *n.* a machine on which woollen yarn or other thread is woven into cloth.

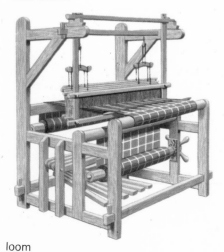
loom

loom² (lŏom) *vb.* (often + *up*) to seem huge and frightening: *the examinations loomed ahead.*

loop (lŏop) *n.* 1. a circle formed by bending one end of a piece of string, wire, etc., over the other. 2. something like a loop in shape: *her writing had many loops.* —*vb.* to make a loop. **loop the loop** to fly an aeroplane in a vertical circle.

loophole ('lŏophōl) *n.* 1. a narrow opening in a castle wall through which shots were fired. 2. a legal chance of escaping control: *he found a loophole in the tax laws.*

loose (lŏos) *adj.* 1. able to move freely; at liberty: *a loose dog.* 2. not firmly fixed in place: *loose teeth.* 3. not packaged up: *loose sweets.* 4. inaccurate; not exact: *a loose account.* —*vb.* **loosing, loosed.** 1. to set (someone, something) free. 2. to shoot (an arrow). '**loosen** *vb.* 1. to make or become loose or looser. 2. (+ *up*) to make one's body supple by exercises. —'**loosely** *adv.* —'**looseness** *n.*

loot (lŏot) *n.* 1. property taken by an army or rioters; plunder. 2. goods stolen by a thief.

lord (lôd) *n.* 1. a male ruler, esp. in the Middle Ages. 2. (Britain) **Lord** the ceremonial or courtesy title of bishops and certain noblemen. **the Lords** the members of the House of Lords. **Lord God** Jesus Christ.

lorry ('lori) *n.,pl.* **lorries.** a large motor vehicle or truck used for transporting goods.

lose (lŏoz) *vb.* **losing, lost.** 1. to fail to keep (something) and then not be able to find it: *he lost his coat.* 2. to fail to win: *they lost the game.* 3. to be without (someone or something) as the result of death, accident, etc.: *he has lost his grandfather.* 4. to be or become totally absorbed in something: *he lost himself in the music.* 5. to waste (money, time). 6. (of a clock) to show a time earlier than the real time; be slow. **lose one's head** to panic. **lose out on** (informal) to miss a chance to enjoy: *he lost out on the cakes by arriving late.* **loss** *n.,pl.* **losses.** 1. act of losing. 2. something lost: *they had a loss of £50.* 3. soldiers dead and wounded: *heavy losses in the battle.* **cut one's losses** to get out of a bad situation before losses become too great. **at a loss** not knowing what to do or say. **lost** *adj.* 1. no longer practised or known: *lost customs.* 2.

ruined: *a lost hope.* 3. helpless; bewildered: *he is lost without his glasses.* 4. to be blind to: *he is lost to any sense of right or wrong.*

lot (lot) *n.* 1. a large amount: *a lot of noise.* 2. a thing or a group of things to be sold at an auction. 3. a small unit of land. 4. something that happens to one as the result of fate: *he had an unhappy lot in life.* 5. one of a set of marked papers, pebbles, etc., used to decide something by chance: *they drew lots.* **throw in one's lot with** to share one's fate and fortune with (someone else).

lottery ('lotəri) *n.,pl.* **lotteries.** a competition in which those taking part buy tickets that are finally mixed together and one or more drawn out at random to win prizes.

loud (loud) *adj.* 1. having a great volume of sound; noisy: *a loud bang.* 2. tasteless or vulgar: *loud colours.* —'**loudly** *adv.* —'**loudness** *n.*

lounge (lounj) *vb.* **lounging, lounged.** to relax or move lazily. —*n.* a room with comfortable seats, esp. in a hotel, where people can relax.

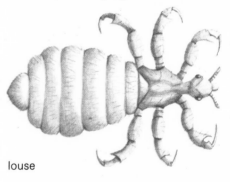
louse

louse (lous) *n.,pl.* **lice** (līs). a small insect that lives on man and some animals, and sucks their blood. **lousy** ('louzi) *adj.* **lousier, lousiest.** 1. infested by lice. 2. (slang) very bad.

love (luv) *n.* 1. the emotion that one feels for people one is very fond of. 2. a strong liking: *she has a great love of reading.* 3. someone beloved: *he wrote a letter to his love.* 4. a zero score in tennis. **for love** as a favour, not for money. **no love lost** dislike: *there is no love lost between Sue and Tom.* —*vb.* **loving, loved.** 1. to feel a strong affection for (someone or something). 2. to like very much. '**lovable** *adj.* causing a feeling of affection: *a lovable baby.*

lovely ('luvli) *adj.* **lovelier, loveliest.** beautiful; delightful: *a lovely garden.*

lunar module

low¹ (lō) *adj.* 1. not high; not far off the ground: *a low ceiling.* 2. less in quantity, value, etc., than is usual: *low prices.* 3. not loud or shrill: *a low whisper.* 4. miserable; suffering from ill-health: *he felt very low.* 5. not having enough: *low on food.* 6. vulgar; morally base: *a low act.* —*n.* 1. lowest point: *the market reached a new low.* 2. (cars) first gear. **'lower** *vb.* to make or become low or lower.

low² (lō) *vb.* to make a deep throaty noise as cattle do. —*n.* the sound of lowing.

loyal ('loiəl) *adj.* faithful; true to one's country, friends, etc. —**'loyally** *adv.* —**'loyalty** *n.,pl.* **loyalties.**

luck (luk) *n.* 1. chance. 2. good fortune: *she was in luck.* **down on one's luck** *or* **out of luck** unfortunate, esp. in money matters. —**'luckily** *adv.* —**'lucky** *adj.* **luckier, luckiest.**

luggage ('lugij) *n.* a traveller's cases, bags, etc., and their contents.

lugger ('lugə) *n.* a type of sailing ship with a square sail.

lukewarm ('look'wôm) *adj.* 1. between hot and cold; tepid: *lukewarm soup.* 2. not enthusiastic; reserved: *a lukewarm welcome.*

lullaby ('luləbī) *n.,pl.* **lullabies.** a quiet, gentle song meant to lull children to sleep.

lump (lump) *n.* 1. a shapeless mass; blob: *there are lumps in the gravy.* 2. a swelling on one's body. **lump sum** single large payment. **lump in the throat** difficulty in speaking because of great emotion. **lump sugar** sugar sold in small cubes. —*vb.* (often + *together*) to put, treat, or bring (different things) together. **lump it** (slang) to put up with (something unpleasant). —**'lumpy** *adj.* **lumpier, lumpiest.**

lunacy ('loonəsi) *n.* 1. madness. 2. great stupidity: *it was lunacy to swim in the flooded river.* **'lunatic** *n.* 1. a foolish person. 2. a mentally ill person. *adj.* 1. very stupid. 2. mad.

lunar ('loonə) *adj.* of or relating to the moon: *lunar exploration.* **lunar module** a small spacecraft, part of a larger one, that can be put into a separate orbit round the moon, land on its surface, and return to the parent spacecraft.

lunch (lunch) *n.* a midday meal. —*vb.* to eat lunch.

lung (lung) *n.* one of the two spongy inflatable organs in the chests of people and animals, used for breathing and taking air into the body.

lurk (lûk) *vb.* to lie in wait; hide: *the thief lurked in the shadows.*

luxury ('lukshəri) *n.,pl.* **luxuries.** 1. expensive and very comfortable way of life: *the rich old countess lived in luxury.* 2. an expensive and unnecessary comfort or pleasure: *a private yacht is a luxury few can afford.* **luxuriate** (lug'zyooəriāt) *vb.* **luxuriating, luxuriated.** to enjoy very greatly. —**lux'urious** *adj.*

lynch (linch) *vb.* to put to death without trial: *an angry mob threatened to lynch the suspected murderer.* **lynch law** rule by mob violence.

M

macaroni (makə'rōni) *n.* food made from flour paste shaped into small hollow tubes. It originally came from Italy, and is often eaten with a sauce of tomatoes, meat, and cheese.

machine (mə'shēn) *n.* a device made up of a number of different parts and used to apply power to do a particular job: *a sewing machine.* **ma'chinery** *n.* machines collectively.

mackerel ('makrəl) *n.,pl.* **mackerel** or **mackerels.** a small silvery fish that lives in the ocean and is caught for food.

mad (mad) *adj.* **madder, maddest.** 1. out of one's mind; crazy. 2. feeling or expressing rage. 3. very foolish. 4.

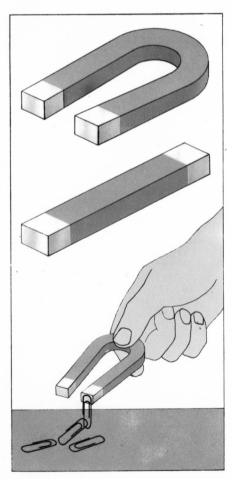

magnet

very keen. 5. wild or dangerous. —'**madly** *adv.* —'**madness** *n.*

magazine (magə'zēn) *n.* 1. a collection of stories and articles by different authors, bound in paper covers and printed at regular intervals. 2. the part of a gun that holds the ammunition. 3. a storehouse for ammunition.

maggot ('magət) *n.* the small white wormlike grub of an insect in the stage of its life history just after it has come out of the egg.

magic ('majik) *n.* 1. the art of using or appearing to use mysterious hidden powers to control events. 2. the skill of performing tricks to entertain people. **black magic** harmful magic, using wicked spirits or demons. **white magic** magic intended to do good. —*adj.* (also **magical**) used in or caused by magic. **magician** (mə'jishən) *n.* a conjurer; one who is skilled in magic. —'**magically** *adv.*

magistrate ('majistrāt) *n.* a person who acts as a judge in minor court cases.

magnet ('magnit) *n.* a piece of metal, esp. iron, that has the power to attract other pieces of iron. **magnetic** (mag'netik) *adj.* 1. having the power of a magnet. 2. attracting attention or admiration: *she has a magnetic personality.* —**mag'netically** *adv.* —'**magnetism** *n.*

magnificent (mag'nifisənt) *adj.* splendid; excellent in beauty, size, quality, etc. —**mag'nificence** *n.* —**mag'nificently** *adv.*

magnify ('magnifī) *vb.* **magnifying, magnified.** to make something seem bigger than it really is. **magnifying glass** a LENS used to make things look bigger.

magpie ('magpī) *n.* a long-tailed black and white bird of the crow family. It is known for its noisy chattering song and habit of stealing small glittering objects.

mahogany (mə'hogəni) *n.* 1. reddish-brown hard wood used in making furniture, planks for boats, etc. 2. the tropical tree from which this wood comes. 3. a reddish brown colour. —*adj.* made from or of the colour of mahogany.

mail[1] (māl) *n.* 1. letters and parcels sent through the postal system: *is there any mail today?* 2. the system by which mail is sent, carried, and delivered. —*vb.* to send by mail.

mail[2] (māl) *n.* body armour made of interlocking steel rings and plates worn for protection by medieval warriors.

main (mān) *adj.* the first or most important: *the main reason for his visit was curiosity.* —*n.* often **mains** (*pl.*) the largest pipe or cable carrying water, gas, electricity, etc. —'**mainly** *adv.*

mainstream ('mānstrēm) *n.* the principal tradition or trend: *the mainstream of art.*

maintain (mān'tān) *vb.* 1. to continue to have or do: *the car maintained a steady speed.* 2. to care for: *he maintained his garden carefully.* 3. to say and continue to say firmly: *he maintained he knew the way.* **maintenance** ('māntənəns) *n.* 1. the act of caring for or maintaining. 2. the

magpie

money to buy things necessary for living: *he earned enough for the maintenance of his family.*

maize (māz) *n.* a tall large-eared corn plant, producing grain that grows in rows on a thick spike (cob). It is also known as sweet corn or as Indian corn.

majesty ('majisti) *n.* 1. grandeur; dignity: *the majesty of a state funeral.* 2. **Majesty,** *pl.* **Majesties** a title used in talking to or about kings and queens. **majestic** (mə'jestik) *adj.* very noble and grand.

mammoth

major ('mājə) *adj.* great in size, age, importance, value, etc.: *the major work in the concert was Beethoven's ninth symphony.* —*n.* an army officer between captain and lieutenant-colonel. **majority** (mə'joriti) *n.,pl.* **majorities.** 1. a larger part or number: *the majority of people enjoy sunshine.* 2. the age of full legal responsibility.

make-believe ('mākbilēv) *n.* fantasy; indulgence in the belief that something obviously false is true: *his idea of himself as a great hero is just make-believe.* —*adj.* not real; imaginary. **make believe** to pretend.

makeshift ('mākshift) *n.* a substitute or replacement, esp. one that is temporary or unsatisfactory. —*adj.* temporary; substitute.

make-up ('mākup) *n.* 1. cosmetics for the face. 2. the way in which something is put together or composed, esp. a person's character: *it is not in her make-up to be rude.* **make up** 1. to put on cosmetics. 2. to invent (a story). 3. to settle (a quarrel) and become friends again.

male (māl) *adj.* 1. of or concerning the sex that can father young: *a male goose is called a gander.* 2. of or concerning men or boys: *the male teachers formed a team to play the school at football.* —*n.* a male person or animal.

malice ('malis) *n.* spitefulness; ill will towards other people.

malicious (mə'lishəs) *adj.* feeling or showing ill will. —**ma'liciously** *adv.*

mallet ('malit) *n.* a heavy wooden hammer used as a tool.

malt (môlt) *n.* a substance made by soaking grain, usu. barley, in water, allowing it to sprout, and then drying it. Malt is used in making beer and other drinks and in cooking.

mammal ('maml) *n.* an animal that has warm blood, a bony SKELETON, and hair or fur on its body. A female mammal feeds its young on milk that it produces from GLANDs in its body. Human beings, sheep, and whales are all mammals.

mammoth ('maməth) *n.* a very large hairy elephant that lived many thousands of years ago. —*adj.* huge; very large: *clearing the minefield was a mammoth task.*

manacle ('manəkəl) *n.* handcuffs or chains to restrain the hands. —*vb.* **manacling, manacled.** to put manacles on (someone).

manage ('manij) *vb.* **managing, managed.** 1. to control or handle: *she managed the galloping horse skilfully.* 2. to succeed, often against difficulties: *in spite of his ill-health, he managed to become a lawyer.* **'management** *n.* 1. act or method of managing. 2. the group of people concerned with running a business, factory, etc. **'manager** *n.* a supervisor of other employees in a company.

mandolin ('mandəlin) *n.* a musical instrument with strings and a pear-shaped body, smaller than a lute.

mane (mān) *n.* the long thick hair that grows on the backs of some animals' necks: *the lion had a fine mane.*

mangle ('manggəl) *vb.* **mangling, mangled.** to damage badly by tearing or crushing: *the heavy lorry mangled the small car.* —*n.* a device with rollers used to squeeze water out of wet clothes.

mania ('māniə) *n.* 1. violent madness. 2. an excessive enthusiasm or craze: *he has a mania for old motorcycles.* **maniac** ('māniak) *n.* a person suffering from mania; a madman. —**manic** ('manik) *adj.*

manner ('manə) *n.* 1. a particular way of doing something: *Tom was whistling in a cheerful manner.* 2. a way of behaving: *she has a sullen manner.* 3. **manners** (*pl.*) polite or correct ways of behaving: *he has good manners.* **'mannerism** *n.* a noticeable and unusual characteristic: *he has a funny mannerism of raising his eyebrows while he talks.*

manoeuvre (mə'noovə) *n.* 1. a clever or crafty movement. 2. often **manoeuvres** (*pl.*) movement of armed forces to gain advantage over an enemy. —*vb.* **manoeuvring, manoeuvred.** to make moves to try to gain an advantage.

mantelpiece

mantelpiece ('mantəlpēs) *n.* the shelf jutting out from the wall or chimney front above a fireplace.

manual ('manyoōəl) *adj.* done by hand: *gardening is mainly manual labour.* —*n.* a book that gives instructions how to do or use something: *I consulted my car manual.*

manufacture (manyoōfakchə) *vb.* **manufacturing, manufactured.** 1. to make (goods) on a large scale by machinery: *the factory manufactures electrical goods.* 2. to invent (an excuse). —*n.* the act or process of manufacturing.

manure (mə'nyoōə) *n.* animal waste, e.g. from horses, cows, and sheep, used to enrich the soil. —*vb.* **manuring, manured.** to spread and dig in manure.

manuscript ('manyŏŏskript) *n.* 1. books, letters, etc., in handwritten form. 2. a book as it is first written out by hand or typed, before it has been printed.

map (map) *n.* an outline drawing of the surface of the earth or part of it, showing towns, rivers, roads, or other features. —*vb.* **mapping, mapped.** 1. to make a map of. 2. (+ *out*) to plan thoroughly.

marathon ('marəthən) *n.* 1. a long-distance running race. 2. a long and exhausting struggle, task, etc.

marble ('mabəl) *n.* 1. a hard stone, often handsomely marked, that is cut and polished for buildings, statues, and furniture. 2. a small glass ball used in games.

march (mach) *vb.* to walk at a regular even pace as soldiers do. —*n.* 1. the steady walking pace of soldiers. 2. the act of marching. 3. a piece of music to accompany marching.

mare (meə) *n.* a female horse, pony, donkey, or zebra.

margarine (mâjə'rēn) *n.* a mixture of edible vegetable oils and skimmed milk used instead of butter.

margin ('mâjin) *n.* 1. the edge of something, esp. the area around the written or printed part of a page. 2. an amount in addition to what is thought to be necessary: *leave a margin of an hour for your journey.* '**marginal** *adj.* 1. in or of the margin: *marginal notes.* 2. small: *the delay is of marginal importance.* —'**marginally** *adv.*

marine (mə'rēn) *adj.* 1. of or found in the sea: *marine animals.* 2. concerned with shipping or naval matters: *a marine insurance company.* —*n.* a soldier serving on a warship.

mark (mâk) *n.* 1. a spot, scratch, etc., made accidentally: *the muddy dog left marks on the carpet.* 2. a sign made as a reminder, to help identification, etc. 3. a letter or figure indicating the standard of a person's performance: *the pupil got the best mark in the class.* 4. a line or object showing position: *the horses passed the two-mile mark.* —*vb.* 1. to put a mark or marks on. 2. to indicate (position). 3. to give marks (def. 3) to.

market ('mâkit) *n.* 1. the open or covered area where people meet to buy and sell goods or animals. 2. the demand for something that is for sale: *there is a poor market for fresh fruit now.* —*vb.* to sell or put up for sale.

marmalade ('mâməlād) *n.* jam made from oranges or other citrus fruit.

maroon[1] (mə'roon) *vb.* 1. to abandon (someone) on a lonely island. 2. to leave (someone) without transport or means of moving from a place: *when the car broke down we were marooned on the lonely road.*

maroon[2] (mə'roon) *n.* a dark crimson colour with a brownish tinge. —*adj.* having the colour maroon.

marrow ('marō) *n.* 1. the soft fatty substance inside the hollows of bones. 2. (also **vegetable marrow**) a vegetable like a large swollen cucumber that grows on a vinelike trailing plant.

marry ('mari) *vb.* **marrying, married.** to join or unite legally as husband and wife. '**marriage** *n.* 1. the state of living together as husband and wife. 2. a wedding.

marsh (mâsh) *n.* an area of low-lying wet ground on which reeds and grasses grow.

marshal ('mâshəl) *n.* 1. a high ranking officer in an army or air force. 2. a person who arranges important public ceremonies. —*vb.* **marshalling, marshalled.** to gather together and arrange in proper order.

marsupial (mâsoopiəl) *n.* one of a class of animals (e.g. opossum, kangaroo) found in Australia and America, whose young are carried by their mothers in a pouch until they are fully developed.

martial ('mâshəl) *adj.* of warfare; military: *martial music.*

martyr ('mâtə) *n.* a person who dies or suffers for a cause: *St. Stephen was an early Christian martyr.* **be a martyr to** to suffer intense pain from: *he is a martyr to rheumatism.* —*vb.* to put (someone) to death or torture for his beliefs.

marvellous ('mâvələs) *adj.* 1. astonishing: *the Grand Canyon is a marvellous sight.* 2. (informal) excellent. —'**marvellously** *adv.*

marzipan ('mâzipan) *n.* paste with an almond and sugar base used in making sweets.

mascara (ma'skârə) *n.* dark dye used as an eye cosmetic.

mascot ('maskət) *n.* a person, animal, or thing reputed to bring good luck.

masculine ('maskyŏŏlin) *adj.* of or like the male sex. —**mascu'linity** *n.*

mash (mash) *n.* 1. animal feed, esp. a mixture of boiled bran given warm. 2. any soft pulp, esp. one produced by crushing potatoes. —*vb.* to make into a soft pulp.

mask (mâsk) *n.* 1. a covering worn to protect or hide the face. 2. anything that conceals or covers up. —*vb.* 1. to put on or wear a mask. 2. to hide.

mass[1] (mas) *n.* 1. a quantity of matter without a specific shape: *a mass of snow slid off the roof.* 2. a large number: *a mass of people.* 3. the quantity of matter in a body: *a feather has a low mass.* —*vb.* to gather or be gathered into a mass.

mass[2] (mas) *n.* the principal religious ceremony of the Roman Catholic Church.

massacre ('masəkə) *n.* the brutal killing of many people. —*vb.* **massacring, massacred.** to kill (many people) brutally.

massage ('masâzh) *n.* the rubbing of body muscles and joints in order to improve their function. —*vb.* **massaging, massaged.** to give a massage to.

massive ('masiv) *adj.* very big; on a very large scale: *the movement had massive public support.* —'**massively** *adv.*

mast (mâst) *n.* 1. the tall pole of timber or iron supporting the sails of a ship. 2. an upright metal pole or pylon used to transmit radio or television broadcasts.

master ('mâstə) *n.* 1. a man who controls or has power. 2. a male school-teacher. 3. a skilled craftsman or person with great knowledge of a particular thing. 4. **Master** the title used on letters as a form of address for a young boy. —*vb.* to achieve control of: *he mastered his anger.*

mastermind ('mâstəmīnd) *n.* a person of superior intelligence. —*vb.* to plan and direct (a scheme, etc.): *she masterminded the publicity campaign.*

marsupials

numbat

opossum

kangaroo

wombat

masterpiece ('mâstəpēs) *n*. a work of expert skill or craftsmanship.

match[1] (ma͟ch) *n*. 1. a person or thing exactly equal to another: *Jane is Carol's match at tennis*. 2. a contest of skill between individuals or teams: *a cricket match*. 3. a marriage. —*vb*. 1. to be the equal of. 2. to correspond to something else: *the pieces of the puzzle don't match*. 3. to harmonize with in colour, quality, etc.: *her gloves match her handbag.*

match[2] (ma͟ch) *n*. a small piece of wood tipped with a substance that bursts into flame when rubbed on a treated surface.

mate (māt) *n*. 1. one of a pair. 2. the male or female of a pair of animals. 3. fellow-worker or assistant. 4. an officer on a ship below the rank of captain. —*vb*. **mating, mated.** to join together as a pair for breeding.

material (mə'tiəriəl) *n*. anything used to make something, esp. a fabric: *she used a light material for her dress.* —*adj*. 1. physical: *material well-being.* 2. important: *a material wit-*ness. **ma'terialism** *n*. the stressing of physical rather than spiritual values. **ma'terialize** *vb*. **materializing, materialized.** to become or cause to become a fact: *our holiday plans materialized.* —**ma'terialist** *n*. —**material'istic** *adj*. —**ma'terially** *adv.*

maternity (mə'tûniti) *n*. the state of being a mother.

mathematics (ma͟thə'matiks) *n*. the study of numbers, quantities, sizes, and shapes. Algebra, arithmetic, geometry, and trigonometry are all branches of mathematics. —**mathematician** (ma͟thəmə'ti͟shən) *n.*

matinee ('matinā) *n*. a performance at a theatre or cinema given in the afternoon.

matrimony ('matriməni) *n*. marriage. —**matri'monial** *adj.*

matron ('mātrən) *n*. 1. the chief nurse in a hospital. 2. a woman in charge of housekeeping in a school or other institution. **'matronly** *adj*. like a matron; dignified.

matter ('matə) *n*. 1. substance having weight and taking up space; substance of which all physical things are made. 2. a subject of interest, importance, discussion, etc. 3. printed or written material. 4. trouble; difficulty. 5. the subject of a book. —*vb*. to be of interest or importance: *it mattered to him that his team should win the cup.*

mattress ('matris) *n*. a thick pad, usu. made to fit a bed frame, and made up of a fabric case containing either stuffing or springs.

mature (mə'tyo͞oə) *adj*. 1. fully grown; adult. 2. ready for use. —*vb*. **maturing, matured.** 1. to develop fully. 2. to ripen. —**ma'turely** *adv*. —**ma'turity** *n.*

mauve (mōv) *n*. a delicate purple colour —*adj*. of this colour.

maximum ('maksiməm) *n*. the greatest or highest point or value: *the temperature reached its maximum at noon.* —*adj*. greatest possible: *the maximum number of schoolchildren should be vaccinated against polio.*

mayor (meə) *n.* the head of the council or government of a town or city.

maze (māz) *n.* 1. a confusing layout of passageways. 2. a series of paths with high hedges on either side, forming a sort of puzzle in which people can wander and lose themselves for amusement.

maze

meadow ('medō) *n.* a field of grass used for hay or as grazing.

meal[1] (mēl) *n.* a type or quantity of food served and eaten at any one time: *fried chicken is my favourite meal.*

meal[2] (mēl) *n.* the edible part of wheat, corn, or any other grain ground into a coarse powder as food.

mean[1] (mēn) *vb.* **meaning, meant** (ment). 1. to want to say or do; intend: *she meant to leave at six o'clock.* 2. to signify: *mensa means table in Latin.* **'meaning** *n.* something that is meant or intended. —**'meaningful** *adj.* —**'meaningfully** *adv.*

mean[2] (mēn) *adj.* 1. unkind: *he played a mean trick on his brother.* 2. selfish; ungenerous: *he is too mean to buy his nephew a present.* 3. poor in quality or social position: *a mean dwelling.*

means (mēnz) *pl.n.* 1. the way in which a particular result is obtained: *she won by honest means.* 2. property or money: *only a man of means can afford to keep racehorses.*

meant (ment) *vb.* the past tense and past participle of MEAN[1].

measles ('mēzəlz) *n.* a VIRUS disease that causes a high fever and a rash of bright red spots all over the body. It can be passed from one person to another.

measure ('mezhə) *vb.* **measuring, measured.** 1. to find or show the size, degree, weight, etc., of something: *I measured the table and found it was six feet five inches long.* 2. to be a certain size: *the car measured fourteen feet in length.* 3. (+ *off* or *out*) to separate (a measured amount of something) from the rest: *I measured out four yards of material for the curtains.* —*n.* 1. the size, amount, weight, etc., of something. 2. a standard or unit of measuring: *a yard is a measure of length.* 3. a device used for measuring: *I found a pint measure in the kitchen.* 4. often **measures** (*pl.*) a proposed law or course of action: *the police take strong measures against drunkenness.* **'measurement** *n.* 1. the act of measuring. 2. the size, weight, etc., shown by measuring. —**'measurable** *adj.*

mechanic (mi'kanik) *n.* a person who is skilled at repairing or operating machinery: *Tom is a motor mechanic.* **me'chanical** *adj.* of or like machinery. **mechanism** ('mekənizəm) *n.* 1. the working parts of a machine or other device. 2. any kind of mechanical device or system that operates like a machine.

medal ('medəl) *n.* a flat piece of metal, usu. on a ribbon and with words or a design on it, given as a reward for an achievement. **medallion** (mi'daliən) *n.* 1. a large medal. 2. a circular ornamental design, esp. one set in a wall or carpet.

medal

meddle ('medəl) *vb.* **meddling, meddled.** to interfere in other people's affairs. —**'meddlesome** *adj.*

medicine ('medsin) *n.* 1. a substance used to prevent or cure disease. 2. the science and skill of preventing or curing disease or injury: *he studied*

medicine for six years. **medical** ('medikəl) *adj.* of the science of medicine.

medieval *or* **mediaeval** (medi'ēvəl) *adj.* of the Middle Ages (usu. reckoned to be between 1000 and 1500 A.D.).

medium ('mēdiəm) *n.,pl.* **media** ('mēdiə). something through or by which something is done or acts: *radio is an important medium of communication.* —*adj.* halfway between extremes of size, amount, etc.: *Chris is of medium weight.*

megaphone ('megəfōn) *n.* a funnel-shaped device used to make one's voice sound louder.

melancholy ('melənkoli) *n.* sadness; lowness of spirits. —*adj.* 1. sad; gloomy: *he was melancholy after his wife's death.* 2. causing sadness: *her departure was a melancholy event.*

melody ('melədi) *n.,pl.* **melodies.** the sequence of musical notes that make up a tune: *she played a gay melody on the flute.* **melodious** (mi'lōdiəs) *adj.* tuneful; sweet-sounding.

melon ('melən) *n.* one of several kinds of large juicy sweet-tasting fruits with a hard outer covering that grow on a creeping vinelike plant.

melt (melt) *vb.* 1. to become or cause to become liquid as a result of heating: *the butter melted in the hot kitchen.* 2. (often + *away*) to change form and disappear: *the crowd melted away after the parade.*

member ('membə) *n.* 1. an individual that is part of a group: *only members can use the club's swimming pool.* 2. (old-fashioned) a part of the body. **'membership** *n.* 1. the state of belonging to a society, club, etc. 2. the total number of members: *the society has a membership of 147.*

membrane ('membrān) *n.* a very thin soft layer of skin or similar tissue that covers, lines, or connects parts of the body.

memorial (mi'môriəl) *n.* something that acts as a reminder of a person or event: *she put up a memorial to her mother in the church.*

memory ('meməri) *n.,pl.* **memories.** 1. the power of storing information in the mind for future use: *Jane has a better memory than John or Mary.*

for figures. 2. a person, thing, or event that is remembered: *our holiday gave us many very happy memories.* '**memorize** *vb.* **memorizing, memorized.** to learn (something) by heart. '**memorable** *adj.* worthy of being remembered: *a memorable dance.* —'**memorably** *adv.*

menace ('menəs) *n.* a danger; threat: *the savage dog was a menace.* —*vb.* **menacing, menaced.** to threaten.

mental ('mentəl) *adj.* 1. of or in the mind: *mental arithmetic.* 2. diseased in the mind: *a mental patient.* —'**mentally** *adv.*

mention ('menshən) *vb.* to speak or write briefly about. —*n.* a reference (to a subject): *he made no mention of his illness.*

menu ('menyōō) *n.,pl.* **menus.** a list of the food that can be obtained in a restaurant, cafe, etc.

melon

merchant ('mûchənt) *n.* a person whose work is buying and selling things, esp. in large quantities: *Simon's father is a grain merchant.*

mercury ('mûkyōōri) *n.* a heavy silver-coloured metallic chemical element that is liquid at normal temperatures and is used in thermometers and barometers. Chemical symbol: Hg.

mercy ('mûsi) *n.,pl.* **mercies.** 1. the treating of wrong-doers or enemies with more forgiveness or kindness than is deserved or expected: *the judge had a reputation for mercy.* 2. a piece of good luck; relief: *it was a mercy that no one was killed in the crash.* '**merciful** *adj.* showing mercy. '**merciless** *adv.* showing no mercy.

mere (miə) *adj.* no more than; only: *the dog that Tom had told us was so savage turned out to be a mere puppy.* '**merely** *adv.* only; simply.

merge (mûj) *vb.* **merging, merged.** to become or cause to become one: *the roads merged in the valley.* '**merger** *n.* the combining of two or more small business companies into one large one.

meringue (mə'raṅg) *n.* a mixture of whites of eggs and sugar baked until it is crisp and eaten as small cakes or used as a topping for desserts.

merit ('merit) *n.* 1. value; excellence: *his work has the merit of thoroughness.* 2. **merits** (*pl.*) the facts or particular circumstances of something: *we consider each case on its merits.* —*vb.* to deserve.

mermaid ('mûmād) *n.* an imaginary sea-creature that was believed to have the head and body of a woman and the tail of a fish.

message ('mesij) *n.* a request, piece of news, information, etc., passed in written form or by word of mouth from one person to another.

messenger ('mesinjə) *n.* a person who takes messages or runs errands.

metal ('metəl) *n.* a substance, such as iron, silver, lead, bronze, etc., that conducts heat and electricity and usually has a shiny surface. —**metallic** (mi'talik) *adj.*

meteor ('mētiə) *n.* a lump of matter from space that falls into the earth's atmosphere and burns up, causing the bright fiery streak in the sky that is known as a shooting star. '**meteorite** *n.* a meteor that has fallen to earth.

meteorology (mētiə'roləji) *n.* study of the weather and the changes and conditions of the atmosphere. —**meteorological** (mētiərə'lojikəl) *adj.*

meter ('mētə) *n.* a device that measures and records the amount of electricity used, the distance travelled by a taxi, etc., so that correct payment can be made.

method ('methəd) *n.* 1. a way of doing something: *which method shall I use?* 2. system; orderliness in actions or speech: *the letters were filed without method.* **methodical** (mi'thodikəl) *adj.* orderly and thorough.

metre[1] ('mētə) *n.* a unit for measuring length in the metric system. A metre is equal to about 39·37 inches. **metric** ('metrik) of or measured in metres. **metric system** the decimal measuring system that has the metre as the basic unit of length. The KILOGRAM is the unit of weight and the LITRE the unit of capacity.

metre[2] ('mētə) *n.* verse rhythm or a particular form of this: *the poem was written in a very complicated metre.* —**metrical** ('metrikəl) *adj.*

metropolis (mi'tropəlis) *n.* a very large city, esp. the largest in a country, state, etc. —**metropolitan** (metrə'politən) *adj.*

mice (mīs) *n.* the plural of MOUSE.

microbe ('mīkrōb) *n.* a very small living creature that can be seen only through a microscope. Some microbes cause disease; others are useful.

microphone ('mīkrəfōn) *n.* an instrument that changes sound waves into changing electrical currents so that they can be recorded, made louder, etc.

microscope ('mīkrəskōp) *n.* an instrument with a LENS or lenses, used to make very small things appear larger. **microscopic** (mīkrə'skopik) *adj.* too small to be seen, except under a microscope.

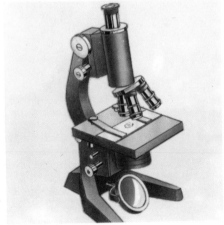

microscope

middle ('midəl) *adj.* 1. halfway between two ends, sides, times, etc.: *ours is the middle house in the row.* 2. medium: *he bought a middle-sized car.* —*n.* a point halfway between two edges, ends, times, etc.: *Jane arrived in the middle of the meal.*

midget ('mijit) *n.* a very small person.

midwife ('midwīf) *n.,pl.* **midwives.** a woman who helps and cares for another woman when she is giving birth to a baby.

might (mīt) *n.* strength; force: *he threw the ball with all his might.* '**mighty** *adj.* **mightier, mightiest.** great in size, force, or amount.

migrate (mī'grāt) *vb.* **migrating, migrated.** 1. to move from one place to go to live in another. 2. to move according to the seasons: *European swallows migrate to South Africa in the winter.* **migrant** *n.* a person or animal that migrates. —**mi'gration** *n.* —**mi'gratory** *adj.*

mild (mīld) *adj.* not severe or harsh; not strong: *in a mild winter we have little frost or snow.* —'**mildly** *adv.*

mile (mīl) *n.* a measure of distance equal to 1760 yards (1.6093 kilometres). '**mileage** *n.* distance travelled measured in miles.

milestone ('mīlstōn) *n.* 1. a stone or other marker set up beside a road to show how many miles one has to travel to reach certain places. 2. an important happening: *Magna Carta was a milestone in English history.*

militant ('militant) *adj.* actively supporting the use of force to achieve political or other ends. —*n.* an active supporter of force or violent tactics.

military ('militari) *adj.* of or for soldiers, land warfare, or an army: *military uniform.*

milk (milk) *n.* 1. white liquid produced by female MAMMALs to feed their young. 2. a similar liquid found in some plants: *coconut milk.* —*vb.* to take milk from (a cow, goat, or sheep).

mill (mil) *n.* 1. a building containing machinery for grinding grain: *a flour mill.* 2. a factory producing certain materials: *a paper mill.* 3. a device for grinding: *a pepper mill.* —*vb.* to put something through a mill.

milligram ('miligram) *n.* a very small unit of weight in the metric system; one-thousandth part of a GRAM.

millimetre ('milimētə) *n.* a very short unit of length in the metric system; one-thousandth part of a METRE[1].

millinery ('milinəri) *n.* 1. womens' hats. 2. the business of making womens' hats. **milliner** *n.*

million ('milyən) *n. adj.* one thousand thousand (1,000,000). **millionaire** (milyə'neə) *n.* a person who owns money and property worth over a million pounds.

mime (mīm) *n.* 1. a play or method of acting in which the actors do not use their voices but tell the story by means of facial expression and hand and body movements. 2. an actor who specializes in this form of acting.

mimic ('mimik) *vb.* **mimicking, mimicked.** to imitate, esp. in order to mock at. —*n.* a person that mimics.

minaret

minaret (minə'ret) *n.* a tall thin tower close to a MOSQUE from the top of which a mosque official summons Muslims to come and pray.

mince (mins) *vb.* **mincing, minced.** to cut up (meat) into tiny pieces with a knife or a special machine. —*n.* minced meat.

mincemeat ('minsmēt) *n.* a sweet mixture of dried fruit, sugar, apples, and spices, used as a pie filling.

mind (mīnd) *n.* 1. a person's ability to think, understand, remember, learn, etc.: *he cannot keep his mind on his work.* 2. something that is thought; an intention, wish, or opinion: *I changed my mind about buying the dress.* —*vb.* 1. to dislike or be unhappy about something: *she minded being left behind.* 2. to pay attention to; be careful about: *mind what you say.* 3. to take care of: *Jill minds her baby sister while her mother is out.* '**mindless** *adj.* lacking or not needing intelligence.

mine (mīn) *n.* 1. a series of holes, pits, and passageways dug underground so that people can reach and get out valuable substances from the earth. 2. a bomb placed underground or underwater. —*vb.* **mining, mined.** 1. to dig out from under the ground. 2. to place bombs in.

mineral ('minərəl) *n.* a natural substance, such as silver or salt, that is found in the ground or in rocks. —*adj.* belonging to or containing this class of substances. **mineral water** water containing natural salts. **mineralogy** (minə'ralǝji) *n.* the study of minerals.

mingle ('minggəl) *vb.* **mingling, mingled.** to mix in together with: *the robbers mingled with the crowd.*

miniature ('minəchə) *adj.* very small in size. —*n.* something made in a very small size, esp. a painted portrait.

minimum ('minimǝm) *n.* the least possible amount: *she does the minimum of work.* —*adj.* lowest; smallest. '**minimal** *adj.* very little.

mink (mingk) *n.,pl.* **mink** or **minks.** a small animal with a soft thick fur that is highly valued for making fur coats.

minor ('mīnə) *adj.* small in size, age, importance, value, etc.: *it was a minor accident and no one was hurt.* —*n.* a person who has not yet reached the age of full legal responsibility. **minority** (mi'noriti) *n.,pl.* **minorities.** 1. a smaller part or number: *a minority of people own motorcycles.* 2. the years before a person reaches the age of full legal responsibility.

mint[1] (mint) *n.* 1. one of several plants producing strongly smelling leaves that are used for flavouring, e.g. peppermint, spearmint. 2. a mint-flavoured sweet.

mint[2] (mint) *n.* 1. a place where coins are made. 2. (informal) a lot of money: *repairs to the house have cost me a mint.* —*vb.* to make coins.

minus ('mīnəs) *prep.* 1. less: *ten minus five equals five.* 2. without: *a table minus one leg.* —*adj.* denoting subtraction or a negative quantity: *minus seven.*

minute[1] (minit) *n.* 1. a sixtieth part of an hour. 2. a very short space of time: *wait a minute.* 3. (geometry) a sixtieth part of a DEGREE. 4. **minutes** (*pl.*) the detailed record of an official meeting or committee.

mint

minute[2] (mī'nyoot) *adj.* 1. very small; tiny. 2. very detailed: *they made a minute investigation of the evidence.*

miracle ('mirəkəl) *n.* 1. an event that cannot be explained by natural causes. 2. something to be amazed at: *he was a miracle of politeness.* **miraculous** (mi'rakyooləs) *adj.* 1. wonderfully unexpected. 2. able to work miracles. 3. caused by a miracle.

mirror ('mirə) *n.* a sheet of glass coated with silvery paint on the back so that it reflects the image of whatever is in front of it. —*vb.* to reflect an image as a mirror does: *the pond mirrored the surrounding trees.*

mischief ('mischif) *n.* 1. playful malice or annoying behaviour: *the little boy was full of mischief.* 2. trouble; damage: *the rats caused mischief in the barns.* —**mischievous** ('mischəvəs) *adj.* —'**mischievously** *adv.*

miser ('mīzə) *n.* a person who hoards money and refuses to spend it. —'**miserly** *adj.*

misery ('mizəri) *n.,pl.* **miseries.** 1. unhappiness. 2. distress caused by poverty or illness. 3. (slang) someone who is always complaining and gloomy. '**miserable** *adj.* 1. very sad. 2. valueless; bad. 3. causing misery or distress. —'**miserably** *adv.*

misfit ('misfit) *n.* a person or thing that does not fit properly into an intended role, situation, etc.

misfortune (mis'fôchən) *n.* 1. bad luck. 2. an unlucky event.

mislay (mis'lā) *vb.* **mislaying, mislaid.** to put (something) away and then forget where it is.

mislead (mis'lēd) *vb.* **misleading, misled.** 1. to cause (someone) to go wrong. 2. to give the wrong idea: *you misled me with your description.*

miss[1] (mis) *vb.* **missing, missed.** 1. to fail to do, hear, see, etc.: *I missed the next words.* 2. to feel the loss of: *I shall miss you.* 3. to avoid; escape: *I just missed bumping into him.* —*n.* the failure to hit a target or achieve an aim.

miss[2] (mis) *n.* 1. **Miss** the title of an unmarried woman or girl. 2. title used for addressing a woman whose name is unknown, e.g. a waitress.

missile ('misīl) *n.* anything that can be thrown or shot through the air: *bricks, bottles, and other missiles were thrown at the police during the riot.*

missing ('mising) *adj.* lost; absent.

mission ('mishən) *n.* 1. the sending out of a group of people specially trained to perform a particular task, esp. people sent to teach the heathen. 2. the buildings these people live or work in. 3. a purpose or duty in life: *she felt she had a mission to teach.* '**missionary** *n.,pl.* **missionaries.** a person sent out to preach and convert unbelievers to Christianity. *adj.* of missions and their work.

mist (mist) *n.* 1. a cloud of tiny water droplets at or near ground level; thin fog. 2. anything that blurs or obscures. —*vb.* (often + *over*) to be or become misty. —'**misty** *adj.* **mistier, mistiest.**

mistake (mi'stāk) *n.* 1. a fault; unintentional error. —*vb.* **mistaking, mistook, mistaken.** 1. to understand wrongly. 2. to think a person or thing is another person or thing: *I mistook her for Sue.*

misunderstand (misundə'stand) *vb.* **misunderstanding, misunderstood.** 1. to interpret (a person's behaviour) wrongly. 2. to fail to understand (the true meaning of words, etc.).

mitre ('mītə) *n.* the tall official headdress of a bishop.

mix (miks) *vb.* 1. to combine two or more different things. 2. (+ *up*) to confuse. '**mixture** *n.* 1. the result of mixing things together. 2. a liquid medicine. 3. an assortment: *there was a strange mixture of things on the floor.*

moan (mōn) *n.* 1. a low sound expressing pain or sadness. 2. (informal) complaint; fuss. —*vb.* to make a soft, pained sound.

moat (mōt) *n.* a deep ditch, usu. filled with water, surrounding a castle or town as a defence against attack.

mobile ('mōbīl) *adj.* able to move or be moved easily. —*n.* a decorative arrangement of light objects attached to strings made so that it can be hung up and left free to move in air currents. —**mo'bility** *n.*

mock (mok) *vb.* 1. to laugh at in a contemptuous way. 2. to imitate (a person, manner, etc.) so as to make seem ridiculous; mimic. —*adj.* false; imitation. '**mockery** *n.,pl.* **mockeries.** 1. mocking behaviour. 2. a feeble imitation: *a mockery of justice.*

mock-up ('mokup) *n.* a full-scale model of something that is being built: *we saw the designer's mock-up of the new racing car.*

model ('modəl) *n.* 1. a particular style or pattern. 2. an exact copy of something on a much smaller scale: *he collects models of ships.* 3. someone or something worthy of imitation. 4. a person who poses for an artist or photographer or who demonstrates clothes. —*vb.* **modelling, modelled.** 1. to shape or construct according to a model. 2. to make an object out of clay or wax. 3. to act as an artist's or fashion model. —*adj.* excellent.

moderate *adj.* ('modərit) 1. not extreme in opinions, wishes, or needs: *a moderate eater.* 2. fairly good: *a moderate success.* —*n.* a person who holds moderate (def. 1) views. —*vb.* ('modərāt) **moderating, moderated.** to make or become less extreme, violent, loud, etc. —**moder'ation** *n.*

mitre

modern ('modən) *adj.* to do with the present or recent times. '**modernize** *vb.* **modernizing, modernized.** to make modern. **moderni'zation** *n.* the process of making modern or more modern.

modest ('modist) *adj.* 1. having a fairly humble opinion of oneself. 2. just adequate; not excessive: *he earned a modest wage.* —'**modestly** *adv.* —'**modesty** *n.*

modify ('modifī) *vb.* **modifying, modified.** 1. to make slight changes to: *I modified the dress by removing the sleeves.* 2. to moderate; make less extreme: *he modified his demands.* —**modifi'cation** *n.*

moist (moist) *adj.* damp; slightly wet. **moisten** ('moisən) *vb.* to make damp or damper. '**moisture** *n.* dampness; slight wetness. —'**moistly** *adv.* —'**moistness** *n.*

mole[1] (mōl) *n.* a small animal with dark grey-brown fur and tiny eyes that lives in tunnels which it makes just under the surface of the ground, using its strong feet for digging.

mole

mole[2] (mōl) *n.* a permanent brown spot on a person's skin.

molecule ('molikyōol) *n.* the smallest particle, consisting of one or more ATOMS, into which a substance can be broken down without undergoing a change in its chemical make-up. —**molecular** (mə'lekyōolə) *adj.*

mollusc ('moləsk) *n.* one of the many soft-bodied boneless animals that live in or near water and usu. have a hard outer shell to protect their bodies. Oysters, snails, and octopuses are all molluscs.

moment ('mōmənt) *n.* 1. a tiny space of time: *I won't be gone a moment.* 2. a particular point in time: *it is the right moment to start.* —'**momentarily** *adv.* —'**momentary** *adj.*

monarch ('monək) *n.* the supreme single ruler of a state; king; queen. '**monarchy** *n.* 1. a country ruled by a monarch. 2. the government or rule of a monarch.

monastery ('monəstəri) *n.,pl.* **monasteries.** the building in which monks live and work. —**monastic** (mə'nastik) *adj.*

money ('muni) *n.* 1. coins and banknotes; cash. 2. the system of coinage used in any country for buying and selling. **monetary** ('munitəri) *adj.* concerning money.

mongrel ('munggrəl) *n.* a dog having parents of different breeds.

monk (munk) *n.* a man who has joined a religious society and lives his life in obedience to its rules.

monkey ('munki) *n.* one of a large group of very intelligent animals closely related to man. They live mainly in trees in the warm areas of the world. —*vb.* (+ *around*) to interfere with and mess up.

monopoly (mə'nopəli) *n.,pl.* **monopolies.** the complete control of trade in a product or service by one person or firm. **mo'nopolize** *vb.* **monopolizing, monopolized.** to gain or hold exclusive control over: *he monopolized everyone's attention.* —**monopoli'zation** *n.*

monotonous (mə'notənəs) *adj.* dull; lacking in interest or variety and therefore boring. —**mo'notonously** *adv.*

monsoon (mon'sōon) *n.* a strong steady seasonal wind that governs the climate in the Indian Ocean and South Asia, bringing either dry weather (dry monsoon) or heavy rains (wet monsoon). It blows from the southwest for half the year and from the northeast for the other half.

monster ('monstə) *n.* 1. any huge imaginary beast, usu. ugly and terrifying. 2. a grotesque or deformed animal or plant. 3. a cruel and inhuman person. —*adj.* extraordinarily large. '**monstrous** *adj.* 1. abnormally or frighteningly large. 2. evil; horrible: *he was accused of monstrous crimes.* 3. (informal) outrageous. —'**monstrously** *adv.*

month (munth) *n.* one of the twelve divisions of the year. '**monthly** *adj.* 1. happening once a month. 2. of the period of a month. —*adv.* once a month.

monument ('monyōomənt) *n.* a statue, building, ornamental slab, etc., erected to keep alive the memory of some person, event, or discovery. **monu'mental** *adj.* 1. connected with monuments: *monumental sculpture.* 2. enduring: *a monumental achievement.* 3. (informal) enormous: *he made a monumental blunder when he bought that car.*

mood (mōod) *n.* an emotional state of mind: *the crowd was in a gay mood.* '**moody** *adj.* **moodier, moodiest.** likely to have fits of depression. —'**moodily** *adv.* —'**moodiness** *n.*

moon (mōon) *n.* 1. often **Moon** the heavenly body that moves round the earth once every 29.5 days and shines by reflected light from the sun. 2. a similar body moving round another planet; SATELLITE: *Mars has two moons.*

moor[1] (mŏoə) *n.* a wide expanse of wild land with heather and grass but few trees.

moor[2] (mŏoə) *vb.* to tie up (a boat) to a fixed place by rope or chain. '**mooring** *n.* a place where boats can be safely tied up.

mop (mop) *n.* an absorbent wad of material on the end of a stick or pole, used for washing up or cleaning floors. —*vb.* **mopping, mopped.** 1. to clean with a mop. 2. (+ *up*) to clean up (spilt liquid) with an absorbent tissue or cloth.

moral ('morəl) *adj.* 1. concerning the choice between right and wrong and how to apply it in life: *whether to fight or not was a moral decision.* 2. of or following the rules for right conduct: *moral life.* —*n.* 1. the moral teaching of a story or event. 2. **morals** (*pl.*) a person's moral character or conduct. **morality** (mə'raliti) *n.* standards of morally right behaviour. '**moralize** *vb.* **moralizing, moralized.** to talk on moral subjects, esp. in a tedious way.

moreover (môr'ōvə) *adv.* besides; in addition; furthermore: *she is pretty; moreover, she's very intelligent.*

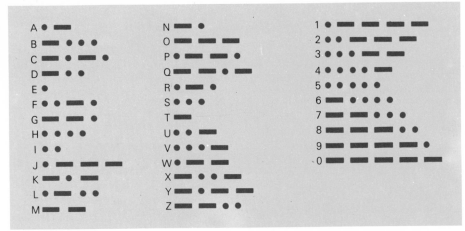

Morse code

Morse code (môs) a code invented by Samuel Morse in 1837 and used for sending messages by wire, radio, or flashlight. Each letter of the alphabet is represented by combinations of long or short buzzes or flashes (dots and dashes).

mortal ('môtəl) *adj.* 1. not living forever. 2. causing death: *a mortal blow.* —*n.* a human being.

mortgage ('môgij) *n.* a loan of money given in exchange for property which is paid off over a fixed time. —*vb.* **mortgaging, mortgaged.** 1. to give (property) as security for a money loan. 2. to lose (future freedom of action) in exchange for a present advantage.

mosaic (mō'zāik) *n.* a design made up of tiny coloured pieces of stone, ceramic, or some other durable material cemented together to make floor or wall decorations. —*adj.* made of or decorated with mosaics: *a mosaic floor.*

mosque (mosk) *n.* a place of worship for Muslims.

mosquito (mə'skēto) *n.,pl.* **mosquitoes.** a long-legged thin-bodied fly found in most countries. The female sucks animals' blood, causing an itching sensation. Some kinds pass on MALARIA.

moss (mos) *n.* a small soft green plant that grows in damp places, on stones, tree trunks, and similar surfaces, in dense spongy clumps. —'**mossy** *adj.* **mossier, mossiest.**

moth (moth) *n.* an insect like a butterfly with large often beautifully coloured wings. Most moths are active at night.

motion ('mōshən) *n.* 1. the act of changing position; movement. 2. a suggestion made formally at a meeting. —*vb.* to show or indicate by a movement: *the stewardess motioned us to go out to the aircraft.*

motive ('mōtiv) *n.* a reason or emotion that causes or influences an action, decision, wish, etc. —*adj.* capable of causing motion or setting something going: *the engine provides the motive power in a car.* '**motivate** *vb.* **motivating, motivated.** to give a motive (for doing something). **moti'vation** *n.* force, reason, etc., encouraging one to act.

motor ('mōtə) *n.* a machine that uses fuel or electricity to produce the power to make another machine or a vehicle work. —*adj.* having to do with or powered by a motor: *Carol bought a motor scooter.* —*vb.* to travel by motorcar. '**motorist** *n.* a person who drives a motorcar.

motto ('motō) *n.,pl.* **mottos** or **mottoes.** a short sentence or phrase that sums up a practical belief or course of action, e.g. *deeds not words* and *do as you would be done by.*

mould[1] (mōld) *n.* a hollow form in a particular shape into which liquid is poured to harden into the shape of the mould: *a jelly mould.* —*vb.* 1. to shape with the hands: *she moulded the clay.* 2. to form (someone else's opinions or character). '**moulding** *n.* an ornamental raised pattern round a wall or ceiling.

mould[2] (mōld) *n.* a fungus growth that flourishes in damp conditions and ruins food or plants. It has a blue, grey, or green woolly appearance. —'**mouldy** *adj.* **mouldier, mouldiest.** —'**mouldiness** *n.*

moult (mōlt) *n.* the seasonal shedding of old fur or feathers to make way for new growth. —*vb.* to pass through this process.

mound (mound) *n.* a heap or small hill of rocks, earth, or other material.

mount (mount) *vb.* 1. to climb onto (a horse, motorcycle, etc.). 2. to go up (steps); get onto (a platform). 3. to increase: *his debts mounted daily.* 4. to arrange or set up: *the art class mounted an exhibition of paintings.* —*n.* 1. something ridden. 2. the cardboard surround or backing for a photograph, painting, etc. 3. a hill or mountain.

mountain ('mountən) *n.* 1. a very large mass of land that rises steeply from the surrounding country. 2. (informal) a large amount or heap. —'**mountainous** *adj.*

mourn (môn) *vb.* to be sorrowful over someone who has died or over some loss. '**mournful** *adj.* sad; gloomy. —'**mournfully** *adv.*

mouse (mous) *n.,pl.* **mice.** a small furry brownish-grey animal with large ears, beady eyes, and a long almost hairless tail.

moustache (mə'stâsh) *n.* the hair growing above a man's upper lip.

mouth *n.* (mouth), *pl.* **mouths** (moudhz). 1. the opening in a person's or animal's face that contains the teeth and tongue. 2. any mouthlike opening, esp. the place where a river joins the sea.

mow (mō) *vb.* **mowing, mowed, mown.** to cut down (grass or grain). '**mower** *n.* a machine for cutting the grass on lawns.

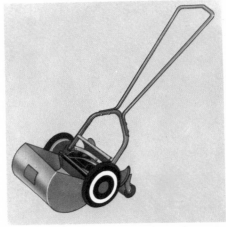

mower

muffle ('mufəl) *vb.* **muffling, muffled.** 1. to wrap up in order to keep warm. 2. to deaden sound (of engines, traffic, etc.). '**muffler** *n.* 1. a woollen scarf to wear round the neck. 2. a device for quietening engine noise.

mummy

mug (mug) *n.* 1. a straight-sided cup with a handle. 2. (informal) someone who is easily deceived. 3. (slang) face or mouth. —*vb.* **mugging, mugged.** 1. to attack and rob someone in the street. 2. (+ *up*) (informal) to study hard.

mule (myōōl) *n.* an animal that has a horse as its mother and a donkey as its father.

multiply ('multiplī) *vb.* **multiplying, multiplied.** 1. to repeat (a given number) a certain number of times: *if we multiply 8 by 5, we get 40.* 2. to increase in number: *the gambler's debts quickly multiplied.* **multiple** ('multipəl) *adj.* with or concerning many parts. —*n.* a number that exactly contains a smaller number multiplied a given number of times: *40 is a multiple of 8.* —**multi-pli'cation** *n.*

mumble ('mumbəl) *vb.* **mumbling, mumbled.** to speak unclearly, jumbling one's words together. —*n.* an unclear way of speaking.

mummy ('mumi) *n.,pl.* **mummies.** a dead body, prepared and wrapped for burial by a special method to preserve it from decay. This practice was common in Egypt in former times. '**mummify** *vb.* **mummifying, mummified.** to preserve (something dead) in perfect condition.

municipal (myōō'nisipəl) *adj.* owned by, or employed by, local government: *municipal workers care for the town parks.* **munici'pality** *n.,pl.* **municipalities.** a town or area that is self-governing, under the central government.

murder ('mûdə) *n.* the intentional and unlawful killing of a person. —*vb.* to kill a person on purpose. —'**murderous** *adj.* —'**murderously** *adv.*

murmur ('mûmə) *n.* 1. a quiet steady sound, rising and falling: *we heard the murmur of a brook in the distance.* 2. a subdued protest. —*vb.* to make a murmuring sound.

muscle ('musəl) *n.* a thick ropelike fibrous tissue in the body that can be tightened or relaxed to cause movement: *long bicycle rides developed his leg muscles.* **muscular** ('muskyōōlə) *adj.* 1. having large muscles. 2. of or concerning muscles.

museum (myōō'zēəm) *n.* a building where things of historic or scientific interest are displayed for people to see.

mushroom ('mushrəm) *n.* a fungus that is umbrella-shaped with a stout central stem. Some mushrooms are edible, but other kinds are very poisonous. —*vb.* to grow rapidly.

music ('myōōzik) *n.* 1. the art or skill of arranging sounds or combinations of sounds to produce a special effect. 2. the sounds thus produced. 3. written symbols representing these sounds; notes or a score. '**musical** *adj.* 1. referring to or using music. 2. showing a feeling, talent, or ability regarding music. **mu'sician** *n.*

Muslim ('muzlim) *adj.,n.* (of) a person who believes in and follows the teachings of the prophet Mohammed, which are embodied in the religion known as Islam.

mussel

mussel ('musəl) *n.* an edible shellfish with a dark-blue or purplish shell.

mustard ('mustəd) *n.* a hot-tasting sauce, used as a relish with meat and made from the tiny bright yellow seeds of the mustard plant.

mute (myōōt) *adj.* 1. silent. 2. not able to speak. —*n.* 1. a person who is unable to speak. 2. a device to soften the sound of a musical instrument.

mutiny ('myōōtini) *n.,pl.* **mutinies.** a rebellion against authority. —*vb.* **mutinying, mutinied.** to join a rebellion. **muti'neer** *n.* a person who takes part in a mutiny.

mutter ('mutə) *vb.* to speak low; grumble. —*n.* a quiet unclear way of speaking.

mutton ('mutən) *n.* the meat from a full-grown sheep.

muzzle ('muzəl) *n.* 1. the nose and mouth of an animal. 2. a device to fit over an animal's muzzle to prevent it from biting. 3. the open end of a gun. —*vb.* **muzzling, muzzled.** to put a muzzle (def. 2) on (an animal).

mystery ('mistəri) *n.,pl.* **mysteries.** something strange, hidden, or inexplicable. **mysterious** (mi'stiəriəs) *adj.* difficult to understand; arousing curiosity. —**mys'teriously** *adv.*

myth (mith) *n.* 1. a story relating to a people's beliefs about their distant past, their ancestors, etc.: *the myths of ancient Greece include many stories about Zeus and the other gods.* 2. a story, belief, etc., that is totally untrue. **my'thology** *n.* 1. the study of myths and legends. 2. the myths of a particular people. —'**mythical** *adj.* —**mytho'logical** *adj.*

N

nail (nāl) *n.* 1. a metal spike with a flattened head and pointed tip, used for fastening together pieces of wood. 2. (also **fingernail** *or* **toenail**) the hard protective covering on the upper tips of fingers and toes. —*vb.* to fasten with nails.

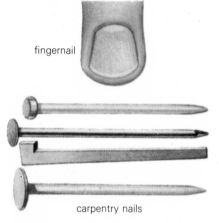

fingernail

carpentry nails

nail

naked ('nākid) *adj.* 1. without clothes or covering. 2. unaided: *I could see the comet with my naked eye.* —'**nakedly** *adv.* —'**nakedness** *n.*

name (nām) *n.* 1. the word or words given to people, places, or things, by which they are spoken of or addressed: *my dog's name is Simba.* 2. character or reputation: *his cheating gave him a bad name.* —*vb.* **naming, named.** 1. to give a name to. 2. to put into words or state: *name a price for your old skates.* '**namely** *adv.* that is to say: *three of us went, namely Donna, Pete, and Ed.*

napkin ('napkin) *n.* 1. a piece of cloth or paper that is used at mealtimes to protect clothing and for wiping fingers and lips. 2. (also **nappy**) a piece of towel or other absorbent cloth wrapped round a baby's bottom.

narrate (nə'rāt) *vb.* **narrating, narrated.** to tell or relate (a series of events). **narrative** ('narətiv) *n.* a story. *adj.* of a story; telling a story: *a narrative poem is one that tells a story.* —**nar'ration** *n.* —**nar'rator** *n.*

narrow ('narō) *adj.* 1. not wide: *a narrow path.* 2. with little to spare: *a narrow escape.* —'**narrowly** *adv.* —'**narrowness** *n.*

nasty ('nâsti) *adj.* **nastier, nastiest.** 1. showing spite or hatred: *that horse has a nasty temper.* 2. unpleasant; disagreeable: *a nasty mess.* 3. severe or dangerous: *there was a nasty accident between two cars.* —'**nastily** *adv.*

nation ('nāshən) *n.* a country and the people who live there and share the same government and culture.

national ('nashənəl) *adj.* of or concerning a nation. —*n.* a person belonging to a particular country: *Henri is a Belgian national.* '**nationalism** *n.* a powerful feeling of loyalty to one's country. '**nationalist** *n.* a patriot. **nation'ality** *n.,pl.* **nationalities.** 1. the condition of belonging to a particular nation. 2. a large number of people who have the same language, history, and culture. '**nationalize** *vb.* **nationalizing, nationalized.** to make (an industry, service, etc.) the property of the nation. —**nationali'zation** *n.*

native ('nātiv) *n.* 1. someone born in a particular place: *she is a native of Rome.* 2. a person, plant, or animal belonging naturally in a certain place. —*adj.* 1. natural: *native wit.* 2. belonging to a person's place of birth: *one's native land.* 3. living or growing naturally in a certain place: *eagles are native to wild and mountainous regions.*

nativity (nə'tiviti) *n.,pl.* **nativities.** the time of one's birth. **the Nativity** the birth of Jesus Christ at Bethlehem.

natural ('nachərəl) *adj.* 1. not artificial; produced or caused by nature: *she has great natural beauty.* 2. normal; expected: *Ed's failure was the natural result of his laziness.* 3. closely imitating nature: *his photograph of the baby looks very natural.* —*n.* a person born with some particular skill: *she is a natural at ballet.*

nature ('nāchə) *n.* 1. creation; the physical world. 2. a person's character or temperament; the essential qualities of a thing: *it is in his nature to keep busy.* 3. type; kind: *she hates work of that nature.*

naughty ('nôti) *adj.* **naughtier, naughtiest.** badly behaved; very mischievous or disobedient. —'**naughtily** *adv.* —'**naughtiness** *n.*

nautical ('nôtikəl) *adj.* having to do with sailors, ships, or the sea.

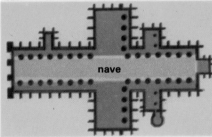

nave

nave (nāv) *n.* the main central part of a church, where the congregation sits, usu. separated from the side AISLEs by pillars.

navel ('nāvəl) *n.* the little hollow in the middle of the abdomen, where the cord joining a newborn baby to its mother was once attached.

navigate ('navigāt) *vb.* **navigating, navigated.** 1. to steer a ship or aircraft by means of instruments and charts. 2. to sail. '**navigable** *adj.* suitable for shipping: *a navigable river.* **navi**'**gation** *n.* 1. the science of navigating. 2. the act of steering. —'**navigator** *n.*

navy ('nāvi) *n.,pl.* **navies.** 1. the whole fleet of warships possessed by a state, together with their officers and crews. 2. (also **navy blue**) the very dark blue colour used for naval uniforms.

near (niə) *adj.* 1. close in space or time: *the near future.* 2. on the lefthand side: *the horse is lame in its near foreleg.* 3. close in relationship or feeling: *a near friend.* —*adv.* not far: *the time draws near for our departure.* —*prep.* close to; not far from: *we have a house near the city.* —*vb.* to approach: *the boat neared the beach.* '**nearby** *adj.* close at hand: *we walked to the nearby village. adv.* not far off: *we waited nearby until she finished taking photos.* '**nearly** *adv.* almost.

neat (nēt) *adj.* 1. orderly; carefully arranged. 2. skilful: *a neat dive.* '**neaten** *vb.* to make neat or neater. —'**neatly** *adv.* —'**neatness** *n.*

necessary ('nesisəri) *adj.* 1. essential or needful. 2. unavoidable; not governed by one's free will: *prison was the necessary result of his crimes.* **necessitate** (ni'sesitāt) *vb.* **necessitating, necessitated.** to make (something) necessary: *the car's breakdown necessitated a change in our plans.* **ne**'**cessity** *n.,pl.* **necessities.** something that cannot be avoided or done without.

neck (nek) *n.* 1. the part of the body connecting the head to the trunk. 2. a narrow part of anything: *the neck of a bottle.*

necklace ('nekləs) *n.* an ornament of beads or jewels threaded or linked together and worn round the neck.

nectar ('nektə) *n.* a sweet substance produced by plants to attract the insects and birds required for pollination.

need (nēd) *vb.* 1. to be in want; lack: *the plant needed water.* 2. to have to: *need we go now?* —*n.* 1. a want or necessity. 2. poverty: *need drove him to steal.* 3. a time of crisis or danger. '**needy** *adj.* **needier, neediest.** very poor. —'**needful** *adj.*

needle ('nēdəl) *n.* 1. a small slender sharp-pointed instrument with a hole at one end, used to draw thread through fabric. 2. any object of similar shape used for various purposes: *knitting needle.* 3. the leaf of a pine tree. —*vb.* **needling, needled.** (informal) to irritate; annoy.

negative ('negətiv) *adj.* 1. expressing denial or refusal. 2. not enthusiastic or helpful; uncomplimentary: *he made some negative comments on her work.* 3. having a particular type of electrical charge. 4. of numbers that are less than zero. —*n.* 1. a word or statement by which something is denied or refused. 2. a photographic plate on which areas of light and

nests

swallow

hummingbird

bowerbird

chaffinch

grebe

shade are reversed. **negate** (ni'gāt) *vb.* **negating, negated.** to cancel; imply the non-existence of: *his one blunder negated his past successes.* —**ne'gation** *n.* —'**negatively** *adv.*

neglect (ni'glekt) *vb.* 1. to fail to take care of: *Tom neglected his hamster.* 2. to fail to do: *he neglected to fetch the newspaper.* —*n.* the lack of proper care or attention.

negotiate (ni'gōshiāt) *vb.* **negotiating, negotiated.** 1. to settle by discussions or bargaining. 2. to pass over or through: *the driver negotiated the track in low gear.* —**negotiable** (ni'gōshəbəl) *adj.* —**negoti'ation** *n.* —**ne'gotiator** *n.*

neighbour ('nābə) *n.* a person who lives in the next house, or nearby. '**neighbourhood** *n.* 1. a particular small area. 2. the people in the area where one lives. '**neighbourly** *adj.* friendly; helpful.

nephew ('nevyōō) *n.* the son of one's brother or sister.

nerve (nûv) *n.* 1. a fibre that carries messages between the brain and parts of the body. 2. bravery: *have you the nerve to jump off the high diving board?* 3. (informal) cheek; impudence: *he had the nerve to try to borrow money again.* '**nervous** *adj.* fearful: *I am nervous of swimming.* —'**nervously** *adv.*

nest (nest) *n.* 1. a structure built by birds and some other animals for shelter for themselves and their young. 2. a cosy home or retreat. 3. a cluster or group occupying a nest: *a nest of ants.* —*vb.* to make, have, or settle in a nest.

net[1] (net) *n.* a fabric of loose open meshes, knotted at the points where the strands of thread, wire, cord, etc., cross. —*vb.* **netting, netted.** 1. to catch with a net. 2. to cover with a net.

net[2] (net) *adj.* 1. remaining after all necessary deductions have been made: *after tax his net income was enough to live on.* 2. (of weights) not including packaging. —*vb.* **netting, netted.** to make as clear profit: *he netted a hundred pounds on the sale.*

nettle ('netəl) *n.* a wild plant with hairs on the leaves and stalk that cause a stinging and burning sensation to the human skin. —*vb.* **nettling, nettled.** to irritate.

network ('netwûk) *n.* 1. a system of many crossing and connecting lines: *the highway network.* 2. a system of radio or television stations, stores, warehouses, offices, etc., under the same ownership. 3. a group of interacting people: *a spy network.*

neutral ('nyōōtrəl) *adj.* 1. not taking sides in a dispute. 2. not distinctively marked or coloured: *the wallpaper was a neutral shade.* 3. (chemistry) neither ACID nor ALKALI. —*n.* 1. a person or group that does not take sides in a dispute. 2. the position of a car's gears in which the engine cannot send power to the wheels. **neu'trality** *n.* a state of not taking sides. '**neutralize** *vb.* **neutralizing, neutralized.** to make or become neutral. —**neutrali'zation** *n.*

new (nyōō) *adj.* 1. only recently existing, made, or done: *a new lamb.* 2. unknown or undiscovered before: *a new star.* 3. modern; different from that which has gone before: *a new style.* 4. beginning again: *a new moon.* 5. unaccustomed; strange: *a new pupil at the school.* —'**newly** *adv.*

news (nyōōz) *n.* information not heard before; recent and interesting events.

newsagent ('nyōōzājənt) *n.* a shopkeeper who sells newspapers, magazines, etc.

newspaper ('nyōōzpāpə) *n.* sheets of paper published daily or weekly to give the latest news.

newt (nyōōt) *n.* a small creature that looks like a lizard and spends most of its time in water.

nice (nīs) *adj.* **nicer, nicest.** 1. pleasant; attractive: *a nice day.* 2. having good social qualities: *a nice woman.* 3. delicate; calling for care or accuracy: *he kept a nice balance between the disputing groups.* **nicety** ('nīsiti) *n.,pl.* **niceties.** exact or perfect detail. —'**nicely** *adv.*

nickel ('nikəl) *n.* a hard silvery metal much used in industry. Chemical symbol: Ni.

nickname ('niknām) *n.* a name given to someone and used instead of his real name: *Paul's nickname was Freckles.* —*vb.* **nicknaming, nicknamed.** to give a nickname to.

nicotine ('nikətēn) *n.* an oily poisonous substance that is found in tobacco plants.

niece (nēs) *n.* the daughter of one's brother or sister.

night (nīt) *n.* the period of darkness between sunset and sunrise. '**nightly** *adj.* of or happening in the night. *adv.* every night.

nightingale

nightingale ('nītinggāl) *n.* a small reddish-brown bird famous for its beautiful song that is heard mainly by night.

nightmare ('nītmeə) *n.* 1. a very unpleasant dream. 2. any horrible experience causing terror or frustration. —'**nightmarish** *adj.*

nil (nil) *n.* nothing; zero: *the final score was five–nil (5–0).*

nimble ('nimbəl) *adj.* **nimbler, nimblest.** moving or working lightly and quickly; agile. —'**nimbleness** *n.* —'**nimbly** *adv.*

nipple ('nipəl) *n.* 1. the small tip in the centre of a breast or udder through which a mammal's young can suck milk from its mother. 2. any similar small projection, e.g. one used for oiling a machine.

nitrogen ('nītrəjən) *n.* a colourless odourless gas that makes up about four-fifths of the world's atmosphere. Chemical symbol: N.

noble ('nōbəl) *adj.* **nobler, noblest.** 1. having or showing high ideals: *her noble action saved her friend's life.* 2. of high social rank. **no'bility** *n.,pl.* **nobilities.** the state or quality of being noble.

noise (noiz) *n.* 1. loud, unpleasant, and continuous sound. 2. any sound. —'**noisily** *adv.* —'**noisy** *adj.* **noisier, noisiest.**

nomad ('nōmad) *n.* a person who has no settled home but wanders from place to place.

nominal ('nominəl) *adj.* 1. existing in name only, not in fact: *he was the nominal leader of the group.* 2. very slight: *the damage was only nominal.* —'**nominally** *adv.*

nonsense ('nonsəns) *n.* something that lacks sense or reason. —**non-sensical** (non'sensikəl) *adj.*

noon (nōon) *n.* twelve o'clock in the daytime; midday.

noose (nōos) *n.* a loop of rope with a knot that can slide along the rope to make the loop smaller or larger.

normal ('nôməl) *adj.* fitting in with accepted standards; typical: *she is of normal height.* —'**normally** *adv.*

north (nôth) *n.* 1. the point on the compass that is on your right if you stand facing towards the sunset. 2. (often **North**) a region lying in this direction: *Cumbria is in the north of England.* —*adj.* towards, from, or in the north. —*adv.* towards the north: *we turned north.* **northern** ('nôdhən) *adj.* of or in the north.

nose (nōz) *n.* 1. the part of a human's or animal's head used for breathing air in and out and for smelling. 2. the front end of something: *the nose of an aeroplane.* —*vb.* **nosing, nosed.** 1. (+ *out*) to find out or discover. 2. to move very slowly and carefully. '**nosey** or '**nosy** *adj.* **nosier, nosiest** (slang) inquisitive.

nostril ('nostril) *n.* one of two openings in the nose through which air passes to and from the lungs.

note (nōt) *n.* 1. a short written record made to help a person remember: *we took notes in the lecture.* 2. a short letter or message. 3. a short explanation or comment: *does your Latin textbook have notes in the back?* 4. a single sound or the sign that stands for that sound in music. 5. importance: *he is an actor of note.* —*vb.* **noting, noted.** 1. to record in writing or in the mind. 2. to pay close attention to. '**noted** *adj.* famous.

notice ('nōtis) *n.* 1. a written or printed poster giving information or warning. 2. attention: *the broken window escaped his father's notice.* —*vb.* **noticing, noticed.** to observe. '**noticeable** *adj.* easily noticed.

notify ('nōtifī) *vb.* **notifying, notified.** to give notice to; inform: *she notified the police about her lost handbag.* —**notifi'cation** *n.*

notion ('nōshən) *n.* a vague idea or general impression: *he had a notion it would rain.*

notorious (nō'tôriəs) *adj.* well-known and generally disapproved of; infamous: *a notorious criminal.* —**no'toriously** *adv.*

noun (noun) *n.* a word belonging to a class of words in a language that express the names of things, people, ideas, etc., e.g. *sheep, Peter, botany, inflation.*

nourish ('nurish) *vb.* to feed and cause (an animal, plant, person, etc.) to keep healthy and grow. '**nourishment** *n.* food and other things necessary for life.

novel[1] ('novəl) *adj.* new; unusual: *she has some novel ideas for raising money for the homeless.* '**novelty** *n.,pl.* **novelties.** 1. a new experience, esp. an enjoyable one. 2. a small cheap toy, ornament, etc.

novel[2] ('novəl) *n.* a long story written about the lives of imaginary people. '**novelist** *n.* a person who writes novels.

novice ('novis) *n.* a beginner or inexperienced person, esp. a new member of a religious order. —*adj.* inexperienced.

nucleus ('nyōokliəs) *n.,pl.* **nuclei** ('nyōoklii). 1. the centre of an atom, made up of protons and neutrons. 2. the centre of a plant or animal cell. '**nuclear** *adj.* 1. of a nucleus. 2. of or coming from atomic energy.

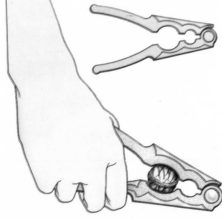
nutcracker

nude (nyōod) *adj.* naked; not wearing clothes. —*n.* a person who is wearing no clothes. —'**nudity** *n.*

nudge (nuj) *vb.* **nudging, nudged.** to push slightly. —*n.* a slight push, usu. given with the elbow.

nuisance ('nyōosəns) *n.* something that causes trouble, annoyance, etc.

numb (num) *adj.* without feeling in the body or mind, often as a result of cold or shock. —*vb.* to make numb.

number ('numbə) *n.* 1. the total of a quantity of things or people: *a large number attended the concert.* 2. a NUMERAL. 3. an issue of a magazine. 4. a song or melody: *the band rehearsed the number.* —*vb.* 1. to count: *he numbers me among his friends.* 2. to count out; assign numerals to: *number these pages from 1 to 125.* '**numberless** *adj.* consisting of an enormous quantity.

numeral ('nyōomərəl) *n.* a figure or sign standing for a number: *the numeral for six is 6.*

numerous ('nyōomərəs) *adj.* 1. many. 2. containing a large number: *a numerous flock of birds.*

nun (nun) *n.* a woman who has joined a religious order and has taken vows to live in poverty and not to marry.

nurse (nûs) *n.* 1. a person who is trained to help doctors to care for sick people in hospitals. 2. a woman whose job is to care for young children. —*vb.* **nursing, nursed.** to care for.

nursery ('nûsəri) *n.,pl.* **nurseries.** 1. a room in which babies and children sleep and play. 2. a place where young plants are reared.

nut (nut) *n.* 1. a dry often edible fruit in a hard, woody shell, e.g. walnut, brazil nut. 2. a small piece of metal with a ridged central hole made so as to screw on to BOLTs. 3. (slang) a person who behaves in a crazy way.

nutcracker ('nutkrakə) *n.* often **nutcrackers** (*pl.*) a pair of pincers for breaking the hard shells of nuts.

nutmeg ('nutmeg) *n.* 1. a hard spicy seed ground up to flavour food. 2. the tropical tree on which this seed grows.

nylon ('nīlon) *n.* a tough manmade material used to make thread, textiles, parachutes, etc.

O

oak (ōk) *n.* 1. one of a large group of DECIDUOUS or EVERGREEN trees that grow in temperate climates and produce acorns. 2. the wood of this tree. —*adj.* made of this wood.

oar (ô) *n.* 1. a long wooden pole with a flattened end, used to row a boat. 2. (also **oarsman**) a rower.

oasis

oasis (ō'āsis) *n.,pl.* **oases** (ō'āsēz). 1. a fertile area with water in the middle of a desert. 2. a place of safety or comfort; haven.

oat (ōt) *n.* 1. a type of cereal plant yielding grain used for food. 2. **oats** (*pl.*) the grains used as food.

oath (ōth) *n.* 1. a solemn formal promise, usu. involving calling God as a witness, to tell the truth, be loyal, etc. 2. the use of a sacred word or the name of God to curse or show anger; swear word.

obey (ə'bā) *vb.* to act in accordance with an order, rule, etc. **obedient** (ə'bēdiənt) *adj.* yielding willingly to the orders of someone else. —**o'bedience** *n.* —**o'bediently** *adv.*

object[1] ('objekt) *n.* 1. a real physical thing; something that can be seen or touched. 2. aim; goal: *his object was to get home.* 3. a person or thing towards which a feeling or action is directed: *she was the object of their pity.* 4.

(grammar) a word or phrase that follows a verb or preposition.

object[2] (əb'jekt) *vb.* 1. (+ *to*) to disapprove of or disagree with: *I object to such rudeness.* 2. to express a reason for not favouring or agreeing: *she objected to his plans.* **ob'jection** *n.* the reason for not doing or favouring something; drawback.

objective (əb'jektiv) *adj.* impartial; not taking sides: *an objective opinion.* —*n.* goal; target; purpose: *my objective was to win.*

oblige (ə'blīj) *vb.* **obliging, obliged.** 1. to do something in order to help or as a favour to. 2. to force; compel: *we were obliged to leave at 10 o'clock.* 3. to cause (someone) to feel that he has a duty to do something: *his mother's illness obliged him to stay at home.* **obligation** (obli'gāshən) *n.* a duty to do something, e.g. to help someone who has helped one. **obligatory** (ə'bligətəri) *adj.* necessary; compulsory. **o'bliging** *adj.* willing to help.

oblong ('oblong) *n.* a geometric figure like a square but having two opposite sides shorter than the other two sides; rectangle. —*adj.* of this shape.

oboe ('ōbō) *n.* a musical instrument of the woodwind family, having a double reed and a high-pitched tone. —'**oboist** *n.*

oboe

obscure (əb'skyōō) *adj.* 1. difficult to understand. 2. dim; dark; gloomy. 3. unclear; indistinct. 4. not well known; hidden: *an obscure poet.* —*vb.* **obscuring, obscured.** 1. to darken or hide from view: *clouds obscured the moon.* 2. to make the meaning of (something) less clear or understandable. —**ob'scurely** *adv.* —**ob'scurity** *n.*

observe (əb'zûv) *vb.* **observing, observed.** 1. to regard; look at; watch carefully. 2. to obey; follow; take notice of: *he observed the speed limit.* 3. to remark on; notice: *he observed that the weather was fine.* **ob'servance** *n.* 1. the keeping (of a custom, etc.). 2. a custom or usual celebration. **ob'servant** *adj.* noticing small things; alert and watchful. **obser'vation** *n.* 1. watch; study. 2. the state of being observed. 3. remark; comment. **ob'servatory** *n.,pl.* **observatories.** a building, usu. containing a large telescope, from which the stars, etc., are observed.

obsolete ('obsəlēt) *adj.* no longer used, done, or made; out-of-date: *an obsolete car.*

obstacle ('obstəkəl) *n.* something that stands in the way of someone's progress; hindrance: *there were mountains, rivers, and other obstacles on the journey.*

obstinate ('obstinət) *adj.* unmoving in opinion, habits, behaviour, etc.; stubborn: *the obstinate donkey refused to move.* —'**obstinacy** *n.* —'**obstinately** *adv.*

obstruct (əb'strukt) *vb.* 1. to block; get in the way of: *the new building obstructed the view.* 2. to be a hindrance or obstacle to: *he obstructed our plans.* —**ob'struction** *n.*

obtain (əb'tān) *vb.* 1. to get; acquire. 2. to be in use or be suitable or appropriate: *the speed limit obtained all over the country.*

obtuse (əb'tyōōs) *n.* 1. stupid. 2. (of an ANGLE) between 90° and 180°.

obvious ('obviəs) *adj.* clear; easily seen or understood. —'**obviously** *adv.* —'**obviousness** *n.*

occasion (ə'kāzhən) *n.* 1. the time when a particular event happens. 2. a special event. 3. a cause or reason for something: *he had no occasion to be upset.* —*vb.* to cause. **oc'casional** *adj.* on or for a particular occasion. —**oc'casionally** *adv.*

occupy ('okyŏopī) *vb.* **occupying, occupied.** 1. to take up time or space; fill: *the visit occupied an hour.* 2. to live in: *he occupies the top storey of the house.* 3. to seize and keep possession of: *the Germans occupied Paris in 1940.* **occu'pation** *n.* 1. a job or profession; business. 2. the act or an instance of occupying. —**occu'pational** *adj.*

occur (ə'kû) *vb.* **occurring, occurred.** 1. to come to pass; happen. 2. to come into someone's mind: *it occurs to me that I have heard his name before.* 3. to be found; exist: *tigers occur in India.* **oc'currence** *n.* a happening.

ocean ('ōshən) *n.* 1. the mass of salt water that covers about 70% of the earth's crust. 2. one of the five main divisions of this mass of water (Indian, Pacific, Antarctic, Arctic, Atlantic). —**oceanic** (ōshi'anik) *adj.*

octave ('octəv) *n.* (music) the interval of eight notes in the basic scale of Western music. In the key of C, it runs C, D, E, F, G, A, B, C.

octopus

octopus ('oktəpəs) *n.,pl.* **octopuses.** a sea creature, ranging in size from 6 inches to 32 feet, with a soft rounded body and eight arms, each bearing rows of suckers.

odd (od) *adj.* 1. unusual; different; peculiar. 2. not important; extra: *an odd job.* 3. (arithmetic) not capable of being exactly divided by two: *3, 5, and 9 are odd numbers.* 4. part of a set now incomplete; the only remaining one of a pair: *an odd glove.* '**oddity** *n.,pl.* **oddities.** a peculiar or unusual person or thing. —'**oddly** *adv.* —'**oddness** *n.*

odds (odz) *pl.n.* the chances of something happening: *the odds are against our team winning.*

odour ('ōdə) *n.* a smell.

offence (ə'fens) *n.* 1. the breaking of a law, rule, etc.; crime. 2. the act of hurting, disgusting, or annoying someone. 3. something that causes disgust or annoyance. **of'fend** *vb.* 1. to make (someone) angry, upset, etc. 2. to cause disgust. 3. to break the law. **of'fensive** *adj.* 1. causing offence; displeasing. 2. used for attacking: *offensive weapons.* *n.* an attitude or policy of attack. —**of'fensively** *adv.*

offer ('ofə) *vb.* to put forward or present (something) to be accepted or refused: *I offered £18 for the radio.* —*n.* 1. the act of offering. 2. something that is offered, such as money.

offhand ('ofhand) *adj.* uncaring; unconcerned; insincere: *an offhand apology.*

office ('ofis) *n.* 1. a room or suite of rooms where business is carried out. 2. a responsible position, esp. in government: *the office of mayor.* 3. **offices** (*pl.*) acts done to help someone: *his friend's kind offices got him the job.*

officer ('ofisə) *n.* 1. someone who holds a responsible position in government, a police force, etc. 2. someone in the army, navy, or air force with a certain rank.

official (ə'fishəl) *n.* someone who is authorized to carry out particular duties. —*adj.* 1. holding a position of authority: *an official agent.* 2. authorized: *an official statement.* 3. formal: *an official banquet.*

offspring ('ofspring) *n.,pl.* **offspring.** 1. child or children. 2. result or development: *the new plan was the offspring of Ed's original idea.*

often ('ofən) *adv.* many times; frequently.

oil (oil) *n.* a thick greasy liquid that will not mix with water. There are many different kinds of oil. —*vb.* to put oil into or on, esp. to make a machine work easily. —'**oily** *adj.* **oilier, oiliest.**

ointment ('ointmənt) *n.* a soft greasy paste used as a medicine to heal or protect sore places on the skin.

old (ōld) *adj.* 1. not young; having existed, grown, developed, etc., for a long time. 2. of a certain age: *Sally is twelve years old.* 3. belonging to the past; former. **the old** old people.

olive ('oliv) *n.* 1. an evergreen southern European tree. 2. the small oval fruit of this tree, from which oil is extracted. —*adj.* dark yellowish-green.

olive

omelette *or* **omelet** ('omlət) *n.* a food made of eggs beaten together and fried in a flat pan.

omen ('ōmən) *n.* an event or thing that is thought to indicate good or bad luck in the future: *it was an ill omen for our team when our mascot was stolen.*

ominous ('ominəs) *adj.* giving an advance warning, esp. of something evil or threatening: *ominous clouds.* —'**ominously** *adv.*

omit (ə'mit) *vb.* **omitting, omitted.** 1. to leave out: *he omitted chapter six.* 2. to fail to make or do: *he omitted to turn the lights off.* **o'mission** *n.* 1. the act of omitting. 2. something left out.

onion ('unyən) *n.* the edible bulb of a vegetable with a strong taste and smell, often used in cooking.

onslaught ('onslôt) *n.* a vigorous attack.

ooze (ōōz) *vb.* **oozing, oozed.** to leak very slowly; seep: *the mud oozed through his boots.* —*n.* liquid mud found on ocean and river beds.

opal

opal ('ōpəl) *n.* a beautiful semi-precious stone much valued as a gem-stone because of its quality of displaying colours in shifting patterns.

opaque (ō'pāk) *adj.* not allowing light to pass through.

opera ('opərə) *n.* a form of stage play in which all or most of the words are sung. —**ope'ratic** *adj.*

operate ('opərāt) *vb.* **operating, operated.** 1. to act; carry out a function. 2. to work or control (a machine). 3. to perform surgery on a person. **oper'ation** *n.* 1. the act of working. 2. a task; project. 3. an act of surgery. **operative** ('opərətiv) *adj.* 1. in working order: *the machine is operative.* 2. effective: *the new law is now operative. n.* a worker: *a machine operative.* '**operator** *n.* a person who works a machine, etc.

opinion (ə'pinyən) *n.* a view or judgment held by someone about a subject: *in my opinion it will rain.*

opossum (ə'posəm) *n.* (also **possum**) a small furry American animal that lives in trees and carries its young in a pouch.

opponent (ə'pōnənt) *n.* someone who is on the opposite side in a war, game, argument, etc.

opportunity (opə'tyōōniti) *n.,pl.* **opportunities.** a good, and often lucky, chance coming at a convenient time. **oppor'tunist** *n.* a person who makes clever use of opportunities. —**oppor'tunism** *n.*

oppose (ə'pōz) *vb.* **opposing, opposed.** 1. to argue, vote, or fight against. 2. to be in contrast or opposition to. **opposite** ('opəzit) *adj.* 1. on the other side of. 2. completely different; contrary. 3. similar in function, character, etc.: *the sales manager spoke to his opposite number in Paris. n.* someone or something that is contrary or opposing: *the opposite is true. prep.* facing; in front of: *the car stood opposite the house.*

oppress (ə'pres) *vb.* **oppressing, oppressed.** 1. to keep down by force; to treat cruelly. 2. to overwhelm: *the heat oppressed us.* —**op'pression** *n.* —**op'pressive** *adj.*

optical ('optikəl) *adj.* of or concerning the sense of sight. **op'tician** *n.* a person who makes or sells spectacles, binoculars, etc.

optimist ('optimist) *n.* a person who looks on the bright side of things and believes that they will turn out well. —'**optimism** *n.* —**opti'mistic** *adj.*

option ('opshən) *n.* 1. the power or ability to make a choice: *as I had no money for the bus fare I had no option but to walk.* 2. something chosen or available to be chosen. '**optional** *adj.* left to one's choice.

orange ('orinj) *n.* 1. a round sweet juicy CITRUS fruit with a tough skin. 2. a reddish-yellow colour.

orange

orbit ('ôbit) *n.* the path along which a planet, satellite, or other body travels when revolving round another body in space. —*vb.* to move round in an orbit: *the satellite orbited the earth.*

orchard ('ôchəd) *n.* a place where fruit trees are grown.

orchestra ('ôkistrə) *n.* a group of musicians who play together, esp. for the performance of large-scale musical works such as symphonies. —**orchestral** (ô'kestrəl) *adj.*

orchid ('ôkid) *n.* one of many types of flower prized on account of their strange and beautiful shapes and brilliant colours.

ordeal (ô'dēl) *n.* an experience that is painful or unpleasant: *the storm was an ordeal for the passengers.*

order ('ôdə) *n.* 1. a rule or command. 2. a condition in which things are neat, in their proper places, etc.: *keep your room in good order.* 3. the way in which things are arranged: *alphabetical order.* 4. working condition: *my watch is out of order.* 5. peace and quiet: *the army restored order after the riot.* 6. an instruction to buy or sell goods or send money. 7. an organized group of people or things. —*vb.* 1. to command. 2. to request (food, goods, etc.) to be supplied: *they ordered 400 nails.* 3. to put in order; arrange. '**orderly** *adj.* 1. neatly arranged: *an orderly room.* 2. well-behaved: *an orderly class. n.,pl.* **orderlies.** 1. a person who keeps things clean and tidy in a hospital. 2. a soldier who runs errands or does other small jobs for an officer. —'**orderliness** *n.*

ordinary ('ôdinəri) *adj.* 1. common; normal. 2. below average quality; poor: *a very ordinary play.* —'**ordinarily** *adv.* —'**ordinariness** *n.*

ore (ô) *n.* a rock, soil, or mineral containing a metal or other useful substance: *iron ore.*

organ ('ôgən) *n.* 1. a musical keyboard instrument in which the sound is made by air forced through a number of pipes. 2. a part of the body of an animal: *the liver is an essential organ.* **organic** (ô'ganik) *adj.* of, obtained from, or concerned with living plants or animals. '**organism** *n.* a living plant or animal.

organize ('ôgənīz) *vb.* **organizing, organized.** 1. to put together in an orderly way: *Ed is organizing his history notes.* 2. to arrange for something to happen: *Susan organized a picnic.* **organi'zation** *n.* an organized group of people or things.

origin ('orijin) *n.* the source or cause of something. **original** (ə'rijinəl) *adj.* 1. first; earliest. 2. new or fresh. *n.* something which is not a copy or translation of anything else: *the painting was an original by Rubens.* **o'riginate** *vb.* **originating, originated.** to begin; start.

ornament *n.* ('ônəmənt) something that adds beauty; decoration. —*vb.* ('ônəment) to add beauty to; decorate. —**orna'mental** *adj.*

orphan ('ôfən) *n.* a child whose parents have died. —*vb.* to deprive of parents: *many young children were orphaned in the war.* **orphanage** *n.* a home for orphans.

ostrich ('ostrich) *n.* a long-legged two-toed bird that cannot fly but runs very quickly. It lives in Africa and Arabia and is the largest bird.

otter

otter ('otə) *n.* a web-footed fish-eating animal. It lives in or near water.

ounce (ouns) *n.* (usu. shortened to **oz.**) a unit of weight equal to one-sixteenth of a pound. **fluid ounce** a liquid measure equal to one-twentieth of a pint.

outcome ('outkum) *n.* a result.

outlaw ('outlô) *n.* a person who does not benefit from the protection of the law. —*vb.* 1. to make unlawful: *people have tried to outlaw alcohol.* 2. to make an outlaw of: *the sheriff outlawed Robin Hood.*

outlet ('outlet) *n.* 1. a point at which water, electrical current, etc., can come out. 2. a means of getting rid of something: *football is a good outlet for his energy.*

outline ('outlīn) *n.* 1. a line around the edge or limits of an object. 2. a drawing on which only the main lines or features are marked. 3. the main features of something; a summary. —*vb.* **outlining, outlined.** 1. to draw the outer lines of. 2. to give the main features of.

output ('outpŏot) *n.* the quantity produced: *the factory has a very high output.*

outrage ('outrāj) *n.* 1. great fury. 2. a shockingly cruel or violent act. —*vb.* **outraging, outraged.** to cause to feel great anger. —**out'rageous** *adj.*

outskirts ('outskûts) *pl.n.* an area on the edge of a town or city.

outspoken (out'spōkən) *adj.* not hiding one's thoughts; frank.

outstanding (out'standing) *adj.* 1. excellent; distinguished: *an outstanding athlete.* 2. not yet dealt with: *John has some outstanding debts.*

oval ('ōvəl) *adj.* egg-shaped. —*n.* a shape like that of an egg.

oven ('uvən) *n.* an enclosed cupboard-like space, usu. part of a stove, in which food is cooked.

overboard ('ōvəbôd) *adv.* over the side of a boat or ship into the water: *the sailor tripped and fell overboard.*

overcoat ('ōvəkōt) *n.* a long coat made of warm material, worn over one's other clothes in cold weather.

overcome (ōvə'kum) *vb.* **overcoming, overcame, overcome.** to be too strong for: *the heat overcame the firemen.*

overhaul *vb.* (ōvə'hôl) to examine carefully: *the garage overhauled our car before we took it on holiday.* —*n.* ('ōvəhôl) a thorough examination.

overhear (ōvə'hiə) *vb.* **overhearing, overheard** (ōvə'hûd). to hear something by chance without the knowledge of the speaker: *I overheard my parents saying they would give me a fishing rod for Christmas.*

overlook (ōvə'lŏok) *vb.* 1. to have a view of: *my window overlooks the river.* 2. to ignore; excuse: *he overlooked his son's faults.* 3. to fail to see, think of, etc.: *in his hurry, the thief overlooked the radio.*

overpower (ōvə'pouə) *vb.* to be too strong for; overwhelm.

oversee (ōvə'sē) *vb.* **overseeing, oversaw, overseen.** to control or organize (work, workers). '**overseer** *n.* a person who is responsible for overseeing; foreman.

overtake (ōvə'tāk) *vb.* **overtaking, overtook, overtaken.** 1. to catch up and pass: *the sports car overtook the bus.* 2. to happen to or come upon suddenly: *disaster overtook the aircraft.*

overtime ('ōvətīm) *n.* time spent working outside normal working hours. —*adv.* after the usual hours.

overture ('ōvətyŏoə) *n.* a piece of music played before an opera, ballet, etc.

overwhelm (ōvə'welm) *vb.* crush; destroy by too much force or weight.

owe (ō) *vb.* **owing, owed.** 1. to have to give or pay: *he owes me an apology.* 2. to be grateful to: *I owe my aunt a great deal for her kindness.*

owl (oul) *n.* a bird with big staring eyes and strong beak and talons. It hunts small animals by night. '**owlish** *adj.* like an owl, esp. looking solemn or wise.

own (ōn) *adj.* relating to or belonging to oneself: *my own bag.* —*pron.* something that belongs to one: *this book is my own.* —*vb.* to have or possess: *do you own a bicycle?* **own up** to admit one's guilt: *Jane owned up to breaking the window.* '**owner** *n.* a person who owns or possesses.

oxygen ('oksijin) *n.* a colourless odourless gas that makes up about one-fifth of the world's atmosphere. Oxygen is necessary for animals to breathe and for combustion. Chemical symbol: O.

oyster ('oistə) *n.* a soft-bodied shellfish with an irregularly shaped shell, split into two halves.

P

pace (pās) *n.* 1. a single step: *she took a pace forwards.* 2. a rate or tempo of movement: *he drove at a rapid pace.* 3. a way of moving: *a horse's fastest pace is the gallop.* —*vb.* **pacing, paced.** 1. to move or walk with regular steps: *he paced up and down.* 2. to set the speed for: *I'll pace you for five lengths of the swimming pool.*

pack (pak) *n.* 1. a number of objects tied or wrapped together for carrying; bundle. 2. a group with something in common: *a pack of wolves.* 3. a set of playing cards. 4. a large number; lot: *a pack of nonsense.* —*vb.* 1. to put together into a bundle. 2. to fill (a container): *he packed his suitcase.* 3. to crowd tightly together: *hundreds of people packed into the hall.*

package ('pakij) *n.* 1. one or more objects wrapped or tied together; parcel. 2. a container in which objects can be packed, esp. for sale. **package tour** *or* **holiday** a tour or holiday arranged in every detail by a travel agent and sold at a fixed price. —*vb.* **packaging, packaged.** to make or put into a package.

packet ('pakit) *n.* a small package or bundle.

pad¹ (pad) *n.* 1. a soft thick piece of any material used for protection or as stuffing: *I slept on a foam rubber pad on the floor.* 2. a number of sheets of paper fastened together along one edge. 3. the soft spongy underneath part of the feet of certain animals, e.g. dogs. 4. (also **launching pad**) the area from which a rocket is launched. 5. (slang) a room or apartment of one's own. —*vb.* **padding, padded.** to stuff or protect with a pad.

pad² (pad) *vb.* **padding, padded.** to move so that one's feet make only a quiet dull sound.

paddle¹ ('padəl) *n.* 1. a short oar with a wide flat blade at one or both ends, used esp. for moving a canoe. 2. any other implement with a wide flat blade: *a table tennis paddle.* 3. any of the wide boards on the outside of a water wheel. —*vb.* **paddling, paddled.** 1. to move (a boat) with paddles; row. 2. to beat, stir, mix, etc., with or as with a paddle.

paddle² ('padəl) *vb.* **paddling, paddled.** to play or wade about in shallow water.

padlock ('padlok) *n.* a lock with a curved movable bar that can be snapped shut and opened with a key. —*vb.* to fasten with a padlock.

padlock

page¹ (pāj) *n.* one side of a sheet of paper, with or without printing or writing on it.

page² (pāj) *n.* 1. a servant, usu. a boy, who runs errands for guests in a hotel. 2. (in the Middle Ages) a boy who was training to become a knight. —*vb.* **paging, paged.** to try to contact (someone) by calling out his name.

pageant ('pajənt) *n.* 1. a colourful and exciting parade. 2. a kind of play about historical events or legends.

paid (pād) *vb.* the past tense and past participle of PAY.

pail (pāl) *n.* a cylindrical metal or plastic container for liquids, granular substances, etc.

pain (pān) *n.* 1. suffering in body or mind: *my broken arm caused me great pain.* 2. **pains** (*pl.*) effort: *John took pains over his work.* —*vb.* to cause to suffer. —'**painful** *adj.* —'**painfully** *adv.*

paint (pānt) *n.* a mixture of colouring matter and oil, water, or some other liquid that can be spread on a surface to colour or protect it. —*vb.* 1. to apply paint to. 2. to make (a picture) by using paint.

pair (peə) *n.* 1. two people, objects, or animals that are alike, are used together, or are related in some way; set of two: *a pair of shoes.* 2. something made up of two similar parts: *a pair of scissors.* —*vb.* to arrange or form into a pair or pairs.

palace ('paləs) *n.* a large impressive building, esp. one where a king, queen, prince, archbishop, or other important person lives. —**palatial** (pə'lāshəl). *adj.*

pale (pāl) *adj.* **paler, palest.** having a whitish complexion, e.g. from illness, shock, or lack of sunshine. —*vb.* **paling, paled.** 1. to become white: *she paled when she heard the bad news.* 2. to fade: *the prince's reputation paled in comparison with the king's.*

palm¹ (pâm) *n.* the area on the front of the hand between the fingers and the wrist. —*vb.* 1. to hide in the hand: *the gambler palmed an extra card.* 2. (+ *off*) to get rid of (an undesirable object): *she palmed off her old radio on her brother.*

palm² (pâm) *n.* any of various tropical trees with tall unbranched stems topped by bunches of large leaves.

pamphlet ('pamflit) *n.* a thin printed book with few pages and paper covers; booklet.

panda ('pandə) *n.* a large bearlike animal that lives in Tibet and Southern China and has a white coat with black legs, shoulders, and ears.

pane (pān) *n.* a sheet of glass set in a window or door.

panel ('panəl) *n.* 1. an area or part of something that is raised, sunk, or otherwise distinct from the rest: *her blue dress has panels of red on the skirt.* 2. a body of people selected for a special task, e.g. a jury. 3. a surface or board with the controls of a machine: *an instrument panel.* —*vb.* **panelling, panelled.** to furnish with panels: *they panelled the hall with oak.*

panic ('panik) *n.* a sudden unreasoning fear often spreading rapidly through a group: *when the fire broke out, panic struck the people in the cinema.* —*vb.* **panicking, panicked.** to affect or be affected by panic. —'**panic-stricken** *adj.*

panorama (panə'râmə) *n.* a view over a wide expanse of territory: *from the hill top we could see a panorama of unbroken forest.*

pant (pant) *vb.* 1. to breathe in quick gasps: *he panted after the long run.* 2. to speak in gasps because of lack of breath. —*n.* a short quick breath.

panther ('panthə) *n.* 1. a leopard, esp. one that has a black coat. 2. a jaguar or other large wild cat.

pantomime ('pantəmīm) *n.* 1. a type of play, usu. based on a fairy tale. 2. a play without words, in which the actors use movements and expressions of the face instead of speech.

pantry ('pantri) *n.,pl.* **pantries.** a small room for storing food, tableware, or glass; larder.

paper ('pāpə) *n.* 1. a flexible material, usu. made in very thin sheets from wood pulp, rags, or other matter, and used for writing, printing, wrapping, etc. 2. a piece of paper that provides information, often officially; document: *a secret paper was stolen from the office.* 3. a newspaper. 4. wallpaper. 5. an essay or article. —*vb.* to decorate with wallpaper.

paprika ('paprikə) *n.* a red spice that is not as strong as red pepper. It is made from the dried fruit of certain sweet peppers.

parachute ('parəshōōt) *n.* an umbrella-like apparatus of silk or nylon with ropes attached to it, used to slow down something or someone falling through the air. —*vb.* **parachuting, parachuted.** to use a parachute to come or send down: *supplies were parachuted to the soldiers.*

parade (pə'rād) *n.* 1. a march or procession. 2. a place where soldiers regularly parade; parade ground. —*vb.* **parading, paraded.** 1. to march or cause to march in a parade. 2. to display or show off: *he is always parading his cleverness.*

paradise ('parədīs) *n.* 1. heaven. 2. a condition of extreme happiness.

paraffin ('parəfin) *n.* a strong-smelling oil obtained from petroleum and used as fuel in lamps and stoves.

paragon ('parəgən) *n.* someone who is a model of excellence or good behaviour.

paragraph ('parəgrâf) *n.* 1. a group of sentences in a piece of writing that deals with one topic. A paragraph begins on a new line and its first word is usu. set in from the margin. 2. a short article or note.

parallel ('parəlel) *adj.* 1. pointing in the same direction and keeping the same distance apart: *the gymnast did stunts on the parallel bars.* 2. similar: *we had parallel experiences.* —*n.* 1. a parallel line, esp. a line of LATITUDE. 2. something that is similar. —*vb.* to develop or move in a similar direction. **paral'lelogram** *n.* (geometry) a four-sided figure, the opposite sides of which are parallel.

canopy

shrouds

parachute

paralyse ('parəlīz) *vb.* **paralysing, paralysed.** to destroy the power to move or feel: *the accident paralysed her right leg.* **paralysis** (pə'ralisis) *n.* loss of feeling or motion. —**paralytic** (parə'litik) *adj.*

parasite ('parəsīt) *n.* 1. a plant or animal that lives on or in a plant or animal of a different kind and takes its food from its host: *fleas are parasites on cats, dogs, and humans.* 2. a person who is supported by other people without doing anything in return. —**parasitic** (parə'sitik) *adj.*

parasol ('parasol) *n.* a sunshade.

paratroops ('paratrōōps) *n.* soldiers who are taken by aircraft to the site of a battle where they are dropped by parachute.

parcel ('pâsəl) *n.* 1. a single item or a number of objects wrapped in paper or put in a box. 2. a part or section, esp. of land. —*vb.* **parcelling, parcelled.** (usu. + *out*) to divide into sections; distribute.

pardon ('pâdən) *n.* 1. forgiveness; an excusing: *I beg your pardon.* 2. a release from punishment. —*vb.* 1. to forgive or excuse. 2. to free from punishment: *the queen pardoned four prisoners.* —'**pardonable** *adj.*

parent ('peərənt) *n.* 1. a father or mother. 2. a plant or an animal that produces offspring. —**parental** (pə'rentəl) *adj.*

parish ('parish) *n.* 1. a small area with its own church and minister. 2. the people who live there.

park (pâk) *n.* an area of land set aside for the public's use and pleasure. —*vb.* to leave (a car, luggage, etc.) in a certain place for a time.

parliament ('pâləmənt) *n.* an assembly or assemblies of elected representatives of the people that in many countries has the power to make all the laws of the land. —**parlia'mentary** *adj.*

parlour ('pâlə) *n.* 1. a room used for receiving guests. 2. a room or rooms used as a shop: *a beauty parlour.*

parole (pə'rōl) *n.* the release of a prisoner before the end of his sentence on condition that he keeps certain promises about his behaviour or obeys certain rules. —*vb.* **paroling, paroled.** to free (someone) on parole.

parrot

parrot ('parət) *n.* a tropical bird with a hooked bill and brightly coloured feathers. Some parrots can learn to copy human words.

parsley ('pâsli) *n.* a garden herb with crinkly leaves that give off a fragrant aroma and are used to flavour food.

parsnip ('pâsnip) *n.* 1. a plant, related to the carrot, that has a long whitish root. 2. the root of this plant, eaten as a vegetable when cooked.

part (pât) *n.* 1. a division or section of a whole: *we saw only part of his face.* 2. one of the sides in an argument, arrangement, etc.: *on our part, we will sell the car at the agreed price.* 3. a share: *we did our part in the work.* 4. a replacement section: *parts for a car.* 5. a role in a play, opera, etc. **take part** to have a share in. —*vb.* 1. to separate or cause to separate; divide. 2. to go one's separate ways: *we parted in Athens and I never saw him again.* 3. to make a dividing line in one's hair. **part with** to be separated from or let go: *Jane would not part with her dog.* —*adj.* incomplete; not all: *part payment.* —*adv.* to a certain extent, not completely. **'parting** *n.* 1. a separation from another person. 2. a line in the hair caused by combing it in opposite directions. —**'partly** *adv.*

partial ('pâshəl) *adj.* 1. not complete: *a partial victory.* 2. biased; prejudiced: *a partial reporter.* 3. (often + to) fond (of): *partial to cream.* —**partiality** (pashi'aliti) *n.* —**'partially** *adj.*

participle ('pâtisipəl) *n.* the form of a verb that can be used as an adjective or noun or with a helping verb, such as *has* or *was,* to form certain tenses, e.g. *working* (present participle), *worked* (past participle).

particle ('pâtikəl) *n.* 1. a very small bit or item: *a particle of dust.* 2. a short word, such as a preposition.

particular (pâ'tikyŏōlə) *adj.* 1. relating to one and not to all; not general: *the particular problem we are discussing.* 2. individual; separate: *her particular job.* 3. to a high degree; special: *Ronald is his particular friend.* 4. very careful; precise: *Sheila is very particular about doing a good job.* 5. hard to please; fussy: *she is most particular about her tea.* —*n.* often **particulars** (*pl.*) details: *please give me the particulars of the job.*

partner ('pâtnə) *n.* 1. a person who shares in an activity; colleague: *a partner in crime.* 2. one of several people who together own a business, sharing its profits and losses. 3. a husband or wife. 4. the person with whom one dances. 5. (games) a player on the same side. **'partnership** *n.* a business or venture in which partners work together.

partridge ('pâtrij) *n.* any of various wild birds that belong to the same family as the chicken and are hunted as food.

party ('pâti) *n.,pl.* **parties.** 1. a gathering of people for the purpose of enjoying themselves. 2. a body of people who join together because they have common political goals. 3. a person or group taking part in some activity: *he was a party to the crime.* —*adj.* of or relating to a party.

pass (pâs) *vb.* 1. to go by, over, beyond, through, etc.: *I passed him in the street.* 2. to go from one place or state to another: *she passed into unconsciousness.* 3. to send, move, or deliver: *pass the salt.* 4. to undergo or complete satisfactorily: *to pass an examination.* 5. (+ for) to be regarded as: *in his disguise he was able to pass for Indian.* 6. to spend (time, etc.). **pass out** to lose consciousness. **pass the buck** (informal) to shift responsibility to someone else. —*n.* 1. a narrow way by which one may travel: *a mountain pass.* 2. a ticket or permit for travel or entry: *a bus pass.* 3. (games) the movement of the ball from one player to another. 4. a success in an examination, etc.

passage ('pasij) *n.* 1. the act of going from one place or state to another. 2. a narrow corridor or hallway. 3. a progress (of time, events, etc.). 4. an extract from a book, etc., or a piece of music.

passenger ('pasinjə) *n.* 1. a person who travels by bus, train, aeroplane, etc. 2. (informal) a member of a team, group, etc., who does not do his fair share of work: *in tomorrow's match we can't afford to carry passengers.*

passion ('pashən) *n.* 1. a powerful emotion or agitation of the mind, e.g. rage, hate, etc. 2. a very strong enthusiasm or desire for anything: *he has a passion for reading poetry.* —**'passionate** *adj.* —**'passionately** *adv.*

passive ('pasiv) *adj.* not reacting to something that might be expected to produce some response; inactive. —**'passively** *adv.* —**pas'sivity** *n.*

passport ('pâspôt) *n.* an official document serving as a means of identification and permitting a person to travel to foreign countries and to re-enter his own country.

past (pâst) *adj.* gone by; in time already over. **past tense** the construction of a verb that refers to action, etc., in time gone by. —*n.* that which has happened in earlier times; history. —*adv.* so as to go by: *he hurried past.* —*prep.* beyond or farther than in amount, position, time, etc.: *it is past three o'clock.*

paste (pāst) *n.* 1. a mixture used for sticking things together. 2. any material in a similar soft thick form: *salmon paste.* —*vb.* **pasting, pasted.** to cover, fasten, or stick with paste or a similar substance.

pasteurize ('pâstyŏōərīz) *vb.* **pasteurizing, pasteurized.** to kill harmful germs in (milk or other food) by a process of heating.

pastry ('pāstri) *n.,pl.* **pastries.** 1. flour dough. 2. a food item made of baked sweetened flour dough, usu. filled with jam, fruit, or cream.

pasture ('pāstyŏōə) *n.* land covered with grass, used for the grazing of cattle, sheep, etc. —*vb.* **pasturing, pastured.** to feed animals by allowing them to graze on grassland.

pat (pat) *vb.* **patting, patted.** 1. to strike gently with something flat in order to smooth or flatten: *he carefully patted the sandcastle into shape.* 2. to tap or stroke gently with the hand as a sign of affection or approval: *she patted the dog.* —*n.* 1. a gentle tap. 2. a small shaped lump of butter.

patch (pach) *n.* 1. a piece of material used to cover a hole or worn place. 2. a small area of ground. —*vb.* 1. to mend with a patch. 2. (usu. + *up*) to repair in a makeshift way. **not a patch on** not comparable with. —'**patchiness** *n.* —'**patchy** *adj.* **patchier, patchiest.**

patent ('pātənt) *n.* a government permit to an inventor giving him the sole right to manufacture and sell his invention. —*vb.* to obtain a patent for (something). —*adj.* 1. protected by a patent: *patent medicines.* 2. obvious: *his irritation was patent.* —'**patently** *adv.*

path (pâth) *n.,pl.* **paths** (pâdhz). 1. a way for passing on foot: *a path through the woods.* 2. the direction in which something moves: *the path of the storm.*

pathetic (pə'thetik) *adj.* 1. arousing pity. 2. (informal) very incompetent or unsuitable: *the team played a pathetic game.*

patient ('pāshənt) *adj.* 1. putting up with trouble, misfortune, etc., without complaint. 2. careful: *her patient work produced splendid results.* —*n.* a person undergoing medical treatment. '**patience** *n.* 1. quality of waiting or enduring without complaint. 2. diligence. 3. a card game for one person only. —'**patiently** *adv.*

patrol (pə'trōl) *vb.* **patrolling, patrolled.** to go round (a town, district, etc.) in order to watch and protect. —*n.* 1. a man or group of men who patrol. 2. a small scouting party of soldiers.

pattern ('patən) *n.* 1. a decorative design arranged in a regular manner. 2. a thing or person to be copied.

pause (pôz) *n.* a temporary ceasing of speech or action; rest. —*vb.* **pausing, paused.** to make a short stop.

pavilion (pə'viliən) *n.* 1. an ornamental building used for exhibitions, concerts, etc. 2. a clubhouse on a games field.

paw (pô) *n.* the foot of an animal with claws.

pawn[1] (pôn) *vb.* to deposit (something) as security for money borrowed. —*n.* the state of being pledged for money: *my watch is in pawn.*

pawn[2] (pôn) *n.* one of the sixteen pieces of the lowest value in chess.

pawnbroker ('pônbrōkə) *n.* a person who lends money in return for articles deposited with him.

pay (pā) *vb.* **paying, paid.** 1. to give money in return for goods or services, as a reward, etc. 2. to yield profit or advantage: *it pays to be careful.* 3. to make (a call, visit, etc.). —*n.* salary; wages. —'**payment** *n.*

pea (pē) *n.* 1. a small, round, green seed that is eaten as a vegetable. 2. the climbing plant on which peas grow.

peace (pēs) *n.* 1. freedom from war or civil disturbance. 2. state of quiet, stillness, or tranquillity. —'**peaceful** *adj.* —'**peacefully** *adv.* —'**peacefulness** *n.*

peach (pēch) *n.* a sweet, juicy, velvety-skinned fruit, yellow and red in colour, with a rough stone inside.

peacock ('pēkok) *n.* the male peafowl. It is a large bird with splendid feathers and a tail that can be spread out like a fan.

peacock

peak (pēk) *n.* 1. a high point: *a mountain peak.* 2. the highest level: *the peak of his achievements.* 3. the projecting front of a cap.

pear (peə) *n.* a sweet juicy fruit that has a smooth yellow, green, or brownish skin and a shape that gets narrower towards the stalk.

pearl (pûl) *n.* a smooth rounded object, white or grey with a beautiful lustre, formed within the shells of oysters and valued as a gem. —'**pearly** *adj.* **pearlier, pearliest.**

peasant ('pezənt) *n.* a farmer who owns or rents a small farm or works on one for wages.

peat (pēt) *n.* decayed vegetable matter that is found in ancient marshy regions and is dug up and dried for fuel and for garden use.

pebble ('pebəl) *n.* a small rounded stone, esp. one worn smooth by water.

peck (pek) *vb.* 1. to strike or pick up with the beak: *Jane's parrot pecked me.* 2. to eat small quantities without enjoyment: *Stan pecked at his meal.* 3. to give a hasty kiss. —*n.* 1. a stroke with the beak. 2. a hasty kiss.

peculiar (pi'kyōōliə) *adj.* 1. strange or unaccustomed. 2. belonging characteristically to: *a method of cookery peculiar to the Chinese.* 3. special: *a book of peculiar interest.* —**peculiarity** (pikyōōli'ariti) *n.,pl.* **peculiarities.**

pedal ('pedəl) *n.* 1. a lever pressed by the foot in order to drive a machine. 2. a foot-operated lever on a musical instrument, e.g. a piano. —*vb.* **pedalling, pedalled.** to operate a pedal.

peddle ('pedəl) *vb.* **peddling, peddled.** to take small goods from place to place, offering them for sale.

pedestrian (pi'destriən) *n.* a person who travels on foot. —*adj.* 1. of walkers and walking: *a pedestrian crossing.* 2. dull; ordinary: *the writer's pedestrian style bored me.*

pedigree ('pedigrē) *n.* a line of ancestors that can be traced and recorded: *the dog had a good pedigree.*

peel (pēl) *vb.* to remove skin or bark from (something): *he peeled an orange.* —*n.* the skin of fruit and vegetables. **keep one's eyes peeled** (informal) to keep a close watch.

peep (pēp) *vb.* 1. to look secretly, esp. through a narrow opening: *I peeped through the railings.* 2. to be just showing: *the sun peeped through the mist.* —*n.* a quick sly look.

peer[1] (piə) *n.* 1. a person of the same rank; an equal. 2. a nobleman.

peer[2] (piə) *vb.* to look narrowly or closely: *he peered at the page.*

pelican ('pelikən) *n.* a large water bird with a long beak under which is an enormous pouch for storing the fish that it catches.

pellet ('pelit) *n.* 1. a small hard ball or pill: *he fed food pellets to the goldfish.* 2. a small lead shot used in a gun.

pen[1] (pen) *n.* a small slender instrument used for writing or drawing with ink. —*vb.* **penning, penned.** to write: *she penned a letter.*

pen[2] (pen) *n.* a small enclosure, esp. one for animals. —*vb.* **penning, penned.** to confine within a small space.

pedal

penal ('pēnəl) *adj.* concerned with punishment, esp. legal punishment. **'penalize** *vb.* **penalizing, penalized.** to impose a punishment or penalty upon. **penalty** ('penəlti) *n.,pl.* **penalties.** 1. a punishment enforced because of the breaking of the law or a rule or agreement. 2. (in games) a free shot, kick, etc., awarded to one side if the other breaks the rules.

pencil ('pensəl) *n.* 1. an instrument for writing or drawing, usu. consisting of a core of GRAPHITE enclosed in a thin tube of wood. 2. anything shaped like a pencil. —*vb.* **pencilling, pencilled.** to write, draw, or mark with a pencil.

pendulum

pendulum ('pendyo͝oləm) *n.* a weight hung from a fixed point by a string, rod, etc., so that it swings freely to and fro. Pendulums are sometimes used as part of a clock's mechanism.

penetrate ('penitrāt) *vb.* **penetrating, penetrated.** to pierce or force a way into: *the enemy penetrated our defences.* —**penetrable** ('penitrəbəl) *adj.* —**pene'tration** *n.*

penguin ('peńggwin) *n.* a flightless black and white sea bird found only in the southern hemisphere. They are good swimmers and feed on fish.

penicillin (peni'silin) *n.* a powerful drug that is made from a type of mould and is widely used by doctors to kill harmful bacteria.

peninsula (pe'ninsyo͝olə) *n.* a piece of land jutting out from a larger mass of land and almost completely surrounded by water: *the Malay Peninsula.* —**pen'insular** *adj.*

pension ('penshən) *n.* a regular payment of money from a former employer or the government to a person who has stopped working because of old age or illness. —*vb.* (often + *off*) to cause to retire.

people ('pēpəl) *n.* 1. all the persons making up a community, nation, or race: *the American people.* 2. human beings in general. —*vb.* **peopling, peopled.** to stock with human beings.

pepper ('pepə) *n.* 1. a seasoning for food obtained from the dried berries of certain plants, either used whole (**peppercorns**) or ground into a powder. 2. the red or green fruit of the capsicum plant. —*vb.* to sprinkle or spray. —**'peppery** *adj.*

peppermint ('pepəmint) *n.* 1. a plant cultivated for its strong-tasting oil. 2. a sweet flavoured with this oil.

perceive (pə'sēv) *vb.* **perceiving, perceived.** 1. to become aware of or (something) through the senses. 2. to understand; grasp. **perception** (pə'sepshən) *n.* understanding.

per cent (pə 'sent) (often represented by the symbol %) one hundredth part: *three per cent of £100 is £3.* **per'centage** *n.* a rate or amount per hundred.

perch (pûch) *n.* 1. a bar or rod on which birds alight. 2. any high seat or position. —*vb.* to settle or rest in some high place.

percussion (pə'kushən) *n.* 1. the class of musical instruments that make a sound by striking or clashing together. 2. the effect of hitting together two hard objects.

perennial (pə'reniəl) *adj.* 1. lasting for a long time. 2. (of plants) living for more than two years. —*n.* a perennial plant. —**per'ennially** *adv.*

perfect *adj.* ('pûfikt) absolutely without fault; beyond improvement. **perfect tense** the construction of a verb expressing an act completed, e.g. *I have returned.* —*vb.* (pə'fekt) to make perfect. —**per'fection** *n.* —**'perfectly** *adv.*

perform (pə'fôm) *vb.* 1. to do. 2. to act in a play, sing, or play music, etc. **per'formance** *n.* 1. a theatrical or musical entertainment. 2. the act of doing or fulfilling.

perfume *n.* ('pûfyo͝om) 1. a pleasant smelling liquid: *she wore an expensive perfume.* 2. a sweet smell: *the perfume of flowers.* —*vb.* (pə'fyo͝om) **perfuming, perfumed.** to give a pleasant smell to.

perimeter (pə'rimitə) *n.* the distance around a flat object or surface or a line describing this distance; circumference: *the perimeter of a 40 by 60 foot rectangle is 200 feet.*

period ('piəriəd) *n.* 1. an interval or portion of time. 2. a full stop at the end of a sentence. **periodical** (piəri'odikəl) *n.* a magazine or other publication that appears at regular intervals. *adj.* 1. published at regular intervals. 2. (also **periodic**) happening at regular intervals of time. —**peri'odically** *adv.*

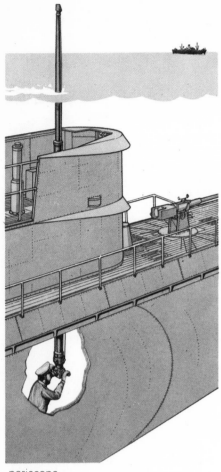

periscope

periscope ('periskōp) *n.* a tube with an arrangement of mirrors or prisms for looking at objects above the direct line of vision, e.g. in a submarine.

perish ('perish) *vb.* 1. to die: *the crew perished when the ship sank.* 2. to decay; rot: *the rubber tubes had perished in the heat.* '**perishable** *adj.* liable to decay. *n.* usu. **perishables** (*pl.*) food that is liable to decay.

permanent ('pûmənənt) *adj.* remaining or intended to remain for an indefinite period; everlasting. —'**permanence** *n.* —'**permanently** *adv.*

permit *vb.* (pə'mit) **permitting, permitted.** to allow. —*n.* ('pûmit) an official document allowing a person to do something: *you will need a permit to visit the bird sanctuary.* **per'mission** *n.* consent granted to do something. **per'missive** *adj.* 1. granting permission. 2. allowing great freedom of action and behaviour. —**per'missively** *adv.*

perpendicular (pûpən'dikyoŏlə) *adj.* 1. straight up and down: *perpen-*

dicular walls. 2. set at right angles to a line or surface. —*n.* a line that forms a right angle with another line or surface. —**perpen'dicularly** *adv.*

perpetual (pə'petyoŏəl) *adj.* lasting forever without stopping or changing. —**per'petually** *adv.*

perplex (pə'pleks) *vb.* to bewilder; puzzle. —**per'plexity** *n.,pl.* **perplexities.** 1. bewilderment. 2. a confusing problem.

persevere (pûsi'viə) *vb.* **persevering, persevered.** to continue steadfastly with an activity despite any discouragement or difficulties.

persist (pə'sist) *vb.* 1. to continue obstinately with a course of action despite opposition or warning. 2. to last; survive: *belief in magic still persists.* —**per'sistence** *n.* —**per'sistent** *adj.* —**per'sistently** *adv.*

person ('pûsən) *n.* 1. a single human being. 2. the living body of a human being: *she had no money on her person.* '**personal** *adj.* 1. relating to, belonging to, or coming from a particular person; private: *do not interfere in my personal affairs.* 2. done by a particular person, not a substitute. **person'ality** *n.,pl.* **personalities.** 1. the impression made on others of all the aspects of a person's character: *she has a very pleasant personality.* 2. a well-known person: *a television personality.* —'**personally** *adv.*

personnel (pûsə'nel) *n.* the body of people engaged in some particular work or activity, e.g. the workers in an office.

perspective (pə'spektiv) *n.* the art of drawing so as to give the appearance of depth and distance.

perspire (pə'spīə) *vb.* **perspiring, perspired.** to sweat; give out moisture through the skin. **perspi'ration** *n.* 1. sweat. 2. the act of sweating.

persuade (pə'swād) *vb.* **persuading, persuaded.** to convince or win over to a point of view, usu. by polite arguments: *surely you can persuade him to come to the party.* —**per'suasion** *n.* —**per'suasive** *adj.*

pessimist ('pesimist) *n.* a person who always looks on the gloomy side, convinced that the worst will happen: *the pessimist insisted on taking an umbrella to the beach.* —'**pessimism** *n.* —**pessi'mistically** *adv.*

pet (pet) *n.* 1. a tame animal kept for company. 2. a spoiled or favourite child. —*adj.* 1. tame: *a pet squirrel.* 2. favourite: *the scientist proved his pet theory.* —*vb.* **petting, petted.** to treat as a pet; cuddle and stroke.

petal ('petəl) *n.* one of the coloured leaflike parts of a flower.

petition (pi'tishən) *n.* a formal request addressed to a court, employer, or other authority, asking for a reform or favour. —*vb.* 1. to present a petition. 2. to ask.

petrol ('petrəl) *n.* the liquid refined from an oily substance known as **petroleum,** which is found under the earth. It is used as a fuel for motorcars.

petticoat ('petikōt) *n.* a garment worn by women under an outer skirt, dress, etc.

petty ('peti) *adj.* **pettier, pettiest.** 1. minor; unimportant. 2. spiteful in a narrow-minded way. **petty cash** small amounts of money. **petty officer** a junior officer in the navy.

pew (pyoō) *n.* a long seat or bench in a church.

phantom ('fantəm) *n.* 1. a ghost. 2. anything that appears to exist but does not really: *the boy's story that he was an astronaut was just a phantom.*

phase (fāz) *n.* 1. a stage in development or growth. 2. the shape and appearance of the moon at a given time. —*vb.* **phasing, phased.** 1. to separate (a plan, activity, etc.) into its different stages. 2. (+ *out*) to do away with or get rid of gradually.

pheasant ('fezənt) *n.* a large bird with a long tail that is hunted for sport and for food. The male birds have brightly coloured feathers. Pheasants came originally from Asia.

photograph ('fōtəgrâf) *n.* often **photo** ('fōtō), *pl.* **photos.** a picture made by recording the action of light on a specially prepared film or plate. —*vb.* to take such a picture of (something) with a camera. **photography** (fə'togrəfi) *n.* art of making pictures with a camera. —**photographic** (fōtə'grafik) *adj.*

phrase (frāz) *n.* 1. a group of words forming part of a sentence, e.g. *in the boat* in the sentence *six men sat in the boat.* 2. (music) a group of notes.

physical ('fizikəl) *adj.* 1. of the body: *he suffers poor physical health.* 2. of or concerning material things, forces, etc.: *what are the physical characteristics of these metals?* 3. of nature: *the mountain was the chief physical feature of the region.* —'**physically** *adv.*

physician (fi'zishən) *n.* a doctor.

physics ('fiziks) *sing.n.* science of energy and matter that studies the nature of light, heat, motion, electricity, etc. '**physicist** *n.* a person who studies physics.

piano

piano (pi'anō) *n.,pl.* **pianos.** a large musical instrument. The player produces sounds by pressing keys that cause small felt-covered hammers to strike metal strings. —'**pianist** *n.*

pick[1] (pik) *vb.* 1. to choose. 2. to poke or probe, esp. with the fingers or a sharp pointed tool. 3. to gather, esp. by hand. 4. to open (a lock) without a key. 5. to start (a fight) on purpose. **pick at** to eat only a small amount of. **pick holes in** to find fault with. **pick on** to criticize repeatedly and unfairly. **pick one's way** to move very carefully. **pick out** to select. **pick up** 1. to raise. 2. to call for and collect. 3. to make friends with (someone) casually. '**pickup** *n.* 1. a small truck for carrying light loads. 2. a casual friend. **the pick** the best.

pick[2] (pik) *n.* a large tool having a heavy curved metal head with pointed ends, used for breaking up stones, concrete, etc.

picket ('pikit) *n.* 1. a striker or group of strikers, standing outside a factory, mine, etc., to persuade other workers to join a strike. 2. a pointed stake driven into the ground, esp. as part of a fence. —*vb.* to act as a picket (def. 1).

pickle ('pikəl) *vb.* **pickling, pickled.** to preserve (food) in vinegar or salt water. —*n.* often **pickles** (*pl.*) vegetables pickled and spiced and used as a sauce.

picnic ('piknik) *n.* a meal eaten out of doors, usu. in the country, for fun. —*vb.* **picnicking, picnicked.** to take part in a picnic.

picture ('pikchə) *n.* 1. a drawing, painting, or photograph representing a person or thing. 2. an image seen on a television or cinema screen. 3. a type or symbol: *Tom is the picture of misery.* —*vb.* 1. to describe (something) in words. 2. to imagine. **pictorial** (pik'tôriəl) *adj.* of or like pictures. **picturesque** (pikchə'resk) *adj.* pretty or interesting enough to be the subject of a picture.

piece (pēs) *n.* 1. a part, portion, or fragment. 2. a literary, artistic, or musical composition. 3. an individual thing that is part of a set or large number: *a chess piece.* **a piece of cake** (slang) a very easy task. **give (someone) a piece of one's mind** to speak frankly and critically to (someone). —*vb.* **piecing, pieced.** (often + *together*) to join up scattered fragments, clues, etc., to make a whole.

pier (piə) *n.* 1. a seaside structure extending into the water used for amusement. 2. a landing place for boats. 3. a pillar supporting a bridge, jetty, etc.

pierce (piəs) *vb.* **piercing, pierced.** to make a hole in or through. '**piercing** *adj.* penetrating; perceptive: *he gave her a piercing stare.*

pigeon ('pijin) *n.* a common bird of the dove family that lives wild and in cities and is capable of flying great distances. Tame pigeons are often used for racing.

pigeonhole ('pijinhōl) *n.* a small box-like compartment of a desk, that is used for storing documents. —*vb.* **pigeonholing, pigeonholed.** 1. to classify: *the boy was pigeonholed as a trouble-maker.* 2. to put off or postpone.

pigmy ('pigmi) *n.,pl.* **pigmies.** See PYGMY.

pile[1] (pīl) *n.* 1. a heap. 2. (informal) a very large amount, esp. of money. —*vb.* **piling, piled.** (often + *on* or *up*) to heap up.

pile[2] (pīl) *n.* the thick fibres on the surface of velvet, carpeting, etc.

pilgrim ('pilgrim) *n.* 1. a person who travels to a holy place as an act of religious devotion. 2. **Pilgrim** one of the people who left England in 1620 to settle in America. '**pilgrimage** *n.* a pilgrim's journey.

pill (pil) *n.* a small tablet of medicine made to be swallowed whole.

pillar ('pilə) *n.* a tall column supporting a building or standing as a monument.

pillow ('pilō) *n.* a soft cushion used to support the head of someone who is asleep or resting.

pilot ('pīlət) *n.* 1. a person who drives an aeroplane or spacecraft. 2. a person who guides ships in and out of harbour. —*vb.* to act as a pilot.

pincers ('pinsəz) *n.* (*pl.* or *sing.*) 1. a tool for gripping and pulling or twisting: *she pulled the rusty nails from the plank with pincers.* 2. the claws of crabs, lobsters, etc.

pinch (pinch) *vb.* 1. to nip or squeeze painfully, esp. between finger and thumb. 2. (slang) to steal. —*n.* 1. a squeeze. 2. the amount that can be held between the finger and thumb. **pinched** *adj.* ill-looking.

pigeon

pine[1] (pīn) *n.* a widespread, hardy, evergreen tree with needle-shaped leaves, whose wood is used for telegraph poles, building, furniture, etc. —*adj.* made of pinewood.

pine[2] (pīn) *vb.* **pining, pined.** 1. to suffer because of sorrow or illness. 2. to long for (something): *I pine for sunshine in winter.*

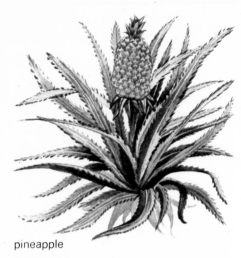
pineapple

pineapple ('pīnapəl) *n.* the large sweet juicy fruit of a tropical plant, with a rough skin and yellow flesh.

pinnacle ('pinəkəl) *n.* 1. a tall pointed structure on a building. 2. a natural rock formation with a similar shape. 3. the highest point.

pint (pīnt) *n.* a liquid measure equal to one eighth of a gallon or 20 fluid ounces.

pioneer (pīə'niə) *n.* 1. a person who explores and settles in new territory. 2. a person who develops new fields of research methods, etc.

pipe (pīp) *n.* 1. a tube of metal, glass etc., used for carrying fluids or gas. 2. a wooden tube with a little bowl at one end used for smoking tobacco. 3. a tubelike musical instrument played by blowing into the end. —*vb.* **piping, piped.** 1. to play a pipe. 2. to send (oil, water, etc.) through a pipe. **pipe down** (informal) to stop talking; become quiet. **pipe up** (informal) to begin to speak, often unexpectedly. '**piping** *n.* 1. the sound of pipe-playing, birdsong, etc. 2. a narrow cord or strip used as decoration on clothes, furniture, etc.

pipeline ('pīplīn) *n.* a long continuous line of pipes transporting something a great distance, e.g. oil from a desert oil-well.

pirate ('pīrət) *n.* 1. a robber who plunders ships at sea. 2. a person who illegally takes over another's rights of trading, broadcasting, etc. —*vb.* **pirating, pirated.** to publish illegally a version of another's writings, records, etc. —'**piracy** *n.*

pistil ('pistəl) *n.* the seed-bearing part of a flower.

pistol ('pistəl) *n.* a small gun held in one hand for firing.

piston ('pistən) *n.* a metal disc or cylinder that fits closely inside a tube in which it moves backwards and forwards.

pit (pit) *n.* 1. a hole dug in the earth. 2. an open mine for chalk, gravel, etc. 3. a natural hollow in the body or skin, e.g. armpit. 4. an area sunk below that of the surroundings: *we looked down into the snake pit at the zoo.* —*vb.* **pitting, pitted.** 1. to make holes (in something). 2. (+ *against*) to set or match against: *the wrestlers pitted their strength against each other.*

pitch[1] (pich) *vb.* 1. to toss; throw. 2. to set up (a tent, camp, etc.). 3. to plunge violently forwards. —*n.* 1. a throw or way of throwing in some sports. 2. an area or space where business is performed or some sports played. 3. a degree or extent: *we were in a high pitch of excitement.* 4. the highness or lowness of a musical note.

pitch[2] (pich) *n.* a sticky black substance made from tar and used to make roofs, ships' decks, etc., waterproof.

pitfall ('pitfôl) *n.* a hidden trap or danger.

pith (pith) *n.* 1. a spongy material in the centre of the stems of some plants. 2. a similar white tissue under the skins of some fruits, e.g. oranges. 3. the essential part: *the pith of her argument was sound.* '**pithy** *adj.* **pithier, pithiest.** of or like pith.

pity ('piti) *n.,pl.* **pities.** 1. a feeling of sympathy for those in trouble. 2. something to be regretted. —*vb.* **pitying, pitied.** to feel sympathy for (someone in distress). '**pitiful** *adj.* 1. arousing pity. 2. arousing scorn: *pitiful cowardice.* —'**pitifully** *adv.*

placard ('plakâd) *n.* a written or printed announcement that is publicly displayed.

place (plās) *n.* 1. a particular position; area of space. 2. one's home. 3. a position or rank. 4. duty; job. —*vb.* **placing, placed.** 1. to put or be in a particular spot or position. 2. to identify: *I can't place her, but I have seen her somewhere else.*

placid ('plasid) *adj.* calm; serene: *the placid baby never cried.* —'**placidly** *adv.* —'**placidness** *n.*

plague (plāg) *n.* 1. a very serious outbreak of an infectious disease, causing widespread deaths, esp. in the Middle Ages. 2. a persistent nuisance: *a plague of mosquitoes.* —*vb.* **plaguing, plagued.** to annoy repeatedly.

plaice (plās) *n.* an edible flatfish with red spotted scales, found in northern seas, esp. around Iceland.

plain (plān) *adj.* 1. clear; easy to understand or see: *I made it plain that I was cross.* 2. undecorated; simple: *a plain grey dress.* 3. of no great beauty, luxury, or richness: *a rather plain girl.* —*n.* a flat stretch of land without hills or valleys. —'**plainly** *adv.* —'**plainness** *n.*

plait (plat) *n.* three strands of hair, rope, straw, etc., woven into one thick strand. —*vb.* to weave or twist into a plait.

plan (plan) *n.* 1. a method of doing or achieving something that is worked out beforehand; scheme. 2. often **plans** (*pl.*) a large-scale diagram, chart, or detailed drawing of the layout or design of a house, ship, etc. —*vb.* **planning, planned.** 1. to make a plan or plans. 2. to intend. 3. to design.

plane

plane[1] (plān) *n.* 1. a completely level surface. 2. a standard of achievement or a stage of development: *his work often reached a very high plane.* 3. an aeroplane. 4. a tool for smoothing wood by scraping off very thin layers. —*vb.* **planing, planed.** to smooth with a plane (def. 4).

plane[2] (plān) *n.* a tree of the SYCAMORE family with thin bark that flakes off in patches. It is often planted in cities.

planet ('planit) *n.* a celestial object orbiting around a star and made visible only by reflecting starlight. **planetoid** ('planitoid) *n.* (also **minor planet**) a small planet.

plank (plaῆgk) *n.* a long narrow piece of sawn wood. —*vb.* to cover with planks.

plankton ('plaῆgktən) *pl.n.* tiny plants and animals that float in the sea or fresh water.

plant (plânt) *n.* 1. a living organism that manufactures food from air, water, and soil, using sunlight and a green substance called chlorophyll. 2. a complete set of equipment including machinery, instruments, etc., esp. for a factory. —*vb.* 1. to set a plant, seed, bulb, etc., in the soil to grow. 2. to set down firmly; establish: *she planted herself near the entrance.* 3. to place a person or object to provide information etc.: *detectives were planted in the crowd.* **plan'tation** *n.* 1. an area planted with trees. 2. a large farm on which single crops such as tea, sugar, or cotton are cultivated, often employing resident workers.

plaster ('plâstə) *n.* 1. a combination of lime, sand, and water used to give walls a smooth surface. 2. a sticky protective covering for a wound. 3. bandages soaked in a white paste that sets hard to form a cast to keep broken limbs in a fixed position. —*vb.* 1. to cover with plaster. 2. to cover over with or supply in abundance: *his boots were plastered with mud after the walk through wet fields.*

plastic ('plastik) *n.* a manmade substance that can be easily shaped when hot. —*adj.* 1. able to be shaped: *warmed wax is plastic.* 2. made of plastic: *plastic raincoats.*

plate (plāt) *n.* 1. a flat dish on which food is eaten or served. 2. a sheet or thin, smooth piece (of metal, glass, etc.). 3. an illustration in a printed book. 4. a structure for supporting false teeth or correcting badly positioned teeth. 5. silver and gold covered objects, esp. cutlery and household articles. —*vb.* **plating, plated.** to coat with metal.

plateau ('platō) *n.,pl.* **plateaus** *or* **plateaux** ('platōz). an expanse of land raised above the surrounding country.

platform ('platfôm) *n.* 1. a raised area of floor; stage. 2. the part of a railway station next to which trains stop. 3. a political programme.

platinum ('platinəm) *n.* a precious metal that looks like silver and is used for making watch parts and jewellery. Chemical symbol: Pt.

play (plā) *vb.* 1. to amuse oneself. 2. to take part in (a game or sport): *do you play tennis?* 3. to compete against (someone) in a game or sport: *England is playing Brazil.* 4. to produce sound from: *will you play your violin?* 5. to act as: *who is playing Cinderella?* 6. to have one's turn (at a game). —*n.* 1. a story written for the theatre; drama. 2. the act or activity of playing. 3. scope for freedom of movement and development: *he gave free play to his fears.* **'playwright** *n.* a person who writes dramas.

plea (plē) *n.* 1. an appeal or earnest entreaty. 2. an excuse: *she made the plea that she had too much work to do.* 3. a statement in a court of law.

plead (plēd) *vb.* **pleading, pleaded** *or* **plead** (pled). 1. to beg; implore. 2. to give as an excuse: *she pleaded a headache.* 3. to make a legal declaration: *do you plead guilty or not guilty?*

pleasant ('plezənt) *adj.* 1. enjoyable. 2. agreeable; likable.

please (plēz) *vb.* **pleasing, pleased.** 1. to give pleasure to; make happy. 2. to choose or desire: *he does as he pleases.* —*adv.* kindly; if you please.

pleasure ('plezhə) *n.* 1. a feeling of deep enjoyment; delight. 2. anything causing pleasure. —**'pleasurable** *adj.* —**'pleasurably** *adv.*

pleat (plēt) *n.* a fold made by doubling cloth. —*vb.* to make pleats in.

pleat

plenty ('plenti) *n.* 1. a large quantity; good supply. 2. riches. —**'plentiful** *adj.*

pliers ('plīəz) *pl.n.* a TOOL for gripping, bending, and cutting.

plod (plod) *vb.* **plodding, plodded.** to walk with a slow heavy regular tread. **'plodder** *n.* 1. a person who plods. 2. a person who works hard but slowly.

plot[1] (plot) *n.* 1. a secret plan: *the Gunpowder Plot.* 2. the main story (of a book, film, etc.). —*vb.* **plotting, plotted.** 1. to make a plot. 2. to plan (something) secretly. 3. to record on a chart or graph: *he plotted the ship's progress.*

plot[2] (plot) *n.* a small area of land, esp. one on which a house is built: *there are very few plots left in the town.*

plough (plou) *n.* 1. a farming implement used for making furrows in the earth before sowing seed. 2. a machine for clearing a way through snow. —*vb.* 1. to use a plough on (land). 2. to move heavily or with difficulty.

pluck (pluk) *vb.* 1. to pull sharply or pick. 2. to remove feathers from (birds). —*n.* 1. the internal parts of a dead animal. 2. (informal) bravery: *Tom has plenty of pluck.*

plug (plug) *n.* 1. something used to close a hole. 2. a pronged object used for connecting an electrical appliance to the power supply. —*vb.* **plugging, plugged.** 1. to stop up by means of a plug. 2. (informal) to recommend or advertise heavily: *they're plugging the new record.* 3. (+ *in*) to connect (an electrical appliance) to a power supply.

plum (plum) *n.* the fruit of the plum tree, which can be purple, red, orange, or yellow in colour, with sweet edible flesh and a hard flat stone.

plumber ('plumə) *n.* a person whose job is to fit and repair the water pipes and equipment associated with them in buildings.

plume (plōōm) *n.* 1. a large fluffy feather, esp. when worn as a decoration. 2. a feather-like streak, e.g. of smoke.

plump (plump) *adj.* rounded; fat in a pleasing way. —*vb.* (+ *up*) to make nicely rounded: *she plumped up the cushions.*

159

plunge (plunj) *vb.* **plunging, plunged.** 1. to jump or dive (into water). 2. to move violently and suddenly sideways, forwards, or downwards: *the car plunged into the ravine.* —*n.* the act of plunging.

plural ('plo͞oərəl) *adj.* of or expressing more than one; not singular. —*n.* the plural grammatical form: *fungi is the plural of fungus.*

plus (plus) *prep.* 1. increased by: *three plus two equals five.* 2. with the addition of; with: *she shows intelligence plus tact.* —*adj.* 1. showing addition: *a plus sign.* 2. higher than: *his grade in the exam was B plus.* —*n.* 1. a sign (+) showing addition. 2. something extra.

pneumonia (n̬yo͞o'mōniə) *n.* a serious disease in which the victim's lungs become swollen, thus making breathing difficult.

poach[1] (pōc̱h) *vb.* to steal game, e.g. rabbits, pheasants, salmon, etc., from territory owned by someone else.

poach[2] (pōc̱h) *vb.* to cook in gently boiling liquid.

pocket ('pokit) *n.* 1. a small pouch or bag, esp. one attached to a garment for holding small objects. 2. a small area that is different in some way from that surrounding it: *there are pockets of sand between the rocks.* —*vb.* to put in one's pocket.

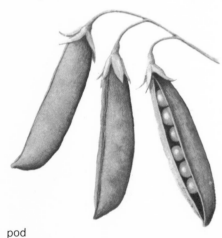
pod

pod (pod) *n.* the small case that contains the seeds of such plants as peas, beans, etc. —*vb.* **podding, podded.** 1. to develop pods. 2. to remove from the pod.

poem ('pōəm) *n.* an arrangement of words using rhythm, imaginative forms of expression, and sometimes rhyme to convey an important idea or intensely felt experience in a relatively short space. '**poet** *n.* a writer of poetry. **poetic** (pō'etik) *or* po'etical *adj.* relating to, like, or suitable for a poem. '**poetry** *n.* 1. the art and practice of writing poems. 2. poems in general.

point (point) *n.* 1. a sharp end or tip. 2. a dot, esp. in punctuation or expressing decimals. 3. a specific position on a scale, course, compass, etc.: *a good starting point.* 4. a time or moment: *we were interrupted at that point.* 5. an argument or opinion: *the speaker made several good points.* 6. a basic fact: *did you get the point of the joke?* 7. purpose or use: *there's no point in continuing.* 8. a narrow strip of land jutting into the sea or water. 9. an electric socket usu. on a wall. 10. a unit used in counting, scoring, or rating. —*vb.* to indicate or show position or direction by stretching out a hand and forefinger. '**pointed** *adj.* 1. having a point. 2. (of remarks) deliberately wounding; meaningful. '**pointless** *adj.* useless; futile.

poison ('poizən) *n.* a substance that injures or kills living plants or animals. —*vb.* 1. to give poison to. 2. to kill with poison. —'**poisonous** *adj.*

poker[1] ('pōkə) *n.* a metal rod used for moving lighted coals in a fire.

poker[2] ('pōkə) *n.* a card game in which the players make bets on the real, pretended, or imagined value of the cards in their hands.

polar ('pōlə) *adj.* of or relating to a pole, esp. the North or South Pole: *a polar expedition.* **polar bear** a large white bear that lives in the regions of the North Pole.

pole[1] (pōl) *n.* a long straight rod of metal, wood, etc.

pole[2] (pōl) *n.* 1. either end of the axis about which the earth rotates, i.e. the North Pole and South Pole. 2. either end of a magnet. 3. either end of the terminals in a battery. '**polar** *adj.* of, at, or near the North or South Pole.

police (pə'lēs) *pl.n.* an organization of men and women responsible for seeing that the law is obeyed and preventing crime and violence during peace time. —*vb.* **policing, policed.** to guard or control. —po'**liceman** *n.,pl.* **policemen.** —po'**licewoman** *n.,pl.* **policewomen.**

policy ('polisi) *n.,pl.* **policies.** a plan of action or declaration of principles and aims, esp. by an institution or government.

polish ('polis̱h) *vb.* 1. to make shiny by rubbing. 2. to make elegant or stylish: *the president polished his speech.* —*n.* 1. shine; glossiness. 2. material used to produce a shine. 3. elegance or refinement.

polite (pə'līt) *adj.* having good manners; courteous. —po'**litely** *adv.*

politics ('politiks) *pl.n.* 1. the work, management, or structure of a government or political party. 2. the tactics and schemes involved in the management of power: *business politics are often complicated.* 3. political opinions or beliefs: *what are your politics?* **political** (pə'litikəl) *adj.* relating to the affairs of government or the management of any kind of power. **politician** (poli'tis̱hən) *n.* a person involved in government, esp. as a member of a political party. —po'**litically** *adv.*

pollen ('polən) *n.* the fine, usu. yellow powder produced by flowering plants and carried by the wind, birds, insects, etc., to fertilize plants of the same species. —'**pollinate** *vb.* **pollinating, pollinated.**

pollute (pə'lo͞ot) *vb.* **polluting, polluted.** to make impure or dirty: *the factory polluted the river with chemicals.* —pol'**lution** *n.*

pomegranate ('pomigranit) *n.* a reddish fruit the size of an orange with a hard rind covering a mass of seeds in an edible semi-sweet jelly.

pomegranate

pomp (pomp) *n.* splendid ceremonious display: *the royal funeral was an*

ponies

Australian Waler

Appaloosa

Exmoor

Highland

occasion of great pomp. **'pompous** *adj.* self-important and full of one's own dignity. —**'pompously** *adv.*

pond (pond) *n.* a pool of still water smaller than a lake.

pony ('pōni) *n.,pl.* **ponies.** a horse of a small breed.

pool[1] (pōol) *n.* 1. a puddle. 2. a small pond. 3. a deep part of a river. 4. a large tank of water for swimming in.

pool[2] (pōol) *n.* an arrangement by which resources are combined and shared: *a typing pool.* **the pools** a form of gambling on the results of football matches that gives a small chance of winning a large amount of money. —*vb.* to put together in a pool.

poor (pōoə) *adj.* 1. not rich; needy. 2. unfortunate; pitiful. 3. inferior; not good. —**'poorly** *adv.*

pope (pōp) *n.* the head of the Roman Catholic Church.

poppy ('popi) *n.,pl.* **poppies.** a plant that grows wild and in gardens and

has red, yellow, or pink flowers.

popular ('popyōolə) *adj.* 1. liked and appreciated by many people: *he is a popular lecturer.* 2. of, for, or in connection with the majority of people: *popular taste.* —**popu'larity** *n.* —**'popularly** *adv.*

population (popyōo'lāshən) *n.* 1. the number of people living in a town, country, etc. 2. people: *the population fled from the earthquake.*

porch (pôch) *n.* 1. a roofed and sometimes enclosed doorway or entrance built onto a house; lobby. 2. (U.S.) a veranda.

porcupine ('pôkyōopīn) *n.* a smallish, short-legged animal whose body is covered in spines that it can raise when attacked. Different kinds of porcupine live in Asia, Africa, and America.

pore (pô) *n.* a tiny opening in the skin or some other surface through which liquid can pass. —**'porous** *adj.*

pork (pôk) *n.* fresh meat from a pig.

porpoise ('pôpəs) *n.* a warm-blooded fish-eating animal the North Atlantic and North Pacific Oceans.

port[1] (pôt) *n.* 1. a harbour used for trading or passenger ships. 2. a town or city with a harbour.

port[2] (pôt) *n.* the left-hand side of a ship or aeroplane from the point of view of someone on board who is facing towards the front or bows.

porcupine

port[3] (pôt) *n.* a sweet rich red or white wine from Portugal.

porter (pôtə) *n.* 1. a person employed to carry goods or baggage. 2. a doorkeeper in a hotel, block of flats, etc.

porthole ('pôthōl) *n.* a small, often circular window in the side of a ship.

portion ('pôshən) *n.* a part of a whole, esp. a helping of food: *a portion of ice cream.* —*vb.* to divide into parts.

portrait ('pôtrāt) *n.* a painting, photograph, or account that depicts or describes a person or group. **portray** (pô'trā) *vb.* to make a portrait.

pose (pōz) *vb.* **posing, posed.** 1. to take up a position consciously, esp. when having one's picture taken. 2. to appear to be something that one is not. 3. to state or present a problem or question: *the breakdown posed a great problem for us.* —*n.* 1. a way of sitting or standing. 2. a pretence: *a pose of self-confidence.*

position (pə'zishən) *n.* 1. a place. 2. an arrangement, posture, or state of affairs: *he was sitting in an uncomfortable position.* 3. someone's social status, occupation, rank, or role in a sports team. 4. a point of view; opinion. —*vb.* to put in place.

positive ('pozitiv) *adj.* 1. without doubt. 2. self-confident; optimistic. 3. greater than zero. 4. (of a photographic print) having the areas of light and dark in their normal relation to one another. —*n.* a photographic print showing objects either light or dark, as they appear in nature. —'**positively** *adv.*

postmark

possess (pə'zes) *vb.* **possessing, possessed.** 1. to have (an object or quality). 2. to own. 3. to influence strongly: *he was possessed by fear.* —**pos'session** *n.* **pos'sessive** *adj.* 1. jealously guarding one's property or treating other people as if they were one's property. 2. (of a part of speech) expressing the relation of possession, e.g. *his, Jim's.* —**pos'sessively** *adv.* —**pos'sessiveness** *n.*

possible ('posibəl) *adj.* 1. capable of being; capable of happening. 2. reasonable; able to be considered: *he is a possible leader for the expedition.* —**possi'bility** *n.,pl.* **possibilities.** —'**possibly** *adv.*

post[1] (pōst) *n.* 1. the institution for the collection and delivery of parcels and letters. 2. letters and parcels sent and delivered by this system. 3. a collection or delivery of parcels or letters. —*vb.* to send a letter or parcel through the post. '**postage** *n.* the amount charged for sending an item through the post. '**postal** *adj.* of the post (def. 1). **post office** a place at which stamps can be bought, parcels sent off, etc.

post[2] (pōst) *n.* a stake of wood or metal placed upright in the ground and used as a support or marker.

poster ('pōstə) *n.* a large notice or advertisement usu. put up in a public place for people to read.

postmark ('pōstmâk) *n.* a mark stamped on a letter or parcel, recording the place and time of mailing.

postpone (pəs'pōn) *vb.* **postponing, postponed.** to arrange (something) at a later time than originally planned: *the match was postponed because of rain.* —**post'ponement** *n.*

postscript ('pōstskript) *n.* (often shortened to **P.S.**) a message added to the end of a letter, after the writer's signature.

posture ('poschə) *n.* the characteristic position of a person's body. —*vb.* **posturing, postured.** to pretend; adopt vain or false attitudes.

potato (pə'tātō) *n.,pl.* **potatoes.** the swollen starchy underground stem (tuber) of the potato plant, cultivated as a vegetable.

pothole ('pothōl) *n.* 1. a small pit in the surface of a road. 2. an underground cave. '**potholing** *n.* the sport of exploring underground caves.

pottery

pottery ('potəri) *n.,pl.* **potteries.** 1. vases, pots, bowls, etc., collectively, shaped in moist clay and hardened by baking. 2. the practice or craft of making such vessels. 3. a workshop where pottery is made. '**potter** *n.* a person who makes pottery.

pouch (pouch) *n.* a small bag or sack, such as the pocket in which a kangaroo carries its young.

poultry ('pōltri) *n.* chickens, turkeys, geese, ducks, and other domestic birds reared to produce flesh and eggs.

pound (pound) *n.* 1. a unit for measuring weight, equivalent to 16 ounces. 2. a unit of British currency equivalent to one hundred pence.

pour (pô) *vb.* 1. to flow or cause to flow in a stream: *he poured the tea into the cup.* 2. to rain hard.

poverty ('povəti) *n.* 1. a lack of money. 2. any lack or deficiency: *the poverty of his education prevented him from getting a good job.*

powder ('poudə) *n.* a dry material of fine particles. —*vb.* 1. to apply fine particles to a surface. 2. to break up into fine particles. —'**powdery** *adj.*

power ('pouə) *n.* 1. ability to act; authority. 2. working energy: *a motorcar with little power.* 3. a person or state with strength and influence. 4. the amount of times a number is multiplied by itself: *3 to the power of 4 is 81* (i.e. $3 \times 3 \times 3 \times 3$). —'**powerful** *adj.* —'**powerfully** *adv.*

practice ('praktis) *n.* 1. an action. 2. a habit or customary action. 3. the repeated performance of some action as a way of learning or perfecting a skill. 4. a professional person's business: *a doctor's practice.* **practicable** ('praktikəbəl) *adj.* capable of being done. '**practical** *adj.* 1. concerned with action rather than theory. 2. good at doing things or carrying out ideas. 3. useful; functional. '**practically** *adv.* 1. almost; virtually. 2. in a practical manner.

practise ('praktis) *vb.* **practising, practised.** 1. to perform some action repeatedly as a way of learning a skill. 2. to be engaged in a profession: *Mary practises law.*

praise (prāz) *vb.* **praising, praised.** to show approval of. —*n.* an expression of approval or admiration. —'**praiseworthy** *adj.*

prawn (prôn) *n.* one of several kinds of small edible SHELLFISH. They resemble shrimps and their flesh is pale pink when cooked.

pray (prā) *vb.* 1. to communicate, through speech or thought, with God or other holy beings. 2. to ask earnestly. **prayer** (preə) *n.* the message of one who prays.

preach (prēch) *vb.* **preaching, preached.** 1. to deliver a sermon. 2. to give moral advice in a patronizing or tedious manner.

precaution (pri'kôshən) *n.* something done in advance in order to prevent troublesome consequences: *when I go out I take the precaution of locking the door.* —pre'**cautionary** *adj.*

precious ('preshəs) *adj.* of great value: *gold and silver are precious metals.*

precipice ('presipis) *n.* a high vertical, or very nearly vertical, cliff. —pre'**cipitous** *adj.*

predator ('predətə) *n.* an animal that lives by hunting and eating other living creatures. —'**predatory** *adj.*

predict (pri'dikt) *vb.* to tell in advance: *it was impossible to predict the outcome of the final game.* —pre'**dictable** *adj.* —pre'**dictably** *adv.* —pre'**diction** *n.*

prefer (pri'fû) *vb.* **preferring, preferred.** to like better: *I prefer dogs to cats.* **preference** ('prefərəns) *n.* 1. the act of preferring: *I have a preference for jazz.* 2. something chosen because liked better: *my preference is skiing.* **preferential** (prefə'renshəl) *adj.* treated with preference.

prefix ('prēfiks) *n.* a part of a word placed before a word, and usu. joined to it, to affect its meaning, e.g. *un-* in *unable.* —*vb.* **prefixing, prefixed.** to put before or at the beginning.

pregnant ('pregnənt) *adj.* 1. (of a woman or female animal) having a child or young developing inside the body. 2. implying more than is expressed: *a glance pregnant with warning.*

prehistoric (prēhi'storik) *adj.* concerning or belonging to a period in time before the existence of written historical documents. —**prehistory** (prē'histəri) *n.*

prejudice ('prejŏodis) *n.* 1. an opinion formed beforehand without reasonable consideration; bias. 2. unreasonably hostile feelings or attitudes: *racial prejudice.* 3. damage or harm. —*vb.* **prejudicing, prejudiced.** 1. to bias the mind of: *they prejudiced her against him.* 2. to injure: *you are prejudicing your chances of success.* **prejudicial** (prejŏo'dishəl) *adj.* harmful.

premier ('premiə) *n.* the prime minister of a government. —*adj.* first in position, importance, etc.

premium ('prēmiəm) *n.* 1. payment for insurance: *what is the annual premium on your car?* 2. reward: *a premium for extra work.* **at a premium** in great demand or in short supply.

prepare (pri'peə) *vb.* **preparing, prepared.** to make ready: *he prepared a delicious meal.* **preparation** (prepə'rāshən) *n.* 1. the act of preparing. 2. something made ready for a purpose, e.g. a medicine.

preposition (prepə'zishən) *n.* a word

precipice

placed before a noun or pronoun to show its relationship to another word, e.g. *at* in *Pete stood at the door.*

prescribe (pri'skrīb) *vb.* **prescribing, prescribed.** to advise or order the use of a particular medicine, treatment, etc.: *these tablets were prescribed for me by my doctor.* **prescription** (pri'skripshən) *n.* 1. instructions written by a doctor regarding the preparation and use of a medicine. 2. a rule to be followed: *a prescription for success.*

presence ('prezəns) *n.* 1. the fact of being in a particular place at a particular time. 2. immediate vicinity. 3. striking personal appearance and manner: *the actor had great presence on the stage.*

present[1] ('prezənt) *adj.* 1. being in a particular place at a particular time: *he was present at the party.* 2. existing, dealt with, or occurring at this time: *our present headmaster is more popular than the last one.* **present tense** the construction of a verb that refers to action, etc., now going on, e.g. *he walks.* —*n.* this time; now. '**presently** *adv.* 1. soon. 2. at the present time.

present[2] *vb.* (pri'zent) 1. to give, often formally: *they presented him with a gold watch.* 2. to introduce (one person) to another: *may I present my son?* 3. to show: *they will present a new play.* 4. to send or put forward for consideration or examination: *I will present my proposals.* —*n.* ('prezənt) a gift. pre'**sentable** *adj.* fit to be seen. **presentation** (prezən'tāshən) *n.* 1. a formal act of giving. 2. something that is presented.

preserve (pri'zûv) *vb.* **preserving, preserved.** 1. to keep safe or in existence: *we must preserve our rights.* 2. to keep food from decay by treating it in a particular way. —*n.* 1. a place set apart for the protection of animals or birds. 2. usu. **preserves** (pl.) jam, chutney, etc. pre'**servative** *n.* a chemical substance used for preserving foodstuffs from decay. *adj.* tending to preserve. —**preservation** (prezə'vāshən) *n.*

preside (pri'zīd) *vb.* **presiding, presided.** to be at the head or in charge of. **president** ('prezidənt) *n.* 1. the head of a republic: *the President of the United States.* 2. the head of an organization, committee, institution, etc. —'**presidency** *n.,pl.* **presidencies.** —presi'**dential** *adj.*

press

press (pres) *vb.* 1. to push with force. 2. to squeeze or clasp. 3. to trouble. 4. to urge strongly: *he pressed me to come.* 5. to iron. —*n.* 1. an apparatus for pressing, shaping, etc. 2. a printing machine. 3. the profession of journalism; newspapers and periodicals collectively: *the story was reported in the press.* 4. the act of pressing: *I gave my trousers a press.*

pressure ('preshə) *n.* 1. force caused by one thing pushing on or against something else: *the pressure of the air makes the barometer rise and fall.* 2. the force divided by the area over which it acts. 3. strong influence. 4. strain and stress: *he is working under very great pressure.* **'pressurize** *vb.* **pressurizing, pressurized.** to regulate the air pressure in an aircraft or submarine. —**pressuri'zation** *n.*

presume (pri'zyōōm) *vb.* **presuming, presumed.** 1. to take as true without proof; suppose: *I presume that you are hungry.* 2. to take liberties; venture: *he presumed to complain about his father's smoking.* **pre'sumably** *adv.* as one can take for granted; probably: *she will presumably be late on account of the train strike.* —**presumption** (pri'zumpshən) *n.* —**pre'sumptuous** *adj.* —**pre'sumptuously** *adv.*

pretend (pri'tend) *vb.* to speak or act falsely in order to deceive: *he pretended he could not hear his father's shout.* **pre'tender** *n.* a claimant to a throne. —**pre'tence** *n.*

pretty ('priti) *adj.* **prettier, prettiest.** pleasing to the eye or ear. —*adv.* quite: *it hit him pretty hard.* —**'prettiness** *n.*

prevail (pri'vāl) *vb.* 1. to be general or common: *cheerfulness prevailed among the people.* 2. to succeed: *our armies prevailed over the enemy.* 3. to persuade: *he prevailed upon me to stop.* —**prevalent** ('prevələnt) *adj.*

prevent (pri'vent) *vb.* to keep from happening; hinder. —**pre'vention** *n.*

prey (prā) *n.* 1. an animal that is killed and eaten by another. 2. a victim: *Steve fell prey to the big bully.* —*vb.* (+ on or upon) 1. to hunt, kill, and eat. 2. to plunder. 3. to distress or trouble: *his problems preyed on his mind.*

price (prīs) *n.* the amount of money for which something is bought or sold. —*vb.* **pricing, priced.** to fix or find out the price of something. **'priceless** *adj.* too valuable to be priced.

pride (prīd) *n.* 1. pleasure or self-esteem derived from achievements, possessions, etc.: *he took great pride in his garden.* 2. self-respect: *have you no pride?* 3. arrogant behaviour; exaggerated opinions of one's qualities, abilities, etc. 4. the best or most highly regarded: *the painting was the pride of his collection.* 5. a group of lions. See also PROUD.

priest (prēst) *n.* a person whose duty it is to perform religious ceremonies.

primary ('prīməri) *adj.* 1. chief or most important. 2. first or original; basic. **primary school** a school for young children, usu. up to the age of 10 or 11. **'primarily** *adv.* in the first place.

prime (prīm) *adj.* 1. first in order of time, rank, value, etc. 2. of the highest quality: *prime beef.* —*n.* the best or most flourishing part of anything: *the prime of life* —*vb.* **priming, primed.** to make ready for a purpose: *the woodwork was primed with its first coat of paint.*

primitive ('primitiv) *adj.* 1. belonging to the earliest times: *primitive man.* 2. simple or crude: *a primitive hut.* —**'primitively** *adv.*

primrose ('primrōz) *n.* a plant with a pale yellow flower, common in woodland and meadows and often planted in gardens.

prince (prins) *n.* 1. a male member of a royal family. 2. the ruler of a principality or other small state. **princess** (prin'ses) *n.* 1. a female member of a royal family. 2. the wife of a prince. —**'princely** *adj.*

principal ('prinsipəl) *adj.* chief; highest in rank or achievement: *the principal dancer.* —*n.* 1. the most important person in an organization, esp. the head of a school or college. 2. anyone who plays a chief part in some activity. 3. invested or borrowed money on which interest is paid. —**'principally** *adv.*

principle ('prinsipəl) *n.* 1. a fundamental truth or basic law: *his argument was based on sound principles.* 2. a settled rule of conduct: *I make it a principle never to borrow money from anyone.*

print (print) *vb.* 1. to produce a book, newspaper, pictures, etc., by pressing inked type, blocks, or plates onto paper or some other surface. 2. to write in letters like those made by type. 3. to mark by pressure. 4. (photography) to produce a positive picture from a negative. —*n.* 1. printed lettering; printed matter, such as a newspaper. 2. a picture or design produced by printing. 3. a mark made by pressure. 4. a photographic picture made from a negative. **'printable** *adj.* suitable to be printed.

primrose

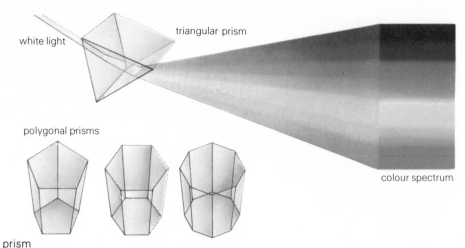

white light

triangular prism

colour spectrum

polygonal prisms

prism

prism ('prizəm) *n.* a solid transparent object that bends and breaks up rays of white light into the colours of the rainbow.

prison ('prizən) *n.* a building where criminals are locked up. **'prisoner** *n.* 1. a person sent to prison. 2. any person kept locked up by others.

private ('prīvit) *adj.* belonging to or concerning some particular person or persons: *my private room.* —*n.* a soldier of the lowest rank. —**privacy** ('privəsi) *n.* —**'privately** *adv.*

privilege ('privilij) *n.* a special right or advantage enjoyed by one person or a few: *the privilege of a good education.* **'privileged** *adj.* enjoying special rights or advantages.

prize (prīz) *n.* 1. a reward for success in a sport, competition, etc. 2. anything that is highly valued or worth striving for. —*vb.* **prizing, prized.** to value something highly.

probable ('probəbəl) *adj.* likely to happen; expected: *the probable result.* —**proba'bility** *n.* —**'probably** *adv.*

probe (prōb) *vb.* **probing, probed.** to investigate or search thoroughly. —*n.* 1. a thorough investigation. 2. a fine surgical instrument. 3. a space vehicle designed to send information back to earth.

problem ('probləm) *n.* a matter or question that is difficult to solve.

process ('prōses) *n.* 1. a series of actions carried out for a purpose: *the process of making steel.* 2. a sequence of changes: *the process of growing up* —*vb.* to treat by some series of operations, as in manufacturing goods, preparing foods for storage, etc.

procession (prə'seshən) *n.* a company of people or vehicles moving forward in a formal or ceremonious manner. **process** (prō'ses) *vb.* to move in a procession.

proclaim (prə'klām) *vb.* to announce formally in public. —**proclamation** (proklə'māshən) *n.*

produce *vb.* (prə'dyōōs) **producing, produced.** 1. to make, provide, or yield: *the factory produces high quality furniture.* 2. to bring out for inspection: *please produce your passport.* 3. to bring before the public (a play, film, etc.). —*n.* ('prodyōōs) things produced on farms, such as eggs, fruit, etc. **product** ('prodəkt) *n.* 1. a thing produced; a result: *a product of his imagination.* 2. the result of mathematical multiplication. **pro'duction** *n.* 1. the act or process of producing. 2. the presentation of a play or other entertainment to the public. **pro'ductive** *adj.* producing abundantly; fertile: *productive land.* —**productivity** (produk'tiviti) *n.*

profession (prə'feshən) *n.* 1. an occupation requiring a lengthy process of training, e.g. law or medicine. 2. declaration: *a profession of love.* —**pro'fessional** *adj.*

professor (prə'fesə) *n.* a university teacher of the highest rank.

profile ('prōfīl) *n.* 1. the outline of an object seen from the side. 2. a short written account of a person's life and career.

profit ('profit) *n.* 1. financial gain: *the firm made a profit of £2000.* 2. advantage; benefit. —*vb.* to benefit; gain advantage: *he profited from the experience.* —**'profitable** *adj.* —**'profitably** *adv.*

programme ('prōgram) *n.* 1. a scheme or plan. 2. an entertainment, esp. on radio or television. 3. a booklet giving details about a ceremony, concert, or theatrical performance. 4. usu. **program.** instructions given to a computer.

progress *n.* ('prōgres) 1. a forward movement. 2. improvement. —*vb.* (prə'gres) 1. to go forward. 2. to improve. **pro'gression** *n.* a growth or development in successive stages. **pro'gressive** *adj.* 1. of a progression. 2. favouring new methods, attitudes, etc. —**pro'gressively** *adv.*

prohibit (prə'hibit) *vb.* to prevent or forbid. **prohi'bition** *n.* an order that forbids.

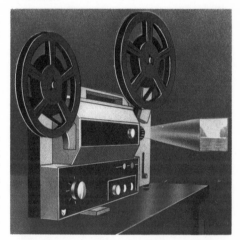

projector

project *vb.* (prə'jekt) 1. to stick out: *the nail projects from the surface.* 2. to cause light, shadows, images, etc., to fall on a surface: *she projected the movie.* 3. to predict what will happen. —*n.* ('projekt) a scheme for a new undertaking. **pro'jectile** *n.* something that is thrown or shot from a gun. **pro'jection** *n.* 1. the act of projecting. 2. something that sticks out. **pro'jector** *n.* a machine used for showing films and picture slides.

promise ('promis) *vb.* **promising, promised.** 1. to give one's word; vow. 2. to look likely to be or have: *this book promises to be interesting.* —*n.* 1. a vow. 2. the indication of future excellence: *this actor shows great promise.*

promote (prə'mōt) *vb.* **promoting, promoted.** 1. to advance (someone) to a better job, higher rank, etc. 2. to give active support 3. to advertise (a product). —**pro'motion** *n.*

prompt (prompt) *adj.* quick and punctual: *he was always prompt in paying.*

—*vb.* 1. to urge (someone) into action. 2. to supply (an actor) with lines that he has forgotten. —**'promptly** *adv.* —**'promptness** *n.*

pronoun ('prōnoun) *n.* a word used in place of a noun, e.g. *he, she, it, who.*

pronounce (prə'nouns) *vb.* **pronouncing, pronounced.** 1. to utter (words, etc.) in a certain way. 2.to declare formally: *the judge pronounced sentence.* **pro'nouncement** *n.* a formal declaration. **pronunciation** (prənunsi'āshən) *n.* a way of pronouncing.

proof (prōof) *n.* the evidence establishing the facts of an action, incident, etc. —*adj.* able to withstand: *the castle was proof against attack.*

propeller

propel (prə'pel) *vb.* **propelling, propelled.** to drive or cause to move forward. **propeller** *n.* a device made of two or more spinning blades, used to drive a ship or aircraft. See also PROPULSION.

property ('propəti) *n.,pl.* **properties.** 1. the things belonging to a person. 2. a house with its land. 3. a distinctive quality: *steel has the property of great strength.*

prophecy ('profisi) *n.,pl.* **prophecies.** a statement that foretells a future event.

prophesy ('profisī) *vb.* **prophesying, prophesied.** to say what will happen in the future. **'prophet** *n.* a person who prophesies. —**prophetic** (prə'fetik) *adj.*

proportion (prə'pôshən) *n.* the relation of one thing to another: *the proportion of oil to vinegar in a salad dressing is three to one.*

propose (prə'pōz) *vb.* **proposing, proposed.** 1. to put forward (a suggestion) for consideration. 2. to nominate (someone) for office. 3. to make an offer of marriage. **pro'posal** *n.* 1. a suggested plan or scheme. 2. an offer of marriage. **proposition** (propə'zishən) *n.* a scheme, plan, etc., put forward for approval.

proprietor (prə'priitə) *n.* the owner of something, esp. a business.

propulsion (prə'pulshən) *n.* force causing a forward motion.

prosecute ('prosikyōot) *vb.* **prosecuting, prosecuted.** to take legal proceedings against (someone). —**prose'cution** *n.*

prospect *n.* ('prospekt) 1. a view over a landscape. 2. the outlook for the future. 3. usu. **prospects** (*pl.*) expectations of success. —*vb.* (prə'spekt) to explore for gold or oil. **pro'spective** *adj.* relating to the future: *a prospective candidate.* **pros'pector** *n.* a person who explores for gold, oil, etc.

prosper ('prospə) *vb.* to do well, esp. financially. **prosperity** (pros'periti) *n.* financial success. **'prosperous** *adj.* financially well off. —**'prosperously** *adv.*

protect (prə'tekt) *vb.* to shield from danger, etc.—**pro'tection** *n.* —**pro-'tective** *adj.* —**pro'tectively** *adv.*

protein ('prōtēn) *n.* a chemical compound that forms an essential part of the bodies of plants and animals.

protest *vb.* (prə'test) to express an objection or disapproval. —*n.* ('prōtest) an objection or complaint.

proud (proud) *adj.* 1. very pleased with one's possessions, etc.: *she was proud of her new car.* 2. having too great an idea of one's own importance. 3. having a sense of self-respect: *he was too proud to accept charity.* See also PRIDE. —**'proudly** *adv.*

prove (prōov) *vb.* **proving, proved.** 1. to show to be true. 2. to be found to be: *the visitor proved to be my brother.*

proverb ('provûb) *n.* a short well-known saying illustrating a popular belief, e.g. *too many cooks spoil the broth.* **pro'verbial** *adj.*

provide (prə'vīd) *vb.* **providing, provided.** to make ready; supply. **pro-**

vide for to support: *parents should provide for their children.* **provident** ('providənt) *adj.* careful; thrifty.

province ('provins) *n.* 1. a division of a country *the Transvaal is a province of South Africa.* 2. an area of knowledge, experience, etc.: *mathematics is not my province..* **provincial** (prə'vinshəl) *adj.* of, relating to, or coming from the provinces.

provision (prə'vizhən) *n.* 1. the act of providing. 2. a condition: *we made the provision that we were to be paid in cash.* 3. **provisions** (*pl.*) a supply of food. **pro'visional** *adj.* conditional; not definitely settled or permanent. —**pro'visionally** *adv.*

provoke (prə'vōk) *vb.* **provoking provoked.** 1. to irritate; annoy. 2. to cause (action or response): *his remarks provoked a heated discussion.* **provocative** (prə'vokətiv) *adj.* likely to cause interest, anger, etc. —**provocation** (provə'kāshən) *n.* the act or an instance of making somebody angry, etc.

prow

prow (prou) *n.* the pointed front part of a ship.

prune[1] (prōon) *n.* a dried plum.

prune[2] (prōon) *vb.* **pruning, pruned.** to cut back (a tree or plant) to encourage better growth.

pry (prī) **prying, pried.** to try to discover other people's plans or secrets.

psalm (sâm) *n.* a sacred song or hymn, esp. one of those in the Bible.

psychology (sī'koləji) *n.* the study of the mind and the way it works. **psy'chologist** *n.* a person who studies the mind. —**psycho'logical** *adj.* —**psycho'logically** *adv.*

public ('publik) *adj.* of, concerning, open to, or owned by the whole community. —*n.* people in general: *open to the public.* **publicity** (pu'blisiti) *n.* 1. state of being widely known; fame. 2. advertising matter. —'**publicly** *adv.*

publication (publi'kāṣhən) *n.* 1. the act of publishing. 2. something that is published, e.g. a magazine.

publish ('publish) *vb.* 1. to print and sell to the public: *his music was published after his death.* 2. to make known to the public.

pulley ('poŏli) *n.* a wheel with a grooved outer edge for a rope or chain that is used to raise heavy loads.

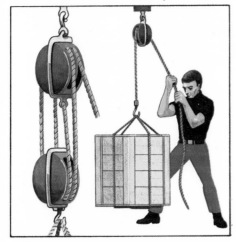
pulley

pulp (pulp) *n.* 1. a soft damp mass of material: *paper is made from pulp.* 2. the soft juicy part of a fruit.

pulpit ('poŏlpit) *n.* a raised boxed-in stand from which a priest preaches and reads the lesson in church.

pulse (puls) *n.* the regular throbbing of the blood in the arteries as it is pumped round the body by the heart, e.g. as felt at a person's wrist.

pump (pump) *n.* a machine or device for forcing fluids, gases, or air through a tube or pipe, e.g. a petrol pump. —*vb.* 1. to use a pump. 2. (+ *up*) to force air into: *Jane pumped up the bicycle tyres.*

pumpkin ('pumpkin) *n.* 1. a large round yellow fruit eaten as a vegetable. 2. the vine on which it grows.

pun (pun) *n.* the witty use of words that sound similar but have different meanings, e.g. they went and *told* the sexton, and the sexton *tolled* the bell.

pumpkin

punch[1] (punch) *vb.* to hit hard with the fist. —*n.* a sharp blow from a fist.

punch[2] (punch) *n.* a tool for making holes through paper, etc., or for impressing a design on a surface. —*vb.* to make holes in or imprint a design on.

punch[3] (punch) *n.* a drink made from wines or spirits, mixed with fruits and spices.

punctual ('pungktyoŏəl) *adj.* arriving or acting on time. —**punctu'ality** *n.* —'**punctually** *adv.*

punctuate ('pungktyoŏāt) *vb.* **punctuating, punctuated.** to break up a piece of writing into sentences and clauses by means of commas (,), stops (.), colons (:), etc., in order to make the sense clearer. —**punctu'ation** *n.*

puncture ('pungkchə) *vb.* **puncturing, punctured.** to make a hole in (something) with a sharp object; pierce: *the broken glass punctured my bicycle tyres.* —*n.* a hole made by a pointed object.

punish ('punish) *vb.* 1. to make (someone) suffer for wrongdoing. 2. to treat roughly: *the desert track punished the car.* '**punishable** *adj.* likely to be punished. —'**punishment** *n.*

pupa ('pyoŏpə) *n.,pl.* **pupae** ('pyoŏpē). an insect at the stage in its life during which it rests, e.g. in a cocoon, and changes into the adult form.

pupil[1] ('pyoŏpil) *n.* a person who is learning from a teacher; student.

pupil[2] ('pyoŏpil) *n.* a hole in the centre of the eyeball through which light enters the eye. It is small in bright light and enlarges in dim light.

puppet ('pupit) *n.* a small doll with movable parts that is fitted over the hand or controlled by strings.

purchase ('pûchis) *vb.* **purchasing, purchased.** to buy. —*n.* 1. something bought. 2. a firm grip: *he got a good purchase on the rope.*

pure (pyoŏə) *adj.* 1. unmixed with anything else: *a coat of pure wool.* 2. nothing but: *pure luck.* **purify** ('pyoŏərifī) *vb.* **purifying, purified.** to make pure. —**purifi'cation** *n.*

purpose ('pûpəs) *n.* 1. plan; intention. 2. use; function: *what is the purpose of the dial on this machine?*

pursue (pə'syoō) *vb.* **pursuing, pursued.** 1. to chase. 2. to carry on; continue: *he pursued his career as a dentist.* **pursuit** (pə'syoōt) *n.*

pus (pus) *n.* a thick yellow fluid formed in a sore, infected wound, etc.

puzzle ('puzəl) *n.* 1. anything that is hard to understand. 2. a game or problem that tests a person's skill, knowledge, etc. —*vb.* **puzzling, puzzled.** 1. to confuse or be hard to understand. 2. (+ *over*) to think hard about.

pygmy *or* **pigmy** ('pigmi) *n.,pl.* **pygmies** *or* **pigmies.** a member of one of the races of very small people (between 4 and 5 feet tall) who live in Africa and certain islands off Asia.

pyramid

pyramid ('pirəmid) *n.* 1. an object with a square base and four triangular sides that meet in a point at the top. See GEOMETRY. 2. a structure shaped like this, esp. one of the tombs in ancient Egypt.

python ('pīthən) *n.* a large snake that coils around and suffocates its prey.

Q

quack (kwak) *n*. 1. the cry of a duck. 2. (informal) an unqualified doctor. —*vb*. to make a noise like a duck's quack.

quadrangle ('kwodraꞑggəl) *n*. 1. a plane figure with four sides, esp. a square or rectangle. 2. an open space or courtyard surrounded by buildings.

quadrant ('kwodrənt) *n*. 1. the fourth part of a circle or its circumference. 2. an instrument used by sailors to find the position of their ship at sea.

quadrilateral (kwodri'latərəl) *n*. a plane figure with four sides. —*adj*. four-sided.

quadruped ('kwodrŏŏped) *n*. a four-footed animal.

quadruplet (kwo'drŏŏplit) *n*. (usu. shortened to **quad**) one of four babies born to one mother at the same time.

quail[1] (kwāl) *vb*. to feel or show fear; flinch: *the sick man quailed at the thought of the long journey.*

quail

quail[2] (kwāl) *n*. a small plump game bird that is valued as food.

quaint (kwānt) *adj*. pleasingly unusual or odd, esp. in an old-fashioned way. —'**quaintness** *n*. —'**quaintly** *adv*.

quake (kwāk) *vb*. **quaking, quaked.** to tremble; shiver, esp. with fear, strong emotion, illness, etc. —*n*. (informal) earthquake.

qualify ('kwolifī) *vb*. **qualifying, qualified.** 1. to obtain the necessary training or standard to fit oneself for a job, career, competition, etc.: *she qualified as a doctor.* 2. to limit or impose restrictions or conditions (on something): *he qualified his offer to such an extent that few people benefited from it.* **qualifi'cation** *n*. 1. something that makes someone or something fit to undertake a task. 2. a restriction.

quality ('kwoliti) *n.,pl.* **qualities.** 1. a degree of excellence; high grade, standard, etc.: *the workmanship is of very high quality.* 2. a personal characteristic, esp. a moral or mental virtue: *she has the qualities of gentleness and generosity.* 3. the basic character of a thing. **qualitative** ('kwolitətiv) *adj*. relating to quality.

quantity ('kwontiti) *n.,pl.* **quantities.** 1. a known or measurable amount, number, weight, etc. 2. often **quantities** (*pl.*) large amounts; plenty: *they supplied quantities of food at their party.*

quarantine ('kworəntēn) *n*. a stretch of time during which people or animals that may be carrying infectious diseases are kept completely cut off from others to prevent the infection from spreading. —*vb*. **quarantining, quarantined.** to isolate to prevent disease spreading.

quarrel ('kworəl) *n*. an angry or unfriendly argument; dispute. —*vb*. **quarrelling, quarrelled.** 1. to argue; fight. 2. (+ *with*) to find fault with: *he quarrelled with our method of working.* '**quarrelsome** *adj*. fond of quarrelling.

quarry[1] ('kwori) *n.,pl.* **quarries.** a large open pit in the ground from which stone, sand, flint, etc., is dug. —*vb*. **quarrying, quarried.** to dig out from a quarry.

quarry

quarry[2] ('kwori) *n.,pl.* **quarries.** a person or animal that is being hunted or chased: *the dog pounced on its quarry, a small rabbit.*

quart (kwôt) *n*. a measurement of liquid equal to one quarter of a gallon or 2 pints.

quarter ('kwôtə) *n*. 1. one of four equal parts. 2. a point in time fifteen minutes before or after an hour: *a quarter past six.* 3. a period of three months; a quarter of a year: *we pay our gas bill every quarter.* 4. a district of a city: *Plaka is the old Turkish quarter of Athens.* 5. source; direction from which something comes: *children ran from every quarter to see the parade.* 6. **quarters** (*pl.*) a place to stay; lodgings: *the soldiers returned to their quarters.* —*vb*. 1. to divide into four equal sections. 2. to find lodgings for (soldiers).

quarterly *adj.,adv.* once every three months. *n.,pl.* **quarterlies.** a magazine published four times a year.

quartet or **quartette** (kwô'tet) *n*. 1. a piece of music written to be performed by four musicians or singers. 2. a group of four musicians or singers who perform together.

quay (kē) *n*. a manmade landing place, usu. built of stone, alongside which ships can be tied; wharf.

queen (kwēn) *n.* 1. a woman ruler. 2. the wife or widow of a king. 3. a woman or thing of particular beauty or importance: *the aircraft carrier was queen of the fleet.* 4. an egglaying bee, ant, wasp, or termite. 5. the most powerful piece in the game of chess. —'**queenly** *adj.*

queer ('kwiə) *adj.* peculiar; unusual; differing from normal.

quench (kwench) *vb.* 1. to put an end to: *I quenched my thirst.* 2. to put out; extinguish: *the firemen quenched the flames.*

query ('kwiəri) *n.,pl.* **queries.** a question, esp. one that expresses doubt about the truth of something. —*vb.* **querying, queried.** to express doubt or uncertainty about: *she queried her bank statement.*

quest (kwest) *n.* a search or hunt, esp. of an adventurous sort: *the explorers went in quest of tigers.*

question ('kweschən) *n.* 1. a sentence that demands an answer; enquiry. 2. a matter to be talked about; something doubtful or uncertain: *the chairman raised the question of money.* —*vb.* 1. to ask questions of (someone). 2. to express doubt about: *she questioned his fitness for the job.* '**questionable** *adj.* doubtful; likely to be challenged. **question mark** a punctuation mark (?) placed at the end of a written question.

queue (kyōō) *n.* a line of people or vehicles waiting one behind the other for their turn to do something. —*vb.* **queueing, queued.** to form or wait in a queue.

quick (kwik) *adj.* 1. happening or done in a short space of time: *quick results.* 2. understanding or working easily and swiftly: *a quick intelligence.* —*n.* sensitive flesh, esp. that in which fingernails and toenails are set. '**quicken** *vb.* to make or become quick or quicker. —'**quickly** *adv.* —'**quickness** *n.*

quiet ('kwīət) *adj.* 1. making little or no noise: *quiet footsteps.* 2. having little or no movement; peaceful; inactive: *a quiet day.* 3. subdued; not too bright or loud: *a quiet colour.* —*n.* state of calm or silence. '**quieten** *vb.* to make or become quiet or quieter. —'**quietly** *adv.* —'**quietness** *n.*

quilt (kwilt) *n.* a warm bedcover made of two pieces of cloth stitched together with thick padding between them. —*vb.* to make a quilt.

quintet *or* **quintette** (kwin'tet) *n.* 1. a piece of music written to be performed by five musicians or singers. 2. a group of five musicians or singers who perform together.

quintuplet (kwin'tyōōplit) *n.* (usu. shortened to **quin**) one of five babies born to one mother at the same time.

quit (kwit) *vb.* **quitting, quit** *or* **quitted.** 1. to leave: *Bill quit school to find work.* 2. (informal) to stop; cease doing something: *he would not quit working even when he was ill.*

quiver[1] ('kwivə) *vb.* to tremble; shake slightly with fear, excitement, etc. —*n.* the act of quivering.

quiver[2] ('kwivə) *n.* a long narrow case for carrying arrows.

quiver

quiz (kwiz) *n.* a test or contest, esp. one in which short questions are asked to test one's general knowledge. —*vb.* **quizzing, quizzed.** to examine or test by asking questions.

quota ('kwōtə) *n.* the limited portion that each person receives after whatever is to be shared out has been divided.

quote (kwōt) *vb.* **quoting, quoted.** 1. to repeat (something that someone else has said or written): *the president quoted Shakespeare in his address.* 2. to give an estimate of the cost of something: *to quote a price.* —*n.* (informal) quotation. **quo'tation** *n.* 1. someone else's words repeated in a speech, article, etc. 2. an estimate of the current cost of anything. **quotation mark** a punctuation mark placed at the beginning (' or ') and end (' or ') of a written quotation.

quotient ('kwōshənt) *n.* the answer obtained when one number is divided by another.

R

rabbi ('rabī) *n.* the religious head of a Jewish community, who is usu. also a teacher of Jewish law. —**rabbinical** (rə'binikəl) *adj.*

rabbit ('rabit) *n.* a small burrowing furry animal with large ears and a short tail.

rabies ('rābēz) *n.* a disease caused by a VIRUS that can affect people and all warm-blooded animals. Infection is passed on by the bite of an animal that already has the disease, and it nearly always causes death.

race[1] (rās) *n.* a competition to find out who or which is the fastest at a sport or other activity. —*vb.* **racing, raced.** 1. to compete or cause to compete in a race: *he races pigeons.* 2. to move at speed: *Jane raced for the bus.*

race[2] (rās) *n.* one of the main divisions of mankind, with its own origins and physical characteristics. '**racial** *adj.* of or concerning a race of people.

racket[1] ('rakit) *n.* 1. a very loud and confusing noise; din. 2. (informal) a scheme, often of a criminal nature, for making money.

racket[2] ('rakit) *n.* a wooden or metal device with a long handle and a round or oval head supporting a tight network of gut or nylon. Rackets are used to hit the ball in tennis, squash, etc.

radar

racket

radar ('rādâ) *n.* electronic apparatus used to find and mark the positions of distant objects, e.g. aircraft, ships at sea, etc., by sending out very short radio waves and measuring the time taken for the rays reflected by the objects to return.

radiant ('rādiənt) *adj.* 1. shining brightly; showing joy or excitement: *the bride's face was radiant.* 2. sending out or given out in waves: *radiant heat is given off by the sun.*

radiate ('rādiāt) *vb.* **radiating, radiated.** 1. to give off or be given off in rays. 2. to move or spread out from the centre like the spokes of a bicycle wheel: *streets radiate from the central square.* **radi'ation** *n.* the sending out of energy, light, etc., in rays. '**radiator** *n.* 1. an apparatus that heats a room. 2. a device for cooling the water that cools a car's engine.

radio ('rādiō) *n.,pl.* **radios.** 1. means of sending and receiving sounds through the air or space by means of waves that are similar to light waves but have a much longer wavelength. 2. an apparatus for receiving these sounds. —*vb.* **radioing, radioed.** to send a message by radio.

radioactive (rādiō'aktiv) *adj.* having atoms that break up and give out energy in the form of rays consisting of very short radio waves or of electrically charged particles that are capable of penetrating solid bodies. —**radioac'tivity** *n.*

radish ('radish) *n.* the red and white root of a small plant. It has a strong taste and is eaten raw in salads.

radius ('rādiəs) *n.,pl.* **radii** ('rādiī) *or* **radiuses.** 1. a straight line from the centre to the outside of a circle or sphere. See GEOMETRY. 2. an area measured in terms of radius: *there are no trees within a radius of fifty yards.*

raffle ('rafəl) *n.* a competition in which each person buys a ticket and a prize is awarded to the holder of the ticket that is picked out at random. —*vb.* **raffling, raffled.** (usu. + *off*) to sell (something) in a raffle.

raft (râft) *n.* a flat floating structure usu. made from lengths of wood fastened together.

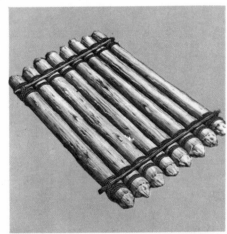
raft

rag (rag) *n.* 1. a torn piece of material. 2. **rags** (*pl.*) old shabby clothes. 3. (slang) a cheap, poorly written newspaper or magazine.

rage (rāj) *n.* 1. violent anger; fury: *Alan flew into a rage.* 2. (informal) someone or something that is currently very fashionable: *straw hats are all the rage this year.* —*vb.* **raging, raged.** to feel and express great anger.

ragged ('ragid) adj. 1. torn in tatters; shabby: *a ragged suit.* 2. rough; not well put together: *a ragged piece of music.*

raid (rād) *n.* 1. a sudden attack in wartime. 2. a sudden invasion of people looking for something: *a police raid.* —*vb.* 1. to attack. 2. to search.

rail (rāl) *n.* 1. a strong metal or wooden bar. 2. one of a pair of parallel steel tracks along which train wheels run. —*vb.* 1. to fence with rails. 2. to send by train. '**railing** *n.* a fence made from rails (def. 1).

railway ('rālwā) *n.* 1. a track made from two parallel steel rails on which trains, trams, etc., run. 2. usu. **railways** (*pl.*) the system of transportation that uses trains.

rain (rān) *n.* 1. water condensed from the water vapour in the clouds to form drops that fall to earth. 2. a shower of this water. —*vb.* to fall as rain. '**rainy** *adj.* **rainier, rainiest.** having much rain.

rainbow ('rānbō) *n.* an arc of seven colours seen in the sky when it rains on a sunny day.

raise (rāz) *vb.* **raising, raised.** 1. to move or cause to move to a higher level; increase the amount of: *he raised their wages.* 2. to produce; grow: *he raised a good crop of potatoes.* 3. to stir up; cause: *the joke raised a laugh.* 4. to collect; gather together: *we raised money for charity.* 5. to suggest (something) for discussion or consideration: *Mike raised some questions.*

raisin ('rāzən) *n.* a dried grape often used in cooking.

rake (rāk) *n.* a tool with many teeth and a long handle, used to level soil and scrape together grass. See IMPLEMENT. —*vb.* **raking, raked.** to use a rake. **rake up** (*or* **out**) to drag up (or out): *he raked up the old quarrel.*

rally ('rali) *vb.* **rallying, rallied.** 1. to bring (soldiers) together and encourage them to further efforts. 2. to revive; recover health, spirits, etc. 3. to come together or assemble for a common purpose. —*n.,pl.* **rallies.** 1. the act of gathering and preparing for further action. 2. a recovery or attempt at recovery made by a sick person. 3. a number of people who have assembled for a common purpose. 4. (tennis) an exchange of several strokes before the point is won. 5. a competition to test a driver's skill over a difficult course.

ram (ram) *n.* 1. a fully grown male sheep. 2. a device for driving repeated and heavy blows: *the battering ram broke through the city gates.* —*vb.* **ramming, rammed.** 1. to hit (something) repeatedly with heavy blows. 2. to crash into (something) violently. 3. to cram; stuff: *he rammed the clothes into the suitcase.*

ramble ('rambəl) *vb.* **rambling, rambled.** 1. to walk for pleasure; rove. 2. (often + *on*) to wander aimlessly in speech: *he rambled on about golf.* —*n.* a walk taken for pleasure.

ramp (ramp) *n.* a sloping roadway, passageway, etc., connecting different levels: *we walked up the ramp into the aircraft.*

rampart ('rampât) *n.* a bank of earth or a thick wall as part of a fort's defences.

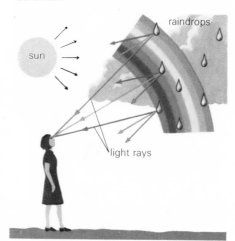
rainbow

ramshackle ('ramshakəl) *adj.* falling to pieces through age or neglect; badly built: *a ramshackle old bus.*

ranch (rânch) *n.* a big farm where horses, cattle, sheep, etc., are reared in large numbers. —*vb.* to work on, manage, or own a ranch.

random ('randəm) *adj.* haphazard; relying on chance: *as she did not know the answer, she made a random guess.* **at random** relying on chance, haphazardly. —'**randomly** *adv.*

rang (rang) *vb.* the past tense of RING².

range (rānj) *n.* 1. the area, scope, or extent over which anything can reach or operate: *the missile's range was 450 miles.* 2. the extent or scope of something: *the range of a subject.* 3. a large kitchen stove. 4. a row, line, or group: *mountain ranges.* 5. a large open area on which livestock can roam. —*vb.* **ranging, ranged.** 1. to arrange in a line, row, etc. 2. to roam. 3. to extend between limits: *their ages ranged from six to nine.* '**ranger** *n.* a person who guards a forest or park.

rank (rangk) *n.* 1. high social position; degree of standing or excellence. 2. a position of authority: *the rank of Captain.* 3. **ranks** (*pl.*) or **rank and file** all soldiers below the rank of officer. —*vb.* to have the position or status of; be considered as: *she ranked high in our estimation.*

ransom ('ransəm) *n.* the price paid to obtain the release of a person or thing in captivity. —*vb.* to pay a ransom to obtain (someone's release).

rap (rap) *vb.* **rapping, rapped.** 1. to tap or strike sharply and quickly; knock: *she rapped on the door.* 2. (+ *out*) to say something sharply: *he raps out orders.* —*n.* a sharp quick blow: *a rap on the door.*

rapid ('rapid) *adj.* moving at great speed; very quick. **rapids** *pl.n.* a part of a river where the current is very swift. —**rapidity** (rə'piditi) *n.* —'**rapidly** *adv.*

rare¹ (reə) *adj.* unusual; not frequent in occurrence and therefore highly valued. '**rarity** *n.,pl.* **rarities.** 1. the state of being rare. 2. something that is rare.

rare² (reə) *adj.* not thoroughly cooked: *a rare steak.*

rascal ('râskəl) *n.* rogue; mischievous person.

rash¹ (rash) *adj.* hasty; lacking in caution. —'**rashly** *adv.* —'**rashness** *n.*

rash² (rash) *n.* an outbreak of red spots or blotches on the skin: *measles causes a rash.*

raspberry

raspberry ('râzbəri) *n.,pl.* **raspberries.** 1. a small soft juicy red fruit. 2. the prickly plant that bears this fruit. **raspberry cane** a long woody shoot of a raspberry bush.

rasping ('râspiñ) *adj.* harsh: *the teacher has a rasping voice.*

rat (rat) *n.* 1. an animal like a mouse but larger, often inhabiting buildings where grain and other foodstuffs are kept. See RODENT. 2. (informal) a person who deserts a cause or his friends in time of difficulty. **rat race** ruthless and unceasing competition for success, esp. in one's career: *he left the rat race to become a farmer.* —*vb.* **ratting, ratted.** 1. to hunt rats. 2. (+ *on*) to desert; betray.

rate (rāt) *n.* 1. a standard or proportion by which a quantity or value may be fixed: *the rate for the job is £3 an hour.* 2. speed: *the mountaineers climbed at a rate of 1000 feet a day.* 3. quality or standard: *his work is first rate.* 4. **rates** (*pl.*) taxes paid by the owner or occupier of a property to the local authority or government to help pay for public services such as water supplies and drainage. —*vb.* **rating, rated.** 1. to estimate (value, rank, class, etc.) or to be placed in such a class or position. 2. to set a value on (property) for the purpose of paying rates to the local authority. **'rating** *n.* 1. the process of assessing rates on property. 2. the class of any member of a ship's crew; an ordinary sailor. 3. the tonnage of a racing yacht. 4. the degree of popularity of TV or radio programmes.

ratify ('ratifī) *vb.* **ratifying, ratified.** to confirm or approve: *now that he has ratified the plan, we can go ahead.* —**'ratification** *n.*

ration ('rashən) *n.* 1. a fixed allowance or portion of something. 2. usu. **rations** (*pl.*) a fixed quantity of food to last for a certain length of time. —*vb.* 1. to share out (food, etc.) in fixed portions, esp. when supplies are limited. 2. to limit or restrict.

rational ('rashənəl) *adj.* reasonable and sensible; involving reason and sound judgment.

rattle ('ratəl) *vb.* **rattling, rattled.** 1. to make or cause to make a rapid series of short sharp sounds. 2. to move briskly and noisily: *the bus rattled along.* 3. (+ *on*) (informal) to speak fast: *he rattled on about his garden.* 4. (slang) to cause alarm to; fluster. —*n.* 1. a rapid series of sharp noises. 2. a baby's toy or other device that will make such noises when shaken.

raucous ('rôkəs) *adj.* harsh; hoarse: *the parrot gave a raucous cry.* —**'raucously** *adv.*

rave (rāv) *vb.* **raving, raved.** 1. to talk wildly and uncontrollably. 2. (+ *about*) to praise enthusiastically.

raven ('rāvən) *n.* a large glossy black bird of the crow family, that has a harsh voice and feeds chiefly on flesh.

ravenous ('ravənəs) *adj.* intensely hungry; greedy. —**'ravenously** *adv.*

ravine (rə'vēn) *n.* a deep narrow gorge or valley.

raw (rô) *adj.* 1. uncooked: *raw meat.* 2. in the natural state; not manufactured: *raw material.* 3. having the skin rubbed off: *a raw spot on the heel.* 4. chilly and damp: *a raw February morning.* 5. untrained: *raw recruits.* 6. without a smooth finish: *a raw edge.* **a raw deal** unfair treatment.

ray[1] (rā) *n.* 1. a narrow beam of light, heat, etc. 2. one of a number of lines or parts spreading out from a central point.

ray[2] (rā) *n.* one of several kinds of deep-sea fish with a broad flattened body and fins.

rayon ('rāon) *n.* an artificial fabric with a fine silky texture, made from a substance called cellulose that is obtained from plants.

razor ('rāzə) *n.* an implement with a sharp blade or cutters used for shaving off hair.

reach (rēch) *vb.* 1. to get as far as; arrive at. 2. to achieve: *the singer reached fame in a year.* 3. to be long enough or go far enough to touch, pierce, etc.; extend: *the bookshelves reached from floor to ceiling.* 4. to stretch out one's hand or arm; touch, take or hand over with outstretched arm: *he reached out to take the book from me.* 5. to try to attain: *he reached for the presidency.* —*n.* 1. the act of stretching out. 2. range or scope of someone's abilities. 3. a stretch or portion between defined limits: *a reach of smooth water between the rapids.*

react (ri'akt) *vb.* 1. to act in return; respond to a stimulus: *he did not react to the bully's threats.* 2. (chemistry) (+ *on* or *with*) to cause or be involved in change: *how does this acid react on silver?* **re'action** *n.* 1. an action in response to another action: *the audience's reaction to his speech was enthusiastic.* 2. resistance to revolution or progress. 3. (chemistry) chemical change. **re'actionary** *n.,pl.* **reactionaries.** a person who opposes change, esp. in politics. **re'actor** *n.* an apparatus for producing controlled atomic energy.

read (rēd) *vb.* **reading, read** (red). 1. to interpret (written or printed words). 2. to utter aloud (something written or printed). 3. to study; learn about, esp. for a university degree. 4. to interpret or understand: *can you read Spanish?* 5. to record or show (information or measurement): *the speedometer read 80 m.p.h.* —*n.* 1. the act of reading. 2. (informal) something that is read. **'reader** *n.* 1. a person who reads. 2. a senior university teacher. 3. a textbook designed to teach children and learners of a foreign language to read. **'readable** *adj.* 1. able to be read easily. 2. worth reading.

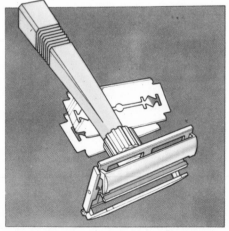

razor

ready ('redi) *adj.* **readier, readiest.** 1. prepared; fit to act or be used at once. 2. willing. 3. likely; inclined: *he was ready to desert at a moment's notice.* 4. quick: *a ready reply.* 5. near at hand: *he had no ready cash.* —*adv.* prepared beforehand. **at the ready** in position to be used or to start. —'**readily** *adv.* —'**readiness** *n.*

real[1]('riəl) *adj.* 1. actually existing; not imaginary. 2. not false; genuine: *are these spoons real silver?* '**realism** *n.* 1. ability or willingness to face facts or to concentrate on the practical. 2. (in art or literature) the attempt to convey life accurately, without hiding unpleasant aspects. '**realist** *n.* a person who concentrates on practical issues and claims to be without illusions. **real'istic** *adj.* 1. practical; clear-sighted. 2. lifelike; true to the object or situation represented. **re'ality** *n.* actual fact. —'**really** *adv.*

realize ('riəlīz) *vb.* **realizing, realized.** 1. to understand clearly; become aware: *he realized it was raining.* 2. to make real; achieve: *she realized her ambition to be a singer.* —**reali'zation** *n.*

realm (relm) *n.* 1. a kingdom. 2. an area of interest or knowledge: *the realm of science.*

reap (rēp) *vb.* 1. to cut (crops) with a sickle, scythe, or reaping machine; harvest. 2. to obtain (penalties or rewards) for past actions: *he reaped the results of his idleness.*

rear[1] (riə) *n.* part or position at the back. **bring up the rear** to be or come last. —*adj.* hind; at the back: *rear wheels.*

rear[2] (riə) *vb.* 1. to bring up; breed (children, plants, etc.). 2. to rise on the hind legs: *the horse reared in fright.* 3. to rise or cause to rise steeply.

reason ('rēzən) *n.* 1. a cause; motive. 2. excuse; logical argument. 3. the mind's power of thinking logically. —*vb.* 1. to think clearly and step by step. 2. to persuade or try to persuade by argument. '**reasonable** *adj.* 1. acting according to reason. 2. sensible; moderate. —'**reasonably** *adv.*

reassure (rēəshŏŏə) *vb.* **reassuring, reassured.** to restore confidence: *your promises reassure me.*

rebate ('rēbāt) *n.* 1. a discount; deduction from the full price. 2. the repayment of part of the money paid as tax.

rebel *n.* ('rebəl) 1. a person who resists social pressures or authority. 2. a person who tries to overthrow the legal government by force. —*vb.* (ri'bel) **rebelling, rebelled.** 1. to resist authority. 2. to try to overthrow a government. 3. to feel or show extreme dislike or resentment. **re'bellion** *n.* an organized open resistance to authority; act of rebelling. —**re'bellious** *adj.* —**re'belliously** *adv.* —**re'belliousness** *n.*

rebound *vb.* (ri'bound) 1. to bounce back after a collision. 2. to react against. —*n.* ('rēbound) the act of rebounding.

rebuke (ri'byōok) *vb.* **rebuking, rebuked.** to scold; reprimand. —*n.* a reproof; a scolding.

recall (ri'kôl) *vb.* 1. to call back. 2. to remember; bring back to mind. —*n.* 1. a message ordering return. 2. the power to remember.

recant (ri'kant) *vb.* to say that one's former beliefs are wrong.

rear

receipt (ri'sēt) *n.* 1. the act of receiving or being received. 2. a written acknowledgment that money or goods have been received. 3. **receipts** (*pl.*) the money taken by a business. —*vb.* to make out a written receipt.

receiver

receive (ri'sēv) *vb.* **receiving, received.** 1. to get; accept. 2. to take in as a guest; greet. **re'ceiver** *n.* 1. a person or thing that receives. 2. the earpiece of a telephone. 3. the apparatus in a TV or wireless set for transforming electrical waves into pictures or sounds.

recent ('rēsənt) *adj.* begun or happening not very long ago; modern. —'**recently** *adv.*

receptacle (ri'septəkəl) *n.* a container in which things may be put away or hidden from sight.

reception (ri'sepshən) *n.* 1. the act or manner of receiving or being received. 2. the way in which radio or TV signals are received: *radio reception was poor because of the thunderstorm.* 3. a formal party or receiving of guests. **re'ceptionist** *n.* a person employed to greet and make arrangements for hotel guests, hospital patients, etc. **re'ceptive** *adj.* quick and eager to receive new ideas, impressions, etc. —**re'ceptively** *adv.* —**re'ceptiveness** *n.*

recess (ri'ses) *n.* 1. an alcove; part of a room or wall set back from the rest. 2. a temporary halt to work.

recipe ('resipi) *n.* 1. a list of ingredients and instructions for making something to eat or drink. 2. a well-known way of achieving a particular result: *the recipe for success.*

recite (ri'sīt) *vb.* **reciting, recited.** 1. to repeat aloud from memory. 2. to quote (a list) item by item. **re'cital** *n.* 1. a detailed account or story. 2. the performance of music by a soloist or a small group of musicians. **recitation** (resi'tāshən) *n.* 1. the act of reciting, esp. from memory to an audience. 2. the repeating of a prepared lesson.

reckless ('reklis) *adj.* not thinking of the consequences; careless; —**recklessly** *adv.* '**recklessness** *n.*

reckon ('rekən) *vb.* 1. to count or estimate: *we reckoned the repairs would cost £90.* 2. to suppose; consider: *I reckon I'll get there in time.* **reckon on** to depend on. **reckon with** to take into account; consider seriously.

recline (ri'klīn) *vb.* **reclining, reclined.** to lie back or down so as to rest comfortably.

recognize ('rekəgnīz) *vb.* **recognizing, recognized.** 1. to be or become aware that one knows (someone or something). 2. to acknowledge or accept (a fact): *Dave recognized that he had to help his father.* —**recognition** (rekəg'nishən) *n.*

recoil (ri'koil) *vb.* 1. to jump or move back from; shrink. 2. (of a gun) to kick back sharply when fired. —*n.* the kicking of a gun when fired.

recommend (rekə'mend) *vb.* 1. to speak well of: *she recommended her dentist to her friend.* 2. to advise: *the doctor recommends a long rest.* **recommen'dation** *n.* 1. the act of recommending. 2. a favourable statement about someone or something.

record *n.* ('rekəd) 1. a permanent account in writing, on film or tape, etc., of facts or events. 2. a person's known previous behaviour: *she has a record of lateness.* 3. an achievement, esp. in sport, that surpasses everything previously achieved: *Joanna broke the school's high jump record.* 4. a thin disc on which music or other sounds have been registered to be played back later. —*vb.* (ri'kôd) 1. to put down in writing. 2. to show or indicate. 3. to make a musical record. **re'corder** *n.* 1. a person or machine that records. 2. a small wooden musical instrument, shaped like a pipe, with finger holes.

recover (ri'kuvə) *vb.* 1. to get well again. 2. to return to normal. 3. to get back: *the police recovered the stolen car.* —**re'covery** *n.,pl.* **recoveries.**

recreation (rekri'āshən) *n.* any sport, hobby, or other activity that a person does in his free time.

recruit (ri'krōot) *n.* a new member of an organization, esp. of the army, navy, or air force. —*vb.* to get (people) to join an organization. **re'cruitment** *n.* the process of obtaining recruits.

rectangle ('rektanggəl) *n.* a figure with four sides with right angles between them. See GEOMETRY. —**rectangular** (rek'tanggyoolə) *adj.*

redeem (ri'dēm) *vb.* 1. to buy or get back. 2. to exchange: *she redeemed her trading stamps for a clock.* 3. to make up for: *the excellent food redeemed the slow service at the restaurant.* 4. to save; rescue; retrieve. —**redemption** (ri'dempshən) *n.*

reduce (ri'dyōos) *vb.* **reducing, reduced.** (often + *to*) 1. to lessen or bring down in amount, size, strength, or position. 2. to change the form of: *reduce this number to decimals.* —**reduction** (ri'dukshən) *n.*

redundant (ri'dundənt) *adj.* 1. unnecessary; of no more use. 2. (of workers) removed or dismissed from work because they are no longer needed. —**re'dundancy** *n.,pl.* **redundancies.**

reed (rēd) *n.* 1. one of many tall moisture-loving grasses with hollow stems. 2. a thin vibrating piece of wood or metal in the mouth of certain wind instruments.

reef (rēf) *n.* a ridge of rock, coral, etc., at or just above the surface of the sea or other stretch of water.

reel

reel[1] (rēl) *n.* a cylinder or spool around which rope, fishing line, film, etc., is wound for storage. —*vb.* to wind or unwind using a reel. **reel off** to recite without hesitation.

reel[2] (rēl) *vb.* 1. to move unsteadily; sway. 2. to be severely shaken physically or mentally. —*n.* 1. a lively Scottish dance. 2. the music played for this dance.

refer (ri'fû) *vb.* **referring, referred.** (+ *to*) 1. to mention. 2. to indicate or concern. 3. to consult for information: *you are now referring to a dictionary.* 4. to send or pass on: *her doctor referred her to a specialist.* **referee** (refə'rē) *n.* 1. a person who acts as a judge, esp. in certain sports; umpire. 2. a person who supports or recommends another by making a statement about his character, abilities, financial status, etc. —*vb.* to act as a referee. **reference** ('refərəns) *n.* 1. an act or instance of referring. 2. the source of a piece of information. 3. a written recommendation of a person.

refine (ri'fīn) *vb.* **refining, refined.** to make (oil, sugar, etc.) pure by removing other substances. **re'fined** *adj.* 1. made pure. 2. behaving in an elegant or polite way. **re'finement** *n.* 1. elegant or delicate manners. 2. improvement: *the latest model of this car has several refinements.* **re'finery** *n.,pl.* **refineries.** a factory that refines oil, sugar, etc.

reflect (ri'flekt) *vb.* 1. to throw back (light, heat, etc.). 2. to throw back (an image of something): *the calm lake reflected the hills.* 3. to think deeply and carefully. 4. (+ *on* or *upon*) to hurt the reputation of: *his disgrace reflected badly upon his parents.* **re'flection** *n.* 1. an image that is reflected. 2. the act of reflecting. —**re'flector** *n.*

reflex ('rēfleks) *n.* an action that is carried out by the muscles without thinking about it: *the doctor tested his reflexes by tapping his knee.* —*adj.* of or by a reflex. **reflex angle** an ANGLE greater than 180°.

reform (ri'fôm) *vb.* to make or become better; improve by making changes. —*n.* a change for the better, esp. the removal of injustices in society.

refract (ri'frakt) *vb.* to cause (rays of sound, light, etc.) to bend aside: *the curved surface of the telescope lens refracts the light.* —**re'fraction** *n.*

refresh (ri'fresh) *vb.* to restore strength and energy, esp. by giving or consuming food or drink. **re'freshment** *n.* food and drink.

refrigerate (ri'frijərāt) *vb.* **refrigerating, refrigerated.** to make or keep cold, esp. for purposes of preservation. **re'frigerator** *n.* (often shortened to **fridge**) a cupboard or box that preserves food by keeping it cold.

refuge ('refyo͞oj) *n.* a place of shelter or safety. **refugee** (refyo͞o'jē) *n.* a person who has been forced by war or other disaster to leave his home.

refund *vb.* (ri'fund) to pay back money paid out for a purpose: *the cost will be refunded.* —*n.* ('rēfund) a repayment.

refuse[1] (ri'fjo͞oz) *vb.* **refusing, refused.** 1. to turn down or reject (something offered). 2. to be unwilling to do or give (something): *he refuses permission.* —**re'fusal** *n.*

refuse[2] ('refyo͞os) *n.* rubbish; waste matter.

regard (ri'gâd) *vb.* 1. to consider. 2. to think well of; esteem: *we all highly regard the new priest.* 3. to stare at. —*n.* 1. a stare or look. 2. admiration; respect. 3. careful thought; concern. 4. **regards** (*pl.*) best wishes; greetings. **re'gardless** *adj.* without any concern for.

regatta (ri'gatə) *n.* a meeting for sailing boat or rowing boat races.

regiment *n.* ('rejimənt) a large military unit, usu. made up of several battalions and commanded by a colonel. —*vb.* ('rejiment) to organize strictly.

region ('rējən) *n.* an area or part of a country or the world, often without any precise boundaries: *the Arctic region.* —**'regional** *adj.*

register ('rejistə) *n.* 1. an official book or list containing a record, e.g. of marriages, voters, etc. 2. a machine or device used to record amounts, e.g. a cash register. 3. a part of the range of a human voice or musical instrument. 4. a device that controls the flow of air in a heating or air-conditioning system. —*vb.* 1. to make an entry in a register. 2. to put one's name in a register. 3. to realize. 4. to show or indicate. 5. to pay a fee for (mail) in order to have it officially recorded. **registrar** ('rejistrâ) *n.* an official responsible for making registrations and keeping records. **'registry** *n.,pl.* **registries.** the place where registers are kept. —**regis'tration** *n.*

regret (ri'gret) *vb.* **regretting, regretted.** to feel sorry or repentant about. —*n.* a feeling of sadness or disappointment. **re'gretful** *adj.* feeling regret. **re'grettable** *adj.* causing regret; unfortunate. —**re'gretfully** *adv.* —**re'grettably** *adv.*

regular ('regyo͞olə) *adj.* 1. evenly set out in time or space: *he walked with a regular step.* 2. usual; according to habit: *a regular customer.* —*n.* 1. a professional soldier. 2. (informal) a person who habitually goes to the same shop, church, etc. —**regu'larity** *n.* —**'regularly** *adv.*

regulate ('regyo͞olāt) *vb.* **regulating, regulated.** 1. to check by means of rules or controls: *the factory regulates the quality of its products.* 2. to adjust in order to make regular or accurate: *the alarm clock needs regulating.* **regu'lation** *n.* 1. the act of regulating. 2. a rule or law. —*adj.* as demanded by the rules; standard.

rehearse (ri'hûs) *vb.* **rehearsing, rehearsed.** 1. to practise (a play, speech, etc.) before a public performance. 2. to recite or relate: *he rehearsed the sad tale to his friends.* —**re'hearsal** *n.*

reign (rān) *vb.* 1. to rule as sovereign or supreme power. 2. to be the main influence; prevail. —*n.* the period during which someone or something rules or prevails.

rein (rān) *n.* often **reins** (*pl.*) the long narrow strap forming part of a horse's bridle, used for guiding and controlling the animal. —*vb.* to control with a rein.

reindeer

reindeer ('rāndiə) *n.,pl.* **reindeer.** a large deer with branched antlers found in Arctic regions and sometimes kept in herds for its milk, meat, and hide.

reinforce (rēin'fôs) *vb.* **reinforcing, reinforced.** to give support or added strength to. **rein'forcement** *n.* 1. the act of reinforcing. 2. something that reinforces, esp. military support.

reject *vb.* (ri'jekt) to turn down; refuse to allow or accept (something offered or proposed). —*n.* ('rējekt) something that is rejected because it is damaged, unwanted, or worthless. —**re'jection** *n.*

rejoice (ri'jois) *vb.* **rejoicing, rejoiced.** to be delighted; to express great joy.

relate (ri'lāt) *vb.* **relating, related.** 1. to tell the story of; describe: *he related his holiday experiences.* 2. to concern; to have, make, or find a connection with: *the description relates to someone else.*

related (ri'lātid) *adj.* connected with, esp. connected by blood ties or marriage.

relation (ri'lāshən) *n.* 1. a person connected with another by blood ties or marriage; relative. 2. a connection or point of similarity: *this problem has no relation to the previous one.* 3. the telling of a story. 4. **relations** (*pl.*) the feelings that exist between people or groups dealing with each other. **re'lationship** *n.* 1. the way in which one person deals with and interacts with another: *a stormy relationship.* 2. the state of being related. 3. the points of connection.

relative ('relətiv) *n.* a person connected to another by blood ties or marriage; relation. —*adj.* 1. comparative: *relative calm was restored.* 2. (+ to) strictly connected with: *state only the details relative to the problem.* 3. (grammar) describing a kind of connecting pronoun, e.g. *who, which,* used to begin a clause. **'relatively** *adv.* comparatively; fairly.

relax (ri'laks) *vb.* 1. to make or become less tense in body and mind. 2. to make easier or less strict: *discipline has slowly been relaxed.* **relaxation** (rēlak'sāshən) *n.* 1. the act or instance of relaxing. 2. a means of relaxing; pastime.

relay *n.* ('rēlā) 1. a fresh group or supply of material that takes over from another: *clearing the wreckage will be done in relays.* 2. an electrical apparatus for increasing the strength and range of radio messages. **relay race** a race in which each member of competing teams covers only part of the course and is then replaced by another member. —*vb.* (rē'lā) 1. to pass on (information). 2. to receive and transmit (a radio message, broadcast, etc.) to a wider area.

release (ri'lēs) vb. **releasing, released.** 1. to let go; set free. 2. to make (information, a record, film, etc.) available to the public. —n. 1. the act of releasing. 2. freedom from something. 3. a discharge from prison. 4. a device for unfastening: *seat belts have easy release mechanisms.* 5. a current record, film, etc.

reliable (ri'līəbəl) adj. dependable; trustworthy. —**relia'bility** n. —**re'liably** adv.

relieve (ri'lēv) vb. **relieving, relieved.** 1. to ease or remove (pain, anxiety, etc.). 2. to free (a besieged town, castle, etc). 3. to take over (duties) from another person. 4. to provide a break from or a contrast to: *no sunshine relieved the foggy day.* **re'lief** n. 1. the act of relieving. 2. someone or something that relieves. 3. a method of carving designs, figures, etc., so that the pattern stands out from the background. **relief map** a map showing hills, valleys, and different heights on the earth's surface by shading, contour lines, etc.

religion (ri'lijən) n. 1. a particular system of belief, worship, etc.: *the Christian religion.* 2. belief in and worship of a supernatural power or powers. —**re'ligious** adj. —**re'ligiously** adv.

relish ('relish) n. 1. spicy or strongly flavoured food, e.g. pickles, used to improve the taste of other food. 2. a liking. —vb. to enjoy.

reluctant (ri'luktənt) adj. unwilling; not enthusiastic. —**re'luctance** n. —**re'luctantly** adv.

rely (ri'lī) vb. **relying, relied.** (+ *on* or *upon*) to depend on; be able to trust. —**re'liance** n.

remain (ri'mān) vb. 1. to be left after the rest or a part has gone away or been changed. 2. to continue; go on being. **re'mainder** n. the remaining portion. **re'mains** pl.n. 1. a thing or things left over. 2. ruins.

remark (ri'māk) vb. 1. to say or state briefly or casually. 2. (+ *on*) to mention specially. —n. a short statement. **re'markable** adj. out of the ordinary; unusual or unexpected.

remedy ('remədi) n.,pl. **remedies.** something that heals or improves. —vb. **remedying, remedied.** to put right, heal, or improve.

remember (ri'membə) vb. 1. to bring back to mind. 2. to keep in mind. —**re'membrance** n.

remind (ri'mīnd) vb. to cause to remember or think of: *remind me to buy some eggs.*

remnant ('remnənt) n. a small number or amount left behind.

remote (ri'mōt) adj. 1. distant; isolated. 2. very slight: *he has only a remote chance of winning the race.* —**re'motely** adv. —**re'moteness** n.

remove (ri'mōv) vb. **removing, removed.** 1. to take or move away. 2. to get rid of. **re'moval** n. the act or process of removing, esp. moving the contents of a house.

rent (rent) n. regular payment for the use of a house or other property belonging to another person. —vb. 1. to have the right to use (something) in return for payment: *we rented a villa for our holiday.* 2. to give the right to use (something) in return for payment: *the farmer rents his cottages to holidaymakers.*

repair (ri'peə) vb. to mend; put in working order again. —n. 1. the act of repairing. 2. the condition of something: *Simon kept his bicycle in good repair.*

repeat (ri'pēt) vb. to say, make, or do (something) again: *she repeated her question.* —n. something that is repeated: *this broadcast is a repeat of last week's concert.* **repetition** (repi'tishən) n. the act of repeating. —**re'peatable** adj.

repel (ri'pel) vb. **repelling, repelled.** 1. to drive away; force back. 2. to cause a feeling of disgust in: *the smell of the rotting fish repelled them.* 3. to keep out: *the raincoat repels rain.* **re'pellent** adj. 1. able to repel. 2. disgusting. n. something that repels, esp. a spray or ointment that drives away insects.

repent (ri'pent) vb. to feel sorrow, guilt, or shame about (something one has done). —**re'pentance** n. —**re'pentant** adj.

replace (ri'plās) vb. 1. to provide a substitute for: *for many uses plastics have replaced leather.* 2. to return or restore (something) to its proper place: *Tony replaced the hammer in his father's workshop when he had finished with it.*

reply (ri'plī) vb. **replying, replied.** to say or do (something) in answer to something else; respond. —n.,pl. **replies.** an answer.

report (ri'pôt) n. 1. a statement, description, or account often set out in a formal way: *the policeman wrote a report on the accident.* 2. a bang: *the report of a gun.* —vb. 1. to make or give a report about: *she reported the faulty telephone.* 2. to present oneself: *Michael reported for work late.* **re'porter** n. a person who reports news for a newspaper or for radio or television.

represent (repri'zent) vb. 1. to stand for; be a symbol of. 2. to act on behalf of: *his lawyer represented him in court.* **represen'tation** n. the act of representing. **repre'sentative** adj. characteristic or typical: *we saw a representative selection.* n. a person who acts or speaks for others, esp. a salesman.

reproach (ri'prōch) vb. to make (someone) feel ashamed or guilty about. —n. 1. sorrowful disapproval or accusation. 2. disgrace; shame. —**re'proachful** adj. —**re'proachfully** adv.

reproduce (rēprə'dyōōs) vb. **reproducing, reproduced.** 1. to produce an exact copy. 2. to produce young.

reproduction (rēprə'dukshən) n. 1. the process of reproducing. 2. a copy; something reproduced from an original, e.g. a painting.

reptile ('reptīl) n. one of a large group of cold-blooded animals that have scaly or horny skins and generally reproduce by laying eggs. —**reptilian** (rep'tiliən) adj.

republic (ri'publik) n. 1. a form of government in which power is held by the people and their elected representatives. 2. a state with this form of government. **re'publican** adj. of or favouring a republic. n. a person who favours the republican system.

reputation (repyōō'tāshən) n. the general public opinion of a person, place, or thing.

repute (ri'pyōōt) n. public opinion; reputation. vb. **reputing, reputed.** to be said or generally thought to be: *he is reputed to be rich.* **'reputable** adj. well-known to be trustworthy, respectable, etc.

request (ri'kwest) *n.* 1. the act of asking for something. 2. something asked for. —*vb.* to ask for politely.

require (ri'kwīə) *vb.* **requiring, required.** 1. to need; demand: *juggling requires a steady hand.* 2. to order: *the court required him to tell the truth.* **re'quirement** *n.* something that is needed.

rescue ('reskyōo) *vb.* **rescuing, rescued.** to save from danger, captivity, or death. —*n.* the act of setting free or saving.

research (ri'sûch) *n.* detailed investigation to discover fresh facts: *she was doing research into new cures for cancer.* —*vb.* to carry out research.

resemble (ri'zembəl) *vb.* **resembling, resembled.** to be like or similar to, either in general appearance or in some detail: *he resembles you in his love of dogs.* —**re'semblance** *n.*

resent (ri'zent) *vb.* to be angered or hurt by another's action: *I resent your interference.* —**re'sentful** *adj.*

reserve (ri'zûv) *vb.* **reserving, reserved.** 1. to keep aside for a special purpose. 2. to save up for future use. —*n.* 1. something reserved or stored for future use. 2. the habit of not expressing one's thoughts or feelings. 3. a price set on goods at an auction below which they are not to be sold. 4. land set aside as a protected area for animals: *game reserve.* 5. emergency forces, players, etc., only to be used if really necessary. **re'served** *adj.* 1. shy; quiet: *a reserved person.* 2. kept for a special purpose: *reserved for the officers only.* **reservation** (rezə'vāshən) *n.* 1. act of reserving. 2. something that is reserved, e.g. a booked seat on a train. 3. doubt or uncertainty: *I have reservations about his honesty.*

reservoir ('rezəvwâ) *n.* an artificial lake or tank where water supplies are stored.

resign (ri'zīn) *vb.* 1. to give up (a job, position, etc.). 2. to submit patiently to something unpleasant. **resignation** (rezig'nāshən) *n.* 1. the act of giving up. 2. calm acceptance.

resist (ri'zist) *vb.* to stand up to or fight against. **re'sistance** *n.* 1. the act of resisting. 2. an opposing force: *water resistance slows down a boat's speed.* —**re'sistant** *adj.*

resolution (rezə'lōoshən) *n.* 1. firm determination. 2. a decision: *the council approved the resolution to buy extra buses.* '**resolute** *adj.* very determined; showing will power. —'**resolutely** *adv.*

resolve (ri'zolv) *vb.* **resolving, resolved.** 1. to make up one's mind; decide. 2. to solve or settle: *the difficult situation was resolved by his departure.* —*n.* a firmly fixed purpose.

resort (ri'zôt) *n.* 1. a place popular with holiday-makers. 2. a person or thing that one goes to for advice, protection, etc. —*vb.* to turn to: *we ran out of milk so we had to resort to using water.*

resound (ri'zound) *vb.* to make a loud or echoing sound; re-echo: *the crash resounded through the room.*

reptiles

chameleon

tortoise

rattlesnake

resource (ri'sôs) *n.* 1. usu. **resources** (*pl.*) supplies of minerals, power, etc., that form the basis of a country's wealth. 2. a person or thing from which one can seek support or help. 3. skill; powers of invention. —**re'sourceful** *adj.* —**re'sourcefully** *adv.*

respect (ri'spekt) *vb.* 1. to honour; admire. 2. to treat with attention or consideration: *he respected his grandfather's need for peace and quiet.* —*n.* 1. admiration. 2. consideration; politeness. **respecta'bility** *n.* the condition of having an assured and respected social position. **re'spectable** *adj.* 1. decent; well-behaved. 2. deserving admiration. **re'spective** *adj.* referring individually or singly to particular people or things: *at the bell the relay runners went to their respective starting positions.*

respond (ri'spond) *vb.* 1. to reply or answer. 2. to react. **re'sponse** *n.* an answer or reaction. **re'sponsive** *adj.* quick to respond. —**re'sponsively** *adv.* —**re'sponsiveness** *n.*

responsible (ri'sponsibəl) *adj.* 1. accountable; having the job of caring for something: *the guide was responsible for our safety.* 2. trustworthy: *Julie is responsible enough to look after the dog.* 3. being the cause of: *the drought was responsible for the bad harvest.* —**responsi'bility** *n.* —**re'sponsibly** *adv.*

rest[1] (rest) *n.* 1. a pause for relaxation, sleep, or refreshment. 2. a prop or support, e.g. a head rest. 3. a silent interval in music. —*vb.* 1. to have or cause to have a rest. 2. to lean on or place something on: *rest the load on the step.* —**'restful** *adj.* —**'restfully** *adv.* —**'restfulness** *n.* —**'restless** *adj.* —**'restlessly** *adv.* —**'restlessness** *n.*

rest[2] (rest) *n.* 1. the remainder; that which is left: *take what you want, they can have the rest.* 2. all the others: *I'm going today, the rest will go tomorrow.*

restaurant ('restəront) *n.* a place where meals are sold and eaten.

restore (ri'stô) *vb.* **restoring, restored.** 1. to give or bring back: *the lost child was restored to his parents.* 2. to repair or renew: *Tim's father restores old furniture.* **restoration** (restə'rāshən) *n.* 1. the act of giving or bringing back. 2. the work of putting old buildings, paintings, etc., into their original condition.

restrain (ri'strān) *vb.* to hold in or back; check: *the boy was restrained from diving into the lake after his dog.*

restrict (ri'strikt) *vb.* to limit; confine: *her diet restricts her to one biscuit daily.* —**re'striction** *n.*

result (ri'zult) *vb.* to have or follow as a consequence: *his carelessness resulted in an accident.* —*n.* outcome; consequence: *the results of the tests were good.* —**re'sultant** *adj.*

resurrect (rezə'rekt) *vb.* 1. to bring back to use after disuse: *she resurrected her grandmother's shawl for the play.* 2. to bring back to life. **resur'rection** *n.* 1. act of resurrecting. 2. the Christian doctrine that Christ rose from the dead, as will all men at the Last Judgment.

retail ('retāl) *n.* sale of goods in small quantities direct to the customer. —*adj.* selling goods by retail: *a retail chemist's shop.* —*vb.* 1. to sell or be sold to the consumer. 2. to repeat in detail: *she retailed the whole incident to everyone she met.*

retain (ri'tān) *vb.* 1. to keep hold of: *though poor, she retained her dignity.* 2. to reserve (someone's services) by paying a fee: *the racehorse trainer retains two jockeys.* **re'tainer** *n.* a fee paid to secure services. —**retention** (ri'tenshən) *n.* —**re'tentive** *adj.*

retaliate (ri'taliāt) *vb.* **retaliating, retaliated.** to take vengeance; give as good as one gets. —**retali'ation** *n.*

retina ('retinə) *n.* the layer of cells at the back of the eyeball that are sensitive to light and transmit images of things seen to the brain. See EYE.

retire (ri'tīə) *vb.* **retiring, retired.** 1. to give up full-time work because of age. 2. to withdraw; go away: *the runner retired from the race with a strained leg muscle.* **re'tirement** *n.* 1. the act of giving up work. 2. the state of being retired.

retort (ri'tôt) *vb.* to answer back quickly, esp. in anger. —*n.* a quickly made angry or witty reply: *Joy made a sharp retort to my complaint.*

retreat (ri'trēt) *vb.* to go back or withdraw, esp. under attack. —*n.* 1. the act of retreating. 2. a place of safety or peace. 3. a period of prayer and meditation: *he attended a retreat in a monastery.*

retrieve (ri'trēv) *vb.* **retrieving, retrieved.** 1. to fetch or recover. 2. to make good or repair: *he retrieved his losses by hard work.* **re'triever** *n.* a breed of dog that is often trained to fetch game that has been shot. —**re'trievable** *adj.*

return (ri'tûn) *vb.* 1. to go, come, give, send, take, or answer back: *please return the books to the library.* 2. to make an official statement or election: *the town returned four women to the council.* —*n.* 1. the act of returning. 2. an official statement, e.g. an income tax return. 3. a return ticket, i.e. a ticket enabling a person to go to a place and return to his starting point. 4. **returns** (*pl.*) proceeds or profit. —**re'turnable** *adj.*

reunion (rē'yōoniən) *n.* a meeting of family members, old friends, etc., after separation: *Carol goes to her college reunion every year.* **reunite** (rēyōo'nīt) *vb.* **reuniting, reunited.** to come or bring together again.

reveal (ri'vēl) *vb.* 1. to cause or allow to be seen. 2. to make known. **revelation** (revə'lāshən) *n.* 1. the act or instance of revealing. 2. something that is revealed.

revenge (ri'venj) *vb.* **revenging, revenged.** to do harm in return for an injury suffered. —*n.* the act of revenging. —**re'vengeful** *adj.*

reverse (ri'vûs) *vb.* **reversing, reversed.** 1. to turn upside down, the other way round, back to front, etc. 2. to change to the opposite. 3. to move or be moved backwards: *the car reversed into the garage.* —*n.* 1. the opposite: *he thought she was rich but the reverse was true.* 2. a setback or defeat: *the army suffered a reverse.* 3. the back or opposite side. —*adj.* opposite; back. —**re'versible** *adj.*

revolver

review (ri'vyōo) *vb.* 1. to look at again; reconsider. 2. to write a critical report of (a play, book, opera, etc.) for a newspaper or magazine. 3. to inspect (troops, ships, etc.). —*n.* 1. a critical report of a play, book, etc. 2. a general reconsideration or summing-up. 3. an inspection of troops, ships, etc.

revise (ri'vīz) *vb.* **revising, revised.** 1. to reconsider and change for the better. 2. to study (previously learnt material) for examinations. —**revision** (ri'vizhən) *n.*

revive (ri'vīv) *vb.* **reviving, revived.** 1. to bring or come back to life, health, popularity, etc. 2. to put on a new production of an old play, opera, etc. —**re'vival** *n.* anything revived, esp. a play, opera, film, etc.

revolt (ri'volt) *vb.* 1. to rebel or rise up against authority. 2. to disgust: *your table manners revolt me.* —*n.* a rebellion or uprising. **re'volting** *adj.* disgusting; loathsome.

revolution (revə'lōoshən) *n.* 1. a rebellion or violent upheaval that overthrows the government. 2. a complete movement or rotation around a central point. **revo'lutionary** *n.,pl.* **revolutionaries.** a person who promotes revolution. *adj.* causing great or violent changes.

revolve (ri'volv) *vb.* **revolving, revolved.** 1. to turn or rotate about a centre. 2. to turn over in one's mind; ponder.

revolver (ri'volvə) *n.* a small hand-held gun that has ammunition placed in a revolving cylinder, so that it does not need reloading after every shot.

reward (ri'wôd) *n.* 1. something given in return for help or merit. 2. a sum of money offered in return for a lost person, thing, etc. —*vb.* to give a reward to.

rheumatism ('rōomətizəm) *n.* a painful disease with stiffness and swelling in the joints and muscles. —**rheumatic** (rōo'matik) *adj.*

rhinoceros (rī'nosərəs) *n.,pl.* **rhinoceroses.** a large heavily built African or Indian animal with a thick skin and one or two upright horns on its snout.

rhombus ('rombəs) *n.,pl.* **rhombuses** *or* **rhombi** ('rombī). a figure with four sides of equal length and angles that are not right angles.

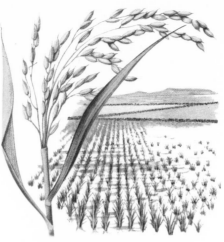
rice

rhubarb ('rōobâb) *n.* a plant whose reddish leaf stalks are cooked and eaten as a sweet or used for jam.

rhyme (rīm) *n.* 1. the similarity of sounds in words, esp. at the ends of lines of verses, e.g. *take, make, bake.* 2. verse or verses containing rhymes. —*vb.* **rhyming, rhymed.** to make a rhyme or rhymes.

rhythm ('ridhəm) *n.* a regular sequence of sounds: *the rhythm of a waltz.* —'**rhythmic** *adj.*

rib (rib) *n.* 1. one of the slender curved bones extending from the backbone to the front of the chest. 2. something resembling a rib in shape: *the ribs of an umbrella.*

ribbon ('ribən) *n.* a flat narrow band or strip of material, paper, etc.

rice (rīs) *n.* 1. a type of grain used as food. 2. the plant that grows in warm countries and produces this grain.

rich (rich) *adj.* 1. wealthy; owning a lot of money, property, etc. 2. fertile: *the desert is rich in oil.* 3. containing much nourishment: *a rich cake.* 4. splendid: *rich paintings.* **the rich** wealthy people. '**riches** *pl.n.* great wealth.

rid (rid) *vb.* **ridding, rid.** to make free from.

riddle¹ ('ridəl) *n.* a puzzling question that is made deliberately difficult to understand, e.g. *what is black and white and re(a)d all through?* Answer: *a newspaper.*

riddle² ('ridəl) *vb.* **riddling, riddled.** to pierce with many holes: *the attackers riddled the car with bullets.*

ridge (rij) *n.* 1. the raised line made by the meeting of two sloping surfaces: *the ridge of a tent.* 2. a long line of hills or high ground.

ridicule ('ridikyōol) *vb.* **ridiculing, ridiculed.** to make fun of; mock. —*n.* mockery; scorn. **ridiculous** (ri'dikyōoləs) *adj.* laughable; absurd. —**ri'diculously** *adv.*

rifle¹ ('rīfəl) *n.* a gun with spiral grooves inside its long barrel that spin the bullet and increase its speed.

rifle² ('rīfəl) *vb.* **rifling, rifled.** to search thoroughly in order to steal from: *the burglar rifled all the drawers in the house.*

rift (rift) *n.* 1. a split; crack: *the sun came through a rift in the clouds.* 2. a quarrel or lack of understanding.

rig (rig) *vb.* **rigging, rigged.** 1. to arrange (something) to benefit oneself: *the race was rigged so that Brown would win.* 2. (usu. + *out*) to provide with necessary equipment. 3. (+ *up*) to make hastily or in a makeshift way. —*n.* 1. the tall drilling tower used in mining and oil extraction. 2. an outfit of clothing, equipment, etc., for a special purpose: *diving rig.* 3. (also **rigging**) the arrangement of ropes, chains, etc., that supports the masts and works the sails of a sailing boat.

right (rīt) *adj.* 1. fair; just. 2. correct; true. 3. proper; suitable: *it was only right to help.* 4. on the east side of your body as you face north. 5. good; advantageous: *this is the right place to see birds.* 6. normal: *the right way up.* **right angle** an ANGLE of 90 degrees. —*n.* 1. that which is naturally just and fair. 2. a just, moral, or legal claim to possess something or act in a

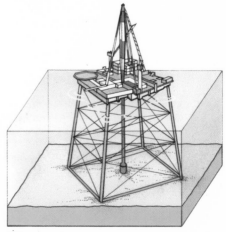
rig

179

certain way. 3. the right side or direction. —*vb.* 1. to recover an upright or normal position after being upset or overturned. 2. to set right; correctly. —*adv.* 1. straight; directly; all the way: *he went right up to him.* 2. correctly; properly. '**rightful** *adj.* legal; legitimate.

righteous ('rīchəs) *adj.* of a morally upright character; virtuous; just. **the righteous** people who devoutly follow moral and religious principles. —'**righteously** *adv.* —'**righteousness** *n.*

rigid ('rijid) *adj.* 1. firm and unbending; stiff: *a rigid iron bar.* 2. severe; inflexible in character: *rigid rules.* —ri'**gidity** *n.* —'**rigidly** *adv.*

rim (rim) *n.* the curved and raised outer edge of something, e.g. a wheel or glass.

rind (rīnd) *n.* the coarse protective outer skin of fruit, vegetables, bacon, and cheese.

rind

ring[1] (riṅg) *n.* 1. a circle; closed curved line or arrangement. 2. a circular metal band, esp. one worn on a finger as an ornament. 3. an enclosed piece of ground used for boxing, circus events, etc. —*vb.* 1. to form the shape of a ring around. 2. to fix a ring onto (an animal or bird).

ring[2] (riṅg) *vb.* **ringing, rang, rung.** 1. to make a clear vibrating sound like a bell. 2. to cause a bell or bells to sound. 3. to re-echo; be full of sound. 4. (+ *up*) to call (someone) on the telephone. 5. (+ *off*) to finish a telephone call. —*n.* a ringing sound.

rink (riṅgk) *n.* an artificial sheet of ice used for skating and playing ice hockey.

rinse (rins) *vb.* **rinsing, rinsed.** 1. to wash out soap from (something) in clean water. 2. to clean quickly in water. —*n.* 1. the act of rinsing. 2. a semi-permanent hair dye.

riot ('rīət) *n.* violent and uncontrolled disorder caused by a crowd. —*vb.* to make or join in a riot. —'**riotous** *adj.* —'**riotously** *adv.*

ripe (rīp) *adj.* 1. ready for eating or harvesting; mature. 2. prepared; ready: *the children were ripe for mischief.* '**ripen** *vb.* to make or become ripe or riper. —'**ripeness** *n.*

ripple ('ripəl) *n.* a small smooth wave; small disturbance on the surface of water. —*vb.* **rippling, rippled.** to make or move in ripples.

rise (rīz) *vb.* **rising, rose, risen** ('rizən). 1. to move or slope upwards. 2. to get up onto the feet from a seated or lying position. 3. to gain higher rank, office, or social position. 4. to increase; reach a higher level: *the tide rose up the beach.* 5. to rebel. 6. to spring up; begin: *the river rises in those hills.* —*n.* 1. an upward movement. 2. an upward slope. 3. (informal) an increase in wages.

risk (risk) *n.* the likelihood of danger. —*vb.* to do or use something knowing there is a chance of failure, danger, etc.; take a chance on. —'**risky** *adj.* **riskier, riskiest.**

rite (rīt) *n.* a formal or customary act or ceremony, esp. as part of religious worship. **ritual** ('rityŏŏəl) *n.* 1. the official order of words and actions at sacred ceremonies. 2. habitual or generally expected actions and words. —*adj.* ceremonial or customary.

rival ('rīvəl) *n.* a competitor; someone who strives against another person for the same object. —*vb.* **rivalling, rivalled.** to claim to be as good as; compete against. —'**rivalry** *n.,pl.* **rivalries.**

river ('rivə) *n.* a large natural body of fresh water that flows between banks towards the sea, a lake, or another river.

road (rōd) *n.* 1. a way used by people and wheeled vehicles to get from one place to another. 2. a course towards some end or goal: *determination and hard work was his road to success.*

roam (rōm) *vb.* to wander; walk about without a fixed purpose.

roar (rô) *n.* 1. a loud throaty sound made by a large animal. 2. any loud deep prolonged sound. —*vb.* to make a roaring sound.

roast (rōst) *vb.* to cook steadily in an oven or before a fire, usu. with fat.

rob (rob) *vb.* **robbing, robbed.** to steal; take someone else's property by force, fraud, or threat. '**robbery** *n.,pl.* **robberies.** an act of robbing.

robe (rōb) *n.* 1. a long loose flowing garment. 2. often **robes** (*pl.*) a garment of a particular colour, cut, and material to show the wearer's rank or office: *the judge put on his scarlet robes.* —*vb.* **robing, robed.** to dress in robes.

robin ('robin) *n.* a small brown bird with a red breast, widespread in Europe and known for its boldness.

robot ('rōbot) *n.* a machine that looks like a man and is able to do certain jobs that a man can do.

robust (rō'bust) *adj.* strong; healthy.

rock[1] (rok) *n.* 1. a large mass of stone; boulder. 2. the dense hard mineral substance of varying kinds and characteristics that composes the earth's surface. 3. a hard stick-shaped sweet sold at seaside resorts. —'**rocky** *adj.* **rockier, rockiest.**

rock[2] (rok) *vb.* 1. to move gently from side to side in order to soothe or lull to sleep. 2. to cause to sway violently.

rocket ('rokit) *n.* a device that is driven forward by a powerful stream of hot gases that are released when the fuel is burnt in the oxygen supply carried in the rocket. —*vb.* to move or rise very rapidly.

river

rodents

rat

squirrel

rod (rod) *n.* 1. a thin straight flexible cane, e.g. a fishing rod. 2. a long metal bar that links moving parts of a machine.

rodent ('rōdənt) *n.* one of a large family of warm-blooded animals with large strong front teeth that are used for gnawing. Rats, mice, beavers, and hamsters are rodents.

rodeo ('rōdiō, rō'dāo) *n.,pl.* **rodeos.** an exhibition in which cowboys show off their skills in riding unbroken horses, roping calves, etc.

roe (rō) *n.* the eggs of a fish.

rogue (rōg) *n.* 1. a dishonest person. 2. a mischievous person. '**roguish** *adj.* playful.

role (rōl) *n.* 1. the part of a character in a play: *John had the role of Othello.* 2. someone's function in a particular situation.

roll (rōl) *vb.* 1. to move by turning over and over: *the ball rolled away.* 2. to move on wheels or by means of a wheeled vehicle: *he rolled along on his bicycle.* 3. to curl or wind up into a ball or cylindrical shape. 4. to press out flat with a cylinder: *she rolled out the pastry.* 5. to trill the letter 'r' in speech. 6. to sweep along with a gentle rising and falling motion. 7. to rumble or reverberate. —*n.* 1. material rolled up into a cylindrical bale: *a blanket roll.* 2. a small bread loaf. 3. a rolling movement or sound. 4. an official list of names. '**roller** *n.* 1. a metal or wooden cylinder that rolls on its axis and has many uses in machines for crushing and smoothing (e.g. a steam roller), for moving loads, processing continuous sheets of paper, etc. 2. a long swelling ocean wave.

romance (rə'mans) *n.* 1. a love affair. 2. the quality of mystery, adventure, or excitement: *the romance of wild desert scenery.* 3. a story or poem dealing with love and adventure. —**ro'mantic** *adj.*

roof (roof) *n.* 1. the protective outer covering on top of a building. 2. the topmost part of anything: *the hot soup burned the roof of my mouth.* —*vb.* to provide with a roof.

rook[1] (rook) *n.* a European bird of the crow family, with black plumage and a strong sharp beak. It builds its nests in colonies and has a deep hoarse voice.

rook[2] (rook) *n.* a chess piece, also known as a castle, that can move in a straight line in any direction except diagonally.

room (room) *n.* 1. a space enclosed by walls inside a building. 2. sufficient space: *there is room for five people in my car.* 3. scope for doing something; opportunity: *his words left no room for argument.* 4. **rooms** (*pl.*) lodgings. '**roomy** *adj.* **roomier, roomiest.** with plenty of space.

roost (roost) *vb.* to perch and settle down for sleep or rest. —*n.* the place where birds settle for the night. '**rooster** *n.* a male farmyard chicken.

root[1] (root) *n.* 1. the part of a plant that grows underground, serving both to anchor it in the soil and to absorb water and mineral salts. 2. a part resembling a root in function or structure: *the roots of one's hair.* 3. the source; origin: *love of money is the root of all evil.* 4. a word from which other words are formed, e.g. *truth* in *truthful, truthfully,* and *truthfulness.* —*vb.* 1. to grow or put down roots. 2. to fix firmly.

root[2] (root) *vb.* 1. to turn up the soil with the snout when looking for food: *the pigs rooted for acorns.* 2. to search around.

rope (rōp) *n.* 1. a length of thick cord made by twisting together strands of hemp, wire, etc. 2. a number of objects strung or twisted together like a rope: *a rope of beads.* —*vb.* **roping, roped.** to tie or fasten with rope.

rose[1] (rōz) *n.* a garden flower that grows on a thorny bush or climbing plant, and has perfumed blooms in shades of red, pink, yellow, or white. '**rosy** *adj.* **rosier, rosiest.** 1. having a pinkish-red colour. 2. promising well; bright: *she has rosy prospects as an actress.*

rose[2] (rōz) *vb.* the past tense of RISE.

rosette (rō'zet) *n.* an imitation rose made of paper, ribbon, etc., used as a decoration or emblem.

rosette

rota ('rōtə) *n.* a list of duties to be carried out in turn by various people.

rotate (rō'tāt) *vb.* **rotating, rotated.** 1. to move round a centre or axis. 2. to change regularly; take turns in a fixed order: *the farmer rotates beans and potatoes with barley in his large field.* —**ro'tation** *n.*

rough (ruf) *adj.* 1. not smooth; uneven. 2. showing force or violence: *a rough game of hockey.* 3. unfinished; not perfectly made or finished off: *a rough sketch.* 4. unpleasant: *he had a rough time when he had measles.* —*vb.* 1. (+ *up*) to beat violently. 2. (+ *out*) to plan or make in an uncomplete way: *he roughed out a plan of the house.* —'**roughly** *adv.* —'**roughness** *n.*

rouse (rouz) *vb.* **rousing, roused.** 1. to cause to get up; awaken from sleep, rest, etc. 2. to stir up: *his rudeness roused the teacher's anger.*

route (rōot) *n.* the road or way one follows from one place to another. —*vb.* **routing, routed.** to send by or arrange a particular route.

routine (rōo'tēn) *n.* 1. a regular pattern or schedule for doing things. 2. dull sameness in work or other actions: *Betty hated school routine.* —*adj.* regular; habitual.

row[1] (rō) *n.* 1. a number of people or things set side by side in a line. 2. a line of seats.

row[2] (rō) *vb.* 1. to propel a boat with oars. 2. to transport in a rowing-boat: *she rowed her parents upstream.* —*n.* a journey in a rowing boat.

row[3] (rou) *n.* 1. a quarrel; noisy argument. 2. an uproar; din: *he shouted above the row of the pneumatic drill.*

royal ('roiəl) *adj.* 1. of, concerning, or belonging to a king or queen. 2. like or suitable for a king or queen: *Sarah's grandparents gave her a royal welcome.* '**royalist** *n.* a loyal supporter of kings and kingship. '**royalty** *n.,pl.* **royalties.** 1. a royal person or persons. 2. the office or power of a king or queen. 3. usu. **royalties** (*pl.*) money paid to a writer for each copy of his work that is sold.

rubber ('rubə) *n.* 1. a strong, flexible, waterproof substance made from the sap of a tree that grows in hot countries and used in manufacturing many products. 2. a small piece of this substance used to remove pencil marks. —'**rubbery** *adj.*

rubber

rubbish ('rubish) *n.* 1. waste material. 2. anything that is inferior or worthless.

ruby ('rōobi) *n.,pl.* **rubies.** 1. a rare precious stone with colours ranging from deep crimson to pale pink. 2. a dark red colour. —*adj.* dark red.

rucksack

rucksack ('ruksak) *n.* a canvas bag that is carried on straps over the shoulders and is used by hikers, soldiers, etc.

rudder ('rudə) *n.* 1. a flat broad movable piece of wood or metal that is attached to the back of a boat and used for steering. 2. a similar structure on the tail of an aeroplane.

rude (rōod) *adj.* 1. bad-mannered; impolite. 2. roughly or crudely made: *the shepherd slept in a rude hut.* —'**rudely** *adv.* —'**rudeness** *n.*

ruffian ('rufiən) *n.* a cruel rough man.

ruffle ('rufəl) *vb.* **ruffling, ruffled.** 1. to disturb the smoothness of: *the wind ruffled his hair.* 2. to upset: *her laughter ruffled them.* —*n.* a strip of material gathered into a frill and used as decoration, e.g. on curtains or clothes.

rug (rug) *n.* 1. a woollen blanket. 2. a small carpet used to cover part of a floor.

rugby football ('rugbi) a football game in which an oval ball is used and players are allowed to pick up the ball and run with it.

rugged ('rugid) *adj.* 1. rough and uneven in surface or outline: *rugged cliffs.* 2. tough; strong: *a rugged fighter.* 3. harsh; uncomfortable: *a rugged life in the Arctic.*

ruin ('rōoin) *n.* 1. downfall; collapse. 2. often **ruins** (*pl.*) the remains of decayed or destroyed buildings. —*vb.* 1. to cause the downfall of. 2. to reduce to ruins; destroy. —'**ruinous** *adj.*

rule (rōol) *n.* 1. a principle or instruction, either formally set out or generally accepted, that controls action or behaviour: *do you know the rules of chess?* 2. government; control: *the rule of a king.* 3. (also **ruler**) a marked strip of wood, plastic, etc., used for measuring and drawing straight lines. —*vb.* **ruling, ruled.** 1. to govern; exercise control over. 2. to make a decision from a position of authority: *the judge ruled that the trial should continue.* 3. to draw lines with the aid of a rule (def. 3).

rumble ('rumbəl) *vb.* **rumbling, rumbled.** to make a dull rolling sound like distant thunder. —*n.* a dull rolling noise.

rumour ('rōomə) *n.* a report or story that is based on gossip and may be totally untrue. —*vb.* to spread (information) by rumour: *it is rumoured that he is bankrupt.*

rump (rump) *n.* 1. the hind end or buttocks of an animal. 2. a joint of meat cut from this part of the body.

rung[1] (rung) *n.* a short piece of wood or metal fitted between the uprights of a ladder to form one of a series of footholds.

rung[2] (rung) *vb.* the past participle of RING[2].

rush[1] (rush) *vb.* 1. to hurry. 2. to make a sudden violent move against: *the police rushed the armed criminal.* 3. to move very fast: *water rushed from the cracked pipe.* —*n.* 1. the act of rushing. 2. intense activity.

rush[2] (rush) *n.* a tall grasslike plant with straight hollow stems that grows near water.

rut (rut) *n.* 1. a track or groove worn into the ground by the passage of wheels. 2. a dull routine: *he got out of the rut by changing jobs.*

ruthless ('rōothlis) *adj.* merciless; without pity. —'**ruthlessly** *adv.* —'**ruthlessness** *n.*

rye (rī) *n.* a grain that grows on a grasslike plant and is used to make bread and whisky and to provide fodder for cattle.

S

sabbath ('sabəth) *n.* the day of the week on which God said to have rested after creating heaven and earth; the day when people rest from their work. For Christians the sabbath falls each Sunday and for Jews it falls each Saturday.

sabotage ('sabətâzh) *n.* the deliberate destruction or damage of machinery, etc., esp. as carried out by enemy agents in wartime. **—sabotaging, sabotaged.** *vb.* to damage or destroy (something) by sabotage.

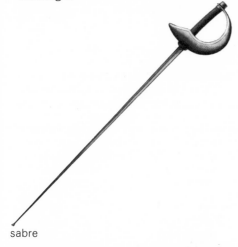
sabre

sabre ('sābə) *n.* 1. a heavy, slightly curved sword with one sharpened edge, used by cavalry soldiers. 2. a light sword used in fencing.

sac (sak) *n.* a bag-like organ or structure in an animal or plant.

saccharine ('sakərin) *n.* also **saccharin.** a sweet chemical compound, used istead of sugar by people who are trying to lose weight. **—adj.** sickly sweet: *she gave him a saccharine smile.*

sachet ('sashā) *n.* 1. a small waterproof packet, usu. plastic, in which shampoos, etc., are often sold. 2. a small, usu. decorated bag, for holding sweet-smelling dried flowers, etc.

sack[1] (sak) *n.* 1. a large bag made from a rough cloth or heavy plastic, used

for carrying bulky things. 2. the amount a sack holds. 3. a baggy, loose-fitting item of clothing, esp. a woman's dress. 4. (informal) dismissal from one's job: *he was given the sack for laziness.* **hit the sack** (slang) to go to bed. **—vb.** 1. to put (something) in a sack. 2. (informal) to dismiss (someone) from his job.

sack[2] (sak) *vb.* to steal from and destroy or burn (a town captured in war). **—n.** 1. the act of sacking a captured town. 2. valuable things stolen from a captured town.

sacrament ('sakrəment) *n.* an act, ceremony, or object that is regarded as especially holy, esp. the bread and wine taken by Christians as symbols of Jesus's body and blood.

sacred ('sākrid) *adj.* 1. concerned with God or a god; holy. 2. deserving respect or reverence: *a sacred law.* 3. devoted to, in honour of, or used for a certain purpose, esp. a religious one: *this gravestone is sacred to his father's memory.* **—'sacredly** *adv.*

sacrifice ('sakrifīs) *n.* 1. the act of deliberately giving up or losing something dear to one as part of one's duty or in order to get something better. 2. the thing given up. 3. an offering made to god. 4. the ritual killing of an animal or other victim in honour of a god. **—vb. sacrificing, sacrificed.** to make a sacrifice of (an animal or thing).

saddle ('sadəl) *n.* 1. a rider's seat, usu. of leather, strapped to a horse's back. 2. a bicycle seat. 3. that part of an animal between the shoulders and the lower back from which a joint of meat may be taken: *saddle of lamb.* **in the saddle** in control. **—vb. saddling, saddled.** 1. to put a saddle on (a horse). 2. (+ *with*) to load with: *she was saddled with heavy responsibilities.*

safari (sə'fâri) *n.,pl.* **safaris.** a journey or expedition carried out in order to hunt or study wild animals. **safari park** (Britain) a type of open

zoo through which people may drive in order to see uncaged wild animals.

safe (sāf) *adj.* **safer, safest.** 1. not in danger; not hurt or damaged: *they were safe at home.* 2. not dangerous; unlikely to cause damage or injury: *that swing is not safe.* 3. reliable; sure; trustworthy. **—n.** 1. a strong metal box or secure room in which money, jewels, etc., are locked away for safety. 2. a cool place or container for storing food, esp. meat. **—'safely** *adj.* **—'safety** *n.*

sag (sag) *vb.* **sagging, sagged.** 1. to bend downwards because of pressure, weight, etc. 2. to weaken; lose force or strength because of tiredness, lack of determination, etc.: *after walking a mile Tom began to sag and fall behind.* **—n.** the state of sagging or the amount of sagging.

said (sed) *vb.* the past tense and past participle of SAY.

sail (sāl) *n.* 1. a large piece of canvas or similar material attached to the mast of a yacht, ship, etc., to catch the wind and thus move the boat. 2. a trip in a sailing boat. 3. anything like a sail, e.g. the arm of a windmill. **set sail** to begin a voyage or trip. **—vb.** 1. to manage a sailing boat. 2. to begin a voyage or trip: *they sailed at dawn.* 3. to move like a sailing boat; glide smoothly. **'sailor** *n.* a person who sails, esp. a seaman in the navy.

saint (sānt) *n.* 1. a person of almost divine goodness whose holiness is officially recognized by the Church after his or her death. 2. any very good, gentle, and kind person. **'saintly** *adj.* **saintlier, saintliest.** like a saint; good and kind.

salad ('saləd) *n.* a dish usu. consisting of raw lettuce, cucumber, tomatoes, etc., often served with a spicy dressing. **—adj.** relating to salads.

salary ('saləri) *n.,pl.* **salaries.** a payment of money made monthly or yearly in return for skilled or professional services.

sale (sāl) *n.* 1. the act or process of selling. 2. an auction. 3. the selling of goods at very cheap prices. 4. demand; market: *there is no sale for swimwear in winter.*

saliva (sə'līvə) *n.* liquid formed in the mouth; spit. It helps to digest food that is being chewed.

salmon ('samən) *n.* a large edible fish having a delicate pink flesh and a brownish skin that lives in the North Atlantic, travelling up rivers to lay eggs. **salmon pink** having the colour of a salmon.

salmon

salt (sôlt) *n.* a naturally occurring white substance that is found esp. in the sea and used for flavouring food. —*vb.* to flavour with salt.

salute (sə'lōot) *n.* 1. a sign of greeting or respect, esp. as given by a soldier to another of higher rank. 2. a sign of respect to a king or queen, etc., usu. involving the firing of a gun. —*vb.* **saluting, saluted.** 1. to make a salute. 2. to give (someone) a salute.

salvation (sal'vāshən) *n.* 1. the act of saving or the person or thing that saves. 2. (Christianity) the rescue of someone's soul. **Salvation Army** a religious organization that gives practical and spiritual help to those in need.

sample ('sâmpəl) *n.* a piece or part of something representing the whole object, etc., from which it was taken. —*vb.* **sampling, sampled.** to test a sample from (something).

sanctuary ('saṅgktyŏŏəri) *n.,pl.* **sanctuaries.** 1. a place of safety or protection: *a wildlife sanctuàry.* 2. the altar of a Christian church or the area in which it is placed.

sand (sand) *n.* 1. a natural substance consisting of small particles of worn rock. 2. also **sands** (*pl.*) a beach, shore, or desert. —*vb.* 1. to spread sand upon or around: *the men sanded the icy roads.* 2. to rub or smooth (wood, metal, etc.) with sandpaper. —'**sandiness** *n.* —'**sandy** *adj.* **sandier, sandiest.**

sandal ('sandəl) *n.* a shoe made of a sole fastened on the foot by straps.

sandpaper ('sandpāpə) *n.* stiff paper that has sand particles stuck to it, used for rubbing down and smoothing wood, metal, or other materials. —*vb.* to rub down or smooth (wood, etc.) with sandpaper.

sandwich ('sandwich) *n.* two slices of bread and butter with any of a number of fillings placed between them: *a jam sandwich.* —*vb.* to place (a person or thing) between two others.

sane (sān) *adj.* not suffering from mental illness; not mad. —'**sanely** *adv.* —**sanity** ('saniti) *n.*

sanitary ('sanitəri) *adj.* 1. healthy: *sanitary conditions.* 2. connected with health, cleanness, and prevention of disease: *he is a sanitary inspector.* —'**sanitarily** *adv.* —'**sanitariness** *n.*

sank (saṅgk) *vb.* the past tense of SINK.

sap (sap) *n.* the juice of a plant carrying the minerals and water necessary for it to live. —*vb.* **sapping, sapped.** 1. to remove sap from (a plant). 2. to remove or exhaust (a person's strength or energy).

sapphire ('safīə) *n.* a hard clear MINERAL used as a gemstone, usu. deep blue in colour. —*adj.* having the colour of a sapphire.

sardine (sâ'dēn) *n.* the young of a pilchard or similar small fish, often preserved in oil for food. **packed (in) like sardines** very close together.

sash (sash) *n.* 1. a strip of cloth worn around the waist as decoration or over one shoulder, e.g. as part of a uniform, etc. 2. a metal or wooden window frame which opens by sliding up or down.

satellite ('satəlīt) *n.* 1. a natural or artificial object that orbits around a larger object in space, esp. a planet: *the moon is a natural satellite of the*

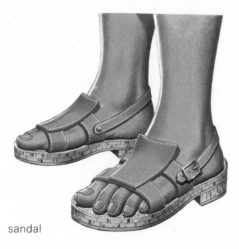
sandal

earth. 2. a person or country associated with a more powerful person or country and copying his or its views, opinions, policies, etc.

satin ('satin) *n.* a fabric made from silk, cotton, or manmade fibres, having a shiny, slippery surface. —*adj.* 1. made of satin. 2. glossy; smooth: *satin skin.*

satisfy ('satisfī) *vb.* **satisfying, satisfied.** 1. to supply (someone or something) with what is wanted, needed, or expected; make content. 2. to fulfil (a desire, need, or demand). 3. to convince: *I satisfied myself that he was telling the truth.* 4. to pay (debts or people to whom they are owed). 5. to meet the needs or requirements of. —**satisfaction** (satis'fakshən) *n.* —**satis'factory** *adj.*

sauce (sôs) *n.* 1. one of many pleasantly flavoured liquid or creamy mixtures served with different foods to improve their tastes. 2. (informal) cheek; impertinence. '**saucy** *adj.* **saucier, sauciest.** 1. impertinent. 2. slightly arousing feelings of sexual interest: *a saucy joke.* —'**saucily** *adv.* —'**sauciness** *n.*

saucer ('sôsə) *n.* 1. a small shallow dish in which a cup stands. 2. anything shaped like a saucer: *some people believe that flying saucers come from outer space.*

sauna ('sônə) *n.* (also **sauna bath**) (originally in Finland) a place where one takes a steam bath followed by a cold shower or swim.

sausage ('sosij) *n.* a type of food consisting of chopped pork or other meat seasoned with herbs and spices and stuffed into a skin. **sausage roll** a baked pastry roll containing sausage meat.

savage ('savij) *adj.* 1. dangerous, untamed, or wild: *a savage beast.* 2. cruel, vicious, or brutal: *a savage crime.* —*n.* anyone who is uncivilized, wild, or cruel. —*vb.* **savaging, savaged.** to bite and tear viciously: *the lion savaged the boy.* —'**savagely** *adv.* —'**savagery** *n.*

save (sāv) *vb.* **saving, saved.** 1. to preserve, rescue, or keep safe from harm, destruction, or loss. 2. (often + *up*) to keep or store up for future use: *Pete saves money to buy books.* 3. (Christianity) to rescue from sin. 4. (football) to prevent the scoring of (a goal): *the goalkeeper saved three penalties.* —*n.* an instance of saving, esp. in football. '**savings** *pl.n.* money that has been saved.

saviour ('sāviə) *n.* 1. a person who saves or rescues. 2. **Saviour** Jesus Christ, as the Son of God who saved men from sin.

savoury ('sāvəri) *adj.* 1. tasty in flavour, but not sweet: *cheese is a savoury food.* 2. respectable: *the less savoury part of the town.* —*n.,pl.* **savouries.** a savoury dish or food.

saw[1] (sô) *n.* a cutting tool with a sharp-toothed blade used to cut wood, metal, etc. —*vb.* **sawing, sawed, sawn.** to cut wood, metal, etc., with a saw. **circular saw** an electrically operated cutting tool consisting of a sharp-toothed fast spinning disc. '**sawdust** *n.* the wood particles produced when a piece of wood is sawn.

saw[2] (sô) *vb.* the past tense of SEE[1].

saxophone ('saksəfōn) *n.* a brass wind instrument having a single reed set in its mouthpiece, used mainly in jazz and pop music.

saxophone

say (sā) *vb.* **saying, said.** 1. to speak, tell, state, or express by word of mouth: *he said he was going away.* 2. to decide or give an opinion. 3. to repeat or recite: *to say a poem.* 4. to suppose; assume: *let us say that he will come.* **go without saying** to be completely obvious. **I dare say** I expect or agree: *I dare say he will go but he hasn't told me.* —*n.* the right or chance to express a view or make a decision: *I insist on having my say.* '**saying** *n.* a well-known or often repeated sentence or phrase, e.g. *as bold as brass.*

scab (skab) *n.* 1. a crust that forms over a wound to protect the new skin being produced underneath. 2. (slang) a contemptible person, esp. one who continues to work after an industrial strike has been called. '**scabby** *adj.* **scabbier, scabbiest.** 1. covered with a scab or scabs. 2. contemptible. **scab labour** people who do work while other workers are on strike.

scaffold ('skafôld) *n.* 1. (also **scaffolding**) a temporary structure of platforms and metal bars, used by workers as a base for building work, etc. 2. a platform from which criminals were executed by hanging.

scald (skôld) *vb.* 1. to burn with boiling hot liquid or steam. 2. to kill all the germs on (something) by putting it in boiling water. 3. to heat (liquid) almost to boiling point. —*n.* a burn caused by scalding.

scale[1] (skāl) *n.* 1. a range of measurements as marked in a scientific instrument. 2. a group of musical notes in ascending or descending order. 3. any system consisting of gradual steps: *a scale of charges.* 4. also **scales** (*pl.*) a balance for weighing things. 5. the size of a drawing, map, etc., as compared with the thing it represents. 6. amount; size; extent: *his business was on a small scale.* —*vb.* **scaling, scaled.** to climb or climb over. **scale up** (or **down**) to increase (or decrease) some quantity or value: *he scaled up prices by 10 per cent.*

scale[2] (skāl) *n.* any of the hard flat horny plates making up the skin covering on certain animals, e.g. fishes and lizards. —'**scaly** *adj.* **scalier, scaliest.**

scallop ('skaləp) *n.* sea animal whose body is enclosed in two curved ridged shells hinged together. The body of the scallop is good to eat.

scalp (skalp) *n.* the skin on top of the head, usu. covered by hair. —*vb.* (esp. among certain American Indian tribes) to tear or cut the scalp from (the head of a person) as a sign of victory.

scalpel ('skalpəl) *n.* a small very sharp knife used in surgical operations.

scampi ('skampi) *n.* a dish consisting of very large prawns fried in batter.

scan (skan) *vb.* **scanning, scanned.** 1. to look over; survey: *he scanned the horizon.* 2. to look rapidly through something; read quickly: *he scanned the newspapers.* 3. to separate (verse) into metrical feet. 4. (of verse) to conform to a consistent metrical pattern. '**scanner** *n.* a thing that scans, esp. a radar transmitter surveying the area near it. **scansion** ('skanshən) *n.* the art of scanning verse.

scandal ('skandəl) *n.* 1. gossip or talk about a person, esp. when untrue and damaging to his reputation. 2. a disgraceful act or event that causes angry talk or gossip among the public: *the disappearance of the money was a scandal.* '**scandalize** *vb.* **scandalizing, scandalized.** to cause shame or embarrassment to. '**scandalous** *adj.* causing scandal. —'**scandalously** *adv.*

scant (skant) *adj.* not enough: *John could not understand the maths problem as he had paid scant attention to the lesson.* '**scanty** *adj.* **scantier, scantiest.** of small size or amount: *the food seems very scanty for a party of this size.*

scapegoat ('skāpgōt) *n.* a person or thing that bears the blame for others' faults, mistakes, etc.

scar (skâ) *n.* 1. a mark left on the skin when a wound, cut, etc., has healed up. 2. a permanent effect left by experience, suffering, etc. —*vb.* **scarring, scarred.** to mark with a scar.

scarce (skeəs) *adj.* not plentiful; rare: *strawberries are scarce in winter.* **make oneself scarce** (informal) to go away. '**scarcely** *adv.* hardly; not much: *I scarcely saw him after that night.* —'**scarcity** *n.,pl.* **scarcities.**

scare (skeə) *vb.* **scaring, scared.** 1. to frighten (a person or animal). 2. (+ *off* or *away*) to drive (someone or something) away by frightening them. —*n.* the state of being scared; sudden fear.

scarecrow

scarecrow ('skeəkrō) *n.* a model of a man dressed in old clothes and placed in the fields to frighten birds away from crops.

scarf (skåf) *n.,pl.* **scarves.** a square or long narrow strip of cloth worn around the neck or on the head for warmth, decoration, or protection from rain.

scarlet ('skålit) *adj.* a very bright orange-red colour. **scarlet fever** an infectious illness characterized by a red rash, sore throat, etc.

scatter ('skatə) *vb.* 1. to throw around: *Betty scatters seeds for the birds.* 2. to send or be sent off in different directions; disperse. —*n.* the act of scattering.

scene (sēn) *n.* 1. the place where something happens; the background of an event. 2. a view or landscape: *a country scene.* 3. a section of an act in a play. 4. a display of anger, etc.: *Sam made a scene about having to stay at home.* **behind the scenes** not in view; secretly. **'scenery** *n.* 1. beautiful landscape. 2. the painted screens, etc., used on stage for a play in a theatre.

scent (sent) *n.* 1. a smell, usu. a pleasant one: *the scent of flowers.* 2. perfume. 3. the smell left by an animal as it moves, which dogs and other animals can detect and follow. 4. any trail of clues, etc. —*vb.* 1. to detect the scent of. 2. to detect, as if by smell: *he scented danger.* 3. to cover, sprinkle, etc., with scent.

sceptre ('septə) *n.* a staff usu. made of precious metals and decorated with jewels and carried by a king or queen on important occasions as a symbol of royal power.

schedule ('shedyŏŏl) *n.* a list of things to be done and the times at which they are to be done; timetable. —*vb.* **scheduling, scheduled.** 1. to make out a schedule. 2. to arrange (something) according to a schedule.

scheme (skēm) *n.* 1. a plan or arrangement. 2. a design made according to a definite plan: *a colour scheme.* 3. a dishonest plan; plot. —*vb.* **scheming, schemed.** 1. to make plans; work out a scheme. 2. to make a secret or dishonest plan.

scholar ('skolə) *n.* 1. a well-educated or learned person. 2. a student, esp. one awarded a special grant of money because of merit, etc. **'scholarship** *n.* 1. the state of being a scholar. 2. a special grant of money given to certain students, usu. because of merit. —**'scholarly** *adj.*

school[1] (skŏŏl) *n.* 1. a place of education attended by children, usu. up to the age of 16. 2. a department in a college or university teaching a particular subject or subjects: *a school of medicine.* 3. a group of writers, artists, etc., all using the same methods, style, etc. —*vb.* to educate; train.

school[2] (skŏŏl) *n.* a large group of fish, porpoises, etc., swimming along together; shoal.

schooner ('skŏŏnə) *n.* a type of sailing ship with two masts.

science ('sīəns) *n.* 1. knowledge about the physical character of things and events occurring in nature or the universe. 2. knowledge concerning a special subject connected with this: *the science of physics.* 2. skill; aptitude. **scientific** (sīən'tifik) *adj.* 1. relating to science. 2. skilled or expert. **'scientist** *n.* a student of science. —**scien'tifically** *adv.*

scissors ('sizəz) *pl.n.* a cutting instrument in which two blades with finger and thumb holes at their ends are pivoted about a central point so that their cutting edges work against each other.

scold (skōld) *vb.* to blame (someone) in a rough and angry manner: *she scolded the naughty boy.*

scoop (skŏŏp) *n.* 1. an instrument similar to a shovel or ladle used to lift or move things. 2. (informal) a news story of great public interest obtained and published before other news-

papers get it. —*vb.* 1. (often + *up*) to move or pick up with a scoop or something similar. 2. (+ *out*) to make (a hollow) with or as if with a scoop. 3. (informal) to get hold of a good news story before rival newspapers.

scooter ('skŏŏtə) *n.* 1. (also **motor scooter**) a lightweight motorcycle. 2. a child's wheeled toy moved by standing on the footboard and pushing against the ground with one foot, while holding on to the handlebars.

scorch (skôch) *vb.* to burn (something) slightly and leave a mark: *he scorched the cloth with the iron.* —*n.* a mark made by scorching.

score (skô) *n.* 1. the record of points gained by competitors in a match, game, etc. 2. a groove or mark made by scratching or cutting, often used to mark points gained, money owed, etc. 3. a group of twenty items. 4. a music copy showing each part and the instrument or voice performing it. 5. a debt; grudge: *he settled an old score.* **to know the score** to know the facts of a situation. —*vb.* **scoring, scored.** 1. to get points, runs, etc., in a game or match. 2. to record such points. 3. to make cuts or grooves in. 4. to cross out (writing, etc.). 5. (music) to write a score for. 6. to gain an advantage.

scorn (skôn) *n.* an attitude of contempt or mockery; act of regarding people or things as inferior and thus unworthy of notice. —*vb.* to show scorn or contempt for. —**'scornful** *adj.* —**'scornfully** *adv.*

scorpion ('skôpiən) *n.* a creature related to the spider, having an armoured body and a long tail ending in a poisonous sting. It is found in the warmer regions of the world.

scorpion

scour ('skouə) *vb.* to clean thoroughly by scrubbing, often with a rough cleaning pad.

scout (skout) *n.* 1. a person sent out to get information, esp. about an enemy before a battle. 2. **Scout** (also **Boy Scout**) a member of an international organization that teaches boys to look after themselves and to help others. —*vb.* to act as a scout or Boy Scout.

scowl (skoul) *vb.* to lower the eyebrows and pull them together in an angry frown. —*n.* the action of scowling; angry frown.

scrap (skrap) *n.* 1. a bit broken off; fragment: *scraps of food.* 2. (informal) a fight. **scrap metal** old metal that can be used again. —*vb.* **scrapping, scrapped.** 1. to throw away something broken or old. 2. (informal) to fight or quarrel.

scrape (skrāp) *vb.* **scraping, scraped.** 1. to rub or scratch (something) with a sharp or rough edge. 2. to remove (an outer layer) by scraping: *he scraped the mud off his shoes.* 3. (+ *up* or *together*) to collect or obtain (money, friends, etc.) with difficulty. **scrape through** to succeed at something with difficulty: *she scraped through her exams.* **bow and scrape** see at BOW[1]. —*n.* 1. the act, the sound, or an instance of scraping. 2. (informal) a difficult situation; muddle.

scratch (skrach) *vb.* 1. to make a mark on (the surface of something) with a sharp object: *he scratched the desk with his knife.* 2. to wound or injure slightly: *the cat scratched him.* 3. to rub with the fingernails to relieve itching. 4. to cancel a contest; withdraw or cause to withdraw from a competition: *the horse was scratched from the race.* **up to scratch** up to standard. **start from scratch** to start at the beginning. —*n.* 1. a mark made by scratching. 2. a cut or slight skin wound. —*adj.* collected hastily: *a scratch team.*

scream (skrēm) *vb.* to make a loud shrill cry or noise: *she screamed with terror.* —*n.* 1. a loud shrill cry. 2. (informal) someone who makes people laugh.

screech (skrēch) *vb.* to give a harsh shrill cry or yell; scream. —*n.* a shrill harsh cry or scream.

screen (skrēn) *n.* 1. a light and easily movable covered frame protecting things from light, heat, etc., dividing rooms, or concealing things. 2. a smooth white surface on which films are shown. 3. the glass front of a television set forming the area on which the picture is formed. —*vb.* 1. to protect, divide, or hide by means of a screen. 2. to project a film onto a screen. 3. to show on television.

screw (skrōō) *n.* 1. a piece of metal resembling and functioning as a nail with a spiral ridge running around its body and a groove in its head allowing it to be driven into wood or metal by the turning action of a **screwdriver.** 2. anything similar to a screw in form or purpose. 3. the action or an instance of screwing. 4. (slang) a prison guard. **have a screw loose** to be slightly mad or eccentric. —*vb.* 1. to fit (a screw) or fasten with a screw.

screwdriver

2. to tighten by turning: *she screwed a top on the bottle.* 3. (+ *up*) to twist out of shape: *Jane screwed up the newspaper.* 4. (informal) to obtain by force, blackmail, etc. **to have one's head (well) screwed on** to be sensible. **'screwdriver** *n.* a tool that fits into the slot on the head of a screw in order to turn the screw.

scribble ('skribəl) *vb.* **scribbling, scribbled.** 1. to make meaningless marks with a pen, pencil, etc. 2. to write hurriedly: *David was scribbling notes.* —*n.* 1. meaningless marks. 2. hasty or poor handwriting.

script (skript) *n.* 1. handwriting, esp. when in a special or elegant style. 2. the text of a play, film, etc. 3. an answer paper in an examination.

scroll (skrōl) *n.* 1. a roll of stiff paper or parchment, bearing writing and usu. very old. 2. anything shaped like a scroll.

scrub[1] (skrub) *vb.* **scrubbing, scrubbed.** 1. to clean or wash (clothes, a floor, etc.) by means of very hard rubbing, usu. with a brush. 2. (informal) to cancel: *they scrubbed the idea.* —*n.* the action or an instance of scrubbing.

scrub[2] (skrub) *n.* 1. low-growing trees, shrubs, and bushes collectively, usu. growing on poor soil. 2. an area covered with this.

scruple ('skrōōpəl) *n.* a doubt or hesitation caused by an uneasy conscience: *I had scruples about borrowing his bicycle without asking him.* —*vb.* **scrupling, scrupled.** to feel such doubts. **scrupulous** ('skrōōpyōōləs) *adj.* 1. avoiding doing anything morally wrong. 2. paying great attention to details. —**'scrupulously** *adv.*

scrutiny ('skrōōtini) *n.,pl.* **scrutinies.** a very careful and close inspection, check, or examination. **'scrutinize** *vb.* **scrutinizing, scrutinized.** to carry out such an examination.

sculpture ('skulpchə) *n.* 1. the art of creating figures and models of people, animals, etc., by carving stone or wood, or modelling clay. 2. the work of art created by sculpting. **sculpt** *vb.* to create or make as a sculpture. **'sculptor** *n.* a person who makes sculpture.

scum (skum) *n.* the impure or filthy material that floats on top of a liquid or a pond.

sea (sē) *n.* 1. an ocean or part of an ocean; extensive body of salt water. 2. a very large freshwater or saltwater lake: *the Dead Sea.* 3. anything like a sea in appearance: *from the stage he looked down on a sea of faces.* **at sea** 1. out on the sea in a ship, etc. 2. confused; not knowing what to do.

seagull ('sēgul) *n.* See GULL.

seal[1] (sēl) *n.* 1. a stamp or ring, esp. a personal or official one, which, when pressed into soft wax, leaves a clear mark as an indication of authority or genuineness. 2. the mark made in this way. 3. a piece of wax placed over a letter, etc., in such a way that it must be broken before the letter can be opened. 4. anything that closes another thing or keeps it secret. —*vb.* 1. to fix a seal to a paper, letter, etc. 2. to fasten or stick (something) down: *she sealed the envelope.*

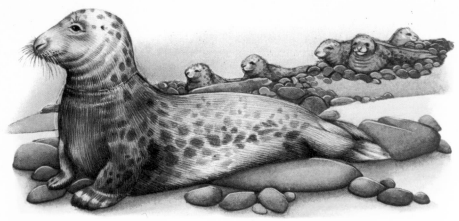
seal

seal² (sēl) *n.* 1. a flesh-eating sea animal having flippers instead of feet and bearing its young on land. 2. the fur or skin of this animal used to make clothes, shoes, etc.

seam (sēm) *n.* 1. the line along which two pieces of material have been joined together. 2. a long thinnish underground layer of mineral, rock, etc.: *a coal seam.* —*vb.* to join two pieces of material by means of a seam.

search (sûch) *vb.* 1. to examine carefully the contents of (a room, etc.), looking for something. 2. to look through the clothing and home of (a person) looking for weapons, evidence, etc. **search me** (informal) I have no idea. —*n.* the action or an instance of searching.

season ('sēzən) *n.* 1. one of the four main parts of the year, each marked by its own weather conditions; spring, summer, autumn, and winter. 2. the time when certain animals and birds may be hunted: *the grouse-shooting season.* 3. the appropriate time for a sport or other activity: *the cricket season.* **in season** 1. (of animals) ready for shooting. 2. (of animals) ready for mating. 3. (of vegetables, fruits, etc.) ready for picking and eating. **season ticket** a ticket that may be used any number of times over a stated time period. —*vb.* 1. to spice or flavour with herbs, etc. 2. to make more mature or tougher by exposing to weather, by drying etc.: *to season wood.* **'seasonable** *adj.* suitable for a particular occasion or season. —**'seasonably** *adv.*

seat (sēt) *n.* 1. a chair, bench, stool, or other object upon which one may sit. 2. the buttocks or bottom. 3. a way of sitting, esp. on horses: *the rider had a good seat.* 4. a central point: *the seat of government.* 5. the area or town rep-resented by a Member of Parliament. —*vb.* 1. to cause to sit down. 2. to be able to provide seats for: *this car seats six people.*

seaweed ('sēwēd) *n.* a plant growing in the sea. Seaweeds are often ALGAE.

second¹ ('sekənd) *adj.* 1. following after the first: *a second glass of milk.* 2. the same as; identical to in function, behaviour, purpose, etc.: *a second Hitler.* —*adv.* after the first: *he came second in the competition.* —*n.* 1. someone or something that comes second in rank, position, quality, etc. 2. a person helping or assisting a boxer, etc. —*vb.* 1. to support or encourage (a boxer, etc.). 2. to support (an idea put forward by someone else) at a meeting.

second² ('sekənd) *n.* 1. a period of time lasting one sixtieth of a minute. 2. (in geometry) an angle equal to one sixtieth of a MINUTE¹.

secondary ('sekəndəri) *adj.* second in rank, importance, authority, etc. **secondary school** a school for children over the age of 11 (or sometimes over the age of 13).

secondhand ('sekəndhand) *adj.* 1. not new; owned or used by someone else: *secondhand furniture.* 2. not fresh or original: *a secondhand report.* 3. dealing in secondhand goods.

secret ('sēkrit) *adj.* kept hidden by the few people who know of it; not widely known: *a secret passage.* —*n.* something known to only a very few people. **'secrecy** *n.* the habit of having and keeping secrets.

secretary ('sekritəri) *n.,pl.* **sec-retaries.** 1. a person who deals with the daily work of a business or other organization, writing or typing let-ters and keeping records. 2. a minister looking after a government depart-ment.

section ('sekshən) *n.* 1. a part; divi-sion: *a section of a book.* 2. a thin slice of something, put under a microscope for examination. 3. a diagram or drawing of an object or animal as if part of it had been cut away to show the inside of it. —*vb.* to cut or slice into sections. —**'sectional** *adj.* —**'sectionally** *adv.*

secure (si'kyōōə) *adj.* 1. safe; pro-tected from danger. 2. firmly in place; fixed. 3. preventing escape, failure, etc.; strong: *a secure prison.* —*vb.* **sec-uring, secured.** 1. to make secure. 2. to obtain for oneself: *Julie secured a good teaching job.* —**se'curely** *adv.* —**se'curity** *n.*

see¹ (sē) *vb.* **seeing, saw, seen.** 1. to experience (something) with the sense of sight; view with one's eyes. 2. to understand: *he saw what they meant.* 3. to meet either by chance or by appointment: *she went to see her mother.* 4. to accompany (someone): *he saw her home.* 5. to make sure: *see that you do your homework.* **see about** to attend to; find out about. **see off** 1. to watch the departure of. 2. to send away roughly; drive off. **see through** 1. to help (a person) through a difficulty. 2. to be undeceived by: *he saw through the trick.*

see² (sē) *n.* the authority of a pope, archbishop, or bishop or the area con-trolled.

seed (sēd) *n.* 1. the tiny object from which a plant grows. 2. an embryo. 3. (tennis) a player who is seeded (vb. def. 3). **go** (*or* **run) to seed.** 1. to stop producing flowers, etc., making only seed. 2. to become shabby; lose fresh-ness. —*vb.* 1. to sow or plant seed. 2. to remove seeds from. 3. (tennis) to put competitors in groups so that the best players do not meet until the later events. **'seedy** *adj.* **seedier, seediest.** 1. gone to seed. 2. shabby; without freshness. 3. (informal) ill; unwell.

seek (sēk) *vb.* **seeking, sought.** 1. to look for; search for: *he sought his brother.* 2. to try to get: *he sought his fortune.* 3. to attempt: *they sought to escape.*

seem (sēm) *vb.* to appear to be; give the impression of being: *this salesman seems honest.*

segment ('segmənt) *n.* a small part of something, esp. a part that can be easily separated from the whole: *an orange can be divided into segments.*

seize (sēz) **seizing, seized.** *vb.* 1. to grab suddenly; grasp. 2. to attack or affect suddenly: *horror seized them.* 3. to capture. 4. to take away; confiscate. **seize up** to get jammed: *the machine seized up.* —**seizure** ('sēzhə) *n.*

seldom ('seldəm) *adv.* not often.

select (si'lekt) *vb.* to choose; pick out: *he selected the best apple.* —*adj.* most desirable; best. —**se'lective** *adj.* —**se'lection** *n.*

self (self) *n.,pl.* **selves.** 1. the individual character or identity of a person or thing; identity. 2. personal interest. —*pron.* (combined with *my-, your-, him-, her-, it-, our-, them-*): *I myself did it; Bill hurt himself.*

self-centred (self'sentəd) *adj.* concerned only with oneself and one's own interests; not caring about other people and their affairs.

self-control (selfkən'trōl) *n.* the ability to keep one's temper, emotions, feelings, actions, etc., under control.

self-defence (selfdi'fens) *n.* 1. the act of defending oneself, esp. by means of some form of unarmed combat. 2. (law) the use of reasonable force against an attacker.

selfish ('selfish) *adj.* caring only for oneself and one's own interests, comfort, pleasure, etc., without caring about anyone else. —**'selfishly** *adv.* —**'selfishness** *n.*

self-service (self'sûvis) *adj.* (of shops, restaurants, etc.) having all the goods, food, etc., set out on shelves so that customers can help themselves and pay when they have collected all they want.

sell (sel) *vb.* **selling, sold.** 1. to transfer (property) to someone else in return for money. 2. to offer for sale. 3. to betray or surrender (something) for a price. **sell off** to get rid of by selling cheaply. **sell out** 1. to have no more of a certain article for sale. 2. to desert one's friends in favour of an enemy. **sell up** to give up one's business by selling all one's goods.

semicircle ('semisûkəl) *n.* half a circle.

segment

semicolon ('semikōlən) *n.* a punctuation mark (;) indicating a longer pause than a comma, but a shorter pause than a full stop.

semifinal ('semifīnəl) *n.* a sporting event coming immediately before the final one in a competition, which decides who shall compete in that final event. **semi'finalist** *n.* a player or team in a semifinal.

senate ('senit) *n.* 1. a political council, esp. the higher division of parliament in certain countries, such as the U.S.A., where laws are discussed, proposed, and made into law or rejected. 2. the chief political body in ancient Rome. **'senator** *n.* a member of a senate. —**senatorial** (seni'tôriəl) *adj.*

send (send) *vb.* **sending, sent.** 1. to cause (someone or something) to go or be carried somewhere: *he sent the parcel by airmail.* 2. to bring into a particular state or condition: *the flies sent the horses mad.* **send for** ask for (someone) to come or for (something) to be brought. **send packing** (informal) to get rid of (someone) very quickly and often roughly. **send up** (informal) to make fun of. **'sendup** *n.* a mocking imitation.

senior ('sēniə) *adj.* 1. higher in rank: *a senior officer.* 2. superior in age, experience, length of service, etc.: *Jones is senior to Lewis.* 3. the older of two people, esp. the father of a man who has the same name: *John Smith, Senior.* —*n.* someone who is senior. —**seniority** (sēni'oriti) *n.*

sensation (sen'sāshən) *n.* 1. an impression of something received by any or all of the senses: *a sensation of warmth.* 2. something which creates great excitement, interest, curiosity, etc.: *the circus was a sensation.* **sen'sational** *adj.* creating great excitement. —**sen'sationally** *adv.*

sense (sens) *n.* 1. one of the five abilities connected with certain organs in the body by which external things are observed; sight, smell, touch, hearing, and taste. 2. intelligence and good judgment; wisdom. 3. knowledge of something and of its proper use: *a sense of justice.* 4. the meaning of something. 5. **senses** (*pl.*) intelligent or responsible behaviour; awareness: *his father's warning brought him to his senses.* **common sense** practical ability or intelligence. **make sense** to have a meaning. **make sense of** to work out the meaning; understand. **common sense** practical ability or intelligence. **sixth sense** the mental ability that makes some people think they are aware of an event or situation that they cannot observe with any of the ordinary five senses. **'senseless** *adj.* unreasonable. —*vb.* **sensing, sensed.** to have a feeling or impression: *he sensed it would rain.*

sensible ('sensibəl) *adj.* having or showing good judgment, common sense, or understanding; reasonable. —**'sensibly** *adv.*

sensitive ('sensitiv) *adj.* 1. easily affected, stimulated, or stirred by something: *people's eyes are sensitive to light.* 2. showing gentleness or consideration: *the sick puppy needed sensitive treatment.* 3. sharp; keen: *bats have very sensitive hearing.* —**sensi'tivity** *n.*

sentence ('sentəns) *n.* 1. a word or group of words that makes sense if read alone and expresses a statement, command, question, etc. 2. a legal punishment pronounced by a court upon a convicted criminal. —*vb.* **sentencing, sentenced.** to condemn; pass sentences upon: *he was sentenced to five years in prison.*

sentiment ('sentimənt) *n.* 1. emotion or feeling, or an instance of this. 2. one of the finer emotions, such as joy, love, or pity. 3. appeal to the emotions as expressed in literature, music, or art. 4. often **sentiments** (*pl.*) opinion; feeling: *he expressed his sentiments.* **senti'mental** *adj.* appealing to the emotions, esp. in an unnecessarily extreme way. —**sentimen'tality** *n.* —**senti'mentally** *adv.*

sentry ('sentri) *n.,pl.* **sentries.** a soldier acting as a guard or watchman.

separate *vb.* ('sepərāt) **separating, separated.** 1. to divide or become divided; split up. 2. to stand between, often as a barrier: *a hedge separates the two gardens.* —*adj.* ('seprit) separated; independent: *the teachers sat at separate tables.* —'**separately** *adv.* —sepa'**ration** *n.*

septic ('septik) *adj.* (of a wound) poisoned or infected by germs.

serene (sə'rēn) *adj.* 1. calm; at peace and untroubled. 2. bright and clear: *serene light.* —se'**renely** *adv.* —**serenity** (sə'reniti) *n.*

sergeant ('sâjənt) *n.* 1. a policeman just below the rank of inspector and above that of constable. 2. a military officer one rank higher than a corporal.

serial ('siəriəl) *n.* a story published or broadcast in regular parts. —*adj.* relating to, arranged in, or belonging to a series. '**serially** *adv.* one after the other.

series ('siərēz) *n.,pl.* **series.** a succession of people, events, things, etc., arranged in a logical order.

serious ('siəriəs) *adj.* 1. grave; thoughtful: *a serious boy.* 2. sincerely or earnestly meant: *a serious suggestion.* 3. not easily or lightly dealt with: *a serious problem.* 4. having important and often dangerous results: *a serious car crash.* —'**seriously** *adv.* —'**seriousness** *n.*

sermon ('sûmən) *n.* 1. a speech delivered by a priest in a church service, usu. based on the Bible and making a moral or religious point. 2. any speech on a serious subject, esp. one that is long and tedious.

serpent ('sûpənt) *n.* 1. a snake. 2. the Devil. 3. any treacherous, cunning, or sly person.

serum ('siərəm) *n.* 1. the thin clear liquid forming part of the blood. 2. a dose of this fluid used to make another person or animal immune from a disease.

servant ('sûvənt) *n.* a person who serves, esp. a person employed to do domestic work in return for wages and a place to live. **civil servant** see under CIVIL.

serve (sûv) *vb.* **serving, served.** 1. to work for (someone): *he served the firm loyally for 35 years.* 2. to wait at table.

3. to obey and submit to: *to serve God.* 4. to be useful to; help: *to serve one's country.* 5. to carry out the duties of an office, membership of something, etc.: *he served as President.* 6. to go through (a prison sentence). 7. (in tennis, etc.) to put (the ball) into play. **it serves him right** he got just what he deserved. —*n.* (tennis) the action or an instance of putting the ball into play.

service ('sûvis) *n.* 1. the work or actions of a person who serves. 2. help, assistance, or use. 3. an action or piece of work carried out for someone in return for money, esp. such work done by an official governmental organization: *the railway service.* 4. duty carried out as part of one's office, as a member of the armed forces, etc., or the time during which one occupies such a position. 5. a religious ceremony at a church. 6. the action or an instance of serving in tennis. 7. **services** (*pl.*) the army, navy, or air force. **senior service** the Royal Navy. —*vb.* **servicing, serviced.** to repair or check (machinery, a car, etc.).

serviette (sûvi'et) *n.* a table napkin, esp. one made of paper.

session ('seshən) *n.* 1. the period of time occupied by some activity, such as a meeting, game, or part of a game, etc. 2. a single meeting of parliament. 3. the part of the year during which a school, university, parliament, or law court is in operation.

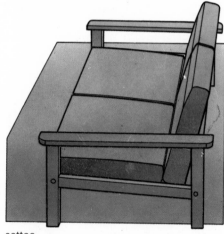
settee

settee (se'tē) *n.* a long seat with a back and arms; couch.

settle ('setəl) *vb.* **settling, settled.** 1. to make final: *they settled an agreement on prices.* 2. (often + *up*) to pay (a bill). 3. to go and live or cause to go and live in (a country, district, etc.). 4.

to make or become calm. 5. to come to rest. **settle down** 1. to become less agitated. 2. to adopt regular habits in life, esp. after marrying. '**settlement** *n.* 1. the act of settling. 2. something settled, e.g. a legal agreement. 3. a small colony or group of dwellings.

sever ('sevə) *vb.* to cut or be cut off; separate. —'**severance** *n.*

several ('sevərəl) *adj.* 1. many; three or more. 2. separate; distinct: *they went their several ways.* '**severally** *adv.* separately; distinctly.

severe (si'viə) *adj.* 1. strict; stern. 2. harsh; hard to bear: *severe punishment.* 3. serious; grave: *a severe illness.* —se'**verely** *adv.* —**severity** (si'veriti) *n.,pl.* **severities.**

sew (sō) *vb.* **sewing, sewed, sewn.** 1. to use needle and thread, esp. to join one piece of material to another. 2. to make or repair by sewing. 3. (often + *up*) to fasten or close with stitches.

sewer ('sōōə) *n.* an underground pipe or passage through which waste material is carried away. '**sewerage** *n.* the system of sewers serving a town or city.

sex (seks) *n.* 1. the quality or character of being either male or female. 2. men or women considered collectively: *equality of the sexes.* 3. (also **sexual intercourse**) the act of making physical love. '**sexy** *adj.* **sexier, sexiest.** physically attractive to someone of the opposite sex. —**sexual** ('seksyōōəl) *adj.* —**sexu'ality** *n.* —'**sexually** *adv.*

shabby ('shabi) *adj.* **shabbier, shabbiest.** 1. showing signs of wear; in a bad state of repair: *a shabby office.* 2. (of a person) wearing worn-out clothes. 3. mean or unfair: *a shabby swindle.* —'**shabbily** *adv.* —'**shabbiness** *n.*

shade (shād) *n.* 1. an area of relative darkness or coolness, esp. as produced by something standing in the way of the full light and heat from the sun. 2. something that shields a source of light: *that lamp needs a shade.* 3. a variation in colour: *a deep shade of pink.* 4. a tiny amount: *move it a shade more to the right.* —*vb.* **shading, shaded.** 1. to protect from strong light and heat. 2. to make darker or add colour to (a drawing, etc.). '**shady** *adj.* **shadier, shadiest.** 1. producing or positioned in shade. 2. dishonest: *a shady character.*

shadow ('shadō) *n.* 1. the dark image of an opaque object produced on a surface when the object stands between the surface and a light shining onto it. 2. shade. 3. a person following somebody. —*vb.* 1. to cast a shadow upon. 2. to follow closely, esp. secretly. **shadow cabinet** (in British politics) a group of opposition M.P.'s who would, if in power, be members of the CABINET. '**shadowy** *adj.* 1. full of shadow. 2. secret, often dishonest. 3. vague; not clear: *a shadowy idea.*

shaft (shâft) *n.* 1. a long smooth rod forming the body of a spear or arrow. 2. the handle of an axe, etc. 3. a pole attached to the front of a cart, carriage, etc., to which the animal pulling the vehicle is harnessed. 4. a beam of light. 5. a long, narrow, vertical passage in a coal mine, etc.

shaggy ('shagi) *adj.* **shaggier, shaggiest.** 1. having long, untidy hair: *a shaggy dog.* 2. (of hair) long and untidy: *a shaggy beard.* **shaggy dog story** a long story with a silly or pointless joke at the end.

shake (shāk) *vb.* **shaking, shook, shaken.** 1. to move or cause to move up and down or from side to side very quickly. 2. to cause to tremble; upset. —*n.* the action or an instance of shaking or being shaken. '**shaky** *adj.* **shakier, shakiest.** 1. trembling. 2. unsteady; unsafe.

shallow ('shalō) *adj.* 1. not deep. 2. superficial; lacking seriousness or thoughtfulness: *a shallow person.* '**shallows** *pl.n.* a shallow part of a body of water: *children were swimming in the shallows.*

shame (shām) *n.* 1. an unpleasant emotion caused by the thought that one has done something wrong. 2. a disappointment: *it's a shame the weather is bad.* —*vb.* **shaming, shamed.** to cause a feeling of shame or embarrassment in (someone). —'**shameful** *adj.* —'**shamefully** *adv.* —'**shamefulness** *n.* —'**shameless** *adj.* —'**shamelessly** *adv.* —'**shamelessness** *n.*

shampoo (sham'pōō) *n.* 1. a soapy liquid or cream preparation for washing the hair. 2. the process of washing hair with shampoo. —*vb.* **shampooing, shampooed.** to wash with shampoo.

shape (shāp) *n.* 1. a physical form or the outline of something. 2. the appropriate or original outline of something: *this old sweater has lost its shape.* 3. a condition, state, or way of being: *his bank balance was in poor shape.* —*vb.* **shaping, shaped.** 1. to mould or give a particular shape to. 2. to decide or determine. '**shapely** *adj.* **shapelier, shapeliest.** having a pleasing or attractive shape. —'**shapeless** *adj.*

share (sheə) *vb.* **sharing, shared.** 1. to divide (something) up and give out the parts: *she shared the cake between the children.* 2. to have or use with another person or persons: *we shared a taxi to the station.* —*n.* 1. a portion; part. 2. one of the equal parts into which the ownership of a company is divided.

shark (shâk) *n.* 1. a large and dangerous fish with several rows of sharp teeth and a tough skin. 2. a person who cheats; swindler.

sharp (shâp) *adj.* 1. suitable for cutting or piercing: *a sharp blade.* 2. having an acute angle; not gradual: *a sharp bend.* 3. sudden; unexpected: *a sharp rise in prices.* 4. (of a taste) acid; bitter. 5. (of a musical note) raised by half a TONE above its normal pitch: *F sharp.* 6. out of tune by being too high in pitch. 7. bright; keen; alert. —*n.* a note that is raised by half a tone above its normal pitch. —*adv.* precisely; exactly: *she came at 10.30 sharp.* '**sharpen** *vb.* to make or become sharp or sharper. —'**sharply** *adv.* —'**sharpness** *n.*

shatter ('shatə) *vb.* 1. to break or cause to break suddenly into pieces. 2. to destroy suddenly: *the bad news shattered her hopes.*

shave (shāv) *vb.* **shaving, shaved.** 1. to remove (hair, bristles, etc.) with a razor or similar cutting implement: *to shave one's face.* 2. to cut off thin slices of (wood, etc.). —*n.* the action or an instance of shaving. **a close shave** a narrow escape. '**shaver** *n.* an electric razor. '**shavings** *pl.n.* thin layers of wood, etc., cut away, e.g. by a chisel, plane, etc.

shawl (shôl) *n.* 1. a square, oblong, or triangular covering for the head, neck, and shoulders, worn by a woman. 2. a similar, usu. woollen, covering in which babies are wrapped.

sheaf (shēf) *n.,pl.* **sheaves** (shēvz). 1. a tied bundle of harvested wheat, rye, or other type of corn. 2. a bundle of anything: *a sheaf of papers.*

shawl

shear (shiə) *vb.* **shearing, sheared, shorn.** to remove wool from (a sheep). **shears** *pl.n.* 1. a large scissor-like tool for cutting garden hedges, etc. 2. a similar instrument for clipping the wool from a sheep.

sheath (shēth) *n.* a protective covering for the blade of a knife or other sharp instrument; anything that fits closely around something else. **sheathe** ('shēdh) *vb.* **sheathing, sheathed.** to put in a sheath; provide with a protective covering.

sheaves (shēvz) *n.* the plural of SHEAF.

shed[1] (shed) *n.* 1. a small building, esp. one outside a house used for storing coal, garden tools, etc. 2. a large building, often open-sided, used for temporary storage or repair work: *a railway shed.*

shed[2] (shed) *vb.* **shedding, shed.** 1. to drop; let go of: *some trees shed their leaves every year.* 2. to throw off: *a duck's oily feathers shed water.*

sheep (shēp) *n.,pl.* **sheep.** an animal related to the goat and often horned, some of whose species are bred for meat, milk, and wool. '**sheepish** *adj.* feeling foolish or embarrassed. '**sheepskin** *n.* the skin of a sheep used for clothing, esp. a coat made of this.

sheer (shiə) *adj.* 1. steep: *a sheer drop from the top of a cliff.* 2. fine; almost transparent: *she wore sheer nylons.* 3. complete; total: *sheer stupidity.*

sheet[1] (shēt) *n.* 1. a large rectangular piece of cotton, linen, nylon, or other cloth that is spread on a bed. 2. a thin, flat, usu. rectangular piece of metal, paper, glass, etc.

sheet² (shēt) *n.* a rope or chain attached to the corner of a sail on a boat in order to control the sail.

sheikh *or* **sheik** (shāk) *n.* (in Arab countries) 1. the head of a family or tribe. 2. a political or religious leader. **'sheikhdom** *or* **'sheikdom** *n.* the area ruled by a sheikh.

shelf (shelf) *n.,pl.* **shelves.** 1. a horizontal piece of wood, metal, etc., fixed to a wall or in a cupboard and used as a place of storage. 2. anything resembling a shelf, e.g. a surface of rock or ice. **shelve** *vb.* **shelving, shelved.** 1. to place on a shelf. 2. to put off dealing with (something): *to shelve a problem.*

shell (shel) *n.* 1. the hard outer covering of some animals, eggs, seeds, or fruits, or the material of which this is made. 2. a discarded animal shell found on the sea shore. 3. a metal case packed with explosives and fired from a cannon or large gun. 4. the frame of anything: *only the shell of the house remained after the fire.* —*vb.* 1. to remove the shell (def. 1) from. 2. to fire shells (def. 3) at.

shellfish ('shelfish) *n.* any sea or river animal with a shell, such as a crab, lobster, oyster, etc.

shelter ('sheltə) *n.* something that gives protection against bad weather, danger, etc. —*vb.* to take or give shelter.

shelve (shelv) *vb.* See under SHELF.

shepherd ('shepəd) *n.* a person employed to look after a flock of sheep. —*vb.* to guide in the manner of someone driving sheep: *the tourists were shepherded around the museum.*

sheriff ('sherif) *n.* 1. the chief official of an English county, who carries out ceremonial duties and takes charge of parliamentary elections. 2. a law officer in a county or other administrative area in any of the states of the U.S.A.

sherry ('sheri) *n.,pl.* **sherries.** a type of wine with extra alcohol added, made mainly in Spain. It varies in colour from pale gold to dark brown.

shield (shēld) *n.* 1. a handheld piece of protective armour formerly carried in battle by soldiers. 2. anything that protects or looks like a shield: *the hedge was a shield for the sheep in the blizzard.* —*vb.* to protect; guard.

shells

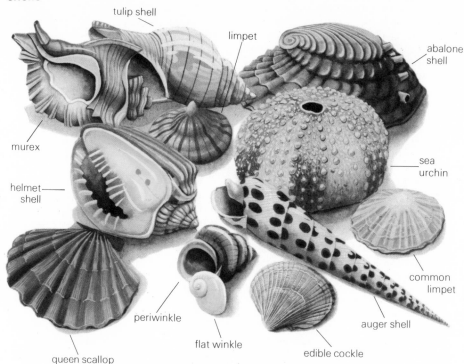

tulip shell
limpet
abalone shell
murex
sea urchin
helmet shell
periwinkle
flat winkle
common limpet
auger shell
queen scallop
edible cockle

shift (shift) *vb.* to move or change or cause to move or change: *he shifted the furniture.* —*n.* 1. a change or movement. 2. a group of workers that takes turns at work with other groups during the day or night. 3. the period worked by such a group: *the night shift is from 10 p.m. till 6 a.m.* 4. a woman's straight loose dress. 5. a clever or dishonest trick. **'shifty** *adj.* **shiftier, shiftiest.** sly; untrustworthy; dishonest.

shin (shin) *n.* the front part of the leg between the knee and the ankle. —*vb.* **shinning, shinned.** to climb by gripping and pulling oneself up, using the hands and legs: *Jack shinned up the tree in no time at all.*

shield

shine (shīn) *vb.* **shining, shone.** 1. to give out or reflect light. 2. to clean and polish (an object) so that it reflects light. 3. to do well: *he shines at swimming.* —*n.* the quality of a reflection: *the shine on the silverware.*

shirt (shût) *n.* a garment of light cloth covering the top half of the body, usu. having buttons down the front. **'T-shirt** *n.* a short-sleeved shirt without buttons, often having a design or writing on the front.

shiver ('shivə) *vb.* to shake or tremble, esp. because of cold or fright. —*n.* a shivering feeling: *a shiver ran down his spine.* **'shivery** *adj.* experiencing or producing shivers.

shoal¹ (shōl) *n.* a large group of fish swimming along close together in the same direction: *a shoal of herring.*

shoal² (shōl) *n.* often **shoals** (*pl.*) a very shallow place in the sea or a river, esp. a bank of sand visible only at low tide.

shock (shok) *n.* 1. a sudden surprise. 2. a violent impact: *shock absorbers.* 3. the sensation caused when an electric current passes through one's body. 4. a medical condition produced as a reaction to fear, injury, etc.: *she's in shock.* —*vb.* 1. to cause a sudden great and usu. unpleasant surprise to (somebody). 2. to cause to suffer an electric shock.

shoe (shoo) *n.* 1. a protective covering for the foot made of leather, wood, plastic, etc. 2. anything resembling a shoe in function or shape. —*vb.* **shoeing, shod.** to supply or fit with shoes.

shone (shon) *vb.* the past tense and past participle of SHINE.

shook (shook) *vb.* the past tense of SHAKE.

shoot (shoot) *vb.* **shooting, shot.** 1. to fire (a gun or similar weapon). 2. to fire (an arrow) from a bow. 3. to kill or wound with a gun, bow, etc. 4. to photograph and make a film of (a scene). 5. to hunt (game). —*n.* 1. a young plant or new part of a plant. 2. an area of land where game is kept for hunting.

shop (shop) *n.* 1. a place where things are bought and sold. 2. a workshop; place where things are made or repaired. —*vb.* **shopping, shopped.** 1. to visit a shop and buy things. 2. to inform the police, etc., about the activities of (a criminal). **'shopping** *n.* 1. the activity of visiting a shop. 2. the things bought at a shop, esp. groceries.

shoplifter ('shoplifta) *n.* a person who steals goods from a shop while pretending to be a customer.

shore (shô) *n.* the land lying next to a large stretch of water such as a lake or sea.

shorn (shôn) *vb.* the past participle of SHEAR.

short (shôt) *adj.* 1. having little length, height, etc. 2. not lasting long: *a short trip.* 3. having less than an appropriate or required length, height, amount, etc.: *our team is two men short.* 4. impolitely abrupt in manner. —*n.* 1. an alcoholic drink, such as gin or whisky, served in a small glass. 2. **shorts** (*pl.*) a pair of short trousers covering the thighs and sometimes extending to the knees. **'shortage** *n.* a lack: *there's a shortage of paper.* **'shorten** *vb.* to make shorter; reduce. **'shortly** *adv.* in a little space of time; very soon. —**'shortness** *n.*

shortcoming ('shôtkuming) *n.* a failure to come up to certain standards; defect.

shot (shot) *vb.* the past tense and past participle of SHOOT. —*n.* 1. the act of firing a gun, shooting an arrow, etc. 2. the sound made by this. 3. an attempt: *he had a shot at becoming president.* 4. the act or result of taking a photograph. 5. an injection. 6. tiny lead balls contained in a cartridge to be fired from a shotgun. **like a shot** (informal) very quickly: *he came like a shot when she called.*

shotgun ('shotgun) *n.* a short-range gun with a long barrel that fires cartridges filled with lead shot.

shoulder ('sholdǝ) *n.* 1. the part of the body between the neck and the top of the arm; the joint that connects the arm to the body. 2. the part of a garment covering the shoulder. 3. the part of an animal where its foreleg joins the rest of its body. 4. a ridge or border at the side of some roads: *the driver stopped on the hard shoulder.* —*vb.* 1. to take or carry on or push with the shoulder. 2. to accept (blame or responsibility).

shout (shout) *vb.* to speak loudly; yell. —*n.* a loud cry.

shove (shuv) *vb.* **shoving, shoved.** to push hard. —*n.* a hard push.

shovel ('shuvǝl) *n.* 1. a tool with a broad blade at the end of a handle, used for moving loose material such as coal, dirt, snow, sand, etc. 2. an instrument resembling this in function. —*vb.* **shovelling, shovelled.** to move by using a shovel.

show (shō) *vb.* **showing, showed, shown.** 1. to cause to be seen; display, esp. to the public. 2. to guide; conduct: *show him out.* 3. to explain; teach: *she showed me how to drive a car.* 4. to prove: *the evidence shows he died yesterday.* **show off** to act in a boastful way. **show up** 1. to embarrass. 2. to arrive or be present. 3. to be seen. —*n.* 1. the act of showing. 2. a public entertainment, esp. one produced at a theatre using much music and dancing. 3. an outdoor event, such as an aircraft display. 4. an appearance; pretence: *he made a show of being poor.* **'showy** *adj.* **showier, showiest.** 1. showing off. 2. visually attractive: *showy flowers.*

shower ('shouǝ) *n.* 1. a sudden brief fall of rain, hail, or snow. 2. (also **shower bath**) a form of bath in which the bather stands under a spray of water. 3. the equipment or place used for this. —*vb.* 1. to cover in the manner of a shower: *he showered me with praise.* 2. to take a shower bath.

shrank (shrangk) *vb.* the past tense of SHRINK.

shred (shred) *n.* 1. a small piece torn or cut from something. 2. a small amount: *there wasn't a shred of proof.* —*vb.* **shredding, shredded** *or* **shred.** to tear or cut into pieces.

shrew (shroo) *n.* 1. a small mouselike animal with a long pointed nose. 2. a bad-tempered woman. **'shrewish** *adj.* (esp. of a woman) bad-tempered; scolding. —**'shrewishly** *adv.* —**'shrewishness** *n.*

shrewd (shrood) *adj.* clever; intelligent; crafty. —**'shrewdly** *adv.* —**'shrewdness** *n.*

shriek (shrēk) *n.* a shrill cry or scream. —*vb.* to utter or say with such a cry.

shrill (shril) *adj.* high-pitched and piercing: *a shrill cry.* —**'shrillness** *n.* —**'shrilly** *adv.*

shrimp (shrimp) *n.* a type of small shellfish, having pale pink edible flesh. —*vb.* to catch shrimps.

shovel

shrine (shrīn) *n.* 1. a building, container, etc., holding a holy object. 2. a place sacred to a person, esp. the place where a saint is buried.

shrink (shringk) *vb.* **shrinking, shrank, shrunk.** 1. to make or become smaller: *my sweater shrank in the washing machine.* 2. to draw back: *he shrank from the idea of hurting the dog.*

shrivel ('shrivǝl) *vb.* **shrivelling, shrivelled.** to make or become smaller, with the surface wrinkling in the process: *the flowers shrivelled in the summer heat.*

shroud (shroud) *n.* 1. a cloth in which a dead body is wrapped. 2. something that covers and conceals: *a shroud of fog.* 3. **shrouds** (*pl.*) ropes holding up a ship's mast or linking a parachutist's harness to the parachute canopy. —*vb.* 1. to wrap (a dead body) in a shroud. 2. to hide: *darkness shrouded the scene.*

shrub (shrub) *n.* any fairly small woody plant with no central stem, such as a bush.

shrug (shrug) *vb.* **shrugging, shrugged.** to raise (the shoulders) as an expression of indifference, doubt, ignorance, helplessness, etc. —*n.* the action or an instance of shrugging.

shrunk (shrungk) *vb.* the past participle of SHRINK.

shrunken (shrungkən) *adj.* made or become less in size: *during the drought the shrunken river could not supply the town with enough water.*

shudder ('shudə) *vb.* to shake or tremble; shiver. —*n.* the action or an instance of shuddering.

shuffle ('shufəl) *vb.* **shuffling, shuffled.** 1. to mix up (playing cards, dominoes, etc.) randomly. 2. to drag or slide the feet along the ground while walking. 3. to fidget from one position to another. —*n.* the action or an instance of shuffling.

shunt (shunt) *vb.* 1. to move (a tram or train) from one line of track to another. 2. (of a train or tram) to move in this way.

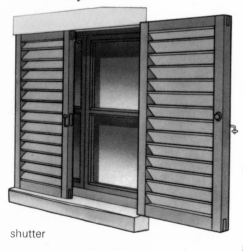
shutter

shut (shut) *vb.* **shutting, shut.** 1. to close or be closed. 2. to secure with a lock, catch, etc. 3. to confine: *she shut the dog in the kitchen.* '**shutter** *n.* 1. a window cover, usu. of wood or metal,

fixed on the outside to keep out sunlight and cold and prevent anyone climbing in. 2. a device in a camera that opens and closes to allow light to pass through the lens to the film.

shy[1] (shī) *adj.* **shyer, shyest** *or* **shier, shiest.** 1. nervous or uncomfortable when with other people. 2. timid or embarrassed: *a shy giggle.* 3. (of animals) very easily frightened. —*vb.* **shying, shied.** (esp. of horses) to move suddenly to one side or rear up when startled.

shy[2] (shī) *vb.* **shying, shied.** (informal) to throw (a stone, ball, etc.). —*n.,pl.* **shies.** (informal) 1. a sudden throw. 2. an attempt; try.

sick (sik) *adj.* 1. unwell; unhealthy. 2. having an attack of vomiting. 3. weary; tired: *he was sick of work.* 4. in bad taste: *a sick joke.*

side (sīd) *n.* 1. any surface of an object that is not the front, back, top, or bottom. 2. any of the surfaces of a solid object: *a cube has six sides.* 3. any of the lines enclosing a square, triangle, etc. 4. either of the two surfaces of a piece of paper or cloth. 5. the area or part of something considered as being to the right or left, east or west, etc., of some central line or point: *the south side of the city.* 6. the right-hand or left-hand part of the human body: *he was shot in the side.* 7. a group, team, or party in competition or disagreement with another one: *our side won the match.* 8. a line of descent: *she has many cousins on her father's side.* —*vb.* **siding, sided.** (+ *with*) to support (one group or party rather than another): *he sided with the Liberals.* '**siding** *n.* a section of railway track branching out from the main line, used for shunting trains, storing goods trains, etc.

sideboard ('sīdbôd) *n.* 1. a piece of dining-room furniture, usu. with cupboards and drawers, used for storing crockery, cutlery, etc. 2. **sideboards** (*pl.*) whiskers on the side of the face.

siege (sēj) *n.* a process used in war in which a fortified position, esp. a town, is surrounded and its supplies are cut off by enemy forces wishing to capture it.

sieve (siv) *n.* a tight net stretched within a frame for separating solids from liquids or large particles from small. **have a head like a sieve** to be very forgetful. —*vb.* **sieving, sieved.** to sift.

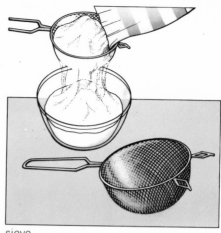
sieve

sift (sift) *vb.* 1. to separate by passing through a sieve. 2. to examine carefully and thoroughly: *the police sifted the evidence.*

sigh (sī) *vb.* to take a deep breath and let it out slowly and with a sound expressing relief, weariness, sadness, etc. —*n.* the action or an instance of sighing.

sight (sīt) *n.* 1. the ability to see; the sense through which the world is observed by means of the eyes. 2. something seen or worth seeing; view: *the snowy mountains were a fine sight.* 3. the appearance of something to the eyes: *I'm sick of the sight of you.* 4. also **sights** (*pl.*) a device on a gun to assist the user's aim. 5. an odd, unusual, or funny appearance: *what a sight she looks in that dress.* —*vb.* 1. to see: *after six days at sea they sighted land.* 2. to aim (a gun) by means of a sight.

sign (sīn) *n.* 1. a gesture, symbol, or mark standing for something or pointing the way to some place. 2. an event indicating a present or future happening: *a red sky at night is a sign of good weather.* 3. an indication; trace: *there was not a sign of damp in the room.* 4. a traffic notice, type of advertisement, etc.: *an inn sign.* —*vb.* 1. to write one's name by hand on (a paper). 2. to gesture; indicate. 3. (+ *on* or *up*) to enter into employment, esp. in the army, navy, or air force.

signal ('signəl) *n.* 1. a sign or message passed by signs. 2. a radio transmission. —*vb.* **signalling, signalled.** to indicate by means of a signal. —*adj.* noteworthy; outstanding: *a signal failure.* **signature** ('signəchə) *n.* the name, initials, or mark of a person written by himself, by which he is identified.

silent ('sīlənt) *adj.* 1. having or making no sound; still. 2. not speaking; not mentioning a particular subject: *he kept silent about his play.* —'**silence** *n.* —'**silently** *adv.*

silhouette (silōō'et) *n.* the shape of an object seen as dark against a bright background.

silk (silk) *n.* the soft shiny fabric made from the thread produced by the caterpillar (**silkworm**) of a certain moth. —*adj.* made of silk. '**silky** *adj.* **silkier, silkiest.** soft and smooth, like silk. —'**silkiness** *n.*

sill (sil) *n.* a ledge made of timber or stone at the base of a window.

silo ('sīlō) *n.,pl.* **silos.** an airtight tower, pit, or other chamber in which green grass is stored for winter food for animals, or in which grain is kept. '**silage** *n.* the grass kept in a silo.

silt (silt) *n.* a fine mass of earth or mud particles that settles to the bottom in water, as in a river. —*vb.* to block or be blocked up with silt.

silver ('silvə) *n.* 1. a greyish-white shiny metal used for making coins, jewellery, spoons, etc. Chemical symbol: Ag. 2. coins, household articles, etc., made of silver. —*adj.* made of, producing, or having the colour of silver.

similar ('similə) *adj.* (often + *to*) like; resembling: *Bob's house is very similar to Jason's.* **similarity** (simi'lariti) *n.,pl.* **similarities.** the condition of being similar or something that is similar. —'**similarly** *adv.*

simmer ('simə) *vb.* 1. to boil gently. 2. to be at a high pitch of emotion, anger, or excitement. **simmer down** to calm down; be less agitated. —*n.* the process of simmering.

simple ('simpəl) *adj.* **simpler, simplest.** 1. easy to do or understand; not difficult: *a simple problem.* 2. ordinary; plain: *simple food.* 3. not clever; easily deceived or tricked. —**simplicity** (sim'plisiti) *n.* —'**simply** *adv.*

simplify ('simplifī) *vb.* **simplifying, simplified.** to make simple or less difficult. **simplifi'cation** *n.* the action or an instance of simplifying.

sin (sin) *n.* 1. the action or an instance of breaking a moral or religious law, esp. one considered to have been given by God. 2. wickedness; immoral behaviour. —*vb.* **sinning, sinned.** to commit a wicked deed. —'**sinful** *adj.* —'**sinfully** *adv.* —'**sinner** *n.*

sincere (sin'siə) *adj.* 1. honest; true. 2. genuine; real: *sincere friendship.* —**sincerity** (sin'seriti) *n.* —**sin'cerely** *adv.*

sinew ('sinyōō) *n.* 1. a strong cordlike part of the body that connects a muscle to a bone; TENDON. 2. (also **sinews**) strength; muscle. '**sinewy** *adj.* 1. of or like a sinew; stringy. 2. strong; powerful; vigorous.

singe (sinj) *vb.* **singeing, singed.** 1. to burn slightly; scorch. 2. to remove (hair) by scorching. —*n.* a slight superficial burn.

single ('singgəl) *adj.* 1. for, used by, or consisting of one only or one part only; not double or complex. 2. separate; individual. 3. unmarried. —*n.* a single ticket; a ticket for a journey in one direction only. '**single-'handed** *adj.,adv.* working alone; without help from anyone. '**single-'minded** *adj.* having one aim or purpose in view. —**single-'mindedly** *adv.*

singular ('singgyōōlə) *adj.* unusual; odd; strange. —*n.* a grammatical form indicating that a word refers to only one person, concept, or thing. —**singularity** (singgyōō'lariti) *n.* —'**singularly** *adv.*

sinister ('sinistə) *adj.* indicating or threatening future evil; unlucky.

sink (singk) *vb.* **sinking, sank, sunk.** 1. to fall or move or cause to fall or move slowly downwards, esp. below the surface of a liquid. 2. to go (into the mind); penetrate. 3. to pass to a lower or worse state: *my spirits sank.* —*n.* a fixed kitchen basin with water taps and a waste-water outlet.

siphon ('sīfən) *n.* 1. a bent tube or channel for transferring liquid from one level to a lower level by way of a higher level. 2. a bottle equipped with a lever and tube for squirting out soda water or similar liquid using the pressure of gas. —*vb.* to draw off by means of a siphon.

siren ('sīrən) *n.* a device for producing a loud warning or signalling sound.

site (sīt) *n.* 1. an area of ground on which a building is to be erected or where something is to be found or is being dug up. 2. a position; situation: *the hill is a good site for a picnic.*

situate ('sityōōāt) *vb.* **situating, situated.** to put in a special area, position, or set of circumstances. **situ'ation** *n.* 1. a position; place. 2. a state or condition.

size (sīz) *n.* 1. the largeness or smallness of a thing. 2. specific measurements of clothes, gloves, shoes, etc. —*vb.* **sizing, sized.** (+ *up*) to make a judgment about (a situation, etc.).

skate[1] (skāt) *n.* 1. a special boot or sandal mounted on a blade (ice skate) or on rollers (roller skate). 2. a period of skating. —*vb.* **skating, skated.** to move on skates.

skate[2] (skāt) *n.* an edible fish of the ray family.

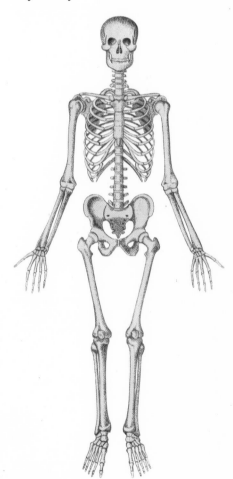

skeleton

skeleton ('skelitən) *n.* 1. the bony frame supporting a person's or animal's body and covered by skin, hide, etc. 2. the basic part of something. —*adj.* consisting of the smallest number necessary for handling something: *a skeleton crew.*

sketch (skech) *n.* 1. a drawing made in preparation for a painting, model, construction of a building, etc. 2. an artistic drawing often intended to catch a temporary effect of light, movement, mood, etc. 3. a short piece of writing giving a brief idea or outline of something. 4. a short humorous stage entertainment or play. —*vb.* (sometimes + *out*) to make a sketch of. '**sketchy** *adj.* **sketchier, sketchiest.** lacking detail; slight. —'**sketchily** *adv.* —'**sketchiness** *n.*

skewer ('skyo͞oə) *n.* a long pointed metal or wooden pin for keeping meat together as it is being cooked. —*vb.* to stick a skewer through (meat).

ski (skē) *n.* 1. either of two long flat strips of wood or metal strapped to boots and used for moving over snow. 2. similar strips used for gliding over water. —*vb.* **skiing, skied.** to slide over snow or water on skis, esp. as a sport.

skid (skid) *vb.* **skidding, skidded.** (of a car, motorcycle, etc.) to slide sideways out of control. —*n.* the action or an instance of skidding.

skies (skīz) *n.* the plural of SKY.

skill (skil) *n.* 1. the knowledge of or ability connected with a particular science, sport, etc. 2. the ability needed to do something to a high standard. —'**skilful** *adj.* —'**skilfully** *adv.* —'**skilfulness** *n.*

skim (skim) *vb.* **skimming, skimmed.** 1. to glide rapidly along or just above the surface of: *the seagull skims the waves.* 2. to remove floating matter from the surface of: *Ann skimmed the soup.* 3. (often + *through*) to read or examine quickly or hurriedly. **skimmed milk** milk with the fat removed.

skin (skin) *n.* 1. the outer covering of the body. 2. the outer covering of an animal's body with or without the hair growing on it, esp. after being removed from the dead animal. 3. a water container, form of clothing, etc., made from an animal skin. 4. the outer covering of a banana and certain other fruit. —*vb.* **skinning, skinned.** to take the skin off: *I skinned my knee when I fell.* '**skinny** *adj.* **skinnier, skinniest.** very thin.

skip (skip) *vb.* **skipping, skipped.** 1. to make small jumps on one spot over a swinging rope. 2. to leave out (something), esp. when reading hastily: *she skipped the third chapter.* 3. to move about quickly, esp. by small jumps. 4. (informal) to escape: *the thief skipped with the money.* —*n.* a small jump or leap.

skirt (skût) *n.* 1. a woman's outer garment fitting round the waist and covering all or part of the legs. 2. the lower part of a dress. 3. **skirts** (*pl.*) the edge of something: *the skirts of the city.* —*vb.* to be on or move along or around the border or edge of: *he skirted around the subject of marriage.*

skull (skul) *n.* the bony framework of the head enclosing the brain.

skunk (skungk) *n.* a small North American animal similar to the weasel that gives out an evil-smelling liquid when attacked.

skunk

sky (skī) *n.,pl.* **skies.** the apparent rooflike space above the earth, where the sun, moon, stars, and clouds are seen. **the sky's the limit** there is no limit. —*vb.* **skying, skied.** to raise or throw high into the air. '**skylight** *n.* a glass window set into a roof to let in light. '**skyline** *n.* the apparent boundary between the earth and the sky; horizon, esp. as seen in a city. '**skyscraper** *n.* an extremely tall building, having many floors.

slab (slab) *n.* 1. a flat piece of stone or concrete. 2. a large heavy piece or chunk. 3. a large thick slice of bread, cake, etc.

slack (slak) *adj.* 1. not tight; loose; limp. 2. lazy; relaxed; inactive. 3. not strict. 4. not busy. —*n.* 1. the loose part of a rope, garment, etc. 2. **slacks** (*pl.*) loose trousers for informal wear. —*vb.* 1. (also **slacken**) to make or become slack. 2. to be idle; fail in one's work, duty, etc.

slam (slam) *vb.* **slamming, slammed.** 1. to shut noisily or violently. 2. to throw down or strike forcefully. 3. (informal) to blame or criticize very harshly. —*n.* 1. the action or an instance of slamming. 2. the sound of a slam.

slang (slang) *n.* a form of language different from standard speech, often thought to be unacceptable in dignified conversation. —*vb.* (informal) to scold or insult roughly.

slant (slânt) *vb.* 1. to slope or cause to slope. 2. to change (a discussion, report, etc.) slightly, usu. to prove a point. —*n.* 1. a sloping line, surface, or movement. 2. a point of view; way of looking at a thing.

slap (slap) *vb.* **slapping, slapped.** to strike with the palm of the hand. **slap down** 1. (informal) to speak sharply to (someone): *she slapped him down for interrupting.* 2. to put (something) down sharply and noisily: *he slapped the papers down on the table.* —*n.* a blow of the open hand or the noise of this. —*adv.* straight; directly: *her bicycle ran slap into the hedge.*

slapstick ('slapstik) *n.* (also **slapstick comedy**) a noisy, zany form of comedy gaining its humour from physical effects.

slash (slash) *vb.* 1. to make long cuts in with a knife, sword, whip, etc. 2. to reduce a great deal: *prices were slashed in the sale.* 3. to criticize harshly. —*n.* 1. a long cut or gash. 2. the act of slashing.

slate (slāt) *n.* 1. a dense grey rock easily split into thin plates. 2. a piece of this used in covering roofs or formerly as a writing tablet. 3. a dark grey-blue colour. **a clean slate** a fresh beginning. —*vb.* **slating, slated.** 1. to cover (a roof) with slates. 2. to criticize; find fault with: *the critic slated the new film.*

slaughter ('slôtə) *vb.* 1. to kill (an animal) for food. 2. to kill (large numbers of people). —*n.* the act or an instance of slaughtering, esp. large numbers of people.

slave (slāv) *n.* 1. a person legally owned by another. 2. a person forced to work for and obey another against his will, or in bad conditions for little or no pay. —*vb.* **slaving, slaved.** to work like a slave. '**slavery** *n.* the condition of being a slave or the system of owning slaves.

sledge

sledge (slej) *n.* (also **sled**) 1. a vehicle mounted on smooth strips of wood or metal and often drawn by horses or dogs, used for travelling or carrying goods over snow. 2. a toboggan. —*vb.* **sledging, sledged.** (also **sled**) to carry on or travel by sledge.

sledgehammer ('slejhamə) *n.* a large heavy hammer.

sleek (slēk) *adj.* 1. (of hair or an animal) smooth; glossy. 2. having a neat well-groomed appearance or smooth manner. —*vb.* to make sleek; smooth.

sleep (slēp) *n.* 1. a natural regularly occurring state of unconsciousness or complete rest with the eyes closed, usu. at night. 2. a period of this: *a good sleep.* —*vb.* **sleeping, slept.** 1. to take rest; be in the state of sleep. 2. to provide sleeping accommodation for: *we can sleep five in our house.* '**sleeper** *n.* 1. a person who sleeps. 2. a horizontal wooden support for railway lines. 3. a train carriage that provides sleeping accommodation. —'**sleepless** *adj.* —'**sleepy** *adj.* **sleepier, sleepiest.**

sleet (slēt) *n.* rain mixed with snow or hail. —*vb.* to send down sleet.

sleeve (slēv) *n.* 1. a part of a garment covering the arm. 2. an envelope-like cover for a record. **laugh up one's sleeve** to be amused secretly. **up one's sleeve** ready for future use. —'**sleeveless** *adj.*

sleigh (slā) *n.* a sledge.

slender ('slendə) *adj.* 1. gracefully slim: *a slender girl.* 2. slight; insufficient: *a slender income.*

slept (slept) *vb.* the past tense and past participle of SLEEP.

slice (slīs) *n.* 1. a thin flat piece cut from something: *a slice of bread.* 2. a flat or broad-bladed type of knife for slicing cake, serving fish, etc. 3. a slash; slicing stroke. —*vb.* **slicing, sliced.** 1. to cut into thin flat pieces. 2. to cut a slice from. 3. to slash.

slick (slik) *adj.* 1. sleek; smooth. 2. smooth in speech or manner. 3. clever, esp. too clever. —*n.* (also **oil slick**) a patch of oil on the surface of the sea.

slide (slīd) *vb.* **sliding, slid.** 1. to move or send in one smooth movement along a surface. 2. to glide in a standing position. 3. to use a playground slide. 4. to allow to become worse: *to let things slide.* —*n.* 1. the action or an instance of sliding. 2. a polished slippery track on an icy surface or a sloping apparatus used for sliding, e.g. at a playground. 3. a bed, groove, or rail on which a thing slides. 4. a piece of extra tubing in a trombone that can be extended or detached. 5. a picture for projecting on a screen. 6. a piece of glass for mounting objects to be examined under a microscope. 7. a hair clip.

slight (slīt) *adj.* 1. of small size, amount, strength, power, importance, etc. —*vb.* 1. to treat as unimportant. 2. to insult. —*n.* an insult. '**slightly** *adv.* rather; somewhat: *he's slightly mad.*

slim (slim) *adj.* **slimmer, slimmest.** 1. gracefully thin; slender: *a slim waist.* 2. slight; small: *he only had a slim chance of winning.* —*vb.* **slimming, slimmed.** to lose or cause to lose fatness. '**slimmer** *n.* a person on a diet trying to slim.

slime (slīm) *n.* 1. a sticky slippery substance such as mud. 2. a slippery substance produced by snails. '**slimy** *adj.* **slimier, slimiest.** 1. covered with slime. 2. (of a person) offensively humble or flattering. —'**sliminess** *n.*

sling (sling) *n.* 1. a loop of leather and cord for throwing, casting, or shooting a stone; catapult. 2. a rope or chain looped round something to lift or support it. 3. a strip of cloth supporting an injured arm or foot. —*vb.* **slinging, slung.** 1. to throw. 2. to shoot or cast with a sling.

slip[1] (slip) *vb.* **slipping, slipped.** 1. to slide without meaning to; lose balance and fall. 2. to move or cause to move into or out of place. 3. to fall suddenly from the hand. 4. to slide: *the key slipped easily into the lock.* 5. (often + *away, by,* etc.) to move

rapidly, quietly, or unnoticed. 6. to hand over, esp. secretly. 7. (sometimes + *up*) to make a mistake. —*n.* 1. the action or an instance of slipping; a sliding fall. 2. a mistake. 3. a woman's petticoat. 4. a pillowcase. **give (someone) the slip** to escape cleverly from (someone). '**slippery** *adj.* 1. causing sliding because of being too smooth, wet, etc.: *slippery roads.* 2. cunning: *he's a slippery character.* —'**slipperiness** *n.*

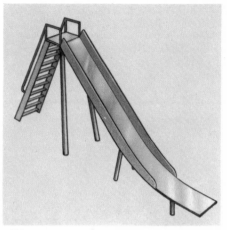
slide

slip[2] (slip) *n.* 1. a narrow strip of paper. 2. a strip; anything thin or narrow. 3. a cutting from a plant.

slipper ('slipə) *n.* a loose soft shoe worn indoors.

slipshod ('slipshod) *adj.* careless or untidy; rough.

slit (slit) *vb.* **slitting, slit.** to make a long cut or tear; split. —*n.* a long narrow opening, tear, or split.

slogan ('slōgən) *n.* an easily remembered phrase or word used to advertise a product or arouse interest in and support for a political party, movement, or action.

slope (slōp) *n.* 1. a piece of ground or a surface rising or falling gradually from the horizontal. 2. the degree of this rise or fall. —*vb.* **sloping, sloped.** to place at an angle to the horizontal; be in an inclined position. **slope off** (informal) to go away secretly.

slot (slot) *n.* a long narrow opening, esp. one able to take a coin. —*vb.* **slotting, slotted.** 1. to make a slot in. 2. (+ *in* or *into*) to fit: *the final clue slotted into place and the detective's case was complete.* **slot machine** a machine operated by inserting a coin.

slow (slō) *adj.* 1. not quick; taking a long time. 2. moving at low speed. 3. (of a clock) showing a time earlier than the correct time. 4. stupid; unintelligent. 5. boring; uninteresting. —*vb.* (often + *down*) to cause to move more slowly. —'**slowly** *adv.* —'**slowness** *n.*

slug[1] (slug) *n.* 1. a small slow-moving black or grey animal related to the snail but having no shell, usu. found in gardens. 2. a lump of metal, esp. that used in a gun. '**sluggish** *adj.* slow-moving; not responding or acting quickly. —'**sluggishly** *adv.* —'**sluggishness** *n.*

slug[2] (slug) *vb.* **slugging, slugged.** (informal) to knock or hit violently. —*n.* a violent blow.

sluice

sluice (slōōs) *n.* 1. a manmade channel fitted with a gate for stopping or regulating the flow of water. 2. a trough for washing gold from sand. —*vb.* **sluicing, sluiced.** 1. to let out or drain by a sluice. 2. to wash thoroughly by means of or as if by means of a sluice.

slum (slum) *n.* 1. a street or district of overcrowded houses in poor condition. 2. a single house in bad condition. —*vb.* **slumming, slummed.** (informal) to visit a slum or any other place considered to be of low or bad character.

slumber ('slumbə) *vb.* to sleep. —*n.* sleep.

slump (slump) *n.* a sudden fall in prices or demand; financial depression involving poor trade and causing much unemployment. —*vb.* 1. to collapse in a heap. 2. to sit down heavily and wearily. 3. (of prices) to fall suddenly.

slung (sluñg) *vb.* the past tense and past participle of SLING.

slur (slû) *n.* 1. a statement or action having a bad effect on someone's reputation. 2. a blurred or unclear quality, as in speech when words are run together. 3. (music) a curved line joining notes to be played with a smooth gliding effect or sung to one syllable. —*vb.* **slurring, slurred.** 1. to pronounce indistinctly by running words together. 2. to sing or play (a number of notes) without a break.

slush (slush) *n.* 1. half-melted snow, esp. when mixed with mud. 2. something sentimental and silly. —'**slushy** *adj.* **slushier, slushiest.**

sly (slī) *adj.* 1. cunning; crafty; dishonest. 2. mischievous; showing humour: *a sly wit.* **on the sly** secretly; without being observed. —'**slyly** *adv.* —'**slyness** *n.*

smack (smak) *vb.* 1. to hit with the palm of the hand; slap. 2. to make a smacking noise. 3. to make a sound by pressing one's lips together and releasing quickly. —*n.* 1. a blow of the open hand. 2. a sharp noise; crack.

small (smôl) *adj.* not great in size, amount, value, power, or importance. **small talk** casual or meaningless talk. **smalls** *pl.n.* underclothes. **the small hours** the hours between midnight and dawn. **the small of the back** the narrow part of the back.

smallpox (smôlpoks) *n.* a highly infectious disease characterized by fever and a violent rash that often leaves permanent marks and pits in the skin.

smart (smât) *adj.* 1. clever; intelligent; quick-witted. 2. tidy, neat, and fashionable: *smart clothes.* **smart-aleck** ('smâtalik) *n.* an annoying person claiming to be clever. —*vb.* 1. to feel a sharp tingling pain. 2. to feel resentful. —*n.* a sharp pain, distress, or irritation. '**smarten** *vb.* (often + *up*) to make or become smart. —'**smartly** *adv.* —'**smartness** *n.*

smash (smash) *vb.* 1. to shatter violently or fall in pieces. 2. to ruin or be ruined. 3. (often + *into*) to collide violently with; crash. —*n.* the action or an instance of smashing; destruction or ruin. '**smashing** *adj.* (informal) especially good; wonderful: *it was a smashing party.*

smear (smiə) *n.* 1. a greasy or stain or mark. 2. a slandering statement; insult; slur. —*vb.* 1. to stain, mark, or spread with dirt or grease. 2. to blur by rubbing. 3. to spread slander about (someone).

smell (smel) *n.* 1. the sense through which things are observed by means of the nose. 2. a pleasant or unpleasant sensation produced in the nose; odour, scent, or stink. —*vb.* **smelling, smelt** *or* **smelled.** 1. to detect the smell of (something). 2. to give off a smell, often an unpleasant one. '**smelly** *adj.* **smellier, smelliest.** giving off an unpleasant smell.

smile (smīl) *n.* a facial expression in which the mouth is stretched sideways and the corners are turned upwards, usu. indicating pleasure, amusement, etc. —*vb.* **smiling, smiled.** to make a smile.

smock (smok) *n.* a loose outer garment usu. worn over other clothes to protect them. —*vb.* to gather material in small folds and sew it in place with a decorative stitch.

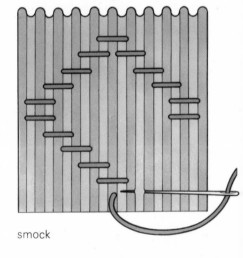
smock

smoke (smōk) *n.* 1. the visible gases given off by a fire. 2. anything resembling smoke. 3. (informal) a cigarette or cigar. 4. the action or an instance of smoking a cigarette, cigar, or pipe. —*vb.* **smoking, smoked.** 1. to give off smoke. 2. (of a house fire) to give off excessive smoke because of incomplete burning. 3. to preserve (meat or fish) by exposing it to smoke: *kippers are made by smoking herring.* 4. to breathe in and blow out the fumes of tobacco, etc., from (a cigarette, pipe, cigar, etc.). 5. to do this regularly. '**smoker** *n.* 1. a person who smokes. 2. a railway carriage, etc., where smoking is allowed. —'**smokeless** *adj.* —'**smoky** *adj.* **smokier, smokiest.**

smooth (smoodh) *adj.* 1. flat, level, or even; without roughness or bumps: *a smooth surface.* 2. without disturbance or difficulty: *a smooth journey.* 3. too polite, pleasing, or persuasive; insincere. —*vb.* to make smooth. **smooth over** to settle (a quarrel, argument, etc.). —'**smoothly** *adv.* —'**smoothness** *n.*

smother ('smudhə) *vb.* 1. to deprive of air; suffocate. 2. to put out (a fire). 3. to cover densely: *apple pie smothered with custard.*

smoulder ('smōldə) *vb.* 1. to burn slowly with smoke but no flame. 2. to show strong emotion: *she smouldered with anger.*

smudge (smuj) *vb.* **smudging, smudged.** to blot; blur; smear. —*n.* a smear; blot.

smug (smug) *adj.* **smugger, smuggest.** too satisfied with oneself. —'**smugly** *adv.* —'**smugness** *n.*

smuggle ('smugəl) *vb.* **smuggling, smuggled.** 1. to bring or take (something) into or out of a country illegally or in secret, esp. without paying the required taxes. 2. to transport secretly: *the spy was smuggled into the room in a basket.*

snag (snag) *n.* 1. a difficulty or unexpected obstacle that holds up or endangers an action, plan, etc. 2. a hole or pulled thread in a garment: *a snag in a stocking.* —*vb.* **snagging, snagged.** to tear on something sharp: *he snagged his jersey on a thorn.*

snail

snail (snāl) *n.* any of a number of small slimy limbless animals that move with a slow wavelike motion and carry a spiral-shaped shell on their backs into which they can withdraw completely.

snake (snāk) *n.* 1. a long-bodied slender scaly legless reptile, some species of which have a poisonous bite. 2. (informal) a treacherous deceitful person. —*vb.* **snaking, snaked.** 1. to move like a snake. 2. to wind along with many twists and turns.

snap (snap) *vb.* **snapping, snapped.** 1. to break with a sudden sharp movement. 2. to make or produce a sharp sound, as of something breaking. 3. to say or speak sharply or angrily. 4. to take an informal photograph of. **snap up** to take eagerly; grab. —*n.* 1. the sound or action of snapping or an instance of snapping. 2. (also **snapshot**) an informal photograph.

snatch (snach) *vb.* 1. to make a sudden grab for; seize suddenly or violently. 2. to take while one has the chance: *they snatched some sleep.* —*n.* 1. the act of snatching. 2. a small fragment: *a snatch of conversation.*

sneak (snēk) *vb.* 1. to creep secretly or unnoticed. 2. to tell tales about someone. 3. to steal or take away secretly. —*n.* a person who sneaks. '**sneaky** *adj.* **sneakier, sneakiest.** dishonest; underhand. —'**sneakily** *adv.* —'**sneakiness** *n.*

sneer (sniə) *vb.* to smile or speak in a contemptuous mocking way: *he sneered at my muddy boots.* —*n.* the action or an instance of sneering.

sneeze (snēz) *n.* a sudden uncontrollable release of air through the nose and mouth, usu. caused by a cold. —*vb.* **sneezing, sneezed.** to make a sneeze.

sniff (snif) *vb.* 1. to breathe in sharply and noisily through the nose, usu. indicating contempt or because one has a cold. 2. to smell by sniffing: *the deer sniffed the air for danger.* —*n.* the action or an instance of sniffing.

snip (snip) *vb.* **snipping, snipped.** to cut out with scissors. —*n.* 1. a small piece of cloth snipped off. 2. a small cut made with scissors.

snipe (snīp) *vb.* **sniping, sniped.** 1. (often + *at*) to shoot at a person, usu. with a rifle, from a hiding place. 2. to criticize in an indirect way. '**sniper** *n.* a person who shoots at people from a hiding place.

snivel ('snivəl) *vb.* **snivelling, snivelled.** to cry in a complaining or feeble way.

snob (snob) *n.* a person who respects the opinions, customs, etc., of those who have wealth and are considered to be of high social rank, while showing contempt for everyone else. —'**snobbery** *n.* —'**snobbish** *adj.* —'**snobbishly** *adv.* —'**snobbishness** *n.*

snoop (snoop) *vb.* to make secret, unwanted, or sly investigations into something; pry.

snore (snô) *vb.* **snoring, snored.** to make a regular grunting sound while asleep by breathing through the mouth and nose. —*n.* the action or an instance of snoring.

snort (snôt) *vb.* 1. to make an abrupt noise indicating contempt, etc., by vigorously forcing air out through the nose. 2. to say with a snort. —*n.* the noise made by a person or animal snorting: *he gave a snort of rage.*

snout (snout) *n.* 1. the nose of an animal, esp. a pig. 2. anything resembling this.

snow (snō) *n.* frozen water vapour that falls from the air in white flakes and lies on the ground in cold weather. —*vb.* to fall as snow. —'**snowy** *adj.* **snowier, snowiest.**

snowflake

snowball ('snōbôl) *n.* a lump of snow pressed together into a ball. —*vb.* 1. to throw snowballs. 2. to increase quickly in size, force, etc.: *support for the new playground snowballed.*

snub (snub) *vb.* **snubbing, snubbed.** to treat coldly or with contempt: *he snubbed our offer of help.* —*n.* snubbing behaviour or words.

snuff[1] (snuf) *n.* powdered tobacco that is sniffed up the nose.

snuff[2] (snuf) *vb.* to put out (a flame).

snug (snug) *adj.* **snugger, snuggest.** 1. cosy and warm. 2. closely fitting. —'**snugly** *adv.* —'**snugness** *n.*

snuggle ('snugǝl) *vb.* **snuggling, snuggled.** to settle down warmly and comfortably, esp. close to someone or something: *the kittens snuggled up to their mother.*

soak (sōk) *vb.* 1. to make completely wet: *the storm soaked my overcoat.* 2. (+ *up*) to absorb; take in (liquid): *blotting paper soaks up ink.* 3. to submerge in liquid: *she soaked the dirty shirts.* 4. to ooze through; penetrate: *the mud soaked through our shoes.* —*n.* the act of soaking.

soap (sōp) *n.* a substance for washing and cleaning, made in the form of blocks, powder, or liquid. —*vb.* to wash or cover with soap. —'**soapy** *adj.* **soapier, soapiest.**

soar (sô) *vb.* 1. to rise into the air with apparent lack of effort: *the eagle soared over the cliffs.* 2. to go up sharply: *food prices soared last winter.*

sober ('sōbǝ) *adj.* 1. not drunk or often under the influence of alcohol. 2. not bright or gay; subdued: *grey is a sober colour.* —'**soberly** *adv.* —**sobriety** (sǝ'brīǝti) *or* '**soberness** *n.*

soccer ('sokǝ) *n.* a football game between two teams of eleven players each, in which players can kick the ball but are not allowed to touch it with hands or arms.

society (sǝ'sīǝti) *n.,pl.* **societies.** 1. human beings as a group: *pollution is a threat to society.* 2. a particular way of organizing human beings as a group: *this country has a democratic society.* 3. a club or organization for people who share the same interest. 4. rich or fashionable people considered as a group.

sock (sok) *n.* a short knitted covering for the foot and lower leg.

socket ('sokit) *n.* a hollow opening into which something fits, e.g. an eye socket.

soda ('sōdǝ) *n.* 1. a common white chemical substance that has many uses in industry, e.g. in making soap. 2. a soft drink.

sodium ('sōdiǝm) *n.* a silvery white chemical element found in many compounds, e.g. ordinary table salt. Chemical symbol: Na.

soft (soft) *adj.* 1. not hard: *a soft bed.* 2. smooth; delicate to the touch: *a soft velvet curtain.* 3. not loud, harsh, or sharp: *a soft melody.* **soften** ('sofǝn) *vb.* to make or become soft or softer. —'**softly** *adv.* —'**softness** *n.*

soggy ('sogi) *adj.* **soggier, soggiest.** wet through; soaked: *it was hard work walking across the soggy ground.* —'**sogginess** *n.*

soil[1] (soil) *n.* the upper layers of the ground in which plants grow: *heather grows well in an acid soil.*

soil[2] (soil) *vb.* to make or become dirty: *my hands are soiled with paint.*

solar ('sōlǝ) *adj.* of or from the sun: *solar energy is used to heat water in some parts of the world.*

sold (sōld) *vb.* the past tense and past participle of SELL.

soldier ('sōljǝ) *n.* a person who belongs to an army. —*vb.* to be or act as a soldier.

sole[1] (sōl) *adj.* 1. single; only one: *the boy was the sole heir.* 2. belonging to only one person or group: *the sole responsibility of the committee.* —'**solely** *adv.*

sole[2] (sōl) *n.* the flat bottom or underside of a foot or shoe.

sole[3] (sōl) *n.* a dark brown flatfish found in the sea and much valued as food.

solemn ('solǝm) *adj.* 1. impressive or dignified: *the solemn procession entered the church.* 2. serious: *a solemn face.* —'**solemnly** *adv.* —**solemnity** (sǝ'lemniti) *n.*

solid ('solid) *adj.* 1. not hollow or mixed with other material: *solid oak.* 2. firm; hard: *the solid surface of the concrete.* 3. not weak or unsettled: *a solid foundation.* 4. without a break: *the noise lasted five solid hours.* —*n.* a form of matter that is not a liquid or a gas and has a definite shape and hardness. **solidarity** (soli'dariti) *n.* unity or a feeling of sympathy caused by shared interests. **solidify** (sǝ'lidifī) *vb.* **solidifying, solidified.** to make or become solid or more solid. **so'lidity** *n.* the state or quality of being solid. —'**solidly** *adv.*

solitary ('solitǝri) *adj.* 1. lonely; without companions: *a solitary life.* 2. single; only one: *a solitary goat was the only animal in sight.* **solitude** ('solityōōd) *n.* the state of being alone.

solo ('sōlō) *n.,pl.* **solos.** 1. a piece of music or a dance written to be performed by one person. 2. a performance by one person. —*adj.* made for one person or instrument.

solstice ('solstis) *n.* the time of the year at which the sun is furthest from the equator, i.e. about 21 June and about 22 December.

solution (sǝ'lōōshǝn) *n.* 1. the answer to a problem. 2. the mixture formed by dissolving a substance in a liquid. **soluble** ('solyōōbǝl) *adj.* able to be dissolved in a liquid.

solve (solv) *vb.* **solving, solved.** to find the meaning of or the answer to (something).

sombre ('sombǝ) *adj.* dark and gloomy: *the sombre sky threatened rain.* —'**sombrely** *adv.*

somersault ('sumǝsôlt) *n.* a movement in athletics in which one rolls one's body quickly forwards or backwards, heels over head. —*vb.* to perform this or a similar movement.

sonata (sǝ'nâtǝ) *n.* a piece of music in three or four movements, written to be performed by one instrument, with or without the accompaniment of other instruments.

soot (sōōt) *n.* the black greasy dust left after burning. —'**sooty** *adj.* **sootier, sootiest.**

soothe (sōōdh) *vb.* **soothing, soothed.** to calm; relieve or comfort: *the lotion soothed the pain of the burn.*

sore (sô) *adj.* **sorer, sorest.** 1. painful. 2. angry; resentful: *she was sore because of his undeserved success.* —*n.* a cut, boil, or other infected wound on the skin. '**sorely** *adv.* seriously; deeply: *he was sorely troubled by guilt.* —'**soreness** *n.*

sorrow ('sorō) *n.* misery; regret. —*vb.* to feel grief or sadness; mourn. '**sorrowful** *adj.* —'**sorrowfully** *adv.*

sorry ('sori) *adj.* **sorrier, sorriest.** 1. apologetic; regretful: *I am sorry to have interrupted you.* 2. miserable: *her clothes were in a sorry state.*

sort (sôt) *n.* a group of things that are alike; type or class: *what sort of biscuits do you like?* —*vb.* 1. to arrange by type; classify: *letters are sorted at the Post Office.* 2. (+ *out*) to tidy; arrange: *I sorted out my desk.* 3. (+ *out*) to find a solution to: *could you sort out this problem?*

sought (sôt) *vb.* the past tense and past participle of SEEK.

soul (sōl) *n.* 1. the spiritual part of a human being, believed to be able to survive after death. 2. sensitivity; sympathy: *a brutal man with no soul.*

sound[1] (sound) *n.* something that is heard by the ears; noise. —*vb.* 1. to make or cause to make a sound. 2. to seem to be: *that price sounds fair.*

sound[2] (sound) *adj.* 1. healthy; in good condition: *her injured leg is sound again.* 2. sensible; well-founded: *his advice is sound.* 3. thorough; complete: *a sound training in arithmetic.*

sound[3] (sound) *n.* a narrow stretch of water between two larger areas of water, e.g. between two islands or an island and the mainland.

soup (sōōp) *n.* a liquid food made by cooking meat, vegetables, etc., slowly in water until they are very soft.

sour (souə) *adj.* 1. sharp-tasting; not sweet. 2. bad-tempered; gloomy. —'**sourly** *adv.* —'**sourness** *n.*

source (sôs) *n.* 1. origin; starting-point: *Betty was the source of the rumour.* 2. the spring or origin of a river.

south (south) *n.* 1. the point on the compass that is on your left if you stand facing towards the sunset. 2. often **South** a region lying in this direction: *Cannes is in the south of France.* —*adj.* towards, from, or in the south. —*adv.* towards the south: *they turned south.* **southern** ('sudhən) *adj.* of or in the south.

souvenir (sōōvə'niə) *n.* a keepsake; something that is kept to remind one of a person, place, or event.

sovereign ('sovrin) *n.* 1. a monarch or supreme ruler. 2. a gold coin used in former times. —*adj.* 1. having supreme power. 2. effective: *sovereign remedies.* —'**sovereignty** *n.*

sow[1] (sō) *vb.* **sowing, sowed, sown.** to plant (seeds).

sow

sow[2] (sou) *n.* an adult female pig.

space (spās) *n.* 1. the limitless area in which the whole universe exists. 2. the zone beyond the earth's atmosphere; outer space. 3. distance between objects: *there is too little space between the houses.* **spacious** ('spāshəs) *adj.* having a lot of space (def. 3); roomy. —'**spaciously** *adv.*

spade (spād) *n.* 1. a garden tool with a long handle and a flat metal blade, used for digging. See IMPLEMENT. 2. a playing card marked with one or more small black pointed leaf shapes.

span (span) *vb.* **spanning, spanned.** to form an arch, link, bridge, etc., over time or space: *the bridge spanned the valley.* —*n.* 1. a stretch of time or space, esp. a lifetime. 2. the distance or part between the piers of a bridge, the pillars of an arch, the tips of a bird's wings, etc.

spanner ('spanə) *n.* a metal TOOL for gripping and tightening or loosening bolts, nuts, etc.

spare (speə) *adj.* 1. extra; more than is needed: *I lent Bob my spare coat.* 2. kept in reserve: *a spare tyre.* 3. small in quantity: *a spare meal.* —*n.* something extra. —*vb.* **sparing, spared.** 1. to give: *he spared them only a few minutes.* 2. to avoid hurting; show mercy to: *she spared the boy's feelings.*

spark (spâk) *n.* 1. a tiny burning fragment of material. 2. a small flash of light caused by electricity. —*vb.* 1. to shoot out sparks. 2. (+ *off*) to cause: *his selfishness sparked off a quarrel.*

sparrow ('sparō) *n.* one of many kinds of small grey or brown birds common in cities and the countryside all over the world.

spastic ('spastik) *adj.* lacking control of the muscles because of damage to the brain, generally suffered at birth. —*n.* a person suffering from this condition.

spat (spat) *vb.* the past tense and past participle of SPIT[1].

spawn (spôn) *n.* the eggs of fish, frogs, etc., laid in water. —*vb.* 1. to lay eggs in water. 2. to breed in very large numbers.

spear (spiə) *n.* 1. a weapon, formerly widely used for hunting, fighting, etc., having a long handle with a sharp pointed head, usu. made of metal. 2. the thin straight stalk of a plant. —*vb.* to kill, pierce, etc., with a spear.

special ('speshəl) *adj.* 1. exceptional; uncommon: *a special treat.* 2. particular to one person or thing: *the queen travelled on a special train.* —*n.* something special or out of the ordinary, e.g. a policeman enrolled for a particular occasion, an extra edition of a newspaper, etc. '**specialist** *n.* a person who knows a great deal about a particular science, skill, etc. **speci'ality** *n.,pl.* **specialities.** 1. something in which one is particularly skilled or interested: *knitting is her speciality.* 2. a special product: *chocolate cake is the baker's speciality.* '**specialize** *vb.* **specializing, specialized.** to give particular time or attention to one branch of a science, skill, etc. —**speciali'zation** *n.* —'**specially** *adv.*

species ('spēshēz) *n.,pl.* **species.** 1. a group of plants or animals whose members resemble each other sufficiently to be able to breed together: *dogs and cats are different species.* 2. a type; kind.

sparrow

specimen ('spesimən) *n.* an example of a group that shows the characteristics of the whole group: *the bull was a fine specimen of its breed.*

speck (spek) *n.* a tiny particle: *there was a speck of dust in her eye.*

spectacles

spectacle ('spektəkəl) *n.* 1. a sight; something to be gazed at: *the school pageant was a fine spectacle.* 2. **spectacles** (*pl.*) glasses made of framed lenses worn in front of the eyes to correct one's eyesight. **spectacular** (spek'takyŏŏlə) *adj.* 1. very impressive to a watcher: *a spectacular performance on the tightrope.* 2. amazing and praiseworthy: *a spectacular achievement.*

spectator (spek'tātə) *n.* a watcher; onlooker.

spectre ('spektə) *n.* 1. a ghost. 2. a threat of something unpleasant: *the spectre of illness.* —'**spectral** *adj.*

spectrum ('spektrəm) *n.* a band of colours formed by the breaking up of white light as it passes through a PRISM, raindrops, etc. A spectrum contains the colours red, orange, yellow, green, blue, indigo, and violet.

speech (spēch) *n.* 1. the ability, or manner of speaking: *the tired man's speech was slurred.* 2. a public talk: *the bridegroom's speech was rather long.* '**speechless** *adj.* unable to speak, esp. because of strong emotion.

speed (spēd) *n.* 1. great quickness: *the speed of his thinking amazed them.* 2. rate of movement: *what speed was the car doing?* —*vb.* **speeding, sped** *or* **speeded.** 1. to go or cause to go fast or too fast. 2. (+ *up*) to increase the rate of work, progress, production, etc. —'**speedy** *adj.* **speedier, speediest.**

speedometer (spi'domitə) *n.* the instrument on a train, car, etc., that measures and shows its speed.

spell[1] (spel) *vb.* **spelling, spelt** *or* **spelled.** to say or write in their correct order the letters that form (a word). '**spelling** *n.* 1. the act of spelling. 2. the way a word is spelt.

spell[2] (spel) *n.* 1. a series of words, e.g. a charm or curse, that is thought to have a magical effect. 2. a fascination or attraction.

spell[3] (spel) *n.* 1. a period of time. 2. a period of activity, duty, etc.: *he took a spell at the lawn-mower.*

spellbound ('spelbound) *adj.* having one's attention held as if by magic; enchanted.

spend (spend) *vb.* **spending, spent.** 1. to pay out (money). 2. to pass (time): *he spent eleven years at school.* 3. to use up: *she spent her energy in caring for the sick.*

sphere (sfiə) *n.* 1. a round object shaped like a ball; globe. See GEOMETRY. 2. area of interest; range of knowledge: *computers are outside his sphere.*

sphinx

sphinx (sfingks) *n.,pl.* **sphinxes.** an imaginary creature with the body of a lion and the head of a human being.

spice (spīs) *n.* a seed or other strongly tasting part of a plant used to add to the flavour of food. Pepper, nutmeg, and cinnamon are spices. —*vb.* **spicing, spiced.** to flavour with spice. —'**spicy** *adj.* **spicier, spiciest.**

spider ('spīdə) *n.* a small insect-like animal with eight legs and no wings that spins a web in which to trap insects for food.

spike (spīk) *n.* 1. a sharp pointed object. 2. a large heavy nail. —*vb.* **spiking, spiked.** to pierce with a spike.

spill (spil) *vb.* **spilling, spilt** *or* **spilled.** 1. to cause or allow (liquid, powder, etc.) to pour out: *Jane spilt the water.* 2. to flow out: *water was spilling over the dam wall.* —*n.* a fall, esp. from a bicycle or horse.

spin (spin) *vb.* **spinning, spun** *or* **span, spun.** 1. to twist (fibres of wool, cotton, etc.) into thread. 2. to make by means of threads: *the spider spun a web.* 3. to move or cause to move rapidly round and round: *Steve spun a coin.* —*n.* 1. a rapid turning movement. 2. a short pleasure ride.

spinach ('spinich) *n.* a common garden plant with large leaves that are eaten as a vegetable.

spine (spīn) *n.* 1. the series of bones in the centre of the back that supports the rest of the body. 2. a needle-like projection from the body of an animal or plant. 3. the narrow back of a book. '**spineless** *adj.* 1. having no spine or spines. 2. timid; unable to make decisions or act vigorously. —'**spiny** *adj.* **spinier, spiniest.**

spiral ('spīrəl) *n.* a continuous winding curve; coil: *a chair spring is a spiral.* —*adj.* having the form of a spiral: *a spiral staircase.* —*vb.* **spiralling, spiralled.** to move in a spiral: *smoke spirals up from the bonfire.*

spire (spīə) *n.* a tall pointed structure in the shape of a cone or pyramid on top of a building, esp. a church.

spirit ('spirit) *n.* 1. the part of a person that is thought to be able to exist independently of the body; soul. 2. a ghost or other supernatural being. 3. vigour; liveliness: *they sang with spirit.* 4. **spirits** (*pl.*) state of one's feelings: *he was in low spirits after the car accident.* 5. **spirits** (*pl.*) strong alcoholic drink, e.g. gin. —*vb.* (usu. + *away*) to take away quickly and mysteriously. '**spiritual** *adj.* 1. of the soul. 2. of religious matters. —*n.* a popular religious song, sung originally by the Negroes of the southern U.S.A. '**spiritualism** *n.* the belief that it is possible to receive messages from the spirits of the dead. '**spiritualist** *n.* a believer in spiritualism. '**spirituous** *adj.* containing alcohol. —'**spiritually** *adv.*

spit[1] (spit) *vb.* **spitting, spat.** to force

out (SALIVA, food, etc.) from the mouth; spurt out violently: *he spat out the bitter medicine.* —*n.* the liquid formed in the mouth; saliva.

spit² (spit) *n.* a thin metal rod to which food is attached for cooking over or under a grill.

spite (spīt) *n.* the desire to cause harm; malice. **'spiteful** *adj.* showing or expressing spite. —**'spitefully** *adv.* —**'spitefulness** *n.*

splash (splash) *vb.* 1. to cause (liquid) to fly about in drops. 2. to fly about and fall in drops: *the rain splashed from the roof.* —*n.* 1. the act or sound of splashing. 2. a small mark: *a splash of red paint.*

splendid ('splendid) *adj.* 1. very beautiful: *a splendid sunset.* 2. very good: *a splendid party.* **'splendour** *n.* great beauty; grandeur; magnificence. —**'splendidly** *adv.*

splice

splice (splīs) *vb.* **splicing, spliced.** to join (two pieces of rope, wood, etc.) by fastening the ends together.

splint (splint) *n.* a piece of wood, metal, etc., that is firmly tied to a broken bone or part of a plant to prevent it moving and so enable it to heal correctly.

splinter ('splintə) *n.* a thin sharp fragment that has broken off from a larger piece of material, esp. wood. —*vb.* to break or cause to break off in splinters: *the mirror splintered when it fell on the floor.*

split (split) *vb.* **splitting, split.** to break or cause to break apart; divide: *the old cushion split and its stuffing fell out.* —*n.* the act or result of splitting; division.

spoil (spoil) *vb.* **spoiling, spoilt** *or* **spoiled.** 1. to damage or make useless: *he spoilt the carpet by dropping paint on it.* 2. to go bad: *the cheese spoiled in the hot weather.* 3. to harm a person's character by allowing him to have his own way too much. —*n.* usu. **spoils** (*pl.*) stolen goods.

spoke (spōk) *n.* one of the rods joining the outer rim to the centre of a wheel.

spokesman ('spōksmən) *n., pl.* **spokesmen.** a person who speaks on behalf of another person or group.

sponge (spunj) *n.* 1. a colony of sea animals that form together into an irregular mass interspersed with holes. 2. the absorbent skeleton of this used for washing, cleaning, or mopping up. 3. a piece of manmade material similar in texture and uses to a natural sponge (def. 2.). 4. (also **sponge-cake**) a light yellow soft cake. —*vb.* **sponging, sponged.** 1. to clean with a damp sponge. 2. (informal) to live by taking advantage of the kindness or generosity of others: *Bob deliberately avoided work and managed to sponge off his friends.*

sponsor ('sponsə) *n.* a person who proposes an idea, provides the money for a show, or in some other way accepts responsibility for someone or something. —*vb.* to act as sponsor.

spontaneous (spon'tāniəs) *adj.* 1. not planned beforehand; done on impulse: *the men broke into spontaneous singing.* 2. having no outside cause; self-acting: *spontaneous combustion.* —**spon'taneously** *adv.*

spool (spool) *n.* a wooden, metal, or plastic cylinder round which wire, thread, etc., is wound.

spoon (spoon) *n.* a small utensil with a shallow bowl on the end of a handle, used for preparing and eating food. —*vb.* to lift up with a spoon.

sport (spôt) *n.* 1. a game or games involving physical exercise. 2. fun: *the boys had great sport with their canoes.* 3. a person who plays fairly and does not mind losing. —*vb.* 1. to wear, esp. in a showy way: *he sported a bright red blazer.* 2. to play. **'sporting** *adj.* willing to play fairly and risk losing. **'sportsman** *n., pl.* **sportsmen** (**sportswoman,** *pl.* **sportswomen**). a person who plays physical games. **'sportsmanship** *n.* fair and generous behaviour in sport.

spot (spot) *n.* 1. a small dirty mark. 2. a small area differing from its background. 3. a small blemish on the skin. 4. (informal) a small amount: *we had a spot of trouble with the car.* 5. a place. —*vb.* **spotting, spotted.** 1. to see. 2. to mark with spots.

spout (spout) *vb.* to come or force out through a small opening. —*n.* a narrow tube or opening through which liquid comes or is forced.

sprain (sprān) *vb.* to twist or wrench a part of the body, causing injury. —*n.* an injury caused by spraining.

sponge

sprang (sprang) *vb.* the past tense of SPRING¹.

sprawl (sprôl) *vb.* 1. to lie or sit in an ungainly way. 2. to spread out untidily: *the housing development sprawled across the fields.*

spray¹ (sprā) *n.* 1. a cloud or jet of liquid in the form of very small drops. 2. a device for applying liquid in this form. 3. a mass of small objects, e.g. bullets, flying through the air. —*vb.* 1. to apply a spray (def. 1). 2. to direct a spray (def. 2) on.

spray² (sprā) *n.* a small branch of a tree or plant with flowers or leaves, esp. one used for decoration.

spread (spred) *vb.* **spreading, spread.** 1. to stretch out; extend: *please spread the tablecloth.* 2. to make a thin layer of (something) on the surface of something else: *he spread jam on the toast.* 3. to become or cause to become widely distributed: *gossip spreads quickly.* —*n.* 1. the extent to which something is stretched out or open. 2. a type of soft food that is spread on bread or toast. 3. a cloth cover for a bed.

spring[1] (spring) *vb.* **springing, sprang, sprung.** 1. to jump. 2. to snap or jerk quickly: *the car door sprang open.* 3. to appear or grow up suddenly: *grass sprang from the broken paving.* 4. to cause to happen unexpectedly: *the teacher sprang a spelling test on us.* —*n.* 1. a jump. 2. a place where water appears from underground. 3. a coiled metal object that can be stretched or squashed and still returns to its original shape. **'springy** *adj.* **springier, springiest.** elastic. —**'springiness** *n.*

spring[2] (spring) *n.* the season of the year between winter and summer.

sprinkle ('springkəl) *vb.* **sprinkling, sprinkled.** to scatter in tiny drops or particles: *he sprinkled some pepper on the steaks.*

sprint (sprint) *vb.* to run very fast for a short distance. —*n.* a short fast race.

sprout (sprout) *vb.* to start growing. —*n.* a young growth or shoot of a plant. **Brussels sprouts** the small round shoots of a cabbage-like plant, eaten as a vegetable.

sprung (sprung) *vb.* the past participle of SPRING[1].

spun (spun) *vb.* the past tense and past participle of SPIN.

spur (spû) *n.* a pointed metal object attached to the heel of a rider's boot and used to urge a horse to go faster. —*vb.* **spurring, spurred.** 1. to use spurs on a horse. 2. to urge on; encourage: *his sister's success spurred Ken to work harder.*

spurt (spût) *vb.* 1. to burst out suddenly in a stream. 2. to make a sudden intense effort. —*n.* 1. a sudden burst: *a spurt of flame.* 2. a sudden effort: *the horse's spurt near the finish enabled him to win the race.*

spy (spī) *n.,pl.* **spies.** a person who keeps watch secretly on the activities of other people, esp. someone employed by a government to obtain secret information. —*vb.* **spying, spied.** 1. to act as a spy. 2. to see.

squabble ('skwobəl) *vb.* **squabbling, squabbled.** to quarrel noisily about a small matter: *Ed and Sue squabbled over who should have the last bun.* —*n.* a noisy quarrel.

squad (skwod) *n.* a small group of people who train or work together.

squadron

squadron ('skwodrən) *n.* a division of the army, navy, or air force containing a fairly small number of men, ships, or aircraft.

squall (skwôl) *n.* 1. a sudden violent wind. 2. a loud harsh cry, esp. of pain or fear. —*vb.* to cry loudly.

squander ('skwondə) *vb.* to waste money or time in an extravagant way.

square (skweə) *n.* 1. a shape that has four sides of equal length and four right angles. See GEOMETRY. 2. an area with the shape of a square: *we bought a square of carpet for the hall.* 3. an open area surrounded by buildings in a town. 4. the number that results when a number is multiplied by itself: *the square of 3 is 9 (3 × 3).* —*adj.* 1. having the shape of a square (defs. 1 and 2). 2. having or forming a right angle: *the table has square corners.* 3. honest; fair: *a square deal.* —*vb.* **squaring, squared.** 1. to bring into the form of a square or right angle. 2. (+ *off*) to mark off in squares. 3. to multiply (a number) by itself.

squash[1] (skwosh) *vb.* to press flat; crush: *he stood on a beetle and squashed it.* —*n.* 1. a game played with rackets and a small rubber ball on a walled court. 2. a fruit drink.

squash[2] (skwosh) *n.* one of several types of fruits that grow on creeping plants and are eaten as vegetables.

squat (skwot) *vb.* **squatting, squatted.** 1. to crouch down with one's knees close to one's body. 2. to move in to live on unoccupied property that is not one's own. —*adj.* short and thick. **'squatter** *n.* a person who occupies land or buildings without the owner's permission.

squeak (skwēk) *n.* a shrill short sound: *the squeak of a mouse.* —*vb.* to make such a sound.

squeal (skwēl) *n.* a shrill noise: *the squeal of brakes.* —*vb.* to make such a noise, esp. indicating pain, fear, or excitement: *the pigs squealed.*

squeeze (skwēz) *vb.* **squeezing, squeezed.** 1. to pinch or press hard: *Tim's fingers were squeezed in the door.* 2. to get by pressing hard: *can you squeeze any more juice from the lemon?* —*n.* the action or an instance of squeezing.

squid (skwid) *n.,pl.* **squid** *or* **squids.** a soft-bodied animal that lives in the sea and has ten long arms. Squid vary in size from a few inches to many feet in length.

squint (skwint) *vb.* 1. to have eyes that turn in different directions. 2. to peer through half-closed eyes: *the strong light made him squint.* —*n.* uneven or crooked position of the eyeballs.

squirm (skwûm) *vb.* 1. to twist and wriggle. 2. to feel embarrassed or uncomfortable.

squirrel ('skwirəl) *n.* a small tree-climbing animal that has a bushy tail and reddish-brown or grey fur. See RODENT.

squirt (skwût) *vb.* 1. to force out (liquid) in a thin stream. 2. to come out in a thin stream.

stab (stab) *vb.* **stabbing, stabbed.** to wound or pierce with a weapon or pointed instrument. —*n.* 1. the act of stabbing. 2. a brief sharp sensation; pang. 3. (informal) an attempt: *Mike made a stab at mending the gate.*

stable[1] ('stābəl) *adj.* steady; not easily upset, changed, or moved. '**stabilize** *vb.* **stabilizing, stabilized.** to make steady. '**stabilizer** *n.* a device that keeps a ship or aircraft steady.

stable[2] ('stābəl) *n.* a building in which horses are kept and fed. —*vb.* **stabling, stabled.** to put or keep in a stable: *we stabled the horses after our ride this morning.*

stack (stak) *n.* 1. a pile of objects: *a stack of books.* 2. (informal) a large amount: *I have a stack of homework to do.* —*vb.* to arrange in a pile.

stadium ('stādiəm) *n.,pl.* **stadiums** or **stadia** ('stādiə). a structure in which sports contests are held, usu. consisting of a flat area surrounded by stands for large numbers of spectators.

staff (stâf) *n.* 1. a strong stick or pole, esp. one used as a support. 2. a group of people who work together for an organization or individual: *Lyn's mother is on the staff at our school.* 3. *pl.* **staves** (stāvz) the set of five parallel lines on which musical notes are written.

stag (stag) *n.* an adult male deer.

stage (stāj) *n.* 1. a raised platform in a theatre on which plays, etc., are performed. 2. the profession of acting in theatres. 3. the scene or setting for an event. 4. a step, section, or particular period in a process: *the last stage of the journey.* 5. a STAGECOACH. —*vb.* **staging, staged.** 1. to present a play, etc., before an audience. 2. to arrange or organize in order to obtain a certain effect: *she staged a fainting fit.*

stagecoach ('stājkōch) *n.* (also **stage**) a large horse-drawn coach, that formerly carried people.

stagger ('stagə) *vb.* 1. to move or stand unsteadily. 2. to arrange at different times: *school lunch hours are staggered as the hall is too small for all the children to get in at once.* 3. to surprise greatly: *we were staggered when Bob came to the party as we thought he was still on holiday.* —*n.* the act of walking or moving unsteadily.

stagnant ('stagnənt) *adj.* 1. without a current: *a stagnant puddle.* 2. inactive; sluggish: *the stock market was stagnant last year.* **stag'nate** *vb.* **stagnating, stagnated.** to be or become inactive.

stain (stān) *vb.* 1. to mark or make dirty. 2. to colour with a dye. 3. to spoil or damage: *the lie stained his reputation for honesty.* —*n.* 1. a dirty mark. 2. a dye, esp. one used on wood. 3. a cause of shame.

stair (steə) *n.* 1. usu. **stairs** (*pl.*) a series of fixed steps between different levels. 2. an individual step in such a series.

stake[1] (stāk) *n.* a post with one end sharpened to a point so that it can be hammered into the ground. —*vb.* **staking, staked.** 1. to fasten or make secure by a stake or stakes. 2. to mark out by means of stakes. **stake a claim** to declare one's right to something.

stake[2] (stāk) *n.* 1. money, jewels, etc., that are put at risk in a gambling game or bet. 2. a share or interest: *he has a large stake in his father's business.* —*vb.* **staking, staked.** to risk (something), esp. money in betting or gambling.

stalactite ('staləktīt) *n.* a stick or cone of limestone that hangs from the roof of a cave and is formed by the continuous dripping of water.

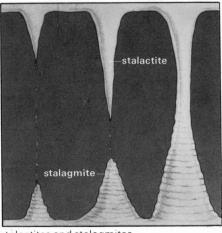

stalactites and stalagmites

stalagmite ('staləgmīt) *n.* a stick or cone of limestone that grows upwards from the floor of a cave.

stale (stāl) *adj.* **staler, stalest.** 1. not fresh: *stale bread.* 2. out of condition, esp. because of too little or too much practice.

stalemate ('stālmāt) *n.* 1. (chess) a draw occurring when one player cannot move without putting his king into CHECK. 2. any position from which no further move seems possible.

stalk[1] (stôk) *n.* the fleshy main stem of a plant that supports the leaves and flowers.

stalk[2] (stôk) *vb.* 1. to follow (someone or something) very quietly: *the cat stalked the sparrows.* 2. to walk in a very stiff and haughty way.

stall (stôl) *n.* 1. a space in a barn or stable in which one horse, cow, etc., is kept. 2. a stand in a street or market on which goods are displayed for sale. 3. a theatre or cinema seat near the stage or screen. —*vb.* 1. to come to a standstill: *the car's engine stalled as we drove through the water.* 2. to delay; fail to act for as long as possible.

stallion ('staliən) *n.* an adult male horse.

stamina ('staminə) *n.* toughness, strength, and energy necessary to overcome physical or mental trials: *his stamina enabled him to win the ten-mile race.*

stammer ('stamə) *n.* a speech habit in which sounds are often repeated several times at the beginnings of words. —*vb.* to speak with a stammer.

stagecoach

stamp (stamp) *n.* 1. a small piece of paper that is stuck on letters to indicate that postage has been paid. 2. a device that makes an imprint or mark. 3. the mark made by such a device. 4. the act of bringing down one's foot with force. —*vb.* 1. to bring one's foot or feet down forcefully. 2. (+ *out*) to destroy. 3. to mark (paper, etc.) with an inked block, pad, or other device. 4. to stick a postage stamp on (a letter, etc.).

stampede (stam'pēd) *n.* a sudden uncontrolled rush by many people or animals. —*vb.* **stampeding, stampeded.** to make a sudden rush in a group.

standard ('standəd) *n.* 1. a person, practice, or thing set up as a good model for other people to copy. 2. a flag or symbol. —*adj.* 1. normal; in accordance with accepted practices, models, etc. 2. of recognized importance, authority, or value: *a standard textbook.* '**standardize** *vb.* **standardizing, standardized.** to make according to fixed rules or patterns.

stank (stangk) *vb.* the past tense of STINK.

staple ('stāpəl) *n.* 1. a piece of bent metal wire that is driven through papers to fasten them together. 2. a U–shaped loop of metal driven into wood, etc. —*vb.* **stapling, stapled.** to fasten with staples.

star (stâ) *n.* 1. one of the many bright heavenly bodies that resemble the sun but are so far away from the earth that they look like tiny dots of light in the night sky. 2. a shape with five or more points arranged around a centre. 3. a person who is outstandingly successful in a particular activity, esp. a famous and popular actor or actress. —*vb.* **starring, starred.** to play the leading part in a play, film, etc. —'**starry** *adj.* **starrier, starriest.**

starboard ('stâbəd) *n.* the righthand side of a ship or aircraft from the point of view of someone on board who is facing towards the front.

starch (stâch) *n.* 1. a white food substance produced and stored in many plants, e.g. potatoes, corn. 2. a substance used to stiffen fabrics. —*vb.* to apply starch (def. 2) to (fabrics).

stare (steə) *vb.* **staring, stared.** to look or gaze very steadily. —*n.* a long steady look.

starfish

starfish ('stâfish) *n.* a sea animal with a star-shaped flattish body.

starling ('stâling) *n.* a common bird with shiny black feathers and a chattering voice, usu. found living in large flocks.

startle ('stâtəl) *vb.* **startling, startled.** to cause fright or surprise to: *the noisy car startled the horse.*

starve (stâv) *vb.* **starving, starved.** 1. to die or suffer severely from lack of food: *the crops failed and the people starved.* 2. to cause to suffer or die from lack of food: *the cruel man starved his dog.* 3. to be very hungry: *the children were starving after the long walk.* —**star'vation** *n.*

state (stāt) *n.* 1. condition: *the stray cat was in a terrible state.* 2. a people or nation organized under one government. 3. a region or part of a country which is recognized as a separate part of the whole: *how many states are there in the United States?* 4. ceremony; grandeur: *the king rode in state through the streets.* —*vb.* **stating, stated.** to say clearly and plainly; declare: *she stated her objections to the plan.* '**statement** *n.* 1. the act of stating. 2. something that is declared or set out plainly.

statesman ('stātsmən) *n.,pl.* **statesmen.** a man who has a high reputation for his skill in government and international affairs.

station ('stāshən) *n.* 1. a building or other place at which trains, buses, etc., stop and pick up passengers and goods. 2. a building or other place where special tasks or services are performed or organized: *fire engines are kept at the fire station.* 3. a place or position in which one stands for a particular purpose or duty: *the doorman was at his station near the main entrance.* 4. social position. 5. a radio or TV broadcasting channel. —*vb.* to place or be placed in a particular position: *the soldiers were stationed abroad.*

stationary ('stāshənri) *adj.* 1. standing still: *a long queue of stationary cars.* 2. not able to be moved: *there was a large stationary crane on the building site.*

stationery ('stāshənri) *n.* writing paper, envelopes, and other materials used for writing.

statue ('statyoo) *n.* a large, often life-size figure made of stone, bronze, etc., that has been carved or moulded to represent a person or animal.

stay (stā) *vb.* 1. to remain or wait in a particular place. 2. to live for a short period away from one's home. 3. to continue; keep on being: *the weather stayed fine.* —*n.* a visit.

steadfast ('stedfâst) *adj.* unchanging; firm; fixed; constant: *a steadfast companion.* —'**steadfastly** *adv.* —'**steadfastness** *n.*

steady ('stedi) *adj.* **steadier, steadiest.** 1. not shaking or trembling: *a very steady hand.* 2. regular; unchanging: *a steady stride.* 3. reliable; not easily upset: *steady nerves.* —*vb.* **steadying, steadied.** to make or become steady. —'**steadily** *adv.* —'**steadiness** *n.*

steak (stāk) *n.* a slice of meat or fish that is usu. fried or grilled.

steal (stēl) *vb.* **stealing, stole, stolen.** 1. to take (something belonging to someone else) without permission: *he stole the money.* 2. to do or move very quietly and secretly: *she stole downstairs without waking anyone.* **steal a march on** to win an advantage over (someone) by cunning and stealth.

steam (stēm) *n.* the gas or vapour formed by boiling water. It is used, under pressure, to work engines. **let off steam** to release suppressed emotions, temper, etc. —*vb.* 1. to give off water vapour. 2. to treat or cook with steam. 3. to move by steam power: *the ship steamed away.* 4. (+ *up*) to be covered with steam. '**steamer** *n.* 1. a ship powered by steam. 2. a kind of pan in which food is cooked by steam. **steam engine** an engine powered by steam.

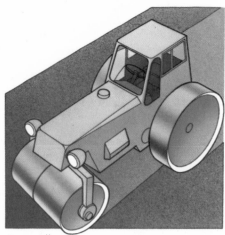
steamroller

steamroller ('stēmrōlə) *n.* a large piece of machinery with heavy rollers instead of wheels, used to crush down and smooth the surface of roads that are being made.

steel (stēl) *n.* a hard tough metal usu. made of iron and a chemical element called carbon, and used for making machinery, cars, and many other products.

steep (stēp) *adj.* sloping upwards or downwards at a very sharp angle: *the path to the top of the cliff was very steep.*

steeple ('stēpəl) *n.* a tall pointed structure in the shape of a cone or pyramid often built on top of church towers.

steer[1] (stiə) *vb.* 1. to drive or guide a car, ship, etc., in a certain direction. 2. to guide: *he steered his son out of danger.* **steer clear of** to avoid.

steer[2] (stiə) *n.* a young male ox, reared for its meat.

stem (stem) *n.* 1. the main stalk of a plant or the smaller stalks supporting the flowers or leaves. 2. any slender support: *the stem of a wineglass.* 3. a branch of a family descended from the same ancestor. —*vb.* **stemming, stemmed.** (+ *from*) to descend or originate from: *the idea stemmed from an old picture.*

stencil ('stensil) *n.* 1. a sheet of metal or card that has holes cut through it to form words, patterns, etc. The cut-out areas allow the penetration of ink or paint so that they can be used to print or mark surfaces. 2. the pattern or words produced by using a stencil. —*vb.* **stencilling, stencilled.** to use a stencil.

step (step) *n.* 1. the act of raising and putting down one foot when walking, running, or dancing; a stride. 2. a single stage in a series of stages: *he was a step nearer his aim.* 3. a ledge, rung, or stair on which one puts one's foot in moving from one level to another. 4. the sound made by putting down one's foot. —*vb.* **stepping, stepped.** 1. to walk. 2. to put one's foot down.

stepfather ('stepfâdhə) *n.* the man whom one's mother marries after the death or divorce of one's real father.

stepladder ('steplad ə) *n.* a small ladder with a support that can be folded away for carrying and having steps instead of rungs or bars.

stepmother ('stepmudhə) *n.* the woman whom one's father marries after the death or divorce of one's real mother.

sterling ('stûling) *n.* 1. British money. 2. (also **sterling silver**) a fine quality silver, used to make jewellery, tableware, etc. —*adj.* 1. of or connected with British money. 2. having genuine moral worth: *he is a sterling character.*

stern[1] (stûn) *adj.* strict; severe: *a very stern teacher.* —**'sternly** *adv.* —**'sternness** *n.*

stern[2] (stûn) *n.* the back end of a ship or aircraft.

stethoscope ('stethəskōp) *n.* a device used by doctors to enable them to listen to the sound of the heart, lungs, etc.

stew (styoo) *n.* a dish of meat and vegetables cooked slowly together. —*vb.* to cook (meat, vegetables, etc.) slowly and gently.

steward ('styooəd) *n.* 1. a man who attends to the passengers on a ship or aircraft. 2. a man in charge of the day-to-day management of a large property or institution. 3. someone who helps organize meetings, entertainments, etc. **'stewardess** *n.* a woman who attends to the passengers on a ship or aircraft.

stick[1] (stik) *n.* 1. a thin stiff rod, esp. of wood. 2. anything shaped like a stick of wood: *a stick of liquorice.* **a cleft stick** a difficult situation for which one cannot find a satisfactory solution. **get (hold of) the wrong end of the stick** to misunderstand.

stick[2] (stik) *vb.* **sticking, stuck.** 1. to push (a pointed object) firmly into something; stab; pierce. 2. to fasten (paper, ribbon, tiles, etc.) to something else with glue, sticky tape, etc.: *he stuck a stamp on the envelope.* 3. to be unable to move or go on any further: *they were stuck in the heavy traffic.* 4. to hold or follow close to: *the dog stuck to the trail of the fox.* 5. to be or become fixed in place: *the nail stuck in the tyre.* 6. to put in a particular place: *she stuck the clothes in the drawer.* 7. (+ *up* or *out*) to stand out from the surrounding area; project: *the nail was sticking out from the wood.* 8. (+ *to* or *at*) to persevere: *sh stuck to her tennis classes for two years.* **'sticker** *n.* a label that can be glued on. **'sticky** *adj.* **stickier, stickiest.** 1. able to stick (def. 2) to things. 2. feeling like damp glue to the touch. 3. (slang) difficult to manage or cope with: *a sticky problem.* —**'stickily** *adv.* —**'stickiness** *n.*

stiff (stif) *adj.* 1. not easily bent or moved: *a stiff muscle.* 2. formal; not friendly or relaxed: *stiff manners.* 3. difficult; needing much effort, skill, etc.: *a stiff examination.* 4. strong; powerful: *a stiff breeze.* 5. harsh: *stiff penalties.* —*adv.* (informal) very much; greatly: *I was scared stiff.* **'stiffen** *vb.* to make or become stiff or stiffer. —**'stiffly** *adv.* —**'stiffness** *n.*

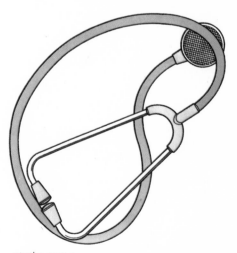
stethoscope

stifle ('stīfəl) *vb.* **stifling, stifled.** 1. to smother; choke by not allowing to breathe: *the thick smoke was stifling the firemen.* 2. to find it difficult to breathe, esp. because of heat, crowds, etc. 3. to hold back: *Jim stifled a laugh.*

stile (stīl) *n.* a part of a fence that has steps on either side so that people can climb over it.

still (stil) *adj.* 1. not moving. 2. quiet; silent. —*n.* one photograph from a series that together form a film. —*vb.* to make calm and quiet. —*adv.* 1. without moving: *she stood still.* 2. up to and including a certain time: *he is still ill.* 3. even more; to a higher degree or greater extent: *her plan was better still.* —*conj.* all the same; nevertheless: *although it was raining heavily, still she insisted on going.*

stilt

stilt (stilt) *n.* one of a pair of long poles with a block on which the foot is placed. People use stilts to raise them above the ground for walking.

stilted ('stiltid) *adj.* stiff; not relaxed: *a stilted conversation.*

stimulate ('stimyŏŏlāt) *vb.* **stimulating, stimulated.** to arouse (somebody) to action: *we were stimulated to work harder by our teacher's praise.* —**stimu'lation** *n.* **'stimulus** *n.* something that stimulates.

sting (sting) *vb.* **stinging, stung.** 1. to pierce with a sharp point: *he was stung by a wasp.* 2. to cause or feel sharp burning pain: *the salt water stung her eyes.* 3. to make (someone or something) act by rousing sharply: *he was stung into action by her scorn.* 4. (slang) to overcharge: *the dealer stung him for £80 for that old carpet.* —*n.* 1. the organ of a bee, wasp, etc., which pierces the skin of its victim and leaves poison in the flesh. 2. the pain or wound caused by this. 3. sharp mental or physical pain.

stingy ('stinji) *adj.* **stingier, stingiest.** mean; unwilling to spend or give.

stink (stiñgk) *vb.* **stinking, stank** *or* **stunk.** to give off a strong unpleasant smell. —*n.* 1. a strong unpleasant smell. 2. (slang) a fuss.

stir (stû) *vb.* **stirring, stirred.** 1. to cause (a liquid, mixture, etc.) to be mixed up or set in motion by moving a spoon, etc., in it. 2. (often + *up*) to rouse (someone) into action; excite: *he stirred the crowd into a frenzy.* 3. to move slightly: *he stirred in his sleep.* —*n.* 1. the act of stirring. 2. excitement: *his news caused a stir.*

stirrup ('stirəp) *n.* 1. one of two metal or wooden foot-rests hanging from either side of a saddle, used by the rider of a horse. 2. one of the three small bones in the middle ear that transmit sounds to the inner ear.

stoat (stōt) *n.* a small furry animal related to the WEASEL. See also ERMINE.

stock (stok) *n.* 1. the supply of goods available for sale, distribution, etc.: *the shop had a good stock of new records.* 2. line of descent; ancestry: *she is of French stock.* 3. the handle or support of a gun, whip, etc. 4. shares in a business company. 5. a thin soup made from stewed bones, etc. —*vb.* to keep (goods) available for sale, distribution, etc.

stockade (sto'kād) *n.* 1. a fence made of tall upright posts. 2. the area enclosed by this fence.

stoke (stōk) *vb.* (often + *up*) to add fuel to (a fire, furnace, etc.). **'stoker** *n.* a person whose job it is to put fuel into a furnace or boiler and keep it working.

stole[1] (stōl) *vb.* the past tense of STEAL.

stole[2] (stōl) *n.* a long scarf or shawl worn round a woman's shoulders.

stolen ('stōlən) *vb.* the past participle of STEAL.

stomach ('stumək) *n.* 1. the baglike part of the body, inside the ribs, into which food passes when it is swallowed and where it is then digested. 2. the lower front part of the body below the chest. 3. inclination; desire: *I have no stomach for violent films.* —*vb.* to endure or accept: *I can't stomach his rudeness.*

stoop (stoop) *vb.* to bend (the body) downwards and forwards. —*n.* a forward and downward curve of a person's head and shoulders.

stopwatch ('stopwoch) *n.* a watch with a hand that can be started and stopped as required, used esp. to time races.

store (stô) *n.* 1. a supply of goods for future use. 2. a large shop. —*vb.* **storing, stored.** to keep (food, goods, etc.) for future use. **'storage** *n.* the storing of food, goods, information, etc.

storey ('stôri) *n.* a floor or level in a building.

stork (stôk) *n.* a large long-legged mainly white bird, often found near water. It sometimes builds nests on houses.

storm (stôm) *n.* a violent outbreak of bad weather with rain, hail, wind, or snow. **a storm in a teacup** a fuss about an unimportant matter. —*vb.* 1. to show anger by shouting, etc. 2. to attack (a building, town, etc.) with violence in order to capture it: *the police stormed the house.*

story ('stôri) *n.,pl.* **stories.** 1. an account of past or imaginary happenings. 2. (informal) lie: *he told stories to make his friends believe that his father was rich.*

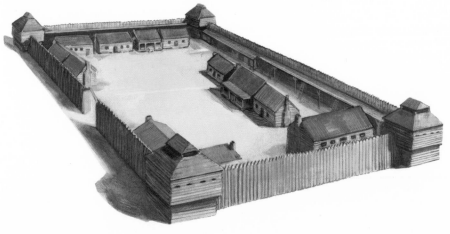

stockade

stout (stout) *adj.* 1. rather fat. 2. strong; not easily worn out: *stout shoes.* 3. (formerly) brave and determined: *a stout friend.* —*n.* strong dark beer.

stove (stōv) *n.* an apparatus with an enclosed source of heat used for cooking food, heating a room, etc.

stow (stō) *vb.* (often + *away*) to pack (something) neatly and carefully.

stowaway ('stōəwā) *n.* a person who hides aboard a ship or aircraft so as to travel without paying.

stork

straggle ('stragəl) *vb.* **straggling, straggled.** 1. to grow in an untidy manner: *the hedge straggled along the roadside.* 2. to wander away from or fall behind other people on the move. **'straggly** *adj.* **stragglier, straggliest.** scattered or growing in an untidy manner.

straight (strāt) *adj.* 1. not crooked or curved. 2. in good order; tidy: *I put the room straight.* 3. (informal) honest: *a straight man will not cheat you.* —*adv.* 1. directly: *he looked straight ahead.* 2. without turning aside or delaying: *they went straight home.* **'straighten** *vb.* to make or become straight or straighter. —**'straightness** *n.*

straightforward (strāt'fôwəd) *adj.* 1. simple to understand or do. 2. direct. —**straight'forwardly** *adv.* —**straight'forwardness** *n.*

strain[1] (strān) *vb.* 1. to make a great effort. 2. to injure (a muscle, limb, etc.) by making too great an effort, e.g. when lifting something. 3. to stretch (a rope, etc.) tightly. 4. to pass (a liquid) through a cloth, strainer, etc., so as to separate the solids in it.

—*n.* 1. pressure or force: *will the rope take the strain?* 2. conditions in a person's life that cause worry or tiredness; STRESS: *she was under great strain during her husband's illness.* 3. an injury caused by too great effort. **'strainer** *n.* a device with a fine mesh or many small holes used to strain (def. 4) liquids.

strain[2] (strān) *n.* 1. breed; stock. 2. a quality in a person's character: *a strain of generosity.* 3. usu. **strains** (*pl.*) sounds, esp. of music, usu. heard only very faintly: *the strains of a waltz.*

strait (strāt) *n.* often **straits** (*pl.*) a narrow channel of water joining two seas: *the Bering Strait.*

strand[1] (strand) *n.* 1. a single thread, fibre, wire, etc., twisted with others to form a rope or cable. 2. a lock of hair.

strand[2] (strand) *vb.* to leave (a person) in a difficult position, without money, transport, etc.

strange (strānj) *adj.* **stranger, strangest.** 1. extraordinary; odd: *a strange thing happened yesterday.* 2. unfamiliar; foreign: *I don't like strange food.* 3. shy; awkward: *he felt strange when he first went to school.* **'stranger** *n.* 1. a person whom one does not know. 2. a person in a place he does not know: *I am a stranger in Rome.*

strangle ('stranggəl) *vb.* **strangling, strangled.** to kill by squeezing the throat so as to prevent breathing. —**'strangler** *n.* —**strangulation** (stranggyōo'lāshən) *n.*

straw (strô) *n.* 1. the dry cut stalks of grain plants, e.g. barley, used as bedding for cattle. 2. a single such stalk. 3. a long thin paper or plastic tube for sucking up liquids; drinking straw. **the last straw** the single extra item that makes a task too difficult or a situation unbearable.

strawberry ('strôbəri) *n.,pl.* **strawberries.** 1. a small juicy red fruit. 2. the plant on which it grows.

stray (strā) *vb.* 1. to wander away (from a group, the path, etc.). 2. (of thoughts) to wander idly over different subjects. —*n.* an animal that has strayed from its usual home, field, herd, etc. —*adj.* 1. unattended; loose: *a stray dog.* 2. occasional: *a stray bullet.*

streak (strēk) *n.* 1. a thin irregular line or mark. 2. a small amount: *a streak of good luck.* —*vb.* to move very quickly.

stream (strēm) *n.* 1. a small river. 2. an even flow (of air, people, liquid, etc.). —*vb.* 1. to flow. 2. to move steadily in a mass. **'streamer** *n.* a long narrow flag, ribbon, etc.

strength (strength) *n.* 1. the quality or condition of being strong. 2. a strong point: *arithmetic is his strength.* **'strengthen** *vb.* to make or become strong or stronger.

stress (stres) *n.* 1. pressure or force. 2. conditions of hardship, trouble, etc. 3. emphasis: *the stress on a word.* —*vb.* 1. to insist on the importance of: *I stressed this point.* 2. to emphasize (a part of a word or sentence).

stretch (strech) *vb.* 1. to make tighter or bigger by pulling. 2. to make larger or extend (one's arm, abilities, etc.). —*n.* a period of time. **'stretcher** *n.* a light folding bed for carrying a sick or injured person.

strict (strikt) *adj.* 1. stern; demanding obedience. 2. clearly limited and with no additions: *she told the strict truth.* —**'strictly** *adv.* —**'strictness** *n.*

strike[1] (strīk) *vb.* **striking, struck.** 1. to hit. 2. (of a clock) to mark (the time) by striking. 3. to light (a match). 4. to arrive at; find. 5. to lower (a flag, sail, etc.). 6. to attack suddenly. —*n.* an attack: *our bombers made a strike against the enemy.*

strike[2] (strīk) *vb.* **striking, struck.** to refuse to work so as to obtain better pay, conditions, etc. —*n.* the refusal to work.

strawberry

stroke

string (string) *n.* 1. a fine cord. 2. the taut lengths of cord, wire, etc., that produce the sounds in a musical instrument, e.g. a piano. 3. a series of things threaded on a string or in a line: *a string of beads.* —*vb.* **stringing, strung.** to thread (items) on a string.

strip (strip) *vb.* **stripping, stripped.** 1. to remove a covering, skin, etc., from (something). 2. to remove one's clothes. 3. to remove furnishings from (a place). 4. (+ *of*) to take away the possessions, rights, etc., of (somebody): *the judge stripped him of his unlawful gains.* 5. to remove (paint) from a surface. —*n.* a long narrow piece of land, paper, cloth, etc.

stroke[1] (strōk) *vb.* **stroking, stroked.** to move one's hand gently along or over (something). —*n.* the act of doing this.

stroke[2] (strōk) *n.* 1. a blow; the act of striking. 2. a sudden attack of illness that injures the brain and so causes part of the body to stop working. 3. one of a series of movements in swimming, e.g. breaststroke. 4. a sudden, unexpected chance: *a stroke of luck.*

strong (strong) *adj.* 1. having great physical strength. 2. not easily broken or damaged: *a strong door.* 3. powerfully felt: *a strong wish.*

struck (struk) *vb.* the past tense and past participle of STRIKE.

struggle ('strugəl) *vb.* **struggling, struggled.** 1. to fight, usu. with a violent effort. 2. to try hard. —*n.* 1. a fight. 2. a great effort.

strung (strung) *vb.* the past tense and past participle of STRING. **highly strung** (of a person or animal) nervous; likely to get excited.

strut[1] (strut) *vb.* **strutting, strutted.** to walk in a stiff proud way. —*n.* a stiff way of walking.

strut[2] (strut) *n.* a piece of wood or metal used to support or strengthen a framework or building.

stub (stub) *n.* 1. the short end of a pencil or cigarette left after the rest has been used. 2. part of a cheque, invoice, etc., kept as a record. —*vb.* **stubbing, stubbed.** to hit (one's foot or toe) against something.

stubble ('stubəl) *n.* 1. the short stalks of grain left in the field after the harvest. 2. the short bristly growth of a man's beard when he has not shaved.

stubborn ('stubən) *adj.* determined not to alter one's own opinions, course of action, habits, etc.; obstinate. —'**stubbornness** *n.* —'**stubbornly** *adv.*

stuck (stuk) *vb.* the past tense and past participle of STICK[2]. '**stuck-**'**up** *adj.* (informal) proud; conceited.

stud[1] (stud) *n.* 1. a small knob or button used on clothing, esp. collars and cuffs. 2. a large-headed nail sticking out from a surface: *studs in car tyres help them to grip on ice.* —*vb.* **studding, studded.** to cover with studs or studlike objects for ornament or protection: *the crown was studded with jewels.*

stud[2] (stud) *n.* 1. a number of animals (esp. horses) kept for breeding. 2. a farm for animal breeding.

student ('styoodənt) *n.* a person who studies, esp. in a university or other place of further education.

studio ('styoōdiō) *n.,pl.* **studios.** 1. the room in which a painter, sculptor, or photographer works. 2. the place in which cinema films are made. 3. the room from which TV and radio broadcasts are made. 4. the place in which music is recorded for making gramophone records, etc.

study ('studi) *vb.* **studying, studied.** 1. to learn (something) by working steadily over a period of time. 2. to gaze at (something) closely. —*n.,pl.* **studies.** a room used for studying. **studious** ('styoōdiəs) *adj.* having the habit of studying. —'**studiously** *adv.* —'**studiousness** *n.*

stuff (stuf) *n.* 1. the material or substance from which other articles are made. 2. (informal) something that the speaker thinks is of poor quality: *do you call this stuff fresh?* 3. (informal) a person's belongings: *she left her stuff in my house while she looked for somewhere to live.* —*vb.* 1. to fill (something) tightly with something else. 2. to force (something) into a small space or container. '**stuffing** *n.* substance used for stuffing, e.g. feathers for pillows, sausagemeat for turkeys, etc. '**stuffy** *adj.* **stuffier, stuffiest.** 1. (of a room) without fresh air. 2. (informal) (of a person) stiff in manner.

stumble ('stumbəl) *vb.* **stumbling, stumbled.** to move unsteadily; stagger or fall, e.g. because one is ill or has tripped over something. —*n.* the act of stumbling.

stump (stump) *n.* 1. the part of a tree left just above the ground after the top and trunk have been removed. 2. anything left behind after the larger part has been removed or worn out: *the stump of a pencil.* 3. one of three wooden sticks forming the wicket in cricket. —*vb.* 1. (often + *about*) to walk about heavily and clumsily. 2. (informal) to be too difficult for: *your question stumped him.* '**stumpy** *adj.* **stumpier, stumpiest.** short and thick.

stung (stung) *vb.* the past tense and past participle of STING.

stunk (stungk) *vb.* the past tense and past participle of STINK.

stunt[1] (stunt) *vb.* to halt or hamper the growth of (a child, plant, etc.). —'**stuntedness** *n.*

stunt[2] (stunt) *n.* an action done to gain publicity, e.g. to advertise something.

'**stuntman** *n.,pl.* **stuntmen.** a person who performs dangerous actions in films, etc.

stupid ('styoōpid) *adj.* foolish and slow-witted; silly. —**stu'pidity** *n.* —'**stupidly** *adv.*

sturdy ('stûdi) *adj.* **sturdier, sturdiest.** strong and solid. —'**sturdily** *adv.* —'**sturdiness** *n.*

stutter ('stutə) *vb.* to talk in jerks: *"p-p-please", stuttered Tom.* —*n.* a jerky way of talking.

sty[1] (stī) *n.,pl.* **sties.** the place where pigs are kept.

sty[2] (stī) *n.,pl.* **sties** *or* **styes.** a swollen sore on an eyelid.

style (stīl) *n.* 1. the manner in which something is done: *he has a clumsy style of writing.* 2. the particular quality that marks something out from other things: *that dress was in the latest style.* 3. the general form or design: *a modern style of building.* '**stylish** *adj.* fashionable; smart.

subject *n.* ('subjikt) 1. any person who is not the ruler of a state; citizen. 2. (in grammar) the word or words in a sentence that rule the verb, e.g. *the dog* in the sentence *the dog ate the meat.* 3. the thing to be studied or talked about: *she talked on the subject of travel.* —*adj.* ('subjikt) 1. under the control of somebody else. 2. (+ *to*) likely to have: *he is subject to headaches.* —*vb.* (səb'jekt) 1. to get (something) under one's control. 2. (+ *to*) to cause (someone) to undergo an experience. —**sub'jection** *n.*

submarine (səbmə'rēn) *n.* a ship able to travel under the surface of the water. —*adj.* of things below the surface of the sea.

submerge (səb'mûj) *vb.* **submerging, submerged.** to go or cause to go under water. —**submersion** (səb'mûshən) *n.*

submit (səb'mit) *vb.* **submitting, submitted.** 1. to put oneself under the control of another. 2. to put forward (e.g. a plan for discussion). —**sub'mission** *n.*

subside (səb'sīd) *vb.* **subsiding, subsided.** 1. (of water) to sink to a lower or more usual level. 2. (of land) to sink. 3. (of emotions or the wind) to become calm. —'**subsidence** *n.*

substance ('substəns) *n.* 1. material, particularly the material out of which something is made. 2. the most important part: *the substance of a plan.* 3. firmness; solidity; body. **substantial** (səb'stanshəl) *adj.* 1. having importance. 2. having solidity.

substitute ('substityoōt) *vb.* **substituting, substituted.** to put or use one thing in the place of another. —*n.* the person or thing substituted. —**substi'tution** *n.*

subterranean (subtə'rāniən) *adj.* underground.

subtle ('sutəl) *adj.* 1. difficult to understand, explain, or sense because very delicate: *a subtle perfume.* 2. with the ability to understand subtle points: *a subtle thinker.* 3. cunning: *a subtle thief.* —'**subtlety** *n.,pl.* **subtleties.** —'**subtly** *adv.*

subtract (səb'trakt) *vb.* to take (something) away from some larger whole. —**sub'traction** *n.*

suburb ('subûb) *n.* an area on the edge of a town. **sub'urban** *adj.* of or in the area between town and country. **sub'urbia** *n.* the suburbs.

submarine

subway ('subwā) *n.* 1. an underground passage, often under a busy street. 2. (U.S.) underground railway.

succeed (sək'sēd) *vb.* 1. to do what one has been trying to do. 2. to do well. 3. to follow next in order. **success** (sək'ses) *n.* 1. an achievement. 2. a person who does well. **suc'cessful** *adj.* of a person or activity that succeeds (defs. 1 and 2). **suc'cession** *n.* the following of one thing after another in time or position. **suc'cessive** *adj.* following one after another. —**suc'cessor** *n.*

suck (suk) *vb.* 1. to draw (liquid) into the mouth by using the lip muscles. 2. to hold (something) in the mouth to melt it. **'sucker** *n.* 1. a device that sticks to a surface by suction. 2. an offshoot from a plant. 3. (slang) a person who is easily cheated.

suction ('sukshən) *n.* 1. the action of sucking (def. 1). 2. force produced by a vacuum, causing something to stick or be drawn into something else: *the rubber disc is attached to the wall by suction.*

sudden ('sudən) *adj.* happening or carried out quickly or abruptly: *the car made a sudden turn in the road.* —**'suddenly** *adv.*

suede (swād) *n.* leather with a soft unpolished surface, often used for jackets and shoes.

suet ('sōoit) *n.* the thick hard fat surrounding the kidneys of sheep and cattle. It is used in cooking, e.g. for suet pudding.

suffer ('sufə) *vb.* 1. to feel or endure pain, injury, etc. 2. to be harmed: *his work suffered because of his illness.* 3. to allow. **on sufferance** allowed but not definitely wanted.

suffix ('sufiks) *n.* the letter(s) or syllable(s) added to the end of a word to make another word, e.g. in the word *strongly, -ly* is the suffix. —*vb.* to add a suffix to.

suffocate ('sufəkāt) *vb.* **suffocating, suffocated.** 1. to kill by preventing breathing. 2. to have or cause difficulty in breathing; stifle. —**suffo-'cation** *n.*

sugar ('shŏogə) *n.* sweet substance found in various plants, e.g. sugarcane and sugarbeet, and used to sweeten food. —*vb.* to sweeten (something) with sugar. —**'sugary** *adj.*

suggest (sə'jest) *vb.* 1. to put forward an idea, etc., to be considered: *I suggest we go to the cinema.* 2. to bring an idea, etc., into the mind: *his behaviour suggests that he is very generous.* **sug'gestion** *n.* 1. an idea, etc., that is suggested. 2. a hint or trace: *there was a suggestion of a smile on her lips.* **sug'gestive** *adj.* tending to bring ideas, etc., into the mind.

suit (sōot) *n.* 1. a set of clothing made of the same material. 2. a case in a law court; lawsuit. 3. (formerly) a formal request. 4. one of the four sets in a pack of cards (spades, hearts, clubs, diamonds). —*vb.* 1. to satisfy. 2. (of clothing) to look well when worn. **'suitable** *adj.* right for a purpose or occasion. **'suitor** *n.* 1. a person who starts a lawsuit. 2. a man who courts a woman. —**'suitably** *adv.*

suitcase

suitcase ('sōotkās) *n.* a rather flat oblong box with a handle, used by travellers to carry their clothes.

sulk (sulk) *vb.* to be in a bad temper, usu. showing this by refusing to talk. —**'sulkily** *adv.* —**'sulkiness** *n.* —**'sulky** *adj.* **sulkier, sulkiest.**

sullen ('sulən) *adj.* 1. (of a person) gloomy and bad-tempered, usu. in a silent way. 2. (of the sky or weather) dark. —**'sullenly** *adv.*

sulphur ('sulfə) *n.* a pale yellow chemical element that burns with a blue flame and smells strongly when mixed with other substances. Chemical symbol: S.

sultan ('sultən) *n.* a MUSLIM ruler.

sultana (sul'tânə) *n.* 1. a dried seedless grape, like a RAISIN, used in cooking. 2. the wife, daughter, or sister of a SULTAN.

sultry ('sultri) *adj.* **sultrier, sultriest.** (of the weather) hot and sticky.

summer ('sumə) *n.* the warmest season of the year, between spring and autumn. —**'summery** *adj.*

summit ('sumit) *n.* the top; highest level.

summon ('sumən) *vb.* 1. to send for or call. 2. (+ *up*) to gather together: *she summoned up her courage to jump off the high wall.* **'summons** *sing.n.* a formal order or demand, esp. to attend a case in a law court.

sun (sun) *n.* the heavenly body that gives warmth and light to the earth. —**'sunnily** *adv.* —**'sunny** *adj.* **sunnier, sunniest.**

sunbathe ('sunbādh) *vb.* **sunbathing, sunbathed.** to sit or lie in the sunlight for pleasure.

sunburn ('sunbûn) *n.* the reddening and blistering of the skin caused by strong sunlight. —**'sunburnt** *adj.*

sunglasses ('sunglâsiz) *pl.n.* spectacles with darkened glass, used to protect the eyes against strong sunlight.

sunk (suñgk) *vb.* the past participle of SINK.

sunrise ('sunrīz) *n.* 1. the time of the sun's appearance above the horizon. 2. the sun's appearance in the morning.

sunset ('sunset) *n.* 1. the time of the sun's disappearance below the horizon. 2. the sun's disappearance in the evening.

sunstroke ('sunstrōk) *n.* an illness caused by too much exposure to the sun's rays, esp. on the head.

superior (sōo'piəriə) *adj.* 1. better. 2. higher in position. 3. greater in number. —*n.* a person who is higher in rank or abilities than another: *Margaret is my superior at chess.* —**superiority** (sōopiəri'oriti) *n.*

superlative (sōo'pûlətiv) *adj.* of the highest quality or degree: *he is a superlative singer.* —*n.* (grammar) a form of an adjective, e.g. *biggest* is the superlative of *big.* —**su'perlatively** *adv.*

supermarket ('sōopəmâkit) *n.* a big self-service store, usu. selling a wide range of food and household items.

supersonic (sōopə'sonik) *adj.* faster than the speed of sound.

superstition (sōopə'stishən) *n.* an unreasonable fear, esp. a belief that certain actions or things are unlucky: *there are many superstitions about black cats.* —**super'stitious** *adj.* —**super'stitiously** *adv.*

supervise ('sōopəvīz) *vb.* **supervising, supervised.** to direct or oversee (work or workers); superintend. —**supervision** (sōopə'vizhən) *n.* —'**supervisor** *n.*

supper ('supə) *n.* the last meal of the day, often a light one.

supple ('supəl) *adj.* easily bent; not stiff. —'**suppleness** *n.*

supply (sə'plī) *vb.* **supplying, supplied.** 1. to provide or give (something) to somebody. 2. to provide (someone or something) with necessary things. 3. to produce some goods or services, usu. for sale. —*n.,pl.* **supplies.** the goods on hand to be supplied or used.

support (sə'pôt) *vb.* 1. to hold up (a weight, etc.). 2. to provide the money to enable (other people) to eat, be clothed, etc. 3. to encourage or help (somebody). 4. to endure. —*n.* 1. a person who supports (def. 2). 2. something that takes the weight of something else. **sup'porter** *n.* a person who supports (esp. def. 3).

suppose (sə'pōz) *vb.* **supposing, supposed.** 1. to take (something) as a fact: *let's suppose he is telling the truth.* 2. to guess or think: *we supposed he would do his share of the hard work.* **sup'posing** *conj.* if. **sup'posed** *adj.* thought to be so: *the supposed prince was really a spy in disguise.* **supposition** (supə'zishən) *n.* 1. the act of supposing. 2. something supposed.

supreme (sōo'prēm) *adj.* 1. highest in rank or quality. 2. of greatest importance. **supremacy** (sōo'preməsi) *n.* highest position, authority, or power. —**su'premely** *adv.*

sure (shōoə) *adj.* 1. positive that something is so: *are you sure of these figures?* 2. certain: *be sure to bring your swim-suit.* 3. trustworthy: *primroses are a sure sign that spring has arrived.* '**surely** *adv.* 1. certainly. 2. if things work out as expected: *surely your parents will not forget your birthday.*

surfboard

surf (sûf) *n.* large waves of the sea breaking on the seashore or on rocks. —*vb.* to ride such waves as a sport, usu. on a **surfboard.**

surface ('sûfis) *n.* 1. the outside of something. 2. the upper layer of a liquid: *bubbles broke through the surface of the water.* —*adj.* appearing or happening on a surface, esp. of the land or sea: *he will never fly anywhere—he always goes by surface transport.* —*vb.* **surfacing, surfaced.** to rise to the surface.

surge (sûj) *vb.* **surging, surged.** to move forwards and upwards with a movement like waves: *the crowd surged against the barrier.* —*n.* a forward rush like that of waves.

surgeon ('sûjən) *n.* a doctor who performs surgery (def. 1). '**surgery** *n.,pl.* **surgeries.** 1. treatment of disease or injury by repairing or removing parts of the body. 2. a doctor's room to which patients come to get advice, treatment, etc. '**surgical** *adj.* of or by surgery (def. 1).

surname ('sûnām) *n.* the part of a person's name that he shares with all his family; family name: *Adams is the surname of Sarah Adams.*

surplus ('sûpləs) *n.* an extra amount of goods, money, etc., over and above the basic or necessary amount: *the country produced a surplus of grain this year.*

surprise (səprīz) *n.* 1. something unexpected. 2. the feeling caused by an unexpected happening. —*vb.* **surprising, surprised.** 1. to cause a feeling of surprise (def. 2) to. 2. to find, unawares come upon, or catch (someone): *we surprised the thief as he was breaking open the door.*

sur'prising *adj.* causing surprise.

surrender (sə'rendə) *vb.* 1. to give oneself up to an enemy, etc.: *the general surrendered to the enemy.* 2. to give up possession of: *he surrendered his gun to the police.* 3. to give way to; yield: *he surrendered to despair.* —*n.* the action or an instance of surrendering.

surreptitious (surəp'tishəs) *adj.* done secretly or by stealth. —**surrep'titiously** *adv.*

surround (sə'round) *vb.* to be or move round (something) on every side; encircle: *the army surrounded the fortress.* **sur'roundings** *pl.n.* the place and conditions in which a person lives or works.

survey *vb.* (sə'vā) 1. to take a general look at. 2. to measure (a piece of land, coastline, etc.) in order to make a map or chart. —*n.* ('sûvā) 1. an overall or general view: *he made a rapid survey of the scene.* 2. the measuring and mapping of the earth. **sur'veyor** *n.* a person whose occupation is surveying land.

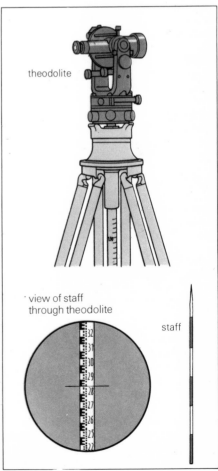

theodolite

view of staff through theodolite

staff

survey

survive (sə'vīv) *vb.* **surviving, survived.** 1. to live longer than. 2. to remain alive, esp. after an accident. **sur'vivor** *n.* a person who lives through a disaster.

suspect *vb.* (sə'spekt) 1. to have an idea that something is so, without being certain: *I suspect that he is wrong.* 2. to be doubtful about: *I suspect this cake—it may be stale.* 3. to believe (somebody) to be guilty of a crime, etc.: *the police suspect him of theft.* —*n.* ('suspekt) a person who is thought to be guilty of a crime.

suspend (sə'spend) *vb.* 1. to hang (something) from a support above. 2. to put off for a time: *the race was suspended because of rain.* 3. to shut out for a time: *they suspended him from the club.* **sus'pension** *n.* the act of suspending or being suspended.

suspense (sə'spens) *n.* uncertainty about the outcome of a story, etc.

suspicion (sə'spishən) *n.* 1. the feeling that something is wrong, or that someone is guilty, without having definite proof. 2. a hint: *there was a suspicion of a smile on her face.* **sus'picious** *adj.* having or causing suspicion: *he is a suspicious character.* —**sus'piciously** *adv.*

swallow¹ ('swolō) *n.* a small fast-flying bird with long wings and a double-pointed tail.

swallow² ('swolō) *vb.* 1. to move food, drink, etc., from the mouth through the throat to the stomach. 2. to accept, usu. too easily: *I swallowed his lies.*

swam (swam) *vb.* the past tense of SWIM.

swamp (swomp) *n.* an area of soft ground with patches of water; marsh. —*vb.* 1. to flood with water. 2. to have too much of: *the teacher was swamped with work.* —**'swampy** *adj.* **swampier, swampiest.**

swan (swon) *n.* a large waterbird, with a long graceful neck.

swarm (swôm) *n.* 1. a large gathering of insects, esp. honeybees. 2. a big crowd of people. —*vb.* 1. (of bees) to move in a swarm with the queen bee. 2. to move or be present in a crowd: *the children swarmed into the street.*

swear (sweə) *vb.* **swearing, swore, sworn.** 1. to promise, esp. on oath. 2. to use bad language.

sweat (swet) *n.* the moisture that comes from the body through the skin, particularly if one is hot or worried. —*vb.* to produce sweat.

sweep (swēp) *vb.* **sweeping, swept.** 1. to clean (a room, floor, etc.) by brushing with a broom. 2. to move swiftly: *the galloping horses swept past.* —*n.* a person whose job is sweeping chimneys. **'sweeping** *adj.* having a great effect: *sweeping changes.*

sweet (swēt) *adj.* 1. tasting like sugar. 2. pleasant; attractive. —*n.* 1. something sweet to eat. 2. a sweet-tasting course in a meal. **'sweeten** *vb.* to make sweet. —**'sweetness** *n.*

swept (swept) *vb.* the past tense and past participle of SWEEP.

swift¹ (swift) *adj.* fast; rapid; quick. —**'swiftly** *adv.* —**'swiftness** *n.*

swift² (swift) *n.* a small fast-flying insect-eating bird.

swim (swim) *vb.* **swimming, swam, swum.** to move through the water by using arms, fins, etc. —*n.* an instance of swimming.

swindle ('swindəl) *vb.* **swindling, swindled.** to cheat or get something by cheating, usu. in money matters. —*n.* 1. an instance of swindling. 2. something by which one is swindled. **'swindler** *n.*

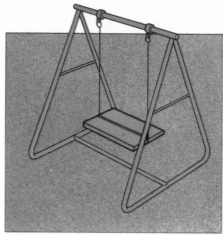

swing

swing (swing) *vb.* **swinging, swung.** 1. (esp. of an object with one fixed end) to move from side to side. 2. to move along a curve: *the car swung round the corner.* —*n.* 1. a swinging movement. 2. a seat on which people, usu. children, swing back and forth for pleasure.

switch (swich) *n.* a device for turning electric current on or off. —*vb.* (+ *on* or *off*) to use a switch to control electric current.

swollen ('swōlən) *vb.* the past participle of SWELL.

sword (sôd) *n.* a weapon with a long sharp-edged pointed steel blade.

swore (swô) *vb.* the past tense of SWEAR.

sworn (swôn) *vb.* the past participle of SWEAR.

swum (swum) *vb.* the past participle of SWIM.

swung (swung) *vb.* the past tense and past participle of SWING.

sycamore ('sikəmô) *n.* one of several types of tall tree that loses its leaves in winter and is valued for its wood.

syllable ('siləbəl) *n.* a part of a word (or a whole word) that is pronounced as a single unit. *Tennis* is a word with two syllables.

symbol ('simbəl) *n.* a sign, object, etc., used to represent something else. **'symbolize** *vb.* **symbolizing, symbolized.** to be or be used as a symbol of. —**symbolic** (sim'bolik) *adj.*

sympathy ('simpəthi) *n.,pl.* **sympathies.** a sharing in or understanding of the feelings of others. **sympathetic** (simpə'thetik) *adj.* having or showing sympathy. **'sympathize** *vb.* **sympathizing, sympathized.** to feel sympathy.

symphony ('simfəni) *n.,pl.* **symphonies.** a piece of music, usu. in four sections (movements), for a full orchestra. —**symphonic** (sim'fonik) *adj.*

symptom ('simptəm) *n.* 1. a change or outward sign in the body showing that it has an illness. 2. a sign that a certain condition exists: *overheating is a symptom of a faulty engine.*

synagogue ('sinəgog) *n.* a building in which Jews worship.

system ('sistəm) *n.* 1. a group of parts working together in an ordered way: *the solar system.* 2. an ordered set of ideas, principles, methods, etc.: *a system of government.* **systematic** (sistə'matik) *adj.* methodical; step-by-step. —**system'atically** *adv.*

T

tabby ('tabi) *n.,pl.* **tabbies.** a cat with grey or brown striped fur.

tablet ('tablit) *n.* 1. a pill. 2. a small hard lump of something, e.g. soap. 3. a writing pad. 4. a flat block with words written on it, e.g. one fixed to a wall in memory of somebody.

tack (tak) *n.* 1. a small flat-headed nail. 2. a long loose temporary stitch. —*vb.* 1. to nail down with tacks. 2. to stitch loosely. 3. to sail against the wind by zigzagging.

tackle ('takəl) *n.* 1. a set of equipment for a certain task or activity: *fishing tackle.* 2. (sport) an attempt to get the ball away from an opponent. —*vb.* **tackling, tackled.** 1. to seize. 2. to deal with (someone or something): *I must tackle him about the money he owes me.* 3. (sport) to attempt to take the ball away from (an opponent).

tact (takt) *n.* the ability to behave towards people in a manner that does not hurt their feelings. —**'tactful** *adj.* —**'tactfully** *adv.*

tactics ('taktiks) *pl.n.* 1. the art of moving soldiers, ships, etc., into a good position for fighting. 2. methods used in carrying out a plan. —**'tactical** *adj.* —**'tactically** *adv.*

tadpole ('tadpōl) *n.* a young frog or toad after hatching and before it is fully developed. It lives in the water and uses its long tail in swimming.

tag (tag) *n.* 1. a metal or plastic tip, e.g. on a shoelace. 2. a label, esp. one showing prices on goods in shops. —*vb.* **tagging, tagged.** to put a price tag on (something).

tail (tāl) *n.* 1. a bodily part, esp. a movable one, at the rear end of an animal. 2. something like a tail in position or function. 3. usu. **tails** (*pl.*) the reverse side of a coin.

tailor ('tālə) *n.* a maker of outer clothing, esp. men's suits.

take-off ('tākof) *n.* 1. the start of an aircraft's flight. 2. the act of copying a person's speech or behaviour in order to amuse others.

take-over ('tākōvə) *n.* the act of taking control or power away from another and into one's own hands: *that firm carried out two successful take-overs last year.*

tale (tāl) *n.* a story or account.

talent ('talənt) *n.* a special natural ability: *he has great talent as a singer.*

talk (tôk) *vb.* 1. to speak or have a discussion. 2. to talk about: *they talked cricket all evening.* —*n.* 1. general conversation. 2. a speech.

talon ('talən) *n.* a long hooked claw of a bird of prey.

tambourine

tambourine (tambə'rēn) *n.* a small flat drum with circles of metal loosely set in the rim that jingle when it is tapped with the hand or shaken.

tame (tām) *adj.* **tamer, tamest.** 1. (of animals) not wild. 2. dull; uninteresting. —*vb.* **taming, tamed.** to make (a wild animal) tame or manageable.

tamper ('tampə) *vb.* (+ *with*) 1. to meddle with. 2. to damage.

tan (tan) *adj.* light brown. —*n.* 1. a tan colour. 2. a suntan. —*vb.* **tanning, tanned.** 1. to make or become tan, often in the sun. 2. to make (an animal's skin) into leather.

tang (tang) *n.* a strong taste or smell: *the wind had the salt tang of the sea.*

tangerine (tanjə'rēn) *n.* a CITRUS fruit like a small orange with a loose skin.

tangle ('tanggəl) *n.* a confused untidy mass. —*vb.* **tangling, tangled.** to make or become confused or untidy.

tank (tangk) *n.* 1. a large storage container for liquid or gas. 2. a heavily armoured vehicle that is used in battle.

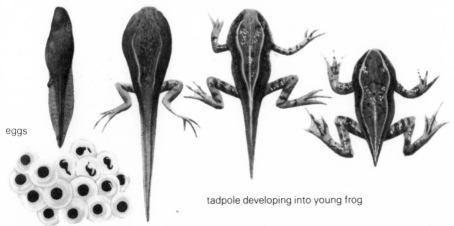
eggs

tadpole developing into young frog

tadpole

tanker

tanker ('taṅkə) *n.* 1. a ship with big tanks for carrying oil. 2. a road vehicle with a large container for carrying liquids, esp. oil or petrol.

tantrum ('tantrəm) *n.* a fit of bad temper, usu. a sudden one about an unimportant matter.

tape (tāp) *n.* 1. a narrow piece of material used in dressmaking, for tying up parcels, etc. 2. a narrow gummed strip of material used for sticking things. 3. the magnetized strip used to record sound in a tape recorder. **tape recorder** an electric machine for recording sound on magnetic tape and playing it back. —*vb.* **taping, taped.** 1. to fasten with a tape. 2. to record (sound) on a tape recorder.

taper ('tāpə) *vb.* to make or become gradually narrower at one end.

tapestry ('tapistri) *n.,pl.* **tapestries.** a cloth into which coloured wools are sewn or woven to make designs, etc.

tar (tâ) *n.* black sticky substance obtained from coal and used on road surfaces. —**tarring, tarred.** to cover with tar.

target ('tâgit) *n.* 1. the mark or object aimed at: *every arrow she shot hit the target.* 2. a person or thing being attacked: *the government is the target these days.*

tariff ('tarif) *n.* 1. a list of taxes on goods brought into a country. 2. a list of prices or charges, esp. at a hotel.

tarpaulin (tâ'pôlin) *n.* a canvas sheet or covering that has been made waterproof by being coated with tar.

tart[1] (tât) *n.* a saucer-shaped pastry base filled with jam, cooked fruit,

etc., and usu. having no top crust.

tart[2] (tât) *adj.* sharp or bitter in taste.

tartan ('tâtən) *n.* 1. Scottish woollen cloth with a design of coloured stripes crossing each other at right angles. 2. a particular pattern of this cloth: *a kilt of the Campbell tartan.*

task (tâsk) *n.* a job of work.

tassel ('tasəl) *n.* a bunch of threads, usu. knotted at one end, hanging from a hat, cushion, etc., as decoration.

taste (tāst) *n.* 1. the sense acting through the tongue that tells us the flavour of food. 2. the quality experienced by this sense: *lemons have a sour taste.* 3. a liking: *a taste for jazz.* 4. the ability to choose and enjoy good things in art, behaviour, dress, etc. —*vb.* **tasting, tasted.** 1. to detect the taste of (something). 2. to have a taste of. 3. to test the taste of.

tattoo[1] (tə'tōō) *n.,pl.* **tattoos.** 1. a continued tapping on a drum or other surface. 2. a public show staged by soldiers.

tattoo[2] (tə'tōō) *n.,pl.* **tattoos.** a permanent marking on the skin, made by pricking it and rubbing on dyes.

taught (tôt) *vb.* the past tense and past participle of TEACH.

taunt (tônt) *vb.* to attack (someone) with unkind words. —*n.* a hurtful remark.

taut (tôt) *adj.* stretched tight: *a taut rope.* —'**tautly** *adv.* —'**tautness** *n.*

tax (taks) *n.* money paid to a government for use on public services,

etc. —*vb.* 1. to raise money by taxes. 2. to put a strain on: *the work taxed his strength.* **tax'ation** *n.* system of collecting money by taxes.

taxi ('taksi) *n.* a motorcar that can be hired, usu. for short journeys in a town. —*vb.* **taxiing, taxied.** (of an aircraft) to move on wheels across the ground.

teach (tēch) *vb.* **teaching, taught.** 1. to give (someone) instruction in (a skill, subject, etc.). 2. to earn one's living by doing this, esp. in a school.

teak (tēk) *n.* 1. a tall tree that grows in southern Asia. 2. the hard wood of this tree, used for furniture.

team (tēm) *n.* 1. a number of people joining together for work or play. 2. two or more animals, e.g. horses, pulling a plough, cart, etc., together.

tear[1] (teə) *vb.* **tearing, tore, torn.** 1. to damage or destroy by pulling sharply apart. 2. to become torn: *paper tears easily.* 3. to move excitedly or at speed: *he tore into the house with the news.* —*n.* a hole caused by tearing.

tear[2] (tiə) *n.* a drop of salty water produced from the eye. '**tear-gas** *n.* a gas that hurts the eyes and makes them produce tears. It is used mainly to control angry crowds. —'**tearful** *adj.*

tease (tēz) *vb.* **teasing, teased.** to make fun of (somebody) either unkindly or playfully. —*n.* a person who teases.

technical ('teknikəl) *adj.* 1. connected with one of the arts or skills used in industry, e.g. printing. 2. connected with the methods used by experts: *technical knowledge.* **tech'nician** *n.*

tartan

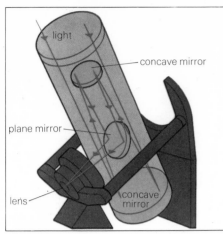
telescope

technique (tek'nēk) *n.* the method or skill connected with doing something: *there are many new techniques in printing these days.*

teenage ('tēnāj) *adj.* of or connected with a person between the ages of 13 and 19. —'**teenager** *n.*

teens (tēnz) *pl.n.* 1. the numbers 13 to 19. 2. the period of someone's life between the ages of 13 and 19: *the girls were in their teens.*

teeth (tēth) *n.* the plural of TOOTH.

teetotal ('tētōtəl) *adj.* not drinking, or forbidding the drinking of, alcoholic liquor. —'**teetotaller** *n.*

telegraph ('teligrâf) *n.* 1. an apparatus in which messages are sent over long distances by means of an electric current running along a wire or by radio. 2. the system using this. —*vb.* to send a message by telegraph. **telegram** ('teligram) *n.* a message sent by telegraph.

telephone ('telifōn) *n.* an instrument used for talking to a person at a distance, using a system similar to a TELEGRAPH but adapted for speech. —*vb.* **telephoning, telephoned.** to make a telephone call.

telescope ('teliskōp) *n.* a tubelike instrument with glass lenses, mirrors, etc., used to make distant objects appear closer. —**telescopic** (teli-'skopik) *adj.*

television ('telivizhən) *n.* 1. process of sending pictures and sound over a distance. 2. (also **television set**) a boxlike apparatus with a screen for receiving television broadcasts. **televise** ('televīz) *vb.* **televising, televised.** to send pictures by television.

temper ('tempə) *n.* 1. a mood or state of mind, esp. an unpleasant one. 2. the degree of hardness, toughness, etc., of a substance, such as steel. —*vb.* to alter the hardness of a substance by heating, moistening, etc.

temperament ('tempərəmənt) *n.* a person's natural condition of mind, feelings, and behaviour: *we work happily together because we have similar temperaments.* **tempera'mental** *adj.* given to rapid changes of mood; moody.

temperate ('tempərət) *adj.* 1. moderate or mild in speech, behaviour, etc. 2. (of climate) neither too hot nor too cold. '**temperance** *n.* 1. self-control in speech, behaviour, etc. 2. avoidance of alcoholic drinks.

temperature ('tempərəchə) *n.* 1. the degree of heat or cold of a thing. 2. a fever: *he had a high temperature when he had measles.*

tempest ('tempist) *n.* a violent storm. —**tempestuous** (tem'pestyōōəs) *adj.* —**tem'pestuously** *adv.*

temple¹ ('tempəl) *n.* a building used for religious worship.

temple² ('tempəl) *n.* one of the two flat parts of the head on each side of the forehead.

tempo ('tempō) *n.,pl.* **tempos** or **tempi** ('tempē). 1. the rate of activity or movement: *work continued at a faster tempo.* 2. the speed at which music is played: *slow waltz tempo.*

temporary ('tempərəri) *adj.* lasting or designed to last for only a short time: *he made a temporary repair to the car.* —'**temporarily** *adv.*

tempt (tempt) *vb.* to encourage, persuade, or try to persuade (someone) to do something. **temp'tation** *n.* 1. the action or an instance of tempting. 2. something that tempts: *the ripe peaches were a temptation to the hungry children.*

tenant ('tenənt) *n.* a person who pays rent for the use of land, rooms, etc., belonging to someone else. '**tenancy** *n.,pl.* **tenancies.** 1. the use of land, buildings, etc., by a tenant. 2. the length of time a tenant can use rented land, rooms, etc.

tender ('tendə) *adj.* 1. easily hurt or injured. 2. (of food) easily chewed; not tough. 3. loving.

tendon ('tendən) *n.* a tough thick cordlike part of the body that joins a muscle to a bone: *the Achilles tendon runs from the back of the leg to the heel.*

tendril ('tendril) *n.* the threadlike part of a climbing plant by which the plant holds onto a support.

tenement ('tenəmənt) *n.* a large building, divided into many flats, often providing poor living conditions for the people who live there.

tennis ('tenis) *n.* a game for two or four players, played with rackets and a ball on a court divided by a net.

tense¹ (tens) *n.* a form of a verb showing the time when an action happened, e.g. *jumped* is the past tense of *jump.*

tense² (tens) *adj.* 1. (of things) tightly stretched. 2. (of people) feeling or showing strain. —*vb.* **tensing, tensed.** to make or become tense. '**tension** *n.* 1. state of being tightly stretched. 2. a state of nervous strain or excitement: *the tension increased as we approached the enemy.*

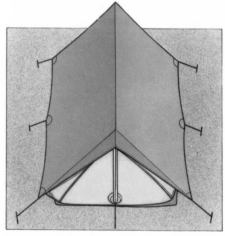
tent

tent (tent) *n.* a temporary shelter, usu. made of canvas sheets supported by poles and stretched by ropes.

tentacle ('tentəkəl) *n.* a long thin boneless outgrowth of certain soft-bodied animals, used for feeling, grasping, or moving: *an octopus has eight tentacles.*

tepid ('tepid) *adj.* slightly warm; not quite cold. —**te'pidity** *n.* —'**tepidly** *adv.*

term (tûm) *n.* 1. a definite period of time. 2. a division of the year during which schools, colleges, etc., are open. 3. a word or phrase expressing a definite or special idea: *scientific terms.* 4. **terms** (*pl.*) the conditions under which something is done or agreed. —*vb.* to call or give a name to: *the arms of an octopus are termed the tentacles.*

terminal ('tûminǝl) *n.* 1. a place where bus routes, railway lines, etc., end. 2. a piece of metal on electrical apparatus, a battery, wire, etc., to which a connection can be made. —*adj.* final: *a terminal illness.*

terminus ('tûminǝs) *n.,pl.* **termin-uses.** the end of a railway line or of a bus, tram, or air route.

termite ('tûmīt) *n.* a tropical insect, sometimes called a white ant, which destroys timber, paper, fabrics, etc., and builds large nests or hills of hardened earth.

terrace

terrace ('terǝs) *n.* 1. a level area of ground formed out of a slope either naturally or by man. 2. a row of houses joined together. —*vb.* **terracing, terraced.** to cut terraces out of (a slope).

terrible ('teribǝl) *adj.* bad, severe, or frightening. —**ter'ribly** *adv.*

terrier ('teriǝ) *n.* a small lively dog, often used for hunting. There are a number of different breeds of terrier.

terrify ('terifī) *vb.* **terrifying, terrified.** to fill with fear. **terrific** (tǝ'rifik) *adj.* 1. very frightening. 2. (informal) very large; excellent. **ter'rifically** *adv.* (informal) very: *I am terrifically pleased you won.*

territory ('teritǝri) *n.,pl.* **territories.** 1. land, esp. land under one govern-

ment. 2. an area of land. **terri'torial** *adj.* 1. of land. 2. belonging to a particular country: *territorial waters.*

terror ('terǝ) *n.* 1. great fear. 2. somebody or something that causes fear. **'terrorize** *vb.* **terrorizing, terrorized.** to cause terror to (someone).

terrorism ('terǝizm) *n.* the policy of causing terror by violence, murder, etc., to get what one wants in politics. —**'terrorist** *n.*

terse (tûs) *adj.* short and concise: *he gave a terse answer to my question.* —**'tersely** *adv.* —**'terseness** *n.*

test (test) *n.* a trial or examination to discover qualities, abilities, etc. —*vb.* 1. to examine: *he tested the strength of the rope.* 2. to be a test of: *the child's crying tested his patience.*

testament ('testǝmǝnt) *n.* 1. a formal written statement, esp. of a person's wishes as to what should be done with his belongings after his death. 2. **Testament** one of the two main parts of the Bible.

testify ('testifī) *vb.* **testifying, testified.** 1. to give evidence, usu. in court. 2. to support; state to be true: *when asked, I will testify to your hard work.*

tether ('tedhǝ) *n.* a rope or chain put on a grazing animal to prevent it from wandering. **at the end of one's tether** at the end of one's powers, patience, etc. —*vb.* to fasten or keep in one place with a tether.

text (tekst) *n.* 1. the main body of writing in a book. 2. a passage, esp. from the Bible, chosen as a subject for discussion. —**'textual** *adj.* —**'textually** *adv.*

textbook ('tekstbŏŏk) *n.* a book used by pupils or students for study: *a textbook of biology.*

textile ('tekstīl) *n.* 1. woven material. 2. thread, fibre, etc., to be spun or woven. —*adj.* of the making of cloth.

texture ('tekschǝ) *n.* 1. the way in which cloth is woven: *tweed has a coarse texture.* 2. the surface of a substance, esp. the way it looks or feels: *his skin has a rough texture.*

thank (thangk) *vb.* to say one is grateful to (someone). **'thankful** *adj.* grateful. **'thankless** *adj.* (of actions) bringing no thanks or gratitude.

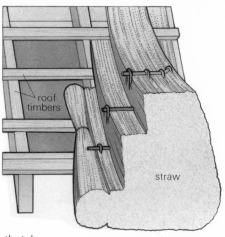

roof timbers

straw

thatch

thatch (thach) *n.* dried straw, reeds, etc., made into a roof covering. —*vb.* to put thatch on (a roof).

thaw (thô) *vb.* to become or cause to become soft or liquid again after being frozen. —*n.* warmer weather causing ice, snow, etc., to melt.

theatre ('thiǝtǝ) *n.* 1. a public building where stage plays are acted. 2. plays in general; drama. **theatrical** (thi'atrikǝl) *adj.* 1. of or for the theatre. 2. behaving like an actor; showy or affected. —**the'atrically** *adv.*

theft (theft) *n.* the action or an instance of stealing: *the boy's theft of the apples made the farmer very angry.*

theme (thēm) *n.* 1. the subject of a talk or piece of writing. 2. a tune that is repeated in a longer piece of music.

theorem ('thiǝrǝm) *n.* (mathematics) a statement that can be shown to be true by logical reasoning.

theory ('thiǝri) *n.,pl.* **theories.** 1. a reason or explanation for something that has not yet been shown to be true: *the scientist had a new theory about the causes of earthquakes.* 2. a general law or principle. **theoretical** (thiǝ'retikǝl) *adj.* based on theory, as opposed to practice. **'theorize** *vb.* **theorizing, theorized.** to form theories. —**theo'retically** *adv.* —**'theorist** *n.*

therm (thûm) *n.* a unit of heat, used in measuring the heat obtained from gas.

thermometer (thǝ'momitǝ) *n.* an instrument for measuring temperature.

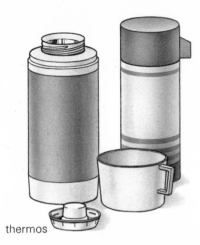
thermos

thistle

thermos ('thûməs) *n.* (trademark) a small container or flask used to keep liquids at a constant temperature.

thermostat ('thûməstat) *n.* a device that turns a heater, furnace, etc., on and off automatically to keep it at a required temperature.

thick (thik) *adj.* 1. big from side to side, back to front, or all round: *a thick plank.* 2. placed close together; dense: *a thick crowd.* 3. not flowing freely: *a thick syrup.* 'thicken *vb.* to make thick or thicker. —'thickly *adv.* —'thickness *n.*

thicket ('thikit) *n.* a group of trees or bushes growing close together.

thief (thēf) *n.,pl.* thieves. a person who steals, esp. in secret and without violence. **thieve** (thēv) *vb.* thieving, thieved. to steal. See also THEFT.

thigh (thī) *n.* the thick part of the leg above the knee.

thimble ('thimbəl) *n.* a small cap of metal or plastic used to protect the top of a finger when pushing a needle through cloth.

thin (thin) *adj.* thinner, thinnest. 1. little in size from front to back, from side to side, or all round: *a thin wire.* 2. (of people) slender. 3. easily poured or watery: *a thin soup.* —*vb.* thinning, thinned. to become or cause to become thin or thinner. —'thinly *adv.* —'thinness *n.*

think (thingk) *vb.* thinking, thought. 1. to use one's mind to deal with a problem or form an opinion. 2. to believe.

thirst (thûst) *n.* 1. feeling of dryness in the mouth and throat caused by lack of moisture. 2. a strong desire: *the thirst for knowledge.* —*vb.* to feel very great thirst. —'thirstily *adv.* —'thirstiness *n.* —'thirsty *adj.* thirstier, thirstiest.

thistle ('thisəl) *n.* a wild plant with prickly leaves and purple, white, or yellow flowers.

thorn (thôn) *n.* 1. a sharp spine or prickle on a plant's stem. 2. a tree or bush with many thorns. 'thorny *adj.* thornier, thorniest. 1. covered with thorns. 2. (of a problem, question, etc.) difficult; tricky.

thorough ('thurə) *adj.* 1. complete: *the party was a thorough success.* 2. (of people) neglecting no detail: *a thorough worker.* —'thoroughly *adv.* —'thoroughness *n.*

thought (thôt) *n.* 1. the process or act of thinking. 2. an idea, opinion, etc., formed by thinking. —*vb.* the past tense and past participle of THINK. 'thoughtful *adj.* 1. thinking. 2. showing care for the needs of others. 'thoughtless *adj.* 1. selfish. 2. without thinking. —'thoughtfully *adv.* —'thoughtlessly *adv.*

thread (thred) *n.* 1. a thin length of cotton, silk, etc. 2. a chain of thought or line in a story: *I lost the thread of my argument.* 3. the ridge running round a bolt or screw. —*vb.* 1. to put thread through (a needle's eye). 2. to put (beads, etc.) on a string. 3. to make one's way in and out of a number of people or things.

threadbare ('thredbeə) *adj.* (of fabrics, carpets, etc.) worn very thin so that the threads show.

threat (thret) *n.* 1. a statement expressing the intention of hurting or punishing. 2. a sign of coming trouble. 'threaten *vb.* 1. to use threats against (someone). 2. to give warning of trouble. 3. to seem likely: *the sky darkened and a storm threatened.*

thresh (thresh) *vb.* to separate (grain) from the stalks or husks of a cereal plant. 'thresher *n.* 1. a machine for threshing grain. 2. a person who threshes grain.

threshold ('threshōld) *n.* 1. the stone, plank, etc., under a door; the bottom part of a door frame. 2. a beginning: *the threshold of a career.*

threw (thrōō) *vb.* the past tense of THROW.

thrift (thrift) *n.* care and economy in handling or using money or goods. —'thriftiness *n.* —'thriftless *adj.* —'thriftlessness *n.* —'thrifty *adj.* thriftier, thriftiest.

thrill (thril) *n.* 1. an experience causing an excited feeling. 2. an excited feeling caused by pleasure, horror, etc. —*vb.* to feel or cause to feel a thrill. 'thriller *n.* something that causes thrills, esp. a story or film.

thrive (thrīv) *vb.* thriving, thrived or throve. 1. to grow strongly. 2. to succeed: *our business has thrived.*

throat (thrōt) *n.* 1. the front part of the neck. 2. the tube in the neck that carries food from the mouth to the stomach. 'throaty *adj.* throatier, throatiest. (of a voice) deep.

throb (throb) *vb.* throbbing, throbbed. (of the heart, pulse, etc.) to beat, esp. to beat faster or harder than usual. —*n.* a throbbing feeling or sound.

throne (thrōn) *n.* the official chair of a king, queen, or bishop.

throne

throng (throng) *n.* a crowd. —*vb.* to move or be present in a crowd.

throttle ('throtəl) *vb.* **throttling, throttled.** to squeeze the throat of (a person or animal) to prevent breathing. —*n.* the part of a motorcar that controls the flow of petrol to the engine.

throw (thrō) *vb.* **throwing, threw, thrown.** 1. to fling (something) through the air. 2. to put (clothing) on or off quickly. 3. to move violently: *he threw himself at the locked door.* 4. (of a horse) to toss off (a rider). —*n.* the act or an instance of throwing.

thrush (thrush) *n.* one of several kinds of small bird noted for their songs.

thrust (thrust) *vb.* **thrusting, thrust.** to push violently and often unexpectedly. —*n.* the action or an instance of thrusting.

thud (thud) *n.* a dull heavy sound: *the book fell on the table with a thud.* —*vb.* **thudding, thudded.** to make a thud.

thug (thug) *n.* a violent, brutal, and dangerous man.

thumb (thum) *n.* the short thick finger of the human hand that is set apart from the other four. —*vb.* 1. (usu. + *through*) to turn over (the pages of a book) rapidly. 2. (of a hitch-hiker) to ask for a lift by signalling with the thumb.

thunder ('thundə) *n.* 1. the loud crash or rumble from the sky usu. heard after lightning is seen. 2. a loud noise like thunder. —*vb.* 1. to produce thunder. 2. to make a loud prolonged noise. '**thunderous** *adj.* (of a noise) loud. '**thundery** *adj.* (of the weather) likely to thunder.

thwart (thwôt) *vb.* to prevent (somebody) from doing something; oppose (intentions, plans, etc.): *the rain thwarted our plans for a picnic.*

tick[1] (tik) *n.* 1. the small regular sound made by a clock or watch. 2. any noise like this. 3. the mark, rather like a V, used to show that something is right or in order. —*vb.* 1. (of a clock) to make a tick-tock sound. 2. to put a tick against (something).

tick[2] (tik) *n.* a small insect like a spider that fastens itself to an animal's skin and sucks its blood.

ticket ('tikit) *n.* 1. a card or slip of paper giving the person who holds it the right to travel on a train, bus, etc., or attend an entertainment. 2. a small label showing the price of goods.

tickle ('tikəl) *vb.* **tickling, tickled.** 1. to touch or rub (a person's skin) lightly, often causing him to laugh. 2. to have the feeling of being tickled: *my back tickles.* 3. to please or amuse. —*n.* the action or an instance of tickling. '**ticklish** *adj.* 1. (of a person) sensitive to tickling. 2. (informal) tricky; requiring skill in handling: *a ticklish problem.*

tide (tīd) *n.* 1. the regular rise and fall in the level of the sea that occurs approximately twice daily. 2. a trend or mass movement of opinion. —*vb.* **tiding, tided.** (+ *over*) to provide money, etc., for (a person's immediate needs): *here is £5 to tide you over until next week.* '**tidal** *adj.*

tidy ('tīdi) *adj.* **tidier, tidiest.** neat; in order. —*vb.* **tidying, tidied.** (often + *up*) to put in order. —'**tidily** *adv.* —'**tidiness** *n.*

tie (tī) *vb.* **tying, tied.** 1. to fasten or secure with string, wire, rope, etc. 2. to make (a knot). 3. to make an equal score in a game: *the teams tied 2-2.* —*n.* 1. a strip of material worn tied round the neck. 2. something that holds people together: *the ties of affection.* 3. an equal score.

tier (tiə) *n.* a row, usu. one of a number rising like steps, esp. of seats in a theatre: *there were empty seats in the upper tiers.*

tiger ('tīgə) *n.* a large fierce animal of the cat family, found in India. It has a golden hide with black stripes. '**tigress** *n.* a female tiger. '**tigrish** *adj.* fierce, like a tiger.

tight (tīt) *adj.* 1. fixed or gripped closely: *a tight cork.* 2. (of knots) difficult to unfasten. 3. stretched; taut: *a tight wire.* 4. (informal) mean about spending money. '**tighten** *vb.* to make or become tight or tighter. **tights** *pl.n.* closely-fitting garment for the feet, legs, and lower part of the body, worn by women, dancers, and acrobats. —'**tightly** *adv.* —'**tightness** *n.*

tightrope ('tītrōp) *n.* a rope on which acrobats balance and perform tricks.

tile (tīl) *n.* 1. a piece of baked clay used for roof covering. 2. a flat usu. square or oblong piece of baked clay, cork, plastic, etc., used for covering floors or walls. —*vb.* **tiling, tiled.** to cover (a roof, wall, etc.) with tiles.

till (til) *n.* the box or drawer in which money is kept in a shop.

tilt (tilt) *vb.* to have or cause to have a leaning position, neither flat nor upright: *he tilted the tray so that the cups slid off.* —*n.* a sloping or leaning position: *the tilt of the mirror.*

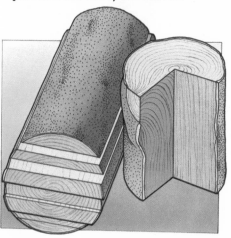

timber

timber ('timbə) *n.* 1. trees cut down and shaped, or about to be shaped, into beams, planks, etc., for use in building and carpentry. 2. a large thick length of wood in a building.

timetable ('tīmtābəl) *n.* a list showing the times at which things are to happen, e.g. school lessons, the arrival and departure of trains, etc.

timid ('timid) *adj.* easily frightened. —ti'**midity** *n.* —'**timidly** *adv.*

tin (tin) *n.* 1. a soft silvery-white metal. Chemical symbol: Sn. 2. a container for food made of tin or some other metal and sealed so as to be airtight. —*vb.* **tinning, tinned.** to put (food) into a tin.

tinge (tinj) *vb.* **tinging, tinged.** 1. (often + *with*) to colour slightly: *the blood tinged the water red.* 2. to affect slightly: *anger tinged his judgment.*

tingle ('tinggəl) *vb.* **tingling, tingled.** to have a slight stinging feeling in the skin. —*n.* a stinging feeling.

tinker ('tingkə) *vb.* (+ *with*) to try to repair or improve (something) without expert knowledge: *he tinkers with his car every weekend.* —*n.* a person who travels from place to place mending pots and pans.

tinsel ('tinsəl) *n.* thin glittering strips of metal used for decoration, esp. on Christmas trees.

tint (tint) *n.* a shade or colour, esp. a pale shade. —*vb.* to give a slight colour to (something): *she tinted her hair red.*

tip[1] (tip) *n.* 1. the narrow or pointed end of something: *the tips of your fingers.* 2. a small piece put on the end of something else: *a filter tip.* —*vb.* **tipping, tipped.** to put a tip on (something). **on tiptoe** on the tips of one's toes.

tip[2] (tip) *vb.* **tipping, tipped.** (often + *up* or *over*) to tilt or cause to tilt, esp. to start a falling or sliding movement: *I tipped over the tray.*

tip[3] (tip) *n.* 1. a small gift of money to a waiter, porter, etc. 2. a piece of useful information often given as a secret. —*vb.* **tipping, tipped.** to give (somebody) a small sum of money, esp. as an extra reward for service, e.g. in a restaurant.

tire (tīə) *vb.* **tiring, tired.** 1. to make or become weary. 2. to make or become uninterested. '**tiresome** *adj.* troublesome. —'**tiredness** *n.* —'**tireless** *adj.*

tissue ('tishoo) *n.* 1. thin light cloth or paper; a piece of this. 2. a substance of a particular nature forming part of an animal or plant, e.g. muscular tissue.

title ('tītəl) *n.* 1. the name of a book, film, etc. 2. a word put in front of a person's name to show rank, e.g. *Professor* or *Sir.* 3. legal right: *do you have a title to this house?*

toad (tōd) *n.* an animal like a large frog that has a cold dry skin. Toads live most of the time on land.

toad

toadstool ('tōdstool) *n.* an umbrella-shaped FUNGUS. Some kinds of toadstool look like mushrooms but are poisonous.

toast (tōst) *n.* 1. sliced bread warmed until it is crisp. 2. a public expression of good wishes confirmed by drinking a glass of wine: *he proposed a toast to the bride.* —*vb.* 1. to heat (bread slices). 2. to wish (somebody) well by making a toast (def. 2).

tobacco (tə'bakō) *n.,pl.* **tobaccos** *or* **tobaccoes.** dried leaves of the tobacco plant, smoked in cigarettes, cigars, and pipes. **tobacconist** (tə'bakənist) *n.* a person who sells tobacco, cigarettes, etc.

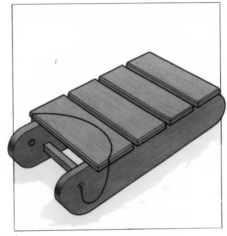
toboggan

toboggan (tə'bogən) *n.* a sledge for sliding down snow-covered slopes, usu. as a sport. —*vb.* to slide across snow on a toboggan.

toe (tō) *n.* 1. one of the five divisions at the front end of the foot. 2. the part of a sock, stocking, etc., covering the toes.

toffee ('tofi) *n.* 1. sticky hard brown sweet made from sugar and butter. 2. a piece of this.

toil (toil) *vb.* 1. to work hard. 2. to move slowly and with difficulty: *the old man toiled up the hill.* —*n.* hard work.

toilet ('toilət) *n.* 1. lavatory. 2. process of washing, doing one's hair, etc., or the results of this process: *he is careless about his toilet.*

token ('tōkən) *n.* 1. a proof or sign of something. 2. a card or disc used instead of money in cash: *milk tokens.*

tolerate ('tolərāt) *vb.* **tolerating, tolerated.** to allow or put up with (something) without protesting. '**tolerance** *or* toler'ation *n.* ability to tolerate other people's behaviour, opinions, etc. '**tolerant** *adj.* possessing tolerance. '**tolerable** *adj.* 1. bearable; able to be tolerated. 2. moderately good: *a tolerable play.* —'**tolerably** *adv.* —'**tolerantly** *adv.*

toll[1] (tōl) *vb.* (of a bell) to ring or cause to ring slowly and steadily. —*n.* the sound of a bell rung in this way.

toll[2] (tōl) *n.* 1. a payment for the use of a road, bridge, etc. 2. cost in loss or damage: *icy roads take a heavy toll in car accidents.*

tomato (tə'mâtō) *n.,pl.* **tomatoes.** 1. a soft juicy red fruit used in salads. 2. the plant on which this fruit grows.

tomb (toom) *n.* the place dug in the ground or built for a dead person's body.

ton (tun) *n.* a measure of weight equal to 2240 pounds (1016·05 kilograms). **tons of** (informal) a lot of.

tone (tōn) *n.* 1. a sound, esp. referring to its quality. 2. a degree or shade of colour, light, etc. 3. the interval between one note of the musical scale and the next. —*vb.* **toning, toned.** 1. to give a particular tone of colour or sound to. 2. (+ *in with* or *with*) (of colours) to blend or be in harmony. 3. (+ *up*) to strengthen; make more healthy.

tongs (tongz) *pl.n.* a household device for gripping and lifting a lump of sugar, a piece of coal, etc.

tongue (tung) *n.* 1. the muscular movable piece of flesh attached to the bottom of the mouth and used for tasting, licking, and, by humans, also for speaking. 2. a language. 3. anything shaped like a tongue: *the tongue of a bell.* '**tongue-tied** *adj.* unable to speak out because of fright, shyness, etc. '**tongue-twister** *n.* a word, phrase, or sentence that is difficult to say, e.g. *she sells sea shells by the sea shore.*

tonic ('tonik) *n.* 1. a medicine to restore one's strength. 2. anything that encourages and gives strength. 3. a fizzy, slightly bitter drink.

tonsil ('tonsəl) *n.* one of two lumps of spongy flesh on either side of the inner wall of the throat. **tonsillitis** (tonsi'lītis) *n.* disease causing a painful swelling of the tonsils.

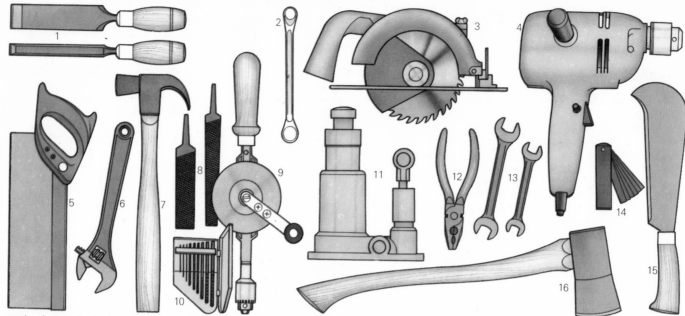

tools: 1 chisels; 2 ring spanner; 3 circular saw; 4 electric drill; 5 tenon saw; 6 adjustable spanner; 7 claw hammer; 8 files; 9 hand drill; 10 drill bits; 11 hydraulic jack; 12 pliers; 13 open spanners; 14 feeler gauge; 15 billhook; 16 axe.

tool (tool) *n.* an instrument used by people to do a job of work.

tooth (tooth) *n.,pl.* **teeth.** 1. one of the small hard white structures in the jaws, used for biting and chewing food. 2. any small sharp object like a tooth: *the tooth of a comb.*

topic ('topik) *n.* a subject for discussion; an essay, a speech, etc. **'topical** *adj.* associated with current affairs. —**'topically** *adv.*

torch (tôch) *n.* 1. a piece of wood with one end soaked in oil and set on fire to give a light. 2. a small handheld electric light operated by a battery.

tore (tô) *vb.* the past tense of TEAR[1].

torn (tôn) *vb.* the past participle of TEAR[1].

tornado (tô'nādō) *n.,pl.* **tornadoes.** a violent destructive whirling wind, usu. travelling along a narrow path.

torpedo (tô'pēdō) *n.,pl.* **torpedoes.** a long metal shell packed with explosives and fired underwater at ships to blow them up. —*vb.* to attack or destroy with a torpedo.

torrent ('torənt) *n.* 1. a violent rush of water, esp. in a small stream. 2. any violent flow: *a torrent of complaints.* —**torrential** (tə'renshəl) *adj.*

tortoise ('tôtəs) *n.* a four-legged slow-moving reptile that lives on land and has a hard shell covering its body.

torture ('tôchə) *vb.* **torturing, tortured.** to cause (somebody) great pain. —*n.* 1. the action of causing great pain. 2. something that causes great pain.

total ('tōtəl) *n.* the complete sum or amount. —*adj.* complete. —*vb.* **totalling, totalled.** to add up to; amount to. **'totally** *adv.* completely.

touch (tuch) *vb.* 1. to put one's hand lightly on. 2. to be in contact with: *the curtains touch the floor.* 3. to affect (somebody's feelings): *his sad story touched me.* **touch down** (of an aircraft, spacecraft, etc.) to land. —*n.* 1. an act of touching. 2. the sensation given by touching.

tough (tuf) *adj.* 1. not easily damaged or worn out. 2. (of meat) not easily chewed. 3. (of people) strong. 4. (of work) difficult. **'toughen** *vb.* to make tough.

tour (tooə) *n.* a journey during which one visits several places. —*vb.* to make a tour. —**'tourist** *n.*

tournament ('tooənəmənt) *n.* an organized series of games between different players.

tow (tō) *vb.* to pull (a boat, car, caravan, etc.) along, esp. by a rope or chain. —*n.* the act of towing.

towel ('touəl) *n.* a piece of cloth or paper used for drying something.

tower ('touə) *n.* a tall building or part of a building. —*vb.* (+ *over* or *above*) to rise to a great height.

town (toun) *n.* 1. a group of houses and

torpedo

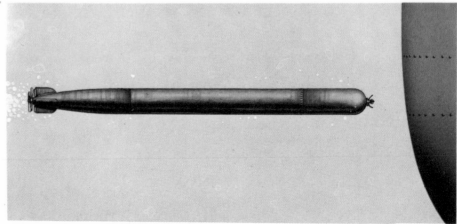

other buildings larger than a village with many people living in it. 2. the people of a town.

toxic ('toksik) *adj.* poisonous. Some gases are toxic.

trace (trās) *vb.* **tracing, traced.** 1. to copy (a drawing, map, etc.) by marking the outline on transparent paper. 2. to follow or discover (somebody or something) by following small bits of evidence: *the police traced him to Paris.* —*n.* 1. a mark or sign made by something that has been present. 2. a very small amount.

track (trak) *n.* 1. a series of marks left by somebody or something moving along. 2. a path made by constant use. 3. a set of rails or a specially prepared course: *a running track.* —*vb.* to pursue (somebody or something) by following the marks or traces left by them.

tractor

tractor ('traktə) *n.* a powerful motor vehicle used esp. by farmers for pulling heavy loads, ploughs, etc.

trade (trād) *n.* 1. the business of buying and selling goods. 2. a way of earning a living, esp. by skilled work in industry. 3. the people involved in a particular trade (def. 2). **trade union** an organized combination of workers formed to obtain better conditions of work. —*vb.* **trading, traded.** to buy, sell, or exchange (goods). '**trader** *n.* a person who trades. '**tradesman** *n.,pl.* **tradesmen.** a shopkeeper.

trademark ('trādmâk) *n.* a special design or name that a company puts on its goods to distinguish them from goods made by other companies.

traffic ('trafik) *n.* 1. movement of people and vehicles along roads and railways; movement of aircraft in and

out of airports. 2. trading, often illegally: *the traffic in drugs.* —*vb.* **trafficking, trafficked.** to trade.

tragedy ('trajidi) *n.,pl.* **tragedies.** 1. a serious stage play with a sad ending. 2. a sad event in real life. '**tragic** *adj.* 1. of a sad play or plays. 2. of a sad event. —'**tragically** *adv.*

trail (trāl) *n.* 1. a line of marks, footprints, etc., left by a person or animal. 2. a path, usu. through rough country. —*vb.* 1. to pull or be pulled along after. 2. to walk wearily. 3. (of plants, hair, etc.) to grow thinly and untidily. '**trailer** *n.* a small vehicle pulled along by another.

train[1] (trān) *n.* 1. a railway engine and a number of coaches joined together. 2. a number of people, animals, etc., moving along in a line. 3. several connected ideas or events. 4. the part of a long formal dress or cloak that trails on the ground.

train[2] (trān) *vb.* 1. to prepare (a child, soldier, animal, etc.) for a particular purpose by instruction and practice. 2. to make a plant grow in a particular direction. '**trainer** *n.* a person who trains sportsmen, animals, etc.

traitor ('trātə) *n.* a person who betrays or is disloyal to his friend, his country, etc. —'**traitorous** *adj.*

tramp (tramp) *vb.* 1. to walk heavily. 2. to walk a long way, esp. over rough ground. —*n.* 1. a person who walks from place to place and has no home or regular job. 2. the sound of heavy footsteps. 3. a long walk.

trampoline ('trampəlēn) *n.* a sheet of strong canvas stretched across a frame, used to enable acrobats, gymnasts, etc., to jump high into the air.

trampoline

trance (trâns) *n.* a state in which a person seems to be asleep but can do and experience some things.

tranquil ('traṅgkwil) *adj.* peaceful; quiet. '**tranquillize** *vb.* **tranquillizing, tranquillized.** to make calm or calmer. —tran'**quillity** *n.*

transfer *vb.* (trans'fû) **transferring, transferred.** 1. to move. 2. to take (something) from one place to another. 3. to hand over (property) to someone else, esp. in a legal sense. —*n.* ('transfə) 1. a move from one place to another. 2. a person or thing transferred.

transform (trans'fôm) *vb.* to alter completely (the appearance or nature of something). **trans'former** *n.* an electrical apparatus for changing electric current from one voltage to another. —**transfor'mation** *n.*

transfusion (trans'fyōōzhən) *n.* the putting of another person's blood into somebody who has lost a lot of his own.

transistor (tran'zistə) *n.* 1. a very small device for controlling the power of an electric current. 2. a small radio set using such devices.

translate (tranz'lāt) *vb.* **translating, translated.** to give the meaning of words in one language in words of another: *she translated the story into German.* —**trans'lation** *n.*

transmit (tranz'mit) *vb.* **transmitting, transmitted.** 1. to send or hand on. 2. to broadcast by radio or television. **trans'mitter** *n.* 1. something that sends or passes something on. 2. a device for sending out radio messages or broadcasts. —**trans'mission** *n.*

transparent (trans'parənt) *adj.* 1. able to be seen through. 2. clear. **trans'parency** *n.,pl.* **transparencies.** a transparent photograph or piece of photographic film.

transplant *vb.* (trans'plânt) 1. to take (a living plant) from one place and plant it in another. 2. (in medicine) to replace a diseased part of the body with a healthy one. —*n.* ('transplânt) an operation to remove and replace a diseased part of the body.

transport *vb.* (tran'spôt) to carry (people, goods, etc.) from one place to another. —*n.* ('transpôt) a vehicle, ship, or aircraft used for transporting.

223

trap (trap) *n.* 1. a device for catching animals, birds, etc. 2. a trick to force someone to do or say something against his wishes. 3. (also **trap door**) a small door in a floor or roof. —*vb.* **trapping, trapped.** to catch (something) in a trap.

trapeze (trə'pēz) *n.* a bar or rod, supported like a swing by two ropes, on which acrobats and gymnasts do exercises and tricks.

travel ('travəl) *vb.* **travelling, travelled.** 1. to make journeys, esp. long ones. 2. to move over a distance: *news travels fast.* —*n.* the experience of making long journeys.

trawler ('trôlə) *n.* a fishing boat that tows a large baglike net known as a **trawl. trawl** *vb.* to fish with a trawl.

treacherous ('trechərəs) *adj.* 1. disloyal; not to be trusted. 2. dangerous; having hazards that are concealed. —'**treacherously** *adv.* —'**treachery** *n.,pl.* **treacheries.**

tread (tred) *vb.* **treading, trod, trodden.** 1. to walk. 2. to crush down or push in with the feet. —*n.* 1. the manner or sound of walking. 2. the level part or step of a stair. 3. the outer patterned part of a rubber tyre.

treason ('trēzən) *n.* the betrayal of one's country or ruler; disloyalty. '**treasonable** *adj.* disloyal.

treasure ('trezhə) *n.* 1. a store of precious things, e.g. jewels, gold; wealth. 2. any highly valued person or thing. —*vb.* **treasuring, treasured.** to value highly. '**treasurer** *n.* a person in charge of a society's money. '**treasury** *n.,pl.* **treasuries.** 1. the government department handling a country's money. 2. any building where treasures are kept.

treat (trēt) *vb.* 1. to behave towards (someone or something) in a particular way: *she treated him kindly.* 2. to give medical attention to. 3. to supply (someone) with food, drink, or entertainment at one's own expense. 4. to put something through a process, esp. in industry. —*n.* an enjoyable event, esp. one that is not often experienced. —'**treatment** *n.*

treaty ('trēti) *n.,pl.* **treaties.** a formal agreement made between nations.

treble ('trebəl) *vb.* **trebling, trebled.** to make or become three times as much. —*n.,adj.* three times as much or as many; three-fold.

tree (trē) *n.* a large long-lived plant with a single woody supporting stem, or trunk.

tremble ('trembəl) *vb.* **trembling, trembled.** to shake or shiver, esp. because of cold, excitement, etc.

tremendous (tri'mendəs) *adj.* 1. very great; powerful. 2. (informal) excellent. —tre'**mendously** *adv.*

tremor ('tremə) *n.* a slight shaking movement lasting only a short time.

trench (trench) *n.* a long narrow hole or ditch dug in the ground.

trend (trend) *n.* a particular direction or inclination: *there has been an upward trend in prices recently.*

trespass ('trespəs) *vb.* (often + *on* or *upon*) 1. to go or be upon private land without right or permission. 2. to make an unfair amount of use of: *business trespasses upon my time.*

trestle

trestle ('tresəl) *n.* a bar with four legs used as a support.

trial ('trīəl) *vb.* 1. a test to find out whether something is suitable, useful, etc.: *they gave the new restaurant a trial.* 2. an examination of facts in a court of law. 3. a nuisance.

triangle ('trīanggəl) *n.* 1. a shape or object having three sides and three angles. See GEOMETRY. 2. a musical instrument made of a metal rod bent into the shape of a triangle. —**triangular** (trī'anggyoolə) *adj.*

tribe (trīb) *n.* a group of people made up of many families that share the same language and customs, esp. in a primitive country. —'**tribal** *adj.*

tributary ('tribyootəri) *n.,pl.* **tributaries.** a river that flows into a larger river.

tribute ('tribyoot) *n.* 1. (in history) a regular payment made by a tribe or small state to its ruler: *many tribes paid tribute to Rome.* 2. something done or said to show respect, gratitude, etc.: *the school gave the headmistress a tribute when she left.*

trick (trik) *n.* 1. something done to cheat or fool somebody: *he escaped his enemies by a trick.* 2. a skilful or clever act: *the magician performs tricks.* 3. a piece of mischief; joke: *Tom plays tricks on his schoolmates.* —*vb.* to cheat or fool. '**tricky** *adj.* **trickier, trickiest.** full of problems; needing careful handling. —'**trickery** *n.* —'**trickster** *n.*

trickle ('trikəl) *vb.* **trickling, trickled.** to flow or cause to flow slowly or drop by drop: *raindrops trickled down the windows.* —*n.* a slow-flowing thin stream.

trawler

tricycle ('trīsikəl) *n.* a vehicle like a BICYCLE but with one wheel in front and two behind.

trifle ('trīfəl) *n.* 1. a thing or happening of little importance or value. 2. (informal) a small amount, esp. of money. 3. a pudding made with sponge cake, jelly, custard, and cream. —*vb.* **trifling, trifled.** 1. to act or talk idly. 2. (+ *with*) to play with.

trigger ('trigə) *n.* the small lever on a gun, pistol, etc., which works on a spring and is pulled to fire the gun. —*vb.* (often + *off*) to start (something) suddenly and violently: *the news of the disaster triggered off a panic.*

trigonometry (trigə'nomitri) *n.* the branch of mathematics that deals with triangles, and the relationship between their angles and sides.

trim (trim) *vb.* **trimming, trimmed.** 1. to make (something) tidy by cutting away uneven or overgrown parts. 2. to decorate (a hat, a cake, etc.). —*adj.* **trimmer, trimmest.** neat. —*n.* 1. (informal) a haircut. 2. an ornament or decoration.

trio ('trēō) *n.,pl.* **trios.** 1. a group of three. 2. a piece of music to be played by three players.

triple ('tripəl) *adj.* made up of three parts. —*vb.* **tripling, tripled** to make or become three times as much or many: *the number of pupils has tripled in two years.*

triplet ('triplit) *n.* one of a set of three, esp. one of three babies born to one mother at the same time.

tripod ('trīpod) *n.* a three-legged support, esp. for a camera.

triumph ('trīumf) *n.* 1. a great success. 2. the joy caused by a success. —*vb.* to win or succeed.

trod (trod) *vb.* the past tense of TREAD.

trolley ('troli) *n.* 1. a handcart with two or four wheels: *the porter loaded our luggage onto a trolley.* 2. a small open cart running on rails.

trombone (trom'bōn) *n.* a brass musical instrument having a sliding U–shaped tube which the player moves to produce different notes.

troop (trōop) *n.* 1. a group of people or animals usu. moving or doing something together. 2. **troops** (*pl.*) sol-

diers. —*vb.* to move in a troop. **'trooper** *n.* a soldier in a cavalry regiment.

trophy ('trōfi) *n.,pl.* **trophies.** something given or kept as a reminder of a success, esp. in sport.

tropic ('tropik) *n.* the line of latitude 23°27' north (**Tropic of Cancer**) or south (**Tropic of Capricorn**) of the Equator. See GLOBE. **the tropics** the hot part of the world between these lines. —**'tropical** *adj.*

trot (trot) *vb.* **trotting, trotted.** 1. (of animals) to move at a pace faster than a walk but slower than a canter. 2. (of people) to move briskly or run, usu. with short steps. —*n.* the pace of an animal faster than a walk.

trouble ('trubəl) *vb.* **troubling, troubled.** 1. to have or cause to have worry, pain, inconvenience, etc. 2. to cause (someone) to make a particular effort: *may I trouble you for the jam?* —*n.* 1. a difficult, worrying, or dangerous situation: *he will be in trouble if he is late.* 2. an extra effort: *he took the trouble to cook dinner.*

trough (trof) *n.* a long narrow open box, esp. one from which animals eat or drink.

trout (trout) *n.,pl.* **trout.** a freshwater fish prized for food and for the sport it provides for those who try to fish it.

trowel ('trouəl) *n.* 1. a small flat-bladed tool used for spreading mortar and plaster. 2. a tool with a scoop-shaped blade used by gardeners. See IMPLEMENT.

truant ('trōoənt) *n.* a child who stays away from school without permission or proper reason.

trombone

truce (trōos) *n.* 1. a pause in fighting. 2. an agreement to stop fighting for a stated period.

truck (truk) *n.* an open railway wagon for bulky loads, e.g. coal.

true (trōo) *adj.* 1. agreeing with facts; not false or made-up. 2. real; genuine: *she is a true friend.* 3. correct: *a true portrait.* **'truly** *adv.* 1. truthfully. 2. sincerely. 3. certainly: *her visit was truly a great surprise.*

trumpet ('trumpit) *n.* 1. a brass musical instrument having a bell-shaped mouth and usu. three keys or valves that are pressed to produce different notes. 2. a sound like that of a trumpet, e.g. an elephant's call.

truncheon ('trunchən) *n.* a short thick heavy stick, esp. one used by policemen.

trunk (trungk) *n.* 1. the main woody stem of a tree. 2. a body without its head, arms, or legs. 3. a large box for holding one's belongings, esp. when travelling. 4. an elephant's long nose.

trust (trust) *vb.* to believe or have faith in: *I trusted his promises.* —*n.* 1. belief; confidence: *he put his trust in the doctor.* 2. an arrangement under which property or money is looked after for someone else's benefit.

truth (trōoth) *n.,pl.* **truths** (trōodhz). 1. the quality of being true or honest: *the truth of his story is very doubtful.* 2. something that is true: *are you telling the truth?* **'truthful** *adj.* 1. (of persons) always telling the truth. 2. giving a true account of the facts.

try (trī) *vb.* **trying, tried.** 1. to make an attempt to do something. 2. to test: *he tried the car's brakes.* 3. to examine in a court of law. 4. to cause a strain on: *the noise tried her nerves.*

tube (tyōob) *n.* 1. a long thin hollow piece of rubber, metal, plastic, etc. 2. a soft metal or plastic container with a screw-cap: *a tooth-paste tube.*

tuck (tuk) *vb.* 1. (+ *in*) to fold or put the edges of (something) in place: *he tucked in his shirt.* 2. (+ *away* or *under*) to put (something) in a safe or covered place: *I tucked the book under my arm.* 3. (+ *up*) to put to bed.

tug (tug) *vb.* **tugging, tugged.** to pull hard. —*n.* 1. a sudden hard pull. 2. a small powerful boat used to help move other boats, esp. in a harbour.

tulip

tulip ('tyōolip) *n.* a cup-shaped flower, often brightly coloured, that grows from a bulb.

tumble ('tumbəl) *vb.* **tumbling, tumbled.** 1. to fall in a clumsy way. 2. to do acrobatic tricks. —*n.* a fall. '**tumbler** *n.* 1. a large flat-bottomed drinking glass without a handle. 2. an acrobat.

tumour ('tyōomə) *n.* a diseased swelling or lump growing in a part of the body.

tumult ('tyōomult) *n.* 1. an uproar. 2. agitation; very great excitement. **tu'multuous** *adj.* violently disturbed or noisy.

tune (tyōon) *n.* a series of notes that make up the melody in a piece of music. **in tune** at correct pitch. —*vb.* **tuning, tuned.** to put or bring into tune. '**tuneful** *adj.* having an attractive tune.

tunnel ('tunəl) *n.* an underground passage. —*vb.* **tunnelling, tunelled.** to make an underground passage.

turban ('tûbən) *n.* a head-dress made of a long strip of cloth wound round and round the head, worn esp. by Arabs and Indians.

turbine ('tûbīn) *n.* an engine that is driven by a stream of water, steam, etc., hitting against the blades of a wheel and forcing it to go round.

turbulent ('tûbyōolənt) *adj.* rough or violent. —'**turbulence** *n.* —'**turbulently** *adj.*

turf (tûf) *n.* 1. surface of the soil with grass growing on it. 2. a piece of this used to make a lawn. **the Turf** the profession of horse-racing.

turkey ('tûki) *n.* a large white or brown bird that is raised for food. The male birds have **large** fan-shaped tails.

turmoil ('tûmoil) *n.* great confusion; uproar.

turnip ('tûnip) *n.* a plant with a round white or yellow root that is used for food.

turnstile ('tûnstīl) *n.* a gate or bar fixed at an entrance or an exit, e.g. to a football stadium, in such a way as to let only one person through at any one time.

turpentine ('tûpəntīn) *n.* an oily, strong-smelling liquid used to mix paints.

turquoise ('tûkwoiz) *n.* a greenish-blue precious stone. —*adj.* of the colour of a turquoise.

turret ('turit) *n.* 1. a small tower on a building, usu. at a corner. 2. a structure on which guns are placed in a warship, tank, etc.

turtle ('tûtəl) *n.* a reptile with a flat body that is protected by a hard shell. Turtles can live in the sea or in fresh water.

tusk (tusk) *n.* a long pointed tooth sticking out of the mouth of certain animals, e.g. walrus, elephant.

tutor ('tyōotə) *n.* 1. a teacher, esp. one who gives private lessons. 2. a university teacher. —*vb.* to teach privately. —**tutorial** (tyōo'tôriəl) *adj.*

tweed (twēd) *n.* a heavy woollen cloth, usu. woven in several colours.

tweezers ('twēzəz) *pl.n.* a small pair of pincers used to pick up and hold very small things: *eyebrow tweezers.*

typewriter

twilight ('twīlīt) *n.* 1. the dim hazy light from the sun soon after sunset or just before sunrise. 2. the time of the day when this light is in the sky, esp. early evening

twin (twin) *n.* one of a set of two, esp. one of two children born to one mother at the same time. —*adj.* of, concerning, or being a twin.

twine (twīn) *vb.* **twining, twined.** to twist or wind. —*n.* string.

twinge (twinj) *n.* a sudden sharp pain.

twinkle ('twiṅkəl) *vb.* **twinkling, twinkled.** to shine with a flickering light. —*n.* 1. a flickering light. 2. a sparkle: *a twinkle in the eyes.*

twirl (twûl) *vb.* to turn or cause to turn around quickly; spin.

twist (twist) *vb.* 1. to wind or turn (something) around another object: *they twisted the rope round the tree.* 2. to turn (something) sharply: *I twisted my ankle.* 3. to curve or turn in different directions: *the path twisted through the hills.* 4. to change the meaning of (something): *she twisted my words to make Tom believe that I was angry with him.* —*n.* 1. the act of twisting. 2. something made by twisting: *a twist of tobacco.* 3. an injury caused by twisting.

twitch (twich) *n.* 1. a quick nervous movement. 2. a sudden pull or jerk. —*vb.* to make a quick or nervous movement.

type (tīp) *n.* 1. a class or group of things that are in some ways the same: *what type of music do you like?* 2. raised letters made on small metal blocks and used for printing. —*vb.* **typing, typed.** to use a typewriter.

typewriter ('tīprītə) *n.* a machine for printing letters on paper.

typhoon (tī'fōon) *n.* a violent storm with strong winds, occurring particularly over the western Pacific Ocean.

typical ('tipikəl) *adj.* having the qualities or characteristics of a certain type: *a typical cat hates water.* —'**typically** *adv.*

typist ('tīpist) *n.* a person who uses a typewriter, esp. in an office.

tyre (tīə) *n.* the outer ring, usu. hollow and made of rubber, that fits round the edge of a wheel.

U

udder ('udə) *n.* the baglike part of the body of certain female animals, e.g. cow, goat, in which milk to feed their young is produced.

ugly ('ugli) *adj.* **uglier, ugliest.** 1. unpleasant in appearance; not beautiful. 2. troublesome, rough, or threatening: *it was ugly weather.* —'**ugliness** *n.*

ulcer ('ulsə) *n.* an open sore, esp. in the stomach or mouth or on the skin. —'**ulcerous** *adj.*

ultimate ('ultimit) *adj.* 1. latest or last: *the ultimate word on a list.* 2. being or coming at the end of an action, etc.: *the ultimate result.* 3. unable to be bettered in quality, effectiveness, etc., by other similar things: *the ultimate weapon.*

ultimatum (ulti'mātəm) *n.* a final demand or order that must be agreed to or obeyed: *the unions have given an ultimatum to the employers.*

ultraviolet (ultrə'vīələt) *adj.* (of light waves) too short to be seen by the human eye; found below violet in the visible colour SPECTRUM.

umbrella (um'brelə) *n.* a portable circular or dome-shaped shade made of cloth, etc., stretched over a light collapsible frame, and used as a shelter from the rain or sun.

umbrella

umpire ('umpīə) *n.* 1. a referee or judge in a game, esp. cricket or tennis. 2. a judge in an argument, dispute, etc.

unanimous (yoo'naniməs) *adj.* accepted or agreed to by everyone: *the vote against his idea was unanimous.* **unanimity** (yoonə'nimiti) *n.* full agreement. —**u'nanimously** *adv.*

unaware (unə'weə) *adj.* 1. not taking any notice. 2. not knowing or realizing. **una'wares** *adv.* unexpectedly; by surprise: *he caught her unawares.*

uncanny (un'kani) *adj.* strange or odd; not normal or reasonable: *an uncanny talent as a detective.* —**un'cannily** *adv.*

unconscious (un'konshəs) *adj.* 1. not conscious; not aware of any sensations, etc.: *the blow knocked him unconscious.* 2. done or said without full awareness; unintentional: *her actions were caused by an unconscious fear.* —**un'consciously** *adv.* —**un'consciousness** *n.*

uncouth (un'kooth) *adj.* clumsy or awkward in manners or behaviour; rough.

underdog ('undədog) *n.* 1. the weaker side in a competition, fight, etc.; a person or side expected to lose. 2. a person who is ignored or continually ill-treated by others.

undergo (undə'gō) *vb.* **undergoing, underwent, undergone.** to experience, endure, or be put through (a test, operation, difficulties, etc.).

undergraduate (undə'gradyooit) *n.* a university student studying for his or her first degree.

underground ('undəground) *adv.* 1. beneath the ground or the earth's surface. 2. in or into hiding or secrecy. —*adj.* 1. used or situated underground. 2. secret; not public because unlawful or against established custom: *an underground organiza-*

tion. —*n.* a secret group or organization, esp. a revolutionary one. **the Underground** London's underground railway.

undergrowth ('undəgrōth) *n.* small bushes or trees growing among larger trees, as in a jungle.

underhand ('undəhand) *adj.* sly, cunning, or secretive. —*adv.* slyly; secretly.

underline (undə'līn) *vb.* **underlining, underlined.** 1. to draw or mark a line underneath (a word, sentence, etc.). 2. to emphasize or stress the importance of (a point in an argument).

undermine (undə'mīn) *vb.* **undermining, undermined.** 1. to weaken (a building, wall, etc.) by digging tunnels underneath it. 2. to weaken (a person's authority, spirit, etc.), esp. by secret methods.

underneath (undə'nēth) *prep.* beneath; in a lower position than; under. —*adv.* in a lower position; beneath. —*n.* the lowest part of something; base.

understand (undə'stand) *vb.* **understanding, understood.** 1. to know or realize the meaning of (a sentence, subject, or problem): *I understand German.* 2. to know about and appreciate the reasons for a person's behaviour or character. 3. to learn or accept (something) as a fact: *I understand that he arrives tomorrow.* **under'standing** *n.* the ability to realize the meaning of something; comprehension. —**under'standable** *adj.* —**under'standably** *adv.*

understudy ('undəstudi) *n.,pl.* **understudies.** an actor or actress who learns another's part in a play or film in order to take over if the other is ill or otherwise unable to perform.

undertake (undə'tāk) *vb.* **undertaking, undertook, undertaken.** 1. to agree or promise (something or to do something): *we undertake to get* you there on time 2. to take on (a job, etc.): *why did you undertake such a difficult duty?* **'undertaker** *n.* a person who prepares dead bodies for burial or cremation, makes coffins, and arranges funerals. **'undertaking** *n.* a job; task.

undertone ('undətōn) *n.* 1. a quiet voice: *he spoke to her in an undertone.* 2. a hint or suspicion: *there was an undertone of sadness in her words.*

underworld ('undəwûld) *n.* 1. the place to which the souls of the dead are taken (in many ancient beliefs). 2. the world of criminals: *the gangster's death shocked the underworld.* —*adj.* connected with the world of criminals.

underwriter ('undərītə) *n.* a person who insures ships, cars, houses, etc., and pays out money if there is a loss.

undo (un'dōō) *vb.* **undoing, undid, undone.** 1. to untie, unfasten, or loosen (clothing, shoelaces, parcels, etc.). 2. to spoil or ruin (what has already been done): *this mistake has undone all my good work.* **un'doing** *n.* the cause of one's ruin, misery, or downfall: *drink was his undoing.* **un'done** *adj.* ruined; finished.

undoubted (un'doutid) *adj.* accepted or undisputed: *Carolyn is the undoubted champion at table tennis.* —**un'doubtedly** *adv.*

undue ('undyōō) *adj.* more or greater than is usual, suitable, or necessary: *he had no undue worries about his exams as he had worked hard all year.* —**un'duly** *adv.*

undulate ('undyōōlāt) *vb.* **undulating, undulated.** to go up and down like waves on the sea; to move in or like waves: *the snake undulated across the floor.* —**undu'lation** *n.*

unearth (un'ûth) *vb.* 1. to dig up out of the ground: *he unearthed a Roman vase.* 2. to discover: *he unearthed a valuable picture in his attic.*

unearthly (un'ûthli) *adj.* unnatural; frightening. **an unearthly hour** an unusually late or early time, esp. an inconvenient one.

uneasy (un'ēzi) *adj.* worried or disturbed in one's mind. —**un'easily** *adv.* —**un'easiness** *n.*

uneven (un'ēvən) *adj.* not even; not level or smooth. —**un'evenly** *adv.*

unfit (un'fit) *adj.* not fit; not suitable or healthy.

unfold (un'fōld) *vb.* 1. to open or roll out (cloth, paper, etc.) that has been folded up. 2. to make or become known; tell or be told: *he unfolded his story to the police.*

unfortunate (un'fôchənit) *adj.* 1. not successful or lucky: *it was unfortunate that he lost the race.* 2. in misery or poverty; deprived. 3. ill-timed or embarrassing; not properly thought about beforehand: *she made an unfortunate comment about the size of his nose.*

unfounded (un'foundid) *adj.* without evidence: *the reports of his death were completely unfounded.*

ungainly (un'gānli) *adj.* awkward or clumsy; not graceful: *Mary has an ungainly walk.*

ungulate ('ungyōōlāt) *n.* an animal that has hooves, such as a horse.

unicorn

unicorn ('yōōnikôn) *n.* a legendary animal resembling a horse and having a single horn growing out of the middle of its forehead.

uniform ('yōōnifôm) *adj.* never different; unchanging, equal, etc. —*n.* official clothing worn by policemen, soldiers, etc.

unify ('yōōnifī) *vb.* **unifying, unified.** unite; make into a single whole or unit.

union ('yōōniən) *n.* 1. the result of joining objects, countries, states, etc., together. 2. a marriage. 3. a group or association organized for a particular aim or purpose: *a trade union.* —**'unionism** *n.* —**'unionist** *n.*

unique (yōō'nēk) *adj.* completely unlike anything else; being the only one of its kind. —**u'niquely** *adv.* —**u'niqueness** *n.*

unison ('yōōnisən) *n.* harmony or agreement. **in unison** 1. together; in agreement; at the same time: *the football supporters chanted in unison.* 2. (of two musical parts) using or performing the same notes.

unit ('yōōnit) *n.* 1. a single person or thing, or a number of people or things considered as a single group: *an army unit.* 2. a fixed quantity used as the basis of measuring length, weight, etc.: *the metre is a unit of length.* 3. piece of equipment: *a sink unit.* 4. the number one (1).

unite (yōō'nīt) *vb.* **uniting, united.** to join or be joined together; make into or become a unit. —**unity** ('yōōniti) *n.*

universe ('yōōnivûs) *n.* all of space containing all the stars and planets and all the matter and energy that exist; the entire total of all things. **uni'versal** *adj.* found, existing, occurring, etc., everywhere.

university (yōōni'vûsiti) *n.,pl.* **universities.** a place of education to which students go after leaving school in order to obtain a degree.

unkempt (un'kemt) *adj.* rough or dirty; having untidy hair and an unshaven face.

unknown (un'nōn) *adj.* not known; strange or unfamiliar. —*n.* something or somewhere that is not familiar: *Tom has gone off into the unknown.*

unravel (un'ravəl) *vb.* **unravelling, unravelled.** 1. to cause (threads of cloth, etc.) to separate, or (of cloth threads) to be separated. 2. to solve or work out (a difficult problem).

unrest (un'rest) *n.* discontentment, esp. when it leads to violence or other troubles.

unruly (un'rōōli) *adj.* badly behaved or rowdy.

untold (un'tōld) *adj.* 1. not told or made known. 2. very many; more than can be counted: *there are untold millions of stars in the universe.*

unwieldy (un'wēldi) *adj.* difficult to handle, use, etc.; awkward; clumsy. —**un'wieldiness** *n.*

urn

upbringing ('upbringing) *n.* the care and education of a child as he or she is growing up.

upheaval (up'hēvəl) *n.* a complete, often violent, change or disturbance.

uphold (up'hōld) *vb.* **upholding, upheld.** to support; keep; preserve.

upholstery (up'hōlstəri) *n.* 1. the cushions, padding, and coverings used in sofas, armchairs, car seats, etc. 2. the work of making and fitting upholstery for furniture. **up'holster** *vb.* to equip (furniture) with upholstery. —**up'holsterer** *n.*

upkeep ('upkēp) *n.* 1. the act of keeping a house, etc., in good order. 2. the cost of doing this.

upright ('uprīt) *adj.* 1. straight; vertical. 2. morally correct; honest: *an upright person.* —*adv.* vertically: *stand upright.* —*n.* something standing vertically, e.g. a pillar or a football post.

uprising ('uprīzing) *n.* an armed rebellion; revolution: *many people were killed in the Hungarian uprising.*

uproar ('uprô) *n.* noisy shouting, as of a crowd of people. **up'roarious** *adj.* noisily happy: *we had an uproarious time at John's New Year's party.* —**up'roariously** *adv.*

upset *vb.* (up'set) **upsetting, upset.** 1. knock over; spill: *she upset a bottle of milk.* 2. to make (someone) sad or angry. —*n.* ('upset) a surprise, esp. an unpleasant one; shock.

upshot ('upshot) *n.* the result (of something): *the upshot of this whole business was that he got to school very late.*

uranium (yōō'rāniəm) *n.* a heavy metallic radioactive chemical element used in producing NUCLEAR power. Chemical symbol: U.

urchin ('ûchin) *n.* a naughty child, esp. a ragged little boy. **sea urchin** a small sea animal that has a round spiked shell.

urge (ûj) *vb.* **urging, urged.** 1. to encourage (someone) to do something. 2. to push or force (someone). —*n.* 1. a strong form of encouragement. 2. an instinct or compulsion: *he had a sudden urge to run away.*

urgent ('ûjənt) *adj.* requiring haste; pressing; needing immediate attention. —**'urgency** *n.,pl.* **urgencies.**

urn (ûn) *n.* 1. a large container for plants. 2. a tall narrow-necked container in which the ashes of a dead person are placed. 3. a tall metal container for tea or coffee.

use *vb.* (yōōz) **using, used.** 1. to apply; employ; utilize. 2. (often + *up*) finish; exhaust the supply of: *I've used (up) all the sugar.* 3. to treat (a person) in a certain way, esp. to mistreat or take advantage of him. **be** (*or* **get**) **used to** be (or become) accustomed to. —*n.* (yōōs) 1. service or employment. 2. purpose. 3. the act of using. 4. the state of being used: *the old car is still in use.* **make use of** to use. **useful** ('yōōsfəl) *adj.* helpful; having value. **useless** ('yōōslis) *adj.* worthless; having no purpose, value, or effect.

usher ('ushə) *n.* a person who shows people to their seats in a theatre, cinema, or church. **usher'ette** *n.* a woman who acts as an usher in a cinema. —*vb.* to act as an usher.

usual ('yōōzhōōəl) *adj.* normal; typical; common. —*n.* something that is normal or customary. —**'usually** *adv.*

usurp (yōō'zûp) *vb.* to take over (a throne, kingdom, or position of authority, etc.) unlawfully or without right: *Tom usurped the form captain's authority.* —**usurp'ation** *n.*

utensil (yōō'tensil) *n.* a thing that one uses, esp. an article used in the kitchen.

utensils: 1 mixing bowl; 2 whisk; 3 kitchen tools; 4 can opener; 5 scales; 6 roasting pan; 7 bun tin.

utility (yōō'tiliti) *n.,pl.* **utilities.** 1. usefulness. 2. something employed by many people; a public service: *the water supply is a public utility.* **utilize** ('yōōtilīz) *vb.* **utilizing, utilized.** to use: *How can we best utilize our resources?*

utmost ('utmōst) *adj.* 1. the greatest, highest, most serious, etc.: *handle those glasses with the utmost care.* 2. the furthest: *from the utmost regions of the north.* —*n.* the most, greatest, best, furthest, etc.

utter[1] ('utə) *vb.* 1. to make (a sound): *she uttered a fearful cry.* 2. to speak: *don't ever utter her name again.* **'utterance** *n.* a word or sentence.

utter[2] ('utə) *adj.* complete; absolute: *you utter fool!* —**'utterly** *adv.*

229

V

vacant ('vākənt) *adj*. 1. not occupied; empty. 2. (of a job, etc.) waiting to be filled or taken on: *the secretary's job is vacant.* 3. uninterested or stupid: *a vacant stare.* '**vacancy** *n.,pl.* **vacancies.** 1. the state of being vacant. 2. a vacant job, room, etc. —'**vacantly** *adv.*

vacation (və'kāshən) *n*. 1. a period during which universities, courts of law, colleges, etc., are closed. 2. a holiday.

vaccinate ('vaksināt) *vb*. **vaccinating, vaccinated.** to inject into (a patient) a modified form of a virus in order to build up his resistance to the usual form. **vaccine** ('vaksēn) *n*. the modified virus injected in this way. —**vacci'nation** *n*.

vacuum ('vakyoom) *n*. a complete absence of air or any other gas; emptiness: *outer space is almost a vacuum.*

vagabond ('vagəbond) *n*. a person who wanders from place to place without a settled home.

vagrant ('vāgrənt) *n*. a beggar or tramp with no settled home; vagabond. —*adj*. of, like, or living as a vagrant.

vague (vāg) *adj*. 1. uncertain; indefinite. 2. unclear in one's thoughts.

vain (vān) *adj*. 1. having no value, use, or success. 2. conceited or proud, esp. about one's appearance. **in vain** unsuccessfully; uselessly. —'**vainly** *adv.*

valiant ('valyənt) *adj*. brave or courageous. —'**valiantly** *adv.*

valid ('valid) *adj*. 1. lawful: *a valid document.* 2. strong or convincing: *valid reasons.* —**validity** (və'liditi) *n*. —'**validly** *adv.*

valley ('vali) *n*. 1. a long narrow piece of low-lying land running between hills or mountains and often having a river running through it. 2. anything resembling a valley.

valour ('valə) *n*. bravery or courage. —'**valorous** *adj.*

value ('valyoo) *n*. 1. usefulness or importance: *the value of literature.* 2. the worth of something, as measured in money, etc.: *the value of a painting.* —*vb*. **valuing, valued.** 1. to think highly of. 2. to work out the value of (something) in money. '**valuable** *adj*. of great value, esp. worth a lot of money: *this painting is valuable.* **valu'ation** *n*. the act of valuing or the value worked out.

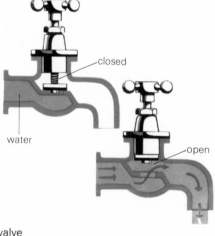
closed
water
open

valve

valve (valv) *n*. 1. a piece of equipment that can be opened or closed to control the flow of a liquid or gas. 2. an organ, esp. in the heart, controlling the flow of blood. 3. a vacuum or gas-filled tube used to control the flow of electricity in a radio, television set, etc.

vampire ('vampīə) *n*. 1. (in legend) a corpse that comes to life at night and sucks the blood of sleeping persons. 2. any of several different species of bat, some of which feed on blood.

vandal ('vandəl) *n*. a person who wilfully destroys something.

vane (vān) *n*. 1. one of the blades of a propeller or other machine. 2. (also **weather vane**) a movable flat metal object mounted on the roof of a building in such a way as to show the direction of the wind.

vanilla (və'nilə) *n*. a substance used in food-flavouring, perfume, etc. It is obtained from the beanlike fruit (**vanilla pods**) of a tropical flowering plant.

vanish ('vanish) *vb*. 1. to become invisible, esp. suddenly; disappear. 2. to stop existing; cease.

vanity ('vaniti) *n.,pl.* **vanities.** 1. the quality of being vain about oneself; conceit or excessive pride. 2. something that one is conceited about. 3. worthlessness; uselessness: *the vanity of human wishes.*

vanquish ('vangkwish) *vb*. to conquer; be victorious over: *our enemies were completely vanquished.*

vapour ('vāpə) *n*. matter in a cloudlike, misty, or gaseous form. '**vaporize** *vb*. **vaporizing, vaporized.** to become or cause to become vapour. —'**vaporous** *adj.*

variety (və'rīəti) *n.,pl.* **varieties.** 1. the quality of not always being the same; variation. 2. a type or kind: *there are several varieties of pony in this country.* 3. a varying collection: *we sell a variety of cars.* **various** ('veəriəs) *adj*. several or different: *we have various pets for sale.*

varnish ('vânish) *n*. a liquid substance that, when dry, produces a hard shiny transparent surface upon wood, metal, etc. —*vb*. to put varnish on pictures (articles of wood, metal, etc.).

vary ('veəri) *vb*. **varying, varied.** to be or cause to be different; change or alter. **vari'ation** *n*. a change or the result of a change. '**varied** *adj*. not equally or always the same; showing change or variation.

vase (vâz) *n*. a container made of glass or pottery, usu. a tall one used for flowers.

vast (vâst) *adj*. of enormous size, proportions, degree, etc.; huge: *a vast amount of money.*

vehicles

truck

coach

car

van

vault[1] (vôlt) *n.* 1. a great curved arch forming a roof. 2. an underground or strongly protected room in which money or other valuable things are stored, corpses are laid, etc.

vault[2] (vôlt) *vb.* to leap or jump, esp. to spring over (a high fence, bar, etc.) with one's hands resting on something or with the aid of a long pole. —*n.* the action of vaulting.

veal (vēl) *n.* the meat of a calf.

veer (viə) *vb.* 1. (esp. of the wind) to change direction. 2. to turn off one's course: *the car veered off the road.*

vegetable ('vejitəbəl) *n.* any of numerous different plants, e.g. cabbage, potato, tomato, lettuce, whose fruits, leaves, seeds, etc., are used for food. —*adj.* of or like a plant or vegetable.

vegetarian (veji'teəriən) *n.* a person who eats only vegetables.

vegetation (veji'tāshən) *n.* plants collectively, esp. the plants of a certain area.

vehicle ('viəkəl) *n.* 1. a cart, car, bus, or other wheeled object used for transport on land. 2. a craft such as a space rocket. —**vehicular** (vi'hikyōōlə) *adj.*

veil (vāl) *n.* a piece of material, usu. thin or delicate, used esp. by women as a covering for the face. **take the veil** to become a nun. **draw a veil over** to hide (something), esp. for reasons of tact. —*vb.* to put on or cover with a veil.

vein (vān) *n.* 1. one of the vessels in the body through which blood flows back to the heart. 2. a layer, streak of colour, etc., appearing in something and resembling a vein: *a vein of silver in rock.* 3. a mood: *music in a sad vein.*

velvet ('velvit) *n.* a cotton or silk cloth having a thick soft pile.

veneer (vi'niə) *n.* 1. a thin layer of fine quality wood glued onto the surface of wooden furniture to give it a pleasant appearance. 2. an outwardly pleasant appearance: *a veneer of charm.* —*vb.* to put a veneer on: *walnut furniture is often veneered.*

vengeance ('venjəns) *n.* injury or suffering caused to someone in return for a past crime or wrong; revenge.

venom ('venəm) *n.* 1. poison, esp. the poison of a snake or other animal. 2. something resembling poison, such as vicious criticism.

vent (vent) *n.* 1. an opening in something allowing the escape of air, smoke, etc. 2. an opening in the back of a coat or jacket. **give vent to** to allow the free expression of (an emotion). —*vb.* to express (an emotion): *to vent one's anger.*

ventilate ('ventilāt) *vb.* **ventilating, ventilated.** 1. to provide (a room, etc.) with fresh air. 2. to allow free discussion or wide knowledge of (a question or subject): *the problems of smoking cigarettes have been ventilated widely in many schools.* —**venti'lation** *n.* —'**ventilator** *n.*

ventriloquist (ven'triləkwist) *n.* an entertainer able to speak without seeming to move his lips, thus making his voice appear to come from somewhere else. —**ven'triloquism** *n.*

venture ('venchə) *n.* a job or task involving risk or uncertainty. —*vb.* **venturing, ventured.** 1. to put at risk; endanger. 2. to go forward without worrying about possible dangers: *the explorer ventured into the jungle.*

veranda *or* **verandah** (və'randə) *n.* a roofed, partially enclosed section built onto a house; porch.

verb (vûb) *n.* a word belonging to a certain class of words in a language that express an action, e.g. *run* and *hit.*

verbal ('vûbəl) *adj.* 1. of or connected with spoken rather than written words. 2. of or concerning verbs.

verbose (vû'bōs) *adj.* containing or using too many words.—**verbosity** (vû'bositi) *n.*

verdict ('vûdikt) *n.* 1. a decision about the guilt or innocence of someone, made on the basis of evidence, as by a jury in a law court. 2. a judgment about something: *what's your verdict on this wine?*

verge (vûj) *n.* 1. the edge of something. 2. the grassy area at the side of a road, etc. —*vb.* **verging, verged.** to border on; touch or come close to.

vermilion (və'miliən) *n.* a bright scarlet or red colour. —*adj.* of or having this colour.

vermin ('vûmin) *pl.n.* rats, mice, insects, and other small animals regarded as a nuisance to man or a danger to his health.

verse (vûs) *n.* 1. a poem or poetry in general. 2. a line or group of lines in a poem or song. 3. a numbered section in a chapter from the Bible.

version ('vûzhən) *n.* 1. an account of an event or situation given from a particular point of view. 2. a form of something different from the original form: *the film version of* Treasure Island.

versus ('vûsəs) *prep.* (esp. used in competitions) against: *John Brown versus Bill Smith.* Abbreviation: **v.**

vertebra ('vûtibrə) *n.,pl.* **vertebrae** ('vûtibrā). any of the several bones or sections that make up the backbone. **'vertebrate** *n.* an animal having a backbone. *adj.* of vertebrae or of an animal that has vertebrae.

vertical ('vûtikəl) *adj.* extending upwards in a straight line; upright.—*n.* something vertical, such as a pillar.

vessel ('vesəl) *n.* 1. a container for liquid. 2. something resembling this: *a blood vessel.* 3. a ship.

vestment

vestment ('vestmənt) *n.* one of the official garments worn by someone at a ceremony, esp. a priest in a church service.

vestry ('vestri) *n.,pl.* **vestries.** a room in a church in which a priest, members of the choir, etc., dress for a service or ceremony.

veteran ('vetərən) *n.* 1. an experienced person. 2. a person who has served for a long time in the army, navy, or air force: *the veterans were on parade last Sunday.* —*adj.* having been in service or use for a long time: *a veteran car.*

veterinary ('vetinəri) *adj.* of or connected with the medical and surgical treatment of animals. **vet** *or* **veterinary surgeon** *n.* a person who provides such treatment as a service to farmers and pet-owners.

vex (veks) *vb.* to make angry or distressed; annoy or worry: *a very vexing problem.*

viaduct ('vīədukt) *n.* a bridge supported by high arches and carrying a road or railway over a valley.

vibrate (vī'brāt) *vb.* **vibrating, vibrated.** to move rapidly back and forth or up and down. —**vi'bration** *n.*

vicar ('vikə) *n.* a clergyman who acts as priest to a parish.

vice[1] (vīs) *n.* 1. wickedness: *a life of vice.* 2. a bad habit: *drinking too much alcohol is a vice.*

vice[2] (vīs) *n.* a device consisting of two adjustable jawlike parts in which an object may be held steady while work is being done on it.

vice versa (vīsə'vûsə) the other way around: *Tony dislikes Mary and vice versa.*

vicious ('vishəs) *adj.* cruel, spiteful, or wicked: *the thief dealt John a vicious blow.*

victim ('viktim) *n.* a person or animal who is killed, injured, or made to suffer by someone or something else: *he became a victim of a crippling disease.*

victory ('viktəri) *n.,pl.* **victories.** 1. the act or fact of conquering an opponent or enemy; conquest. 2. any triumph or success: *this is a victory for common sense.* **victor** ('viktə) *n.* the winner of a victory; conqueror. —**victorious** (vik'tôriəs) *adj.*

view (vyōō) *n.* 1. the action of seeing or the ability to see: *our view was blocked by a car.* 2. the appearance to the eye of a landscape or other scene: *the view from my window was wonderful.* 3. an opinion: *what is your view on education?* —*vb.* 1. to look at or run the eye over. 2. to watch (a television programme). 3. to consider, esp. in a particular way.

vigil ('vijil) *n.* an act of keeping watch or of staying awake. **'vigilance** *n.* watchfulness; awareness. —**'vigilant** *adj.*

vigour ('vigə) *n.* strength; force; energy; power. —**'vigorous** *adj.* —**'vigorously** *adv.*

vile (vīl) *adj.* **viler, vilest.** 1. offensive or disgusting: *a vile smell.* 2. morally bad; worthless: *he's a vile fellow.* 3. thoroughly bad or unpleasant: *vile weather.* —**'vilely** *adv.* —**'vileness** *n.*

villa ('vilə) *n.* a detached house, usu. one at the seaside or in the country.

village ('vilij) *n.* a very small group of houses, shops, etc., usu. in a country area.

villain ('vilən) *n.* 1. an evil person; wrongdoer. 2. (slang) a criminal. —**'villainous** *adj.* —**'villainously** *adv.* —**'villainy** *n.*

vine (vīn) *n.* 1. a creeping or climbing plant, esp. one on which grapes grow. 2. a long branch or stem of such a plant.

vinegar ('vinigə) *n.* a sour liquid, consisting of dilute acetic acid, made from wine, etc., and used to flavour or pickle food.

vintage ('vintij) *n.* 1. the time when grapes are picked for wine-making. 2. the wine made in a particular year: *the 1960 vintage.* —*adj.* 1. especially fine: *1960 was a vintage year.* 2. made in a good year or belonging to a good period in the past: *a vintage wine.*

vinyl ('vīnəl) *n.* a tough plastic used esp. in gramophone records and clothing. —*adj.* made of vinyl.

viola (vi'ōlə) *n.* a stringed musical instrument of the violin family. It is slightly larger and deeper in pitch than the violin.

violate ('vīəlāt) *vb.* **violating, violated.** 1. to break (a promise, treaty, rule, etc.). 2. to disturb or shatter (peace, a pleasant situation, etc.). —**vio'lation** *n.*

violence ('vīələns) *n.* power or force, esp. that which causes destruction or injury. '**violent** *adj.* using or involving violence.

violet ('vīəlit) *n.* 1. a small purple, blue, or white flower. 2. the little round-leaved creeping plant that produces these flowers. 3. a purplish-blue colour. —*adj.* having the colour violet.

violin

violin (vīə'lin) *n.* a four-stringed musical instrument usu. played with a bow. **vio'linist** *n.* a person who plays the violin.

vine

viper ('vīpə) *n.* one of several kinds of poisonous snakes found in Europe, Africa, and Asia.

virtue ('vûtyōō) *n.* moral worth or quality; merit. advantage. **by** (*or* **in**) **virtue of** because of: *he passed his exams by virtue of his hard work.* '**virtuous** *adj.* morally good.

virus ('vīrəs) *n.,pl.* **viruses.** a germ that is smaller than a bacterium and causes such diseases as influenza, chickenpox, mumps, measles, and the common cold.

visa ('vēzə) *n.* a stamp placed on someone's passport by an official from a certain country allowing the holder free passage through the country.

visible ('vizibəl) *adj.* able to be seen. **visi'bility** *n.* 1. the ability to see. 2. the distance over which one can see: *fog cut visibility to forty yards.*

vision ('vizhən) *n.* 1. sight. 2. the visual part of a television transmission. 3. a vivid dream. 4. imagination: *a man of vision.*

visit ('visit) *vb.* 1. to go to see or stay with someone for a short time, esp. to call upon (a friend). 2. to go to (a place) on business or holiday. —*n.* the act or an instance of visiting: *Mary paid her aunt a visit.* —'**visitor** *n.*

visual ('vizyōōəl) *adj.* of, connected with, or involving vision. '**visualize** *vb.* **visualizing, visualized.** to create a picture of (someone or something) in one's mind. —'**visually** *adv.*

vital ('vītəl) *adj.* 1. connected with or necessary for life. 2. very important or urgent: *a vital message.* **vi'tality** *n.* freshness or liveliness. —'**vitally** *adv.*

vitamin ('vitəmin) *n.* any of a number of chemical substances present in various foods and necessary in small amounts for keeping a person alive and healthy.

vivacious (vi'vāshəs) *adj.* lively and animated: *Bill and Carolyn were engaged in vivacious conversation.*

vivid ('vivid) *adj.* 1. very bright: *a vivid colour.* 2. full of life; lively: *a vivid character.* 3. lifelike; believable: *a vivid dream.* 4. strong: *vivid feelings.*

vocabulary (vō'kabyōōləri) *n.,pl.* **vocabularies.** 1. the collection of all the words used in a language, sometimes arranged in alphabetical order to form a dictionary. 2. the number of words in a language known to and used by any person: *Mike's French vocabulary is very limited.*

vocal ('vōkəl) *adj.* of, connected with, or using the voice. —*n.* (informal) a piece of music written for the voice; song. —'**vocally** *adv.*.

vocation (vō'kāshən) *n.* a type of work to which a person feels that he is called, esp. to serve others: *school-teaching is a vocation.* —**vo'cational** *adj.*

vogue (vōg) *n.* 1. a fashion. 2. something that is popular for a short time. **in vogue** popular.

voice (vois) *n.* 1. the sound or sounds made by a person in speaking, singing, shouting, etc. 2. such a sound considered with regard to its quality or condition: *he is in good voice.* 3. something similar to a voice in its effect or function: *the voice of reason.* 4. the right to express an opinion: *everyone should have a voice in the government.* 5. (in some languages) a form of the verb indicating the connection between the subject of a sentence and the action of the verb, e.g. the active voice or passive voice. **give voice to** to express (an opinion). —*vb.* **voicing, voiced.** to put (something) into words.

void (void) *adj.* having no force; not effective: *the law was declared void.* —*n.* space; emptiness.

volatile ('volətīl) *adj.* 1. (of a liquid) giving off a vapour: *a volatile oil.* 2. behaving in a frivolous or changeable way: *Mary was in a volatile mood and refused to make a definite arrangement.*

233

volcano

volcano (vol'kānō) *n.,pl.* **volcanoes.** a mountain with a hole or crater in its top through which hot ash and melted rock (LAVA) are released from inside the earth.

vole (vōl) *n.* a small ratlike animal found in fields.

volley ('voli) *n.* 1. a number of shots, arrows, etc., fired at the same moment. 2. (tennis, cricket, etc.) the way a ball is said to fly if it does not bounce. 3. the act of striking a ball that has not bounced. —*vb.* to strike (a tennis or cricket ball) on the volley.

volt (vōlt) *n.* a unit of electrical force; the electrical force needed to cause a current of one ampere to flow through a resistance of one ohm.

volume ('volyo̅o̅m) *n.* 1. the amount of space taken up by something, measured in cubic units. 2. a book, esp. one of a series. 3. the strength of a sound; loudness. 4. an amount or quantity, esp. a large one.

voluntary ('voləntəri) *adj.* 1. willing; not forced or compelled. 2. not controlled by the state; private: *a voluntary organization.* 3. controlled by one's own mind; deliberate: *a voluntary movement of a part of the body.* **volun'teer** *n.* someone who does something without being asked. *adj.* of or connected with a volunteer. *vb.* to offer to do something without being asked. —'**voluntarily** *adv.*

vomit ('vomit) *vb.* to throw out (food, etc.) from the stomach through the mouth; be sick.

vote (vōt) *vb.* **voting, voted.** (often + *for*) to indicate one's opinion or choice, as at a parliamentary election, committee meeting, etc. —*n.* the act or a result of voting.

vouch (vouch) *vb.* (+ *for*) to declare or guarantee the truth, correctness, honesty, etc., of (someone or something). '**voucher** *n.* a paper showing that something is in order or guaranteeing a person's right to something.

vow (vou) *n.* a serious promise, often made to God or in God's name. —*vb.* to make a vow; promise.

vowel ('vouəl) *n.* 1. a continuous speech sound in which the voice is used. 2. a letter representing such a sound, e.g. *a, e, i, o, u,* or *y.* Compare CONSONANT.

voyage ('voiij) *n.* a journey, esp. a long one, by ship. —*vb.* **voyaging, voyaged.** to travel over the sea in a ship.

vulgar ('vulgə) *adj.* 1. rude; offensive: *vulgar language.* 2. (old-fashioned) common; of or used by the public. —**vul'garity** *n.*

vulnerable ('vulnərəbəl) *adj.* 1. easily hurt or wounded: *Mary is very vulnerable to criticism.* 2. open to attack; not easily defended: *that bridge is very vulnerable to attack by aircraft.*

vulture ('vulchə) *n.* a large bird that feeds on dead animals.

vulture

W

wad (wod) *n.* 1. (also **wadding**) small mass of soft material used for plugging a hole or for packing. 2. a bundle of folded banknotes or papers. 3. (of money) a large amount.

wade (wād) *vb.* **wading, waded.** to walk through water, snow, mud, etc. **wade into** (informal) to attack (someone or something). '**wader** *n.* 1. a bird that wades in water. 2. a high waterproof boot.

wafer ('wāfə) *n.* a very thin crisp biscuit often sweetened and eaten with ice cream.

waft (woft) *vb.* to float or carry along upon or as if upon the air or water: *pleasant smells wafted in from the kitchen.* —*n.* something floating along on the air.

wag (wag) *vb.* **wagging, wagged.** to move or cause to move up and down or from side to side; shake or wave: *the dog wagged his tail.*

wage (wāj) *n.* often **wages** (*pl.*) the sum of money that a person receives in return for work. —*vb.* **waging, waged.** to carry on (a war, battle, etc.).

wagon ('wagən) *n.* 1. a large four-wheeled cart pulled by horses or oxen and now usu. used for carrying goods. 2. a railway truck. '**wagoner** *n.* a person who drives a wagon.

wagon

wail (wāl) *n.* a long loud cry of sadness. —*vb.* to cry out sadly.

waist (wāst) *n.* 1. the middle part of the body, just above the hips. 2. the central narrowest part of something. such as a violin.

wait (wāt) *vb.* 1. (usu. + *for*) to keep oneself or be kept ready for (something expected or hoped for): *there's a message waiting for you.* 2. to do nothing until something expected happens: *we waited all day.* **wait upon** to serve (someone), e.g. at a restaurant. '**waiter** *n.* a man who serves at a restaurant. '**waitress** *n.* a female waiter.

wake (wāk) *vb.* **waking, woke, woken.** (often + *up*) 1. to come or bring out of a state of sleep; become or cause to become awake. 2. to become or cause to become excited or aware.

wallaby ('woləbi) *n.,pl.* **wallabies.** an Australian animal that is very similar to a small kangaroo. See MARSUPIAL.

wallet ('wolit) *n.* a small folding case of leather or similar material used for carrying paper money, etc.

wallow ('wolō) *vb.* to roll or play around, in mud, water, etc.: *the baby seals were wallowing at the edge of the sea.* —*n.* 1. the action or an instance of wallowing. 2. a place for wallowing.

walrus ('wôlrəs) *n.,pl.* **walruses.** a large sea animal related to the seal and living in northern regions. It has flippers and a pair of long tusks.

walrus

waltz (wôls) *n.* 1. a piece of dance music, having three beats in each bar. 2. the ballroom dance performed to this music. —*vb.* to dance a waltz.

wand (wond) *n.* a rod or stick used by a conjurer or magician, or supposedly by fairies.

wander ('wondə) *vb.* 1. to travel about with no real purpose. 2. to move away from the correct course, etc.: *we have wandered away from the subject.*

wane (wān) *vb.* **waning, waned.** to get smaller or less. —*n.* the action of becoming smaller or less. **on the wane** getting smaller or less: *the moon is on the wane.* Compare WAX².

war (wô) *n.* 1. a fight or struggle using weapons, waged between two or more countries or groups within a country. 2. a struggle of any sort: *the war against poverty.* —*vb.* **warring, warred.** to carry on a war.

warble ('wôbəl) *vb.* **warbling, warbled.** to sing sweetly with trills. —*n.* 1. a song produced in this way: *the warble of the nightingale was heard very clearly in the wood.* 2. the act of warbling.

235

ward (wôd) *n.* 1. a room in which people stay when they are in hospital. 2. a division of a town or city having a representative on the local council. 3. a person under the protection of someone else. —*vb.* (+ *off*) to drive or keep away; prevent from causing injury, etc. '**warden** *n.* 1. an official or a person in charge of something: *a traffic warden.* '**warder** *n.* a prison guard.

wardrobe ('wôdrōb) *n.* 1. a tall cupboard for storing clothes. 2. all the clothes belonging to a person. 3. the clothes belonging to a theatrical company.

warehouse ('weəhous) *n.* a building used for storing goods, material, etc.

warn (wôn) *vb.* (often + *of*) to advise or inform (someone) that something is about to happen, esp. something dangerous, important, etc.

warren ('worən) *n.* a place occupied by the tunnels and burrows of a large number of rabbits.

warrior ('woriə) *n.* a person experienced in fighting wars.

warship ('wôship) *n.* a ship equipped with weapons and used in war.

wart (wôt) *n.* a small lump on the skin.

wash (wosh) *vb.* 1. to clean oneself by putting soap and water on one's body. 2. to clean (clothes, dishes, etc.) with water and soap or detergent. —*n.* 1. the action or an instance of washing. 2. the waves left by the passage of a boat. '**washer** *n.* 1. a machine for washing. 2. a small flat metal ring used under a nut or on a bolt. 3. a rubber ring or plug used to stop the flow of water in a tap.

wasp (wosp) *n.* a stinging insect having a yellow and black striped body and transparent wings.

waste (wāst) *vb.* **wasting, wasted.** 1. to lose (something) by using too much of it: *they waste money.* 2. (often + *away*) to become or cause to become weak or thin: *his body was wasting away.* 3. to destroy (land, homes, etc.). —*n.* 1. the action or an instance of wasting: *it's a waste of money.* 2. rubbish; refuse. —*adj.* of no more use: *waste paper.*

watch (woch) *vb.* 1. to look at: *Pete watched television.* 2. to keep guard over: *the cat watched the mouse.* 3. to keep awake or vigilant. **watch out** (often used as a warning) to be careful. —*n.* 1. the action or an instance of watching. 2. a period of watching. 3. someone who watches, such as a guard. 4. a small device for measuring time usually worn on the wrist or carried in a pocket. —'**watchman** *n.,pl.* **watchmen.**

water ('wôtə) *n.* 1. the liquid that forms the seas, rivers, and lakes on the earth. Pure water is a colourless liquid having no smell or taste. 2. a body of water: *a boat was floating on the water.* 3. **waters** (*pl.*) area of the sea: *home waters.* —*vb.* 1. to put water on (flowers, plants, etc.). 2. to give water to (animals). '**watery** *adj.* 1. of or containing water. 2. (of colour) pale.

watercolour ('wôtəkulə) *n.* 1. paint that is mixed with water before use. 2. a picture painted in watercolours. —*adj.* of or connected with watercolours.

waterfall ('wôtəfôl) *n.* a place in a river where there is a steep dip in the riverbed forming a cliff over which the flowing river pours.

waterlogged ('wôtəlogd) *adj.* soaked through by water: *the ground was waterlogged after the heavy rain.*

waterproof ('wôtəproōf) *adj.* specially treated to allow no water to pass through: *a waterproof raincoat.* —*n.* a garment, etc., that is waterproof. —*vb.* to make (a coat, etc.) waterproof.

watershed ('wôtəshed) *n.* an area of high ground separating two low-lying areas from which two different rivers draw off water.

watertight ('wôtətīt) *adj.* keeping water out.

watt (wot) *n.* a unit of electrical power.

wave (wāv) *n.* 1. a curving movement seen on the surface of a liquid, such as on a lake or the sea. 2. anything resembling a wave in movement or shape: *her hair had beautiful waves in it.* 3. an up-and-down or sideways movement of the hand, a flag, etc.: *he gave us a friendly wave.* 4. a sudden rush: *a wave of enthusiasm.* 5. a short period: *a heat wave.* —*vb.* **waving, waved.** to move or cause to move in waves or wavelike motions. —'**wavy** *adj.* **wavier, waviest.**

wavelength ('wāvleṅgth) *n.* the length of waves of light, radio or television signals, etc. The higher the wavelength, the lower the frequency. See under FREQUENT.

wax[1] (waks) *n.* 1. (also **beeswax**) a substance produced by bees for building their honeycombs. 2. a similar substance produced from other things, softened by heat and easy to shape, used for candles, model-making, polish, etc. 3. yellow substance that collects in the ears. —*vb.* to cover with wax polish. —*adj.* made of or from wax: *a wax figure.* —'**waxy** *adj.* **waxier, waxiest.**

wax[2] (waks) *vb.* 1. (esp. of the moon) to appear bigger. 2. to grow; become: *he waxed eloquent about the book.* Compare WANE.

weak (wēk) *adj.* 1. not strong; faint; feeble. 2. not good: *weak at English.* '**weaken** *vb.* to make or become weak or weaker. '**weakling** *n.* a weak person. '**weakness** *n.* 1. the state of being weak. 2. some failure or defect.

wealth (welth) *n.* 1. a great deal of money or valuable things; riches. 2. a large number or amount of something: *a wealth of reasons.*

waterfall

weapon ('wepən) *n.* an instrument or method used in fighting: *his sword was his most trusted weapon.*

wear (weə) *vb.* **wearing, wore, worn.** 1. to be dressed in (clothes, etc.). 2. to have or show: *he wore a frown.* 3. to damage or be damaged by continual use: *he wore a hole in his shoe.* 4. to last a long time despite being in continual use: *this suit has worn well.* —*n.* 1. the act of wearing: *this shirt is suitable for casual wear.* 2. clothes: *children's wear.* 3. damage caused by continual use: *the carpet shows signs of wear.* 4. usefulness: *there's plenty of wear left in this suit.*

weary ('wiəri) *adj.* **wearier, weariest.** 1. tired; exhausted: *weary after a hard day's work.* 2. impatient with: *I'm weary of your excuses.* —*vb.* **wearying, wearied.** (often + *of*) to make or become weary.

weasel ('wēzəl) *n.* a small warm-blooded thin-bodied animal with short legs and a long neck that feeds mainly on rabbits and other small animals.

weather ('wedhə) *n.* atmospheric conditions in a certain area and at a particular time: *the weather is warm.* —*vb.* 1. to be affected, changed, or worn by being left in the open air. 2. to come through safely: *we have weathered the crisis.*

weathercock

weathercock ('wedhəkok) *n.* a device in the shape of a cock mounted on a roof and used as a weather VANE.

weave (wēv) *vb.* **weaving, wove, woven.** 1. to make (cloth, etc.) by interlacing threads together. 2. to follow a winding course or path: *the car wove through the busy streets.* —*n.* a style of weaving.

web (web) *n.* the netlike object of sticky thread spun by a spider to catch the insects on which it feeds.

wed (wed) *vb.* **wedding, wedded** or **wed.** 1. to marry. 2. to combine: *the composer wed beautiful music and beautiful words.* '**wedding** *n.* a ceremony at which a man and a woman are married.

wedge (wej) *n.* 1. a V-shaped object made of metal or wood used for splitting or separating. 2. anything shaped like a V: *a wedge of cheese.* —*vb.* **wedging, wedged.** 1. to drive a wedge between (things) to separate them or keep them steady. 2. to push or be pushed in like a wedge: *she wedged herself into a corner.*

weed (wēd) *n.* an unwanted plant. —*vb.* 1. to remove weeds from (a garden). 2. (+ *out*) to remove unnecessary or unwanted people or things: *he weeded out the troublemakers.*

weep (wēp) *vb.* **weeping, wept.** to cry; shed tears.

weigh (wā) *vb.* 1. to measure the heaviness of (something). 2. to have a particular measurable heaviness. **weight** (wāt) *n.* 1. the heaviness of a person or thing, resulting from the pull of gravity upon him or it. 2. a heavy object: *he used a stone as a weight.* 3. a load: *that's a weight off my mind.* 4. importance: *his opinions carry weight.*

weir (wiə) *n.* a type of dam controlling the flow of a river.

welcome ('welkəm) *vb.* **welcoming, welcomed.** 1. to greet someone in a friendly manner. 2. to receive happily: *he welcomed the news of his son's success.* —*n.* the action of welcoming.

weld (weld) *vb.* to fuse (pieces of metal or plastic) together.

welfare ('welfeə) *n.* 1. a person's state of health or happiness: *I'm thinking only of your welfare.* 2. money provided by the government to people who are ill, out of work, etc.

well¹ (wel) *adv.* **better, best.** 1. in a good way; satisfactorily: *he sings well.* 2. thoroughly; completely: *stir the mixture well.* 3. very much; considerably: *she looks well over 40.* —*adj.* healthy: *I hope you are well.* —*interj.* (used to begin a sentence or express surprise): *well, I haven't seen you for ages.*

well

well² (wel) *n.* a hole dug in the ground in order to obtain water, gas, or oil from beneath the earth.

wept (wept) *vb.* the past tense and past participle of WEEP.

west (west) *n.* 1. the direction one faces to see the sunset. 2. the part of a country lying in this direction. —*adj.* lying in or towards the west: *the west side.* —*adv.* towards the west: *moving west.* '**western** *adj.* of or in the west. *n.* a film, book, etc., about cowboys and Indians.

wet (wet) *adj.* **wetter, wettest.** containing or covered with water.

whale (wāl) *n.* a very large sea animal that resembles a fish but which is warm-blooded and gives birth to live young instead of laying eggs.

wheat (wēt) *n.* a grass that produces grains from which flour is made.

wheel (wēl) *n.* a circular frame, often covered with a tyre and having spokes and a central hub, fitted to a car.

wheel

237

wheelchair ('wēlchēə) *n.* a chair fitted with wheels for use by people who cannot walk.

whelk (welk) *n.* a type of snail found in shallow seawater and used for food.

whimper ('wimpə) *vb.* to cry with weak sounds: *the dog whimpered because he wanted to go out.* —*n.* the sound of whimpering: *the child gave a whimper.*

whine (wīn) *vb.* **whining, whined.** to make complaining or miserable sounds; moan: *the dog was whining for its food.*

whip (wip) *n.* a leather strap used for punishment, for making horses go faster, etc.; lash. — *vb.* **whipping, whipped.** 1. to hit with a whip or rod. 2. to beat or stir (eggs, cream, etc.).

whirl (wûl) *vb.* to spin or cause to spin rapidly: *the dancers whirled their partners round the room.* —*n.* a rapid spin or something like it, e.g. a confused state: *I'm in a whirl.*

whirlpool ('wûlpool) *n.* a water current that spins quickly and sucks down anything or anyone caught in it.

whirlwind ('wûlwind) *n.* a wind that causes a rapid circular motion in the air; hurricane or tornado.

whisk (wisk) *n.* an instrument for beating eggs, cream, etc. —*vb.* to beat (eggs, cream, etc.) with a whisk.

whisker ('wiskə) *n.* usu. **whiskers** (*pl.*) 1. hair growing on a man's face as part of his moustache or beard. 2. one of the long hairs on the face of a cat or other animal.

whiskey *or* **whisky** ('wiski) *n.* a very strong alcoholic drink, made from corn or other grain. When the drink comes from Scotland it is spelt **whisky,** and when it comes from Ireland or elsewhere it is spelt **whiskey.**

whisper ('wispə) *vb.* to speak or talk very quietly. —*n.* a very quiet sound: *the whisper of the breeze.*

whistle ('wisəl) *vb.* **whistling, whistled.** to make a sound by putting one's lips and tongue into a certain position and blowing air through them. Sometimes the fingers are also used. —*n.* 1. a high-pitched sound made by or as if by whistling. 2. an instrument that produces such a sound when blown through.

whitewash ('wītwosh) *n.* a watery white paint used on walls, fences, etc. —*vb.* 1. to paint with whitewash. 2. (informal) to make (something or someone) appear in a favourable way.

whole (hōl) *adj.* complete; total: *the whole bill comes to £2.* —*n.* the complete or entire amount of something: *he ate the whole of the cake before I could stop him.* —*adv.* in one; without being broken up: *the bird swallowed the mouse whole.* '**wholly** *adv.*

wholehearted ('hōl'hâtid) *adj.* not holding anything back; complete: *you have our wholehearted agreement.* —'**whole'heartedly** *adv.*

wholesale ('hōlsāl) *n.* the selling of goods in large quantities to shopkeepers who then sell (RETAIL) them to individual customers. —*adj.* in large amounts; on a large scale: *there was wholesale destruction by the bulldozer.* —*adv.* 1. by wholesale. 2. completely: *he dismissed my ideas wholesale.*

wick (wik) *n.* a piece of cotton or similar material in a candle, oil lamp, etc., through which the melted or liquid fuel is drawn up to be burnt.

wicked ('wikid) *adj.* 1. evil; not good in character: *the devil is wicked.* 2. naughty: *you wicked boy!* 3. showing evil or naughtiness: *a wicked smile.* —'**wickedness** *n.*

wicket ('wikit) *n.* 1. (cricket) either of the two sets of three sticks in front of which a batsman stands. 2. the part of a cricket pitch between these sticks. 3. (also **wicket gate**) a small gate.

wide (wīd) *adj.* **wider, widest.** 1. extending over a large area. 2. having a certain distance from one side to the other: *six feet wide.* 3. far away from something: *his shot went wide.* 4. great; considerable: *a wide variety of articles.* —*adv.* 1. (also **far and wide**) over a large area. 2. as much as possible: *open your mouth wide.* —*n.* (cricket) a ball bowled beyond the batsman's reach. —'**widely** *adv.*

widow ('widō) *n.* a woman whose husband has died and who has not married again. —*vb.* to make (someone) a widow. '**widower** *n.* a man whose wife has died and who has not married again.

width (width) *n.* the distance of something measured from one side of it to the other; breadth.

wife (wīf) *n.,pl.* **wives.** a married woman.

wig (wig) *n.* a head covering made of hair or artificial hair.

wild (wīld) *adj.* 1. living or existing outside human control; natural: *wild flowers.* 2. out of control; disorderly, untidy, etc. —*adv.* without being controlled: *flowers growing wild.*

wilderness ('wildənis) *n.* an area having no trace of human existence.

will (wil) *n.* 1. a person's wish, intention, or command, esp. as expressed in the legal document left by someone who has died. 2. control over one's own mind: *Luke has a strong will to win.* —*vb.* (used with infinitive to express intention or the future tense in English): *I will come tomorrow.* '**wilful** *adj.* 1. intentional. 2. obstinate or unmanageable.

willing ('wiliñg) *adj.* ready; prepared: *I'm willing to come.* —'**willingly** *adv.*

willow ('wilō) *n.* a tree with long, easily bent branches, from which one obtains wood for cricket bats, etc.

willow

wind[1] (wind) *n.* 1. a current of moving air in the earth's atmosphere. 2. one's breath or energy: *the race took all the wind out of him.*

wind[2] (wind) *vb.* **winding, wound** (wound). 1. to turn: *the boy winds the handle of the musical box.* 2. to wrap or roll up with a circular motion: *she wound the bandage around his finger.* 3. to twist along or follow a curving path: *the road wound up the hill.* 4. (often + *up*) to tighten the spring of (a clock or watch).

windfall ('windfôl) *n.* 1. a fruit or fruits brought off a tree by the wind. 2. something that one obtains by unexpected good fortune, as in a competition.

windmill ('windmil) *n.* a mill powered by the wind.

windpipe ('windpīp) *n.* the tubelike air passage in the body leading down from the throat to the lungs.

windscreen ('windskrēn) *n.* a protective pane of glass or clear plastic in the front of a car or other vehicle, through which the driver views the road ahead.

wine (wīn) *n.* any of several different kinds of alcoholic drink made from the juice of grapes or other fruit, flowers, etc.

wing (wing) *n.* 1. either of two movable limbs of a bird, bat, or insect specially adapted for flying. 2. one of two structures situated on either side of an aircraft. 3. a side section of a house, stage, etc.: *the actors waited in the wings before making their entrance.* —*vb.* to move by using wings; fly. **'wingspan** *n.* the distance between the two wing-tips of a bird or aircraft.

winter ('wintə) *n.* the coldest season of the year. —*vb.* to spend the winter in a place.

wire (wiə) *n.* 1. a long thin strand of metal. 2. a telegram or cable. —*vb.* **wiring, wired.** 1. (often + *up*) to fit out with wires for carrying electricity: *my brother wired the house.* 2. to send a telegram. —*adj.* made of wire.

wise (wīz) *adj.* **wiser, wisest.** clever or sensible. **wisdom** ('wizdəm) *n.* 1. the condition of being wise. 2. cleverness or good sense: *the wisdom of Solomon.*

wish (wish) *vb.* 1. (+ *for* or *to*) to need or desire greatly; want: *I wish to go out.* 2. to hope strongly for (something): *I wish I had more money.* —*n.* a need, hope, or desire.

wisp (wisp) *n.* a tiny or thin bit of something: *a wisp of smoke.*

wit (wit) *n.* 1. the ability to make clever or humorous remarks. 2. a person who has this ability. 3. often **wits** (*pl.*) sense or intelligence. —**'witty** *adj.* **wittier, wittiest.**

witch (wich) *n.* a woman supposed to have magic powers, esp. evil ones.

withdraw (with'drô) *vb.* **withdrawing, withdrew, withdrawn.** 1. to take or be taken away: *the commander withdrew his men.* 2. to leave. 3. to take back: *he withdrew his offer.*

wither ('widhə) *vb.* to become less, die off, or shrivel up.

withhold (with'hōld) *vb.* **withholding, withheld.** to keep (something) back; refuse to give: *his father withheld his permission for the young man to get married.*

withstand (with'stand) *vb.* **withstanding, withstood.** 1. to stand up to; refuse to give in under: *he can withstand a lot of pain.* 2. to bear without giving way; support: *the plank can withstand a weight of 500 pounds.*

witness ('witnis) *n.* a person who has seen or heard an event, esp. a crime or accident. —*vb.* to act as a witness to (something).

wives (wīvz) *n.* the plural of WIFE.

wizard ('wizəd) *n.* 1. a man supposed to have magic powers. 2. someone who is very clever at something: *John is a wizard at model-making.*

woke (wōk) *vb.* the past tense of WAKE.

woken ('wōkən) *vb.* the past participle of WAKE.

wolf (woolf) *n.,pl.* **wolves.** a large wild animal of the dog family living in cold regions and hunting in large groups called packs. —*vb.* to eat quickly: *don't wolf your food.*

woman ('woomən) *n.,pl.* **women** ('wimin). a female human being. —*adj.* female: *a woman doctor.*

wonder ('wundə) *vb.* 1. to be curious to know: *I wonder where my mother has gone.* 2. to be or feel amazed or surprised at something: *I wonder how you can be so silly.* —*n.* 1. something strange, unusual, or surprising. 2. a feeling of awe or admiration: *he was filled with wonder at the view.* **'wonderful** *adj.* excellent: *we had a wonderful time.*

wood (wood) *n.* 1. the substance from which trees are formed, lying just below the bark. 2. a place where there are a number of trees; forest. **'wooden** *adj.* made of wood. **'wooded** *adj.* (of land) having lots of trees.

woodpecker ('woodpekə) *n.* a bird with a strong pointed beak that can make a hole in a treetrunk.

woodpecker

woodwind ('woodwind) *n.* any of a group of musical wind instruments originally made of wood but now usu. made of metal. They include flutes, oboes, and clarinets.

wool (wool) *n.* the outer covering of soft curly hair on a sheep's body, spun into yarn and made into cloth. —**'woollen** *adj.*

wore (wô) *vb.* the past tense of WEAR.

work (wûk) *n.* 1. something done or to be done, esp. as a job in return for wages. 2. a great effort: *running up the hill was hard work.* 3. a piece of writing, painting, or music: *Shakespeare's works.* —*vb.* to do a job.

world (wûld) *n.* 1. the whole of the earth; our planet. 2. a part of this: *the western world.* 3. everyone on the earth: *the world knows his name.* 4. a field of activity or interest: *the sporting world.*

worm (wûm) *n.* an animal having a long thin soft body and no legs. —*vb.* to get (something) usu. by sly methods and without being noticed.

worn (wôn) *adj.* damaged through long use. —*vb.* the past participle of WEAR.

worry ('wuri) *vb.* **worrying, worried.** to be or cause to be anxious or distressed —*n.,pl.* **worries.** something that makes a person worry.

worship ('wûship) *vb.* **worshipping, worshipped.** 1. to praise or honour (God or a god). 2. to love deeply: *they worship their mother.* —*n.* the action of worshipping.

worth (wûth) *n.* value: *it costs a pound but that is not its true worth.* —*prep.* 1. having the value of: *it's worth a lot of money.* 2. good enough for: *this party was worth coming to.* —**worthiness** ('wûdhinis) *n.* —'**worthy** *adj.* **worthier, worthiest.**

wound[1] (woond) *n.* an injury; cut or other hurt. —*vb.* to hurt; injure.

wound[2] (wound) *vb.* the past tense and past participle of WIND[2].

wove (wōv) *vb.* the past tense of WEAVE.

woven ('wōvən) *vb.* the past participle of WEAVE.

wrap (rap) *vb.* **wrapping, wrapped.** 1. (often + *up*) to cover, pack, or enclose (something): *she wrapped the presents in paper.* 2. to place (something) around another object: *she wrapped her arms around his neck.*

wreath

wreath (rēth) *n.* a bunch of leaves or flowers woven together to form a circle. **wreathe** (rēdh) *vb.* **wreathing, wreathed.** to bind or wrap round with or as if with a wreath: *fog wreathed the tree tops.*

wreck (rek) *vb.* 1. to destroy or ruin: *the rain wrecked the picnic.* 2. to destroy or damage (a ship at sea). —*n.* something that has been wrecked, esp. a ship. —'**wreckage** *n.*

wrench (rench) *n.* 1. a sudden sharp twist. 2. a type of spanner. —*vb.* to give (something) a sudden twist.

wrestle ('resəl) *vb.* **wrestling, wrestled.** 1. to struggle with (an opponent) and try and force him to the groun. 2. to struggle: *she is wrestling with the problem.* '**wrestler** *n.* a person who takes part in the sport of wrestling.

wriggle ('rigəl) *vb.* **wriggling, wriggled.** to twist and turn like a snake or worm.

wring (ring) *vb.* **wringing, wrung.** 1. to remove (liquid) from something by twisting it. 2. to dry (something) by squeezing the water out. 3. to get (information) from someone by using force. 4. to press and twist (the hands) together.

wrinkle ('ringkəl) *vb.* **wrinkling, wrinkled.** to form or cause to form creases: *her face wrinkled into a smile.* —*n.* a small fold or crease in a surface: *the old lady's face is full of wrinkles.*

wrist (rist) *n.* the lower part of the arm, just above the hand.

write (rīt) *vb.* **writing, wrote, written.** 1. to form letters, words, or other marks on paper. 2. to send a letter to someone. 3. to put down (stories, articles, etc.) on paper and have them printed and sold. '**writer** *n.* a person who writes stories, articles, etc. '**writing** *n.* 1. letters, words, etc., written by hand: *his writing is very difficult to read.* 2. usu. **writings** (*pl.*) the work of a writer: *we study the writings of Shakespeare.*

writhe (rīdh) *vb.* **writhing, writhed.** to twist or turn: *he was writhing in pain.*

wrong (rong) *adj.* 1. not right; not true, correct, morally good, or suitable. 2. out of order: *there is something wrong with my car. n.* an action that is wrong (def. 1); moral harm. *vb.* to treat (someone) badly or unjustly.

wrote (rōt) *vb.* the past tense of WRITE.

wrung (rung) *vb.* the past tense and past participle of WRING.

X Y Z

xenon ('zēnon) *n.* a rare gas, which makes up a tiny proportion of air. Chemical symbol: Xe.

xenophobia (zenə'fōbiə) *n.* a fear or dislike of people who come from abroad. —**xeno'phobic** *adj.*

xerophyte ('ziərəfīt) *n.* a plant that grows in dry conditions.

Xerox ('ziəroks) *n.* a trade name for a machine that copies documents without touching the originals.

Xmas ('eksməs) *n.* a short way of writing CHRISTMAS.

xylophone

x-ray ('eksrā) *n.* 1. a type of ray that can pass through substances that ordinary light rays cannot penetrate. x-rays have very short wavelengths. 2. a photograph taken with x-rays: *the x-ray of her arm showed a small break in the bone.* —*vb.* to take a photograph of (a person, part of the body, etc.) using x-rays.

xylophone ('zīləfōn) *n.* a musical instrument that is made of a row or rows of wooden bars of different lengths on a frame. The player hits these bars with a pair of sticks to make a tune.

yacht

yacht (yot) *n.* 1. a ship, generally with space on board for people to eat and sleep, used for pleasure cruising. 2. a small light sailing vessel for racing, pleasure sailing, etc.

yak (yak) *n.* a long-haired ox found in central Asia.

yard[1] (yâd) *n.* 1. a unit of length equal to 3 feet or 36 inches (0·9144 metre). 2. a rod fixed to a ship's mast and used to support a sail.

yard[2] (yâd) *n.* a small enclosed area of ground near or around buildings.

yarn (yân) *n.* 1. a thread, esp. a woollen thread, prepared for weaving or knitting. 2. (informal) a story, esp. a long, made-up one.

yawn (yôn) *vb.* 1. to open the mouth wide and draw in breath involuntarily because one is sleepy or bored. 2. to be wide open: *the pit yawned in front of them.* —*n.* the act of yawning.

year (yiə) *n.* the period of time that it takes for the earth to make one complete revolution round the sun; 365 days or 366 in a **leap year.**

yeast (yēst) *n.* a substance made of tiny FUNGUS plants and used in making bread, brewing beer, etc.

yew

yew (yoo) *n.* an evergreen tree with small dark spiny leaves and red berries. Yew trees are poisonous to cattle. Their wood was formerly used to make bows for archers.

yield (yēld) *vb.* 1. to produce or give forth: *the orchard yields a heavy crop of apples.* 2. to give way, esp. as a result of pressure or force: *the door yielded to their push.* 3. to surrender or give oneself up: *they yielded to the enemy.* —*n.* the amount produced: *the farm's yield of wheat was greatly improved.*

yodel ('yōdəl) *vb.* **yodelling, yodelled.** to sing or shout in a musical way, in the manner of Swiss mountain-dwellers, making one's voice travel over a great distance. —*n.* a yodelled song or cry.

yoga ('yōgə) *n.* an Indian religious practice involving breathing control, body postures, and mental training. **yogi** ('yōgi) *n.* a person who practises yoga.

yoghurt ('yogət) *n.* clotted liquid food made from sour milk.

yoke (yōk) *n.* 1. a wooden frame placed across the necks of oxen or other working animals. 2. a pair of animals joined together by a yoke. 3. the part of a dress, coat, shirt, etc., that fits across the shoulders. —*vb.* **yoking, yoked.** to put (animals) in a yoke.

yolk (yōk) *n.* the yellow part of an egg.

young (yung) *adj.* not old; having existed, grown, developed, etc., for only a short time. —*n.* young offspring.

youth (yōōth) *n.* 1. the condition of being young. 2. the time of life between being a child and being grown up. 3. a young man. —'**youthful** *adj.*

yoyo ('yōyō) *n.,pl.* **yoyos.** (trademark) a toy like a disc with a string wound around a groove on the rim. The disc runs up and down the string.

---

zebra ('zebrə) *n.* a wild animal from Africa that looks rather like a donkey but has a black and white striped skin.

zebra crossing a place in a street marked by white stripes in the road. People on foot can cross there and wheeled traffic must wait for them.

zero ('ziərō) *n.,pl.* **zeros.** 1. the figure 0; nought. 2. the point between + and – on a scale, e.g. on a thermometer, from which a measurement is taken: *the temperature was eight degrees below zero.*

zest (zest) *n.* enthusiasm, pleasure, and interest: *he worked with zest at his model railway.*

zigzag ('zigzag) *n.* a pattern, line, path, etc., that goes in a series of short sharp turns from one side to another. —*vb.* **zigzagging, zigzagged.** to move in a zigzag: *lightning zigzagged across the sky.*

zoo

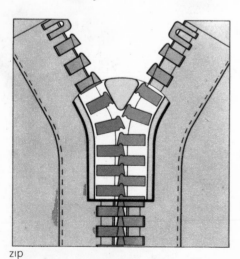

zip

zinc (zingk) *n.* a greyish white metallic chemical element used in electric batteries and for coating steel used in roofing, buckets, etc. Chemical symbol: Zn.

zip (zip) *n.* a device made of two rows of interlocking metal or plastic teeth, used for fastening clothes, suitcases, etc. —*vb.* **zipping, zipped.** (often + *up*) to close (something) with a zip.

zircon ('zûkon) *n.* a mineral that occurs in various colours. Transparent varieties are used in jewellery.

zodiac ('zōdiak) *n.* 1. an imaginary area of space going around the earth like a belt and divided into twelve parts known as the signs of the zodiac. 2. a diagram of these divisions.

zone (zōn) *n.* 1. one of the five regions of the earth's surface, called after the type of climate found there, e.g. the arctic zone. 2. any region or area that has some special quality, feature, or purpose: *there is a new factory zone in our town.*

zoo (zōō) *n.* a park or area where animals are kept for show.

zoology (zōō'oləji) *n.* the study of animals and the animal kingdom. —**zoological** (zōōə'lojikəl) *adj.* —**zoologist** (zōō'oləjist) *n.*

zoom (zōōm) *vb.* to move suddenly and at speed, often noisily: *the motorcyclist zoomed past the cars.*

zygote ('zīgət) *n.* a fertilized egg cell.

ABCDE
abcdefg
KLMNO
nopqrst
TUVW
zabcdef
CDEFG